ALTERNATIVE PROTEINS

ALTERNATIVE PROTEINS
Safety and Food Security Considerations

Edited by
Alaa El-Din A. Bekhit, William W. Riley, and
Malik A. Hussain

CRC Press is an imprint of the
Taylor & Francis Group, an **informa** business

First edition published 2022
by CRC Press
6000 Broken Sound Parkway NW, Suite 300, Boca Raton, FL 33487-2742

and by CRC Press
2 Park Square, Milton Park, Abingdon, Oxon, OX14 4RN

© 2022 Taylor & Francis Group, LLC

CRC Press is an imprint of Taylor & Francis Group, LLC

Reasonable efforts have been made to publish reliable data and information, but the author and publisher cannot assume responsibility for the validity of all materials or the consequences of their use. The authors and publishers have attempted to trace the copyright holders of all material reproduced in this publication and apologize to copyright holders if permission to publish in this form has not been obtained. If any copyright material has not been acknowledged please write and let us know so we may rectify in any future reprint.

Except as permitted under U.S. Copyright Law, no part of this book may be reprinted, reproduced, transmitted, or utilized in any form by any electronic, mechanical, or other means, now known or hereafter invented, including photocopying, microfilming, and recording, or in any information storage or retrieval system, without written permission from the publishers.

For permission to photocopy or use material electronically from this work, access www.copyright.com or contact the Copyright Clearance Center, Inc. (CCC), 222 Rosewood Drive, Danvers, MA 01923, 978-750-8400. For works that are not available on CCC please contact mpkbookspermissions@tandf.co.uk

Trademark notice: Product or corporate names may be trademarks or registered trademarks and are used only for identification and explanation without intent to infringe.

Library of Congress Cataloging-in-Publication Data
Names: Bekhit, Alaa El-Din, editor. | Riley, William Walter, 1954- editor. | Hussain, Malik A., editor.
Title: Alternative proteins : safety and food security considerations / Alaa El-Din A. Bekhit, William W. Riley, Malik A. Hussain.
Description: First edition. | Boca Raton : CRC Press, 2022. | Includes bibliographical references and index.
Identifiers: LCCN 2021031872 (print) | LCCN 2021031873 (ebook) | ISBN 9780367281298 (hbk) | ISBN 9781032161600 (pbk) | ISBN 9780429299834 (ebk)
Subjects: LCSH: Food--Technological innovations. | Artificial foods. | Wild foods. | Food--Safety measures. | Food security. | Proteins.
Classification: LCC TX353 .A58 2022 (print) | LCC TX353 (ebook) | DDC 363.19/26--dc23
LC record available at https://lccn.loc.gov/2021031872
LC ebook record available at https://lccn.loc.gov/2021031873

ISBN: 978-0-367-28129-8 (hbk)
ISBN: 978-1-032-16160-0 (pbk)
ISBN: 978-0-429-29983-4 (ebk)

DOI: 10.1201/9780429299834

Typeset in Times
by MPS Limited, Dehradun

Dedication

Alaa El-Din dedicates this book to Mona, the first member of the Bekhit family that consumed alternative proteins.

William dedicates this book to his four children and eight grandchildren – their future depends on a safe and sustainable food supply.

Malik dedicates this book to his father (late), mother, wife and three children (Afeef, Hassan and Zahra).

Contents

Preface ix
About the Editor xi
Contributors xiii

Chapter 1 Trends and Motivations for Novel Protein Sources and Contribution towards Food Security 1

Malik Altaf Hussain, William Riley, and Alaa El-Din Bekhit

Chapter 2 Plant Proteins 17

William W. Riley

Chapter 3 Single-Cell Protein – A Group of Alternative Proteins 49

Marzieh Hosseininezhad and Malik Altaf Hussain

Chapter 4 Algae as an Alternative Source of Protein 65

Neda Irvani, Alan Carne, Dominic Agyei, and Indrawati Oey

Chapter 5 Insect-Derived Protein as Food and Feed 85

Parinaz Hobbi, Alaa El-Din Ahmed Bekhit, Frederic Debaste, Nei Lei, and Amin Shavandi

Chapter 6 Snails 133

Alaa El-Din Bekhit, Jinlin Shi, Zhijing Ye, Isam A. Mohamed Ahmed, Fahad Y. Al-Juhaimi, William W. Riley, and Ravi Gooneratne

Chapter 7 Keratin as an Alternative Protein in Food and Nutrition 173

Thirawat Tantamacharik, Alan Carne, Amin Shavandi, and Alaa El-Din Ahmed Bekhit

Chapter 8 Non-traditional Meat Sources, Production, Nutritional and Health Aspects, Consideration of Safety Aspects and Religious Views 215

Isam A. Mohamed Ahmed, Fahad Y. Al-Juhaimi, Zuhaib F. Bhat, Alan Carne, and Alaa El-Din Bekhit

Chapter 9 Cultured Meat: Challenges in the Path of Production and 3D Food Printing as an Option to Develop Cultured Meat-Based Products 271

Zuhaib F. Bhat, James D. Morton, Alaa El-Din Ahmed Bekhit, Sunil Kumar, and Hina F. Bhat

Chapter 10 Bioconversion of Marine By-products into Edible Protein 297

Abdo Hassoun, Turid Rustad, and Alaa El-Din Ahmed Bekhit

Chapter 11 Meat Co-products 329

*Reshan Jayawardena, James David Morton, Charles S. Brennan,
Zuhaib Fayaz Bhat, and Alaa El-Din Ahmed Bekhit*

Chapter 12 Food Safety Risks Associated with Novel Proteins 361

Malik Altaf Hussain

Chapter 13 Allergenicity Risks Associated with Novel Proteins and Rapid Methods of Detection 379

Mostafa Gouda and Alaa El-Din Bekhit

Chapter 14 Novel Protein Sources: An Overview of Food Regulations 407

Malik Altaf Hussain

Index 429

Preface

Over the last decade, substantial research activities in food science have been dedicated towards prospecting and investigating physiochemical, nutritional and health properties of novel protein sources. This trend was fueled by predictions of increased human population and lack of a parallel increase in traditional animal protein sources (land and marine sources). These predictions should be revised in the light of the recent COVID-19 pandemic and an increase in civil unrest in many hotspots worldwide. One of the main drivers for the rise in novel proteins/novel foods research activities is linked to significant changes in young consumers' attitudes towards red meat consumption and their interest in new alternative protein products. This has led to important changes in the food market. For example, significant market growth has been observed in plant milk imitations (almond, rice, oat and soy varieties) instead of traditional cow, buffalo, sheep and goat milks. Similarly, several plant-based meat analogues and meat-free small goods have been developed and marketed (e.g., Impossible Foods, Quorn, Beyond Meat, and so on). Various novel protein sources have emerged at different levels of commercial uptake (e.g., edible insects, algae, microbial single cell and *in vitro* meat). Many of the new technologies investigating novel proteins are still at the concept stage with issues surrounding upscaling, safety and biosecurity, cost, waste management and consumer issues being major challenges to overcome before these products find their way to our dining tables. Cost and consumer acceptability are probably the most important factors that will influence the purchasing of these new protein products. It is expected that the protein shortage is likely to be more significant in low-income societies and thus affordability will be a key factor for accessibility and purchase of these products. A commonly unaccountable factor in scientific research, but very important for marketability of foods, is the religious status and permissibility of consumption and the cultural acceptability of such food products. This issue appears to be of significant importance to large portions of followers of certain faiths that may have declared restrictions on certain food sources (e.g., certain insects and animals) and in cultures where insects represent emotions of disgust, fear and disease-bearing. This book aims to provide a holistic evaluation of novel proteins by covering processing, nutritional, safety and, where necessary, the consumer and religious aspects of protein type. Chapter 1 introduces the drivers and motivations for novel proteins to examine the humanistic, environmental and epidemiological changes that underline the need for alternative sources to complement, and in some cases, replace traditional protein sources. Several chapters have been dedicated to some of the well-known protein sources, such as plants (Chapter 2), single-cell proteins (Chapter 3), non-traditional meat sources (Chapter 8) and marine wastes (Chapter 10). Other chapters are dedicated to protein sources that have been known and consumed in certain localities and now are being heavily investigated and proposed for international markets, such as algae (Chapter 4), edible insects (Chapter 5) and meat co-products (Chapter 11). Chapter 9 examines the recent updates on *in vitro* meat, a technology that enjoys large publicity worldwide. A special focus has been placed on the religious aspects of this technology. This book also reviews two novel protein sources that have not been considered previously (snails in Chapter 6 and keratin in Chapter 7). Comprehensive accounts of their nutrition and potential utilization have been provided as well as their safety and health aspects. Separate information has been presented on the safety requirements (Chapter 12) and risks associated with novel proteins (Chapter 13).

It was the aim of the editors to provide industry and academia up-to-date views on opportunities and considerations of hindrances that face these novel proteins. While several options are available for the international community to tackle the predicted future protein shortage and address several ethical and sustainability issues, we believe the current situation is as Linus Pauling described: *'The picture is, however, still very far from definite - she suggests various alternatives and does not make any definite predictions.'*

Alaa El-Din A. Bekhit
William W. Riley
Malik A. Hussain

About the Editor

Alaa El-Din A. Bekhit, PhD, earned his PhD in Biochemistry from Lincoln University, New Zealand in 2004. His PhD research investigated the role of metmyoglobin reducing activity in the maintenance of fresh meat colour. He obtained his MSc in Food Process Engineering from the University of Reading, UK, in 1994.

Dr. Bekhit is an Associate Professor at the Food Science Department, University of Otago, New Zealand. He also holds an Honorary Distinguished Professor post in the Food Science and Pharmacy College, Xinjiang Agricultural University; and the Chinese Academy of Agricultural Sciences (CAAS); Honorary Associate Professor in College of Food and Agricultural Sciences, King Saud University, Kingdom of Saudi; and Adjunct Associate Professor in Faculty of Agriculture and Life Sciences, Lincoln University, New Zealand. He has been active in studying meat quality and muscle foods for 29 years. He published more than 200 research articles, 50 review articles and >40 book chapters. Aladin led several major research projects that aimed at understanding composition, biochemistry, functionality and potential applications of proteins from oilseed cakes, whey, blood, snails and wool. He also carried out several projects on the quality of muscle foods and the processing of co-products such as animals offal and fish roe.

William W. Riley, PhD, was awarded his PhD in Nutritional Biochemistry from Cornell University, his MSc in Exercise Physiology from the University of Tennessee and his BSc in Physical Education from the University of Massachusetts.

Dr. Riley worked as a National Institutes of Health Postdoctoral Fellow in Biochemistry at the University of Minnesota, in Austin, Minnesota. Since then, he has served as an Assistant Professor in the Department of Food and Nutrition at North Dakota State University, a Senior Clinical Research Associate in the Medical Department, at Ross Laboratories in Columbus, Ohio, and as a Research Associate and Lecturer in the Department of Zoology, University of Manitoba, Winnipeg, Canada. From 1993–95, Dr. Riley held the position of Adjunct Professor in the Department of Food and Nutrition at the University of Manitoba while serving as Vice President, Research and Development with the Canola Council of Canada in Winnipeg.

In 2006, Dr. Riley moved to China and assumed the position of Professor, Food Quality and Safety in the International School at Jinan University. He has also worked within the animal feed and veterinary pharmaceutical industries while living in Guangzhou and Nanjing, having served in various technical consulting roles for Chinese and foreign companies. At present, he is serving as Professorial Lecturer in the Department of Food Science and Nutrition at the University of the Philippines-Diliman, and as Technical Consultant to a number of Asian and North American companies.

Malik A. Hussain, PhD, is a food microbiologist and an active food professional. He holds a PhD degree in food microbiology from the University of Melbourne (Australia) and a master's in food technology from the University of Agriculture Faisalabad (Pakistan) with distinction. He was awarded OECD Fellowship 2014 to work on a collaborative research project at Guelph Food Research Centre, Canada. Over more than 20 years, he has worked on several academic, research, technical and industrial positions in different countries including Australia, Canada, New Zealand and Pakistan.

In academia, he has extensive experience in food science teaching and research supervision at world-renowned universities (i.e., the University of Melbourne, Australia; Queensland University of Technology, Australia; Lincoln University, New Zealand, University of Sydney, Australia). As a food safety expert, he worked at world-leading agencies (i.e., NSW Food Authority, Sydney, Australia; Agriculture and Agri-Food, Canada) in food safety regulation, risk assessment, food policy and standards development. He was the former associate director at the Centre for Food Research and Innovation (CFRI) of Lincoln University. Dr Hussain completed a variety of industry-led projects on the development of functional foods (probiotics), food safety and microbial proteomics. His research interests are to improve applications of probiotics through understanding the microbial physiology and stress responses. He has published more than 100 scholarly documents in food science area and over 50 conference abstracts. He is the founder and initiator of Asia-Pacific Probiotics workshops in the region. He is an executive director of Asia-Pacific Institute of Food Professional (APIFP). He maintains memberships of several professional associations and sits on scientific committees of many international conferences and symposiums.

Contributors

Dominic Agyei
Department of Food Science
University of Otago
Dunedin, New Zealand

Isam A. Mohamed Ahmed
Department of Food Science and Nutrition,
    College of Food and Agricultural Sciences
King Saud University
Riyadh, Kingdom of Saudi Arabia

Fahad Y. Al-Juhaimi
Department of Food Science and Nutrition,
    College of Food and Agricultural Sciences
King Saud University
Riyadh, Kingdom of Saudi Arabia

Hina F. Bhat
Animal Biotechnology
SKUAST-Kashmir, India

Zuhaib F. Bhat
Livestock Products Technology
SKUAST-Jammu, India
and
Department of Wine Food and Molecular
    Biosciences
Lincoln University
Lincoln, New Zealand

Charles S. Brennan
Department of Wine Food and Molecular
    Biosciences
Lincoln University
Lincoln, New Zealand

Alan Carne
Department of Biochemistry
University of Otago
Dunedin, New Zealand

Frederic Debaste
Department of Transfers, Interfaces and Processes
Université libre de Bruxelles
Brussels, Belgium

Ravi Gooneratne
Faculty of Agriculture & Life Sciences
Lincoln University
Canterbury, New Zealand

Mostafa Gouda
College of Biosystems Engineering and Food
    Science
Zhejiang University
Hangzhou, China
and
Department of Nutrition & Food Science,
    National Research Centre
Dokki, Giza, Egypt

Abdo Hassoun
Nofima AS, Norwegian Institute of Food,
    Fisheries, and Aquaculture Research
Tromsø, Norway

Parinaz Hobbi
BioMatter-BTL, École interfacultaire de
    Bio-ingénieurs
Université Libre de Bruxelles
Brussels, Belgium

Marzieh Hosseininezhad
Research Institute of Food Science and
    Technology
Mashhad, Iran

Neda Irvani
Department of Food Science
University of Otago Dunedin
Dunedin, New Zealand

Reshan Jayawardena
Department of Wine Food and Molecular
    Biosciences
Lincoln University
Lincoln, New Zealand

Sunil Kumar
Livestock Products Technology
SKUAST-Jammu, India

James D. Morton
Department of Wine, Food and Molecular Biosciences, Faculty of Agriculture and Life Sciences
Lincoln University
New Zealand

Lei Nei
College of Life Sciences
Xinyang Normal University (XYNU)
Xinyang, China

Indrawati Oey
Department of Food Science
University of Otago
Dunedin, New Zealand
and
Riddet Institute
Palmerston North, New Zealand

Turid Rustad
Department of Biotechnology and Food Science
NTNU-Norwegian University of Science and Technology
Trondheim, Norway

Amin Shavandi
BioMatter-BTL, École interfacultaire de Bio-ingénieurs
Université Libre de Bruxelles
Brussels, Belgium

Jinlin Shi
Faculty of Agriculture & Life Sciences
Lincoln University
Canterbury, New Zealand

Thirawat Tantamacharik
Department of Food Science
University of Otago
Dunedin, New Zealand

Zhijing Ye
Eastern Institute of Technology
New Zealand

1 Trends and Motivations for Novel Protein Sources and Contribution towards Food Security

Malik Altaf Hussain[1], William Riley[2], and Alaa El-Din A. Bekhit[3]

[1]Food Safety Unit, The Victorian Department of Health, Melbourne, Australia
[2]International School, Jinan University, Guangzhou, China
[3]Food Science Department, Otago University, Dunedin, New Zealand

CONTENTS

1.1 Introduction 1
1.2 Trends and Motivations for Novel Protein Sources 2
    1.2.1 Health Improvement 3
    1.2.2 Cost and Availability of Protein 3
    1.2.3 Environmental Impact 3
    1.2.4 Food Transition and Justice 4
    1.2.5 Other Factors 4
1.3 Novel Proteins to Improve Food Security and Sustainability 4
    1.3.1 Food Security 4
    1.3.2 Aging Population and Chronic Disease 5
    1.3.3 Alternative Protein Sources and Sustainability 6
    1.3.4 Food Choice Changes 6
1.4 The Challenges of Novel Proteins 7
    1.4.1 Challenges with *In Vitro* Meats as a Protein Source 7
    1.4.2 Challenges with Edible Insects as a Protein Source 9
1.5 Key Aspects of Novel Protein Sources 10
    1.5.1 Food Safety Aspects 11
    1.5.2 Health and Nutritional Aspects 12
    1.5.3 Technological Aspects 13
    1.5.4 Environmental and Ethical Aspects 14
1.6 Conclusion 14
Acknowledgement and Declaration 14
References 15

1.1 INTRODUCTION

Traditionally, only proteins derived from animal sources are considered to be of high quality and value. Even today's food market is heavily loaded with meat and dairy protein products. This is primarily driven by consumer demand and perception around the nutritional and health benefits of these protein sources. However, over the last decade or so, alternative proteins, especially from plant-based sources, have entered the food supply chain. Food markets have begun to display and promote these new protein products due to growing consumer interest in alternative protein sources.

It was challenging and difficult to begin to provide sufficient non-animal sources to meet the growing demand for protein. But there are many excellent non-traditional protein sources, including vegetarian, microbial, insect and others to supply the adequate nutrition needed for good health. Plant-based protein is the most rapidly growing sector within the alternative protein industry, and it offers several dozen of potential high quality protein sources (Chapter 2). Single-cell protein (SCP) includes the edible microbial biomass derived from bacteria, yeasts, filamentous fungi or microalgae that are also considered promising alternative sources of protein (Chapter 3). Many different species of insects are eaten without risk to health throughout the world; however, each edible insect species has a strict culture and historical background behind it (Chapter 5). Table 1.1 lists several alternative proteins and protein products that are available now or that are emerging as potential sources in the future.

Future protein sources will look fundamentally different from the proteins that we consume today. Therefore, rapidly evolving diversity and novelty of protein sources require completion of comprehensive risk assessments prior to regulatory approvals to ensure that public health and safety issues are addressed (Chapters 12 and 13). The innovation and development of alternative protein sources are vital to ensure food security, sustainability, health and nutrition in response to consumer trends in the coming years.

1.2 TRENDS AND MOTIVATIONS FOR NOVEL PROTEIN SOURCES

Alternative proteins are disrupting animal-based food systems and a clear transitioning is seen towards plant-based food systems over the last decade or so. The emerging trends and transitions in food systems towards diversified and novel sources of protein are supported by a range of institutions, organizations, agencies, scientific associations, and industry lobbyists. Several factors including health concerns, nutritional implications, environmental sustainability and economic

TABLE 1.1

Examples of alternative protein sources and new commercial products

Category	Protein Source or Product			
Plant-based	Soybeans	Hemp seed	Pumpkin seed	Sunflower seeds
	Peas	Chickpeas	Seitan	Lentils
	Kidney beans	Navy beans	Black beans	Lima beans
	Flaxseed	Chia seeds	Quinoa	Sun-dried tomatoes
	Almonds	Peanuts	Pistachio	Cashew
	Walnuts	Pine nuts	Amaranth	Wheat
	Wild rice	Oats	Buckwheat	Millet
	Barley	Corn	Sorghum	Buckwheat
Insect	Agave worm	Bamboo borer	Bee	Centipede
	Chapulines (grasshoppers)	Crickets	Dragonfly	Dung beetle
	Mealworms	Mopane worm	Sago grubs	Locust
Microbial	Quorn™	All-G Rich	FeedKind	KnipBio Meal
	Spirulina	Pruteen	Provesta	UniProtein
Technologically produced and other	Cell-cultured meat	Cell-cultured fish	Cell-cultured chicken	Cell-cultured prawn
	3D printed meat	Synthetic eggs	Synthetic milk	

TABLE 1.2
Key driving factors that are influencing growth of alternative proteins

Factor	Ways to Influence Growth
Health	• Improve health by providing varying and high-quality protein sources. • Offer many nutritional benefits. • Healthier than traditional proteins. • Help to reach the recommended daily targets for whole grains, fruits and vegetables. • Less saturated fat than red meat.
Cost and availability	• Plant-based protein offers the least expensive option. • Could be available to everyone at an affordable cost.
Environmental impact	• Alternative proteins are considered more sustainable. • Lower environmental footprint. • Less water usage. • Lower greenhouse gas production.
Food systems transition and innovation	• A successful transition of existing food systems towards more efficient, diverse, resilient and equitable food systems. • The overall efficiency of the entire food production process is improved.
Social impact	• A significant impact on consumer health and safety (real and perceived).
Consumer acceptability and perception	• Consumers are looking for something new and exciting in terms of flavour and texture. • Consumers are looking for a more versatile protein option. • Animal welfare advocates are gaining traction.

challenges are driving movements to introduce novel protein sources in global food systems. This section will discuss some of the key driving factors that substitute alternative proteins for our conventional protein sources (Table 1.2).

1.2.1 HEALTH IMPROVEMENT

Novel proteins, especially plant-based, are gaining popularity due to their diversity and nutritional benefits. For example, lupins, quinoa and hempseed are considered excellent sources of energy, high-quality proteins, fibres, vitamins, and minerals. Many health-improving compounds such as polyphenols and bioactive peptides are present in plant-based protein sources (Pihlanto et al., 2017). Protein consumers equate a high-protein diet with a myriad of health benefits. Likewise, many young consumers perceive alternative or plant-based protein products as a healthy choice.

1.2.2 COST AND AVAILABILITY OF PROTEIN

The increasing cost of animal-based protein is one of the major factors that is encouraging the industry to find alternative protein sources. Plant-based protein sources, such as beans, peas and lentils, offer the lowest-cost options for protein sources. However, currently, many alternative protein products are at the development stage and are more expensive than traditional animal-based protein products. The cost-effectiveness, functionality and taste are key parameters that will have a huge impact on consumer acceptance of any new and novel protein source.

1.2.3 ENVIRONMENTAL IMPACT

The production of animal-based proteins poses serious issues for environmental health. Current animal farming practices to produce protein are adversely impacting the environment due to excess water usage, land clearing and greenhouse gas (GHG) production. Among many trends that are driving consumer demand for plant proteins include concerns related to food security and sustainability. For example, consumer desire for clean labels, compatibility with vegetarian and vegan lifestyles, the carbon footprint and sustainability of plant-based protein sources are important factors in making protein choices in the future.

1.2.4 Food Transition and Justice

The introduction and development of alternative protein sources have multiple barriers, including political, economic, social, cultural, technological and logistic, which must be overcome for a successful transition of food systems (McGregor, 2021). A good understanding of these challenges is useful to assist the transition process. Strategies that rely on 'fit and conform' make innovation competitive within unchanged food systems, whereas 'stretch and transform' convert existing systems into new and more efficient food systems (Smith & Raven, 2012). However, consumer's perception of what constitutes a good protein source is important in the food transition process. Indeed, consumers are more interested in eating protein from diverse sources, but plant-based proteins are gaining more rapid popularity than are lesser-known sources, such as algae and hemp-based proteins. Food justice refers to a social movement that has its roots among people of colour in North America (McGregor, 2021). It is a social categorization based on how food is produced, valued, retailed, accessed and consumed, determined on the basis of race, gender, class and geographical region. According to Broad (2019), food transitions associated with novel proteins must consider issues related to food justice for socially just outcomes of new product development.

1.2.5 Other Factors

Many other factors play a role in driving alternative protein product success. These include the following:

- Development of new technologies to produce and formulate novel proteins.
- Food innovation and marketing tactics to promote alternative protein sources and new products.
- The use of social media to create awareness of the social cost and barriers to the introduction of novel protein sources.
- Engaging with different social groups (race, gender and class) is likely to result in socially just outcomes.

1.3 NOVEL PROTEINS TO IMPROVE FOOD SECURITY AND SUSTAINABILITY

There have been several reliable estimates that global population will reach and exceed 9 billion by 2050, and that ~70% more food will be required to feed humanity. Moreover, there may be a severe shortage of protein if only animal sources are relied upon; therefore, novel protein sources are needed to strengthen global food security efforts. Weindl et al. (2020) described a sustainable approach for the production of food protein to improve global food security (Figure 1.1).

1.3.1 Food Security

Unfettered growth in animal production, particularly in concert with the expected increase in global population not only by 2050 but especially by the turn of this century, will eventually require an amount of plant-based ingredients to produce animal products that may well surpass the production capacity of all available arable land. Independent of this concern, the diversion of available plant products to animal production, where the conversion factors (feed consumed relative to final animal

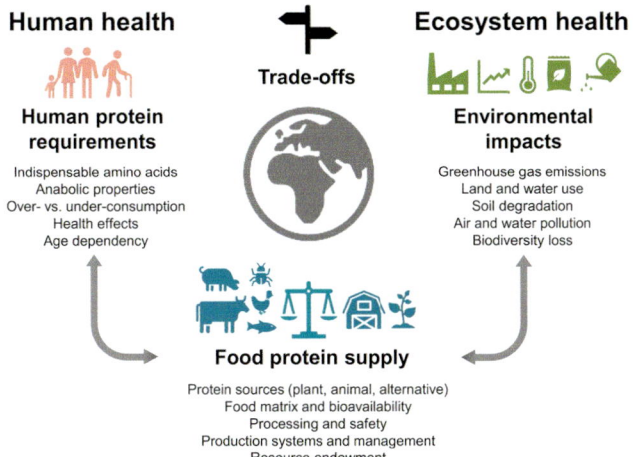

FIGURE 1.1 A sustainable approach for the production of food protein that advocates human and ecosystem health. The image is from Weindl et al. (2020). The image is from an open-access article distributed under the terms of the Creative Commons CC-BY license, which permits unrestricted use, distribution and reproduction in any medium, provided the original work is properly cited.

weight) currently range from 2:1 for poultry and most aquatic species to 5-7:1 for cattle, will become increasingly counterintuitive. Would it not make more sense that as the population increases towards and perhaps exceeds 10 billion by 2200 that increasing amounts of plant proteins be consumed directly, and that other alternative protein sources be sought and utilized for direct human consumption? As of 2018, humans and domesticated animals represent 30 times the living mass of all wild mammals on the planet (Bar-On et al., 2018). Food security depends upon many things, not least of which is the availability of food. There is abundant evidence that we are in the midst of sixth mass extinction of species, primarily due to human endeavours (Ceballos et al., 2020). Further expansion and congestion of domestic animal production is implicated as a factor in the loss of biodiversity both directly and indirectly, as the destruction of tropical forests in Brazil to produce more soybeans to feed animals and in Indonesia and Malaysia to produce more palm oil, in part, to divert to animal production, has had a profound impact on the loss of species (Ledford, 2019). Thirty to eighty more years of the same will do little to enhance food security. Many of the proposed alternative protein sources to be discussed herein are dependent upon the maintenance of biodiversity, so it is to humanities' benefit to consider the consequences of actions taken within any food sector upon others. Sustainability is a simple concept to put forth, albeit a difficult process to enact.

1.3.2 Aging Population and Chronic Disease

Implicit in the expansion of the world population is an alteration in its demographics. Modern medicine and public health efforts have done much to extend the life span of individuals, which adds to the population number at any given time, due to decreased mortality relative to births, even if the number of births is diminished. Unfortunately, commensurate with adaptation of 'developed nation' status has been the co-development of a variety of chronic diseases, including heart disease, insulin-independent diabetes and cancer. The etiology of these diseases can be traced to a great extent to the dietary habits of the developed nations as well as the sedentary characteristics of much of these countries' inhabitants. However, some of the 'blame' for the increased incidence of chronic disease can be put on the increased longevity itself. Cancer is primarily a disease of 'age' and the environment when genetic factors are excluded. This is especially true for specific cancers, such as prostate cancer in males. Cancerous cell development is highly influenced by environmental factors, which include exposure to radiation, chemicals and other toxic compounds, and chronic exposure (over time) is the more important factor than is acute exposure for a vast number of people. By definition, this means that as a population ages, the incidence of cancer can be expected to increase, although those controllable factors that are implicated can be mitigated (e.g., diet, smoking, medical radiation exposure).

It is the category of diet where the topic of alternative proteins may have a key role to play in having a positive impact in controlling chronic disease, as the average age of the population stretches into its 9th and 10th decades. Science understands the role that a plant-based diet can play in decreasing the risk of certain cancers, and research has made clear what risk factors are to be avoided to prevent the scourge of adult-onset diabetes and its consequences. Heart disease is the number one killer in most developed nations, either as a direct cause or as an indirect consequence of diabetic conditions. High levels of animal protein consumption, and the concurrent ingestion of fat and saturated fat, are implicated in most types of heart disease. A shift to lower fat animal protein products, and especially those with predominantly unsaturated fat, or non-animal proteins, is warranted to avoid many of the chronic disease issues associated with the aging process, while at the same time recognizing the importance of maintaining an adequate ingestion of high-quality protein in the elderly to compensate for age-related sarcopenia.

1.3.3 Alternative Protein Sources and Sustainability

Animal-based proteins are likely to remain a significant source of protein for both the developed and developing worlds throughout the 21st century. The challenges of climate change and the health-related risks associated with the consumption of certain types of animal proteins will certainly affect the types of animal proteins that will be consumed in the future. One of the largest growing food sectors at present is the 'Beyond Meat' plant-based meat substitute market, which has seen rapid growth and significant public and private investment in recent years. In fact, there are far more consumers interested in this type of plant-based substitution of animal proteins than there are in switching to any of the vegetarian type diets, including veganism. The alternative protein market, including insect proteins, algae, duckweed, laboratory-grown meats, mycoproteins and plant proteins, is expected to reach US $17.9 billion by 2025, with a compound annual growth rate in value (CAGR) of 9.5%, while in terms of volume, the market is expected to grow at a CAGR of 5.2% by 2025 (Meticulous Research®). This rate of growth is the result of growing urbanization, increased venture capital investments in alternative protein companies, food technology innovation and efforts towards the environmental sustainability of food production.

Among the impediments that remain to be solved are the high cost of some alternative sources of protein, especially those that require further processing (e.g., plant-based 'meats' such as 'The Impossible Burger') or have high developmental costs (e.g., laboratory-grown meats), as well as a general preference worldwide for animal-based protein products. This latter factor is spurred by cultural considerations, where meat consumption is often equated with higher social status, and by persistent and effective lobbying by vested interests within the various animal protein sectors. The long-term sustainability of animal proteins is debatable and depends upon the type of protein that is to be produced, with ruminant-derived proteins imposing the most stress on environmental resources while fish and poultry protein production demands the least, based on feeding requirements and their respective 'carbon footprints'.

1.3.4 Food Choice Changes

Despite numerous advisories from health authorities worldwide for consumers to decrease their consumption of animal proteins and increase the plant-based portion of their diets, including plant proteins, relatively few people choose a vegan or vegetarian lifestyle when they have the option to do so. The reasons for this are manifold and include cultural, historical, organoleptic and nutritional considerations. It's doubtful that animal proteins, including meat, will disappear from the human diet in the foreseeable future, so the reality is that alternative proteins will serve to add to the expanding requirement for protein *per se* as the world population expands through the 21st century and as the developing nations continue to fill the void of their heretofore protein-deficient diets. Likely, for health and environmental considerations, animal proteins will continue to diminish as a percentage of the total proteins consumed, necessitating diligence on the part of alternative protein producers to generate innovative and healthy products over the next 80 years.

1.4 THE CHALLENGES OF NOVEL PROTEINS

It is not foreseeable that a major shift in human diet to plant-based only and adoption of other alternative protein sources will occur in the near future due to several challenges (technical, consumers, financial, environmental and legal issues) that need to be solved before wide industrial uptake. All the novel proteins share common challenges regarding health and safety as well as regulatory issues that may slow their introduction and acceptability by consumers, including unique dogma surrounding them (Yuck factor, religious restrictions or production cost limitation) (La Barbera et al., 2018; Jensen & Lieberoth, 2019). The following section will focus only on challenges for protein coming from two novel sources, i.e., *in vitro* meat and edible insects. Some of the challenges and limitations of other proteins will be available in their respective chapters. In general, some of the challenges faced by all novel protein sources are listed in Table 1.3.

1.4.1 CHALLENGES WITH *IN VITRO* MEATS AS A PROTEIN SOURCE

Despite the great exposure that lab-grown meat has enjoyed during the last 8 years, the technology is still in its infancy. The technology, as discussed in Chapter 9, aims to allow stem cells to proliferate and form a network of myotubes that can be grown on a construct to generate muscle

TABLE 1.3
Major challenges faced by novel proteins

Challenge	Description
Consumer acceptance	It is not clear whether the growth in the plant-based protein sector is a fad or a long-term trend.
	Consumer acceptance may vary for different types of novel proteins.
Cost competitiveness	Alternative proteins are generally more expensive than are their traditional counterparts.
	Costs of some novel proteins may come down in the coming years.
Ingredient supply	New protein sources may face the problem of limited ingredient supply.
	Short supply of ingredients could inhibit growth in the industry.
Distribution	Competing with traditional protein product in distribution channels could be a challenge for novel protein products.
	Visibility of alternative protein options in the store and online shopping is not consistent, and unavailability could be a hurdle to their growth.
Regulatory challenges	Uncertainty around the regulatory framework of many novel proteins and new technologies.
	Labeling is a major challenge as to whether plant-based alternatives can use the words 'meat' or 'milk' on their labels.
Financing	Supply chain is an issue, as there are many companies competing for resources and funding to develop novel protein products.
Transition	Introducing plant-based and other novel protein sources to consumers and the market supply chain is a challenging process.

tissue (Bhat et al., 2014). So far, cultured meat prototypes produced by laboratories and start-up companies are produced in the form of loose cells or tissues that are suitable for processed/ground meat products such as sausages, patties and nuggets (Bhat et al., 2017). This is an important technical limitation since this type of meat product is normally considered to be of low value within conventional meat production systems, where tender intact meat cuts (such as those obtained from fillet and loins) are considered the most valuable (Bekhit et al., 2014), and a change in this perception will require some time to occur. Further, a trade-off occurs between the sensory value of intact meat and perceived humanistic quality of the product. A possible solution to this technical hurdle is to use a 3D structure (either edible constructs made from collagen or keratin as suggested in Chapter 7 or the use of 3D printing technology). These latter technologies are attractive options to produce intact cultured meat and can provide variety and products with complex designs. However, these methods lack a functional circulatory system to deliver oxygen and nutrients to the cells and to eliminate the metabolic waste products, which are major technical hurdles for developing muscle meat at a commercial scale.

During cell culture, the stem cells can proliferate, grow and differentiate on scaffolds under optimal growth conditions that require a continuous supply of specific stimuli to encourage the formation of myofibers and the formation of skeletal muscle that expands within a self-organizing construct. It is unlikely that the static cultural conditions to produce muscle structure resemble meat obtained from conventional farming systems (marbled or have different graining that has important sensory aspects) due to the diffusional limitations of the process. Different meat cuts have different sensory properties and even the connective tissues that are naturally produced in different meat cuts can contribute to different cooking and eating aspects that give conventional meat some variability and utility aspects that are important to certain cultures (e.g., in many Middle Eastern and African countries, meat with a bit of 'a bite' is preferred rather than very tender meat). This will not be easily replicated under *in vitro* conditions. Further, meat produced by current *in vitro* methods lacks other elements such as nerves, blood and adipose tissue and do not possess some of the sensory attributes that are developed during conversion of muscle to meat and are normal parts of the sensory characteristics of the meat.

In terms of production finances, culturing meat is a very expensive process. The growth of cells under extremely hygienic and controlled conditions that is done manually is not only laborious and expensive, but also increases safety risks and the chances of contamination. Thankfully, fully automated systems already exist in tissue engineering facilities for medical purposes where all these steps are done under a sterile and closed environment (Post & Hocquette, 2017). Still, the need to have specialized growth medium with expensive nutrients is a significant challenge for commercial large-scale operations. The treatment of the growth media is not widely discussed. There is no information available about the cost associated with sterilization, recycling or waste management of the tissue culture waste. There are several financial and ethical challenges associated with primary stem cells used for culturing to produce *in vitro* meats.

Other challenges associated with cultured meat are the sourcing of the initial cells, obtaining culture media and the composition of scaffolds. The cell lines raise several concerns, such as subculturing, passaging, misidentification and continuous evolution (Stephens et al., 2018) and the source of the cell line. Some ethical (animal, bird or human) and religious (from clean or unclean animals, according to various faiths as discussed in Chapter 8) could have a great impact on the source of the cells as well as the culture media (use of foetal calf serum or horse serum in the media) (Chiron et al., 2012; Burattini et al., 2004). Further, there are no standards for cultured meat, and this is an important prerequisite for commercialization.

In terms of nutrition, *in vitro* meat has been presented as the solution for future protein needs, but very little is known about its nutritional quality. While it is generally expected that the protein content and possible profile will be very similar to the parent stem cells, meat is not only protein. Meat has always been considered a good source of minerals, including iron and zinc, and vitamins such as the vitamin B complex group. Currently, there is no information about the content of these nutrients in cultured meat. It is expected that cell culture could be 'engineered' to modify the accumulation of nutrients and to tolerate fortification with supplements that cannot be maintained under conventional conditions. Further, potential addition of such nutrients is always a possibility under product formulation guidelines.

A positive advantage that has been highly publicized for cultured meat production is its low environmental impact compared to conventional meat production systems. Recent research (Lynch & Pierrehumbert, 2019) examined the production of carbon dioxide (CO_2), methane (CH_4) and nitrous oxide (N_2O) in a climate model that compared the temperature impact of cattle farming (three beef production systems) and cultured meat production over the next 1000 years. The authors found that the accumulative effects of CO_2 that are associated with cultured meat were more harmful than the non-accumulating CH_4 that will be associated with beef cattle farming. The authors concluded that 'cultured meat is not *prima facie* climatically superior to cattle' and thus challenge some of the perceived environmental positive benefits associated with this technology.

It appears that among all the potential novel sources of protein, *in vitro* meat is the least well-accepted. A survey conducted in the USA to explore consumer acceptability of conventional beef burgers compared to burgers from novel proteins (*in vitro*, pea protein and plant-based with animal-like protein) reported that the *in vitro* meat burger was the least-preferred choice at 5% and farm-raised beef was the most preferred at 72% (Van Loo et al., 2020). The authors characterized potential consumers that accepted the plant-based and *in vitro* meat products as '*vegetarians, male, younger, and more highly educated individuals*'. It was interesting that when the brands of the products were made available to the consumers (Certified Angus Beef, Beyond Meat, Impossible Foods and Memphis Meats), the preference towards the farmed beef burger was increased to 80%, which suggests that meat consumption is not going to be off the menu soon.

1.4.2 Challenges with Edible Insects as a Protein Source

While insect eating has a long history in the human diet and the use of insects as food is still practiced in many nations, consumer acceptance in Western and many Middle Eastern countries is a major challenge due to unfamiliarity with the concept of entomophagy and religious restrictions. Several reports document a lack of acceptability of insects as food (Jensen & Lieberoth, 2019; La Barbera et al., 2018; Verbeke, 2015). The main reasons for the rejection of insects were disgust – the 'Yuck factor' – and food neophobia. Young consumers appear to be more adventurous compared to older consumers (Verbeke, 2015), and some regional differences in acceptability do exist with the EU (Piha et al., 2018), the Indian continent (Chakravorty et al., 2016), and world regions (e.g., entomophagy has been practiced in more African, Asian and South American countries compared to European and North American countries) (van Huis, 2013; van Huis & Oonincx, 2017). Transformation of insects into flours and formulated products will eliminate their aesthetic properties (shape, appearance, colour and so on), and promotion of insects as an alternative source of protein may reduce food neophobia and improve acceptability (La Barbera et al., 2018). In particular, there are strong religious oppositions towards entomophagy in Islam and Judaism. In Islam, only locust is regarded *halal* (permissible) according to the majority of scholars. In Sunan Ibn Majah (Book 29, Hadith 64), it has been reported that '*Abdullah bin Umar narrated that the Messenger of Allah (ﷺ) said: "Two kinds of dead meat and two kinds of blood have been permitted to us. The two kinds of dead meat are fish and locusts, and the two kinds of blood are the liver and spleen*', declaring the halal status of locust only. The consumption of wildly harvested locust is commonly practiced in the Arabian peninsula. With recent advancement and knowledge of potential health benefits of some insects that have no clear prohibition in the Holy Quran and Hadith, the authoritative Dar Al-Ifta Al-Missriyyah (Official Egyptian Fatwa committee that provides religious opinions on matters according to Islamic sharia) provided the following opinion: '*the matter is contingent upon scientific, medical, and pharmaceutical studies which prove either the benefit or harm of these insects. It is permissible to use the insects and consume the substances* manufactured from them for medicinal reasons if it is proven that they treat diseases or malnutrition without producing any harmful side effects. Otherwise, they are forbidden' (https://www.dar-alifta.org/Foreign/ViewFatwa.aspx?ID=6872). This opinion may open more uptake of insect products if health benefit (treatment of allergy or bites by poisonous insects) or avoidance of harm (e.g., famine or malnutrition).

In Judaism, the most explicit declaration regarding the kosher status of insects and the type of insects permissible are given in The Holy Torah in Leviticus 11:20-23: '[20]*All flying insects that creep on all fours shall be an abomination to you.*[21]*Yet these you may eat of every flying insect that creeps on all fours: those which have jointed legs above their feet with which to leap on the earth.* [22]*These you may eat: the locust after its kind, the destroying locust after its kind, the cricket after its kind, and the grasshopper after its kind.* [23]*But all other flying insects which have four feet shall be an abomination to you*'; Leviticus 11:42-43: '[42]*Whatever crawls on its belly, whatever goes on all fours, or whatever has many feet among all creeping things that creep on the earth—these you shall not eat, for they are an abomination.* [43]*You shall not make [a] yourselves [b] abominable with any creeping thing that creeps; nor shall you make yourselves unclean with them, lest you be defiled by them*', New King James Version. Only certain kinds of locust, cricket and grasshopper could be acceptable, but it will require kosher certification.

The main challenge towards the use of insects as ingredients is the lack of information on processing conditions and the variability in their nutritional composition. Much of the information produced regarding protein composition and quality are done under experimental conditions and laboratory settings, and very little is known concerning commercial insect flour/products (Gravel & Doyen, 2020). For insects to be a competitive source of protein, it will require knowledge of protein functionality compared to other conventional protein sources as well as their cost-effectiveness and health and safety profiles. However, there are several environmental factors that could be considered in addition to indirect cost (positive for insects compared to conventional animal farming), such as space requirements, low energy (no heating as they are cold-blooded), feed and water requirements and no cost associated with veterinary care, pesticides and slaughter. The safety of insect products may be the most important issue, several pathogenic bacteria were isolated from bread containing cricket flour. (Gahukar, 2020; Osimani et al., 2018), antinutrients such as phytic acid and tannins (Chakravorty et al., 2016; de Castro et al., 2018) and the presence of allergens (Broekman et al., 2016; 2017; Guiné et al., 2021; Ribeiro et al., 2018), and this will require further investigation concerning possible processing options to ensure insect product safety. Given the already established use of insects for food in many parts of the world, the competition presented by insect predators and parasites, the negative impact of climate change and the lack of legal control over the harvesting of insects, the abundance and diversity of global populations of edible insects in nature has been found to be in decline (Gahukar, 2020; Ledford, 2019). Gahukar (2020) cited several cases as evidence of this phenomenon (such as the black ant *Carebara vidua* in Kenya, termites and ants in the Lake Victoria and declining numbers of edible insects in several localities). Insect farming is likely to provide better control over the safety and productivity of edible insects and reduce the risk associated with the wild collection of insects. This also will contribute to the livelihood and source of income in many localities.

1.5 KEY ASPECTS OF NOVEL PROTEIN SOURCES

Novel proteins are predicted to deliver a wide range of economic, environmental and ethical benefits in support of the world's future protein requirements (Figure 1.2). Some of the technologies that are used to produce novel proteins offer several advantages, such as higher productivity compared with traditional animal protein sources, lower water requirements and diminished GHG production (Cappelli et al., 2020b). Despite the high hopes that have been placed on various potential sources of protein (e.g., *in vitro* meat, algae, plant, microbial, insects and other alternative protein sources), there are key aspects that need to be considered in evaluating their potential to

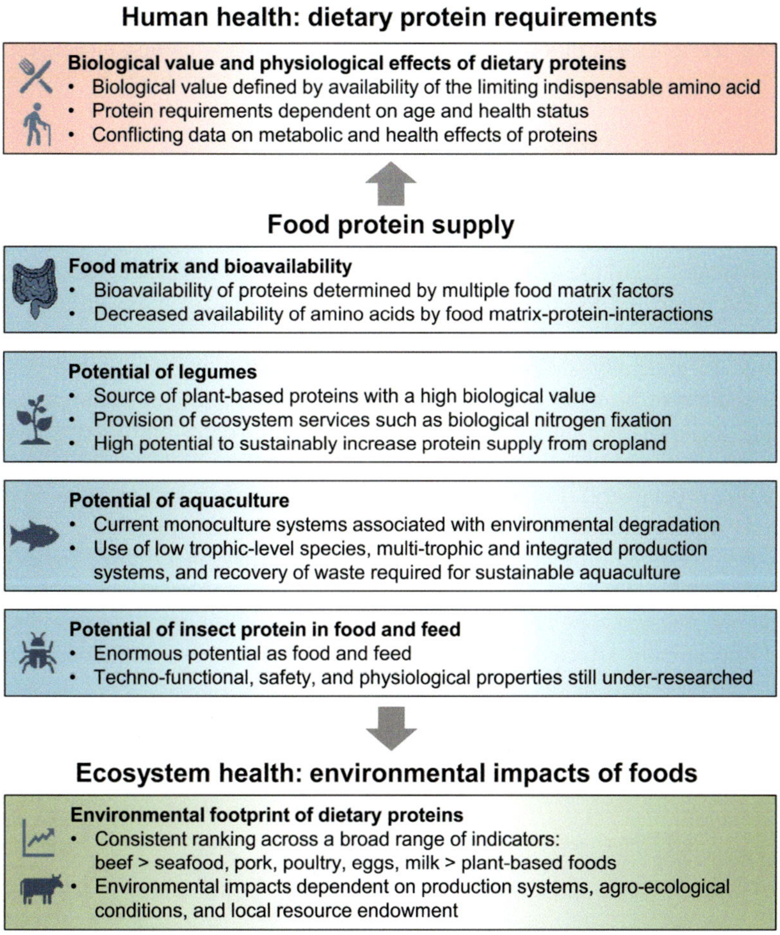

Novel Protein Sources and Food Security 11

Human health: dietary protein requirements

Biological value and physiological effects of dietary proteins
- Biological value defined by availability of the limiting indispensable amino acid
- Protein requirements dependent on age and health status
- Conflicting data on metabolic and health effects of proteins

Food protein supply

Food matrix and bioavailability
- Bioavailability of proteins determined by multiple food matrix factors
- Decreased availability of amino acids by food matrix-protein-interactions

Potential of legumes
- Source of plant-based proteins with a high biological value
- Provision of ecosystem services such as biological nitrogen fixation
- High potential to sustainably increase protein supply from cropland

Potential of aquaculture
- Current monoculture systems associated with environmental degradation
- Use of low trophic-level species, multi-trophic and integrated production systems, and recovery of waste required for sustainable aquaculture

Potential of insect protein in food and feed
- Enormous potential as food and feed
- Techno-functional, safety, and physiological properties still under-researched

Ecosystem health: environmental impacts of foods

Environmental footprint of dietary proteins
- Consistent ranking across a broad range of indicators:
  beef > seafood, pork, poultry, eggs, milk > plant-based foods
- Environmental impacts dependent on production systems, agro-ecological conditions, and local resource endowment

FIGURE 1.2 A schematic presentation for 'The Leibniz Position' on the potential of novel proteins for human and ecosystem health. The image is from Weindl et al. (2020). The image is from an open-access article distributed under the terms of the Creative Commons CC-BY license, which permits unrestricted use, distribution and reproduction in any medium, provided the original work is properly cited.

meet future needs (Burlingame & Dernini, 2010). As it was highlighted more than a decade ago by these authors, future sustainable food sources should be healthy, safe, affordable, accessible and culturally acceptable to people and have a low impact on the environment.

Therefore, the food safety, nutritional and health aspects of the novel proteins need to be established and need to be on par with current conventional sources. Financial constraints and cost associated with production are also extremely important to establish markets and evaluate the competitiveness and affordability of these new proteins. Further, the environmental impact of production systems is crucial to obtain consumer acceptance and to insure the sustainability of these novel proteins.

1.5.1 Food Safety Aspects

Some novel proteins, such as insect and plant proteins, have a long history of consumption, but this does not mean that they are safe (Cappelli, 2020a). The historical consumption of specific insects and plants for food in certain cultures may result in some sort of adaptability that other communities lack, which could expose new consumers to risk. Having systems in place to monitor, reduce and verify an absence of tolerance threshold of allergens, microbial and environmental contaminants is a must to ensure the safety of novel proteins. The use of processing techniques (thermal or non-thermal) will modify the protein structure, bioavailability and digestibility of the proteins, all which are important to their sensory and nutritional qualities.

1.5.2 Health and Nutritional Aspects

The quantity and quality of the protein are the most important characteristics of the novel proteins that are being considered to fill the gap that will emerge in the high-quality protein demand that is expected in the future. Thus, the quality and nutritional aspects of novel sources of proteins need to be evaluated and compared to current conventional sources to gain more insights into their nutritional competitiveness, and to determine the need for any fortifications to meet standard diets. Protein quality is generally determined by the availability of indispensable amino acids. Conventional sources of protein, such as egg, dairy and animal proteins are high quality, as they have digestible indispensable amino acid scores and protein digestibility-corrected amino acid scores of 1.0 and >1.0, respectively, whereas plant materials have wide ranges (from 0.01 to 0.90 and 0.08 to 0.98, respectively). Proper protein intake is very important, as protein deficiency and excessive intake can both lead to disorders (Weindl et al., 2020). Figure 1.3 presents a health impact assessment of three protein sources (animal-based meats, plant-based meats and cultured meats) developed by Ferreira et al. (2020). Novel proteins contain various amino acid profiles that depend on the raw material they come from and processing conditions. For example, their amino acids can be dramatically affected by the method of solubilization (oxidation, reduction, enzymatic, acid hydrolysis, etc.), as discussed in Chapter 7.

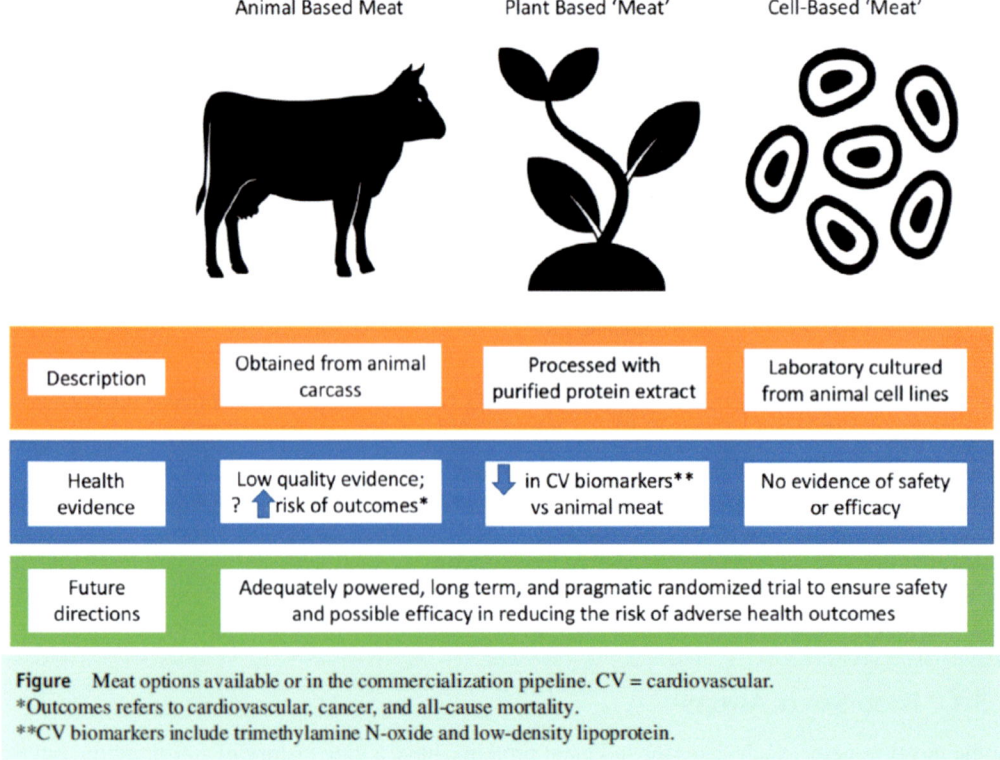

FIGURE 1.3 The future of meat: health impact assessment with randomized evidence. The figure is from Ferreira et al. (2020) published in *The American Journal of Medicine* (https://doi.org/10.1016/j.amjmed.2020.11.007) and is reproduced by kind permission from Elsevier, License Number 5021550933907.

Generally, keratin is very rich in cysteine and has high contents of glycine, proline, serine and various acidic amino acids, such as glutamic acid but has low contents of methionine, histidine and lysine and an undetectable tryptophan content. Keratin extracted using high heat and alkaline treatments can result in the formation of lanthionine, which has a great impact on health and possible toxic side effects. Plant proteins may be deficient in one or more indispensable amino acids, but supplementation with these amino acids can bring the protein quality to that of animal protein. The functional and physiological aspects of insect proteins are scarce (Weindl et al., 2020), probably due to the large number of edible insects that vary widely in their composition and protein structures. The authors of this chapter acknowledge that the use of amino acid composition and even the bioavailability of indispensable amino acid content alone is probably not the right way to determine the nutritional effects of the novel proteins, as in many cases the proteins and/or the food source used as a source of protein contains nutritional (e.g., minerals and vitamins) or antinutrients (e.g., lectins, tannins and phytates) that contribute to the overall healthiness of the food. The amounts of the antinutrients in edible insects can vary widely with phytic acid content in the range of 15.5 mg/100 g in *Macrotermes subhyalinus* to 2482.1 mg/100 g in worker termites, and a similar trend was also reported for plant materials (de Castro et al., 2018).

Recent studies demonstrated that chronic dietary red meat intake increased systemic trimethylamine N-oxide (TMAO) levels (suspected to increase the risk of cardiovascular diseases and several non-communicable degenerative diseases) whereas plant-based diet has much lower levels of TMAO. (Koeth et al., 2019; Mente et al., 2015; Wang et al., 2019). The authors suggested the mechanisms associated with this trend to be: (i) enhanced intake of dietary precursors; (ii) increased microbial TMA/TMAO production from carnitine, but not choline; and (iii) reduced renal TMAO excretion. The authors also found that discontinuation of dietary red meat reduces plasma TMAO within 4 weeks. This highlights the impact of red meat on *in vivo* TMAO production. This research also demonstrated an increased conversion of carnitine to TMAO and that the rate of its production was much higher in omnivore diets as compared to Vegan diets. The rate of TMAO production in Omnivore diet subjects was >20 times that found in Vegan diet subjects. Again, this highlights the importance of meat and its content of carnitine in the production of TMAO. However, plant-based meat substitutes in Table 1.4 are generally high in salt, but they do not contain cholesterol. This could have interesting effects on CVD, but this has not been reported as yet.

1.5.3 Technological Aspects

Alternative proteins (either from edible insects, marine sources, keratin, plant, *in vitro* meat, etc.) are unlikely to be consumed as is and instead will be incorporated in meals or products (e.g. smoothies, protein shake, protein bars, etc.). The obtained protein from these sources needs to have several technological properties (water holding capacity, oil holding capacity, emulsification capacity, rheological properties, etc.) to achieve desirable sensory properties in the final product. Novel proteins could provide an advantage in certain applications. For example, Cappelli et al. (2020a) investigated the rheological properties and the characteristics of dough and bread supplemented with mealworm flour (*Tenebrio molitor*), cricket (*Acheta domesticus*) and chickpea (*Cicer arietinum*) flours at 5%, 10% and 15% substitution levels and compared the products with a control flour (100% wheat). The authors reported that cricket flour at 15% substitution level increased the stability of dough and reduced the degree of softening. The best outcome in terms of dough stability and bread volume was obtained with chickpea flour at a 5% substitution level. The authors concluded that these proteins were useful in improving the nutritional and functional characteristics of the bread.

TABLE 1.4
Nutritional information for burgers from animal and plant-based materials

Characteristics	Beyond Burger	Impossible Burger	Grass-Fed Beef Burger
Serving size	1/4 pound (113 g)	1/4 pound (113 g)	1/4 pound (113 g)
Calories	250	240	240
Total fat (g)	18	14	14
Saturated fat (g)	6	8	6
Cholesterol (mg)	0	0	70
Sodium (mg)	300	370	77
Carbohydrate (g)	3	9	0
Fiber (g)	2	3	0
Protein (g)	20	19	22
Iron	0	4.2	2.7

The table is from Ferreira et al. (2020). The data is reproduced by kind permission from Elsevier, License Number 5021550933907.

1.5.4 Environmental and Ethical Aspects

Modern agricultural systems are characterized by their intensive practices, high inputs (energy, water, nutrients and chemical fertilizers) and the climate changes that have resulted as well as deforestation and competition for land use, all which have had a substantial negative impact on the environment (GHG emissions and pollution, loss of biodiversity, acidification and eutrophication) (Campbell et al., 2017). Red meat production systems (especially beef) have the highest GHG emission intensities, whereas plant-based products have the lowest impact (Clune et al., 2017; Weindl et al., 2020). Current life cycle assessment (LCA) for sheep meat production systems and an evaluation of their environmental footprint may be improved if keratin production as a potential new protein is considered.

1.6 CONCLUSION

The increased demand for new protein sources is primarily driven by the growing global population, socio-economic changes, food consumption patterns, an aging population and a protein shortage. Consumers are increasingly becoming interested in eating more protein from a greater variety of sources. This change in the pattern of protein consumption is seen among consumers of all ages. The health and nutritional aspects of alternative or plant-based proteins are most apparent in younger consumers. Moreover, the sustainability of food is important to many consumers and is likely to play a key role in driving protein demand in the future. Some of the challenges faced include improving taste profiles, consumer acceptability and the cost-effectiveness of novel protein products. Despite current challenges to develop new protein sources, they do fit very well in the overall global campaign to enhance food security and sustainability.

ACKNOWLEDGEMENT AND DECLARATION

The authors declare no conflict of interest. Hussain contributed sections 1.1 and 1.2, Riley contributed section 1.3, and Bekhit contributed sections 1.4 and 1.5. The views and opinions expressed in this chapter are those of the authors and do not reflect the position of the Victorian Department of Health.

REFERENCES

Bar-On, Y. M., Phillips, R., & Milo, R. (2018). The biomass distribution on Earth. *Proceedings of the National Academy of Sciences*, *115*, 6506–6511. doi:10.1073/pnas.1711842115

Bekhit, A. E. D., Carne, A., Ha, M., & Franks, P. (2014). Physical interventions to manipulate texture and tenderness of fresh meat: A review. *International Journal of Food Properties*, *17*, 433–453.

Bhat, Z. F., Bhat, H., & Pathak, V. (2014). Prospects for in vitro cultured meat – a future harvest. In: *Principles of Tissue Engineering*, 4th edition. Lanza, R., Langer, R., & Vacanti, J. (Eds). Boston, MA: Academic Press, 1663–1683.

Bhat, Z. F., Kumar, S. & Bhat, H. (2017). *In-vitro* meat: A future animal-free harvest. *Critical Reviews in Food Science and Nutrition*, *57*(04), 782–789.

Broad, G. 2019. Plant-based and cell-based animal products alternatives: An assessment and agenda for food tech justice. *Geoforum*, *107*, 223–226.

Broekman, H., Knulst, A. C., de Jong, G., Gaspari, M., den Hartog Jager, C. F., Houben, G. F., & Verhoeckx, K. C. M. (2017). Is mealworm or shrimp allergy indicative for food allergy to insects? *Molecular Nutrition & Food Research*, *61*(9). doi: 10.1002/mnfr.201601061. Epub 2017 Jul 18. PMID: 28500661.

Broekman, H., Verhoeckx, K. C., den Hartog Jager, C. F., Kruizinga, A. G., Pronk-Kleinjan, M., Remington, B. C., & Knulst, A. C. (2016). Majority of shrimp-allergic patients are allergic to mealworm. *The Journal of Allergy and Clinical Immunology*, *137*(4), 1261–1263.

Burattini, S., Ferri, P., Battistelli, M., Curci, R., Luchetti, F., & Falcieri E. (2004). C2C12 murine myoblasts as a model of skeletal muscle development: Morpho-functional characterization. *European Journal of Histochemistry*, *48*, 223–233.

Burlingame, B., & Dernini, S. (2010). Sustainable diets and biodiversity. *Proceedings of the International Scientific Symposium Biodiversity and Sustainable Diets United Against Hunger*, 3–5 November 2010, FAO Headquarters, Rome.

Campbell, B. M., Beare, D. J., Bennett, E. M., Hall-Spencer, J. M., Ingram, J. S. I., Jaramillo, F., Ortiz, R., Ramankutty, N., Sayer, J. A., & Shindell, D. (2017). Agriculture production as a major driver of the Earth system exceeding planetary boundaries. *Ecology and Society*, *22*(4). doi:10.5751/ES-09595-220408.

Cappelli, A., Cini, E., Lorini, C., Oliva, N., & Bonaccorsi, G. (2020a). Insects as food: A review on risks assessments of Tenebrionidae and Gryllidae in relation to a first machines and plants development. *Food Control*, *108*, 106877.

Cappelli, A., Oliva, N., Bonaccorsi, G., Lorini, C., & Cini, E. (2020b). Assessment of the rheological properties and bread characteristics obtained by innovative protein sources (*Cicer arietinum*, *Acheta domesticus*, *Tenebrio molitor*): Novel food or potential improvers for wheat flour? *LWT - Food Science and Technology*, *118*, 108867.

Ceballos, G., Ehrlich, P. R., & Raven, P. H. (2020). Vertebrates on the brink as indicators of biological annihilation and the sixth mass extinction. *Proceedings of the National Academy of Sciences*, *117*, 13596–13602. doi:10.1073/pnas.1922686117.

Chakravorty, J., Ghosh, S., Megu, K., Jung, C., & Meyer-Rochow, B. V. (2016). Nutritional and anti-nutritional composition of *Oecophylla smaragdina* (Hymenoptera: Formicidae) and Odontotermes sp. (Isoptera: Termitidae): Two preferred edible insects of Arunachal Pradesh, India. *Journal of Asia-Pacific Entomology*, *19*, 711–720.

Chiron, S., Tomczak, C., Duperray, A., Lainé, J., Bonne, G., Eder, A., Hansen, A., Eschenhagen, T., Verdier, C., & Coirault. C. (2012). Complex interactions between human myoblasts and the surrounding 3D fibrin-based matrix. *PLoS One*, *7*, e36173.

Clune, S., Verghese, K., & Crossin, E. (2017). Systematic review of greenhouse gas emissions for different fresh food categories. *Journal of Clean Production*, *140*, 766–783. doi:10.1016/j.jclepro.2016.04.082

de Castro, R. J. S., Ohara, A., & Aguilar, J. G. S. (2018). Nutritional, functional and biological properties of insect proteins: Processes for obtaining, consumption and future challenges. *Trends in Food Science & Technology*, *76*, 82–89.

Ferreira, J. P., Sharma, A., & Zannad, F. (2020). The future of meat: Health impact assessment with randomized evidence. *The American Journal of Medicine*. doi:10.1016/j.amjmed.2020.11.007.

Gahukar, R. T. (2020). Edible insects collected from forests for family livelihood and wellness of rural communities: A review. *Glob Food Security*, *25*, 100348. doi:10.1016/j.gfs.2020.100348.

Gravel, A., & Doyen, A. (2020). The use of edible insect proteins in food: Challenges and issues related to their functional properties. *Innovative Food Science and Emerging Technologies*, *59*, 102272.

Guiné, R. P. F., Correia, P., Coelho, C., & Costa, C. A. (2021). The role of edible insects to mitigate challenges for sustainability. *Open Agriculture*, 6(1), 24–36. doi:10.1515/opag-2020-0206.

Jensen, N. H., & Lieberoth, A. (2019). We will eat disgusting foods together – Evidence of the normative basis of Western entomophagy-disgust from an insect tasting. *Food Quality and Preference*, 72, 109–115.

Koeth, R. A., Lam-Galvez, B. R., Kirsop, J., Wang, Z., Levison, B. S., Gu, X., Copeland, M. F., Bartlett, D., Cody, D. B., Dai, H. J., Culley, M. K., Li, X. S., Fu, X., Wu, Y., Li, L., DiDonato, J. A., Tang, W. H. W., Garcia-Garcia, J. C., & Hazen, S. L. (2019). L-Carnitine in omnivorous diets induces an atherogenic gut microbial pathway in humans. *Journal of Clinical Investigations*, 129(1), 373–387. doi:10.1172/JCI94601.

La Barbera, F., Verneau, F., Amato, M., & Grunert, K. (2018). Understanding Westerners' disgust for the eating of insects: The role of food neophobia and implicit associations. *Food Quality and Preference*, 64, 120–125.

Ledford, H. (2019). World's largest plant survey reveals alarming extinction rate. *Nature*, 570, 148–149. doi: 10.1038/d41586-019-01810.6

Lynch, J., & Pierrehumbert, R. (2019). Climate impacts of cultured meat and beef cattle. *Frontiers in Sustainable Food Systems*, 3. doi:10.3389/fsufs.2019.00005.

McGregor, A. (2021). Just food transitions? Maximising the social benefits of alternative proteins. *Food Australia*, 73, 32–34.

Mente, A., Chalcraft, K., Handan, A., Davis, D., Lonn, E., Miller, R., Potter, M. A., Yusuf, S., Anand, S. S., & McQueen, M. J. (2015). The relationship between trimethylamine-N-oxide and prevalent cardiovascular disease in a multiethnic population living in Canada. *Canadian Journal of Cardiology*, 31, 1189–1194.

Osimani, A., Milanović, V., Cardinali, F., Roncolini, A., Garofalo, C., Clementi, F., ….. & Aquilanti, L. (2018). Bread enriched with cricket powder (*Acheta domesticus*): A technological, microbiological and nutritional evaluation. *Innovative Food Science & Emerging Technologies*, 48, 150–163.

Piha, S., Pohjanheimo, T., Lahteenmaki-Uutela, A., Kreckova, Z., & Otterbring, T. (2018). The effects of consumer knowledge on the willingness to buy insect food: An exploratory cross-regional study in Northern and Central Europe. *Food Quality and Preference*, 70, 1–10. doi:10.1016/j.foodqual.2016.12.006.

Pihlanto, A., Mattila, P., Mäkinen, S., & Pajari, A. M. (2017). Bioactivities of alternative protein sources and their potential health benefits. *Food Functions*, 18, 3443–3458. doi:10.1039/c7fo00302a. PMID: 28804797.

Post, M. J., & Hocquette, J. F. (2017). New sources of animal proteins: Cultured meat. In: *New Aspects of Meat Quality: From Genes to Ethics*. Purslow, P. (Ed.). Woodhead Publishing, Sawston, UK.

Ribeiro, J. C., Cunha, L. M., Sousa-Pinto, B., & Fonseca, J. (2018). Allergic risks of consuming edible insects: A systematic review. *Molecular Nutrition & Food Research*, 62, 1700030.

Smith, A., & Raven, R. (2012). What is protective space? Reconsidering niches in transitions to sustainability. *Research Policy*, 41, 1025–1036.

Stephens, N., Silvio, L. D., Dunsford, I., Ellis, M., Glencross, A., & Sexton, A. (2018). Bringing cultured meat to market: Technical, socio-political, and regulatory challenges in cellular agriculture. *Trends in Food Science and Technology*, 78, 155–166.

van Huis, A. (2013). Potential of insects as food and feed in assuring food security. *Annual Review of Entomology*, 58, 563–583.

van Huis, A., & Oonincx, D. G. A. B. (2017). The environmental sustainability of insects as food and feed. A review. *Agronomy for Sustainable Development*, 37, 43.

Van Loo, E. J., Caputo, V., & Lusk., J. L. (2020). Consumer preferences for farm-raised meat, lab-grown meat, and plant-based meat alternatives: Does information or brand matter? *Food Policy*, 95(2020), 101931.

Verbeke, W. (2015). Profiling consumers who are ready to adopt insects as a meat substitute in a Western society. *Food Quality and Preference*, 39, 147–155.

Wang, Z., Bergeron, N., Levison, B. S., Li, X. S., Chiu, S., Jia, X., Koeth, R. A., Li, L., Wu, Y., Tang, W. H. W., Krauss, R. M., & Hazen, S. L. (2019). Impact of chronic dietary red meat, white meat, or non-meat protein on trimethylamine N-oxide metabolism and renal excretion in healthy men and women. *European Heart Journal*, 40(7), 583–594. doi:10.1093/eurheartj/ehy799.

Weindl, I., Ost, M., Wiedmer, P., Schreiner, M., Neugart, S., Klopsch, R., Kühnhold, H., Kloas, W., Henkel, I. M., Schlüter, O., Bußler, S., Bellingrath-Kimura, S. D., Ma, H., Grune, T., Rolinski, S., & Klaus, S. (2020). Sustainable food protein supply reconciling human and ecosystem health: A Leibniz Position. *Global Food Security*, 25, 100367.

2 Plant Proteins

William W. Riley
International School, Jinan University, Guangzhou, China

CONTENTS

2.1 Introduction 18
    2.1.1 Development of Hunting Skill and Physiological Adaptation to Dietary Changes 19
    2.1.2 Animal Protein Versus Plant Protein Consumption in the Future 19
2.2 Animal Protein and Plant Protein-Based Diets 19
    2.2.1 Adequacy of Vegetarian Diets 19
    2.2.2 Complementary Plant Proteins to Meet Essential Amino Acids Requirements 20
    2.2.3 A Healthy Rationale for Plant-Based Proteins 20
    2.2.4 Dietary Habits of Related Species 20
        2.2.4.1 Differences in Protein Intake and GI Anatomy between Humans and Other Primates 21
        2.2.4.2 Comparative Diet of Domestic and Feral Pigs to Humans, Given Comparable GI Tracts 21
        2.2.4.3 Commercial Swine Feeding as Evidence of the Efficacy of Plant-Based Proteins 21
2.3 Protein Quality 22
    2.3.1 The Protein Efficiency Ratio 22
    2.3.2 The Protein Digestibility-Corrected Amino Acid Score 22
    2.3.3 Application of the PDCAAS 23
2.4 Legumes (Soybeans and Pulse Crops: Peas, Chickpeas, Common Beans and Faba Beans, Lentils) 23
    2.4.1 World Legume Production 24
    2.4.2 Soybeans 24
        2.4.2.1 Purported Health Benefits of Soy Protein Consumption 25
        2.4.2.2 Amino Acid Composition of Soy Protein 25
        2.4.2.3 Digestibility of Soy Protein 26
    2.4.3 Peas 26
        2.4.3.1 Protein and Amino Acid Composition of Peas 26
        2.4.3.2 Pea Flours, Concentrates and Isolates 27
        2.4.3.3 Pea Protein Digestibility 27
    2.4.4 Chickpeas 27
        2.4.4.1 Culinary Uses of Chickpeas and the Effect of Cooking on Nutrient Availability 28
        2.4.4.2 Protein and Amino Acid Composition of Chickpeas 28
        2.4.4.3 Chickpea Protein Digestibility 28
    2.4.5 Common Beans and Faba Beans 29
        2.4.5.1 Utility of Beans and the Effect of Antinutritional Factors on Protein Digestibility 29
        2.4.5.2 Protein and Amino Acid Composition of Beans 29

DOI: 10.1201/9780429299834-2

		2.4.5.3	The Presence of Antinutritional Factors and Their Effect on Protein Digestibility 29
		2.4.5.4	Processing Methods That Alter Antinutritional Activity 30
	2.4.6	Lentils 30	
		2.4.6.1	The Protein Content of Lentils 31
		2.4.6.2	The Amino Acid Balance of Lentils 31
		2.4.6.3	The Presence of Bioactive Peptides in Lentils.. 31
		2.4.6.4	Antinutritional Factors and Their Effect on Protein Digestibility 31
	2.4.7	Cereals and Pseudo-cereals 32	
		2.4.7.1	Corn Utilization in World Food, Feed and Industrial Markets 32
		2.4.7.2	Wheat Utilization in World Food, Feed and Industrial Markets 32
		2.4.7.3	Rice Utilization in the World Food Market 33
		2.4.7.4	Barley Utilization in World Food and Feed Markets 33
		2.4.7.5	Sorghum Utilization in World Food, Feed and Industrial Markets........... 33
		2.4.7.6	Oats Utilization in the World Food and Feed Markets 33
	2.4.8	The Pseudo-cereals 34	
		2.4.8.1	Consumption of the Pseudo-cereals 34
		2.4.8.2	Complementarity of the Cereal and Pseudo-cereal Protein to Other Plant Protein 34
		2.4.8.3	Protein Content and Limiting Essential Amino Acids in the Cereals and Pseudo-cereals 34
		2.4.8.4	Protein Quality in the Cereals and Pseudo-cereals 35
		2.4.8.5	Antinutritional Factors in the Cereals and Pseudo-cereals 35
2.5	Nuts and Seeds 35		
	2.5.1	Ground Nuts and Tree Nuts 35	
	2.5.2	Chia Seeds and Sunflower Seeds 36	
	2.5.3	Protein Content and Limiting Amino Acids in Nuts 36	
	2.5.4	Protein Content and Limiting Amino Acids in Seeds 37	
	2.5.5	Antinutritional Factors and Their Effect on Protein Digestibility in Nuts and Seeds 37	
2.6	Vegetables 38		
	2.6.1	Antinutritional Factors in Vegetables 38	
	2.6.2	Protein and Limiting Amino Acids in Vegetables 38	
	2.6.3	Vegetable Protein Digestibility 39	
2.7	Summary 39		
References 40			

2.1 INTRODUCTION

Our distant hominin ancestors (genus *Homo*) and their bi-pedal primate neighbours were omnivores (Milton, 1999; Watts, 2008), but given their hunter-gather lifestyles, limited mobility and lack of advanced tools, particularly outside of the Euro-Asian dual continent (Diamond, 2017), it is likely that plant proteins provided a large part of their energy, protein and additional nutrient requirements. Given the relative ease with which plant products could be gathered by a mobile populace compared to hunting, at times, dangerous animals, this premise seems reasonable. As with our closest primate relatives, the chimpanzees (*Pan troglodytes*), and bonobo (*Pan paniscus*), the non-plant protein component of early hominin diets likely consisted of more easily (and safely) obtained insects, small reptiles, amphibians and mammals, rather than the larger mammals that existed at that time. There is evidence that the butchering of animal carcasses by early hominins included at least some scavenging of carcasses to obtain the meat and bone marrow for consumption (Blumenschine & Madrigal, 1993; Domínguez-Rodrigo 1997; Domínguez-Rodrigo et al., 2007).

2.1.1 Development of Hunting Skill and Physiological Adaptation to Dietary Changes

It would have taken considerable time to perfect the hunting techniques necessary to access herds of large animals and even longer to domesticate certain species for their meat (e.g., swine, poultry, goats, cattle) or products (e.g., milk and eggs – cattle, buffalo, goats, yak; chickens, ducks, quail, turkeys). Excavated spear points date back as far as 500,000 years ago, as evidence of primitive hunting capability, but more complicated projectile weapons have been suggested to not have arisen until much later – perhaps 71,000 years ago. Adaptive features of the human gastrointestinal (GI) tract to diets that reflect its greater capacity to process animal proteins than do the GI tracts of other primates (Milton, 1999) are expected; however, it is unclear when these anatomical and physiological changes occurred over the evolutionary lineage of each species of *Homo sapiens* versus chimpanzees, bonobos, gorillas (*Gorilla gorilla*) and other primates.

2.1.2 Animal Protein Versus Plant Protein Consumption in the Future

It is ironic that as the world population has expanded to a level greatly exceeding that of the earliest human inhabitants, and as technology has contributed to humanity's environmental concerns, civilization must now consider the wisdom of continuing to rely on animal protein as the principal means by which it meets its dietary nitrogen requirements. The burden placed on water resources (Hoekstra, 2011), the production of carbon dioxide and methane (smith, 2005), and the direct utilization of plant products to produce animal protein have brought into question the efficacy of large-scale meat and animal product production (i.e., milk, eggs). In addition, medical research has provided evidence of a causative link between the consumption of processed red meat and possibly red meat itself and the development of certain types of cancers (Mehta et al., 2020; Vieira et al., 2017).

2.2 ANIMAL PROTEIN AND PLANT PROTEIN-BASED DIETS

In this chapter, the quality of plant proteins will be assessed; first, by considering their role in the diet of other primates and animals with similar digestive capabilities as humans, and then by considering the quality of plant proteins in the context of providing sole-source or near sole-source nitrogen and other essential nutrients to the diet. Most important plant sources of protein will be reviewed, with an emphasis on protein quality and utility in the diet. The categories of proteins to be covered include legumes, grains and cereals, seeds and nuts, and vegetables.

2.2.1 Adequacy of Vegetarian Diets

An often misunderstood concept is that the human protein requirement, or rather the requirement for the indispensable or essential amino acids plus additional nitrogen to allow for amination of the carbon skeletons of the dispensable amino acids, can only be met with the highest quality dietary proteins. This is incorrect, as it infers that only animal-source proteins, due to their greater 'biological value' (BV; relative to egg protein), rather than plant proteins, which are usually limiting in one or more of the essential amino acids. However, this concern can be minimized or negated when a variety of plant products is consumed within a reasonable time frame. This is known and practiced not only by those who consume 'vegan diets' (diets that contain no food or products derived from animals) but also by the American Dietetic Association (Craig & Mangels, 2009), the Canadian Dietetic Association (ADA/CDA, 2003), the Association of UK Dietitians (Vegan Society, 2021), among other professional and government authorities worldwide (Mariotti & Gardner, 2019). Of the different types of vegetarianism, 'vegans' are the most prone to nutrient deficiency, given the complete exclusion of any animal products in their diets (i.e., meat, fish, eggs, dairy). Other more liberal versions of vegetarianism (Lacto-ovo vegetarian: dairy and eggs allowed, but not meat or fish; Pesco vegetarian: fresh- and saltwater fish and shellfish allowed, as well as dairy and eggs; Pollo vegetarian: all that a Pesco vegetarian can eat, plus chicken; Flexitarian: a diet that is centred on plant foods with the occasional inclusion of meat) do not have these concerns to the same extent, as their diets contain varying levels of complete protein and other essential nutrients, especially iron and vitamin B_{12}.

2.2.2 Complementary Plant Proteins to Meet Essential Amino Acids Requirements

The proper balancing of protein foods consumed by vegans requires both knowledge and diligence, but it is possible to meet the body's essential amino acid needs with a vegan diet (Craig & Mangels, 2009). The most important factor is the concept of variety in choice of both types of plant products consumed (grains, pseudo-grains, legumes, seeds, nuts, vegetables) and the specific food items within each category. This is, in fact, no different from how diets or rations are formulated for domestic livestock, be it poultry, swine, fish or cattle. A variety of ingredients are needed to meet the prescribed nutrient needs of food animals, and a deficiency of nutrients in one major ingredient (e.g., lysine and tryptophan in corn) are met by an excess in another (soybean meal). Conversely, the deficiency of the sulphur amino acids in soybean meal is compensated for by the relatively higher level of methionine and cysteine in corn. In practical animal husbandry, small quantities of synthetic L-lysine are generally still needed in swine diets and DL-methionine in poultry diets, depending upon what other ingredients are included in the diet, to properly balance the diets for essential amino acids.

2.2.3 A Healthy Rationale for Plant-Based Proteins

Not only do we know that sufficient protein and overall nutrient intake in humans is possible with a diet primarily or totally based on plant products, but research suggests that from a health perspective, this may be preferable to a diet that contains high levels of animal protein. A number of national health bodies have made dietary recommendations that emphasize more plant proteins in the diets while decreasing the intake of animal proteins, and especially the intake of red meats (American Heart Association Recommendations, 2017; Craig & Mangels, 2009; World Cancer Research Fund, 1997). Animal proteins have not been vilified *per se*, as they are rightly valued for their highly digestible and high BV protein, iron, vitamin B_{12} and other essential nutrients, as well as the organoleptic contribution that they make to the diet. However, there is a definite trend towards minimizing dietary animal-based proteins, including those from the dairy group, while increasing the amount of protein that is derived from plant proteins, in the form of legumes, grains, cereals, seeds and nuts, fruits and vegetables, and even single-cell proteins. There are valid health and environmental reasons for redirecting the population to plant protein-based food selections. The trend towards minimizing the total and animal protein content of the human diet is consistent with the diets of our phylogenetically most similar primates, the chimpanzee and the bonobo.

2.2.4 DIETARY HABITS OF RELATED SPECIES

Sarusi (2021), from the Jane Goodall Institute of Canada, described the diet of chimpanzees, who are omnivores, yet whose diet is made up primarily of plant products. Normal daily consumption for a chimpanzee (or bonobo) would include fruit, seeds, flowers and blossoms, nuts, leaves, figs, honey, medicinal plants, honey, insects, eggs and some meat. It was pointed out that Dr Jane Goodall was the first person to observe chimpanzees eating other animals (animal by-products and smaller monkeys through hunting endeavours), as well as termites by using sticks to extract them from sand mounds. Estimates are that insects may represent up to 4% of a chimpanzees diet while meat and eggs may represent up to 10% of the diet. This was significant in that previous to Dr Goodall's observations, these smaller apes were considered to be herbivores, similar to most of the larger apes (e.g., gorillas). Relative to developed countries, the 'small ape' meat consumption as a part of their total caloric consumption would likely place them in the category of flexitarian.

2.2.4.1 Differences in Protein Intake and GI Anatomy between Humans and Other Primates

In 2018, the average American ate 100.8 kg of meat (beef and veal, poultry, pork, lamb) or 270 g/day (OECD Data, 2019). Other developed countries had similar intake levels. Obviously, many eat far more meat than this each day, yet it is unlikely that any of the closest primate cousins of relatives come close to consuming those levels of animal protein. They subsist well on significantly lower levels of meat *per se*, by compensating with other animal protein (insects, eggs), but most notably, by ingesting a wide variety of plant proteins. An interesting difference between humans and the apes is the relative capacity of the colon. In the apes (including the chimpanzee), the colon represents 50% of the total gut volume, whereas in humans, it is only 20% of total gut volume (Milton & Demment, 1988). However, this is attributable to the fact that humans have for several hundred thousand years consumed cooked foods, while other primates have not had this luxury (Weaver, 2012; Wrangham & Conklin-Brittain, 2003). Therefore, the ape's hindgut must be far more proficient at the fermentation of plant-based foods and the subsequent release of short-chain fatty acids for energy (Leonard et al., 2007). Hence, evolution has maintained this ability in the apes, while our intestinal tracts have little need for the same auto-catalytic activity since plant fibres are, for the most part, broken down through the cooking process.

2.2.4.2 Comparative Diet of Domestic and Feral Pigs to Humans, Given Comparable GI Tracts

The length and function of the human large intestine lies between that of the pig, which is similar to an omnivore, similar to humans, and the dog, which is primarily a carnivore, but capable of consuming plant products in an omnivore diet (many dry dog food products contain plant-based ingredients) (Furness et al., 2015). The feral or wild pig normally consumes acorns, forbs (an herbaceous flowering plant), grass, tubers, roots, bulbs, fungi, herbaceous vegetation, including water hyssop (*Bacopa monnieri*), as well as agricultural crops (oats, corn, wheat, potatoes, rice, soybeans, melons, peanuts) (Ballari & Barrios-Garcia, 2013). However, they also consume any or all of the following: insects and their larvae, birds, amphibians, snails, crayfish, worms and reptiles. They will hunt and eat small mammals up to the size of rabbits and small livestock on farms or grazing (sheep, goats, cows – especially the frail). Needless to say, they will also feed on the eggs of several of these species and at times on carrion – the remains of deceased animals. In brief, feral hogs are very much omnivores and capable of subsisting on significant levels of animal protein in their diets, as are domestic pigs. Likewise, feral and domestic pigs are able to survive on essentially plant-based diets.

2.2.4.3 Commercial Swine Feeding as Evidence of the Efficacy of Plant-Based Proteins

There is a subtle irony in the observation that swine may survive and, in fact, thrive on markedly different diets, not only because the pig's digestive tract is similar to humans but also due to its commercial emphasis in the marketplace. As the second most commonly consumed meat in the world, only recently surpassed by poultry as number one (ABARES, 2019), pork producers and others involved in the industry encourage increased consumption of the product, with marketing messages that pork is part of a healthy diet (which it certainly can be) and that consumers should eat more pork. The meat industry in general has mirrored this message in encouraging the expanded consumption (and therefore production and sale) of meat and animal proteins, at times offering conflicting viewpoints to recommendations by medical and scientific experts to reduce the consumption of meat in general and red meat in particular. Ironically, although pigs normally consume a balanced diet of meat (animal) protein and plant-based proteins, pork producers feed little if any animal-based protein to their pigs once the piglet has been weaned from the sow. Perhaps 5.0% of the animal's total feed is derived from animal sources during its initial growing period post-wean (up to ~20–25 kg), but then for the rest of the growth cycle until market weight (~90–120 kg), it will essentially be on a plant-based diet. The reason for this is primarily financial, as plant product ingredients (generally corn, soybean meal, wheat and other grains and oilseeds) are lower in price than are animal-based feed ingredients. In other cases, the requirement may be mandated by law, due to safety concerns (e.g., the European Union). Yet, the animals gain sufficiently well on these vegetarian diets, since all their nutrient needs are met through supplementation – much as a 'vegan' is required to do. The same is true in poultry meat production, as chickens are omnivores, and will readily eat meat when provided to them, but as with pigs, they must generally settle for a plant-based diet before they themselves become our 'meat-based' meal.

2.3 PROTEIN QUALITY

Schaafsma (2005) assessed the nutritional quality of several different proteins for human or animal consumption, and these proteins were ranked by their ability to meet the requirements for nitrogen and amino acids in various species. The nutritional quality of proteins may differ widely, depending on essential amino acid composition and protein digestibility, specific to species requirements. For many years, bioassays, predominantly using growing rats, were the preferred means to assess the nutritional quality of proteins. Values were most commonly expressed as the Protein Efficiency Ratio (PER), Net Protein Utilization (NPU) and BV. Although these three measures are still useful, the only true way to measure protein quality in humans is by evaluating nitrogen balance in experiments with human volunteers. Though preferable, nitrogen balance studies might not be performed for ethical reasons or because they are too expensive for routine use.

2.3.1 THE PROTEIN EFFICIENCY RATIO

The PER, the most widely used bioassay, was the first method that was adopted for the routine assessment of the protein quality of foods, and it is still used by the food industry in Canada as the standard for evaluating the food protein quality (Canada.ca; Canadian Food Inspection Agency, 2020). It is a standardized method, wherein weanling rats are fed a casein control diet or a test diet, with both diets containing 10% protein (w/w, N × 6.25), for four (4) weeks, and PER values are calculated as body weight gain (g)/g protein consumed. The values obtained for the given proteins tested are standardized against an assumed value for casein of 2.5. An obvious disadvantage in the use of the PER is that the amino acid requirement pattern of the growing rat is not identical to that of other species tested, including humans (Schaafsma, 2005), and this is particularly true when it comes to evaluating the legumes and the oil-seed proteins (Young & Pellett, 1994). As well, adult human nitrogen requirements are dictated by maintenance needs, rather than by growth, which predominates in the growing rat model used in the PER assay.

2.3.2 THE PROTEIN DIGESTIBILITY-CORRECTED AMINO ACID SCORE

In 1989, a joint Food and Agriculture Organization/World Health Organization (FAO/WHO) Expert Consultation on Protein Quality Evaluation (FAO/WHO Expert Consultation, 1991) concluded that protein quality could also be assessed by expressing the content of the first limiting essential amino acid (i.e., the essential amino acid that first becomes deficient in the diet) in a test protein as a percentage of the content of that same amino acid in a reference pattern of essential amino acids. The FAO/WHO Expert Consultation used a reference pattern that was based on the essential amino acid requirements of preschool-age children, which it had published previously (WHO/FAO/UNU Expert Consultation, 1985). The determined percentage is corrected for true digestibility of the test protein as measured in a rat faecal-based assay. This resultant scoring method is known as the Protein Digestibility-Corrected Amino Acid Score (PDCAAS), and it is accepted as a routine procedure for protein quality evaluation. The PDCAAS is defined using the following formula:

$$\text{PDCAAS}(\%) = (\text{mg of first limiting amino acid in 1 g test protein})/(\text{mg of the same amino acid in 1 g reference protein}) \times \text{TD}(\%)$$

where TD is true faecal digestibility of the test protein, as measured in a rat assay.

True faecal protein digestibility is defined as the difference between intake of protein N and output of faecal N, expressed as a percentage of protein N intake, where faecal N is corrected for metabolic faecal N as measured using a protein-free diet.

A defining feature of the PDCAAS is that proteins with values greater than 100% are lowered to 100%, as it is assumed that there is no additional benefit to humans from this higher value. This assumption is not without controversy, as are other aspects of the PDCAAS, including the validity of the scoring pattern, the use of faecal versus ileal digestibility, the impact of anti-nutritional factors in the protein sources and the suitability of PDCAAS in predicting the quality of amino acid-supplemented proteins (FAO/WHO, 2001; Reeds et al., 2000; Schaafsma, 2005). However, the method remains popular on a worldwide basis. Boye et al. (2012) presented a concise review on the PDCAAS as a method to evaluate protein quality along with a summation of all protein quality evaluation methods and protein intakes used in different countries.

2.3.3 APPLICATION OF THE PDCAAS

According to the formula that is used to calculate the PDCAAS, two primary factors are considered in determining the value. First, the content of the first limiting essential amino acid in a single protein or in a mixture of proteins is the critical factor for the ability of that protein or mixture of proteins to meet the nutritional amino acid requirements, which in fact refers to the body's ability to support optimal protein synthesis. Once the first limiting essential amino acid is exhausted, protein synthesis will be compromised, irrespective of the availability of the other essential or non-essential amino acids. The second consideration of the PDCAAS method is that only absorbed amino acids can meet nutritional requirements, thus, necessitating adequate digestibility of the ingested protein(s) and the subsequent absorption of the constituent amino acids. Schaafsma (2005) summarized these assumptions succinctly as being that the bioavailability of the essential amino acid in question is reflected correctly by its true faecal protein digestibility and that the composition of the reference protein is valid.

2.4 LEGUMES (SOYBEANS AND PULSE CROPS: PEAS, CHICKPEAS, COMMON BEANS AND FABA BEANS, LENTILS)

Leguminous crops have multiple benefits in agriculture, and because of this, they provide unique nutritional benefits when included in human and animal diets. Thanks to a symbiotic relationship that

TABLE 2.1
World Legume Production, Million Metric Tonnes

Legume	Crop Year	Crop Year	Crop Year
Soybeans[1]	361.04 (2018/19)	336.46 (2019/20)	361.00 (2020/21; Proj.)
Peas, green[2]	19.80 (2016)	21.15 (2017)	20.27 (2018)
Chickpeas[2]	12.30 (2016)	14.15 (2017)	16.14 (2018)
Common/faba beans[2]	28.95 (2016)	31.48 (2017)	29.97 (2018)
Lentils[2]	7.08 (2016)	6.81 (2017)	6.29 (2018)

Notes
1 USDA (2021)
2 FAO-FAOSTAT (2018)

legume plants share with nitrogen-fixing bacteria, these plants are able to convert atmospheric nitrogen into a form that the plant can use. The benefit to the plant is further realized in residual nitrogen left in the soil upon harvest and decomposition of the remainder of the plant or of any unharvested plants, which may be used by ensuing crops the following crop cycle. As well, the nitrogen-fixation results in a relatively high protein content in the plant itself, making legumes one of the best dietary protein sources of all plant proteins consumed by humans and animals. Thus, legume proteins are some of the most important sources of amino acid nitrogen, including the essential amino acids, of all the plant proteins. Legumes are depended upon by vegans and other vegetarians to provide the bulk of their daily protein needs. Combined with cereal, pseudo-cereal, nuts, seeds and grain sources, the high lysine content of legumes and relatively low content of the sulphur-containing amino acids cystine and methionine are balanced by the high content of the sulphur amino acids and low lysine of the cereals and grains. This forms the basis for the complementation of plant protein sources in vegetarian diets. But is the relatively high content of crude protein in legumes (~20–30%) that provides the majority of the actual protein in the diet, as this is generally 2–3 times the content of protein that is present in the cereals and nuts. The exception to this is the pseudo-cereals, which will be discussed later, and which have crude protein contents comparable to legume products.

2.4.1 World Legume Production

All the important legumes of human dietary significance will be discussed here, with the exception of ground nuts, which will covered under the separate heading of '10 Nuts and Seeds'. By far, soybean production exceeds the production of all other legumes (combined) (Table 2.1). This is a reflection of the main use of soybeans, which is for crushing purposes to produce meal for feeding livestock and oil for use as both edible oil and, in certain areas, for industrial purposes (biofuels). Only a small quantity of the total world supply of soybeans is used for direct human consumption (~6.0%). All beans at the second most important legume produced in the world, followed by peas. The majority of beans are consumed as food, as is true for peas; however, a significant market has grown for animal feed peas, due to their relatively high content of lysine, which balances quite well with the oilseeds that are used with it, and in particular, rapeseed/canola, which are deficient in lysine, but rather high in the sulphur amino acids – something that peas are particularly lacking in. Chickpeas follow peas in importance, and lentil production volumes lag all others, although their production is projected to increase at a faster rate than the other legumes listed here (Section 2.4.6). If one considers only those soybeans that are used for direct human consumption, then ~21.0–22.0 million tonnes of soybean are were consumed in 2018/19 for this purpose, making them the second most important source of legume protein to the common bean.

2.4.2 Soybeans

The soybean *(Glycine max)* is the most abundantly grown oilseed crop in the world as well as being the most economically important bean of any kind (USDA, 2021). This, however, does not mean that soy protein is widely used in human food applications. In fact, the majority of the solid portion of the soybean, which makes up ~82% of the total mass of the bean, is used to make soybean meal, which is fed to animals. The other ~18% of the mass is soybean oil. Those soybeans are grown specifically for that purpose, while soybeans grown for human food consumption are designated only for that purpose and represent <10.0% of total world soybean production in any given year (Voora et al., 2020). These beans are used in a variety of forms, with differing protein contents (per 100 gm): edamame or whole soybeans (~38–40 gm protein), tofu or soybean curd (~8 gm), tempeh or cooked and fermented soy (~19 gm), soymilk (~3.3 gm), soy flour (~36 gm), miso (fermented soybean paste (nil), soy sauce (~8 gm), and supplemental soy concentrates (~70 gm) and isolates (~81 gm). The largest consumption base for soy products is in Asia, where it has been a staple part of the diet for thousands of years. There is a much smaller consumer base in Europe, the Americas and Africa. Soy consumers outside of Asia, although still representing a market for the traditional products, are also targeted by soy food manufacturers for products made with textured soy protein or 'meat analogue' products, such as soy sausages, burgers, frankfurters and delicatessen meats. These are made from de-fatted soy, which is then compressed and dehydrated and further processed with colourings and flavours to serve as quite remarkable substitutes for animal-based products. Other common 'soy-substitutes' include soy yogurts and cheeses, and flavoured soy milks, which would find little following in Asian markets.

2.4.2.1 Purported Health Benefits of Soy Protein Consumption

Most of these 'analogue' and 'substitute' products made with soy for non-Asian markets are admittedly produced due to the fact that the targeted consumer base will not eat traditional soy products *per se,* but they are trying to obtain the purported health benefits of soy protein. Health benefits have been attested to soy food consumption through both epidemiological evidence (traditionally lower incidence of some forms of cancer in Asian populations that have long consumed soy-based diets, with relatively low animal protein consumption) and by scientific studies on the effects of both the isoflavones in soybeans and the soy protein itself (Friedman & Brandon, 2001). Likely, the turning point in the acceptance by western populations of the benefits of soy consumption was the decision by the United States Food and Drug Administration (FDA) in 1999 to allow the (limited) heath claim that 'a daily diet containing 25 grams of soy protein, also low in saturated fat and cholesterol, may reduce the risk of heart disease'. This guarded recommendation was enough to stimulate a significant section of the population to emulate Asians in adding soy protein to its diet, albeit in a different way. This population, at least in North America, has included the generation known as the 'Baby Boomers' (those born post-World War II through the 1950s), who are now more interested in longevity and good health than were previous generations, the large growth in the Asian population in the United States and Canada that demands traditional soy foods, which has led to increased acceptance of these traditional soy foods by younger indigenous generations. This phenomenon holds true for Europe as well. These younger generations in North America and Europe are also turning more forcefully towards plant-based foods in general, and soy tends to be a regular component of their diets.

2.4.2.2 Amino Acid Composition of Soy Protein

Soybean protein is unique among the plant proteins in being complete in the essential amino acids needed by humans (Cleveland Clinic, 2019). The most limiting amino acid in soybeans for human consumption is methionine; however, the limitation is marginal. Soybean-based infant formulas are supplemented with methionine to account for this limitation, but adults that consume soy food products in the absence of other proteins of higher BV at the same meal (e.g., animal-based proteins), would not normally supplement with synthetic methionine but would likely consume other food items with relatively higher quantities of methionine, such as cereals or grains. Soy protein is especially high in lysine, while marginal in methionine, while grains and cereals as a group are relatively high in the sulphur amino acids (methionine and cystine) and limiting in lysine and either tryptophan (corn) or threonine (most others) (USDA, 2019). Legumes in general, and soybeans in particular are sufficient enough in tryptophan and threonine to complement the deficiencies of these two essential amino acids in cereals, making it relatively easy to consume soybean products within a vegetarian-based meal that provides protein of a high overall BV. It should be noted, however, that for young children and adults, the need to supplement methionine to soybean protein, or to products containing soy protein may not be necessary, particularly when soy is eaten in combination with other plant product that contains sufficient quantities of methionine. Evidence now suggests that the essential amino acid profile of soy protein itself is sufficient to meet the requirements of young children and adults, and consumption of soy in a normal diet further insures the utilization of this protein owing to the complementarity of the other plant and/or animal proteins present in the mixed diet (Cleveland Clinic, 2019).

2.4.2.3 Digestibility of Soy Protein

The value of soy protein is enhanced by cooking (heat treatment) due to the presence of trypsin and chymotrypsin inhibitors and lectins (Adeyemo & Onilude, 2013; Samtiya et al., 2020) which can compromise protein digestibility. These anti-nutritional factors will be inactivated by the heat treatment or they may be eliminated by fractionation during processing. Although the lectins are heat-labile, the inhibitors are more heat-stable than the lectins. Nevertheless, methods are available to reduce the activity of inhibitors to acceptable levels, which would result in higher digestibility and availability of soy protein amino acids. The digestibility of some soy foods have been reported as follows: tofu – 92.7%; soymilk – 92.6%; soy protein isolate – 93–97%; steamed soybeans – 65.3% (FAO/WHO Expert Consultation, 1991). The BV (a value that measures how well the body can absorb and utilize a protein) of soybeans and soybean products has been shown to be comparable to animal proteins, if supplemented with its first-limiting amino acid methionine. Published BVs for soy products are: soybean protein isolate = 74, whole soybeans = 96, soymilk = 91 (National Soybean Research Laboratory, 2012). As described earlier, the US FDA and the Food and Agricultural Organization of the United Nations/World Health Organization (FAO/WHO) uses the PDCAAS as the method of choice in evaluating protein quality based on the amino acid requirements of humans and their ability to digest the protein. The PDCAAS value can be used to compare the quality of soy protein in its various forms to animal proteins: soy protein = 0.92; soy concentrate = 0.99; isolated soy protein = 0.92; egg white = 1.00; beef = 0.92. Proteins with values higher that 1.0 are rounded down (truncated) to 1.0 since these essential amino acids would exceed the human requirement (Schaafsma, 2005). It is little wonder that soy protein enjoys the role as one of the most popular high-quality plant proteins in the world.

2.4.3 PEAS

The pea (*Pisum sativum*) is a legume crop that is grown primarily in cooler latitudes, which is evidenced by the location of its primary producers – Canada, Russia, the United States, China and India (the majority of Indian production occurs in the northern states). Peas grow well in temperate climates or at higher altitudes in more tropical regions. Plant growth is compromised at temperatures above 27 °C, but the plant can survive and germinate at 4–5 °C and even survive mild frost (Dhall, 2017). Peas are a crop with a long history of both food and feed use, with a centre of origin surmised to be in the Fertile Crescent of the Middle East, in what is now Turkey. Evidence of pea cultivation has been traced to the fifth millennium BC, but they could have been in production even prior to these in other parts of the Middle East (Hirst, 2019). The use of the crop spread from there throughout Europe and Asia, and peas can now be found growing on all continents except Antarctica. There are generally three types of peas that are commonly consumed:

garden, field or green (and yellow) peas (*P. sativum*), snow peas (*P. sativum* var. *macrocarpon*) and snap peas (*P. sativum* var. *macrocarpon ser. cv.*). Green or field peas by far encompass the largest volume production, and these two terms refer to the pea in its dry form, which is how most peas are harvested, marketed and exported both for feed use and for human consumption, either in whole form or as components (pea flour, pea protein concentrates and isolates). When peas are sold fresh or in canned or frozen form (in the pod or whole), these are referred to as garden peas. Snow peas and snap peas are usually marketed in a similar manner to garden peas.

2.4.3.1 Protein and Amino Acid Composition of Peas

The crude protein content of peas varies widely, based on the cultivar planted, the climate that they grow in, and a variety of agronomic factors. Values from 18.0% to 28.0% crude protein can be found in the literature, and correspondingly wide ranges in the essential and non-essential amino acids accompany these levels of crude protein. The limiting essential amino acid in peas is methionine but both sulphur-containing amino acids (methionine + cystine) are quite low. In fact, pea protein meals or powders have been used to define the requirement for methionine in animal species due to the low dietary level that it generates in a control feed. In contrast, peas are a very good source of lysine, with a concentration that is higher on a per gm of protein basis than is the lysine in soybeans. Peas contain all other essential amino acids and are a good source of histidine and threonine, in addition to lysine. This makes them a highly valued plant protein source that are consumed intact as a vegetable or condiment, in the form of extruded noodles (yellow peas), or as isolated soy flours, concentrates and isolates. The protein value of pea flours, concentrate and isolate can be improved by the addition of synthetic methionine, and their respective protein contents (per 100 gm) are 27.1 gm (green peas) or 18.6 gm (yellow peas), 75.8–81.4 gm and 85.0–90.0 gm.

2.4.3.2 Pea Flours, Concentrates and Isolates

Flours are derived from both yellow and green peas and, in addition to being ~27% or ~18–19% crude protein (green or yellow peas, respectively), they are also high in dietary fibre (25–27% for green and yellow pea-based flours) as well as in resistant starch and total carbohydrates (~42%) (Pulse Canada, 2017). This makes pea flour a widely used product in food and baking applications, including pancakes, cookies, cakes and pastas. Yellow pea flour, referred to as 'peasemeal', is flour made from ground yellow field peas. The yellow peas are first roasted, which caramelizes some of the sugars present in the peas. This serves to darken the colour and increase the nutritional value of the final product by increasing the protein and starch levels. From there, the peas are ground to the desired texture, and the final brownish-yellow peasemeal powder is most often used to make porridge, coatings for fish and chicken, and added to sauces and pates. Pea concentrates or isolates are made by first grinding dried peas into a fine powder and the removing the starch and fibre. This leaves a concentrated protein powder whose protein content will vary depending upon the initial protein content of the peas and the thoroughness of the aqueous extraction of the carbohydrates and other non-proteinaceous materials. The protein content may range from 75% to 90%. These products are marketed directly to consumers as concentrates or isolates, or they can be further modified to increase their nutritional or functional properties by the addition of limiting amino acids or by extrusion (Pulse Canada, 2017).

2.4.3.3 Pea Protein Digestibility

The digestibility of peas and processed pea products is quite good. This is not surprising given the high level of readily digestible starch in peas (~54%), the low level of crude fibre (~6.9%), and minimal levels of antinutritional factors (trypsin inhibitors, lectins (phyto-haemagglutinins), oligosaccharides) (Dvořák et al., 2005; Kalač and Mika, 1997). The following true protein digestibility (percent) and PDCAAS values have been reported by Canada's Pulse Canada (2017): yellow pea – 87.9, 0.64; green pea – 85.2, 0.50; pea protein isolate (82% protein) – 97.1, 0.53; pea protein concentrate (50% protein) - 92.6, 0.54.

2.4.4 CHICKPEAS

There are two types of chickpeas (*Cicer arietinum*) grown in the world – the desi and the Kabuli, with each having decidedly different uses as food sources. The desi chickpea is the smaller and darker of the two types of chickpea, and it is noted as having a hard rough seed coat. Kabuli chickpeas, also known as garbanzo beans, are larger and lighter in colour, and they have a lighter seed coat than do desi chickpeas. Chickpeas were first domesticated in the Fertile Crescent as long as 10,000 to 12,000 years ago (Hirst, 2020; Redden, 2007). Sustained cultivation of chickpeas did not likely occur prior to ~7500 BC (Hirst, 2020), and it appears that the desi chickpea preceded the Kabuli chickpea, as genetic diversity in the Kabuli is much narrower than it is in the desi chickpea genome. Nevertheless, both desi and Kabuli chickpeas are now grown widely around the world, with an average of 13.08 million tonnes being produced globally during the period 2015–2020 (a high of 16.23 million tonnes in 2018), and 14.32 million tonnes expected to be harvested in 2020 (Clancey Report, 2020). India is by far the leading producer of chickpeas with over 70% of the total. Australia, Pakistan, Myanmar, Ethiopia, Turkey, Iran, Mexico, Canada and Russia are major chickpea producers as well. Chickpea production has seen a steady increase from 2016 to 2018 of 12.3, 14.15 16.16 million tonnes, respectively (Table 2.1).

2.4.4.1 Culinary Uses of Chickpeas and the Effect of Cooking on Nutrient Availability

Chickpeas are a versatile and widely used legume in cuisines in many cultures. Chickpeas can be used fresh or from a dry state, with only the cooking time and method needing to be altered. The cooked chickpeas can be eaten cold as is or in salads, or they can be served hot in a number of mixed vegetable and/or meat dishes. Various types of cooking methods decrease the content of several nutrients in chick peas: fat, total ash, reducing sugars sucrose, raffinose and stachyose, verbascose, mineral and B-vitamins (Alajaji & El-Adawy, 2006). Alajaji and El-Adawy (2006) also showed that cooking (heat) decreased the content of antinutritional factors (trypsin inhibitor, haemagglutinin activity, tannins, saponins and phytic acid) and the concentrations of lysine, tryptophan, total aromatic and sulphur-containing amino acids while increasing *in-vitro* protein digestibility, the protein efficiency ratio and the essential amino acid index. The chemical score and limiting amino acids in chickpeas subjected to the various cooking treatments varied considerably, depending on the type of treatment. Chickpeas can be ground into a flour, which is then used to make besan (gram flour or Channa dal), falafel (a deep fried ball), panelle (Sicilian fritters) or farinata (a pancake). Chickpea flour has a wide variety of uses in Indian and other Asian cuisines. In the Philippines, chickpeas are used somewhat uniquely in an iced, sweetened dessert known as halo-halo. Perhaps the best known application of the chickpea in the western diet is hummus, which is made by cooking and grinding chickpeas into a paste and mixing this with sesame seed paste (Wallace et al., 2016).

2.4.4.2 Protein and Amino Acid Composition of Chickpeas

Chickpeas, like other legumes, are relatively high in crude protein. The crude protein content of uncooked chickpeas varies based on cultivar and environment, but the average is ~20.47% (Wallace et al., 2016). Chick pea gram flour (besan) is ~22.0% protein, and it is valued especially for its relatively high protein and low-calorie content relative to wheat flour, as well as being gluten-free. Chickpeas, as with other legumes, is first limiting in the sulphur amino acids, and particularly in the essential amino acid methionine, while threonine is the second limiting amino acid (Alajaji & El-Adawy, 2006; Nestares et al., 1996).

2.4.4.3 Chickpea Protein Digestibility

The true protein digestibility (percent) and PDCASS value, as reported by Pulse Canada (2017), are 85.0 and 0.52, respectively, for Kabuli chickpeas, determined PDCAAS values of 83.8 for extruded chickpeas, 75.2 for cooked chickpeas, and 80.0 for baked chickpeas (casein truncated to 100.00). Previously, a PDCAAS value for cooked chickpeas was determined to be 51.9% (Tavano et al., 2008), due primarily to a lower amino acid score (0.6) than that determined in the chickpeas that were used in the study (0.86). A PDCAAS value of 75.2 and protein content of 22% place cooked chickpeas in the same category as other legumes relative to quality and quantity of protein and amino acids. The chickpea protein digestibility is adversely affected by the presence of antinutritional factors that are common to other legumes, including phytic acid, oxalates, saponins, cyanide, tannins and trypsin inhibitor (Popova & Mihaylova, 2019). Especially, the tannins and trypsin inhibitors compromise protein digestibility either by binding proteins and precipitating them (tannins) or by inhibiting protease enzymes (trypsin inhibitor) (Blow et al., 1974; Kurhekar, 2016). As with other legumes and plant protein products that contain antinutritional factors, their effects on protein digestibility and, hence, protein quality can be obviated by various cooking methods (Alajaji & El-Adawy, 2006).

2.4.5 COMMON BEANS AND FABA BEANS

Beans represent a broad category of legumes. Various names are used to describe the same type of bean, *Phaseolus vulgaris,* including the kidney bean, black (turtle) bean, navy (white) bean and pinto bean. In contrast, *Vicia faba* describes the broad or faba bean, *Phaseolus lunatus* the lima bean, *Vigna angularis* the Adzuki bean (red mung bean) and *Vigna unguiculata* the cow bean (cow pea or black-eyed pea). The common characteristic of these beans is that they are considered dried beans as normally marketed to the consumer, although they are commonly soaked in water prior to cooking. There are exceptions to this, of course, but in general, whole legume beans are stored and then sold dry for preservation purposes or for further processing into flours. Combined, the various species of common beans and faba beans represent the second most abundant legumes grown in the world, after soybeans (Table 2.1). They serve as a staple food in many cultures and a significant source of protein for vegans and other practitioners of vegetarian diets. In 2016–18, world production totalled 28.95, 31.48 and 29.97 million tonnes.

2.4.5.1 Utility of Beans and the Effect of Antinutritional Factors on Protein Digestibility

The largest group of beans, *P. vulgaris* (common beans) are a good source of protein and a valuable addition to the diet of vegetarians (all types). Dry beans add variety to a plant-based diet as well as heterogeneity to the balance of the essential amino acids that are ingested. Common beans have also been utilized for industrial purposes in the preparation of ice cream (Kebary & Hussein, 1997) and miso (Reiss, 1993). Like other legumes, the common and other beans contain several antinutritional factors (Diouf et al., 2019; Farinde et al., 2018; Jansman et al., 1998; Vogelsang-O'Dwyer et al., 2020) that may have a direct negative impact on the digestibility and utilization of protein. However, these antinutritional factors can be eliminated or reduced by appropriate cooking or other simple technologies (Jansman et al., 1998; Luo & Xie, 2013), albeit with some modification of the nutritive value of the protein (either positive or negative), depending upon the severity of the heat, the duration of the cooking or the technology utilized (Diouf et al., 2019; Farinde et al., 2018; Occena et al., 1997; Udensi et al., 2007; Vogelsang-O'Dwyer et al., 2020).

2.4.5.2 Protein and Amino Acid Composition of Beans

The protein levels of the various beans vary by type, cultivar planted, soil conditions, and even by the method of measurement. Therefore, absolute values and comparisons among species and individual types of beans within the four bean species discussed herein must take this into consideration. However, from highest to lowest, the average protein content of the different beans, per 100 gm are (USDA, 2019): Pinto – 9.0; Black – 8.9; Kidney – 8.7; Black Turtle – 8.2; Navy – 8.2; Lima – 7.8; Cowpeas – 7.7; Adzuki – 7.5; Faba – 7.6; Mung – 7.5. These values are based on cooked portions of each bean, and the differences among the various beans reflect considerable variance primarily in carbohydrate content, as none of these beans have appreciable quantities of fat in them. As with other legumes, beans are first limiting in the sulphur-containing amino acid methionine. This makes methionine a difficult amino acid for vegans to obtain in the diet since other plant sources are second or third limiting in methionine as well. However, all of the beans are good sources of the essential amino acids tryptophan, threonine and histidine (essential in children). In contrast, many of the beans have relatively low levels of the branched-chain amino acids leucine and valine, with adzuki and navy beans being exceptions (USDA, 2019). Overall, faba beans have a low amount of protein and, with it, a low amount of all of the essential amino acids and, in particular, methionine.

2.4.5.3 The Presence of Antinutritional Factors and Their Effect on Protein Digestibility

The presence of antinutritional factors in beans, including indigestible carbohydrate fractions, renders the digestibility of nutrients, including crude protein and individual amino acids, somewhat problematic, as is true with most plant proteins. This is particularly true with the legumes, as described for soybeans. Digestibility in legumes, including beans, is compromised by the indigestible oligosaccharides raffinose, stachyose and verbascose, which have been identified in *P. vulgaris* (Queiroz et al., 2002), *Vicia faba* (Rupérez, 1998), *V. angularis* (Onigbinde & Akinyele, 2006) and *V. unguiculata* (Meredith et al., 1988). Queiroz et al. (2002) determined the levels of raffinose-type oligosaccharides in different common bean preparations, and they observed significant reductions in the contents raffinose (25.0%), stachyose (24.0%) and verbascose (41.7%), as well an in the total sugar (80.6%), reducing sugar (58.2%), non-reducing sugars (90.3%), and starch (26.8%) contents when the beans were soaked prior to cooking and the soaking water that was not absorbed by the beans was discarded. Luo and Xie (2013) utilized a number of physical treatments on green and white faba beans (*Vicia faba*), including soaking, dehulling, cooking, microwaving and autoclaving) to determine their effect on antinutritional factors and *in vitro* protein digestibility. Raw green and white faba bean contain phytic acid, tannins, trypsin inhibitor activity and lectin activity (Popova & Mihaylova, 2019). The tannins and trypsin inhibitors interfere with protein digestion and absorption, while phytic acid and lectins compromise mineral absorption.

2.4.5.4 Processing Methods That Alter Antinutritional Activity

Removal of the outer layer or hull of the bean (dehulling) was found by Luo and Xie (2013) to significantly increase phytic acid and trypsin inhibitor activity and decrease tannins. Lectin activity was unchanged. In this study, the method of cooking was shown to differentially affect the antinutritional factors. The simple act of cooking or autoclaving increased phytic acid, had no effect on tannins, but inactivated both trypsin inhibitor and lectin activities. Combination effects, such as soaking following cooking treatments, significantly decreased phytic acid, tannins, and lectin activity while increasing trypsin inhibitor activity level in both green and white faba beans. When dehulling was followed by soaking and cooking, there was a significant increase in both phytic acid and trypsin inhibitor activity. The *in vitro* protein digestibility of raw green and white faba bean seeds were 72.65 and 73.28%, respectively, which were improved by all processing methods, with soaking-dehulling post-autoclaving proving to be the most effective. While some treatments increased the level of antinutritional factors, they nevertheless improved the *in vitro* protein digestibility. It can be inferred, therefore, that the antinutrients described here are likely not the only responsible factors for lowering *in vitro* protein digestibility in common and other beans. Schaafsma (2005) has reported true protein digestibility (TPD) scores for raw and heated black beans of 71 and 83, respectively, and PDCAAS values of 0 and 83 for the same, respectively (with a truncated PDCAAS value of 100 for casein).

2.4.6 LENTILS

In a recent review by Khazaei et al. (2019), cultivated lentils (*Lens culinaris*) were identified as the most rapidly expanding crop for direct human consumption and, as such, provide a significant potential source of plant protein for direct human consumption and for food processing applications. The average annual global production of lentils during the years 2012–2017 was 5.9 million tonnes, which represented 9.2% of the total average annual global pulse production of 64.2 million tonnes during those same years (lentils, faba beans, peas, chickpeas, common beans; excluding soybeans) (FAO, 2019). Although this was the second lowest production level of the five pulse crops monitored (faba beans represented 7.0% of the average annual global production of pulses), lentils production is projected to grow at an average annual rate of 10.3% over the next 50 years, while faba bean production will decrease by an average 0.2%/year, and peas, chickpeas and the common bean will increase on average annually by 0.5, 2.1 and 2.6%, respectively (FAO, 2019). If these projections hold true, then by the year 2070, global lentil production will approach 30.5 million tonnes and be second only to the ~37 million tonnes of global common bean production of the five pulse crops noted earlier. Table 2.1 gives further details on lentil production during the years 2016–18. Production during this three-year span was relatively static, with 7.08, 6.81 and 6.29 million tonnes of lentils being produced in 2016, 2017 and 2018, respectively.

2.4.6.1 The Protein Content of Lentils

Lentils are higher in total soluble fibre than are peas and chickpeas and higher in dietary fibre than beans and chickpeas. Similar to other legumes, lentils are a good source of protein. Urbano et al. (2007) estimated that the protein content of lentils varies from 20.6% to 31.4%, while Khazaei et al. (2019) more recently reported an average crude protein content in lentil seed of ~26.0%. However, Khazaei et al. (2019) also noted a wide genetic variability in lentil seed protein levels, depending upon species of lentil and the means of measurement, with reported crude protein levels varying from as low as 10.5% (Kumar et al., 2016) to as high as 36.4% (Hawtin et al., 1977). Given the average value of crude protein in the mid 20% range and the projected large increase in lentil production over the next several decades, this plant protein is expected to provide an important source of high-quality, economical protein for human consumption, particularly in areas of protein-energy malnutrition (Khazaei et al., 2019). Most protein in the lentil seed exists in the form of storage proteins (Kiosseoglou & Paraskevopoulou, 2011), located in the cotyledon portion of the seed. Lentil proteins are comprised of ~16% albumins, 70% globulins, 11% glutelins and 3% prolamins (Boye et al., 2010).

2.4.6.2 The Amino Acid Balance of Lentils

The nutritional value of lentil protein depends on its amino acid composition relative to the requirements of a given species, with primary consideration here being human essential amino acid requirements. Khazaei et al. (2019) composed a principal component analysis (PCA) from amino acid data (meta-analysis) which indicated that the amino acid profile of lentils is nearly identical to that of peas, as described previously by Djemel et al. (2005). Like peas (and other legumes), lentils are notably deficient in the sulphur-containing amino acids, methionine and cysteine, while they are relatively high in the essential amino acid lysine. The high lysine content of lentils, combined with the adequate levels of methionine and cysteine in cereal proteins, provides the basis for meeting the nutritional essential amino acid requirements of an individual in a plant-based diet (Gomez et al., 2008).

2.4.6.3 The Presence of Bioactive Peptides in Lentils

Lentils provide not only dietary amino acids but also a source of several bioactive peptides that are purported to provide health benefits. These bioactive peptides have been shown to exhibit anti-hypertensive, antioxidant and antifungal activities (García-Mora et al., 2017; Khazaei et al., 2019; Natesh et al., 2003; Rizzello et al., 2017). Although there are considerable data available on the characterization of bioactive peptides from lentils and their potential use in functional food products, there is a paucity of data on their *in vivo* efficacy, which would justify health claims and regulatory approval (Chalamaiah et al., 2019). This is a barrier to the use of bioactive peptides from plant sources, and it will be a difficult hurdle to overcome, due to the ethical considerations and costs involved in conducting the needed *in vivo* and clinical trials. The favourable functional qualities of lentil proteins have been well described by others (Boye et al., 2010; Khazaei et al.,

TABLE 2.2
World Cereal Production, Million Metric Tonnes[1]

Cereal	2018/19	2019/20	2020/21, Projected
Corn (Maize)	1,123.84	1,116.55	1,134.05
Wheat	730.90	763.93	773.44
Rice	497.32	497.17	504.02
Barley	139.42	156.58	157.36
Sorghum	59.24	57.99	61.62
Oats	22.25	23.01	25.47

Note
1 USDA (2021)

2019), and they include their solubility (Ladjal-Ettoumi et al., 2016), emulsifying properties (Karaca et al., 2011; Ladjal-Ettoumi et al., 2016), and water and fat holding capacities (Aryee & Boye, 2017; Toews & Wang, 2013). These functional characteristics have made lentils a popular plant protein for food applications beyond their direct consumption. Lentil proteins may be used in combination with other plant proteins to take advantage of both their nutritional and favourable functional properties.

2.4.6.4 Antinutritional Factors and Their Effect on Protein Digestibility

The principal antinutritional factors in lentils are tannins (phenolic compounds that precipitate proteins) and trypsin inhibitors, both of which can affect protein digestibility unless lentils are cooked (heat treated) (Davis, 1981). The tannin content of lentils has been reported to be higher than in other legumes, but zero tannin varieties are available (Matus et al., 1993). Trypsin inhibitors impede the activity of the pancreatic enzyme trypsin, a serine protease that is essential to protein digestion in humans and animals (Yu & Ahmedna, 2012). With the exception of peas, the trypsin inhibitor concentration in lentils is lower than are the concentrations in other leguminous seeds (Elkowicz & Sosulski, 1982; Khazaei et al., 2019; Shi et al., 2017).

2.4.7 Cereals and Pseudo-cereals

The cereals constitute the bulk of harvested grains in the world, with corn, wheat, rice, barley, sorghum and oats providing the largest harvested volumes the last three crop years (Table 2.2; USDA, 2021). Corn is the predominant cereal grain grown globally, followed by wheat and rice. Barley is a distant fourth to these three in production, and sorghum and oats are only minor crops in comparison to the three major cereal grains that are planted and harvested each year, and which contribute much of the world's caloric consumption, either directly or indirectly, by being fed first to domesticated livestock.

2.4.7.1 Corn Utilization in World Food, Feed and Industrial Markets

However, the use of cereals differs and may change in any given year due to competing market signals. For example, in the United States in 1980, 83.4% of the corn (*Zea mays*) produced was subsequently used in animal feed production, while 16.2% was used for food, seed and industrial purposes, and only 0.4% was used for ethanol production (Ranum et al., 2014). But government legislation mandating the use of biofuels, of which ethanol was to become a major contributor, changed the corn utilization breakdown dramatically. In 2013, 43.6% of the corn produced in the United States was then used in animal feed production, 12.7% was used for food, seed and industrial purposes, and 43.6% was used to produce ethanol (Ranum et al., 2014). The effect of this marked shift has been felt not just in the United States but around the world, as the United States is the largest producer and exporter of corn, which is primarily used to feed livestock on a global basis. The impact of decreased availability of corn for the animal feed markets has been to increase its market price and thus the price of the meat and animal products that are produced with it. Corn is generally the predominant grain ingredient used in livestock feeds in most of the world, and it is also used in fish and crustacean feeds.

2.4.7.2 Wheat Utilization in World Food, Feed and Industrial Markets

Wheat (*Triticum aestivum*) utilization differs from corn in that the majority of the world's wheat supply is used for food purposes (~70%) (AEGIC, 2017; International Grains Council, 2021). The remainder is used for animal feed, industrial purposes (biofuel) and seed. Particularly in northern Europe, western Canada, the north-central United States, northern Europe and northern China, wheat is a higher protein alternative to corn as the primary grain used to meet the energy requirement of a variety of livestock species. It is also a valuable addition to aquaculture feeds, due to the excellent binding qualities of its gluten proteins, which are needed to form the hard pellets used in these feeds.

2.4.7.3 Rice Utilization in the World Food Market

Rice (*Oryza sativa*) is almost exclusively used in food applications. What is not eaten directly or made into rice-products (e.g., noodles, cakes) is used for seeding purposes (International Grains Council, 2021). However, the bran portion of the rice, when removed to produce the white rice that is generally favoured by consumers, is fed to cattle, swine and other commercial species as a medium-level protein source. As well, broken rice kernels can be fed to animals after being ground into a powder.

2.4.7.4 Barley Utilization in World Food and Feed Markets

Barley (*Hordeum vulgare*) is the direct opposite of rice in that there are several uses for this grain. The main market for barley is in animal feed (Newton et al., 2011). According to data from the FAO (FAO-FAOSTAT, 2018), approximately 70% of all barley grown in the world is used for animal feed, while ~21% is malting barley that is used for brewing and distilling purposes, and only about 6% is actually consumed as human food. In addition, a small amount of barley is diverted to the biofuel sector (Griffey et al., 2010). Barley for food use finds its way into soups, breads, stews, alcoholic beverages and, due to its particularly high content of the β-glucans, into natural health food products (Tricase et al., 2018).

2.4.7.5 Sorghum Utilization in World Food, Feed and Industrial Markets

Sorghum (*Sorghum bicolor*) is the fifth most important cereal grain produced in the world, with 58.0 million, 60.4 million and 57.9 million tonnes being produced globally in 2017, 2018 and 2019, respectively (FAO-FAOSTAT, 2018). Similar to barley and wheat, it has several different uses that vary by location and market conditions (Qi et al., 2019). It is used widely as an animal feed ingredient, for both cattle and monogastric species (i.e., swine and poultry) in the United States, Australia and Mexico, where its drought-tolerant agronomic advantage is consistent with the regions of these countries where it is grown (Kidanemaryam, 2019; Newton et al., 2011). In the United States, >30% of the sorghum is diverted into the biofuel sector, resulting in similar products as are obtained from corn that is used as biofuel (ethanol and distillers dried grains with solubles, with is fed to livestock) (Qi et al., 2019). Sorghum is the preferred grain in the Chinese alcoholic beverage Baijiu, in which the ethyl acetate and ethyl octanoate contents have been positively correlated with the tannin content from the sorghum used when the content of tannin was <1.94% (Xing-Lin et al., 2017). Finally, sorghum is an important staple food in some parts of the world, and it is also a minor food ingredient in others (Deribe & Kassa, 2020; Ratnavathi & Patil, 2013). In the arid and semi-arid regions of Africa and Asia, sorghum is a staple food for much of the population, with most of this grain being grown for human consumption and the remainder for animal feed. Food sorghum is used to produce a flour that is then used to prepare bakery products, such as breads, cakes and biscuits (Ratnavathi & Patil, 2013), while more innovative products such as noodles and pasta, extruded products and syrup have been created using sorghum as the base grain (FAO, 2013).

2.4.7.6 Oats Utilization in the World Food and Feed Markets

Oats (*Avena sativa* L) quantitatively are a small contributor to the world's total cereal grain supply, but they are an important food product for more than just their protein content. Oats are a rich source of soluble fibre (including the β-glucans), which have been shown to lower blood cholesterol levels (Rasane et al., 2015). Specifically, found that the bran component of oats lowered serum cholesterol by 23% with no change in the high-density lipoprotein (HDL) cholesterol level. Oats are consumed whole (granola bars, cereals, infant foods, oatmeal), as a flour to be used to make breads, cookies and biscuits, as an extract to make oat milk, and fractionated into the bran, dextrin and β-glucan components for functional food applications (e.g., stabilizer, fat substitute) (Rasane et al., 2015). Oats are still used as an animal feed, primarily for horses, but this application has diminished as the value of the oat food market has increased. Oat husks may also be used to produce methane for biogas, as a renewable energy source (Kusch et al., 2011).

2.4.8 THE PSEUDO-CEREALS

Pseudo-cereals are a group of plants that produce high-protein, high-starch seeds that are used in food applications similarly to cereal grains, but botanically, they are not true cereals. While cereals are monocotyledonous plants, pseudo-cereals are dicotyledonous plants, i.e., they contain two cotyledons (leaves) in their embryo instead of the single cotyledon in the embryo of the monocot (Schoenlechner & Bender, 2020). The best known of the pseudo-cereals are buckwheat (*Fagopyrum esculentum* Moench and *F. tartaricum* [L.] Gaertn.) (AMRC, 2021a; Izydorczyk et al., 2014), amaranth (*Amaranthus* spp.) (Ballabio et al., 2011) and quinoa (*Chenopodium quinoa* Willd) (Abugoch-James, 2009; AMRC, 2021b).

2.4.8.1 Consumption of the Pseudo-cereals

One of the key attractions of the pseudo-cereals as a food source is the absence of gluten from their protein content, similar to corn, rice, sorghum and oats. Amaranth and quinoa are characterized by their small seed size, while the buckwheat seed is triangular and hard, making it a challenge to process into flour. Quinoa and amaranth can be eaten in their seed form, similar to how other cereals are consumed at meals, or they can be added to snack foods, flours that are subsequently made into breads or biscuits, or to pastas (AMRC, 2021b; FAO, 2011). Buckwheat is most commonly processed into a flour that is used to make pancakes in the western world, or soba noodles in Japan. In Eastern Europe and Russia, buckwheat groats are roasted and sold as kasha, and buckwheat has also found its way into beer and ice cream products (AMRC, 2021a; Schoenlechner & Bender, 2020).

2.4.8.2 Complementarity of the Cereal and Pseudo-cereal Protein to Other Plant Protein

The crude protein contents of the cereals and pseudo-cereals are lower than they are in the legumes, but cereal protein can still contribute significant quantities of medium quality protein to the diet particularly when other sources of higher quality protein are not available. The cereals are generally considered to be complementary to the legume proteins, especially in diets that are based entirely or mainly on plant-based proteins. This is due to the fact that legumes are first limiting in the essential amino acid methionine, yet relatively high in lysine, while the cereals are first limiting in the essential amino acid lysine and relatively high in the sulphur-containing amino acids, especially methionine. This concept forms the basis for how vegans meet their essential amino acid requirements, and it is also the cornerstone of most livestock feeding, where corn, wheat, barley and sorghum are the most commonly used cereals that complement the soybean meal, primarily, that is fed to poultry, swine, cattle and even aquatic species.

2.4.8.3 Protein Content and Limiting Essential Amino Acids in the Cereals and Pseudo-cereals

The average crude protein content and the first and second limiting amino acids for the six cereals and three pseudo-cereals are as follows: corn – 8–11%, lysine/tryptophan (FAO, 1992); wheat – 10–15%, lysine/threonine or tryptophan (Shewry & Hey, 2015; Young & Pellett, 1985); rice – 4–14%, lysine/threonine (Kennedy et al., 2003; Rosenberg et al., 1959); barley – 7–25%, depending on end-use, lysine/threonine (Yilmaz et al., 2018); sorghum – 10–12%, lysine/threonine (Salunkhe et al., 1977; Serna-Salvidar & Espinosa-Ramírez, 2018); oats – 11–15%, lysine/threonine (Litwinek et al., 2013; buckwheat – ~12%, lysine/threonine (Sytar et al., 2016; Luthar et al., 2021); amaranth – 12.5–16%, threonine, methionine, tryptophan (Bressani et al., 1987; 1989), quinoa – 9.1–16.5%, no limiting for eight essential amino acids (Angeli et al., 2020; Vega-Gálvez et al., 2010).

2.4.8.4 Protein Quality in the Cereals and Pseudo-cereals

The pseudo-cereals are remarkable not only in their total crude protein content relative to the 'traditional' six cereals but also in the quality of the protein, with quinoa being the most notable in that it meets the FAO standards for eight essential amino acids (FAO, UN, 2011). Of the six cereals, oats stand out as having, on average, a higher amount of both crude protein and digestible lysine than do the other five cereals (Klose & Arendt, 2012). In general, the cereals and buckwheat are first limiting in lysine and second limiting in threonine, although tryptophan may be limiting as well, depending upon the nature of the other dietary foodstuffs. Data are insufficient to identify the first and second limiting amino acids in amaranth seeds, with conflicting results being found in the literature. Quinoa is an excellent source of all essential amino acids, including lysine and threonine, while it is adequate in tryptophan (FAO, 2019). Buckwheat has similarly high levels of crude protein, lysine, threonine and tryptophan as does quinoa, but protein and nitrogen digestibility in buckwheat is compromised by the presence of tannins and proteolytic enzyme inhibitors (Eggum et al., 1980; Mattila et al., 2018).

2.4.8.5 Antinutritional Factors in the Cereals and Pseudo-cereals

Tannins represent the major antinutritional factor in sorghum, although there are varieties of sorghum with negligible levels of tannins that are now being grown, primarily to improve protein digestibility for feeding to livestock (Nyachoti et al., 1997). However, phytic acid is the most important antinutritional factor found in most cereals. It binds multivalent ions, including zinc, calcium and iron, making them unavailable for absorption from the intestinal tract (Nadeem et al., 2010). Other antinutritional factors that are commonly found in the cereals include protease inhibitors, which decrease protein digestibility, and lectins and haemagglutinins (sugar-binding proteins), which cause agglutination of red blood cells (Samtiya et al., 2020). Saponins are steroidal in structure and most often found in leguminous crops, but they are also the principal antinutritional factors found in quinoa and amaranth seeds. They can form complexes with proteins, lipids and multi-valent minerals, effectively decreasing their bioavailability (Schoenlechner & Bender, 2020). Samtiya et al. (2020) have reviewed the methods available to eliminate or inactivate the antinutritional factors in the cereals and pseudo-cereals, which include milling, soaking, fermentation, germination, autoclaving and cooking.

2.5 NUTS AND SEEDS

Nuts and seeds represent yet another valuable source of plant-based protein and amino acids. True 'nuts' are those grown and harvested above ground ('tree nuts'), while ground nuts or peanuts are actually legumes that are produced below ground level but are usually discussed within this culinary category. Seeds represent a diffuse group of products, which may fall under the realm of other categories, such as cereals and pseudo-cereals, but for the present purposes, the focus will be upon those seeds that are consumed primarily in their native form (i.e., chia [*Salvia hispanica*], sunflower [*Helianthus annuus*]). Within the nut category, peanuts (*Arachis hypogea*), walnuts (*Juglans regia*), almonds (*Prunus dulcis*), cashews (*Anacardium occidentale*), hazelnuts (*Corylus avellana*), macadamias (*Macadamia integrifolia*) and pistachios (*Pistacia vera*) will be discussed herein.

2.5.1 GROUND NUTS AND TREE NUTS

Peanuts are the most diversely used nut products. They are in one sense considered to be an oilseed, as they are crushed to release peanut oil, which is subsequently used as an edible cooking oil, while the by-product is utilized as a high protein feed ingredient in animal feed rations (USDA, 2015). Raw and roasted peanuts are consumed throughout the world, as is peanut paste, peanut sauce, peanut flour, peanut milk, peanut beverage, peanut snacks (salted and sweet bars) and peanut cheese analogue (Arya et al., 2016). The tree nuts are more likely to be consumed in their raw or roasted form.

2.5.2 CHIA SEEDS AND SUNFLOWER SEEDS

Chia seed is sometimes categorized as a pseudo-cereal, and like its cousin quinoa, it has ancient origins in Latin America (Ullah et al., 2016). In reality, the chia seed is an oilseed, as it possesses high levels of omega-3 fatty acids with a concomitant assortment of polyphenolic antioxidants that protect the high levels of polyunsaturated fatty acids in the seed (Ayerza, 1995). Chia seed is also a rich source of protein with a good balance of the essential amino acids (Sandoval-Oliveros & Paredes- López, 2013; Ullah et al., 2016). Sunflower is primarily grown as an oilseed. During the 2019/20 crop year, 54.89 million tonnes of sunflower seed were produced in the world, making it the third most important oilseed crop after soybeans and rapeseed/canola, the fourth largest source of vegetable oil (after palm, soy and rapeseed/canola) and the third oilseed meal among animal feed sources (soybean meal and rapeseed/canola meal) (USDA, 2021). The confectionary sunflower seed market includes those sunflowers that are used in their shells as snacks, or they can be roasted and/or salted seeds, or dehulled, mainly for use with bakery products or to be eaten as such. As well, sunflower seeds are fed to birds and other pets. The exact volume of sunflower seeds that are diverted to the confectionary market is not monitored on an annual basis, but it is a small proportion of the total amount of sunflowers harvested each year. The International Sunflower Association provided an estimate at a Symposium on Confection Sunflower Technology and Production, that was held in Wuyuan, China in August 2018. They estimated that for the crop year

TABLE 2.3
World Nut and Seed Production, Million Metric Tonnes[1]

Nut or Seed	2017/18	2018/19	2019/20
Peanut	–	46.810	46.060
Walnuts	2.071	2.010	2.126
Almonds	1.291	1.347	1.481
Pistachios	0.649	0.780	0.717
Sunflower seeds	–	50.630	54.890

Note
1 USDA (2021)

2016/17, total confection sunflower use on a global basis was ~1.95 million tonnes. As an example, in that same year, total sunflower production worldwide was 48.33 million tonnes (USDA, 2021), meaning that confection sunflower use was 4.0% of total use (Table 2.3).

2.5.3 Protein Content and Limiting Amino Acids in Nuts

The protein content of nuts and seeds vary, as do the limiting essential amino acids in each. However, in the context of a plant-based diet, nuts and seeds may contribute a significant amount of both total protein and complementary essential amino acids to the diet, when measured against other plant protein sources (i.e., legumes, cereals, vegetables). Nonetheless, nuts and seeds are recommended as a valuable contributor to meeting essential amino acid requirements in vegetarian diets (Amit, 2010; Craig & Mangels, 2009). The average crude protein content per 100 gm of the following nuts are as follows: peanuts – 25.8; almonds – 21.3; pistachios – 20.6; cashews – 18.2; walnuts – 15.2; hazelnuts – 15.0; macadamia – 7.9. These absolute values vary by variety of nut measured, regions where they are grown, and measuring methods, but the relative quantities of crude protein per type of nut tend to stay constant. This is evidenced by crude protein data for nuts being sold in Korea, in mg per kg: peanuts – 30.5; almonds – 23.8; pistachios – 24.4; cashews – 20.2; walnuts – 14.4; macadamia – 8.9. The limiting essential amino acids in nuts differ as well. Based on FAO/WHO recommended essential amino acid amounts for a 2- to 5-year-old child, lysine is the first essential limiting amino acid in cashews, hazelnuts and walnuts, while methionine is the first limiting essential amino acid in almonds, tryptophan in macadamia nuts and pistachios, and threonine in Virginia peanuts (Venkatachalam & Sathe, 2006). Based on a rat bioassay, lysine is the first limiting amino acid and threonine the second in peanut protein (McOsker, 1962), but in general terms, for most if not all nuts, lysine is the first limiting amino acid and methionine the second (Cudmore, 2019). Peanuts, pistachios and cashews have the best overall balance of the essential amino acids, while macadamia nuts have the worst balance (Cudmore, 2019).

2.5.4 Protein Content and Limiting Amino Acids in Seeds

Chia seed, in addition to having a high protein content relative to other plant products, also has a favourable balance of the essential amino acids, with lysine being its first limiting amino acid for infants (0.5–1 year old) and adults and threonine and leucine the second limiting amino acid for infants and adults, respectively. However, chia seeds are a very good source of the sulphur amino acids methionine and cysteine for all age groups (Grancieri et al., 2019; Sandoval-Oliveros & Paredes-López, 2013), determined the amino acid composition of sunflower protein isolates and found that lysine was the first limiting amino acid while valine was likely the second limiting amino acid. Sunflower seed protein, similar to chia seed protein, is a very good source of methionine as cysteine (Ivanova et al., 2013). Another commonly consumed seed is pumpkin seed (*Cucurbita maxima*). Lazos (1986) reported a crude protein level of 32.3% for pumpkin seeds on a dry matter basis, while Habib et al. (2015) determined the total protein content of powdered pumpkin seed (4.06% moisture) to be 34.56%, of which 18.1% was soluble protein. Amin et al. (2019) estimated the crude protein content in pumpkin seed to be ~21.0%. Lysine is considered to be the first limiting amino acid in pumpkin seed, while methionine is the second limiting amino acid. Valine may be the second limiting amino acid depending upon the nature of other foods consumed, especially in a vegetarian diet (USDA, 2019) and used an ethanol treatment to prepare concentrates pumpkin protein products, and the products that were produced (meals, concentrates and isolates) had high levels of crude protein in the range 720–960 g/kg. It was further determined that isoleucine and valine were the first limiting amino acids for pumpkin meal and pumpkin protein concentrate, while the sulphur-containing amino acids methionine and cysteine, and valine were first limiting in the two protein isolates tested.

2.5.5 ANTINUTRITIONAL FACTORS AND THEIR EFFECT ON PROTEIN DIGESTIBILITY IN NUTS AND SEEDS

The digestibility and protein quality of the nuts and seeds is determined to a great extent by the presence of antinutritional factors. The most common antinutritional factors in tree nuts (almonds, hazelnut, cashew, pistachio, walnuts, macadamia) are phytic acid, lectins and oxalates (which chelate multivalent ions, similar to phytic acid), while peanuts contain anti-nutritional factors that are similar to other legumes (phytic acid, saponins, cyanide, tannins, trypsin inhibitor, oxalates) (Popova & Mihaylova, 2019). Seeds, including sunflower and pumpkin, are characterized by relatively high levels of phytic acid, alpha-amylase inhibitor and cyanide (Popova & Mihaylova, 2019). Tannins and phytates are present in small quantities in chia seed (Grancieri et al., 2019). Suárez López et al. (2006) reported a PDCASS for peanuts of 56.28%, which is comparable to that of cereal grains. This is a reflection of the presence of tannins and trypsin inhibitors in peanuts, which compromise protein digestibility. *In vitro* measures of peanut protein digestibility (IVPD) have shown more favourable results, with Elsheikh and Mohamedzein (1998) reporting an IVPD of 93.06 ± 0.042% and Abdualrahman (2013) measuring an IVPD of 92.65 ± 0.02. In general, all the tree nuts, as well as peanuts and seeds, are more easily digested when roasted, as this action will destroy the antinutritional inhibitors that are present. Raw nuts and seeds may be very difficult to digest, especially by those individuals who may have compromised gastrointestinal or pancreatic function. The full nutritional value of these food products is therefore best obtained in their various prepared forms, be they in the cooked natural nut and seed shape, in concentrated or isolated proteins, or in flours or other processed food products. Physical methods, such as de-hulling, are used to eliminate the high-fibre component of many nuts and seeds prior to eating or further processing, while cooking methods include autoclaving and roasting.

2.6 VEGETABLES

Vegetables are recognized as an excellent source of vitamins, minerals and dietary fibre, but few recognize that some vegetables also are a good source of protein, particularly the cruciferous and non-cruciferous green vegetables. The green cruciferous vegetables, within the Genus *Brassica*, are rich in the B-vitamin folate as well as vitamins A, C and K (USDA, 2019). They also contain an abundance of phytonutrients, which are compounds (many of which are phenolic antioxidants) found in plants that have been associated with anti-inflammatory and anti-carcinogenic actions in animal models and, by projection, in humans. Vegetables which fall within this category are cabbage *Brassica oleracea* (the word 'brassica' in Latin means 'cabbage'), brussels sprouts (*Brassica oleracea var. gemmifera*), broccoli (*Brassica oleracea var. italica*) and bok choy (*Brassica rapa var. chinensis*). Although not green, cauliflower (*Brassica oleracea var. botrytis*) and turnip (*Brassica rapa var. rapa*) are also *Brassica* vegetables. Interestingly, the oilseeds canola/rapeseed and certain mustards fall under the Crucifer and *Brassica* categories as well.

2.6.1 ANTINUTRITIONAL FACTORS IN VEGETABLES

Of the non-cruciferous vegetables, which include spinach (*Spinacia oleracea*), swiss chard (*Beta vulgaris var. cicla*) and lettuce (*Lactuca sativa*), spinach stands out as a vegetable that is not only a good source of vitamins and minerals (particularly iron) but also protein (USDA, 2019). The non-cruciferous vegetables are recommended for those individuals who may have thyroid gland problems, as cruciferous vegetables contain a specific type of antinutritional factor called glucosinolates, which are sulphur-containing glycosides that, when hydrolysed, form bioactive compounds. These isothiocyanates act as goitrogens, which can interfere with iodine uptake and reduce the production of thyroxine (T4) and triiodothyronine (T3) by the thyroid gland (Felker et al., 2016). This is not a concern with the non-cruciferous vegetables like spinach, as they do not contain glucosinolates.

However, glucosinolates have been linked to a reduction in the incidence of certain types of cancers, including colon, lung, breast, prostate, rectum and thyroid (Fowke et al., 2003; Hayes et al., 2008; London et al., 2000; Plate & Gallaher, 2003; Shankar et al., 2008; Steinbrecher & Linseisen, 2009; Traka & Mithen, 2009; van Poppel et al., 1999; World Cancer Research Fund, 1997).

2.6.2 Protein and Limiting Amino Acids in Vegetables

The legumes, nuts, seeds, meats, dairy and fish as generally considered the principal protein sources in the human diet, but certain cruciferous and non-cruciferous vegetables may contribute significant amounts of protein to the diet. Spinach contains 2.9 gm of protein per 100 gm (91% moisture) (USDA, 2019), and the first and second limiting amino acids have been reported to be methionine and leucine or lysine, respectively (USDA, 2019). For the cruciferous vegetables, broccoli contains 2.5 gm of protein per 91 gm (89% moisture) with the first and second limiting amino acids being methionine and leucine, respectively while brussels sprouts contain 3.0 gm of protein per 88 gm (87% moisture) with the first and second limiting amino acids being methionine and leucine as well (USDA, 2019). Not surprisingly, other green cruciferous vegetables have similar levels of protein and limiting amino acids. Cauliflower, as a representative non-green cruciferous vegetable, contains 6.7 gm of protein in 107 gm (93% moisture), and with similar limiting amino acids as other cruciferous vegetables (methionine first and leucine second) (USDA, 2019).

2.6.3 Vegetable Protein Digestibility

The digestibility of vegetable protein is, as with other plant proteins, dependent upon the presence of dietary fibre and antinutritional factors. Thus, vegetable protein will be more digestible in cooked form than when the vegetables are consumed in raw form. Most cooking methods will destroy the glucosinolates in cruciferous vegetables, which often removes the bitter taste that they impart to the specific foods that they are found in, but at the same time, this will eliminate a component of the *Brassicas* that adds to their value for many consumers – their purported role in reducing the incidence of many different type cancers and some of the anti-inflammatory compounds in these vegetables as well.

2.7 SUMMARY

Plant proteins provide a significant quantity of medium to high-quality protein to the human diet, and in the absence of animal-based proteins, whether by design (vegetarian dietary preference) or through lack of availability, plant proteins may meet the entire essential amino acid needs of all age-groups as well as supply sufficient additional nitrogen in the diet to synthesize the non-essential amino acids (Craig & Mangels, 2009). The different categories of plant proteins provide various nutritional benefits to an individual, in addition to protein, including beneficial fibres, essential fatty acids, vitamins, minerals and a variety of phytochemicals that are being further explored for their potential health-promoting benefits (e.g., glucosinolates, antioxidant phenolics). In some cases, plant proteins are packaged in relatively high-calorie surroundings (e.g., peanuts and other nuts, chickpeas, corn), while in other instances, the protein may be minimal, but it is obtained in conjunction with minimal calories (e.g., cruciferous and non-cruciferous green vegetables, lentils).

Thus, plant proteins in general can be added to the diet as nutrient-dense foods, unless they have been further processed into concentrated, isolated or flour forms, which give them further utility as components of value-added food products. Limiting factors to the addition of plant proteins to the human diet are the presence of various types of antinutritional factors which may compromise protein digestion and amino acid availability (the tannins and protease inhibitors) as well as the availability of dietary trace minerals (phytic acid, oxalates and fibres). However, there are several methods available to improve digestibility and, hence, availability of the protein from plant products, depending upon the nature of the ingredients. Physical processes include milling (dehulling or de-husking), while soaking, fermentation, germination, autoclaving and cooking (e.g., roasting) all are effective in eliminating or degrading antinutritional factors and increasing the utilization of the amino acids from the plant product in question.

In terms of highest levels of crude protein, soybeans stand out in this regard, followed by the pseudo-cereals and other legumes, such as lentils, chickpeas, common beans and peas. These should form the basis for meeting the essential amino acid needs in a vegan diet, with the understanding that despite the excellent amino acid profiles found in soybeans, other legumes and the pseudo-cereals, the diet is likely to be lacking in methionine. Adding significant quantities of the cereal grains as well as nuts will help to 'complement' the legumes and pseudo-cereals, as they are better balanced in regards to the sulphur amino acids, but lacking in the essential amino acid lysine, which is found at adequate levels in the legumes and pseudo-cereals. Of the cereal grains, oats are an excellent source of total protein and balanced essential amino acids, and quinoa is a similar counterpart within the pseudo-cereals. For those vegetarians that include some animal proteins in their diet, be it eggs and dairy products (Lacto-ovo vegetarian), chicken (Pollo vegetarian) or Pesco vegetarian (fish and chicken), the need to be concerned about complementary plant proteins is far less of an issue that with the vegan diet.

Plant proteins have served *Homo sapiens* well for 200,000 years, and as the benefits of plant-based diets become more evident and the possible detrimental effects of high animal protein consumption are exposed, there is currently a seeming revolution in interest in increased plant protein consumption. An added benefit to this trend in the human dietary pattern is the realization that the production of animal-based proteins requires multiple quantities of plant products to be consumed by animals to produce a single kg of animal product. Increased growth in world population and, perhaps more importantly, the increased *per capita* consumption of meat products will inevitably put a tremendous burden on the productive capacity of the world's croplands. One must consider the wisdom of this direction, when the crops themselves may be better used for direct consumption to meet the protein and other nutritional needs of a large portion of the world's population.

REFERENCES

ABARES Agricultural Commodities. (2019). Global trends in meat consumption. https://www.agriculture.gov.au/sites/default/files/sitecollectiondocuments/abares/agriculture-commodities/AgCommodities201903_MeatConsumptionOutlook_v1.0.0.pdf. Accessed February 10, 2021.

Abdualrahman, M. A. Y. (2013). Chemical, *In-vitro* protein digestibility, minerals and amino acids composition of edible peanut seeds (*Arachis hypogaea* L.). *Science International*, *1*(6):199–2020. doi:10.5567/sciint.l.2013.199.202.

Abugoch-James, L. E. (2009). Quinoa (*Chenopodium quinoa* Willd.): Composition, chemistry, nutritional, and functional properties. *Advances in Food and Nutrition Research*, *58*:1–31.

ADA/CDA. (2003). Position of the American Dietetic Association and Dietitians of Canada: Vegetarian diets. *Journal of the American Dietetic Association*, *103*(6), 748–765. doi:10.1053/jada.2003.50142.

Adeyemo, S. M., & Onilude, A. A. (2013). Enzymatic reduction of anti-nutritional factors in fermenting soybeans by *Lactobacillus plantarum* isolates from fermenting cereals. *Nigerian Food Journal*, *31*(2), 84–90.

Agricultural Marketing Resource Center (AMRC). (2021a). Buckwheat, reviewed October 2018. Iowa State University. https://www.agmrc.org/commodities-products/grains-oilseeds/buckwheat. Accessed February 12, 2021.

Agricultural Marketing Resource Center (AMRC). (2021b). Quinoa. Iowa State University. https://www.agmrc.org/commodities-products/grains-oilseeds/quinoa. Accessed February 12, 2021.

Akin-Idowu, P. E., Odunola, A-I. O. A., Gbadegesin, M. A., Oke, A., & Orkpeh Uterdzua, U. (2013). Assessment of the protein quality of twenty nine grain amaranth (*Amaranthus* spp. L.) accessions using amino acid analysis and one-dimensional electrophoresis. *African Journal of Biotechnology*, *12*(15), 1802–1810. doi:10.5897/AJB12.2971.

Alajaji, S. A., & El-Adawy, T. A. (2006). Nutritional composition of chickpea (*Cicer arietinum* L.) as affected by microwave cooking and other traditional cooking methods. *Journal of Food Composition and Analysis*, *19*(8), 806–812. doi:10.1016/j.jfca.2006.03.015.

American Heart Association (AHA) Recommendations. (2017). https://www.heart.org/en/healthy-living/healthy-eating/eat-smart/nutrition-basics/aha-diet-and-lifestyle-recommendations. Accessed February 8, 2021.

Amin, M. A., Islam, I. T., Uddin, M. R., Uddin, M. J., Rahman, M. M., & Satter, M. A. (2019). Comparative study on nutrient contents in the different parts of indigenous and hybrid varieties of pumpkin (*Cucurbita maxima* Linn.). *Heliyon*, *5*(9), e02462. doi:10.1016/j.heliyon.2019.e02462.

Amit, M. (2010). Canadian Paediatric Society, Community Paediatrics Committee. *Paediatrics and Child Health*, *15*(5), 303–314.

Angeli, V., Miguel Silva, P., Crispim Massuela, D., Khan, M. W., Hamar, A., Khajehei, F., Graeff-Hönninger, S., & Piatti, C. (2020). Quinoa (*Chenopodium quinoa* Willd.): An overview of the potentials of the "golden grain" and socio-economic and environmental aspects of its cultivation and marketization. *Foods (Basel, Switzerland)*, *9*(2), 216–236. doi:10.3390/foods9020216.

Arya, S. S., Salve, A. R., & Chauhan, S. (2016). Peanuts as functional food: A review. *Journal of Food Science and Technology*, *53*(1), 31–41. doi:10.1007/s13197-015-2007-9.

Aryee, A. N. A., & Boye, J. I. (2017). Comparative study of the effects of processing on the nutritional, physicochemical and functional properties of lentil. *Journal of Food Processing and Preservation*, *41*, e12824–12839.

Australia Export Grain Innovation Centre (AEGIC). (2017). Feed versus food: Implications for Australian wheat. https://www.grainsinnovation.org/blog/2017/9/4/12-feed-versus-food-implications-for-australian-wheat. Accessed February 12, 2021.

Ayerza, R. (1995). Oil content and fatty acid composition of chia (*Salvia hispanica* L.) from five northwestern locations in Argentina. *Journal of American Oil Chemists Society*, *72*(9), 1079–1081.

Ballabio, C., Uberti, F., Di Lorenzo, C., Brandolini, A., Penas, E., & Restani, P. (2011). Biochemical and immunochemical characterization of different varieties of amaranth (*Amaranthus* ssp. L) as a safe ingredient for gluten-free products. *Journal of Agricultural and Food Chemistry*, *59*, 12969–12974.

Ballari, S., & Barrios-Garcia, M. N. (2013). A review of wild boar *Sus scrofa* diet and factors affecting food selection in native and introduced ranges. *Mammal Review*, *44*(2), 124–134. doi:10.1111/mam.12015.

Blow, D., Janin, J., & Sweet, M. F. S. (1974). Mode of action of soybean trypsin inhibitor (Kunitz) as a model for protein-protein interactions. *Nature*, *249*, 54–57. doi:10.1038/249054a0.

Blumenschine, R. J., & Madrigal, T. C. (1993). Variability in long-bone marrow yields of East African ungulates and its zooarchaeological implications. *Journal of Archaeological Science*, *20*, 555–587.

Boye, J., Ramani, W.-B., & Burlingame, B. (2012). Protein quality evaluation twenty years after the introduction of the protein digestibility corrected amino acid score method. *British Journal of Nutrition*, *108*, S183–S211.

Boye, J., Zare, F., & Pletch, A. (2010). Pulse proteins: Processing, characterization, functional properties and applications in food and feed. *Food Research International*, *43*, 414–431.

Bressani R., Elias, L. G., & Garcia-Soto, A. (1989). Limiting amino acids in raw and processed amaranth grain protein from biological tests. *Plant Foods for Human Nutrition*, *39*(3), 223–234. doi:10.1007/BF01091933.

Bressani, R., Gonzalez, J. M., Zuniga, J., Breuner, M., & Elias, L. G. (1987). Yield, selected chemical composition and nutritive value of 14 selections of amaranth grain representing four species. *Journal of the Science of Food and Agriculture*, *38*, 347–356. doi:10.1002/jsfa.2740380407.

Canadian Food Inspection Agency. (2020). Canada.ca. http://inspection.gc.ca/food/labelling/food-labelling-for-industry/nutrition-labelling/elements-within-the-nutrition-factstable/eng/1389206763218/1389206811747?chap=7. Accessed February 8, 2021.

Chalamaiah, M., Ulug, S. K., Hong, H., & Wu, J. (2019). Regulatory requirements of bioactive peptides (protein hydrolysates) from food proteins. *Journal of Functional Foods*, *58*, 123–129. doi:10.1016/j.jff.2019.04.050.

Cleveland Clinic. (2019). And how much protein do I need, anyway? Do I need to worry about eating 'complete' proteins? https://health.clevelandclinic.org/do-i-need-to-worry-about-eating-complete-proteins/. Accessed February 12, 2021.

Craig, W. J., & Mangels, A. R. (2009). Position of the American Dietetic Association: Vegetarian diets. *Journal of the American Dietetic Association*, *109*(7), 1266–1282. doi:10.1016/j.jada.2009.05.027.

Cudmore, D. (2019). Essential amino acid profiles for all nuts [data]. https://vegfaqs.com/essential-amino-acid-profiles-nuts/. Accessed February 5, 2021.

Davis, K. R. (1981). Effect of processing on composition and Tetrahymena relative nutritive value on green and yellow peas, lentils and white pea beans. *Cereal Chemistry*, 58, 454–460.

Deribe, Y., & Kassa, E. (2020). Value creation and sorghum-based products: What synergetic actions are needed? *Cogent Food & Agriculture*, 6(1), 1722352. doi:10.1080/23311932.2020.1722352.

Dhall, R. K. (2017). *Pea Cultivation. Bulletin No. PAU/2017/Elec/FB/E/29*. Printed and Published by Additional Director of Communication for Punjab Agricultural University and Printed at PAU Printing Press, Ludhiana.

Diamond, J. (2017). *"Guns, Germs and Steel: The Fates of Human Societies". Part Two. The Rise and Spread of Food Production*. W.W. Norton and Company, Inc., New York, NY, 81–183.

Diouf, A., Sarr, F., Sene, B., Ndiaye, C., Fall, S. M., & Ayessou, N. C. (2019). Pathways for reducing antinutritional factors: Prospects for *Vigna unguiculata*. *Journal of Nutritional Health and Food Science*, 7(2), 1–10. doi:10.1007/BF0109193310.15226/jnhfs.2019.001157.

Djemel, N., Guedon, D., Lechevalier, A., Salon, C., Miquel, M., Prosperi, J. M., Rochat, C., & Boutin, J. P. (2005). Development and composition of the seeds of nine genotypes of the *Medicago truncatula* species complex. *Plant Physiology and Biochemistry*, 43, 557–566. doi:10.1007/BF0109193310.1016/j.plaphy.2005.04.005.

Domínguez-Rodrigo, M. (1997). Meat-eating by early hominids at the FLK 22 Zinjanthropus site, Olduvai Gorge (Tanzania): An experimental approach using cut-mark data. *Journal of Human Evolution*, 33, 669–690. doi:10.1006/jhev.1997.0161.

Domínguez-Rodrigo, M., Barba, R, & Egeland, C. P. (Eds.). (2007). *Deconstructing Olduvai: A Taphonomic Study of the Bed I Sites*. Springer, Netherlands.

Dvořák R., A. Pechová, L. Pavlata, J. Filipek, Dostálová J., Z. Réblová, B. Klejdus, K. Kovařcik, & J. Poul (2005). Reduction in the content of antinutritional substances in pea seeds (*Pisum sativum* L.) by different treatments. *Czech Journal of Animal Science*, 50(11), 519–527. doi:10.17221/4257-CJAS.

Eggum, B. O., I. Kreft, & B. Javornik (1980). Chemical composition and protein quality of buckwheat (*Fagopyrum esculentum* Moench). *Plant Food for Human Nutrition*, 30, 175–179. doi:10.1007/BF01091933/10.1007/BF01094020.

Elkowicz, K., F. W. Sosulski (1982). Antinutritional factors in eleven legumes and their air-classified protein and starch fractions. *Journal of Food Science*, 47, 1301–1304. doi:10.1111/j.1365-2621.1982.tb07673.x.

Elsheikh, E. A. E., & Mohamedzein, E. M. E. (1998). Effect of *Bradyrhizobium*, VA mycorrhiza and fertilizers on seed composition of groundnut. *Annals of Applied Biology*, 132, 325–330. doi:10.1111/j.1744-7348.1998.tb05207.x.

FAO. (1992). *Maize in Human Nutrition*. Food and Agriculture Organization of the United Nations, Rome.

FAO. (2013). *Food and Agriculture Organization of the United Nations Database of Agricultural Production*. Sorghum: Post-harvest Operations, Italy, Rome.

FAO. (2019). Dietary protein quality evaluation in human nutrition report of an FAO expert consultation. http://www.fao.org/3/a-i3124e.pdf. Accessed September 24, 2019.

FAO-FAOSTAT (Food and Agriculture Organization of the United Nations). (2018). Crops [Internet]. www.fao.org/faostat/en/#data/QC. Accessed March 19, 2018.

FAO, UN. (2011). Quinoa: An ancient crop to contribute to world food security. Regional Office for Latin America and the Caribbean. http://www.fao.org/3/aq287e/aq287e.pdf. Accessed February 12, 2021.

FAO/WHO Expert Consultation. (1991). *Protein Quality Evaluation. Food and Agricultural Organization of the United Nations*. FAO Food and Nutrition Paper No. 51, Rome.

Farinde, E. O., O. T. Olanipekun, & R. B. Olasupo (2018). Nutritional composition and antinutrients content of raw and processed lima bean (*Phaseolus lunatus*). *Annals of Food Science and Technology*, 19(2), 250–264.

Felker, P., R. Bunch, & A. Leung (2016). Concentrations of thiocyanate and goitrin in human plasma, their precursor concentrations in brassica vegetables, and associated potential risk for hypothyroidism. *Nutrition Reviews*, 74(4), 248–258. doi:10.1093/nutrit/nuv110.

Food and Agriculture Organization/World Health Organization. (2001). *Report of the FAO/WHO Working Group on Analytical Issues Related to Food Composition and Protein Quality*. FAO, Rome, Italy.

Food and Agriculture Organization of the United Nations. (2019). FAOSTAT. http://faostat.fao.org. Accessed September 2019.

Fowke, J. H., F. L. Chung, F. Jin, D. Qi, Q. Y. Cai, C. Conaway, J. R. Cheng ..... (2003). Urinary isothiocyanate levels, brassica, and human breast cancer. *Cancer Research*, 63, 3980–3986.

Friedman, M., & D. L. Brandon (2001). Nutritional and health benefits of soy proteins. *Journal of Agricultural and Food Chemistry*, 49(3), 1069–1086. doi:10.1021/jf0009246.

Furness, J. B., J. J. Cottrell, & D. M. Bravo (2015). Comparative gut physiology symposium: Comparative physiology of digestion. *Journal of Animal Science*, 93(2), 485–491. doi:10.2527/jas2014-8481.

García-Mora, P., M. Martín-Martínez, M. A. Bonache, R. González-Múniz, E. Peñas, J., Frias, & C. Martinez-Villaluenga (2017). Identification, functional gastrointestinal stability and molecular docking studies of lentil peptides with dual antioxidant and angiotensin I converting enzyme inhibitory activities. *Food Chemistry, 221*, 464–472. doi:10.1016/j.foodchem.2016.10.087.

Gerbens-Leenes, P. W., M. M. Mekonnen, & A. Y. Hoekstra (2013). The water footprint of poultry, pork and beef: A comparative study in different countries and production systems. *Water Resources and Industry, 1-2*, 25–36. doi:10.1016/j.wri.2013.03.001.

Gomez, M., B. Oliete, C. M. Rosell, V. Pando, & E. Fernandez (2008). Studies on cake quality made of wheat-chickpea flour blends. *LWT – Food Science and Technology, 41*, 1701–1709. doi:10.1016/j.lwt.2007.11.024.

Grancieri, M., H. S. D. Martino, & E. G. de Mejia (2019). Chia seed (*Salvia hispanica* L.) as a source of proteins and bioactive peptides with health benefits: A review. *Comprehensive Reviews in Food Science and Food Safety, 18*, 480–499. doi:10.1111/1541-4337.12423.

Griffey, C., W. Brooks, M. Kurantz, W. Thomason, F. Taylor, D. Obert, R. Moreau ...... (2010). Grain composition of Virginia winter barley and implications for use in feed, food and biofuels production. *Journal of Cereal Science, 51*, 41–49. doi:10.1016/j.jcs.2009.09.004.

Habib, A., S. Biswas, A. H. Siddique, M. Manirujjaman, B. Uddin, S. Hasan, M. M. H. Khan..... (2015). Nutritional and lipid composition analysis of pumpkin seed (*Cucurbita maxima* Linn.). *Journal of Nutrition and Food Sciences, 5*(4), 374–379. doi:10.4172/2155-9600.1000374.

Hawtin, G. C., K. O. Rachie, & J. M. Green (1977). Breeding strategy for the nutritional improvement of pulses. In: *Nutritional Standards and Methods of Evaluation for Food Legume Breeders*. Hulse, J. H., Rachie, K. O., & Billingsley, L. W. (Eds). Ottawa, ON: IDRC, 43–51.

Hayes, J. D., M. O. Kelleher, & I. M. Eggleston (2008). The cancer chemopreventive actions of phytochemicals derived from glucosinolates. *European Journal of Nutrition, 47*(S2), 73–88. doi:10.1007/s00394-008-2009-8.

Hirst, K. K. (2019). Pea (*Pisum sativum* L.). "Domestication - the history of peas and humans." *ThoughtCo*. April 28, 2019. https://www.thoughtco.com/domestication-history-of-peas-169376?print. Accessed February 8, 2021.

Hirst, K. (2020). The eight founder crops and the origins of agriculture. *ThoughtCo*. August 27, 2020. thoughtco.com/founder-crops-origins-of-agriculture-171203.

Hoekstra, A. Y. (2011). Understanding the water footprint of factory farming. *Farm Animal Voice, 180*, 14–15.

International Grains Council. (2021). Grain market report. https://www.igc.int/en/gmr_summary.aspx. Accessed February 12, 2021.

Izydorczyk, M. S., T. McMillan, S. Bazin, J. Kletke, L. Dushnicky, & J. Dexter. (2014). Canadian buckwheat: A unique, useful and under-utilized crop. *Canadian Journal of Plant Science, 94*, 509–524. doi:10.4141/cjps2013-075.

Jansman, A. J. M., G. D. Hill, J. Huisman, & A. F. B. VanderPoel (Eds). (1998). *Recent Advances of Research in Antinutritional Factors in Legume Seeds*. Wageningen Press, Wageningen.

Karaca, A. C., Low, N., & Nickerson, M. (2011). Emulsifying properties of chickpea, faba bean, lentil and pea proteins produced by isoelectric precipitation and salt extraction. *Food Research International, 444*, 2742–2750. doi:10.1016/j.foodres.2011.06.012.

Kebary, K. M. K., & Hussein, S. (1997). Quality of ice cream as influenced by substituting non-fat dry milk with whey ± bean protein coprecipitates. *Egyptian Journal of Dairy Science, 25*, 311–325.

Kennedy, G., B. Burlingame, & V. N. Nguyen. (2003). Nutritional contribution of rice and impact of biotechnology and biodiversity in rice-consuming countries. Sustainable rice production for food security. Proceedings of the 20th Session of the International Rice Commission Bangkok, Thailand, July 23–26, 2002. Food and Agriculture Organization of the United Nations, Rome.

Khazaei, H., M. Subedi, M. Nickerson, C. Martinez-Villaluenga, J. Frias, & A. Vandenberg. (2019). Seed protein of lentils: Current status, progress, and food applications. *Foods, 8*, 391–414. doi:10.3390/foods8090391.

Kidanemaryam, W. (2019). Review on mechanisms of drought tolerance in sorghum (*Sorghum bicolor* (L.) Moench) basis and breeding methods. *Academic Research Journal of Agricultural Science and Research, 7*(2), 87–99. doi:10.14662/ARJASR2019.007.

Kiosseoglou, V., & A. Paraskevopoulou (2011). Functional and physicochemical properties of pulse proteins. In: *Pulse Foods: Processing, Quality and Nutraceutical Applications*. Tiwari, B. K., Gowen, A., & McKenna, B. (Eds). Cambridge, MA: Academic Press, 57–90.

Klose, C., & E. K. Arendt (2012). Proteins in oats; their synthesis and changes during germination: A review. *Critical Reviews in Food Science and Nutrition, 52*(7), 629–639. doi:10.1080/10408398.2010.504902.

Kumar, J., J. Singh, R. Kanaujia, & S. Gupta. (2016). Protein content in wild and cultivated taxa of lentil (*Lens culinaris* ssp. *culinaris Medikus*). *Indian Journal of Genetics and Plant Breeding*, *76*(4), 631–634. doi:10.5958/0975-6906.2016.00078.X.

Kurhekar, J. (2016). Tannins – antimicrobial chemical components. *International Journal of Technology and Science*, *IX*(3), 5–9.

Kusch S., B. Schumacher, H. Oechsner, & W. Schafer. (2011). Methane yield of oat husks. *Biomass and Bioenergy*, *35*, 2627–2633. doi:10.1016/j.biombioe.2011.02.044.

Ladjal-Ettoumi, Y., H. Boudries, M. Chibane, & A. Romero (2016). Pea, chickpea and lentil protein isolates: Physicochemical characterization and emulsifying properties. *Food Biophysics*, *11*(1), 43–51. doi:10.1007/s11483-015-9411-6.

Lazos, E. S. (1986). Nutritional, fatty acid, and oil characteristics of pumpkin and melon seeds. *Journal of Food Science*, *51*(5), 1382–1383. doi:10.1111/j.1365-2621.1986.tb13133.x.

Leonard, W. R., J. J. Snodgrass, & M. L. Robertson (2007). Effects of brain evolution on human nutrition and metabolism. *Annual Review of Nutrition*, *27*, 311–327. doi:10.1146/annurev.nutr.27.061406.093659.

Litwinek, D., H. Gambuś, B. Mickowska, G. Zięć, & W. Berski. (2013). Amino acids composition of proteins in wheat and oat flours used in breads production. *Journal of Microbiology, Biotechnology and Food Sciences*, *2*(1), 1725–1733.

London, S. J., J. M. Yuan, F. L. Chung, Y. T. Gao, G. A. Coetzee, R. K. Ross, & M. C. Yu (2000). Isocyanates, glutathione S-transferase M1 and T1 polymorphisms, and lung cancer risk: A prospective study of men in Shanghai, China. *Lancet*, *356*, 724–729. doi:10.1016/S0140-6736(00)02631-3.

Luo, Y.-W., & W.-H. Xie (2013). Effect of different processing methods on certain antinutritional factors and protein digestibility in green and white faba bean (*Vicia faba* L.). *CyTA - Journal of Food*, *11*(1), 43–49. doi:10.1080/19476337.2012.681705.

Luthar, Z., M. Zhou, A. Golob, M. Germ (2021). Breeding buckwheat for increased levels and improved quality of protein. *Plants*, *10*, 14–26. doi:10.3390/plants10010014.

Mariotti, F., & C. D. Gardner (2019). Dietary protein and amino acids in vegetarian diets—A review. *Nutrients*, *11*, 2661–2680. doi:10.3390/nu11112661.

Mattila, P. H., J.-M. Pihlava, J. Hellström, M. Nurmi, M. Eurola, S. Mäkinen, T. Jalava, & A. Pihlanto (2018). Contents of phytochemicals and antinutritional factors in commercial protein-rich plant products. *Food Quality and Safety*, *2*(4), 213–219. doi:10.1093/fqsafe/fyy021.

Matus, A., A. E. Slinkard, & A. Vandenberg (1993). The potential of zero tannin lentil. In: *New Crops*. Janick, J., & Simon, J. E. (Eds). New York, NY: Wiley, 279–282.

McOsker, D. E. (1962). The limiting amino acid sequence in raw and roasted peanut protein. *The Journal of Nutrition*, *76*(4), 453–459. doi:10.1093/jn/76.4.453.

Mehta, S. S., W. D. Arroyave, R. M. Lunn, Y.-M. M. Park, W. A. Boyd, & D. P. Sandler (2020). A prospective analysis of red and processed meat consumption and risk of colorectal cancer in women. *Cancer Epidemiology, Biomarkers & Prevention*, *29*(1), 141–150. doi:10.1158/1055-9965.EPI-19-0459.

Meredith, F. I., C. A. Thomas, M. E. Snook, D. S. Himmelsbach, & H. Van Halbeek (1988). Soluble carbohydrates oligosaccharides and starch in lima bean seeds. *Journal of Food Science*, *53*(3), 768–771. doi:10.1111/j.1365-2621.1988.tb08952.x.

Milton, K. (1999). A hypothesis to explain the role of meat-eating in human evolution. *Evolutionary Anthropology*, *8*:11–21.

Milton, K. (2003). The critical role played by animal source foods in human (Homo) evolution. *The Journal of Nutrition*, *133*, 3886S–3892S. doi:10.1093/jn/133.11.3886S.

Milton, K., & M. W. Demment (1988). Digestion and passage kinetics of chimpanzees fed high and low fiber diets and comparison with human data. *The Journal of Nutrition*, *118*, 1082–1088. doi:10.1093/jn/118.9.1082.

Nadeem, M., F. M. Anjum, R. M. Amir, M. R. Khan, S. Hussain, & M. S. Javed. (2010). An overview of antinutritional factors in cereal grains with special reference to wheat-A review. *Pakistan Journal of Food Sciences*, *20*(1-4), 54–61.

Natesh, R., S. L. Schwager, E. D. Sturrock, & K. R. Acharya (2003). Crystal structure of the human angiotensin-converting enzyme-Lysinopril complex. *Nature*, *421*, 551–554. doi:10.1038/nature01370.

National Soybean Research Laboratory. (2012). Nsrl.uiuc.edu. Archived from the original on March 4, 2012. Urbana, IL. https://web.archive.org/web/20120304080126/http://www.nsrl.uiuc.edu/soy_benefits.html. Accessed February 8, 2021.

Nestares, T., López-Frías, M., Barrionuevo, M., & Urbano, G. (1996). Nutritional assessment of raw and processed chickpea (*Cicer arietinum* L.) protein in growing rats. *Journal of Agricultural and Food Chemistry*, *44*, 2760–2765.

Newton, A. C., A. J. Flavell, T. S. George, P. Leat, B. Mullholland, L. Ramsay, C. Revoredo-Giha, J. Russell, B. J. Steffenson, J. S. Swanston, W. T. B. Thomas, R. Waugh, P. J. White, & I. J. Bingham (2011). Crops that feed the world 4. Barley: A resilient crop? Strengths and weaknesses in the context of food security. *Food Security, 3*(2), 141–178. doi:10.1007/s12571-011-0126-3.

Nyachoti, C., Atkinson, J., & Leeson, S. (1997). Sorghum tannins: A review. *World's Poultry Science Journal, 53*(1), 5–21. doi:10.1079/WPS19970002.

Occena, L. G., Bennink, M. R., Uebersax, M. A., & Chung, Y. S. (1997). Evaluation of drum-dried meals prepared from split beans (*Phaseolus vulgaris* L): Protein quality and selected anti nutritional factors. *Journal of Food Processing and Preservation, 21*, 335–344. doi:10.1111/j.1745-4549.1997.tb00787.x.

OECD Data. (2019). Meat consumption. https://oecd.org/agroutout/meat-consumption.htm. Accessed February 5, 2021.

Onigbinde, A., & Akinyele, I. (2006). Oligosaccharide content of 20 varieties of cowpeas in Nigeria. *Journal of Food Science, 48*, 1250–1251. doi:10.1111/j.1365-2621.1983.tb09203.x.

Plate, A. Y. A., & D. D. Gallaher (2003). Breakdown products of glucosinolates and reduced risk of colon cancer. *FASEB Journal, 17*, A1153.

Popova, A., & Mihaylova, D. (2019). Antinutrients in plant-based foods: A review. *The Open Biotechnology Journal, 13*, 68–76. doi:10.2174/1874070701913010068.

Pulse Canada. (2017). Protein quality of cooked pulses. https://www.pulsecanada.com/wp-content/uploads/2017/09/Pulses-and-Protein-Quality.pdf. Accessed February 10, 2021.

Qi, G., Ningbo, L., Sun, X. S., & Wang, D. (2019). Overview of sorghum industrial utilization. In: *Sorghum: A State of the Art and Future Perspectives*, Vol. 58. Ciampitti, I. A., & Vara Prasad, P. V. (Eds). First published on January 11, 2019. doi:10.2134/agronmonogr58.

Queiroz, K. D., de Oliveira, A. C., Helbig, E., Reis, S. M. P. M., & Carraro, F. (2002). Soaking the common bean in a domestic preparation reduced the contents of raffinose-type oligosaccharides but did not interfere with nutritive value. *Journal of Nutritional Science and Vitaminology, 48*(4), 283–289. doi:10.3177/jnsv.48.283.

Ranum, P., Pena-Rosas, J. P., & Garcia-Casal, M. N. (2014). Global maize production, utilization, and consumption. *Annals of the New York Academy of Sciences, 1312*, 105–112. doi:10.1111/nyas.12396.

Rasane, P., Jha, A., Sabikhi, L., Kumar, A., & Unnikrishnan, V. S. (2015). Nutritional advantages of oats and opportunities for its processing as value added foods: A review. *Journal of Food Science and Technology, 52*(2), 662–675. doi:10.1007/s13197-013-1072-1.

Ratnavathi, C. V., & Patil, J. V. (2013). Sorghum utilization as food. *Journal of Nutrition and Food Sciences, 4*, 247–254. doi:10.4172/2155-9600.1000247.

Redden, R. J. (2007). *History and Origin of Chickpea. Australian Temperate Field Crops Collection*. Department of Primary Industries, Horsham, Australia.

Reeds, P., Schaafsma, G., Tome, D., & Young, V. (2000). Criteria and significance of dietary protein sources in humans. Summary of the workshop with recommendations, 16th Ed. *The Journal of Nutrition, 130*(7), 1874S–1876S. doi:10.1093/jn/130.7.1874S.

Reiss, J. (1993). Miso from peas (*Pisum sativum*) and beans (*Phaseolus vulgaris*) of domestic origin. Fermented foods from agricultural products in Europe. II. *Zeitschrift für Ernährungswissenschaft, 32*, 237–241. doi:10.1007/BF01610734.

Rizzello, C. B., Verni, M., Bordignon, S., Gramaglia, V., Gobbetti, M. (2017). Hydrolysate from a mixture of legume flours with antifungal activity as an ingredient for prolonging the shelf-life of wheat bread. *Food Microbiology, 64*, 72–82.

Rosenberg, H. R., Culik, R., & Eckert, R. E. (1959). Lysine and threonine supplementation of rice. *The Journal of Nutrition, 69*(3), 217–228. doi:10.1093/jn/69.3.217.

Rupérez, P. (1998). Oligosaccharides in raw and processed legumes. *European Food Research and Technology, 206*, 130–133. doi:10.1007/s002170050228.

Salunkhe, D. K., Kadam, S. S., & Chavan, J. K. (1977). Nutritional quality of proteins in grain sorghum. *Plant Food for Human Nutrition, 27*, 187–205. doi:10.1007/BF01092359.

Samtiya, M., Aluko, R. E., & Dhewa, T. (2020). Plant food anti-nutritional factors and their reduction strategies: An overview. *Food Production, Processing and Nutrition, 2*(1), 6–19. doi:10.1186/s43014-020-0020-5.

Sandoval-Oliveros, M. R., & Paredes-López, O. (2013). Isolation and characterization of proteins from chia seeds (*Salvia hispanica* L.). *Journal of Agricultural and Food Chemistry, 61*(1), 193–201. doi:10.1021/jf3034978.

Serna-Salvidar, S. O., & Espinosa-Ramírez, J. (2018). Grain structure and grain chemical composition. In:

Sorghum and Millets: Chemistry, Technology and Nutritional Attributes, 2nd Edition. AACC International, Elsevier, Amsterdam, Netherlands.

Sarusi, D. (2021). The Jane Goodall Institute of Canada. University of Toronto Mailroom. https://janegoodall.ca/who-we-are/. Accessed February 10, 2021.

Schaafsma (2005). The protein digestibility-corrected amino acid score (PDCAAS)—A concept for describing protein quality in foods and food ingredients: A critical review. *Journal of the Association of Official Analytical Chemists International*, 88(3), 988–994.

Schoenlechner, R., & Bender, D. (2020). Pseudocereals for global food production. *Cereal Foods World*, 65(2). doi:10.1094/CFW-65-2-0014.

Shankar, S., Ganapathy, S., & Srivastava, R. K. (2008). Sulforaphane enhances the therapeutic potential of TRAIL in prostate cancer orthotopic model through regulation of apoptosis, metastasis and angiogenesis. *Clinical Cancer Research*, 14, 6855–6866. doi:10.1158/1078-0432.CCR-08-0903.

Shewry, P. R., & Hey, S. J. (2015). The contribution of wheat to human diet and health. *Food and Energy Security*, 4(3), 178–202. doi:10.1002/fes3.64.

Shi, L., Mu, K., Arntfield, S. D., & Nickerson, M. T. (2017). Changes in levels of enzyme inhibitors during soaking and cooking for pulses available in Canada. *Journal of Food Science and Technology*, 54, 1014–1022. doi:10.1007/s13197-017-2519-6.

Smith, K. A. (2005). The impact of agriculture and other land uses on emissions of methane and nitrous and nitric oxides. *Environmental Sciences*, 2(2-3), 101–108. doi:10.1080/15693430500370423.

Steinbrecher, A., & Linseisen, J. (2009). Dietary intake of individual glucosinolates in participants of the EPIC-Heidelberg cohort study. *Annals of Nutrition and Metabolism*, 54, 87–96.

Suárez López, M. M., Kizlansky, A., & López, L. B. (2006). Evaluación de la calidad de las proteínas en los alimentos calculando el escore de aminoácidos corregido por digestibilidad [Assessment of protein quality in foods by calculating the amino acids score corrected by digestibility]. *Nutricion Hospitalaria*, 21(1), 47–51.

Sytar, O., Brestic, M., Zivcak, M., & Tran, L. S. (2016). The contribution of buckwheat genetic resources to health and dietary diversity. *Current Genomics*, 17(3), 193–206. doi:10.2174/1389202917666160202215425.

Tavano, O. L., da Silva, S. I. Jr, Demonte, A., & Neves, V. A. (2008). Nutritional responses of rats to diets based on chickpea (*Cicer arietinum* L.) seed meal or its protein fractions. *Journal of Agricultural and Food Chemistry*, 56(22), 11006–11010. doi:10.1021/jf8010799.

Toews, R., & N. Wang (2013). Physicochemical and functional properties of protein concentrates from pulses. *Food Research International*, 52, 445–451. doi:10.1016/j.foodres.2012.12.009.

Traka, M., & Mithen, R. (2009). Glucosinolates, isothiocyanates and human health. *Phytochemistry Reviews*, 8, 269–282.

Tricase, C., Amicarelli, V., Lamonaca, E., & Rana, R. L. (2018). Economic analysis of the barley market and related uses. doi:10.5772/intechopen.78967. Accessed February 5, 2021.

Udensi, E. A., Ekwu, F. C., & Isinguzo, J. N. (2007). Antinutrient factors of vegetable cowpea (Sesquipedalis) seeds during thermal processing. *Pakistan Journal of Nutrition*, 6(2), 194–197. doi:10.3923/pjn.2007.194.197.

Ullah, R., Nadeem, M., Khalique, A., Imran, M., Mehmood, S., Javid, A., & Hussain, J. (2016). Nutritional and therapeutic perspectives of chia (*Salvia hispanica* L.): A review. *J Food Science and Technology*, 53(4), 1750–1758. doi:10.1007/s13197-015-1967-0.

Urbano, G., Porres, J. M., Frias, J., & Vidal-Valverde, C. (2007). Nutritional value. In: *Lentil: An Ancient Crop for Modern Times*, Vol. 3. Yadav, S. S., McNeil, D., & Stevenson, P. C. (Eds). Berlin: Springer, 47–93.

United States Department of Agriculture (USDA). (2015). http://ndb.nal.usda. gov/ndb/foods/show/4800?fgcd=&manu=&lfacet=&format=&count=&max=35&offset=&sort=&qlookup=peanut. Accessed February 5, 2021.

U.S. Department of Agriculture. (2019). Agricultural Research Service. FoodData Central. fdc.nal.usda.gov. Accessed February 5, 2021.

U.S. Department of Agriculture. (2021). Foreign Agricultural Service Global Market Analysis. https://apps.fas.usda.gov/psdonline/circulars/production.pdf. Accessed February 12, 2021.

U.S. Department of Agriculture. (2021). Oilseeds: World Markets and Trade. Foreign Agriculture Service. https://apps.fas.usda.gov/psdonline/circulars/oilseeds.pdf. Accessed February 10, 2021.

van Poppel, G., Verhoeven, D. T., Verhagen, H., & Goldbohm, R. A. (1999). Brassica vegetables and cancer prevention; epidemiology and mechanisms. *Advances in Nutrition and Cancer 2*, 472, 159–168. Part of the *Advances in Experimental Medicine and Biology* book series (AEMB, Vol. 472). doi:10.1007/978-1-4757-3230-6_14.

Vega-Gálvez, A. V., Miranda, M., Vergara, J., Uribe, E., Puente, L., & Martínez, E. A. (2010). Nutrition facts and functional potential of quinoa (*Chenopodium quinoa* willd.), an ancient Andean grain: A review. *Journal of the Science of Food and Agriculture*, *90*(15), 2541–2547. doi:10.1002/jsfa.4158.

Vegan Society. (2021). https://www.vegansociety.com/resources/nutrition-and-health. Accessed February 5, 2021.

Venkatachalam, M., & Sathe, S. (2006). Chemical composition of selected edible nut seeds. *Journal of Agricultural and Food Chemistry*, *54*(13), 4705–4714. doi:10.1021/jf0606959.

Vieira, A. R., Abar, L., Chan, D. S. M., Vingeliene, S., Polemiti, E., Stevens, C., Greenwood, D., & Norat, T. (2017). Foods and beverages and colorectal cancer risk: A systematic review and meta-analysis of cohort studies, an update of the evidence of the WCRF-AICR Continuous Update Project. *Annals of Oncology*, *28*(8), 1788–1802. doi:10.1093/annonc/mdx171.

Vogelsang-O'Dwyer, M., Petersen, I. L., Joehnke, M. S., Sørensen, J. C., Bez, J., Detzel, A., Busch, M., Krueger, M., O'Mahony, J. A., Arendt, E. K., & Zannini, E. (2020). Comparison of faba bean protein ingredients produced using dry fractionation and isoelectric precipitation: Techno-functional, nutritional and environmental performance. *Foods*, *9*, 322–345. doi:10.3390/foods9030322.

Voora, V., Larrea, C., & Bermudez, S. (2020). *Global Report: Soybeans*. International Institute for Sustainable Development, Winnipeg, Manitoba. https://www.iisd.org/system/files/2020-10/ssi-global-market-report-soybean.pdf. Accessed February 8, 2021.

Wallace, T. C., Murray, R., & Zelman, K. M. (2016). The nutritional value and health benefits of chickpeas and hummus. *Nutrients*, *8*, 766–776. doi:10.3390/nu8120766.

Watts, D. P. (2008). Scavenging by chimpanzees at Ngogo and the relevance of chimpanzee scavenging to early hominin behavioral ecology. *Journal of Human Evolution*, *54*, 25–133. doi:10.1016/j.jhevol.2007.07.008.

Weaver, T. D. (2012). Did a discrete event 200,000–100,000 years ago produce modern humans? *Journal of Human Evolution*, *63*, 21–126. doi:10.1016/j.jhevol.2012.04.003.

WHO/FAO/UNU Expert Consultation. (1985). *Energy and Protein Requirements*. WHO Technical Report no. 724. World Health Organization, Geneva.

World Cancer Research Fund. (1997). Food, nutrition and the prevention of cancer: A global perspective. American Institute of Cancer Research, Washington DC. *Nutrition*, *15*(6), 523–526. doi:10.1016/s0899-9007(99)00021-0.

Wrangham, R., & Conklin-Brittain, N. (2003). Cooking as a biological trait. *Comparative Biochemistry and Physiology Part A: Molecular & Integrative Physiology*, *136*(1), 35–46. doi:10.1016/S1095-6433(03)00020-5.

Xing-Lin, H., De-Liang, W., Wu-Jiu, Z., & Shi-Ru, J. (2017). The production of the Chinese baijiu from sorghum and other cereals. *Journal of the Institute of Brewing*, *123*, 600–604.

Yilmaz, S., Ilbas, A., Akbulut, M., & Çetin, A. (2018). Grain amino acid composition of barley (*Hordeum vulgare* L.) cultivars subjected to selenium doses. *Turkish Journal of Biochemistry*, *43*(3), 268–276. doi:10.1515/tjb-2017-0027.

Young, V. R., & Pellett, P. L. (1985). Wheat proteins in relation to protein requirements and availability of amino acids. *The American Journal of Clinical Nutrition*, *41*(5), 1077–1090. doi:10.1093/ajcn/41.5.1077.

Young, V. R., & Pellett, P. L. (1994). Plant proteins in relation to human protein and amino acid nutrition. *The American Journal of Clinical Nutrition*, *59*(Suppl), 1203S–1212S.

Yu, J., & Ahmedna, M. (2012). Functions/applications of trypsin in food processing and food science research. In: *Trypsin: Structure, Biosynthesis and Functions*. Nova Science Publishers, Hauppauge, NY, USA, 75–96.

3 Single-Cell Protein – A Group of Alternative Proteins

Marzieh Hosseininezhad[1] and Malik Altaf Hussain[2]
[1]Research Institute of Food Science and Technology, Mashhad, Iran
[2]Food Safety Unit, The Victorian Department of Health, Melbourne, Australia

CONTENTS

3.1	Introduction	49
3.2	Production of SCP	50
	3.2.1 Suitable Strain Selection	51
	3.2.2 Fermentation	51
	3.2.3 Harvesting	53
	3.2.4 SCP Processing for Food	53
3.3	Major Microbial Sources	53
	3.3.1 Fungi	53
	3.3.2 Yeast	54
	3.3.3 Algae	55
	3.3.4 Bacteria	56
3.4	Applications of SCP	56
	3.4.1 Health and Nutrition	56
	3.4.2 Therapeutic, Natural Medicine and Cosmetic Products	57
	3.4.2.1 Food Production	57
	3.4.2.2 Cosmetic Products and Other Industries	57
3.5	Advantages of SCP	58
	3.5.1 High Rate of Multiplication	58
	3.5.2 Genetic Modification	58
	3.5.3 Variety of Raw Material	58
	3.5.4 Independence of Climatic Conditions and Environment Friendship	58
3.6	Disadvantages of SCP	59
	3.6.1 High Level of Nucleic Acids	59
	3.6.2 Allergic Reactions and Toxic Metabolites	59
	3.6.3 Health Condition Developments	59
	3.6.4 Cost of Production	60
3.7	Conversion of Food Wastes to SCP	60
3.8	Recent Advances in SCP and Future Aspects	61
3.9	Conclusion	62
Acknowledgement and Declaration		62
References		62

3.1 INTRODUCTION

Microorganisms have the ability to upgrade low-quality organic material to highly nutritive protein food, and this has been exploited by industry. An alternative to plant and animal proteins is the

DOI: 10.1201/9780429299834-3

aerobic production of microbial proteins, the dried cells of microorganisms used as food and feed are collectively known as 'single-cell protein' (SCP). The term was coined by Carol L. Wilson in 1966, as most microorganism grows as single or filamentous individuals. Typically, this mode of production involves the supply of nitrogen, an electron donor, a carbon source and an electron acceptor (e.g., oxygen) to a reactor system, enabling highly efficient production and harvesting of the protein.

Although yeasts have been used in food production, mainly bread and beverages, since 2500 BC, the technology of SCP production was developed over the 20th century. The term 'single-cell protein' was first used by a professor at the Massachusetts Institute of Technology, Carol Wilson, and the first industrial production of SCP in nutrition was in Germany during the First World War, where the yeast *Saccharomyces cerevisiae* was developed and molasses were used as sources of carbon, energy and ammonium salts. The yeast *Candela utilis* was first applied as a source of protein in nutrition, and its development on the fluid from paper mills and sugars resulted from acidic decomposition of the wood. This method resulted in the production of about 15,000 tonnes of *C. utilis* protein per year in Germany during World War II (Al-Mudhafr & Al-Garawyi, 2019).

Commercial production of SCP is limited to a small number of processes due to high capital and operating costs and the high cost of nutritional and toxicological assessment (Sadler, 1994). However, besides the nutritional value of SCP, a considerable benefit of SCP technology is that due to their year-round production, only a small area of land is required, and therefore SCP can be produced as needed.

There are several factors that affect the growth of SCP, including the pH of the media, temperature, incubation period, dissolved oxygen, aeration rate, nutritional requirements and the carbon source. The yield (g/l) and productivity (g/l h^{-1}) of SCP production are strongly dependent on culture medium composition and environmental conditions (Reihani et al., 2019).

3.2 PRODUCTION OF SCP

The production of SCP takes place in a fermentation process by selected microbial strains which are multiplied on suitable nutrient media in a technical cultivation process that is directed to the growth of the culture and the cell mass followed by separation processes (Nasseri et al. 2011).

In SCP production, the raw materials are hydrolyzed by physical, chemical and enzymatic methods before being used as substrates. Pre-treatment methods are elementary to reduce the crystallinity of cellulose and to break the resistant layer of lignin, thus increasing the availability of carbohydrates to be used by microorganisms. Physical pre-treatments are mechanical (i.e., grinding, chopping, milling, knife mill, scissors, etc.), as well as by the use of microwave, ultrasound, steam explosion and liquid hot water methods. In contrast, chemical pre-treatments are purely initiated by chemical reactions to disrupt the biomass structure.

Process engineering and apparatus technology adapt the technical performance of the process to prepare the production for large technical scale use. Here is where economic factors (e.g., energy, cost) come into play. Safety demands and environmental protection are also considered in the production of SCP in relation to both the process and to the product. Finally, safety and protection of innovation present legal and control barriers, namely operating licenses, product authorizations for particular applications, and legal protection of new processes and strains of microorganisms (Nasseri et al., 2011).

Looking over the significance of SCP as protein supplements, it is required to develop clean-green technology for SCP production on a large scale to fulfill the future global requirements. The process involved in the production of SCP from any microorganism or substrate would generally include the selection of suitable microbial strains and preparation of nutrient media and raw materials, preferably from waste; cultivation, including solid-state fermentation; separation and concentration, drying and final processing.

SCP production would include the following basic steps (Srividya et al., 2013; Ukaegbu-Obi, 2016):

1. Provision of a carbon source with physical or chemical pre-treatments, if needed.
2. Addition of sources of nitrogen, phosphorus and other nutrients to the carbon source to support optimal growth of the target microorganism.
3. Prevention of contamination by maintaining sterile or hygienic conditions throughout the process. The medium components may be heated or sterilized by filtration, and the fermentation equipment may be sterilized.
4. Inoculation of the selected microorganism in a pure state to carry out the fermentation process.
5. Adequate aeration and cooling, as SCP processes are highly aerobic (except those using algae), and considerable heat is generated.
6. Harvesting the microbial biomass and post-harvesting treatments including filtration, purification and, in some cases, drying of the final product to prepare for marketing or storage.
7. Processing of the biomass into product and ingredients to enhance its usefulness and/or storability.

3.2.1 Suitable Strain Selection

The careful selection of strains is critical, as protein quality depends on the microbial sources that are used. These sources are preferably those which contain more than 30% protein in their biomass and which can provide a healthy balance of the essential amino acids. The SCP process development begins with microbial screening, in which suitable production strains are obtained from soil, water, air or swab samples of inorganic or biological materials which are subsequently optimized by the selection, mutation or other genetic methods. Then, the technical cultivation conditions for the optimized strains are carried out, and all metabolic pathways and cell structures are determined (Nasseri et al., 2011). SCP is currently produced from a limited number of microbial species, particularly when considering human sources, while the range of sources for animal feed is broader. The main characteristics for suitable strain selection include high specific growth rate and biomass yield, low nutritional requirements, the ability to utilize complex substrates with high affinity, the ability to develop high cell density, stability during multiplication, a capacity for genetic modification, high tolerance to pH and temperature, balanced protein and lipid composition, low nucleic acid content, good digestibility and non-toxicity (Upadhyaya et al., 2016).

There are some challenges faced with SCP production that are related to the different microbial sources, including economical scale-up and cell disruption to release microalgae nutrients and the protein and essential amino acid content from yeasts, and there are palatability issues for bacteria. A list of microorganisms used as sources of SCP and their overall characteristics are indicated in Table 3.1.

3.2.2 Fermentation

The production of SCP takes place in a fermenter, where they undergo submerged, semisolid and solid-state fermentation processes. This is done by selected microorganisms that are grown on suitable raw materials in technical cultivation processes directed to the growth of the culture and the cell mass. The fermentation process requires a pure culture of the selected organism and its growth to a correct physiological state, sterilization of the growth medium, which is used for the organism, a production fermenter or bioreactor which is equipped with an aeration system, controlled pH, a thermostat, etc., to draw the culture medium into a steady state. Process development begins with microbial screening, in which suitable production strains are obtained and are subsequently optimized by selection, mutation or other genetic methods. The technical conditions of

TABLE 3.1
Summary of SCP sources and their average proximate compositions and characteristics

Microorganism	Bacteria	Yeast	Fungi	Microalgae	Protists
Specific characteristics	High protein content	Use of a variety of feedstocks		Phototrophic growth	Production of omega-3 fatty acids
Protein content %	50–80	30–50	30–70	60–70	10–20
Fat %	1.5–3	2–6	2–8	7–20	
Ash %	3–7	5–9.5	8–10	4–19	
Free amino acids %	8–12	6–12	3–8	7–10	
Examples of organisms	*Acromobacter delvaevate, A. calcoacenticus, Aeromonas hydrophila, Bacillus megaterium, B. subtilis, Brevibacterium, Corynobacterium ammoniagenes, Cupravidus nectar, Flavobacterium sp., Lactobacillus species, Methylococcus capsulatus, Methylophilus methylitrophus, Methylomonas methylotrophus, Rhodopseudomonas palustris, Rhodopseudomonas capsulata, Pseudomonas fluorescens, Thermomonospora fusca*	*Saccharomyces cerevisiae, Amoco torula, Candida utilis, C. tropicalis, C. intermeia, C. lipolytica,*	*Aspergilus fumigatus, Aspergilus niger, A. oryzae, Cephalosporium, C. cichhorniae, Chaetomium cellulolyticum, Fusarium graminearum, Penicillium cyclopium, Rhizopus chinensis, Scytalidium acidophlium, Tricoderma viride, T. alba*	*Chlorella vulgaris, Desmodesmus sp., Nannochloropsis salina, Auxenochlorella prothecoides, Chlorella pyrenoidosa, Chlorella sorokiana, Chondrus crispus, Porphyrium sp., Scenedesmus acutus, Sprulina maxima, S. platensis*	*Schizochytrium limacinum*

Sources: Jones et al. (2020), Reihani et al. (2019), Ritala et al. (2017), Saeed et al. (2016) and Upadhyaya et al. (2016).

cultivation for the optimized strains are worked out, and any special metabolic pathways and cell structures are determined (Srividya et al., 2013).

3.2.3 Harvesting

Following fermentation, the biomass is harvested with the full development of the cell colonies. Bulks of cells are removed by decantation or centrifugation, and then the process is followed by product purification and effluent treatment. After harvesting, the biomass is subjected to downstream stages, including washing, cell disruption, protein extraction, and purification (Nasseri et al., 2011; Upadhyaya et al., 2016).

Post-harvest treatment, in general, includes steps like the separation and collection of cell-free supernatant by a number of decantation and centrifugation times and washing. Undesirable traces of medium are removed after washing, and these can be recycled for economic reasons. Final harvesting can be performed by a rotary vacuum filter to produce a cake containing 20–40% dry matter, which is then dried to reach 6–10% water content (Riviere, 1977).

3.2.4 SCP Processing for Food

When producing SCP for human food, production processes must be conducted under sterile conditions at the highest standards of hygiene. Also, care should be taken to ensure that the selected strains do not have a toxic effect on the consumer. Processing for food also includes the destruction of indigestible cell walls to release cell proteins. This can be achieved by mechanical methods, such as crushing, grinding or pressure homogenization or by the application of enzymes or by physical methods (e.g., freeze-thawing). It is also important to apply chemical or enzymatic treatments to reduce the nucleic acid content.

3.3 MAJOR MICROBIAL SOURCES

Various microorganisms used for the production of SCP are bacteria (*Cellulomonas*, *Alcaligenes*, etc.), algae (*Spirulina*, *Chlorella*, etc.), molds (*Trichoderma*, *Fusarium*, *Rhizopus*, etc.) and yeasts (*Candida*, *Saccharomyces*, etc.). The choice of microorganism depends on numerous nutritional and technical criteria, such as speed of growth, suitable substrates, energy value, protein content, amino acid balance, type of culture, type of separation, nutritional requirements, etc. (Upadhyaya et al., 2016).

There is a wide range of industries involved in SCP production, with some producing SCP as a by-product of other processes, while several companies report an interest in focusing primarily on SCP production itself. Companies with commercial activities in SCP production include Cellana, Pond Technologies and BioProcess Algae for Microalgae; ADM, Alltech, Flint Hills Resources, ICC Brazil and Pacific Ethanol for Yeasts; Calysta, Kiverdi, KnipBio, NovoNutrients, White Dog Labs for bacteria; and Veramaris for protists (Jones et al., 2020).

Substrates used as the carbon source for SCP production are provided from food wastes, petroleum by-products, natural gas and other organic compounds which include lactose, n-alkaline, methanol, ethanol, hemicellulose, cellulose, maltose, glucose, galactose, pentose, uric acid and other non-protein nitrogenous ingredients as carbon sources. Choice of substrates depends on their cost, ease of availability, oxygen requirement during fermentation, the heat produced and the level of fermented cooling required, and downstream processing costs.

3.3.1 Fungi

SCP is not often produced from fungal sources due to a slower growth rate and lower protein content compared to algae, bacteria and yeasts. The highest reported growth rates for micro-fungi are in the range of 0.36 h^{-1}. However, there are some advantages in producing microbial proteins from micro-fungi, particularly compared to animal sources, mainly:

- Filamentous fungi are capable of using a wide range of substrates and have straightforward nutritional requirements.
- Due to the particle size of the filaments, separation and recovery are easier than for other microorganisms.
- The texture of the final product is desirable.
- The whole micro-fungi can be eaten (whereas only part of an animal carcass can be consumed).
- The flavour is mild and the overall nutritional value is high.
- Micro-fungi are more acceptable as human food since they have played a role in the human diet for centuries.
- One of the main advantages of mycoprotein is its high fibre content and its low fat content.

Although filamentous fungi have advantages in ease of harvesting, they are limited by lower growth rates, lower protein content and consumer acceptability. Therefore, commercial application of micro-fungi as SCP may have some disadvantages as they may produce toxic metabolites, fermentation difficulties may arise due to their rheological properties, and cultures of mycelial fungi are strongly susceptible to yeast contamination, meaning fermentation conditions must be sterile. Thus, for SCP production, it is essential to choose a micro-fungus with optimal growth rate and suitable organoleptic properties.

Fusarium graminearum (Schwabe), which belongs to the sub-division of fungi known as Deuteromycotina, was found to be a good source of microbial protein (Sadler, 1994). This fungus converts 1 kg of glucose into 1 kg of wet cell mass, which represents 136 g of pure protein (Sadler, 1994). The efficiency of conversion on a dry-weight basis is at least 2:1, which is considerably higher than animal conversion rates for protein production.

The exponential growth of micro-fungi in submerged culture occurs, after an initial lag phase, in a medium providing an excess of essential nutrients. Growth continues at the characteristic maximum rate for the organism until one of the nutrients is no longer in excess and thus becomes limiting, as a result of cell composition changes.

For most of the filamentous fungal species, fruit wastes were used as the carbon source, such as lemon pulp for *Aspergillus niger* and date waste for *Fusarium venenatum, Fusarium graminearum* and *Aspergillus oryzae*. In addition to fruit wastes, mono- and disaccharides such as glucose, fructose, sucrose, maltose, and lactose were used for *Fusarium moniliforme* and *Fusarium oxysporum* (Reihani et al., 2019).

Net protein utilization (NPU) for mycoprotein is 60 compared with other protein-rich foods, such as 100 for egg, 83 for fish, 80 for beef, 75 for cow's milk, 52 for wheat flour and 47 for beans (Sadler, 1994).

3.3.2 Yeast

Yeast was the first microorganism whose importance as an animal feed supplement was recognized almost a century ago. During World War I, Germany replaced half of the imported protein sources with yeast. It is probably the most widely used and accepted microorganism for SCP production. Therefore, many researchers and producers focus on yeast SCP rather than other sources. Consumption of baker's yeast (*S. cerevisiae*) as food in Germany during World War I increased its importance, and this strain was known as the first and one of the most widely used eukaryotic microorganisms for application in SCP production.

Yeast cells are small in size (5–8 m), the density of which reaches 1.1 g ml^{-1}. They synthesize amino acids from inorganic acids and supplemented sulphur in the form of salts. Yeast SCPs have played a significant role in the evolution of aquaculture diets. Some yeast strains with probiotic properties, such as *S. cerevisiae* and *Debaryomyces hansenii* (Tovar et al., 2002), boost larval survival either by colonizing the gut of fish larvae, thus triggering the early maturation of the pancreas or via the immune-stimulating glucans that are derived from yeast cell walls (Suman et al., 2015).

From the literature, several yeast strains have been studied for SCP production from a wide range of substrates. Yeast species were mostly exposed to agricultural residues and fruit waste. They get carbon and energy sources from organic wastes (e.g., molasses, starchy materials, milk whey, fruit pulp, wood pulp and sulphite liquor). For instance, *Candida utilis* and *Rhizopus oligosporus* were utilized to produce microbial biomass from fermented wheat bran, which resulted in a maximum crude protein yield of 41.02% (Yunus et al., 2015). Other fruit wastes, such as date, Beles fruit peels, banana skin, mango waste, sweet orange peel, pomegranate rind, apple waste, pineapple waste, orange plantain, beet pulp, cactus pear and virgin grape marc, were used as substrates for *Trichoderma reesei* and *Thermomyces lanuginosus*, *S. cerevisiae*, *C. utilis* and *Candida tropicalis*. Industrial wastes, such as oil-rich manufacturing wastewater, cheese whey, defatted rice polishing, raw glycerol from biodiesel production and wheat flour, were used for *Kluyveromyces marxianus*, *Clavaria versatilis*, *Kluyveromyces lactis*, *S. cerevisiae*, *Mucor hiemalis*, *Kluyveromyces fragilis*, *Torulopsis cremoris* and *Yarrowia lipolytica* (Reihani et al., 2019). From the results of Mondal et al. (2012), it may be said that *S. cerevisiae* is able to grow on a variety of agro-waste substrates without supplementation of inorganic carbon and nitrogen sources.

Yeast strains have been tested for SCP production from whey. The most commonly used has been *K. marxianus*. It was indicated that for the successful production of SCP, from sweet and sour whey with high Yx/s yields and high cell dry weights, up to a 100-l scale, the use of the Crabtree-negative strain *K. marxianus* CBS 6556 was particularly suitable (Schultz et al., 2006). By using this strain, the production of ethanol motivated by the high amount of lactose was avoided (Crabtree effect). After improvement of the whey for *K. marxianus* CBS 6556, dry biomass concentrations of up to 50 g l^{-1} could be reached with Yx/s values of 0.52 for sweet whey and of up to 65 g l^{-1} with Yx/s values of 0.48 for sour whey concentrates (Schultz et al., 2006).

Yeasts have advantages as SCP compared to bacteria, including larger size (easier to harvest), lower nucleic add content, high lysine content and an ability to grow at acidic pH. However, the most important advantages are familiarity and acceptability because of their long history of use in traditional fermentations. Disadvantages are lower growth rates, lower protein content (45–65%) and lower methionine content than in bacteria (Amata, 2013).

3.3.3 ALGAE

Microalgae have typically high amounts of protein and a relatively low nucleic acid content (3–8%) (Ritala et al., 2017). Microalgae are mainly used in the form of food supplements or processed as food product ingredients. Algal SCP needs warm temperatures and a sufficient amount of sunlight and carbon dioxide to grow properly. Also, the algal cell wall is indigestible.

The indigestibility of the cellulosic cell walls is compounded by the presence of concentrations of heavy metals in the algae, and they are also rich in chlorophyll, which is not suitable for human consumption. In the case of algae, it has to be stressed that, due to technical and economic reasons, it is not intended to be isolated and utilized as a sole protein, but the goal is to propagate the whole algal biomass. So, the term SCP is not quite correct, because the micro-algal material is definitely more than just protein. To date, various worldwide technologies are employed for mass production and processing of photoautotrophic microalgae. The annual world production of all microalgae species is estimated to be approximately 10,000 tons year^{-1} (Nasseri et al., 2011).

3.3.4 BACTERIA

Bacterial SCP is primarily restricted to the feed industry. Bacteria are capable of growth on a wide variety of substrates. They are usually high in protein (50–80%) and have a rapid growth rate. For bacterial species such as *Bacillus cereus*, *B. subtilis*, *B. coagulans*, *B. licheniformis*, *B. stearothermophilus*, *Escherichia coli* and *Brevibacterium lactofermentum*, ram horn hydrolysate, beet pulp hydrolysate and molasses, liquid whey, and glucose have been used as the carbon source (Reihani et al., 2019).

Compared to fungi, algae and yeast, bacteria have the advantage of not only growing rapidly on organic substrates but also on gases, such as methane, hydrogen and syngas (i.e., a mixture of CO + H_2). When bacteria are supplied with one of these substrates, they can produce highly concentrated cellular protein up to 75 wt% of the dry microbial biomass at achievable protein production rates of 2–4 kg m^{-3} reactor volume per hour. The latter protein production rates, using naturally available microorganisms, are much higher than plant-based protein production. The fact that bacteria can use hydrogen (in combination with carbon dioxide), methane gas or syngas as their energy source opens up the unique opportunity to completely short-cut agriculture-based feed and food production, enabling virtually land-free production of microbial protein.

The applications of bacteria are limited by reluctant acceptance by consumers of bacteria as food, their small size and difficulty in harvesting, and the high content of nucleic acid on a dry weight basis. According to Nasseri et al. (2011), the principal disadvantages of bacteria as SCPs are as follows:

- Bacterial cells are small in size and have a low density, which makes harvesting them from fermented media a difficult and costly process .
- Bacterial cells have a high nucleic acid content relative to yeast and fungi. To decrease the nucleic acid level, additional processing steps must be introduced, and this increases the cost.
- The general public believes that all bacteria are harmful and produce disease. An extensive education program is required to remove this misconception and to make the public accept bacterial proteins.

3.4 APPLICATIONS OF SCP

According to the literature and practical sources, SCPs have to date exhibited the following applications:

3.4.1 HEALTH AND NUTRITION

SCPs have been used for a long time as a feed or feed supplement, not to mention unintentional traditional and ethnic uses of microorganisms as part of the human diet (Tusé, 1984; Guerrero & Illanes, 2016; Saeed et al., 2016).

Nutritive and food values of SCP vary with the microorganisms used. SCPs from yeast and fungi contain 50–55% crude protein. SCPs produced using bacteria contain more than 80% protein, although they have small amounts of sulphur-containing amino acids and they are high in nucleic acids (Attia et al., 2003). Besides high protein content (about 60–82% of dry cell weight), SCPs also contain carbohydrates, fats, vitamins, minerals, fibres and nucleic acids. They are also rich in certain essential amino acids, including lysine and methionine, which are limiting in many plant and animal foods (Srividya et al., 2013). It has been calculated that 100 lbs of yeast will produce 250 tons of protein in 24 h. Algae grown in ponds can produce 20 tons (dry weight) of protein per acre per year. Bacteria are usually high in protein (50–80%) and have a rapid growth rate (Nasseri et al., 2011).

Microbial proteins are healthy sources of vitamins, carotenoids and carbohydrates. They can be applied in animal nutrition for fattening calves, fattening poultry, feeding laying hens, fish breeding, fattening pigs, and feeding domestic animals, and in the area of food, used as aroma and vitamin carriers, emulsifying aids, and to enhance the nutritive value of bakery products and soups (Srividya et al., 2013; Ukaegbu-Obi, 2016).

Proteins not only provide nutritional value but also perform a number of other functions. SCPs have additional applications in animal nutrition to fatten calves, poultry, pigs and fish, they may be used in the food area as aroma carriers, vitamin carriers, emulsifying aids, and to improve the nutritive value of baked goods, soups, ready-to-serve meals, and diet recipes, and in technical fields such as paper processing, leather processing and as foam stabilizers.

3.4.2 Therapeutic, Natural Medicine and Cosmetic Products

There are reports that suggest the use of SCPs in therapeutic and natural medicines for controlling obesity, lowering blood sugar levels in diabetic patients, reducing body weight, cholesterol and stress, and also preventing the accumulation of cholesterol in the body.

3.4.2.1 Food Production

SCP became of interest during the latter half of the 20th century because of concern about meeting the protein demands of the world's increasing population, although they initially gained importance in human nutrition during times of war, when traditional sources of protein became scarce.

Yeast has been used in bread and beverage production since 2500 BC using protein derived from cultured bacteria. In recent centuries, methods have been discovered to produce high concentrations of yeast; therefore, there is a wide range of industries involved in SCP production, with some producing SCP as a by-product of other processes, and others that focus primarily on SCP. Yeast SCP has been consumed for decades as a cell extract in the form of pastes which can be spread on bread, whereas the fungal SCP was deliberately developed as a product that could be formulated into slices that more closely resemble meat. The products are often formulated as dry powders or flours, which are intended to be mixed with other ingredients to create products in which the individual components are not identified. Such products are suitable for incorporation into protein bars and beverages. SCPs from filamentous fungi and yeast continue to dominate the established markets, particularly when considering SCP for human consumption. Considering that yeast, fungi and algae have long been used as food, the potential for cultured microorganisms to serve as an edible protein source is enormous. SCP for humans from filamentous fungi, however, is likely to remain restricted to *F. venenatum* (Quorn™) and solid-state fermentations with other food fungi, because of the risk of mycotoxins and the long path to regulatory acceptance (Ritala et al., 2017). Additionally, solid-state fermentations continue to be developed which use microbes to upgrade the protein quality and the palatability of low nutrient plant products or ingredients. SCPs can also be used in ready-to-serve meals and in the technical field as foam stabilizers (Ukaegbu-Obi, 2016).

3.4.2.2 Cosmetic Products and Other Industries

SCP is claimed to have applications in cosmetic products to maintain healthy hair and in the production of different herbal beauty products, such as biolipstics, herbal face creams, etc. Microbial proteins can also be used as foam stabilizers and in other industries than food, including paper processing and leather factories (Ukaegbu-Obi, 2016).

3.5 ADVANTAGES OF SCP

The application of microorganisms for the production of biomass and their use as food and feed supplements has several advantages over conventional methods. Large-scale processes for SCP production show interesting features, including a wide variety of methodologies, raw materials and microorganisms that can be used for this purpose; high efficiency in substrate conversion; high productivity derived from the fast growth rate of microorganisms, and independence of seasonal factors (Nasseri et al., 2011).

3.5.1 High Rate of Multiplication

Compared to animals and plants, the rate of multiplication for microorganisms is consistently high (algae: 2–6 h; yeast: 1–3 h; bacteria: 0.5–2 h); therefore, due to the rapid succession of generations, large amounts of protein can be produced in a relatively short time under normal settings.

3.5.2 Genetic Modification

The shorter generation time of microorganisms and their high rate of multiplication make them easily modifiable and allow genetic transformation to alter the amino acid composition and cell characteristics (Yunus et al., 2015). A number of benefits in producing SCP and microbial products by application of genetic engineering have been reported and reviewed by Ritala et al. (2017). These include broadening a range of substrates by the production organism to enable them using different feedstocks or increasing the efficiency of their application; enhancing the nutraceutical value of the biomass by improving the content and composition of amino acids, vitamins, fatty acids and other metabolites, and modification to provide a series of cell wall degrading enzymes or new methods of cell recovery for inclusion in food/feed (Ritala et al., 2017).

3.5.3 Variety of Raw Material

Microbial proteins have the possibility of continuous production on a variety of raw materials in many parts of the world. Conventional substrates such as starch, molasses, agricultural residues and fruit wastes have been used for SCP production, as well as unconventional ones, such as petroleum by-products, natural gas, ethanol, methanol and lignocellulosic biomass. Bioconversion of these available substrates and raw materials (carbon and energy sources) by microorganisms into value-added food and feed products may cause a low environmental footprint and enhance food security and sustainable development (Oshoma & Eguakun-Owie, 2018).

3.5.4 Independence of Climatic Conditions and Environment Friendship

Microorganisms utilize many substrates with no requirements for arable land and specific season of growth. SCPs are a good alternative for replacing protein of plant and animal origin since its production is not characterized by high water consumption, does not cover large areas of land, does not endanger environmental diversity and does not produce high greenhouse gas emissions (Spalvins et al., 2018). Thus, land shortage and environmental calamities (such as drought or flood) cannot be a bottleneck to SCP production.

MP production could help to decrease future pressures on fertile land to the benefit of natural ecosystems since they have no requirements for arable land or any particular season to grow. In addition, agriculture requires major inputs of freshwater, with ~70% of the global freshwater withdrawals used for irrigation. Reactor-based MP production requires very limited amounts of water (~5 m^3/ton MP versus 2364 m^3/ton for soy), which can be further reduced if water is recycled or recycled water is used. In addition, environmental concerns play an important role in the development of SCP production, and in particular from wastes. MP production does not require the use of chemicals to control weeds or insect pests; therefore, it helps to reduce environmental pollution.

3.6 DISADVANTAGES OF SCP

Despite many benefits, there are a few disadvantages to the application of SCP as animal feed and human supplements, which are as follows:

3.6.1 High Level of Nucleic Acids

The concentration of nucleic acids in SCP is higher than in other conventional protein sources (40% in algae, 10–15% in bacteria and 5–10% in yeasts), which makes the use of SCP inappropriate unless the nucleic acids are removed, particularly if SCPs are to be used for human consumption. Purine compounds derived from RNA breakdown may increase the uric acid concentration in plasma, which can cause gout and kidney stones and may lead to gastrointestinal disorders. Therefore, it is important to find yeast strains with optimal properties. For example, yeasts contain lower amounts of nucleic acids (5–12%) than do bacteria (8–14%), which is more beneficial for human food or animal feed ingredient applications. Recent studies have led to yeast biomass production with high protein contents (*circa* 50% w/w) and low nucleic acid contents, plus similar amino acid profiles to those of fishmeal (Lapeña et al., 2020). Endogenous RNA degrading enzymes (ribonucleases) can be exploited to degrade RNA. Also, various methods to decrease the RNA content in SCP have been developed and continue to be used.

3.6.2 Allergic Reactions and Toxic Metabolites

The presence of carcinogenic and toxic substances plus indigestion and allergic reactions are key safety concerns in SCP utilization when they are produced for human consumption. Certain microorganisms produce toxic compounds which have side effects in humans and animals as well as in the environment; therefore, the safety of the product must be tested and guaranteed. Allergic symptoms may also occur by following SCP consumption because the digestive system may recognize this biomass as foreign material and evoke an allergic reaction against them. The challenge of toxins and allergenic material can be overcome by carefully selecting suitable organisms, processing them under proper conditions, and formulation the products correctly. Toxins may be extracellular (exotoxins) or cell-bound (endotoxins); therefore, fractionation and removal of the wall may overcome a part of this problem (Ritala et al., 2017).

3.6.3 Health Condition Developments

Susceptibility of SCP production to contamination can be considered as a detrimental factor that affects the acceptability of SCPs in terms of safety and health. Organisms to be cultured for SCP production should be non-pathogenic to humans and animals, while there is also a high risk of contamination to pathogenic microorganisms during cell growth. Moreover, some strains, mainly filamentous fungi, produce mycotoxins and should be well screened before consumption. Several yeast supplements, lacking sulphur-containing amino acids, and especially methionine, are limited in their use as exclusive protein sources (Upadhyaya et al., 2016)

High nucleic acid-containing proteins (18–25 g/100 g protein dry weight) may result in the production of uric acid in the blood and lead to health disorders, such as gout and kidney stones (Nasseri et al., 2011; Upadhyaya et al., 2016). It should also be noted that the microbial cell wall may be indigestible and gastrointestinal reactions may occur resulting in nausea and vomiting.

3.6.4 COST OF PRODUCTION

Even though much progress has been achieved, commercial production of SCP is still limited to a small number of manufacturers due to high capital and operating costs along with assessment costs. Economic aspects are of importance when the results of any research project are scaled up to an industrial pilot plant scale while higher capital costs are incurred for aseptic processes that are necessary for food-grade SCP products. Therefore, energy consumption, raw material and operation cost for SCP production as well as capital investment and profitability must be at a reasonable level compared to any conventional method of protein production. Production of food-grade SCP is expensive. Utilizing waste biomass is noticed as an approach to reduce the substrate costs to meet economic aspects, provided that the substrate does not compromise the suitability of the final product.

The scale of SCP production is also important to economic viability. As reviewed by Ritala et al. (2017), there is a practical relationship between cost and scale of production; hence, continuous operations have been proven to be the most profitable ones, and the majority of SCP processes which have been implemented at industrial scale have been adjusted to continuous design (Ritala et al., 2017).

3.7 CONVERSION OF FOOD WASTES TO SCP

Many research projects have led to the concept that SCP production can be considered as a reasonable response to both the global protein challenge and waste management. The global intensification of food production has resulted in producing large quantities of food and generating considerable waste, which is rich in organic and nutritional ingredients. Agricultural wastes are plentiful materials containing carbohydrate and cellulose as the major components, which are suited for the growth of microorganisms and the production of microbial biomass. To reduce the cost of SCP production, it is recommended to use biodegradable agro-industrial by-products and waste as a source of nutrients. In this way, the wastes whose disposal otherwise is costly can be utilized as substrates for the production of cell biomass rather than being discarded to the environment and water bodies.

Although it is preferred to produce SCP for human consumption from food-grade substrates, many studies describe attempts to develop processes to produce SCP from various common and inexpensive waste materials from the food industries, forestry and agricultural sources, including whey, molasses, brewer's solid wastes, fruit peels and other residues. After the oil crisis, attention was driven to the use of agricultural and agro-industrial wastes and residues as sources of protein; hence, they are presumed to support a more circular economy and lower costs. Bioconversion of food processing wastes into valuable by-products, such as the production of yeast protein from fruit and confectionary effluents, were the subject of research during previous decades (Nigam, 1998; Mondal et al., 2012). Moreover, using food processing wastes in SCP production alleviates pollution, and the recovery of such by-products could significantly reduce the cost of waste disposal. Wastes could be by-products of industries, agriculture, households from different sources which are generally considered as useless products that must be discarded. However, regulatory issues must always be taken into account.

Nigam (1998) examined the composition of effluent produced by the pineapple cannery as the sole carbon and energy source for growing *C. utilis* and investigated its suitability for the commercial production of SCP. Using batch fermentation, 50 kg of the yeast protein could be produced from the effluent containing 23.2 g carbohydrate/l obtained from a pineapple cannery. A maximum specific growth rate of 0.46 h^{-1} and cell yield coefficient of 0.30 were obtained with 23.2 g carbohydrate/l in the growth medium.

Mondal et al. (2012) studied the bioconversion of fruit wastes, mainly cucumber and orange peels, into SCP using *S. cerevisiae* by submerged fermentation. Their results showed that while both tested fruit wastes were highly susceptible to hydrolysis, cucumber peel generated higher amounts of protein followed by that of orange with 53.4% and 35.5% crude protein per 100 g of substrate, respectively. The addition of glucose to the supplemented fruit hydrolysate medium enhanced the protein content to 60.31% within the yeast cells, showing that SCP production by yeast depends on the growth substrate or media composition. The results of Mondol revealed that fruit peels are capable of yeast production in an appropriate amount of protein content by utilizing various ingredients present in them to convert these wastes to proteinaceous feed and food.

Another investigation clearly indicated that for *S. cerevisiae*, a banana skin was the best substrate, followed by pomegranate peel, apple waste, mango waste and sweet orange peel. Various forms of organic waste such as cellulose, hemicelluloses, hydrocarbon and different types of agricultural waste were used in the production of SCP. *Aspergillus terreus* possesses a high protein value and has been used as a better choice for SCP production using cheap energy sources such as Eichornia and banana peel. Lignocellulosic biomass such as cellulose and hemicellulose waste has been used as a proper substrate for SCP production. However, several compositional and structural characteristics provide resistance to biological degradation, consequently limiting the bioconversion of lignocellulosic substrates (Reihani et al., 2019).

Agricultural wastes are useful substrates for the production of microbial protein; however, they must meet important criteria, such as the following: the waste should be non-toxic, abundant, regenerable, non-exotic, cheap and able to support the growth of the multiplication of organisms, resulting in high-quality biomass (Dhanasekaran et al., 2011). Studies and practical experiences advise deep consideration on capital and processing costs to control and upgrade wastes as feedstocks, along with the potential regulatory challenges.

It is important to make sure that agricultural waste or residues, considered as an appropriate substrate for MP production, should meet a number of criteria to result in biomass of high quality, including non-toxicity, re-generatability, wealthiness, cheap and availability, and ability to support rapid growth and multiplication of organisms.

3.8 RECENT ADVANCES IN SCP AND FUTURE ASPECTS

Microbial protein can be regarded as an important protein reservoir for supplying the nutritional needs of the future. Even though SCP research projects have been conducted for decades and commercialized successfully over many years, study on different perspectives of microbial proteins in terms of optimal fermentation conditions, various potential substrates, quality improvements and a broad range of microorganisms is still being carried out by many researchers.

In recent years, research on genetically modified organisms in SCP production is a concept that has gained interest and acceptance with a wild range of advantages for future possibilities. DuPont has genetically engineered yeast to produce long-chain omega-3 fatty acids, which are essential to human health (Xie et al., 2015). Genetic engineering could also broaden the range of substrates or increase the efficiency of their use, enabling the application of multiple feedstocks and ensuring that all potential carbon in the raw material can be used. This is important as carbon source metabolism is a target for improving SCP processes; hence, it can be a major cost in SCP manufacturing (Ritala et al., 2017). GM could also increase the nutraceutical value of the biomass and may provide new ways of harvesting the proteins for inclusion in food or feed.

To fulfill the protein demands of the future and reach a sustainable environment, it is vital to develop green-clean technology for large-scale production. In parallel to biological investigations, process engineering and apparatus technology adapt the technical performance of the process and the apparatus in which the production of microbial biomass is to be carried out to make them ready for use on a large technical scale. For the future success of SCP, food technology problems need to be solved to make the similar to daily used proteins, and the production should compare well with other protein sources.

The prospect of SCP production will depend on reducing the production cost and on improving quality. Moreover, in the future, dietary protein may also be gained from proteins produced by engineered microbial cells and secreted from animal and plant cell cultures, in which the cells belong to neither microorganisms nor animals or plants. As a consequence, no clear distinction can be observed between SCP and other types of proteins.

3.9 CONCLUSION

SCPs represent the bioconversion of raw materials into edible biomass, rich in protein as well as minerals, vitamins and essential fatty acids. SCPs have been recommended as a solution to the threat of protein shortage and global scarcity caused by the fast-growing population of the world. SCP production is considered an effective alternative for animal and plant cultivation because, unlike conventional agricultural methods, high water consumption is not needed; the process has not characterized the use of large areas of land, it does not threaten environmental conditions, does not contribute to climate change and does not generate high greenhouse gas emissions. However, the quantity and quality of microbial protein along with its function as safe food and feed are of utmost significance.

Microbes are able to grow on waste materials; therefore, with the objective of developing more economical ways to produce SCPs in industry, suitable agricultural wastes can be used as substrate. Therefore, it reduces production costs, environmental pollution and helps in recycling materials.

After many decades, investigations on improving optimal fermentation conditions, more reliable microorganism sources, new and better substrates and possible economical approaches for the quantity, quality and safe enhancement of the products are still being pursued by many researchers.

ACKNOWLEDGEMENT AND DECLARATION

The authors declare no conflict of interest. The views and opinions expressed in this chapter are those of the authors and do not reflect the position of the Victorian Department of Health.

REFERENCES

Al-Mudhafr, A. W., & Al-Garawyi, A. M. A. (2019). Microbiological sources and nutritional value of single cell protein (SCP). *International Journal for Research in Applied Sciences and Biotechnology*, 6(6). https://www.ijrasb.com/DOC/IJRASB2019060601.pdf

Amata, I. (2013). Yeast a single cell protein: Characteristics and metabolism. *International Journal of Applied Biology and Pharmaceutical Technology*, 4, 158–170.

Amr, A. G., & Schoenbach, K. H. (2000). Biofouling prevention with pulsed electric fields. *IEEE Transactions on Plasma Science*, 28, 115–121.

Dhanasekaran, D., Lawanya, S., Saha, S., Thajuddin, N., & Panneerselvam, A. (2011). Production of single cell protein from pineapple waste using yeast. *Innovative Romanian Food Biotechnology*, 8, 26–32.

Guerrero, C., & Illanes, A. (2016). Enzymatic Production of Other Lactose-Derived Prebiotic Candidates, In Illanes, A., Guerrero, C., Vera, C., Wilson, L., Conejeros, R., & Scott, F. (eds). *Lactose-Derived Prebiotics: A Process Perspective* (pp. 229–259). New York: Academic Press.

Jones, S. W., Karpol, A., Friedman, S., Maru, B. T., & Tracy, B. P. (2020). Recent advances in single cell protein use as a feed ingredient in aquaculture. *Current Opinion in Biotechnology*, 61, 189–197.

Lapeña, D., Kosa, G., Hansen, L. D., Mydland, L. T., Passoth, V., Horn, S. J., & Eijsink, V. G. (2020). Production and characterization of yeasts grown on media composed of spruce-derived sugars and protein hydrolysates from chicken by-products. *Microbial Cell Factories*, 19, 19. doi:10.1186/s12934-020-1287-6.

Mondal, A. K., Sengupta, S., Bhowal, J., & Bhattacharya, D. K. (2012). Utilization of fruit wastes in producing single cell protein. *International Journal of Science, Environment and Technology*, 1(5), 430–438.

Nasseri, A. T., Rasoul-Amini, S., Morowvat, M. H., & Ghasemi, Y. (2011). Single cell protein: Production and process. *American Journal of Food Technology*, *6*(2), 103–116.

Nigam, J. N. (1998). Single cell protein from pineapple cannery effluent. *World Journal of Microbiology and Biotechnology*, *14*(5), 693–696.

Oshoma, C. E., & Eguakun-Owie, S. O. (2018). Conversion of food waste to single cell protein using *Aspergillus niger*. *Journal of Applied Sciences and Environmental Management*, *22*(3), 350–355.

Reihani, S. Fatemeh S., & Khosravi-Darani, K. (2019). Influencing factors on single-cell protein production by submerged fermentation: A review. *Electronic Journal of Biotechnology*, *37*, 34–40.

Ritala, A., Häkkinen, S. T., Toivari, M., & Wiebe, M. G. (2017). Single cell protein—State-of-the-art, industrial landscape and patents 2001–2016. *Frontiers in Microbiology*, *8*, 2009.

Riviere, J. (1977). Microbial proteins. In: *Industrial Applications of Microbiology*. Moss, M. O. & Smith, J. E. (Eds). London: Surrey University Press, 105–149.

Sadler, M. J. (1994). Fungal protein. In: *New and Developing Sources of Food Proteins*. Hudson B. J. F. (Ed). London, UK: Chapman & Hall, 343–360.

Saeed, C., Iqra, Y., Murtaza, M. A., Iqra, F., & Shehwar, S. (2016). Single cell proteins: a novel value added food product. *Pakistan Journal of Food Sciences*, *26*, 211–217.

Schultz, N., Chang, L., Hauck, A., Reuss, M., & Syldatk, C. (2006). Microbial production of single-cell protein from deproteinized whey concentrates. *Applied Microbiology and Biotechnology*, *69*(5), 515–520.

Spalvins, K., Ivanovs, K., & Blumberga, D. (2018). Single cell protein production from waste biomass: Review of various agricultural by-products. *Agronomy Research*, *16*, 1493–1508.

Srividya, A. R., Vishnuvarthan, V. J., Murugappan, M., & Dahake, P. G. (2013). Single cell protein: A review. *International Journal for Pharmaceutical Research Scholars*, *2*, 1–4.

Suman, G., Nupur, M., Anuradha, S., & Pradeep, B. (2015). Single cell protein production: A review. *International Journal of Current Microbiology and Applied Sciences*, *4*(9), 251–262.

Tusé, D. (1984). Single-cell protein: current status and future prospects. *Critical Reviews in Food Science & Nutrition*, *19*, 273–325.

Ukaegbu-Obi, K. M. (2016). Single cell protein: A resort to global protein challenge and waste management. *Journal of Microbiology & Microbial Technology*, *1*(1), 5.

Upadhyaya, S. U., Tiwari S. H., Arora N., & Singh D. P. (2016). Microbial protein: A valuable component for future food security. *Microbes and Environmental Management*. Studium Press, New Delhi, 8.

Xie, D., Jackson, E. N., & Zhu, Q. (2015). Sustainable source of omega-3 eicosapentaenoic acid from metabolically engineered Yarrowia lipolytica: From fundamental research to commercial production. *Applied Microbiology and Biotechnology*, *99*(4), 1599–1610.

Yunus, F. U. N., Nadeem, M., & Rashid, F. (2015). Single-cell protein production through microbial conversion of lignocellulosic residue (wheat bran) for animal feed. *Journal of the Institute of Brewing*, *121*(4), 553–557.

4 Algae as an Alternative Source of Protein

Neda Irvani[1], Alan Carne[2], Dominic Agyei[1], and Indrawati Oey[1,3]

[1]Department of Food Science, University of Otago, Dunedin, New Zealand
[2]Department of Biochemistry, University of Otago, Dunedin, New Zealand
[3]Riddet Institute, Palmerston North, New Zealand

CONTENTS

4.1	Introduction	65
4.2	Algal Species Evaluated as Sources of Protein	66
4.3	Protein Quality	68
4.4	Protein Extraction Methods	70
	4.4.1 Cell Disintegration Methods for Protein Extraction	70
	4.4.1.1 Mechanical and Physical Techniques for Protein Extraction	70
	4.4.1.2 Chemical Techniques of Cell Disintegration	76
	4.4.1.3 Cell Disintegration Methods Using Enzymes	76
	4.4.1.4 Cell Disruption Using a Combination of Different Methods	77
4.5	Recovery and Fractionation of Protein from Micro-algae Extracts	77
4.6	Analysis and Quantification of Micro-algae Extracted Protein	78
4.7	Digestibility of Algae Protein	78
4.8	Use of Algae Proteins as Animal Feed	79
4.9	Safety of Micro-algae Extracted Proteins	79
4.10	Conclusion and Future Outlook	79
Acknowledgements		80
References		80

4.1 INTRODUCTION

It is common knowledge that healthy diets are important for health and wellbeing. In recent times, the need to source foods sustainably, and thereby protect the environment has also become an important consideration (Bjarnadóttir et al., 2018). This is particularly important in the face of the expected human population growth in the coming decades. Population numbers of up to 10.2 and 13.2 billion, respectively, by 2030 and 2050 are projected (UNDESA, 2017). Rapid economic development and consequential population growth have resulted in a need to increase the level and the rate of food production. One interesting observation that exacerbates this concern is that, in most countries around the world, an increase in the economic status of individuals is usually accompanied by a reduction in the consumption of plant-based diets and a concomitant increase in the proportion of animal-based protein sources (D'hondt et al., 2017). This phenomenon is in part responsible for the rise in meat consumption globally (Van der Spiegel et al., 2013).

The increase in meat consumption has necessitated an increase in the number of farming systems for meat production. But there are some environmental consequences to this. For example,

DOI: 10.1201/9780429299834-4

over 25% of all global anthropogenic greenhouse gas (GHG) emission is associated with food production systems (Vermeulen et al., 2012). Livestock production alone contributes about 18% of all CO_2 equivalent GHG emissions (Bjarnadóttir et al., 2018). Therefore, to reduce the effect on the environment and energy consumption, it has been suggested that the average meat portion size in diets should be reduced or replaced with meat substitutes, or protein from alternative sources (Bjarnadóttir et al., 2018; Van der Spiegel et al., 2013).

Another benefit to be gleaned from a reduction in meat consumption is the fact that diets containing limited animal products and a higher proportion of other food materials of plant origin, which usually contain phytochemical bioactive compounds such as polyphenols, offer health benefits (Bjarnadóttir et al., 2018; Springmann et al., 2016). It is therefore imperative to identify alternative sources of proteins that fulfil dietary and nutritional requirements, with positive effects on human health, and on the environment (Bjarnadóttir et al., 2018). In this regard, algae are suitable candidates for alternative protein sources that can meet most of the aforementioned requirements (Batista et al., 2013; Postma et al., 2016).

Algae can be divided into micro-algae (those that are unicellular) and macro-algae (those that are multicellular) (Barka & Blecker, 2016). Algae have received a lot of attention as an important source of high-value compounds such as pigments, complex carbohydrates and essential lipids, in addition to proteins (Bjarnadóttir et al., 2018). Algae being an excellent source of protein for food, feed and providing other compounds that can be utilized by chemical industries is well supported in the literature (Safi et al., 2013; Waghmare et al., 2016). In addition to algae protein containing all of the essential amino acids, with appropriate optimization protein expression in algae can be achieved at 20–50 times that of soybean (Tibbetts et al., 2015).

Algae have also attracted increasing interest due to their relatively simple and unconventional growth requirements (Waghmare et al., 2016). Algae can be grown in aquaculture on low-quality farmland as well as in the ocean. Hence, they would not compete with areas suitable for terrestrial agricultural production. Moreover, under optimized conditions, algae can be cultivated at industrial scale in bioreactors, both indoors and outdoors (D'hondt et al., 2017). Some of the parameters that can be selected and/or tuned to improve protein yields from algae are the type of algal species, growth conditions, nutrient supply, harvesting techniques, as well as processing methods (Tibbetts et al., 2015). There are some qualitative and quantitative similarities in the amino acid profiles of micro-algae protein obtained from different species, and the ratio and level of these amino acids is not influenced by the algae growth conditions. These make micro-algae a potentially sustainable and scalable source of protein to supplement the feeding of the growing global population, as well as for use in algal products in various industrial sectors (Waghmare et al., 2016).

However, some form of cell disruption technique is required to break open algal cells to enable the extraction of intracellular components (Safi et al., 2014a). In this context, a number of cell wall disruption techniques have been reported in the literature (D'hondt et al., 2017). In this chapter, an overview of recent trends, main sources investigated and the quality of protein extracted from various macro- and micro-algae are discussed. Moreover, various techniques for algal cell disintegration, protein separation and analytical methods are presented. The application of algal protein in the food, pharmacology and nutraceutical sectors is also reviewed.

4.2 ALGAL SPECIES EVALUATED AS SOURCES OF PROTEIN

On average, micro-algae contain a higher level of proteins than macro-algae (seaweeds). The protein content varies with species, can be influenced by seasonal conditions and the yield of extracted protein depends on the method of extraction and/or additional processing (Samarakoon & Jeon, 2012). The protein content of several macro- and micro-algae are summarized in Table 4.1. Within the macro-algae group, the brown seaweeds are typically low in protein content (3–15% of the dry weight), and the green and red seaweeds contain about 10–47% protein per dry weight of algae (Fleurence, 1999). The protein content of *Undaria pinnatifida* is 11–24% (dry weight), but

TABLE 4.1
The protein contents reported for various macro- and micro-algae

	Species	Protein Content (% Dry Weight)	References
Micro-algae	*Acutodesmus dimorphus*	28.1	Tibbetts et al. (2015)
	Anabaena cylindrica	43–56	Becker (2007)
	Aphanizomenon flosaquae	62	Becker (2007)
	Arthrospira maxima	56–77	Barka and Blecker (2016)
	Botryococcus braunii	39.9	Tibbetts et al. (2015)
	Chlorella ellipsoidea	42.2	Servaites et al. (2012)
	Chlorella ovalis	10.97	Slocombe et al. (2013)
	Chlorella pyrenoidosa	57	Becker (2007)
		42.2	Zhang et al. (2020)
	Chlorella spaerckii	6.87	Slocombe et al. (2013)
	Chlorella vulgaris	51–58	Tibbetts et al. (2015)
		42.2	Zhang et al. (2020)
	Chlorella zofingiensis	35.6	
	Chlorococcum sp.	32.3	Zhang et al. (2020)
	Dunaliella primolecta	12.26	Slocombe et al. (2013)
	Dunaliella salina	57	Becker (2007)
	Dunaliella tertiolecta	11.4	Barka and Blecker (2016)
	Nannochloropsis granulata	33.5	Tibbetts et al. (2015)
	Neochloris oleoabundans	30.1	Tibbetts et al. (2015)
	Phaeodactylum tricornutum	39.6	Tibbetts et al. (2015)
	Porphyridium aerugeneum	31.6	Tibbetts et al. (2015)
	Porphyridium cruentum	3528–39	López et al. (2010) Becker (2007)
	Scenedesmus almeriensis	41.8	García 2012
	Scenedesmus obliquus	4850–55	López et al. (2010) Becker (2007)
	Scenedesmus sp	40.2	Zhang et al. (2020)
	Spirulina platensis	60–7155.863	Barka and Blecker (2016) Tibbetts et al. (2015) Samarakoon and Jeon (2012)
	Tetraselmis	36	Schwenzfeier et al. (2011)
	Tetraselmis chuii	3146.5	Brown (1991) Tibbetts et al. (2015)
Macroalgae	*Ascophyllum nodosum*	3–15	Fleurence et al. (2012)
	Fucus sp.	3–11	Fleurence (1999)
	Gracilaria verrucosa	7–23	Fleurence et al. (2012)
	Grateloupia turuturu	14–27.5	Fleurence et al. (2012)
	Gelidium sesquipedale	2.6	Trigueros et al. (2021)
	Laminaria digitata	8–15	Fleurence et al. (2012)
	Mazzaella japonica	25	Kitade et al. (2018)
	Palmaria palmate	358–35	Burtin (2003), Fleurence et al. (2012), Fleurence (1999, #36)
	Porphyra tenera	4733–47	Burtin (2003)
	Ulva lactuca	8.7–32.7	Fleurence et al. (2012)
	Ulva pertusa	20–26	Fleurence (1999)
	Undaria pinnatifida	11–24	Burtin (2003)

aside from this species, the protein content of other industrially relevant brown seaweeds is typically lower than 15% (dry weight) (Table 4.1). For the most part, brown seaweeds contain a high content of phenolic compounds. In contrast, red and green seaweeds contain a lower level of phenolics and a higher content of protein. For example, the red seaweeds *Porphyra tenera* and *Palmaria palmat* have a protein content of around ~47% and 35% of dry weight, respectively, which is comparable to that of soybean (Samarakoon & Jeon, 2012). Some micro-algae contain a protein content higher than that of some conventional animal and plant protein sources. *Arthrospira platensis* (also called *Spirulina*) contains a protein content in the range on 55.8–77% on dry weight basis, which is higher than the protein content from animal sources such as milk, chicken and beef, and from plant sources such as soybean and peanuts.

4.3 PROTEIN QUALITY

Protein quality is an important parameter used to assess the dietary and nutritional value of food proteins. The quality of protein is based on its solubility in aqueous systems, the degree of hydrolysis achieved in the digestive tract, and the amino acid profile, especially in relation to the number of essential amino acids present. Some parameters used to assess protein quality are the protein efficiency ratio (PER), biological value (BV), protein digestibility coefficient (DC), net protein utilization (NPU) (Becker, 2007; Ursu et al., 2014), Protein Digestibility Corrected Amino Acid Score (PDCAAS) and Digestible Indispensable Amino Acid Score (DIAAS) (Barka & Blecker, 2016). These protein quality indices can be affected by factors such as the source of protein, level of processing (if any), presence of other dietary components and their interaction with the other non-protein compounds and the presence of anti-nutritive factors such as protease inhibitors (Tibbetts et al., 2015).

The high nutritional quality of algae is an important consideration for achieving a wide usage of algae in food and feed (Ursu et al., 2014). Interestingly, the essential amino acid content of algae has been shown to be comparable to that of other sources such as egg and soybean (Barka & Blecker, 2016; Christaki et al., 2011; Kent et al., 2015). The amino acid composition of some micro- and macro-algae are shown in Table 4.2.

For most seaweed protein, aspartic acid and glutamic acid are among the most abundant amino acids present. These acidic amino acids are present at between 22% and 44% in brown seaweeds such as *Fucus* species, and between 26% and 32% of the total amino acid complement in green seaweeds such as *Ulva* species. However, in the red seaweeds such as *P. palmata* and *P. tenera*, the aspartic acid and glutamic acid content is lower, typically between 14% and 19% of total amino acids. Moreover, for most of these algae, the amounts of some essential amino acids such as leucine, valine, methionine, isoleucine and threonine are within the levels found in conventional protein sources such as egg and legumes (Fleurence, 1999). The amino acid composition of different species of macro- and micro-algae compared with that of bean and egg is summarized in Table 4.2.

In red algae and cyanobacteria, the most abundant proteins are the water-soluble pigment-containing proteins called phycobiliproteins (PBPs). PBPs contain covalently attached phycobilin pigments that are involved in harvesting light energy that is transferred to chlorophyll, as part of the photosynthesis process in the algae. Over ten different PBPs have been identified in algae. These PBPs are either blue in color (the phycocyanins), or red (the phycoerythrins), and the phycocyanins can be divided into allophycocyanins and phycocyanins based on the chromophores composition and the data on apoproteins (Stadnichuk & Tropin, 2017). Different algal species have evolved to produce different PBPs. For example, phycocyanins are abundant in *Spirulina* sp., whereas phycoerythrins are produced in red algae. Various PBPs have been isolated from *Anabaena* sp., *Phormidium* sp., *Oscillatoria* sp. and *R. marinus* (Stadnichuk & Tropin, 2017; Tibbetts et al., 2015). PBPs have a range of potential health applications, due to their exhibiting various bioactivities, including antioxidative and neuro- and hepato-protective properties. Moreover, phycocyanins are a highly suitable water-soluble blue dye, but their use as food colorants is limited as consumers are not so accustomed to blue-colored products as there are not

TABLE 4.2
Amino acid composition of different species of macro- and micro-algae as compared with common bean (*Phaseolus vulgaris* cv. Mela) and egg

Species Amino Acid	Common Bean	Egg	Palmaria palmata	Porphyra tenra	Ulvales intestinalis	Alaria esculenta	Phaeodactylum tricornutum	Nannochloropsis granulata	Spirulina platensis	Porphyridium aerugineum	Chlorella
			Macro-algae						Micro-algae		
Essential amino acids (EAA)											
Threonine	3.89	5.0	5.3	4.0	5.8	4.7	4.8	5.4	6.2	5.8	4.7
Valine	4.21	7.2	6.6	6.4	6.5	4.9	5.1	7.1	7.1	7.3	6.1
Methionine	0.69	3.2	2.2	1.1	1.8	1.3	2.7	3.5	2.5	3.7	2.2
Isoleucine	3.72	6.6	4.0	4.0	4.0	5.5	4.6	5.6	6.7	7.1	4.4
Leucine	6.44	8.8	7.0	8.7	7.3	5.2	7	11.0	9.8	11.9	9.2
Phenylalanine	2.61	5.8	5.0	3.9	4.9	3.6	4.8	6.2	5.3	6.3	5.5
Histidine	2.42	2.4	1.6	1.4	1.3	1.4	1.5	2.3	2.2	1.9	2.4
Lysine	5.46	5.3	7.7	4.5	5.4	5.2	6.4	8.5	4.8	8.0	8.9
Arginine	7.59	6.2	6.8	16.4	5.2	3.4	5.7	7.4	7.3	8.6	7.1
Tryptophan	0.61	1.7	3.4	1.3	2.5	2.9	2.6	2.8	0.3	3.3	-
Non-essential amino acids (NEAA)											
Aspartic acid	9.25	11.0	12.5	7.0	14.6	11.9	11.6	11.4	11.8	15.0	9.4
Serine	4.13	6.9	6.0	2.9	5.0	4.8	4.8	5.6	5.1	7.0	4.0
Glutamic acid	16.15	12.6	12.3	7.2	13.2	25.8	18.8	14.1	10.3	15.6	12.9
Proline	3.39	4.2	5.5	6.4	7.3	3.4	7.1	11.2	4.2	5.0	4.8
Alanine	3.45	-	7.6	7.4	9.2	13.3	5.5	7.5	9.5	7.0	8.3
Glycine	4.59	4.2	6.5	7.2	5.9	4.6	7.3	7.1	5.7	8.4	5.4
Cysteine	1.03	2.3	-	-	-	-	1.5	1.6	0.9	2.2	0.4
Tyrosine	2.56	4.2	3.4	2.4	2.5	2.9	3.4	4.2	5.3	5.8	4.2
Reference	Grela et al. (2017)	Barka and Blecker (2016)	Biancarosa et al. (2017)	Fleurence (1999)	Biancarosa et al. (2017)	Biancarosa et al. (2017)	Tibbetts et al. (2015)	Becker (2007)	Christaki et al. (2011)	Tibbetts et al. (2015)	Kent et al. (2015)

many foods that are naturally colored blue. The low lipophilicity of phycocyanins limits their use in fat-containing products such as creams and lipid emulsions (Stadnichuk & Tropin, 2017). Nevertheless, phycocyanins have been used in a range of food products such as fermented milks, chips, crackers, non-alcoholic beverages, chewing gums, marmalades fruit and nut bars, as well as topically applied products for protection from oxidative stress damage (Stadnichuk & Tropin, 2017; Zamani et al., 2020).

4.4 PROTEIN EXTRACTION METHODS

The utilization of algal extracted proteins has not gained substantial interest, as after extraction, algae protein contains high levels of non-protein components such as chlorophyll, which contributes undesirable color and taste in formulated products (Becker, 2007). The presence of algal cell wall hinders the release of intracellular algae biomolecules, which results in low protein extraction recovery (Safi et al., 2014b). An overview of various cell disruption technologies and a review of different separation and analysis methods are presented in the following sections.

4.4.1 Cell Disintegration Methods for Protein Extraction

Effective extraction of proteins from micro-algae first requires the disruption of the rigid cell wall thereby facilitating the release of intracellular proteins. The methods reported in the literature for disruption of algal cells can be grouped into four methods including physical, chemical, enzymes/biochemical and a combination of the aforementioned methods (Figure 4.1). Safi et al. (2014b) reported that some features that make the disruption of micro-algae cell challenging are the cell wall structure, cell size, cell shape and morphology. It is imperative that the cell disruption method must be economical and energy efficient in order to ensure a relatively low cost in the downstream processing of micro-algae (D'hondt et al., 2017). Moreover, an ideal cell disintegration technique should ideally not negatively affect the nutritional and functional properties of the extracted proteins.

4.4.1.1 Mechanical and Physical Techniques for Protein Extraction

Physical-mechanical disruption methods potentially enable the utilization of a wider range of algal species. A description of some of these methods is discussed below.

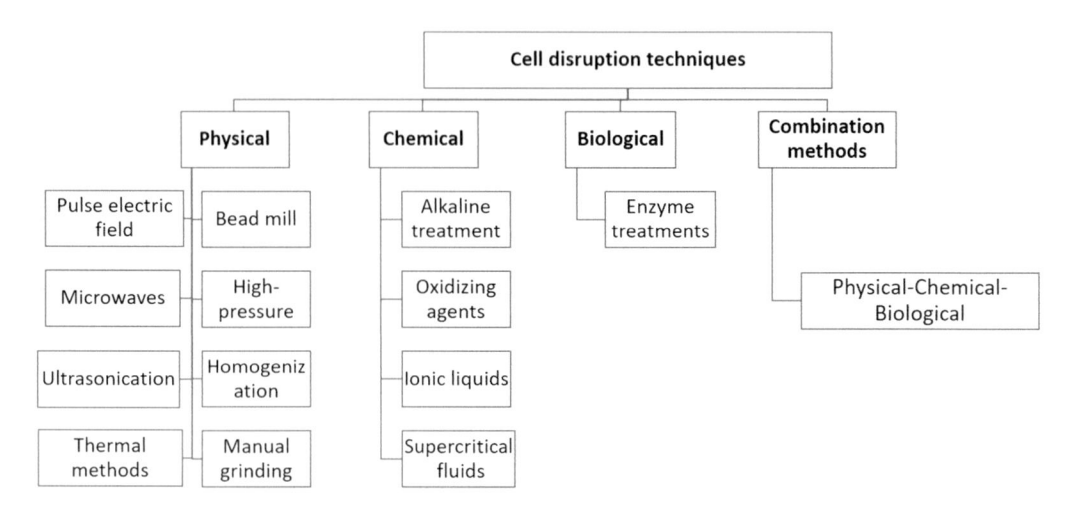

FIGURE 4.1 Flow chart of various cell disruption methods for extraction.

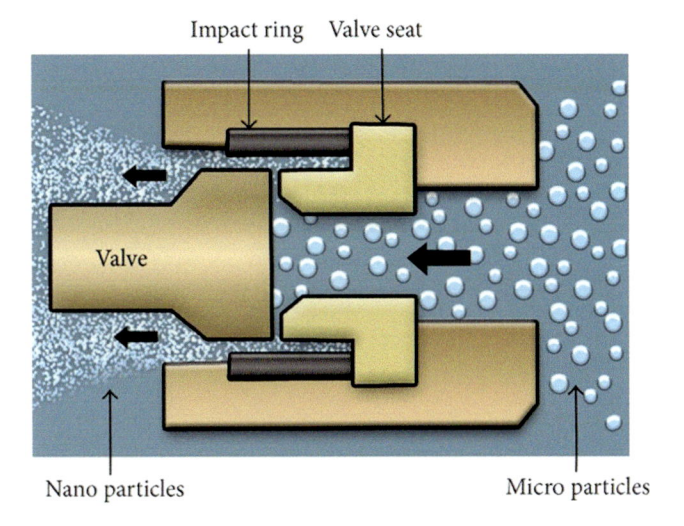

FIGURE 4.2 Schematic indicating the principle of high-pressure homogenization (Sutradhar, Khatun, & Luna, 2013). This figure reproduced under Creative Commons Attribution License (CC BY 3.0). https://www.hindawi.com/journals/jnt/2013/346581/#copyright.

High-pressure homogenization (HPH) has been touted as an effective method for the disruption of algae cells. The suitability of HPH as a disruption method has been demonstrated with algae species such as *Porphyridium cruentum*, *A. platensis*, *Chlorella vulgaris*, *Nannochloropsis oculata* and *Haematococcus pluvialis* (Grimi et al., 2014; Grossmann et al., 2018; Günerken et al., 2015; Safi et al., 2014b). HPH works on the principle that once materials are pressurized in a chamber and passed through a narrow orifice into a chamber at lower pressure, the materials experience pressure-drop shear stress which leads to rupture (D'hondt et al., 2017). A schematic of the HPH technique is presented in Figure 4.2. The extraction and recovery of proteins from various algae species using the HPH technique is presented in Table 4.3. 41–90% dry weight of protein could be recovered by applying 27,000 bar pressure in tow times passing through the HPH machine. They deduced that the HPH is an effective cell disruption technique owing to high capacity of cell wall disruption, also enabling mini HPH is an effective cell disruption technique and able to minimize protein aggregation (Safi et al., 2014a). The HPH technique lends itself to the possibility of re-cycling the same material through the device more than once, to achieve effective cell disruption and protein recovery. For example, in one study, using about 6 times velocity fluid stream passes through the nozzle at pressures of at least 50 MPa was shown to be effective in disrupting 99.9% of *Chlorella protothecoides* cells (Grossmann et al., 2018). Figure 4.2 shows a schematic indicating the principle of HPH.

Ultrasonication is a technique used for disruption of algal cells to achieve protein extraction. During ultrasonication, high-frequency sonic waves are used to generate high pressure that is capable of causing cell disruption through implosion of gas-filled cavitation bubbles around the algae cells (Zhang et al., 2018). Interestingly, the effectiveness of ultrasonication for disruption of micro-algal cell walls depends on algal (biomass) concentration, algal features such as morphology (shape and size) of the micro-algae species. Operational conditions and parameters such as treatment temperature, time, power and the number of cycles of treatment with the high-pressure homogenizer also influence the effectiveness of the technique in disrupting algae cells (Günerken et al., 2015; Passos et al., 2015b). Wang and Zhang (2012) have used ultrasonication to achieve a 16% DW protein yield from *C. pyrenoidosa*. Moreover, ultrasound pretreatment (20 kHz, 30 min, 26.7 MJ/kg Transverse [TS]) has been shown to be effective in increasing the proportion of protein in soluble algae extracts (Passos et al., 2015a). However, other authors such as Safi et al. (2014b)

TABLE 4.3
Protein content obtained from various cell disruption techniques

Species	Treatment	Extracted Protein	References
Arthrospira platensis	High pressure	78.0	Safi et al. (2014b)
	Ultrasonication	47.1	
	Manual grinding	35.0	
	Stirring for 2 h at pH 12 (40 °C)	53.4	
Chlorella fusca	Alkaline extraction + enzyme addition (5% Protex 40XL)	73.6	Sari et al. (2013)
Chlorella pyrenoidosa	Ultrasonication	19.816	Zhang et al. (2018), Wang and Zhang (2012)
	Thermal methods	1.51	Zhang et al. (2018)
	Homogenization	12.1	
	60% (v/v) ethanol-soaking, enzyme digestion, ultrasonication and homogenization extraction	72.41	
	Chemical and enzymatic treatment	78.1	Waghmare et al. (2016)
	Freeze-thawing	3.21.5	Wang and Zhang (2012), Zhang et al. (2018)
	Freeze-thawing and ultrasonication	22.923.52	Wang and Zhang (2012), Zhang et al. (2018)
	Ionic liquid	12.1	Wang and Zhang (2012)
	Low-temperature high-pressure	45.78	
	60% (v/v) ethanol-soaking extraction	27.7	Zhang et al. (2018)
	Distilled water-soaking extraction	28.52	
	Sodium carbonate (5% w/v Na_2CO_3)-soaking extraction	22.5	
	Enzyme digestion extraction	17.0	
	Enzyme digestion and ultrasonication extraction	29.58	
	Enzyme digestion and Homogenization extraction	26.52	
	Enzyme digestion, ultrasonication and homogenization extraction	39.47	
	Distilled water-soaking, enzyme digestion, ultrasonication and homogenization extraction	66.14	
Chlorella protothecoides	High pressure homogenization + ethanol:acetone (1:1) precipitation	67.2	Grossmann et al. (2018)
Chlorella vulgaris	High pressure	52.8	Safi et al. (2014)
	Ultrasonication	18.1	Safi et al. (2014)
	Pulsed electric fields	3.6	Postma et al. (2016)
	Manual grinding	9.0	Safi et al. (2014)
	A combination of alkaline conditions and high-pressure disruption	52	Ursu et al. (2014)
	Combined pulsed electric fields-temperature treatment	3–5%	Postma et al. (2016)
	Stirring for 2 h at pH 12 (40°C)	33.2	Safi et al. (2014)

TABLE 4.3 (Continued)
Protein content obtained from various cell disruption techniques

Species	Treatment	Extracted Protein	References
Haematococcus pluviali	High pressure	41.0	
	Ultrasonication	8.5	
	Manual grinding	7.4	
	Stirring for 2 h at pH 12 (40°C)	15.8	
Nannochloropsis oculata	High pressure	52.3	
	Ultrasonication	13.5	
	Manual grinding	9.7	
	Stirring for 2 h at pH 12 (40°C)	31.1	
Porphyridium cruentum	High pressure	90.0	
	Ultrasonication	67.0	
	Stirring for 2 h at pH 12 (40°C)	73.5	
Tetraselmis sp	Bead milling	21	Schwenzfeier et al. (2011)
Spirulina platensis	High-pressure homogenization + solubilization at alkaline pH followed by precipitation at acidic pH	60.7	Parimi et al. (2015)

did not observe any change in enhanced protein extraction from *H. pluvialis* with the use of ultrasonication. Moreover, they reported only a minor effect on the cell walls of *N. oculata* and *C. vulgaris* with the use of ultrasonication.

Pulsed electric fields (PEF) is a technique with potential application in the disruption of micro-algal cell walls. PEF is considered to be non-thermal if conducted under appropriate conditions. The principle behind this technique is that PEF leads to 'perforation' or electroporation of the cell membranes, which enables the release of intracellular materials. The PEF-induced perforation of the cells can be either reversible or irreversible, depending on the intensity of PEF that is applied (D'hondt et al., 2017). PEF systems can be operated in either batch or continuous mode. Figure 4.3 depicts a schematic of a laboratory-scale continuous mode of PEF system.

PEF has been used for the extraction of proteins from *C. vulgaris* (Postma et al., 2016). Treatment at room temperature at 0.55 and at 1.11 kWh kg/DW led to protein yields of 3.2% DW and 3.6% DW, respectively (Postma et al., 2016). This suggests that an increase in PEF treatment intensity does not necessarily correlate with a proportional increase in extracted product yield from micro-algae. Nevertheless, Goettel et al. (2013) demonstrated the effectiveness of PEF as a technique for the extraction of intracellular macromolecules such as proteins, carbohydrates and lipids from micro-algae. The use of PEF for the extraction of products from various single-cell systems has also been reported (Coustets & Teissié, 2016; Grimi et al., 2014; Lai et al., 2014; Luengo et al., 2015; Parniakov et al., 2015).

Freezing and thermal methods have been used as a treatment for the disruption of micro-algae cell walls (Safi et al., 2014b). In this method, micro-algae cells are disrupted using either heating or cooling regimes that fall into one of two categories: the use of freezing temperatures (below 0 °C), and heat, either between 50 and 100 °C, or above 100 °C (D'hondt et al., 2017). A variant of the freezing method is the freeze-fracture approach which involves the sequential use of freeze-thaw cycles. This approach works on the principle that, during freezing, micro-algae cells expand due to ice crystal formation. The expansion and subsequent formation of large and sharp ice crystals can cause chilling injury when the micro-algae cells are thawed or defrosted that resulted in cell wall

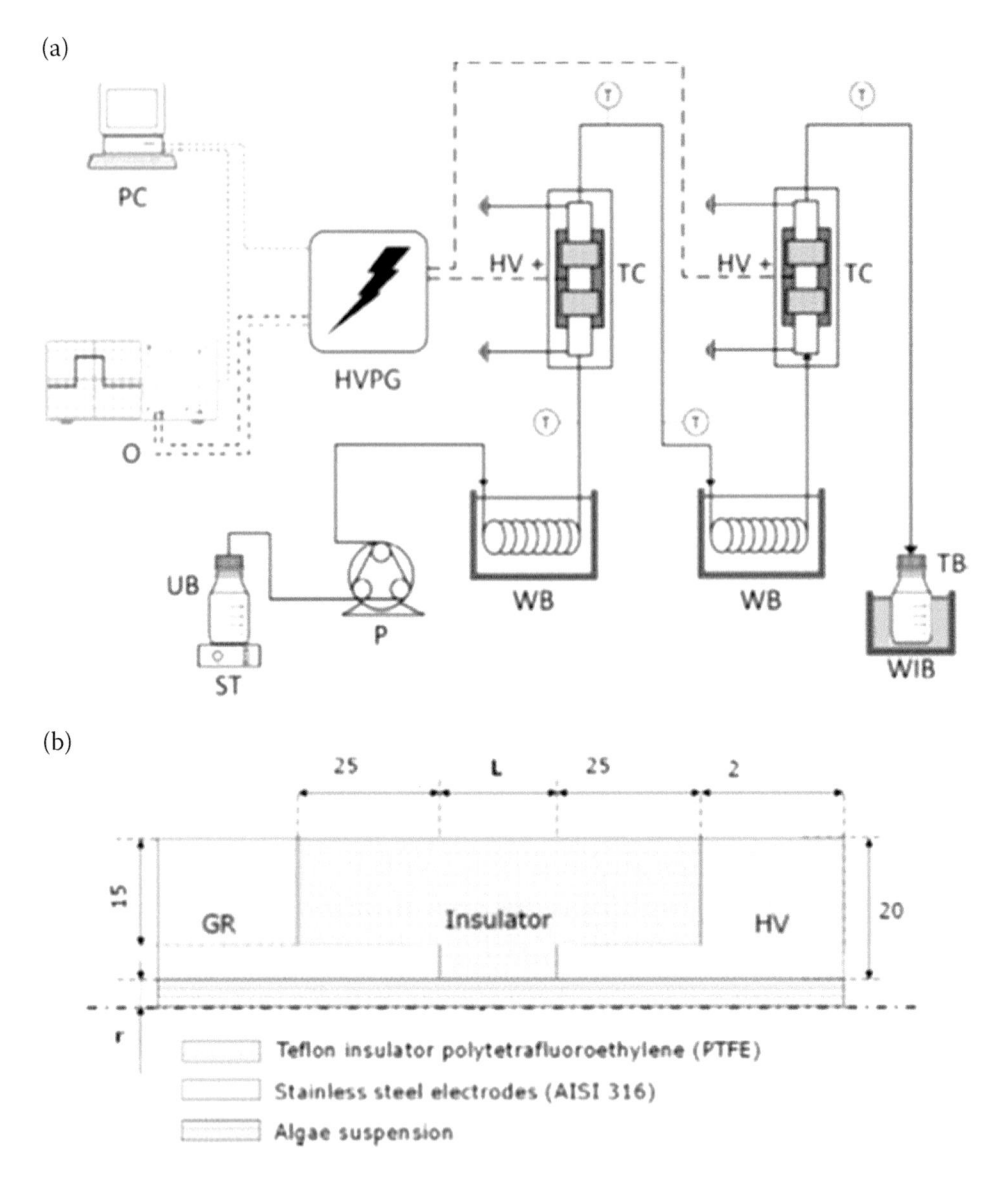

FIGURE 4.3 (A) Schematic overview of a continuous flow PEF system. O: oscilloscope, UB: untreated biomass, ST: magnetic stirrer, HVPG: high voltage pulse generator, P: peristaltic pump, WB: water bath, HV+: high voltage, T: thermocouple, TC: treatment chamber, TB: treated biomass, WIB: water ice bath; and (B) dimensions and geometry of a single co-linear PEF treatment chamber in axis-symmetrical configuration. GR: ground electrode; HV: high voltage electrode; L: gap distance (4 mm); r: inner radius (1.5 mm) (Postma et al., 2016). Figure 3 reproduced with permission from Postma, P.R., Pataro, G., Capitoli, M., Barbosa, M.J., Wijffels, R.H., Eppink, M.H.M., Olivieri, G. and Ferrari, G., 2016. Selective extraction of intracellular components from the microalga Chlorella vulgaris by combined pulsed electric field–temperature treatment. Bioresource technology, 203, pp.80-88. Copyright © 2015 Elsevier Ltd. All rights reserved. License Number: 5001210014847.

disruption. Lyophilization of micro-algae materials also causes some degree of increased porosity of micro-algae cell wall and membrane. The simultaneous freezing, leading to the formation of large ice crystals, and reduced-pressure induce dehydration, leading to sublimation of ice crystals, can result in pore formation in the cell wall and cell membrane of the algae (D'hondt et al., 2017). Zhang et al. (2018) used cycles of freeze-thaw treatment to release proteins from *C. pyrenoidosa*, although the recovery of protein (1.51% dry weight) was very low, indicating this approach alone was not efficient for extracting proteins from this species. A list of techniques that have been used for the extraction of proteins from a number of algae species is shown in Table 4.3. Algae have also been treated with steam which can achieve better heat transfer rates. The latent heat of steam causes disruption of hydrogen bonding in cell walls, leading to disruption of structural integrity micro-algae (D'hondt et al., 2017). The thermal treatment technique is a relatively low-cost method which is applicable for a wide range of algae materials and does not involve the use of chemicals (D'hondt et al., 2017).

Many of the aforementioned physical disruption methods involve harsh conditions of high pressure and/or high temperature. The use of such extreme conditions has the potential to affect the properties, such as solubility and functionalities, of the extracted proteins (Postma et al., 2015). Therefore, physical disruption treatments need to be performed under mild conditions. The challenge however is that extraction yields are very low under mild conditions (Grimi et al., 2014).

Bead milling is a type of homogenization process that uses beads agitated in a chamber to grind materials through shear force and collision of the beads with the material being homogenized (Postma et al., 2015). A number of studies have demonstrated the suitability of bead milling to disrupt micro-algae cell walls (Doucha & Lívanský, 2008; Postma et al., 2016). Bead milling can be operated in batch mode with recirculation of the same material, or in continuous mode that involves a single pass of materials through the milling chamber. A schematic of a bead-milling chamber is shown in Figure 4.4. The main parameters that affect the efficiency of cell disruption are the concentration of biomass, feed rate, process time, agitation speed, design of the agitator and milling chamber, as well as bead diameter and density and number of beads used (Doucha & Lívanský, 2008). Among these, the biomass concentration (C_x) and agitator speed are the most important determinants of disruption efficiency. These two parameters also determine the required process time and amount of energy consumed. Bead milling has been used in the extraction of proteins from *C. vulgaris* and *Tetraselmis* sp. (Postma et al., 2015; Schwenzfeier et al., 2011).

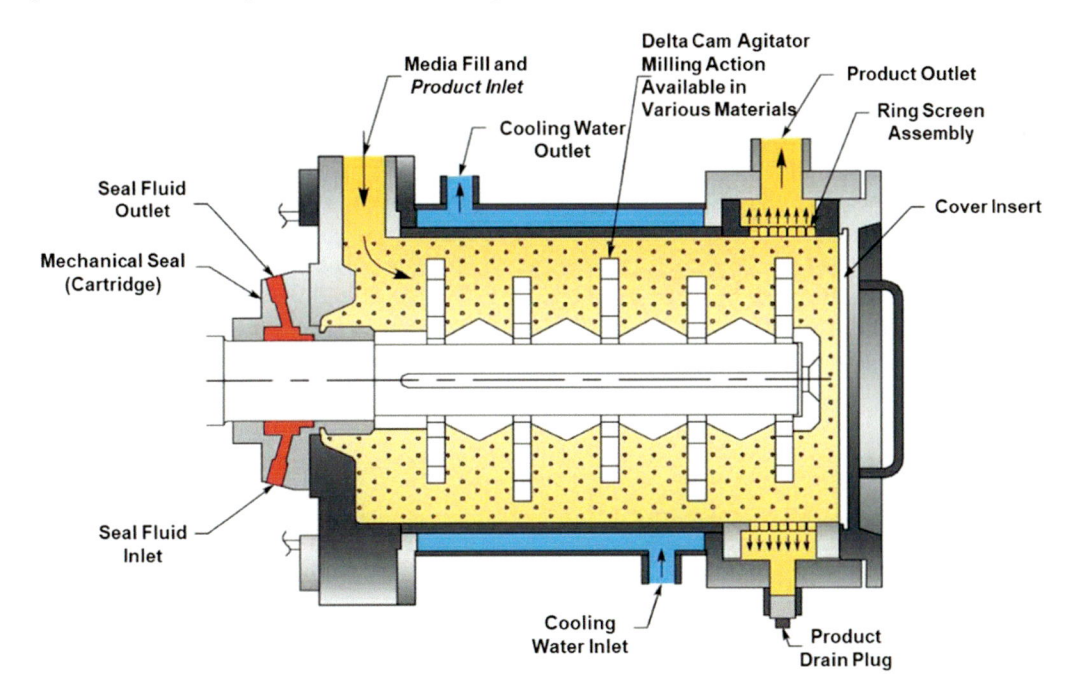

FIGURE 4.4 Schematic structure of a bead mill reproduced with permission from Emery Li, the CEO of Union Process. Available from: AGT-Mining [Internet], 2014.

Microwave energy is a thermal approach to treat algae cells for disruption. This technique has been shown to be effective for both micro-algae and seaweed (D'hondt et al., 2017). During microwave treatment, electromagnetic waves interact with dielectric and polar molecules, thereby stimulating local heating within cells. This in turn increases intracellular pressure and leads to disruption of the cell wall. Biomass concentrations, treatment time and power of the applied microwave treatment are critical operation factors for this technique. As a pre-treatment approach, microwaves are robust, efficient and scalable (Günerken et al., 2015; Passos et al., 2015b).

4.4.1.2 Chemical Techniques of Cell Disintegration

Chemical techniques rely on particular cell wall component interactions and these techniques are more selective than mechanical techniques. Compared to physical techniques, energy consumption in chemical techniques is usually lower with higher efficiency of cell disintegration and up-scaling more easily. However, the cost and safety of chemicals can compromise the aforementioned advantages (D'hondt et al., 2017).

Alkaline treatments: It is widely known that the solubility of proteins within cells and in cell wall structures is influenced by pH. Alkaline pH has been widely used to solubilize micro-algae proteins. As a strong base, NaOH is able to dissolve cellulose, and so allows the disintegration of the cellulose crystalline structure of micro-algae cell walls, and facilitate the release of intracellular components (Barbarino & Lourenço, 2005; Safi et al., 2013). Safi et al. (2014b) demonstrated that NaOH is effective for the extraction of proteins from algae species such as *C. vulgaris* and *N. oculata* (Table 4.3). However, alkaline treatment is not effective with micro-algae such as *H. pluvialis* which is reported to have a very tough cell wall and is highly resistant to disruption by many chemical compounds (Hagen et al., 2002). In addition, there is the possibility that alkaline treatment could denature the protein (Günerken et al., 2015).

Ionic liquids are defined as molten salts that have been used as extraction solvents, but evaluation of their use with micro-algae is relatively new. Ionic liquids have low volatility, can be recycled and usually require relatively short treatment times. However, these advantages are offset by the high cost and potential toxicity of ionic liquids (D'hondt et al., 2017). Wang and Zhang (2012) used ionic liquids to achieve a 12.1% DW recovery of proteins from *Chlorella pyrenoidosa*.

Supercritical fluids have been demonstrated to be effective in the extraction of biomolecules from organic materials, and also have been shown to be effective for micro-algae cell disintegration (Bahadar et al., 2015). The characteristics of supercritical fluids, such as viscosity, diffusivity, surface tension, and density, are reported to be important for the effective extraction of compounds, along with the need for fine tuning of operational parameters such as biomass concentration, pressure and temperature (Bahadar et al., 2015). The major drawback of this method is the high equipment cost, high operational costs (especially energy consumption) and challenges in scaling up the process (D'hondt et al., 2017; Thana et al., 2008).

Oxidizing agents such as hydrogen peroxide (H_2O_2) and ozone (O_3) can react with micro-algae cell wall components resulting in disruption of the cell wall (Concas et al., 2015). The use of oxidizing agents is an effective pre-treatment method to improve the extraction efficiency of intracellular components. However, such pre-treatment needs to be carried out in a very short time to avoid the oxidation of proteins. Some important process parameters that need to be tuned to ensure the efficiency of extraction are the reactor design, amount and type of oxidizing agents used with the algae material, the moisture content of the material, the ratio of ozone to air, and the treatment time (Huang et al., 2016; Travaini et al., 2016). Some disadvantages of the use of oxidizing agents are the high operation cost, potential toxicity, and safety concerns in relation to the corrosive nature of oxidizing agents (Travaini et al., 2016).

4.4.1.3 Cell Disintegration Methods Using Enzymes

The carbohydrate components of cell walls can be hydrolysed by using enzymes, leading to weakening or breakdown of cell wall structure that can facilitate the release of protein and other intracellular compounds. Hydrolytic enzymes that have been used to disrupt cell wall carbohydrate structure include amylases, cellulases, glycosidases and xylanases, as well as lipases for hydrolysis of lipid and proteases for hydrolysis of protein present in cell walls. The use of a combination of hydrolysis enzymes for disruption of cell wall structure has been reported to be effective for extraction of proteins from micro-algae (Bjarnadóttir et al., 2018). The use of enzymes has been shown to be as effective as the use of physical techniques such as ultrasonication for protein extraction from *Chlorella* sp. (Al-Zuhair et al., 2017). The biological specificity, selectivity, moderate operational conditions (leading to low energy demand), low investment cost, potential for scale-up of the process and non-destructive nature are potential benefits of enzymatic hydrolysis. However, enzyme hydrolysis has some disadvantages such as the high cost of enzymes and long incubation times required for hydrolysis (Lam & Lee, 2015).

4.4.1.4 Cell Disruption Using a Combination of Different Methods

A combination of disintegration techniques with various solvent systems can potentially be used to improve the efficiency of the process and reduce energy consumption. A few studies have reported the development of a micro-algae biorefinery system that operates under mild conditions (D'hondt et al., 2017; Passos et al., 2015b; Zhang et al., 2018). Zhang et al. (2018) have demonstrated that a combination of solvent treatment, enzyme hydrolysis, and homogenization was effective for the extraction of proteins from *C. pyrenoidosa*. In their work, *C. pyrenoidosa* was initially soaked in ethanol and then the micro-algae were treated with cellulase to degrade cellulose components of the cell wall, and was then homogenized to disrupt the integrity of the cell wall. This combination treatment was reported to achieve a protein recovery of 72% DW (Zhang et al., 2018). In another study, a combination of alkaline treatment and enzyme hydrolysis was used to improve protein extraction from *Chlorella fusca* (Sari et al., 2013). A three-phase solvent partitioning system involving ammonium sulphate solution, tert-butanol and buffered enzymes has been evaluated and was found to extract about 78% of the protein from *C. pyrenoidosa* (Waghmare et al., 2016). Ursu et al. (2014) combined alkaline treatment and high-pressure shearing and achieved an extraction of 52% of the proteins in *C. vulgaris*.

4.5 RECOVERY AND FRACTIONATION OF PROTEIN FROM MICRO-ALGAE EXTRACTS

Various methods have been used for the recovery of proteins from micro-algae extracts. The methods used include solvent precipitation, pI (isoelectric point) precipitation and salting-out. Some aspects to be considered during protein recovery are typical, the need to preserve the native molecular structure of proteins as much as possible, the method should be scalable, and whether there is a need to remove lipids and pigments (Grossmann et al., 2018). Lipids and pigments are usually extracted from micro-algae extracts using solvents such as acetone, chloroform and hexane. The use of aqueous buffers has been widely used for the recovery of proteins from micro-algae extracts via pI precipitation (Gerde et al., 2013; Safi et al., 2014b; Schwenzfeier et al., 2011; Ursu et al., 2014). Although this approach is highly scalable, it is only suitable for the extraction of soluble proteins. In addition, whether the extracted proteins will retain their native conformation is dependent on the type of protein, and other downstream processing methods used. Some downstream processing steps that are used for protein recovery are protein chromatography and solvent partitioning. For example, ion-exchange chromatography is an efficient technique for the separation of soluble proteins from other cell components in clarified micro-algae extracts. Another technique is expanded bed adsorption (EBA) chromatography which has the ability to directly separate protein from the cellular lysate. EBA chromatography is an attractive technique, as it is scalable and can decrease the cost of production by not requiring additional purification and centrifugation steps (Schwenzfeier et al., 2011). Three-phase partitioning (TPP) is another separation method with potential application in recovering algae proteins. One TPP process has involved the use of tert-butanol and ammonium sulphate to precipitate proteins from aqueous solutions. TPP is reported to be quick, scalable, and applicable for the separation, decontamination, and concentration of proteins from samples (Harde & Singhal, 2012).

4.6 ANALYSIS AND QUANTIFICATION OF MICRO-ALGAE EXTRACTED PROTEIN

The protein content of algae is commonly determined by either the Dumas or Kjeldahl techniques (Dumas, 1831; Kjeldahl, 1883). These methods determine the total nitrogen content, which can then be converted to total protein by using nitrogen to protein conversion factor, such as 6.25, that is commonly used (Bjarnadóttir et al., 2018). One consideration is that cell extracts often contain non-protein nitrogen compounds, and the use of either the Dumas or Kjeldahl techniques will therefore overestimate the protein content. Other protein analysis methods, such as the bicinchoninic acid assay (BCA), and the Bradford and Lowry assays may underestimate the total protein content of algae extracts because other compounds such as polyphenols present in the extracts may interfere with the colorimetric reagents used in the assays (Bjarnadóttir et al., 2018). However, some of these spectrophotometric methods, such as the Lowry assay, have been reported to be reliable for measuring the protein content of algae cell extracts without the need for conversion factors (Safi et al., 2013). However, an appropriate protein standard is necessary to calibrate the assay, and in addition, these assays only measure soluble protein (Safi et al., 2013).

The Kjeldahl and Dumas methods are considered the gold standard methods for establishing the nitrogen content of food materials. As such, a number of researchers have conducted studies to identify a better conversion factor that is suitable for algae materials. López et al. (2010) reported that a conversion factor of 4.44 (based on elemental analysis) and 4.95 (based on the Kjeldahl method) were more appropriate for five micro-algae species studied. In another study, Lourenço et al. (2002) investigated 19 tropical macro-algae and proposed new conversion factors of 5.38 for red macro-algae, 5.13 for green macro-algae and 4.92 for brown macro-algae. In another study, Tibbetts et al. (2015) measured total nitrogen by elemental analysis via combustion and reported that the protein content could be determined from the total nitrogen content of micro-algae, using a factor of 4.78. The differences among conversion factors in the above-mentioned studies could be the result of differences in the protein content of the algae species studied. In addition, the robustness of the cell wall affects how effective the extraction of protein from the algae is going to be. For example, micro-algae with robust cell walls, micro-algae such as *C. vulgaris, H. pluvialis* and *N. oculata* require methods that will enable efficient extraction to avoid underestimation of their total protein contents. Others such as *P. cruentum* and *Spirulina* have less robust cell walls, and thus a relatively mild cell disruption method is sufficient to rupture the cells and release the intracellular contents, including protein (Safi et al., 2013).

4.7 DIGESTIBILITY OF ALGAE PROTEIN

Hitherto, *in vivo* digestion study of algae has not been conducted except using *in vitro* digestion simulation and testing susceptibility of algae protein to the action of digestive protease materials such as pancreatin and pepsin, and other proteases such as pronase (MisurCova et al., 2010). The digestibility of algae protein within intact algae is reported to be hindered by the presence of the cell wall and a high amount of fibre and xylan (Marrion et al., 2003) In this study, mechanical processing and fermentation were found to enhance *in vitro* protein digestibility of *P. palmata,* for example, after liquid nitrogen freezing and fermentation, *in vitro* protein digestibility was 58% and 45–65 % of that of casein, respectively. The increase in digestibility after physical treatment might be linked to a reduction of compounds such as mineral salts and xylan. MisurCova et al. (2010) conducted an *in vitro* digestibility study of red algae such as *P. palmata*, *P. tenera*, brown seaweed including *U. pinnatifida, Laminaria japonica, Eisenia bicyclis* and *Hizikia fusiformis* or green algae such as *C. pyrenoidosa*, *S. platensis* and *S. pacifica*. They found that the *in vitro* protein digestibility of brown algal products was around 60% (compared to 100% digestibility of casein) that was less than what is observed in other algae.

4.8 USE OF ALGAE PROTEINS AS ANIMAL FEED

In addition to the potential for use of algae and algal products in food, algae have been used in animal feed (D'hondt et al., 2017). Digestive enzymes extracted from cattle have been found to hydrolyse proteins isolated from *Chlorella* and *Nannochloropsis* sp. which is comparable to soy protein digestibility (Lodge-Ivey et al., 2014). Various animal studies have shown the benefits of feeding animals with micro-algae. For example, feeding cattle with *A. platensis* was found to increase milk production and the protein content in milk, and to increase the weight of cattle and improve their fertility (Kulpys et al., 2009). Similar findings were observed with sheep and lambs (EL-Sabagh et al., 2014), and they also found that sheep and lambs had a better overall health and immunity status.

A combination of defatted *Desmodesmus* sp. algae with the addition of polysaccharidase and proteases was found to significantly increase the performance of pigs compared to their normal feed (Ekmay et al., 2014). Adding 2 W/W *A. platensis* to normal pig feed was found to not show any negative effect on their growth and food intake (Grinstead et al., 2000) and resulted in an increase in the biosorption of copper (Saeid et al., 2013). Combining feed with *Chlorella* sp. was also found to result in an increase in weight, better ingestion and discharge of microbial fecal matter (Yan et al., 2012).

Similar promising benefits of using algae in feed were observed in fish feeding trials. Gong et al. (2018) fed Atlantic salmon post-smolts with defatted *Desmodesmus* sp. and *Nannochloropsis* sp. in seawater and measured the coefficient of apparent digestibility. They found that adding *Nannochloropsis* sp. in extruded feeds resulted in a higher coefficient of digestibility of dry matter and protein in fishmeal compared to the normal cold pellet; however, when *Desmodesmus* sp. algae was used, it did not have the same effect. Another study (Tibbetts et al., 2017) with European seabass, gilthead seabream, red drum, *Sciaenops ocellatus* and *Sparus aurata* found 25% W/W algae supplementation with *Nannochloropsis salina* resulted in an acceptable digestion based on the targeted parameters measured, such as intestinal histology, nourishing component, the weight of organs, sensorial evaluation, enzyme hydrolysis activity and growth efficiency.

4.9 SAFETY OF MICRO-ALGAE EXTRACTED PROTEINS

The safety risks linked to micro-algae are reported to be due to the potential presence of contaminants such as toxins, heavy metals, pesticides, allergens and pathogens (Caron et al., 2010; Gerssen et al., 2010; Roheim et al., 1996; Van der Fels-Klerx et al., 2012; Vershinin & Orlova, 2008) and natural environment pollution (Van der Spiegel et al., 2013). Algae have the capability to take up and store substantial amounts of heavy metals including chromium, copper, cadmium, and zinc. As algae are at the base of the marine food pyramid web, they can transmit these pollutants over the trophic food chain (Hung et al., 1996; Souza et al., 2012; Van der Spiegel et al., 2013; Wong et al., 1996). Allergenicity risk arising from micro-algae has been reported for *Chlorella*, *Phormidium fragile* and *Nostoc muscorum* (Sharma & Rai, 2008; Tiberg & Einarsson, 1989). However, this was in contrast to another study (Szabo et al., 2012) that reported no food allergy risk for whole algal flour prepared from *C. protothecoides*.

4.10 CONCLUSION AND FUTURE OUTLOOK

From the information currently available in the literature, it is evident that algae have considerable potential as an outstanding source of protein and bioactive, either for food for human consumption or for animal feed applications. Algae have a complete essential amino acid profile and studies have shown positive impact on animal performance when algae are used as a feed supplement. However, the digestibility of algal protein in intact algal cells is relatively low due to the presence of a robust cell wall structure in many algae. Therefore, algae require mechanical, chemical and/or enzyme hydrolysis treatments to enable efficient release of the cell contents, and in processing applications to enable efficient protein extraction, in order to increase the bioaccessibility of algal protein for human digestion. Several studies have started to explore the potential of using emerging processing technologies that have low energy consumption and can achieve chemical-free treatment for protein extraction are showing promise and should be further explored. Extraction of algal protein also results in extraction of a range of other molecules, including pigments and polyphenols which may need to be removed depending on the food use application. Therefore, there needs to be a consideration as to the type and extent of fractionation that algal cell extracts need to be subjected to for the use application. In addition, growth conditions and suitable environment for culturing algae should be properly controlled to achieve industrial-scale algae production that is free from pollutants and contaminants in order to quality assure sustainable and safe algae production. Another advantage is that algae can be cultivated in areas that do not compete for use of high-quality agricultural land. Systematic *in vivo* human studies on algal protein will need to be conducted to obtain a better understanding of how algae protein as an emerging alternative food ingredient can be used safely and efficiently for human consumption.

ACKNOWLEDGEMENTS

The authors acknowledge the University of Otago for awarding a doctoral scholarship to Neda Irvani, and the Riddet Institute, a New Zealand Centre of Research Excellence, funded by the New Zealand Tertiary Education Commission.

REFERENCES

Al-Zuhair, S., Ashraf, S., Hisaindee, S., Darmaki, N. A., Battah, S., Svistunenko, D., ... Chaudhary, A. (2017). Enzymatic pre-treatment of microalgae cells for enhanced extraction of proteins. *Engineering in Life Sciences*, *17*(2), 175–185.

Bahadar, A., Khan, M. B., Asim, M., & Jalwana, K. (2015). Supercritical fluid extraction of microalgae (*Chlorella vulagaris*) biomass. In: *Handbook of Marine Microalgae*. Cambridge, MA, USA: Academic Press. (pp. 317–330).

Barbarino, E., & Lourenço, S. O. (2005). An evaluation of methods for extraction and quantification of protein from marine macro-and microalgae. *Journal of Applied Phycology*, *17*(5), 447–460.

Barka, A., & Blecker, C. (2016). Microalgae as a potential source of single-cell proteins. A review. *Base*, *20*(3), 427–436.

Batista, A. P., Gouveia, L., Bandarra, N. M., Franco, J. M., & Raymundo, A. (2013). Comparison of microalgal biomass profiles as novel functional ingredient for food products. *Algal Research*, *2*(2), 164–173.

Becker, E. (2007). Micro-algae as a source of protein. *Biotechnology Advances*, *25*(2), 207–210.

Biancarosa, I., Espe, M., Bruckner, C., Heesch, S., Liland, N., Waagbø, R., ... Lock, E. (2017). Amino acid composition, protein content, and nitrogen-to-protein conversion factors of 21 seaweed species from Norwegian waters. *Journal of Applied Phycology*, *29*(2), 1001–1009.

Bjarnadóttir, M., Aðalbjörnsson, B. V., Nilsson, A., Slizyte, R., Roleda, M. Y., Hreggviðsson, G. Ó., ... Jónsdóttir, R. (2018). *Palmaria palmata* as an alternative protein source: Enzymatic protein extraction, amino acid composition, and nitrogen-to-protein conversion factor. *Journal of Applied Phycology*, *30*(3), 2061–2070.

Brown, M. R. (1991). The amino-acid and sugar composition of 16 species of microalgae used in mariculture. *Journal of Experimental Marine Biology and Ecology*, *145*(1), 79–99.

Burtin, P. (2003). Nutritional value of seaweeds. *Electronic Journal of Environmental, Agricultural and Food Chemistry*, *2*(4), 498–503.

Caron, D. A., Garneau, M.-È., Seubert, E., Howard, M. D., Darjany, L., Schnetzer, A., ... Jones, B. (2010). Harmful algae and their potential impacts on desalination operations off southern California. *Water Research, 44*(2), 385–416.

Christaki, E., Florou-Paneri, P., & Bonos, E. (2011). Microalgae: A novel ingredient in nutrition. *International Journal of Food Sciences and Nutrition, 62*(8), 794–799.

Concas, A., Pisua, M., & Caoa, G. (2015). Microalgal cell disruption through Fenton reaction: Experiments, modeling and remarks on its effect on the extracted lipids composition. *Chemical Engineering, 43*, 367.

Coustets, M., & Teissié, J. (2016). The use of pulsed electric fields for protein extraction from *Nanochloropsis* and *Chlorella*. In: *1st World Congress on Electroporation and Pulsed Electric Fields in Biology, Medicine and Food & Environmental Technologies*. Singapore: Springer. (pp. 405–408).

D'hondt, E., Martin-Juarez, J., Bolado, S., Kasperoviciene, J., Koreiviene, J., Sulcius, S., ... Bastiaens, L. (2017). Cell disruption technologies. In: *Microalgae-Based Biofuels and Bioproducts*. Kindlington, U.K: Woodhead Publishing, (pp. 133–154).

Doucha, J., & Lívanský, K. (2008). Influence of processing parameters on disintegration of Chlorella cells in various types of homogenizers. *Applied Microbiology and Biotechnology, 81*(3), 431.

Dumas, J. B. A. (1831). Procedes de l'Analyse Organique. *Annales de Chimie et de Physique, 2*(47), 198–215.

Ekmay, R., Gatrell, S., Lum, K., Kim, J., & Lei, X. G. (2014). Nutritional and metabolic impacts of a defatted green marine microalgal (*Desmodesmus* sp.) biomass in diets for weanling pigs and broiler chickens. *Journal of Agricultural and Food Chemistry, 62*(40), 9783–9791.

El-Sabagh, M. R., Abd Eldaim, M. A., Mahboub, D., & Abdel-Daim, M. (2014). Effects of *Spirulina platensis* algae on growth performance, antioxidative status and blood metabolites in fattening lambs. *Journal of Agricultural Science, 6*(3), 92.

Fleurence, J. (1999). Seaweed proteins: Biochemical, nutritional aspects and potential uses. *Trends in Food Science & Technology, 10*(1), 25–28.

Fleurence, J., Morançais, M., Dumay, J., Decottignies, P., Turpin, V., Munier, M., ... Jaouen, P. (2012). What are the prospects for using seaweed in human nutrition and for marine animals raised through aquaculture? *Trends in Food Science & Technology, 27*(1), 57–61.

García, J. R., Fernández, F. A., & Sevilla, J. F. (2012). Development of a process for the production of l-amino-acids concentrates from microalgae by enzymatic hydrolysis. *Bioresource Technology, 112*, 164–170.

Gerde, J. A., Wang, T., Yao, L., Jung, S., Johnson, L. A., & Lamsal, B. (2013). Optimizing protein isolation from defatted and non-defatted Nannochloropsis microalgae biomass. *Algal Research, 2*(2), 145–153.

Gerssen, A., Pol-Hofstad, I. E., Poelman, M., Mulder, P. P., Van den Top, H. J., & De Boer, J. (2010). Marine toxins: Chemistry, toxicity, occurrence and detection, with special reference to the Dutch situation. *Toxins, 2*(4), 878–904.

Goettel, M., Eing, C., Gusbeth, C., Straessner, R., & Frey, W. (2013). Pulsed electric field assisted extraction of intracellular valuables from microalgae. *Algal Research, 2*(4), 401–408.

Gong, Y., Guterres, H., Huntley, M.. Sørensen, M., & Kiron, V. (2018). Digestibility of the defatted microalgae Nannochloropsis sp. and Desmodesmussp. when fed to Atlantic salmon, Salmosalar. *Aquaculture Nutrition, 24*(1), 56–64.

Grela, E. R., Kiczorowska, B., Samolińska, W., Matras, J., Kiczorowski, P., Rybiński, W., & Hanczakowska, E. (2017). Chemical composition of leguminous seeds: Part I—Content of basic nutrients, amino acids, phytochemical compounds, and antioxidant activity. *European Food Research and Technology, 243*(8), 1385–1395.

Grimi, N., Dubois, A., Marchal, L., Jubeau, S., Lebovka, N., & Vorobiev, E. (2014). Selective extraction from microalgae *Nannochloropsis* sp. using different methods of cell disruption. *Bioresource Technology, 153*, 254–259.

Grinstead, G., Tokach, M., Dritz, S., Goodband, R., & Nelssen, J. (2000). Effects of *Spirulina platensis* on growth performance of weanling pigs. *Animal Feed Science and Technology, 83*(3-4), 237–247.

Grossmann, L., Ebert, S., Hinrichs, J., & Weiss, J. (2018). Effect of precipitation, lyophilization, and organic solvent extraction on preparation of protein-rich powders from the microalgae *Chlorella protothecoides*. *Algal Research, 29*, 266–276.

Günerken, E., D'Hondt, E., Eppink, M., Garcia-Gonzalez, L., Elst, K., & Wijffels, R. H. (2015). Cell disruption for microalgae biorefineries. *Biotechnology Advances, 33*(2), 243–260.

Hagen, C., Siegmund, S., & Braune, W. (2002). Ultrastructural and chemical changes in the cell wall of *Haematococcus pluvialis* (Volvocales, Chlorophyta) during aplanospore formation. *European Journal of Phycology, 37*(2), 217–226.

Harde, S. M., & Singhal, R. S. (2012). Extraction of forskolin from *Coleus forskohlii* roots using three phase partitioning. *Separation and Purification Technology, 96*, 20–25.

Huang, Y., Qin, S., Zhang, D., Li, L., & Mu, Y. (2016). Evaluation of cell disruption of *Chlorella vulgaris* by pressure-assisted ozonation and ultrasonication. *Energies, 9*(3), 173.

Hung, K., Chiu, S., & Wong, M. H. (1996). Sludge-grown algae for culturing aquatic organisms: Part I. Algal growth in sludge extracts. *Environmental Management, 20*(3), 361–374.

Kent, M., Welladsen, H. M., Mangott, A., & Li, Y. (2015). Nutritional evaluation of Australian microalgae as potential human health supplements. *PloS One, 10*(2), 1–14.

Kitade, Y., Miyabe, Y., Yamamoto, Y., Takeda, H., Shimizu, T., Yasui, H., & Kishimura, H. (2018). Structural characteristics of phycobiliproteins from red alga *Mazzaella japonica*. *Journal of Food Biochemistry, 42*(1), e12436.

Kjeldahl, J. (1883). A new method for the determination of nitrogen in organic matter. *Zeitschrift für Analytische Chemie, 22*, 366–382.

Kulpys, J., Paulauskas, E., Šimkus, A., & Jerešiūnas, A. (2009). The influence of weed *Spirulina platensis* on production and profitability of milking cows. *Veterinarija ir Zootechnika , 46*(68), 24–29.

Lai, Y. S., Parameswaran, P., Li, A., Baez, M., & Rittmann, B. E. (2014). Effects of pulsed electric field treatment on enhancing lipid recovery from the microalga, *Scenedesmus*. *Bioresource Technology, 173*, 457–461.

Lam, M. K., & Lee, K. T. (2015). Bioethanol production from microalgae. In: *Handbook of Marine Microalgae*. Cambridge, MA, United States: Academic Press. (pp. 197–208).

Lodge-Ivey, S., Tracey, L., & Salazar, A. (2014). Ruminant nutrition symposium: The utility of lipid extracted algae as a protein source in forage or starch-based ruminant diets. *Journal of Animal Science, 92*(4), 1331–1342.

López, C. V. G., García, M. D. C. C., Fernández, F. G. A., Bustos, C. S., Chisti, Y., & Sevilla, J. M. F. (2010). Protein measurements of microalgal and cyanobacterial biomass. *Bioresource Technology, 101*(19), 7587–7591.

Lourenço, S. O., Barbarino, E., De-Paula, J. C., Pereira, L. O. D. S., & Marquez, U. M. L. (2002). Amino acid composition, protein content and calculation of nitrogen-to-protein conversion factors for 19 tropical seaweeds. *Phycological Research, 50*(3), 233–241.

Luengo, E., Martínez, J. M., Bordetas, A., Álvarez, I., & Raso, J. (2015). Influence of the treatment medium temperature on lutein extraction assisted by pulsed electric fields from *Chlorella vulgaris*. *Innovative Food Science & Emerging Technologies, 29*, 15–22.

Marrion, O., Schwertz, A., Fleurence, J., Guéant, J. L., & Villaume, C. (2003). Improvement of the digestibility of the proteins of the red alga *Palmaria palmata* by physical processes and fermentation. *Food/ Nahrung, 47*(5), 339–344.

MisurCova, L., KracMar, S., KLeJduS, B., & VaCeK, J. (2010). Nitrogen content, dietary fiber, and digestibility in algal food products. *Czech Journal of Food Sciences, 28*, 27–35.

Parimi, N. S., Singh, M., Kastner, J. R., Das, K. C., Forsberg, L. S., & Azadi, P. (2015). Optimization of protein extraction from *Spirulina platensis* to generate a potential co-product and a biofuel feedstock with reduced nitrogen content. *Frontiers in Energy Research, 3*, 30.

Parniakov, O., Barba, F. J., Grimi, N., Marchal, L., Jubeau, S., Lebovka, N., & Vorobiev, E. (2015). Pulsed electric field and pH assisted selective extraction of intracellular components from microalgae *Nannochloropsis*. *Algal Research, 8*, 128–134.

Passos, F., Carretero, J., & Ferrer, I. (2015a). Comparing pretreatment methods for improving microalgae anaerobic digestion: Thermal, hydrothermal, microwave and ultrasound. *Chemical Engineering Journal, 279*, 667–672.

Passos, F., Uggetti, E., Carrère, H., & Ferrer, I. (2015b). Algal biomass: Physical pretreatments. In: *Pretreatment of Biomass*. Cambridge, MA, United States: Academic Press. (pp. 195–226).

Postma, P., Miron, T., Olivieri, G., Barbosa, M., Wijffels, R., & Eppink, M. (2015). Mild disintegration of the green microalgae *Chlorella vulgaris* using bead milling. *Bioresource technology, 184*, 297–304.

Postma, P., Pataro, G., Capitoli, M., Barbosa, M., Wijffels, R. H., Eppink, M., ... Ferrari, G. (2016). Selective extraction of intracellular components from the microalga *Chlorella vulgaris* by combined pulsed electric field–temperature treatment. *Bioresource Technology, 203*, 80–88.

Roheim, C. A., Kline, J. D., & Anderson, J. G. (1996). Seafood safety perceptions and their effects on anticipated consumption under varying information treatments. *Agricultural and Resource Economics Review, 25*(1), 12–21.

Saeid, A., Chojnacka, K., Korczyński, M., Korniewicz, D., & Dobrzański, Z. (2013). Effect on supplementation of *Spirulina* maxima enriched with Cu on production performance, metabolical and physiological parameters in fattening pigs. *Journal of Applied Phycology, 25*(5), 1607–1617.

Safi, C., Charton, M., Pignolet, O., Silvestre, F., Vaca-Garcia, C., & Pontalier, P.-Y. J. J. O. A. P. (2013). Influence of microalgae cell wall characteristics on protein extractability and determination of nitrogen-to-protein conversion factors. *Journal of Applied Phycology, 25*(2), 523–529.

Safi, C., Charton, M., Ursu, A. V., Laroche, C., Zebib, B., Pontalier, P.-Y., & Vaca-Garcia, C. (2014a). Release of hydro-soluble microalgal proteins using mechanical and chemical treatments. *Algal Research, 3*, 55–60.

Safi, C., Ursu, A. V., Laroche, C., Zebib, B., Merah, O., Pontalier, P.-Y., & Vaca-Garcia, C. (2014b). Aqueous extraction of proteins from microalgae: Effect of different cell disruption methods. *Algal Research, 3*, 61–65.

Samarakoon, K., & Jeon, Y.-J. (2012). Bio-functionalities of proteins derived from marine algae—A review. *Food Research International, 48*(2), 948–960.

Sari, Y. W., Bruins, M. E., & Sanders, J. P. (2013). Enzyme assisted protein extraction from rapeseed, soybean, and microalgae meals. *Industrial Crops and Products, 43*, 78–83.

Schwenzfeier, A., Wierenga, P. A., & Gruppen, H. (2011). Isolation and characterization of soluble protein from the green microalgae *Tetraselmis* sp. *Bioresource Technology, 102*(19), 9121–9127.

Servaites, J. C., Faeth, J. L., & Sidhu, S. S. (2012). A dye binding method for measurement of total protein in microalgae. *Analytical Biochemistry, 421*(1), 75–80.

Sharma, N. K., & Rai, A. K. (2008). Allergenicity of airborne cyanobacteria *Phormidium fragile* and *Nostoc muscorum*. *Ecotoxicology and Environmental Safety, 69*(1), 158–162.

Slocombe, S. P., Ross, M., Thomas, N., McNeill, S., & Stanley, M. S. (2013). A rapid and general method for measurement of protein in micro-algal biomass. *Bioresource Technology, 129*, 51–57.

Souza, P. O., Ferreira, L. R., Pires, N. R., S Filho, P. J., Duarte, F. A., Pereira, C. M., & Mesko, M. F. (2012). Algae of economic importance that accumulate cadmium and lead: A review. *Revista Brasileira de Farmacognosia, 22*(4), 825–837.

Springmann, M., Godfray, H. C. J., Rayner, M., & Scarborough, P. (2016). Analysis and valuation of the health and climate change cobenefits of dietary change. *Proceedings of the National Academy of Sciences, 113*(15), 4146–4151.

Stadnichuk, I., & Tropin, I. (2017). Phycobiliproteins: Structure, functions and biotechnological applications. *Applied Biochemistry and Microbiology, 53*(1), 1–10.

Sutradhar, K. B., Khatun, S., & Luna, I. P. (2013). Increasing possibilities of nanosuspension. *Journal of Nanotechnology, 2013*, 1–12.

Szabo, N. J., Matulka, R. A., Kiss, L., & Licari, P. (2012). Safety evaluation of a high lipid Whole Algalin Flour (WAF) from *Chlorella protothecoides*. *Regulatory Toxicology and Pharmacology, 63*(1), 155–165.

Thana, P., Machmudah, S., Goto, M., Sasaki, M., Pavasant, P., & Shotipruk, A. (2008). Response surface methodology to supercritical carbon dioxide extraction of astaxanthin from *Haematococcus pluvialis*. *Bioresource Technology, 99*(8), 3110–3115.

Tibbetts, S. M., Milley, J. E., & Lall, S. P. (2015). Chemical composition and nutritional properties of freshwater and marine microalgal biomass cultured in photobioreactors. *Journal of Applied Phycology, 27*(3), 1109–1119.

Tibbetts, S. M., Yasumaru, F., & Lemos, D. (2017). In vitro prediction of digestible protein content of marine microalgae (Nannochloropsis granulata) mealsfor Pacific white shrimp (Litopenaeus vannamei) and rainbow trout (Oncorhynchusmykiss). *Algal Research, 21*, 76–80.

Tiberg, E., & Einarsson, R. (1989). Variability of allergenicity in eight strains of the green algal genus Chlorella. *International Archives of Allergy and Immunology, 90*(3), 301–306.

Travaini, R., Martín-Juárez, J., Lorenzo-Hernando, A., & Bolado-Rodríguez, S. (2016). Ozonolysis: An advantageous pretreatment for lignocellulosic biomass revisited. *Bioresource Technology, 199*, 2–12.

Trigueros, E., Sanz, M. T., Alonso-Riaño, P., Beltrán, S., Ramos, C., & Melgosa, R. (2021). Recovery of the protein fraction with high antioxidant activity from red seaweed industrial solid residue after agar extraction by subcritical water treatment. *Journal of Applied Phycology, 33*(2), 1181–1194.

UNDESA. (2017). World Population Prospects: The 2017 Revision. Retrieved August 26, 2018.

Ursu, A.-V., Marcati, A., Sayd, T., Sante-Lhoutellier, V., Djelveh, G., & Michaud, P. (2014). Extraction, fractionation and functional properties of proteins from the microalgae *Chlorella vulgaris*. *Bioresource Technology, 157*, 134–139.

Van der Fels-Klerx, H., Olesen, J., Naustvoll, L.-J., Friocourt, Y., Mengelers, M., & Christensen, J. (2012). Climate change impacts on natural toxins in food production systems, exemplified by deoxynivalenol in wheat and diarrhetic shellfish toxins. *Food Additives & Contaminants: Part A, 29*(10), 1647–1659.

Van der Spiegel, M., Noordam, M., & Van der Fels-Klerx, H. (2013). Safety of novel protein sources (insects, microalgae, seaweed, duckweed, and rapeseed) and legislative aspects for their application in food and feed production. *Comprehensive Reviews in Food Science and Food Safety, 12*(6), 662–678.

Vermeulen, S. J., Campbell, B. M., & Ingram, J. S. (2012). Climate change and food systems. *Annual Review of Environment and Resources, 37*, 195–222.

Vershinin, A., & Orlova, T. Y. (2008). Toxic and harmful algae in the coastal waters of Russia. *Oceanology, 48*(4), 524–537.

Waghmare, A. G., Salve, M. K., LeBlanc, J. G., & Arya, S. S. (2016). Concentration and characterization of microalgae proteins from *Chlorella pyrenoidosa*. *Bioresources and Bioprocessing, 3*(1), 16.

Wang, X., & Zhang, X. (2012). Optimal extraction and hydrolysis of *Chlorella pyrenoidosa* proteins. *Bioresource Technology, 126*, 307–313.

Wong, M. H., Hung, K., & Chiu, S. (1996) Sludge-grown algae for culturing aquatic organisms: Part II. Sludge-grown algae as feeds for aquatic organisms. *Environmental Management, 20*(3), 375–384.

Yan, L., Lim, S., & Kim, I. (2012). Effect of fermented Chlorella supplementation on growth performance, nutrient digestibility, blood characteristics, fecal microbial and fecal noxious gas content in growing pigs. *Asian-Australasian Journal of Animal Sciences, 25*(12), 1742.

Zamani, N., Fazilati, M., Salavati, H., Izadi, M., & Koohi-Dehkordi, M. (2020). The topical cream produced from phycocyanin of *Spirulina platensis* accelerates wound healing in mice infected with *Candida albicans*. *Applied Biochemistry and Microbiology, 56*(5), 583–589.

Zhang, J., He, Y., Luo, M., & Chen, F. (2020). Utilization of enzymatic cell disruption hydrolysate of *Chlorella pyrenoidosa* as potential carbon source in algae mixotrophic cultivation. *Algal Research, 45*, 101730.

Zhang, R., Chen, J., & Zhang, X. (2018). Extraction of intracellular protein from *Chlorella pyrenoidosa* using a combination of ethanol soaking, enzyme digest, ultrasonication and homogenization techniques. *Bioresource Technology, 247*, 267–272.

5 Insect-Derived Protein as Food and Feed

Parinaz Hobbi[1], Alaa El-Din Ahmed Bekhit[2], Frederic Debaste[3], Nei Lei[4], and Amin Shavandi[1]

[1]BioMatter-BTL, École Interfacultaire de Bioingénieurs, Université Libre de Bruxelles, 1050 Brussels, Belgium
[2]Department of Food Science, University of Otago, Dunedin, New Zealand
[3]Department of Transfers, Interfaces and Processes, Université Libre de Bruxelles, 1050 Brussels, Belgium
[4]College of Life Sciences, Xinyang Normal University (XYNU), Xinyang 464000, China

CONTENTS

5.1 Introduction 86
    5.1.1 Development Challenges of Livestock Production as a Protein Source 86
    5.1.2 Development Challenges of Plant and Poultry Production as Protein Sources 86
    5.1.3 Current Sources of Protein 87
    5.1.4 Insects as an Alternative Food Source 87
5.2 Insect Proteins 89
5.3 Some Important Insect Species and Their Utilization as a Protein Source in Animals Feeding 94
    5.3.1 Black Soldier Fly Larvae (*H. illucens*) and Its Protein 94
        5.3.1.1 Utilization of BSF in Animals Feeding 96
        5.3.1.2 Challenges Associated with the Utilization of BSF in Animals Feed 97
    5.3.2 Housefly and Its Protein 98
        5.3.2.1 Utilization of Housefly in Animals Feeding 98
    5.3.3 Silkworm Pupae and Its Protein 99
        5.3.3.1 Utilization of Silkworm Pupae in Animals Feeding 99
    5.3.4 Mealworm (*T. molitor*) and Its Protein 100
    5.3.5 Cricket and Its Protein 101
        5.3.5.1 Utilization of Cricket in Animals Feeding 102
    5.3.6 Grasshopper and Its Protein 102
        5.3.6.1 Utilization of Grasshopper in Animals Feeding 102
    5.3.7 Locust and Its Protein 103
        5.3.7.1 Utilization of Locust in Animals Feeding 103
5.4 Processing Proteins from Insects and Their Potential Applications 103
5.5 Utilization of the Whole Insect as a Protein Source in Processed Foods 106
5.6 Production of Insect Protein Extracts and Their Techno-functional Properties 108
5.7 Application of Insect Protein Hydrolysates in the Production of Food Product 110
5.8 Biological Activities of Insect Protein Hydrolysates and Peptides 110
5.9 Insect Proteins as a Potential Source of Antimicrobial Peptides 112

DOI: 10.1201/9780429299834-5

5.10	The Importance of Insects' Utilization in Human Food	113
5.11	Safety Issues with Insects as Source of Protein	123
5.12	Challenges Associated with the Consumption of Insects as Human Food	125
References		126

5.1 INTRODUCTION

The world population is predicted to increase to nine billion people by 2050. Based on the estimation by the UN Food and Agricultural Organization (FAO), 70% more food has to be produced to provide the food requirements for this approximately extra two billion people increase in human population (Makkar et al., 2014; Veldkamp et al., 2012). The demand for animal-derived protein is expected to increase by about 60–70%, which will result in 58% and 70% higher demand for meat and milk, respectively, in 2050 compared with 2010 (Cullere et al., 2016; Makkar et al., 2014). In addition to the predicted increase in population, an increased per capita meat consumption from 28 to 42 kg and from 80 to 91 kg in developing and developed countries, respectively, is also anticipated due to economic development and increased purchasing power (van Huis & Oonincx, 2017). Some studies predict a considerable increase in the consumption of poultry meat and eggs, as these protein products are nutritious, relatively cheap, and no religious restrictions are connected with their consumption (Józefiak et al., 2016). The International Feed Industry Federation (IFIF) proposed that the production of meat (poultry, swine and beef) will need to double by 2050 to meet the expected demands (Veldkamp & Bosch, 2015).

Proteins play important roles in growth, health, reproduction and well-being of humans and animals (Stamer, 2015). However, it is not the protein but rather its building blocks, important amino acids, and the bioavailability of amino acids that determine the quality of a protein (Boland et al., 2013). Essential amino acids (EAAs; histidine, isoleucine, leucine, lysine, methionine, phenylalanine, threonine, tryptophan and valine) are important since humans cannot synthesize them in the body, and they must be acquired through diet (Boland et al., 2013; Stamer, 2015).

5.1.1 Development Challenges of Livestock Production as a Protein Source

Livestock production is highly dependent on the provision of sufficient protein in the feed, which normally involves the inclusion of soya bean meal, fish meal and processed animal proteins in the rations (Cullere et al., 2016; Veldkamp & Bosch, 2015). Approximately 80% of agricultural lands are dedicated to animal grazing or feed production (van Huis & Oonincx, 2017). Cultivation of crops, such as soybeans, as the primary protein feed for livestock puts massive pressure on lands with negative environmental impacts, such as the loss of biodiversity, decreased soil fertility and the depletion of water resources (Spranghers et al., 2017; Stamer, 2015). The price for soybeans will increase as the demand for them soars, which will lead to more than a 30% increase in the cost of meat products by 2050, as compared to 2000 (Cullere et al., 2016). It is worth noting that livestock is an important contributor to greenhouse gas emissions and climate change (Rumpold & Schlüter, 2013; van Huis & Oonincx, 2017). Livestock is responsible for 9% of CO_2, 35–40% of CH_4, 65% of N_2O and 64% of NH_3 production (Rumpold & Schlüter, 2013). An agreement signed by 195 countries at the Paris Climate Conference in 2015, where they committed to decrease the global temperature increase to 1.5 °C and, with it, reduce the adverse effects of climate change (van Huis & Oonincx, 2017).

5.1.2 Development Challenges of Plant and Poultry Production as Protein Sources

The transition of livestock farming from ruminant cattle and sheep to pigs and poultry is considered to be relatively more environmentally friendly (Józefiak et al., 2016) due to less greenhouse gas emissions. Poultry production and aquaculture require higher protein intake to cover the EAAs required for their growth, development and egg production. Given that typical vegetable protein sources are inferior in their sulfur-containing amino acid (methionine and cysteine) contents, diets for poultry are often supplemented with animal protein, such as fish meal, feather meal and other meat byproducts (Cullere et al., 2016; Józefiak et al., 2016). There is already a huge demand for seafood products for human consumption and fish oil due to their perceived health benefits. An increase in fish meal for animal feed puts further pressure on fisheries, which will negatively impact the availability of sea products as a result of overharvesting (Riddick, 2013). That being said, fish meal as a leading source of animal protein, is becoming less available, and its price is rising due to various biotechnological options available for its use (Riddick, 2013; Shakil Rana et al., 2015). In this regard, aquaculture and related industries are currently investigating possibilities to replace fishmeal-based feedstuffs with alternative plant and animal-based protein sources, thus allowing aquaculture to remain economically and environmentally sustainable (Shakil Rana et al., 2015; Tran et al., 2015). Plant proteins are the favourite option, and these have been widely investigated. However, the low level of some EAAs, high fibre content, non-starch polysaccharides and the presence of anti-nutritional substances such as oxalates, phytates, tannins, and hydrocyanide as well as inherent palatability issues may limit plant protein applications (Rumpold & Schlüter, 2015; Shakil Rana et al., 2015; Tran et al., 2015). As a result, alternative protein sources are urgently required (Makkar et al., 2014; Spranghers et al., 2017).

5.1.3 CURRENT SOURCES OF PROTEIN

In 2008, the world total protein consumption was estimated to be 150–170 million tons, and this figure is continuously growing due to population growth (Cullere et al., 2016; Makkar et al., 2014). The most used major protein sources in animal nutrition are oilseed meals (soybean meal, rapeseed meal, sunflower meal, and cottonseed meal), animal by-products (meat meal, hydrolysed feather meal, spray dried blood meal, and fish meal) and pulses (peas). Livestock have been estimated to consume 77 million tons of protein supplied by feed each year in which soybean meal is the main source (75%) followed by animal by-products and fishmeal (Boland et al., 2013). Human demand for fish consumption has increased due to its health benefits, where it provides 17% of animal protein intake (Riddick, 2013; Tran et al., 2015). Fish meal is widely used as a feed ingredient since it has an excellent EAAs composition (Tran et al., 2015). More than 90% of the fish meal produced globally is utilized for fish feed, which can later be used as food for humans (Stamer, 2015). The limited available protein resources will be under severe competition for human and animal consumption and thus new protein resources. Among the potential natural resources that could be used as practical sources of protein, insects are at the forefront due to a long history of their utilization as food for humans and animals (Van Huis et al., 2013). It has been suggested that there are more than 2,111 edible insect species worldwide (Jongema, 2017). The protein composition of many insect species fulfils the criteria of high-quality protein that meets the requirements of humans and pets (Table 5.1).

5.1.4 INSECTS AS AN ALTERNATIVE FOOD SOURCE

Several studies have focused on possible alternative solutions to meet the predicted increase in protein demand. Insects are rich in protein and a strong potential choice to be included in future food and feed systems (Akhtar & Isman, 2018). The utilization of insects as a sustainable protein source is very appealing due to numerous potential benefits that could be gained by adapting insects as food (Van Huis, 2017). Several environmental and economic benefits have been suggested by Van Huis et al. (2013), Van Huis (2017) and Williams et al. (2016) that can be summarized as follows:

TABLE 5.1
Essential amino acids, taurine, essential amino acid index of some insects, common protein sources and requirements in humans and pets

Insect	His	Isoleu	Leu	Lys	Met + Cys	Phe + Tyr	Thr	Try	Val	Tau	Sum of EAA	EAA index
American cockroach (*Periplaneta americana*)	16.1	19.6	37.4	36.4	9.3	20.5	21.9	4.9	32.3	1.1	199	0.84
Flesh fly, larva (*Sarcophaga (Neobellieria) bullata*)	35.7	41.6	68.2	85.3	24.3	61.7	41.3	13.6	53.9	1.4	426	0.99
Flesh fly, adult (*Sarcophaga (Neobellieria) bullata*)	31.7	40.8	65.9	78.1	25.3	41.2	36.9	11.5	51.4	4.2	383	1.00
Western harvester ant (*Pogonomyrmex occidentalis*)	22.8	45.7	70.7	42.9	12.1	24.4	36.7	0.0	57.2	9.7	313	0.00
Black soldier fly, larva (*Hermetia illucens*)	33.4	37.0	61.6	61.2	14.9	34.3	35.4	13.4	55.7	0.4	347	0.93
Tenebrio molitor (defatted)	29	43	73	54	26	100	39	12	61	–	437	0.96
Casein	32	54	95	85	35	111	42	14	63	–	531	0.98
Beef	32	42	78	79	33	70	42	10	45	2.0	431	0.96
Egg white	23	53	88	70	66	91	47	15	68	NA	519	1.31
Wheat flour	22	33	69	27	39	78	29	11	43	NA	350	1.05
Soybean	25	47	85	63	24	97	38	11	49	NA	439	0.92
1985 FAO/WHO/UNU	15	30	59	45	22	38	23	6	39	NR	277	1.00
NRC MR Canine for growth	17.2	28.9	57.2	38.9	15.6	28.9	36.1	10.0	30.0	NR	–	–
NRC MR Feline for growth	14.4	23.9	56.7	37.8	19.4	22.2	28.9	7.2	28.3	1.8	–	–

Hist = Histidine; Isoleu = Isolecuine; Leu = Leucine; Lys = Lysine; Met = Methionine; Cys = cysteine; Phe = Phenylalanine; Tyr = tyrosine; Thr = Threonine; Try = Tryptophan; Val = Valine; Tau = Taurine; NA = not available; NR = not require.

Economic Benefits: Excellent feed conversion ratio (FCR) when feeding crickets of ~2.0 (this could vary for other insects), which is similar to the FCR for chickens. This FCR is far superior to that for cattle (6–10) or pigs (2.7–3.5). Aquaculture is the only production option that provides better feed conversion, with the FCR for salmon, tilapia and carp being ~1.2–1.5, while the FCR for catfish is close to 1.0 (Shike, 2013). Insects can produce useful co-products that have economic importance (such as honey and silk). The life cycle of insects is shorter than that of many traditional protein sources. Also, the space required for insect farming and potential vertical expansion is much easier compared to traditional protein production systems. The capital investment required to set up insect farming is much lower, and it will allow smaller scale economic activities. However, it's expected that meeting regulatory and environmental regulatory requirements and insuring safety and security (prevention of unintended release to the environment) will add to overall costs.

Environmental Benefits: Compared with ruminant and other animal protein sources, insects produce less greenhouse gases. Insects have minimal impact on the environment (water pollution, land erosion), and they are capable of biotransformation and waste biodegradation of organic matter (agriculture waste including animal carcases, manure and materials that may have no use). Furthermore, greenhouse emissions generated by insects are lower than emissions from commercial animal protein sources. Thus, insects could effectively utilize food market and processing waste, by-catches from fishing activities, and household and food service leftovers. The use of water by insects is low compared to other protein sources.

Nutritional Benefits: Insect-derived products have a very good nutritional profile. Mealworms have comparable protein, mineral and vitamin contents to muscle foods. Also, mealworms have higher unsaturated fatty acids and omega-3 fatty acid contents than does red meat.

Ethical Issues: Insects farming does not have major issues associated with traditional animal and poultry farming (animal welfare and humane slaughtering) or dogma towards the prohibition of certain meats. Some of these benefits are discussed later. Most insect species contain high amounts of proteins, fatty acids, vitamins, fibres and minerals (calcium, iron and zinc) (Akhtar & Isman, 2018). The insect is also considered a sustainable and environmentally friendly alternative protein source with a low impact on resources and the environment as it emits lower levels of greenhouse gases. Insects can be produced on a large scale by using less space and water; therefore, they can be more easily and quickly produced on a large scale in comparison to other animals, due also to their high reproduction rate (Akhtar & Isman, 2018; Makkar et al., 2014; Van Huis, 2017). More importantly, if insects can be reared on bio-waste and organic matter down streams, they could be used as a protein-rich ingredient in pig, poultry and fish diets, contributing to enhanced recovery of organic matter and better solutions to environmental pollution (Makkar et al., 2014). In this regard, some insect species, such as the black soldier fly (*Hermetia illucens*), the common housefly (*Musca domestica*) and yellow mealworms (*Tenebrio molitor*) have been identified as the most promising species for industrial production. These insect species can valorize a wide range of organic wastes that are not suitable for further applications and thus reduce the negative impacts of them on the environment (Veldkamp et al., 2012). When black soldier fly larvae feed on poultry manure, they are able to reduce phosphorous and nitrogen content in the manure by 61–70% and 30–50%, respectively (Józefiak et al., 2016). These species each have a high feed conversion rate. For example, to produce 1 kg of protein, just 1.7 kg of feed is required for crickets, while 7.7 kg are required for beef, 6.3 kg for sheep, 3.6 kg for pork and 2.2 kg for chicken to produce the same 1 kg of protein (Makkar et al., 2014). Thus, such species would be doubly effective in reducing environmental contamination and producing protein for animal feed.

5.2 INSECT PROTEINS

To date, an estimated 2111 species of insects have been recorded as edible insects, but a mere fraction of them are consumed, primarily the easily accessible ones. It has been reported that the average protein content of 100 insect species ranged from 13% to 77% on a dry matter basis (Akhtar & Isman, 2018). The average protein content was reported to be 57.3% in Blattodea (cockroaches), 40.69% in Coleoptera (beetles), 49.48% in Diptera (flies), 48.33% in Hemiptera (beetles), 46.47% in Hymenoptera (bees, wasps, and ants), 35.34% in Isoptera (termites), 45.38% in Lepidoptera (caterpillars), 55.23% in Odonata (dragonflies) and 61.32% in Orthoptera (grasshoppers, locusts, and crickets) (Rumpold & Schlüter, 2013). The protein content of different insect species varies according to species, sex, development stage, feed consumed, gut contents and environmental factors (day length, temperature, humidity and light intensity) (Makkar et al., 2014). Several insects, such as grasshoppers, termites, weevils, caterpillars and houseflies, are considered to be better sources of protein on a dry weight basis compared to beef, chicken, pork and lamb. The protein content (g/100g) of edible insects on a fresh weight basis ranges from 7% to 48%, with many species having comparable protein content to beef (19–26%), tilapia (16–19%) and shrimp (13–27%) (Churchward-Venne et al., 2017).

To evaluate the suitability of insect protein for application in different food systems, the availability and digestibility of the protein, as well as the content of EAAs, must be determined (Akhtar & Isman, 2018). An analysis of nearly a hundred edible insect species indicated an EAA content of 46–96% of the total amino acids present, with at least 40% of the FAO/WHO recommendation (Liu & Zhao, 2019). Total EAA of insect protein, from the orders of Coleoptera, Hymenoptera, Orthoptera and Lepidoptera, have been reported to meet or exceed the EAA requirements determined for adult humans, which are comparable to the EAA contents of beef, milk, egg and soy. In contrast, some other insect orders, such as Diptera, Hemiptera, Isoptera and Blattodea, have a deficiency of at least one EAA (Table 5.2; Churchward-Venne et al., 2017).

There is limited information on the digestibility of insect proteins since digestibility experiments using human and animal subjects are expensive to conduct. Therefore, *in vitro* approaches for digestibility assessment have generally been used, as they are simple, cheap and rapid (Churchward-Venne et al., 2017).

While the protein digestibility of insect protein is 76–90%, which is lower than it is for egg protein (95%) and beef (98%), it is regarded as superior or comparable to many plant proteins such as rapeseed meal (70%), sunflower meal (77%), cottonseed meal (78%) and peas (74%) (Akhtar & Isman, 2018; Boland et al., 2013). Using an *in vitro* gastric-duodenal digestion model, Yi et al. (2016) determined protein digestibility, protein solubility in the supernatant, and the identity of the insoluble protein fractions in the pellet and the residue for whole mealworm larvae (*T. molitor*). Protein identification was by LC-MS/MS, and the most abundant proteins in the supernatant fraction were hemolymph and the putative allergen alpha-amylase. These proteins had a higher digestibility (80%) in the supernatant than in the pellet protein fraction (50%), which also contained actin, tropomyosin, and troponin T, or in the residue protein fraction (24%). These findings demonstrated that the water-soluble protein fractions of *T. molitor* are more easily digested using the gastric and duodenal digestion model than are the water-insoluble protein fractions.

In another study, *in vitro* digestion by pancreatin and pepsin enzymes was used to evaluate the digestibility of materials from whole homogenized mealworm larvae (*T. molitor*) and its nitrogenous substances (Adámek et al., 2019). Different thermal culinary treatments (drying for 2 min at 120 °C and then 5–7 min at 70–80 °C, roasting for 4 min at 160 °C) were applied to the insects to determine the optimum processing conditions for human digestibility. The findings showed that the digestibility of untreated whole larvae samples (91.5%) using the mixture of digestive enzymes was higher than when the whole samples were roasted (81%). This study confirmed that heat processing can influence the digestion of edible insects (Adámek et al., 2019).

For a better understanding of insect protein quality, more comprehensive studies examining ileal dietary amino acid digestibility (based on the DIAAS method), *in vivo* postprandial protein digestion, amino acid absorption kinetics, and ingestion studies, particularly in humans, are needed (Churchward-Venne et al., 2017). In an effort to fill this gap, a recent study by Vangsoe et al. (2018) investigated the potential of protein isolate of lesser mealworm (*Alphitobius diaperinus*)

TABLE 5.2
Essential amino acid content for selected insect species and common high protein commodities (mg/100 g dry matter)

Insect	Ile	Leu	lys	Met	Cys	SAA	Phe	Tyr	AAA	Thr	Trp	Val	Arg	His	Limiting AAA	Amino acid Score
Diptera																
Copestyla anna and *C. haggi*	40	74	55	19	18	37	54	66	120	49	7	61	63	29	Trp	64
Lepidoptera																
Caterpillar, *Nadurelia oyemensis*	25.6	82.7	79.8	23.5	19.7	43.2	58.6	75.7	134	44.5	16	96	63.5	18.1	ILe	91
Caterpillar, *Imbrasis truncata*	24.2	73.1	78.9	22.2	16.5	38.7	62.2	76.5	139	46.9	16.5	102	55.5	17.4	ILe	86
Caterpillar, *Imbrasia epimethea*	28.6	81	74.2	22.4	18.7	41.1	65	75	140	48	16	102	66.2	19.7	ILe	102
Caterpillar, *Imbrasia ertli*	36	36.7	39.3	15.8	13.4	29.2	17.4	13.2	30.6	40.5	8.1	41.9	–	–	–	49
Caterpillar, *Usta terpsichore*	108.7	91.3	91	11.3	12.9	24.2	55.9	33	88.9	50.8	6.6	75.8	–	–	Trp	60
Maguey worm,*Aegiate sp.*	49	52	36	10	–	–	37	42	79	33	9	47	30	16	Lys	49
Gusano rojo de maguey, *Cossus retenbachi*	51	79	49	8	13	21	40	53	93	47	6	61	60	16	Trp	55
Caterpillar meal,*Bombycomorphasp.*	46.1	62.1	64.5	17.9	29.9	47.8	59.8	81.4	141.3	42.9	13	60.5	41.8	8.31	Leu	94
Caterpillars cooked,*Bombycomorpha sp.*	44.3	77.4	47.8	16.2	21.8	37.9	93.4	63.4	157	49.1	9.4	55	37	16.2	Lys	82
African silkworm larvae, *Anaphe venata*	21.4	13.1	8.8	–	–	–	21.4	24.9	46.4	3.8	–	17.6	3.2	7.8	Trp	–
Spent silkworm pupae	57	83	75	46	14	60	51	54	105	54	9	56	68	25	Trp	82
Xyleutes redtenbacheri	51	79	49	21	13	34	93	53	146	47	6	61	60	16	Trp	55
Ascalapha odorata	41	69	63	23	21	44	95	44	139	40	4	48	28	67	Trp	36
Arsenura armida	43	69	54	24	19	43	93	52	145	42	4	48	63	29	Trp	36
Hylesia frigida	44	71	57	26	54	80	64	52	116	41	5	49	20	68	Trp	45
Phasus triangularis	46	80	57	22	13	35	72	95	167	38	4	57	57	25	Trp	36
Chilecomadia moorei (larvae)	6.5	10	8.7	2.5	0.87	–	5.47	7.95	–	5.74	1.56	9.71	11.7	4.08	–	–
Coleóptera: Curculionidae																
Palm weevil larvae, *Rhynchophorus phoenicis*	77.5	58.9	63.9	12	10.6	22.6	32.8	13.6	46.4	28.6	5.1	54.9	–	–	Trp	46
Larvae of *Sciphophonts acupunctatus*	48.2	78.2	53.5	20.2	26.7	46.9	46.1	63.5	109.6	40.4	8.1	62	44	14.7	Trp	74
Scyphophorus acupunctatus	48	78	55	20	22	42	46	64	110	40	8	62	44	15	Trp	72
Callipogon barbatus	58	100	57	20	20	40	47	42	98	40	9	90	59	22	Trp	64

(Continued)

TABLE 5.2 (Continued)
Essential amino acid content for selected insect species and common high protein commodities (mg/100 g dry matter)

Insect	Ile	Leu	Lys	Met	Cys	SAA	Phe	Tyr	AAA	Thr	Trp	Val	Arg	His	Limiting AAA	Amino acid Score
Orthoptera: Acrididae																
Chapulin, *Sphenarium histrio*	53	87	57	7	13	20	44	73	117	40	6	51	66	11	Trp	55
'Chapulin', *Sphenarium purpurascens*	42	89	57	25	18	43	103	63	166	38	6.5	57	60	22	Trp	59
Mexican 'Chapulines'	46	64	52	8	–	–	36	32	68	49	10	54	42	21	Lys	90
Schistocerca sp.	53	79	51	–	–	–	–	–	–	41	4	51	–	–	–	–
Taeniopoda eques	41	72	31	–	–	–	–	–	–	45	6	54	–	–	–	–
Melanoplus femurrubrum	47	88	27	–	–	–	–	–	–	41	5	52	–	–	–	–
Blattalateralis (nymphs)	7.73	12	12.8	3.35	1.44	–	7.67	14.3	–	7.89	1.66	12.3	14	5.49	–	–
Brachytrupes sp.	3.1	5.5	4.8	1.9	1	2.9	2.9	3.9	–	2.75	–	4.42	3.7	1.94	–	–
House crickets, *Acheta domesticus*	36.4	66.7	51.1	14.6	8.3	–	30.2	44	–	31.1	6.3	48.4	57.3	23.4	–	–
Hymenoptera: Formicidae																
Ants, *Atta mexicana*	53	80	49	19	15	34	41	47	88	43	6	64	47	25	Trp	55
Escamol, *Liometopum apiculatum*	49	76	58	18	14	32	39	68	10	42	8	60	50	29	Trp	73
Atta mexicana	53	80	49	34	15	49	88	47	135	43	6	64	47	25	Trp	55
Trigana sp.	48	73	79	13	23	36	75	64	139	48	6	53	60	22	Trp	55
Apis mellifera	41	66	60	25	9	34	70	41	111	44	7	59	64	33	Trp	64
Parachartegus apicalis	42	77	58	20	24	44	43	71	114	47	5	57	43	29	Trp	45
Brachygastra azteca	51	85	61	14	16	30	41	65	106	44	7	64	44	28	Trp	64
Brachygastra mellifica	44	78	36	18	20	38	40	75	115	44	7	54	57	36	–	–
Vespula squamosal	49	63	51	17	28	45	49	63	112	44	7	57	42	30	Trp	64
Polybia sp.	45	78	74	21	29	50	33	56	99	40	7	59	57	30	Trp	64
Polistes instabilis	64	115	43	21	17	38	42	66	108	49	3	67	34	22	Trp	72
Isoptera: Termitidae																
Termites, *Macrotermes bellicosus*	51.1	78.3	54.2	7.5	18.7	26.2	43.8	30.2	74	27.5	14.3	73.3	69.4	51.4	Thr	81
Termites, mature alates, *Macrotermes subhyalinu*	37.1	79.7	35.4	12.9	9	21.9	43.1	36.8	79.9	41.9	7.7	51.4	–	–	Lys	61

Hemiptera												
'Ahuahutle' or Mexican caviar, eggs of water bugs (Corixidae)	50	80	35	15	–	–	34	111	145	40	11	60	77	33	Lys	60
'Axayácatl', adults and nymphs of water bugs (Corixidae and notonectidae)	59	80	43	16	–	–	32	45	77	44	16	55	55	24	Lys	74
'Jumiles de Taxco', nymphs of *Atizies taxcoensis* (Pentatomidae)	41	77	31	17	10	27	36	66	102	42	1	73	51	18	Trp	9
'Jumiles', nymphs of several species of Pentatomidae	45	62	38	15	–	–	25	40	65	28	15	48	29	30	Lys	66
Edessa petersii	40	71	40	28	10	37	67	115	182	45	5	64	45	23	Trp	45
Umbonia reclinata	38	68	57	19	14	33	59	68	127	47	60	40	46	37	Trp	55
Diptera												
Aquatic insect flour	52	79	78	24	8.5	32.5	47	58	105	46	–	47	69	32	Trp	0
Hermetia illucens	7.6	12	12	3.4	1.02	–	7.56	12.1	–	6.82	3	12.9	12.3	5.9	–	–
Musca domestica (pupa)	8.14	12.4	12.6	5.84	1.4	–	7.91	9.26	–	7.54	2.4	11	12.1	5.71	–	–
Commonly consumed protein sources												
Beef	0.90	1.71	1.85	0.601	0.219	–	0.803	0.731	–	0.933	0.236	0.95	1.39	0.68	–	–
Pork	1.02	1.76	1.92	0.569	0.238	–	0.868	0.786	–	0.927	0.217	1.08	1.37	0.892	–	–
Chicken	0.74	1.36	1.51	0.446	0.188	–	0.683	0.604	–	0.727	0.147	0.83	1.128	0.529	–	–
Egg	0.67	1.09	0.91	0.38	0.272	–	0.68	0.499	–	0.556	0.167	0.86	0.82	0.309	–	–
Salmon	0.91	1.61	1.82	0.587	0.213	–	0.775	0.67	–	0.87	0.222	1.02	1.19	0.584	–	–
Whole milk-dry	1.59	2.58	2.09	0.66	0.243	–	1.27	1.27	–	1.19	0.371	1.76	0.953	0.714	–	–
Whole milk-fluid	0.20	0.32	0.26	0.082	0.03	–	0.158	0.18	–	0.148	0.046	0.22	0.119	0.089	–	–

Ile = Isoleucine; Leu = Leucine; Lys = Lysine; Met = Methionine; Cys = cysteine; SAA = (Met + Cys); Phe = Phenylalanine; Tyr = Tyrosine; AAA = total aromatic amino acid (Phe + Tyr); Thr = Threonine; Trp = Tryptophan; Val = Valine; Arg = Arginine; His = Histidine. Adapted from Williams, J. P., Williams, J. R., Kirabo, A., Chester, D., & Peterson, M. (2016). Nutrient content and health benefits of insects. In *Insects as Sustainable Food Ingredients* (pp. 61–84), with permission from Elsevier (License Number 4822981315653).

compared to whey protein and soy protein to enhance blood amino acid concentrations in humans (*in vivo* postprandial ingestion). In this experiment, six healthy young men were selected and received drinks supplemented with 25 g crude proteins (CPs) from insect, whey or soy. Analysis of blood samples showed that all the protein isolates increased the blood concentration of the branched-chain amino acid (BCAA) leucine over a 120-min period. This increase in amino acid concentration in blood for insect protein was similar to that for soy protein but lower than it was for whey protein. Insect protein was observed to increase the blood amino acid concentration after 120 min, which indicated that it was a slowly digestible protein source. This study also revealed that the total amino acid contents of whey, soy, and insect proteins were 96.2%, 83.2% and 69.1%, respectively, and that the EAA contents of all these protein sources met the requirements for adults based on FAO/WHO/UNU criteria (Vangsoe et al., 2018).

The CP content of some insects, including black soldier fly larvae, housefly maggot meal, mealworm, locust meal, house cricket, Mormon cricket, silkworm pupae meal and silkworm pupae meal (defatted) have been compared with the CP of fishmeal and soymeal (Makkar et al., 2014). The CP contents of these insects were high and varied from 42% for black soldier fly larvae to 63% for house cricket, which was comparable to soymeal (52%) but slightly lower than for fishmeal (71%). If these insects are intended to be used as animal feed and for other applications, they must provide a balanced amino acid composition and in some cases, compensate for a deficiency of amino acids. Black soldier fly larvae, housefly maggot, and silkworm pupae meals have an adequate level of lysine (average 6.5 g/16 g nitrogen). The methionine content, as one of the major limiting amino acids for growing pigs and broilers, in all insect meals was higher than in soymeal (Makkar et al., 2014). Overall, the quality of insect proteins is considered good since it is comparable to soybean meal and beef and much higher than in wheat flour (Van Huis, 2017). The nutritional value of insect proteins is better than what is found in the diets of some countries where EAA deficiencies are common and thus the inclusion of insects would improve the overall diet nutritional quality. For instance, in the Democratic Republic of the Congo, the consumption of lysine-rich caterpillars with traditional lysine-poor grains has compensated the nutritional gap in their livestock rations (Akhtar & Isman, 2018).

5.3 SOME IMPORTANT INSECT SPECIES AND THEIR UTILIZATION AS A PROTEIN SOURCE IN ANIMALS FEEDING

Several insect species are being successfully incorporated into some animal feeding, such as pig, broilers, laying hens, fish species, ruminants and crustaceans as a replacement for soymeal and fishmeal. The amino acids profile of some insects (black soldier fly, mealworm, silkworm, house fly, cricket, locust and grasshopper) has been compared to the amino acid profiles of soymeal and fishmeal as well as the FAO reference protein for 2–5-year-old child, and is described in Table 5.3 (Makkar et al., 2014).

5.3.1 BLACK SOLDIER FLY LARVAE (*H. ILLUCENS*) AND ITS PROTEIN

Black soldier fly (BSF) larva is a well-known insect species that has a rapid feeding rate (from 25 to 500 mg of fresh matter/larva/day). The BSF feed on a wide range of waste substances, such as rotten fruits and vegetables, coffee bean pulp, distillers' grains, fish offal, food service and catering waste, animal manures (swine, poultry and cattle) and human excreta. The disposal of these organic materials is normally difficult and carries a cost. The use of insects to process and convert these valueless materials into protein-rich and fat-rich biomass (Makkar et al., 2014; van Huis & Oonincx, 2017) appears to provide a promising strategy for gaining valuable nutrients from unwanted waste. Due to its efficiency, BSF is one solution to solving the environmental problem associated with organic waste, such as reducing the mass and bad odour of manure and reducing the heavy metals that often accompany organic matters. The resultant protein and fat biomass can

TABLE 5.3
Amino acid composition (g/16 g nitrogen) of insect meals versus FAO reference dietary protein requirement values, soymeal and fishmeal

Insects	Black Soldier Fly Larvae	House Fly Maggot Meal	Mealworm	Locust Meal	House Cricket	Mormon Cricket	Silk Worm Pupae Meal	Silk Worm Pupae Meal (Defatted)	Fish Meal	Soy Meal	FAO Reference Protein for 2–5-Year-Old Child
Amino acids profile											
Essential											
Methionine	2.1	2.2	1.5	2.3	1.4	1.4	3.5	3.0	2.7	1.32	2.50[a]
Cystine	0.1	0.7	0.8	1.1	0.8	0.1	1.0	0.8	0.8	1.38	–
Valine	8.2	4.0	6.0	4.0	5.1	6	5.5	4.9	4.9	4.5	3.50
Isoleucine	5.1	3.2	4.6	4.0	4.4	4.8	5.1	3.9	4.2	4.16	2.80
Leucine	7.9	5.4	8.6	5.8	9.8	8.0	7.5	5.8	7.2	7.58	6.60
Phenylalanine	5.2	4.6	4.0	3.4	3.0	2.5	5.2	4.4	3.9	5.16	6.30[b]
Tyrosine	6.9	4.7	7.4	3.3	5.2	5.2	5.9	5.5	3.1	3.35	–
Histidine	3.0	2.4	3.4	3.0	2.3	3.0	2.6	2.6	2.4	3.06	1.90
Lysine	6.6	6.1	5.4	4.7	5.4	5.9	7.0	6.1	7.5	6.18	5.80
Threonine	3.7	3.5	4.0	3.5	3.6	4.2	5.1	4.8	4.1	3.78	3.40
Tryptophan	0.5	1.5	0.6	0.8	0.6	0.6	0.9	1.4	1.0	1.36	1.10
Non-essential											
Serine	3.1	3.6	7.0	5.0	4.6	4.9	5.0	4.5	3.9	5.18	–
Arginine	5.6	4.6	4.8	5.6	6.1	5.3	5.6	5.1	6.2	7.64	–
Glutamic acid	10.9	11.7	11.3	15.4	10.4	11.7	13.9	8.3	12.6	19.92	–
Aspartic acid	11.0	7.5	7.5	9.4	7.7	8.8	10.4	7.8	9.1	14.14	–
Proline	6.6	3.3	6.8	2.9	5.6	6.2	5.2	–	4.2	5.99	–
Glycine	5.7	4.2	4.9	4.8	5.2	5.9	4.8	3.7	6.4	4.52	–
Alanine	7.7	5.8	7.3	4.6	8.8	9.5	5.8	4.4	6.3	4.54	–

Notes
a Methionine plus cystine.
b Phenylalanine plus tyrosine. Adapted from Makkar, H. P. S., Tran, G., Heuzé, V., & Ankers, P. (2014) Makkar 2014. State-of-the-art on use of insects as animal feed. *Animal Feed Science and Technology, 197*, 1–33, with permission from Elsevier (License Number 4822990168137).
The values are the average of multiple values, collated from several publications.

be used as feed for cattle, pig, poultry and fish as well as for the production of biodiesel and chitin (Moore, 2018). It should be noted that the adult insect does not feed on the waste, as it is only the larvae that utilize waste efficiently, without the need of management. Furthermore, the larvae are not a potential pathogen vector for humans.

The BSF larvae have been reported to contain about 40–44% CP and variable amounts of fat, depending upon the diet consumed, for example, 15–25% for larvae fed on poultry manure and 42–49% on oil-rich food waste (Makkar et al., 2014). Lauric acid, which has been shown to possess antimicrobial activity, is the principal fatty acid present in insect fat (Shockley & Dossey, 2013). The content of most EAAs, including methionine, valine, isoleucine, leucine, phenylalanine, tyrosine and lysine, are higher in BSF larvae than in soymeal. BSF larva also has higher amounts of valine, isoleucine, leucine, phenylalanine, tyrosine, histidine, aspartic acid, proline and alanine amino acids than does fishmeal.

Comparing the amino acid composition of BSF larvae to the FAO reference dietary protein requirement for a 2–5-year-old child shows equal or excess amounts of the EAAs (valine, isoleucine, leucine, phenylalanine, tyrosine, histidine, lysine and threonine) in the BSF larvae (Makkar et al., 2014). This confirms that all EAAs of this insect prepupae meet the standard requirements and exceed the standard for some EAA, with histidine and phenylalanine plus tyrosine being higher in BSF prepupae (Caligiani et al., 2018). The aforementioned results show that BSF protein has the appropriate EAAs profile for application in human diets and animal feed.

5.3.1.1 Utilization of BSF in Animals Feeding

The BSF larvae meal can be a valuable ingredient for inclusion in growing pig diets due to its amino acid, lipid and calcium contents (Newton et al., 1977). Nevertheless, it is deficient in methionine + cystine and threonine and thus cannot be applied as the sole source of protein in the preparation of pig feed. Dried BSF prepupae meal was used as a replacement for dried blood plasma at inclusion levels of 0, 50, or 100% in early-weaned pigs diet, with or without amino acid supplementation (Newton et al., 2005). Better performance (+4% weight gain, +9% feed efficiency) was achieved in a 50% replacement diet without amino acid supplementation. The overall performance of the early-weaned pigs declined by up to 13% when the 100% replacement diet was used. The taste of the diet containing the larvae meal was as acceptable as a soymeal based diet (Newton et al., 2005).

BSF larvae meal can also support chicken growth. Dried BSF larvae as an alternative diet for a soymeal control diet in chicken feed achieved a similar weight gain rate to the soymeal control, and higher feed conversion efficiency was obtained by the larvae meal diet (Cullere et al., 2016).

Supplementation of quail feed with BSF larvae as a partial replacement for maize or soy-based feeds resulted in similar productivity performance, breast meat weight and overall yield (Cullere et al., 2016; Wang & Shelomi, 2017). The amino acid content of the meat was improved, with higher levels of aspartic acid, glutamic acid, alanine, serine, tyrosine and threonine, and meat sensory and flavor values, oxidative status and cholesterol content were not affected by the replacement.

The ability of BSF larvae to partially or fully substitute for fishmeal in fish diets has been investigated in several studies (Makkar et al., 2014; Tran et al., 2015; Zhang et al., 2014). The BSF has an excellent potential to be utilized in fish feed, but factors such as rearing substrate, processing methods and economics must be considered since performance reduction in fish species such as turbot (*Psetta maxima*) have been reported (Tran et al., 2015). Replacing 25% fish meal by BSF larvae meal in yellow catfish diets (*Pelteobagrus fulvidraco*) resulted in no considerable difference in growth and immunity indexes compared with a control group (Zhang et al., 2014).

Conversely, feeding blue tilapia (*Oreochromis aureus*) with dry BSF larvae as the sole component diet did not lead to good growth since sufficient dry matter or protein intake was not achieved; however, chopping the larvae enhanced weight gain by 140% and feed efficiency by 28% (Bondari & Sheppard, 1987). In another experiment by the same group, using chopped BSF larvae grown on hen manure alone or in combination with common diets fed to this fish provided similar performance (body weight and total length) as control diets. The use of BSF larvae did not affect the fish sensory attributes, and consumers were satisfied with the aroma and texture of the tilapia (Bondari & Sheppard, 1981). A mixture of fishmeal and BSF larvae was found to provide optimal growth of mono sex tilapia (*Oreochromis niloticus*) when EAA and mineral availability and increased palatability were the main contributing factors (Shakil Rana et al., 2015). However, poor growth was observed when BSF larvae were the only source of protein in the diet.

The combination of BSF prepupae meal (reared on dairy cattle manure) with 25–50% trout offal was used as placement for up to 50% fish meal protein in rainbow trout (*Oncorhynchus mykiss*) diets. After 8 weeks, no significant changes were observed in fish growth or the sensory quality of trout fillets. These results were confirmed in a subsequent 9-week study in which 25% fish meal was replaced with BSF prepupae meal (reared on pig manure). The result showed that this mixture did not affect the weight gain and FCR of rainbow trout (Sealey et al., 2011).

A diet containing 33% defatted BSF larvae meal was used as a replacement for fishmeal in Juvenile turbots (*Psetta maxima*) (Kroeckel et al., 2012). This level of inclusion did not have a significant effect on feed intake or feed conversion, but higher inclusion resulted in lower acceptance of the diet and thus reduced feed intake and growth performance. A low specific growth rate was observed at all inclusion levels.

The use of BSF in Atlantic salmon (*Salmo salar*) diets resulted in significant benefits. BSF larvae meal replaced 20% fish meal in the ration (the normal inclusion level in salmon feed) at 25%, 50% or 100% of the fish meal (Belghit et al., 2019). Similar growth was achieved, the apparent digestibility of lipid, protein, amino acids, fatty acids and a greater feed conversion efficiency, feed intake, daily growth and sensory evaluation of fillets were not affected by the BSF substitution. More importantly, the whole-body compositions of protein, lipid, and amino acids were not affected by the insect meal diet.

Channel catfish (*Ictalurus punctatus*) fed chopped BSF larvae grown on chicken manure alone or in combination with commercial diets were investigated to examine the efficacy of the BSF as a replacement diet. The results demonstrated that the channel catfish performance, in terms of body weight and total length, was similar to the control diets. The aroma and texture of the fish were also acceptable (Bondari & Sheppard, 1981). In a comparison between menhaden fishmeal and BSF prepupae meal fed to channel catfish, the inclusion of BSF at 7.5% proved to be advantageous (Newton et al., 2005). Complete replacement of fishmeal did not provide sufficient dry matter or CP to produce equivalent growth to the control.

5.3.1.2 Challenges Associated with the Utilization of BSF in Animals Feed

Based on studies to date, the possibility of including BSF in poultry, pig and fish diets, insects can replace traditional protein ingredients such as soymeal; however, several important points have to be considered (Makkar et al., 2014). Supplementation of fish and poultry diets with BSF affects the fatty acid profile of the meat products, with lower polyunsaturated and higher saturated and monounsaturated lipids resulting from the use of insect meals. This may have an adverse effect on the resultant product characteristics, depending upon their intended use. This problem can be solved by manipulating the insect diet, as the protein and fat compositions of the insect are affected by feed composition (Wang & Shelomi, 2017). For example, adding fish offal as part of the BSF larvae's feed resulted in insect meals rich in PUFA, especially EPA and DHA (Rumpold & Schlüter, 2013). Reduced growth of some fishes has been reported when they were fed on BSF protein alone. The researchers concluded that this poor performance was due to the limited digestibility of the chitinous body, as no chitinase activity in fish intestine has been detected (Riddick, 2013; Shakil Rana et al., 2015). The effect of different processing methods on the nutritional or functional qualities of larvae (e.g. chitin removal, rendering or chopping) appears to be necessary to evaluate and determine (Rumpold & Schlüter, 2015; van Huis & Oonincx, 2017). It is important to note that when BSF was used as the sole food ingredient in fish and chicken feeds, reduced performance in some cases was also observed. As a result, many studies recommend that BSF be used as a partial fish meal replacement (Wang & Shelomi, 2017).

5.3.2 Housefly and Its Protein

Housefly (*M. Domestica*) is a well-known insect species. Both its larvae and adults can grow and feed on a wide range of waste materials and convert them into highly nutritious dense feed rich in fat and protein. Unlike BSF, the housefly is recognized as a disease carrier. When housefly larvae are grown on poultry manure, they have shown their capacity to be a beneficial source of protein in poultry diets (Makkar et al., 2014; Pretorius, 2011). The housefly is considered to be a good source of protein and fat. The CP content of housefly larvae is variable and ranges between 40% and 60% (Makkar et al., 2014). Differences in nutrient compositions that have been reported for house fly larvae can be connected to the type of food consumed food during growth, life stage, and methods of processing and storage before utilization. For instance, sun-dried larvae have a lower protein content than do oven-dried larvae. It has also been reported that the protein content of the housefly larvae begins to decrease when the house fly approaches the end of its life cycle, from 55.4% CP at 2 days of age to 47.1% at 4 days (Rumpold & Schlüter, 2015). Housefly larvae meal has been considered a potential replacement for fishmeal, cereal and legume-based diets in poultry and livestock feedstuff due to its high contents of lysine, cysteine, threonine, methionine and tryptophan (Hwangbo et al., 2009). The lysine content in housefly larvae meal, like BSF Larvae, is high. In addition, the EAAs methionine plus cystine, valine, isoleucine, phenylalanine + tyrosine, histidine, lysine, threonine, and tryptophan in larvae can cover the protein requirements of a 2–5-year-old child. The level of tryptophan in housefly larvae is higher than it is in BSF larvae, mealworm, locust meal, house cricket, Mormon cricket and silkworm pupae meal. Larvae also have higher contents of lysine and methionine plus cystine than does pupae (Makkar et al., 2014). Housefly pupae meal contains higher levels of arginine, tyrosine, valine, phenylalanine and leucine in comparison with soya oil cake meal, dehydrated fish meal (common animal feeds) and housefly larvae meal (Pretorius, 2011).

5.3.2.1 Utilization of Housefly in Animals Feeding

Soybean-based weaned piglet diets were supplemented with 10% housefly larvae meal. Data on body weight gain and feed conversion efficiency showed no adverse effects at that supplementation level (Wanasithchaiwat & Saesakul, 1989). In Russia, a diet containing housefly larvae meal was given to sows and their offspring, and the performance, meat organoleptic characteristics, piglet health, and sow physiology and breeding performance were not different from the control group (Bayadina & Inkina, 1980).

Several studies investigated the use of housefly larvae meal on broiler performance (Adeniji, 2007; Bamgbose, 1999; Hwangbo et al., 2009). Results indicated that total or partial replacement of fishmeal was feasible; however, an optimal outcome was accomplished when the inclusion rate was lower than 10% in the diet. A study in South Korea using 0–3 and 4–5 week old broilers employed up to 20% housefly larvae meal in the diet. The best result was obtained at 10–15% larvae supplementation level for 4–5 weeks to broilers since dressing percentage (the percentage of a live animal that results in carcass weight), thigh and breast muscle and lysine and tryptophan levels of muscle were all increased (Hwangbo et al., 2009). A study from Nigeria revealed that larvae meal could replace up to 100% meat and bone meal (added at 8% of the feed) when methionine was supplemented to the diet (Bamgbose, 1999). In the diet of 25-day broilers, substitution of 75 and 100% groundnut cake (added at 22% of the diet) with housefly larvae meal did not have an adverse effect on broiler feed intake, weight gain or performance (Adeniji, 2007). In laying hens, housefly larvae meal can replace 50% of fishmeal protein without any negative influence on egg production and shell strength. It increased egg yield and hatchability when it replaced meat and bone meal in a 7-month feeding trial (Agunbiade et al., 2007).

Many studies have been conducted in which housefly larvae meal was included in the diets of African catfish (Adewolu et al., 2010; Madu & Ufodike, 2003; Aniebo et al., 2009). At 25–30% inclusion, performance was positive, but at higher inclusion rates there was a tendency for performance to decline. The influence of the diet, which consisted of feather meal, chicken offal meal and housefly larvae meal at a 4:3:2 ratio and replaced 0–100% of the fishmeal, on African catfish (*Clariasgariepinus*) fingerlings, indicated that this diet could substitute for up to 50% of the fishmeal without any detrimental effects on specific growth rate, weight gain, the protein efficiency or FCRs (Adewolu et al., 2010). However, at higher substitutions (75–100%), lower performance was observed. Another study demonstrated that between two experimental diets of live larvae meal at 100% of the diet and a 1:1 mixture of larvae and commercial diet at 40% protein, the mixed diet resulted in the best growth performance and economic gain in terms of the relative cost of feed per unit of fish weight gain (Madu & Ufodike, 2003). A diet mixture of wheat bran and live housefly larvae (4:1) was investigated in Nile tilapia (*O. niloticus*) (Ebenso & Udo, 2004). This formulated diet provided better specific growth rate, growth performance, FCR and survival than did a diet containing wheat bran only.

5.3.3 SILKWORM PUPAE AND ITS PROTEIN

Silkworms have acquired fame due to their value in the production of silk. A significant by-product of silk production is silkworm pupae which are produced in large quantities and have the potential to be used as a valuable source of protein. Silkworm pupae meal has been reported to have a high fat content (37%) with predominantly polyunsaturated fatty acids, and an especially high linolenic acid content (Makkar et al., 2014). This insect has a long history of human consumption as food and medicine in Asian silk-producing countries, especially in China, Japan, Thailand and India. Due to its high protein, lipid, and polysaccharide contents, silkworm pupae meal may help to ameliorate diabetes, protect the liver and enhance immune system function (Sun-Waterhouse et al., 2016). Several species of silkworm pupae are consumed in India, with eri (*Attacus ricini*) having the highest level of consumption (87.7%), followed by muga and mulberry at 57.4% and 24.6%, respectively. The Ministry of Health of the Republic of China has approved the consumption of silkworm pupae as a new food source (Zhou & Han, 2006). The nutrient composition and protein quality of eri silkworm (*Samia ricinii*) pupae and prepupae suggest that they are a source of high-quality protein due to their excellent amino acid profile score of 0.99 and true protein digestibility of 87% (based on the protein digestibility-corrected amino acid score (PDCAAS)) (Longvah et al., 2011).

Extracted oil from the pupae can be utilized in various industrial products, such as pharmaceuticals, paints, varnishes, candles, soaps, plastics and biofuels (Trivedy et al., 2008). Silkworm pupae can also produce chitin. Silkworm pupae meal has a CP content ranging from 52% to 72%, and it can reach as high as 80% when defatted. An analysis of the amino acid profile of silkworm pupae meal and a comparison to fishmeal and soymeal amino acids shows that the contents of methionine, valine, isoleucine, phenylalanine, tyrosine, threonine are higher in silkworm than in either fishmeal or soymeal. However, the amounts of lysine in fishmeal and cysteine, leucine and histidine in soymeal are higher than they are in silkworm pupae meal.

Methionine and lysine contents are higher in silkworm than in other insects such as BSF, housefly maggot meal, mealworm, locust meal, house and Marmon crickets. Silkworm pupae meal provides all the EEAs requirements necessary to feed livestock, fish and ruminants (Makkar et al., 2014; Trivedy et al., 2008).

5.3.3.1 Utilization of Silkworm Pupae in Animals Feeding

Non-defatted silkworm meal was used to replace 100% of the soy meal in a diet for growing and finishing pigs (Coll et al., 1992). Growth performance and meat characteristics were not changed, however, at a substitution rate >50%, the diet intake was negatively affected due to the low palatability and high energy density of the diet (Coll et al., 1992). This negative effect was not observed in other studies. For example, silkworm meal was used to fully replace fishmeal in the diet of growing and finishing pigs, and it was reported that carcass and meat quality and blood parameters were not altered by the silkworm meal diet (Medhi et al., 2009).

It has been reported that more than 14 brands of protein concentrate are being imported into Bangladesh to feed livestock and poultry, which is expensive and constrains production due to the need for foreign currency. In a study from Bangladesh, silkworm meal was used at up to 6% in layer chick diets, and this resulted in better growth and egg production and improved profitability compared to the commercial control diet (Khatun et al., 2005). In another study from India, defatted silkworm meal was found to be a useful replacement for 100% fishmeal in a layer chick diet (Virk et al., 1980).

Several studies have been conducted to investigate the use of silkworm meal as a replacement for fishmeal in conventional broiler diets (Jintasatapomr, 2012; Makkar et al., 2014; Sheikh et al., 2006). There are conflicting results regarding total replacement of fishmeal, and its generally accepted that 50% replacement (weight basis) is the maximum acceptable, as this will pre-empt poor performance that may be evident with higher levels of replacement (Makkar et al., 2014). For instance, 100% replacement of fishmeal with silkworm meal did not have any adverse effects on carcass properties (Sheikh et al., 2006). However, the substitution of 50% fishmeal with a mixture of defatted and non-defatted silkworm meal had a slightly unfavourable effect on growth, muscle mass and taste of broiler meat, while higher inclusion levels were shown to have detrimental effects (Jintasatapomr, 2012).

Silkworm pupae meal has been reported to be a good protein source for fish feeds. A diet based on silkworm meal resulted in better nutrient digestibility, nutrient retention, and feed conversion efficiency in carp (*Cyprinus carpio*) than did a diet based on plant leaf meal (alfalfa and mulberry) (Vijayakumar Swamy & Devaraj, 1995). Similar growth performance and feed conversion were achieved by replacing 100% fishmeal with silkworm meal (Nandeesha et al., 1990). Defatted silkworm pupae can be used to replace fishmeal in the diet of common carp since flavor, odour, colour and texture of this fish were not different from those obtained by common standard diet (Riddick, 2013). Tilapia (*Oreochromis mossambicus*) diet containing defatted and non-defatted silkworm meal had high protein digestibility (85–86%) (Hossain et al., 1997). A diet containing 20, 30, 40 and 50% levels of defatted silkworm pupae was investigated as a replacement of fishmeal in Deccan mahseer (*Tor Khudree*) fish feed (Shyama & Keshavanath, 1993). The results from that study demonstrated that the incorporation of silkworm meal did not affect survival and fish quality. Moreover, better nutrient digestibility was observed in all tested diets, and the best growth rate was obtained for the diet containing 50% replacement, which was fish meal-free.

5.3.4 Mealworm (*T. molitor*) and Its Protein

Mealworm is an omnivorous species that can consume all types of plant materials and animal products. The typical feed consumed by the mealworm includes cereal bran, maize flour, wheat and oats supplemented with protein sources, as well as fresh fruits and vegetables (Ramos-Elorduy et al., 2009). This insect species can convert plant waste materials into a high-quality feed rich in energy, fat, and protein. Mealworm meal has been reported to contain high contents of protein (47–60%) and fat (31–43%). This protein content of meal worm has a valuable protein profile and is produced in live, canned, dried and lyophilized form for feeding pets and zoo animals, including reptiles, birds, small mammals, fish and amphibians. Mealworm protein supplies EAAs (lysine, methionine, valine, isoleucine, leucine, tyrosine, threonine, tryptophan and histidine), comparable to the way that soy meal and fishmeal do (Makkar et al., 2014). Considering the amino acid pattern of dietary protein recommended for adult consumption, as issued by the WHO/FAO/UNU (1985), mealworm larvae contains all the EAAs in quantities that meet the requirements for human. Furthermore, the sum of the total EAAs is comparable to that in soybeans, but slightly lower than that in casein. Based on the calculated EAA index (EAAI) of mealworm larvae, the quality of its protein is comparable to conventional food protein sources (Yi et al., 2013). The fatty acid composition of mealworm meal consists primarily of oleic acid, followed by linoleic acid and palmitic acid, which is similar to the fatty acid composition of housefly maggot meal and house cricket meal (Makkar et al., 2014).

Methionine is a critical amino acid for poultry growth and development, and this amino acid can be supplied in sufficient levels by mealworm meal. However, mealworm is deficient in calcium, and this must be added to the diet if mealworm is to be used as the sole protein source (Ramos-Elorduy et al., 2009).

The addition of 10% dried mealworm to a broiler starter feed, which normally contains sorghum or soybean meal, did not show adverse effects on feed efficiency, feed consumption or weight gain (Ramos-Elorduy et al., 2009). Supplementation of broiler feed with ground yellow mealworm at inclusion levels of 0, 0.5, 1, 2 and 10% was assessed (Ballitoc & Sun, 2013). A slight increase in protein content was found in all treatments compared to the control diet, and growth performance and carcass yield were improved at the 2% inclusion level.

It has been determined that fresh and dried mealworm can be an excellent alternative protein source to feed to African catfish (*C. gariepinus*). Replacing up to 80% fishmeal with mealworm resulted in good growth performance, feed utilization efficiency and palatability (Ng, 2001). Feeding rainbow trout (*O. mykiss*) with mealworm, at up to 50% replacement of fishmeal, did not affect growth performance (Gasco et al., 2015). Inclusion of mealworm up to 25% in the diet of European sea bass (*Dicentrarchus labrax*) also did not affect weight gain, while a 50% inclusion reduced the growth, specific growth rate and feed consumption ratio, but it did not influence the protein efficiency ratio, body composition or feed consumption (Gasco et al., 2016). Replacement of fishmeal by up to 25% mealworm in the diet of juvenile Gilthead seabream (*Sparus aurata*) did not cause any adverse effect on growth performance or whole-body composition (Piccolo et al., 2014).

5.3.5 Cricket and Its Protein

In Southeast Asia, particularly in Thailand, edible crickets are consumed as common food. Their popularity has spread worldwide since they were introduced as the standard feeder insect for the pet and research industries. Cricket farming has increased due to consumer acceptance of its taste and texture (Makkar et al., 2014). Crickets are usually processed into flour, which may potentially be employed in human food products as an additive (e.g., bread, pasta (Figure 5.1), crackers and

FIGURE 5.1 Cricket Pasta with 20% cricket flour produced by Bugsolutely Ltd company, adapted from https://www.bugsolutely.com.

cookies) (Van Huis, 2017). Also, cricket flour is utilized in protein bars, food for pets, livestock, carnivorous zoo animals, laboratory animals and in industrial applications (Collavo, 2016). A high percentage of unsaturated fatty acids (oleic acid, linoleic acid and linoleic acid) in field crickets make it a potential source of oil for food and industrial uses (Wang et al., 2004). Crickets have a high CP content. The house cricket (*Acheta domesticus*), the field cricket (*Gryllus testaceus*) and the Mormon cricket (*Anabrus simplex*) have been reported to have average CP contents of 63%, 58% and 60%, respectively. House and Mormon crickets provide the EAAs valine, isoleucine, leucine, histidine, phenylalanine plus tyrosine and threonine, which help to meet the amino acid requirements of a 2–5-year-old child. The content of sulphur-containing amino acids (methionine and cysteine) in the field cricket is higher than in the Mormon cricket, although the level of lysine is higher in the Mormon cricket. The amount of leucine is much higher in the house cricket than in housefly maggot meal, locust meal and silkworm pupae meal (Makkar et al., 2014). The field cricket contains a higher percentage of amino acids than does fishmeal, except for histidine (Wang et al., 2005). The protein derived from house fly, Mormon fly and field crickets is tryptophan deficient. For the EAAs in the field cricket, leucine, tyrosine and lysine do not reach the required level needed for preschoolers based on the WHO/FAO/UNU reference values; however, valine, isoleucine, histidine, and the sulphur-containing amino acids cover their needs (Wang et al., 2004).

5.3.5.1 Utilization of Cricket in Animals Feeding

A diet containing 62% maize grain and 30% cricket meal has been fed to broilers (DeFoliart et al., 1982; Finke et al., 1985). The results showed that this diet could provide better growth for broilers than a control diet that included maize, fishmeal, and meat and bone meal. The maize-cricket diet matched the maize-soymeal diet in feed-to-gain ratio and weight gain, and sensory characteristics of the meat from the maize-cricket-fed birds were not adversely affected by the diet.

5.3.6 GRASSHOPPER AND ITS PROTEIN

Grasshoppers belong to the Orthoptera order of insects, the majority of which contain high levels of protein. Most of its species are edible and are consumed as a normal part of the daily diet in many parts of Asia, Africa and South America. Grasshoppers generally feed on different types of vegetation, particularly cereals; however, some species also consume animal tissue and animal faeces. Farming of grasshoppers, like locusts and crickets, is being developed since they are used as feed for pets, zoo animals and livestock (Makkar et al., 2014). Grasshoppers have been considered as a potential dietary protein source for poultry as they have higher protein content than soymeal and fishmeal, and they are a rich source of Ca, Mg, Zn, Fe and Cu (Rumpold & Schlüter, 2013). Three species of dried grasshopper, *Brachystola magna*, *Melanoplus differentialis* and *Hesperotetti speciosus,* have been found to contain approximately 75%, 71%, and 67% protein, respectively. The EAA content of these species is higher than that of the FAO amino acid pattern, except for methionine, which is the limiting amino acid in grasshopper protein (Ueckert et al., 1972). Among the 20 amino acids that have been analysed in this species, glutamine + glutamic acid are present in the highest amounts, followed by lysine, threonine, cysteine, isoleucine and leucine. In comparison with fish, grasshopper species contain lower amounts of arginine, tyrosine, histidine, methionine, tryptophan and valine. However, except for valine and tryptophan, the EAA requirements for fish can be met by this insect (Ghosh et al., 2016).

5.3.6.1 Utilization of Grasshopper in Animals Feeding

Higher breast meat redness, shear force, and protein content, and lower pH, cooking loss, fat, and moisture contents were observed in chickens reared on lands with a massive population of grasshoppers compared with chickens fed on a soymeal-maize diet (Sun et al., 2013). However, the weights of the breast, wing, thigh and drumsticks were decreased. From a sensory aspect, chewiness, flavor, aroma and overall appreciation were scored the highest, but lower scores for tenderness were observed. Grasshopper-fed broiler meat had higher antioxidative potential and so a longer storage life (Sun et al., 2012).

Adult variegated grasshopper (*Zonocerus variegatus*) meal was used to replace fishmeal in the diet of African catfish (*C. gariepinus*) fingerlings at five inclusion levels (0%, 25%, 50%, 75% and 100%) (Alegbeleye et al., 2012). In terms of growth and nutrient utilization, the 25% replacement level was recommended because it did not create unfavourable effects. However, in the group fed 100% grasshopper meal, weight gain and specific growth rates were significantly lower. The results also indicated high apparent protein and lipid digestibility at all levels of insect inclusion.

5.3.7 Locust and Its Protein

Locusts, like grasshoppers and crickets, belong to the Orthoptera order, which represents 13% of all edible insects. Different species of locusts are consumed as food in Africa, the Middle East and Asian countries. In the Persian Gulf area, locust is used by elders to prevent illness and gain strength. Insects are often prepared fried, grilled, smoked or dried (Makkar et al., 2014). The desert locust (*Schistocerca gregaria*), the migratory locust (*Locusta migratoria*), the red locust (*Nomadacris septemfasciata*) and the brown locust (*Locustana pardalina*) are the best-known species among others that are commonly consumed in Africa due to their wide availability and high protein content (Van Huis et al., 2013). The average CP content in locust meal was reported at 57.3% (Makkar et al., 2014).

Regarding its amino acids profile, the lysine and the methionine plus cystine contents in locust meal are higher than in house cricket meal. Also, levels of cysteine and histidine in locust meal are higher than in fishmeal, and the methionine content in locust meal is higher than it is in soymeal. The glutamic acid content in locust meal is higher than in black soldier fly larvae, housefly maggot meal, mealworm, house and Mormon crickets and silkworm pupae meal as well as fishmeal (Makkar et al., 2014). The protein of locust meal can provide the protein requirements of a 2–5-year-old child due to its content of methionine + cystine, valine, isoleucine, phenylalanine + tyrosine, histidine and threonine. Due to its good nutritional value, locust meal has been used in poultry feed since the 1930s. Locust and other Orthoptera are used to feed broilers, fresh and live for chickens, pets and zoo animals (Makkar et al., 2014).

5.3.7.1 Utilization of Locust in Animals Feeding

Locust has long attracted the attention of animal nutritionists. For example, a study conducted in 1947 showed that a mixed diet containing dried red locust fed to pigs led to a satisfactory growth rate, but fresh meat and bacon produced from the treated animals had a fishy taint (Hemsted, 1947). Substitution of fishmeal with wild migratory locust meal at levels of 25, 50 and 75% in Nile tilapia (*O. niloticus*) fingerling diets was investigated by Sánchez-Muros et al. (2016). Protein and lipid digestibility values at 25% and 50% replacement levels not significantly different from the digestibility values for the control diet containing fishmeal.

5.4 PROCESSING PROTEINS FROM INSECTS AND THEIR POTENTIAL APPLICATIONS

Incorporation of insects into different foodstuffs and products requires appropriate implementation of suitable processing and preparation methods. Proper processing of insect products can retain and boost the functionality, nutritional, organoleptic (taste, aroma, texture, etc.) and colour properties of the product and simultaneously remove the potential safety hazards, which collectively results in a safe insect-based product with high quality and an extended shelf life (Dossey et al., 2016). Functionality is a critical factor that affects the acceptability and sensory properties of finished products, such as mouthfeel, palatability and flavor (Williams et al., 2016). For instance, protein extracts from different insects have shown different functionalities of oil binding, moisture-binding,

FIGURE 5.2 Cricket powder (*Acheta domesticus*) with 78% protein. Cricket powder (*Gryllus bimaculatus*) with 67% protein. Silkworm pupae powder (*Bombyx mori*) with 55% protein, produced by JR Unique Foods Ltd, adapted from https://jrunique.com. The authors acknowledge JR Unique Foods for the kind permission to use the image.

gel formation and emulsification capacity that are dependent on the processing of the insect. Different processing options can lead to diverse effects on the protein charge, surface hydrophobicity, and protein integrity (Mishyna et al., 2019a). Product format is another consideration for the preparation of insect-based products. It has been reported that dry insect powder is the ideal format due to its several advantages (Fig. 5.2) (Dossey et al., 2016). Powder can be effectively blended with many components without disrupting the integrity of structure and texture of the product, and protein powders have a long shelf life. Furthermore, protein powders are compatible with the majority of food processing equipment. Another beneficial format of insect-based material is in the liquid form, including slurries or pastes. Like powder, liquids mix well with other ingredients in food formulations and can be used with diverse food production equipment. However, unlike powder, the shelf life of liquid insect products is much shorter, and more care during storage and handling is needed. When insect product is intended to apply in a liquid form product such as in beverages, processing needs to be done with extreme care, as protein is sensitive to thermal treatment.

Some insect-based products, such as meat analogue and tofu, are available in solid or semisolid forms. In addition to the mentioned products made from whole processed insects, some extracts, such as protein concentrates, protein extracts, protein isolates, oils and chitin, can be obtained from the insect fractionation (Dossey et al., 2016). Protein recovery from some species of insects has

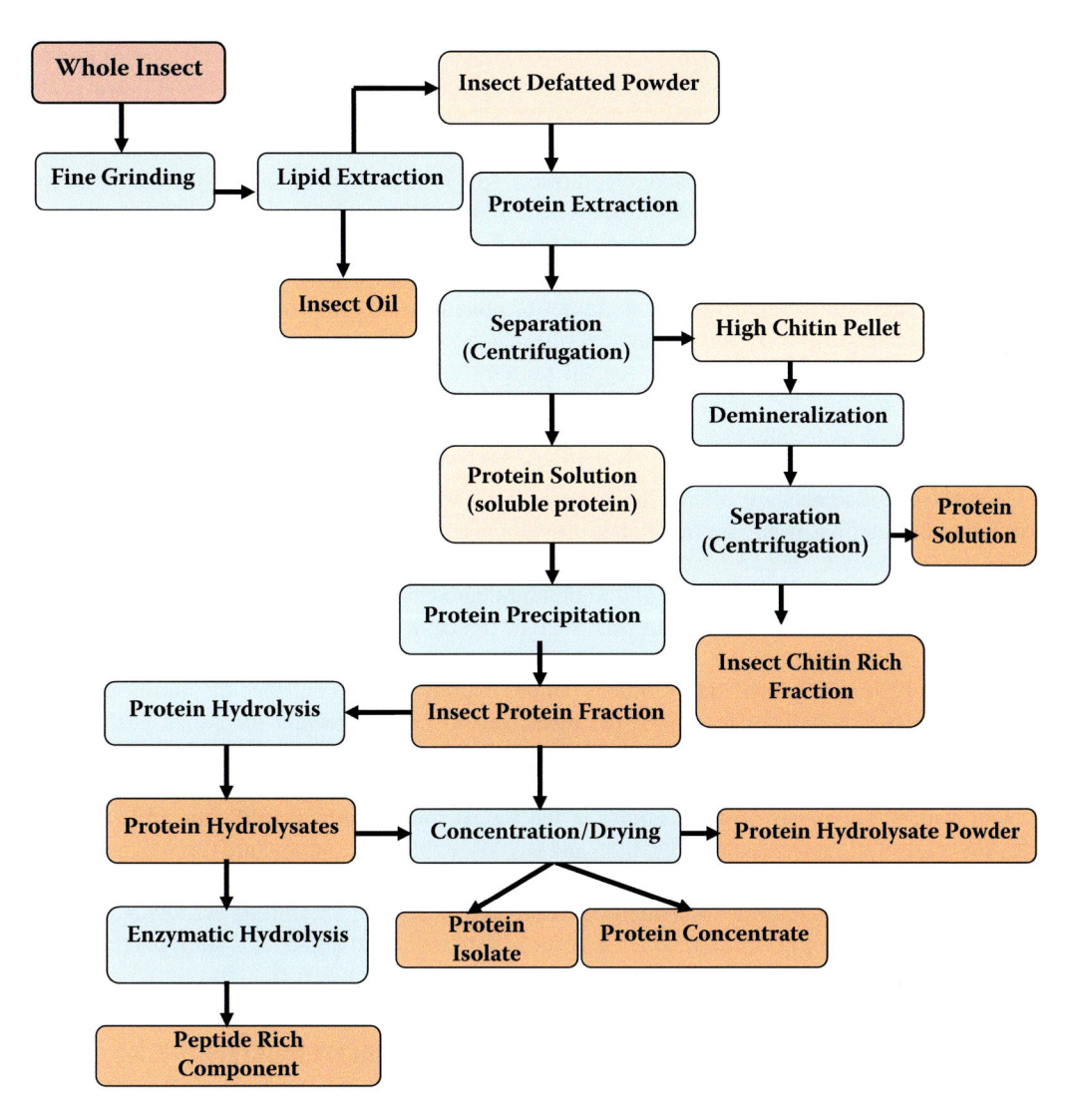

FIGURE 5.3 Schematic representation of the production of insect protein and its fractions (hydrolysate, isolate, concentrate, peptide). Adapted from Caligiani, A., Marseglia, A., Leni, G., Baldassarre, S., Maistrello, L., Dossena, A., & Sforza, S. (2018). Composition of black soldier fly prepupae and systematic approaches for extraction and fractionation of proteins, lipids and chitin. *Food Research International*, *105*, 812–820, with permission from Elsevier (License Number 4822990511494).

been achieved by using several processing steps, including homogenization (cell disruption), defatting, aqueous protein solubilization, protein isoelectric precipitations, mechanical separation of insoluble fractions, protein solubilization followed by a drying step (Figure 5.3), which results in 60–80 g/100 g dry basis protein (Purschke et al., 2018b).

The homogenization step consists of mechanical grinding of the insects, and this is followed by suspension in a suitable solvent (usually water). This process creates small insect particles with high surface area which allows the particles to have more interaction with the solvent leading to an efficient protein extraction (Nongonierma & FitzGerald, 2017).

Defatting has been regarded as a crucial step in the extraction of high content and high purity proteins concentrate and isolates (Laroche et al., 2019). This step has been mostly conducted by employing different traditional solvent extraction methods, but more recently other approaches, such as extraction with supercritical CO_2, which has been suggested to prevent the loss of protein in solvents (Nongonierma & FitzGerald, 2017). To understand the importance of fat removal in the process of protein extraction, Laroche et al. (2019) investigated the effects of several defatting techniques (Soxhlet with different organic solvents (hexane, petroleum ether, ethyl acetate and ethanol), three-phase partitioning and supercritical CO_2) on protein extraction yield and protein purity obtained from house cricket (*A. domesticus*) and mealworm (*T. molitor*). The method of lipid extraction affected protein extraction, and the highest protein purity was found after ethanol lipid extraction of *A. domesticus*. It was suggested that the fat extraction methodology be chosen according to the lipid composition of the insect to obtain maximum protein yield and purity. An interesting outcome from the study was that inferior protein yield and purity were obtained from these two insects compared to some vegetal proteins (pea, lentil, chickpea and flaxseed). The authors suggested that the presence of chitin in insect protein was the main reason for this low quality and yield and concluded that better protein quality could be obtained by removing the chitin and fat (Laroche et al., 2019).

Insect protein isolates are often achieved by alkaline treatment. However, in some cases, extraction with water has been reported to be sufficient, such as in the case of gelatin extraction from melon bugs (*Coridius viduatus*) and sorghum bugs (*Agonoscelis versicoloratus*) (Liu & Zhao, 2019). In order to prevent enzymatic and microbial degradation of insects during storage, prior to protein extraction, some thermal treatments, such as freeze-drying, pasteurization or hot air drying (60 °C) are preferred, to inhibit such reactions (Nongonierma & FitzGerald, 2017). After fat extraction, the protein-rich meal can be utilized in food applications to enhance the nutritional value and bioactive/antioxidative capacity of the meal, and to provide techno-functional attributes of targeted products (Mintah et al., 2019b). Extraction of protein from insects requires that some optimization be designed for each insect species. In an effort to optimize alkaline extraction of protein from yellow mealworm, the effects of the NaOH solution liquid: solid ratio (6:1, 13:1 and 20:1 mL/g), NaOH concentration (0.1, 0.25 and 0.5 M), extraction temperature (20, 50 and 80 °C) and extraction time (30, 75 and 120 min) were evaluated using a defatted mealworm sample. The optimum extraction conditions were achieved using an L:S ratio of 15:1 mL/g, 0.25 M NaOH, and incubation at 40 °C for 60 min, in which protein isolate with 79.0 and 65.1% (dry weight) purity and yield, respectively, was obtained (Nongonierma & FitzGerald, 2017).

5.5 UTILIZATION OF THE WHOLE INSECT AS A PROTEIN SOURCE IN PROCESSED FOODS

In recent years, the incorporation of insect powders into food products, particularly cereal-based products such as bread, pasta, biscuits, cookies and muffins, has resulted in positive technological, nutritional and sensory product properties (Osimani et al., 2018; da Rosa Machado & Thys, 2019; Azzollini et al., 2018; Pauter et al., 2018; Duda et al., 2019). Cricket (*A. domesticus*) powder was used to enhance the nutritional value of bread by blending it with wheat flour at concentrations of 10% and 30% (based on wheat flour) (Osimani et al., 2018). Bread containing cricket powder had more nutritional value due to its high protein and EAA (threonine, tyrosine, valine, methionine and lysine) contents compared to whole wheat flour bread. Furthermore, the addition of 10% cricket powder produced dough with better technological parameters and more favourable and acceptable bread than 30% enriched bread (Osimani et al., 2018). Another species of cricket (*Gryllus assimilis*) was used in powder to evaluate its value in the production of gluten-free bread. The cricket flour was added to the basic ingredients (rice flour and cornstarch) at 10% and 20%. The results confirmed that the cricket powder produced acceptable technological properties in the bread (hardness and chewiness of crumbs) and a high protein content (40% and 100% protein increase in the protein contents at 10% and 20% inclusion, respectively, compared to the control). This insect powder had high water and oil holding capacities, which provided good technological properties to the enriched bakery products during storage (Figure 5.4) (da Rosa Machado & Thys, 2019).

FIGURE 5.4 Images of internal structure of bread slices: (a) control, (b) cricket powder 10%, (c) cricket powder 20%, (d) cricket powder 10% no oil, (e) cricket powder 20% no oil, (f) buckwheat flour 10%, (g) buckwheat flour 20%, (h) lentil flour 10%, (i) lentil flour 20%. Adapted from da Rosa Machado, C., & Thys, R. C. S. (2019). Cricket powder (*Gryllus assimilis*) as a new alternative protein source for gluten-free breads. *Innovative Food Science and Emerging Technologies*, *56*, 102180, with permission from Elsevier (License Number 4822990279529).

Yellow mealworm larvae (*T. molitor*) powder was used for the production of snacks (Azzollini et al., 2018). Snacks such as extruded cereals are very popular, and their consumption has been increasing, especially among Western consumers (Azzollini et al., 2018). Enriched wheat flour with yellow mealworm powder at inclusion levels of 10% and 20% resulted in positive outcomes. Enriched snacks provided higher protein content and net digestible protein contents compared to 100% wheat flour snacks. Textural and microstructural characteristics of the snacks were also affected by the inclusion of mealworm powder. Snacks enriched by 10% exhibited slight differences in expansion properties, viscosity, and mechanical force, whereas 20% inclusion resulted in poor expansion attributes (Azzollini et al., 2018).

Muffins enriched with 2%, 5% and 10% (w/w) cricket powder were investigated for their nutritional value, textural properties, and consumer acceptance compared to the untreated control (Pauter et al., 2018). The treatment group had higher protein content and lower carbohydrate contents in the 5% and 10% cricket powder treatment groups. The mechanical properties (hardness, chewiness, springiness and resilience) of the enriched muffin were significantly decreased. Sensory tests (colour, texture and flavor) confirmed consumer preference for consuming muffins with a lower amount of added cricket powder (2% w/w), which was more similar to the control muffin (Pauter et al., 2018).

Durum wheat pasta was enriched with cricket powder as a valuable protein additive to improve the nutritional value since the quality of pasta protein is low (Duda et al., 2019). The pasta formulation contained 5%, 10% or 15% of cricket powder. Analysis of nutritional value and quality of the pasta showed higher protein content in pasta enriched with cricket powder (increased from 9.96% for the control to 16.92% for 15% enrichment). Cooking weight and cooking loss were decreased, and higher firmness was found in the enriched pasta. However, pasta samples with 5% cricket powder provided better colour and high consumer acceptance (Duda et al., 2019). A study on the functional properties of *Cirina forda* larvae powder demonstrated that this insect powder has high oil and water absorption capacities, which can be beneficial in baked products since these properties can retain flavor and enhance product mouthfeel (Rumpold & Schlüter, 2013). The high emulsion stability of this insect powder suggested a potential use of it as a texturizing agent in insect-processed products.

Two insect flours of mealworm larvae (*T. molitor*) and silkworm pupae (*Bombyx mori*) were subjected to defatting and acid-hydrolysing steps, and the resultant extracts were used for the production of emulsion sausages (Kim et al., 2016). The insect extract was used at 10% replacement of lean pork. The sausage containing insect extract had a higher protein content, cooking yield and hardness of emulsion without affecting protein solubility (Kim et al., 2016). In a recent study (Scholliers et al., 2019), the production of batters from three insect larvae (*A. diaperinus, T. molitor* and *Zophobas morio*) and the effect of different isothermal heating temperatures on the structure of the batters were investigated. The rheological measurements confirmed that the type of insect powder and heating temperature has a significant influence on the structure of the batter. *Z. mori* structure exhibited higher stability than the two other insects. Overall, the structure formation of insect larvae was inferior to meat products but increasing the heating temperature improved the structure and stability of the batter. A heating temperature of 90 °C was the minimum required to obtain a desirable structure and stability in insect batters. However, meat batters require only 70 °C to have a stable and desirable structure (Scholliers et al., 2019). These results support an earlier conclusion that to design high-quality and acceptable formulations, relationships among all textural, microstructural, and digestibility properties need to be considered (Azzollini et al., 2018).

5.6 PRODUCTION OF INSECT PROTEIN EXTRACTS AND THEIR TECHNO-FUNCTIONAL PROPERTIES

Different protein extracts from insects are being considered as high-quality protein ingredients to produce protein supplements like bars, shakes, powders, cereals, etc. To produce these products, plant-derived proteins have been most frequently used. Insect protein extracts can be a potential option in producing different types of protein supplements and products (Dossey et al., 2016).

Water-soluble proteins obtained from two species of grasshoppers, *Patanga succincta* and *Chondracris roseapbrunner,* were investigated for their characteristics, functional properties and antioxidant activities. Extraction efficiencies of 48.77% and 42.86% and protein yields of 7.35% and 7.49% (based on wet weight) were found for *P. succinct* and *C. roeapbrunner,* respectively (Chatsuwan et al., 2018). The protein from both species showed good solubility in strong acidic and alkaline aqueous solutions. The emulsifying and foaming capacities were poor; however, greater foaming stability compared with bovine serum albumin was reported. In addition, protein hydrolysates presented high antioxidant activities (Chatsuwan et al., 2018).

Grasshopper (*S. gregaria*) and honeybee brood (*A. mellifera*) protein powders were prepared by defatting, alkaline extraction and sonication-assisted extractions (Mishyna et al., 2019a). The obtained protein fractions had protein contents of 57.5 and 55.2% for grasshopper and honeybee, respectively. Both protein fractions showed high emulsifying and foaming capacities. High foaming stability was obtained for grasshopper protein fractions after alkaline extraction, and for the honeybee protein fraction, it was found after sonication. The honeybee brood protein fractions exhibited higher protein heat coagulation than did grasshopper and whey proteins. These results demonstrated that defatting, alkaline and sonication extraction methods provide protein-enriched fractions from these insect powders, and the well-balanced profile of essential and non-EAAs from these fractions meet the values recommended by FAO. This study also suggested that *S. gregaria* and *A. mellifera* proteins could be utilized in food, feed or insect-based dietary supplements (Mishyna et al., 2019a). Similarly, the extraction of protein fractions from mealworm larvae (*T. molitor*) was investigated by examining the impact of solubilization pH, centrifugation speed/force and centrifugation time on the efficiency of protein recovery (Purschke et al., 2018b). The optimization process indicated that the centrifugation force and solubilization pH are crucial parameters in the recovery of protein. The protein content was increased from 39 to 56–65 g/100 g dry matter basis, and the recovery ranged from 31% to 58% (Purschke et al., 2018b). To improve the protein extraction from migratory locust (*L. migratoria*) meal, the influence of extraction parameters such as pH and salt concentration on compositional and techno-functional properties of protein was studied (Purschke et al., 2018c). The results indicated that ionic strength and solvent pH had high impacts on protein techno-functionality. The obtained protein concentrates under certain conditions displayed favourable solubility, emulsifying activity (at pH 5), foamability (at pH 3 and 3% NaCl), and foam stability (at pH 9), and that these were comparable with those of commercial egg white protein concentrate.

In a recent study, it was revealed that freeze-dried raw powder of honeybee brood (*Apis mellifera*) has the potential to be applied as gelling material with comparable characteristics to other conventional protein sources and considered as an insect-based gel product (Mishyna et al., 2019b). The soluble proteins also showed their highest aggregation (coagulation) at a maximum temperature of 85 °C, at pH 5 and 7.

An aqueous protein extraction to obtain soluble proteins from five species of insects, *T. molitor* (larvae), *Z. morio* (larvae), *A. diaperinus* (larvae), *A. domesticus* (adult) and *Blapticadubia* (adult), was described by Yi et al.(2013). The proteins obtained showed their ability to form gels at a concentration of 30% w/v at pH 3, 5, 7 and 10 and at a temperature range of 51–63 °C, but their foaming capacities were poor. The *A. domesticus* protein fraction exhibited the most robust gel structure at a concentration of 15% w/v at pH 7 and 10. These techno-functional properties suggested that this insect species has the potential to be used as a gelling material and texturizer in food products.

To understand the effect of domestic cooking methods on protein digestibility (*in vitro*), two insects species, *Eulepidamashona* (beetle) and *Henicuswhellani* (cricket), were selected and subjected to boiling, roasting, or combined boiling and roasting processes, which are common ways to prepare insects in Zimbabwe (Manditsera et al., 2019). The results of this study demonstrated that these traditional methods influence protein content and digestibility. Boiling led to significant protein losses in the two insects due to the leaching of proteins into the water, while roasting best kept protein intact in the insects. Boiling reduced protein digestibility of *Henicus whellani*, but there was no difference between boiling and roasting in *Eulepida mashona*. A maximum reduction in protein digestibility (approximately 25%) was observed in boiled and roasted cricket. The study concluded that roasting is preferred to boiling, and a shorter boiling time is recommended.

To improve the techno-functional characteristics of extracted protein from insects, enzymatic modification has been investigated in some studies. For example, protein flour from migratory locust (*L. migratoria*) was subjected to enzymatic hydrolysis using different hydrolysis settings for a variety of proteases (Alcalase, Neutrase, Flavourzyme and Papain), enzyme-substrate ratios (0.05–1.0% w/w), heat pre-treatments (60–80 °C; 15–60 min), and hydrolysis times (0–24 h) (Purschke et al., 2018a). The results indicated that all the reaction parameters highly influence the extent of enzymatic hydrolysis. The combination of proteases was shown to be very effective in protein hydrolysis, while thermal pre-treatment prior to hydrolysis had a negative effect. Considering the techno-functional properties of the obtained protein isolates, solubility was improved over a wide pH range from 10–22% up to 55% under alkaline conditions. In addition, enhancement of emulsifying activity (54%) at pH 7, foamability (326%) at pH 3 and oil binding capacity were all achieved.

In another research study from the United States, tropical banded cricket (*Gryllodes sigillatus*) protein hydrolysates were achieved by enzymatic (Alcalase) hydrolysis of the whole insect. Different reaction conditions (nine experimental trials) of hydrolysate preparations, consisting of enzyme-substrate (E/S) concentrations (0.5, 1.5% and 3% w/w) and hydrolysing times of 30, 60 and 90 min on functional properties of the obtained protein hydrolysates were evaluated. All samples showed good solubility over a wide pH range compared to the unhydrolysed samples. The emulsifying activity index (EAI) varied among the various trials, and it was highest in the following trials: (0.5% E/S for 30 and 60 min and 3% E/S for 60 min). Non-hydrolysed protein had the lowest foam capacity, and samples obtained at 0.5% E/S and 30 min hydrolysis time exhibited the highest foaming capacity. Reduction in foaming and emulsion stabilities was correlated with extensive enzymatic hydrolysis. The above results suggest that enzymatic hydrolysis is a successful approach for generating protein hydrolysates with improved functional properties that can be applied to different food systems at different pH values (Hall et al., 2017).

5.7 APPLICATION OF INSECT PROTEIN HYDROLYSATES IN THE PRODUCTION OF FOOD PRODUCT

For the suitable application of insect protein hydrolysates in food matrices, assessment of their techno-functional attributes is crucial. Protein hydrolysate of silkworm pupae at concentrations ranging from 0.1% to 0.9% (w/v) was added to a milk formulation for yogurt production (Wang et al., 2017). Evaluation of the rheological properties indicated that the highest firmness and consistency for yogurt was obtained at enrichment with 0.5% (w/w) hydrolysate. The water holding capacity of the yogurt was decreased at hydrolysate concentrations ≥0.7% (w/v). The flavor and mouthfeel of the supplemented yogurts were dependent on the applied hydrolysate concentration, but no visual appearance difference was found among the treatments or the control (with no hydrolysate). Acceptability of the supplemented yogurts was low at high protein hydrolysate concentration (>0.3%) in comparison with the control yogurts.

The applicability of gelatin produced from two species of Sudanese beetles *Aspongubus viduatus* and *Agonoscelis pubescens* as a stabilizer in ice cream production was investigated by Bußler et al. (2016). Compared to commercial gelatin, these insect gelatins received a comparable acceptability score by a taste panel. There were no significant differences in general preferences between insect gelatin-produced ice creams and the commercial gelatin-produced ice creams. Studies on insect protein hydrolysate applications in food systems are rare; therefore, more research is needed in this area (Nongonierma & FitzGerald, 2017).

5.8 BIOLOGICAL ACTIVITIES OF INSECT PROTEIN HYDROLYSATES AND PEPTIDES

Nowadays, the global demand for and the consumption of protein hydrolysates are both increasing. A protein hydrolysate is a mixture of peptides, oligopeptides and free amino acids produced from protein hydrolysis processes which result in the degradation of the protein structure and, thus, produce molecular species with diverse properties of size, amino acid composition, and sequence. Protein hydrolysates have diverse food and biotechnological applications, such as in children's nutritional products, food supplements, energy drinks, cosmetics/toiletries, highly nutritious animal feed mixtures and as ingredients in growth mediums (Firmansyah & Abduh, 2019). Protein hydrolysates may contain bioactive peptides (BAPs) that display special biological activities, such as Angiotensin-converting enzyme (ACE) inhibitory activity, antioxidant activity, antihypertensive, antimicrobial and anticoagulant actions. The principal raw materials used for the production of a protein hydrolysate have traditionally come from animal and plant protein sources (beef, fish, milk, egg, wheat and soybean) (Firmansyah & Abduh, 2019; Nongonierma & FitzGerald, 2017). Substituting these traditional sources with alternative proteins is a necessity in the near future to reduce competition for use of the traditional materials for food against their use for biotechnological applications. Also, alternative proteins have different protein sequences, and they provide an excellent opportunity to generate novel BAPs with novel or more effective activities. Insects have a high protein content and are worthy candidates for BAP production. Therefore, the production of BAPs from several insects has been investigated (Nongonierma & FitzGerald, 2017). In this regard, various processes (acid, alkaline, enzymatic) can be employed to hydrolyse insect proteins to release BAPs. Enzymatic hydrolysis is preferred due to its milder and controllable reaction conditions, high-quality products and availability of a wide range of proteases. Some pretreatments, such as microwave and ultrasound before enzymatic hydrolysis, are useful in inducing protein conformational changes that improve the ability of the proteases to attack specific protein bonds. Published studies suggest that optimum hydrolysis is achieved by using enzymes (different types of proteases) along with pre-treatment methods such as ultrasound (Mintah et al., 2019b). In a recent study, the effect of pretreatment techniques (conventional, fixed-frequency ultrasonic, and sweep-frequency ultrasonic) on the production of protein hydrolysates from *H. illucens* was studied (Mintah et al., 2019b). The findings indicated that protein hydrolysates obtained by sweep-frequency ultrasound had the highest foam expansion over a wide pH ranges (2–12), solubility and antioxidative capacity, whereas alkaline protease hydrolysis without pretreatment damaged the emulsifying property and foam stability of protein isolates. It's clear that the type of treatment has a significant impact on the microstructure, functional properties, and antioxidative activity of protein hydrolysates, and that it improves protein functionality (solubility, foamability, and emulsification).

In order to achieve optimum antioxidant activity in protein hydrolysates from *H. illucens*, the sonication pretreatment parameters were optimized using a three-factor, three-level Box-Behnken's design for pH (7, 8, and 9), temperature (25, 40, and 55 °C) and time (10, 20, and 30 min). The application of these pretreatment parameters was shown to have a considerable effect on producing hydrolysates with the best antioxidant activity. Optimum conditions were obtained at pH = 9, time = 29.84 min and temperature = 54.93 °C, resulting in optimum antioxidant activities, as follows; Ferrous ion chelating activity = 37.84%, cupric ion chelating activity = 68.93%, DPPH-radical scavenging activity = 43.19% and hydroxyl radical scavenging activity = 71.01% (Mintah et al., 2019a).

Silkworm pupae (*Bombyx mori*) has been identified as a good source for producing BAPs with ACE inhibitory activity. Protein extracts (i.e. albumins, globulins, glutelins and prolamins) of *B. mori* were subjected to enzymatic hydrolysis (Nongonierma & FitzGerald, 2017). The obtained hydrolysate from the albumin fraction exhibited the highest degree of hydrolysis (DH) and ACE inhibitory activity. The ACE inhibitory activities of insect BAPs and animal and plant proteins BAPs were of similar potency. The antidiabetic activity of insect BAPs has not been extensively reported in the literature. The *in vitro* α-glucosidase inhibitory activity (indicative of antidiabetic activity) of silkworm BAPs has been reported (Nongonierma & FitzGerald, 2017). In a recent study, lesser mealworm (*A.diaperinus*) peptides obtained by enzymatic hydrolysis of protein concentrate (56.5% protein) and isolate (85.9% protein) were tested against dipeptidyl-peptidase IV(DPP-IV) enzyme for the purpose of treating type 2 diabetes (Lacroix et al., 2019). Different proteases (Alcalase, Flavourzyme, Papain and Thermolysin) were used to produce the peptides. Thermolysin was found to release more active DPP-IV inhibitory peptides (inhibitory activity of 43%) than other enzymes, and this was explained by the production of various peptide sequences resulting from different enzyme specificities. The utilization of ultrafiltration to generate peptides with low molecular weight did not make a significant difference in the inhibitory activity of the peptides. This study suggested that insect peptides may potentially have an antidiabetic effect (Lacroix et al., 2019).

The antioxidant activity of various edible insect protein hydrolysates has been identified and reported to be high compared to other food protein hydrolysates (Nongonierma & FitzGerald,

2017). In a study on BSF larvae, a protein hydrolysate was successfully obtained with different DH values ranging from 10–44% using concentrations of bromelain enzyme (1–5%), hydrolysis times (3–24 hours), and pH values (6–8) (Firmansyah & Abduh, 2019). Optimum conditions for obtaining the highest DH value were achieved using bromelain at a concentration of 3%, pH = 8, and a hydrolysis time of 24 hours. The hydrophobic EAAs lysine, leucine and valine existed in high amounts in the protein hydrolysate. Because of hydrophobic and aromatic amino acids (phenylalanine and tyrosine), BSF larvae protein hydrolysate exhibited high DPPH free radical activity (Firmansyah & Abduh, 2019). In a recent study, the effect of ultrasonication-assisted extraction of protein hydrolysates from *H. illucens* was studied (Mintah et al., 2019b). The findings from that study indicated that improved protein functionalities, solubility, foamability, and emulsification capacities made this protein hydrolysate a suitable option for therapeutic/functional food fortification. Enzymatic hydrolysis of the male silkworm moth (*Bombyx mori*) resulted in a peptide fraction (<3 kDa) with high antioxidant activity, and the power of peptide antioxidant activity was shown to be related to their size (molecular weight), and the presence of certain amino acids, such as lysine and methionine, improved antioxidant activity (de Castro et al., 2018).

The antioxidant activity of peptides obtained by *in vitro* gastrointestinal digestion from 5 species of edible insects, including *Blaptica dubia, L. migratoria, Gromphadorhina portentosa, Z. morio* and *Amphiacusta annulipes,* has been reported (Zielińska et al., 2017b). Peptide antioxidant activity was expressed as free radical scavenging activity, ion chelating activity and reducing power. Results showed that the peptides obtained from all insect samples had high Fe^{2+} and Cu^{2+} chelating activities. The reducing power of peptides obtained from *A. annulipes, Z. morio, G. portentosa* and *B. dubia* was high and even higher than leafy vegetable or legume species, such as *Moringa oleifera, Amaranthus viridis, Tamarindus indica, Spinacia oleracea, Trigonella foenum-graecum* and Black Jamapa bean (*Phaseolus vulgaris*) protein hydrolysates. *L. migratoria* had the highest concentration of peptides before and after digestion, and its antioxidant activity was higher than some plant and animal protein hydrolysates.

Antioxidant and anti-inflammatory activities of the hydrolysates from heat-treated (boiled and baked) mealworm larvae *(T. molitor)*, adult locust (*S. gregaria*), and adult cricket (*G. sigillatus*) were studied under simulated digestion and gastrointestinal absorption conditions (Zielińska et al., 2017a). The results indicated that the digestion and absorption processes increased peptide antioxidant activity (antiradical activity and iron-chelating ability) as well anti-inflammatory activity (lipoxygenase and cyclooxygenase-2 inhibitory activity). This research suggested that heat processing of whole insects could improve insect antioxidant activity since baked cricket and boiled locust had higher activities than did their raw counterparts.

The characteristics of protein hydrolysates obtained from mealworm larvae (*T. molitor*), adult cricket (*Gryllus bimaculatus*) and silkworm pupae (*Bombyx mori*) after enzymatic hydrolysis using Flavourzyme and Alcalase were compared (Yoon et al., 2019). Compared to the control (unhydrolysed protein), enzymatic hydrolysis led to higher solubility but lower foamability of the protein hydrolysates. In terms of hydrolysate bioactivity, the ACE inhibitory activity of all three insect samples was considerably higher, particularly following Alcalase treatment. Moreover, *B. mori* and *T. molitor* exhibited effective α-glucosidase activity using a mixture of enzymes, and *B. mori* displayed anti-inflammatory activity (Yoon et al., 2019).

5.9 INSECT PROTEINS AS A POTENTIAL SOURCE OF ANTIMICROBIAL PEPTIDES

A unique and diverse group of peptides, antimicrobial peptides (AMPs), has attracted wide attention as therapeutic agents due to their ability to destroy Gram-negative and Gram-positive bacteria, viruses, fungi and even transformed or cancerous cells (Józefiak et al., 2016). These beneficial small cationic peptides, of there are estimated to be more than 1500 types, have been recognized in diversified sources, including animals, plants, fungi and bacteria. Nowadays, the global trend is towards a reduction in the use of synthetic antibiotics in veterinary medicine, agriculture and the feed industry since animal product drug residues are harmful to and may lead to drug resistance in humans. AMPs have the potential to be effective alternatives to antibiotics. Several studies have reported that various peptides generated from insects possess antimicrobial activity. Therefore, they are being considered significant sources of AMPs (Józefiak & Engberg, 2017). These interesting insect peptides can be classified into four groups: cysteine-rich peptides (defensin and drosomycin), proline-rich peptides (apidaecin, drosocin and lebocin), glycine-rich proteins (attacin and gloverin) and α-helical peptides (cecropin and moricin) (de Castro et al., 2018; Józefiak & Engberg, 2017). Defensins, as small cysteine-rich peptides, constitute the largest group of insect AMPs, and these have been identified in diverse insect species within the orders Diptera, Hymenoptera, Coleoptera, Lepidoptera, Hemiptera, Isoptera and Odonata. Insect defensins have been reported to have antimicrobial activities against both Gram-positive and Gram-negative bacteria (Józefiak et al., 2016). *H. illucens* larvae extracts have been found to contain antibacterial peptides that inhibit Gram-positive bacteria, like *Staphylococcus aureus*, methicillin-resistant *Staphylococcus aureus* (MRSA), and the Gram-negative bacterium *Pseudomonas aeruginosa* (Park et al., 2014). A methanol extract of *H. illucens* larvae was shown to have an antibacterial effect against *Klebsiella pneumoniae*, *Neisseria gonorrhoeae*, and *Shigella sonnei* bacteria. However, some Gram-positive bacteria, such as *Bacillus subtilis*, *Streptococcus mutans* and *Sarcina lutea* were not affected by the extract (Choi et al., 2012). A novel defensin-like peptide 4 (DLP4) was purified from the immunized hemolymph of *H. illucens* larvae. This molecule showed inhibitory activity against Gram-positive bacteria, such as MRSA, *S. aureus, S. epidermidis* and *B. subtilis*, but it was not effective against Gram-negative bacteria (*E. coli, Enterobacter aerogenes, P. aeruginosa*) (Park et al., 2015). The above studies confirmed the ability of AMPs of *H. illucens* larvae extracts and their potential use as a new source of antibiotic-like compounds for infection control (Józefiak & Engberg, 2017). The protein extract from the larvae of the mealworm (*T. molitor*) has been used as a source of AMPs. Tenascin has shown activity against Gram-positive bacteria, mainly MRSA and fungi. An extracted peptide from the pupae of the house fly (*M. domestica*) demonstrated high activity against Gram-positive bacteria and lower activity against Gram-negative bacteria and fungi (Dang et al., 2010). Clearly, the activity of peptides obtained from various insects demonstrated different affinities towards microorganisms. Insect AMPs could be used as alternatives to antibiotics in livestock production in support of animal growth and therefore human health, as a preservative in food systems, and as a dietary supplement in animal feeds (Józefiak & Engberg, 2017).

5.10 THE IMPORTANCE OF INSECTS' UTILIZATION IN HUMAN FOOD

Some insect species classified as edible have been consumed as food in many cultures for centuries, including approximately 2 billion people in Asia, Africa, Australia and Central and South America (Akhtar & Isman, 2018). Several suborders of Orthoptera, including grasshoppers (*Caliphera*), locust (*Acrididae*) and crickets (*Gryllidae*) are among the most favoured insects consumed worldwide (Halloran et al., 2018). In West Africa, insects have a long history of use as a human and animal food source, and the most common insects for human consumption are grasshoppers and termites (Moore, 2018). In the EU, insects that have been considered for human use are crickets (*Gryllodus sigillatus* and *A. domesticus*), lesser mealworm (*A. diaperinus*) and yellow mealworm (*T. molitor*) (Van der Spiegel et al., 2013). The high nutritional value of insects is the main driver for adopting their use as food in developing and developed countries. Insects are rich in protein (40–70% of the dry matter) and high-quality fat (5–40% of the dry matter and can be as high as 70% in palm weevil larvae; *Rhynchophorus phoenicis*) (Halloran et al., 2018). Also, they are rich in vitamins (A, D, E, K, C and B complex), fibre (mainly chitin, ranging from 2.7 mg to 49.8 mg per kg of wet matter), minerals (K, Na, Ca, Cu, Fe, Zn, Mn and P) and antioxidants (carotenoids and flavonoids) (Kouřimská & Adámková, 2016). Other advantages are that they are palatable and potentially inexpensive foods. Table 5.4 shows the nutritional value of some popular insect species. High levels of minerals, such as iron, zinc, and calcium, in insects have made them a good complement to meals that are deficient in these (Akhtar & Isman, 2018). The deficiencies of

TABLE 5.4
Proximate analysis data (moisture, protein, fat, ash and fibre) for selected insect species and common high protein commodities

Food Insects	Common Name	Preparation	Moisture (%)	Protein (Crude Measured as N × 6.25)	Fat (% Crude Fat)	Fibre (a, Acid Detergent Fibre; b, Crude Fibre)	Ash
Lepidoptera							
Agrotis infusa (larva)	Bogong moth	Roasted	49.2	52.7	39.0	5.3	–
Anaphe panda (larva)	African moth	Intestinal contents and hair removed	73.9	45.6	35.0	6.5b	3.7
Anaphe venata (larva)	African moth	Dried without hairs	6.6	60.0	23.2	3.2	–
Ascalapha odorata (larva)	Black witch moth	Whole raw, not fasted	56.0	15.0	–	12.0b	6.0
Bombyx mori (larva fed artificial diet)	Silkworm	Whole raw, not fasted	82.7	53.8	8.1	6.4a	6.4
Bombyx mori (larva fed mulberry leaves)	Silkworm	Whole raw, not fasted	76.3	64.7	20.8	–	–
Bombyx mori (larva fed mulberry leaves)	Silkworm	Whole raw, intestinal	69.9	62.7	14.2	–	–
Bombyx mori (pupa)	Silkworm	Whole raw (dried)	18.9	60.0	37.1	–	10.6
Callosamia promethea (larva)	Silkworm	Whole raw, freeze dried	4.5	51.7	10.5	11.3b	7.2
Catasticta teutila (larva)	Pure banded Dart white moth	Whole raw, not fasted	60.0	19.0	–	7.0b	7.0
	Tebo worms		60.2	15.5	29.4	1.4	1.2

Insect-Derived Protein as Food and Feed

Chilecomadia Moorei (larva)		Whole raw, fasted			
Conimbrasia belina (larva)	Mopani worm	Intestinal contents removed, dried	62.0	16.0	11.4b	7.6
Galleria mellonella (larva)	Waxworm	Whole raw, fasted	58.5	34.0	8.1a	1.4
Heliothis zea (larva fed broad beans)	Corn earworm	Whole raw, fasted	77.4	18.2	–	–
Heliothis zea (larva fed artificial diet)	Corn earworm	Whole raw, fasted	77.5	30.2	–	–
Hyalophora cecropia (larva)	Cecropia moth	Whole raw, freeze dried	2.6	56.2	15.1b	6.1
Imbrasia epimethea (larva)	African moth larva	Smoked and dried	7.0	62.5	–	4.0
Imbrasia ertli (larva)	African moth larva	Viscera removed then boiled or roasted. Dried and salted	9.0	52.9	–	15.8
Imbrasia truncate (larva)	African moth larva	Smoked and dried	7.3	64.7	–	4.0
Manduca sexta (larva fed artificial diet)	Carolina sphynx moth	Whole raw, freeze dried	4.7	61	9.9b	7.8
Manduca sexta (larva fed fresh plant material)	Carolina sphynx moth	Whole raw, freeze dried	4.7	60.7	8.8b	8.5
Nudaurelia oyemensis (larva)	–	Smoked and dried	7.0	61.1	–	3.8
Porthetria dispar (adult with eggs)	Gypsy moth	Whole raw, not fasted	68.6	44.6	8	–
Army worm			2	55.5	5.1b	7

(Continued)

TABLE 5.4 (Continued)
Proximate analysis data (moisture, protein, fat, ash and fibre) for selected insect species and common high protein commodities

Food Insects	Common Name	Preparation	Moisture (%)	Protein (Crude Measured as N × 6.25)	Fat (% Crude Fat)	Fibre (a, Acid Detergent Fibre; b, Crude Fibre)	Ash
Pseudaletia unipuncta (larva)		Whole raw, freeze dried					
Spodoptera eridania (larva)	Fall army worm	Whole raw, freeze dried	4.5	57.3	14.6	7.4b	10.3
Spodoptera frugisperda (larva fed artificial diet)	Fall army worm	Whole raw, freeze dried	2.1	59	20.6	6.8b	5.7
Spodoptera frugiperda (lkarva fed fresh plant material)	Fall army worm	Whole raw, freeze dried	3.6	59.3	11.7	12.4b	11.6
Usta terpsichore (larva)	African moth	Viscera removed then boiled or roasted, dried and salted	9.2	48.6	9.5	—	13.0
Xyleutes redtenbacheri (larva)	Carpenter moths	Whole raw, not fasted	43.0	48.0		6.0b	2.0
Hylesia frigida	—	—	—	42	10	—	—
Arsenura armida	Giant silk moth	—	52	8	—	—	—
Phasus triangularis	moth	—	—	15	77	—	—
Coleoptera							
Aplagiognathus spinosus (larva)	—	—	—	—	—	—	—

Insect-Derived Protein as Food and Feed

Callipogon barbatus (larva)	—	—	41.0	34.0	—	2.0
Oileus rimator (larva)	Beetle	Whole raw, not fasted	26.0	36.0	23.0b	3.0
Passalus punctiger (larva)	Beetle	Whole raw, not fasted	26.0	44.0	15.0b	3.0
Rhynchophorus ferrugineus (larva)	Red palm weevil	—	70.5	20.7	15.0b	—
Rhynchophorus palmarum (larva)	Red palm weevil	Whole raw, not fasted	71.7	25.8	—	2.1
Rhynchophorus phoenicis (larva)	Red palm weevil	Incised, fried in oil	10.8	22.8	—	2.7
Scyphophorus acupunctatus (larva)	Agave weevil	Whole raw, not fasted	36.0	52.0	46.8	1.0
Tenebrio molitor (adult)	Mealworm beetle	Whole raw, fasted	63.7	65.3	6.0b	3.3
Tenebrio molitor (larva)	Mealworm beetle worm	Whole raw, fasted	61.9	49.1	20.4a	2.4
Zophobas morio (larva)	Darkling beetle	Whole raw, fasted	57.9	46.8	6.6a	2.4
Orthoptera						
Acheta domesticus (adult)	House cricket	Whole raw, fasted	69.2	66.6	6.3z	3.6
Acheta domesticus (nymph)	House cricket	Whole raw, fasted	77.1	67.2	10.2a	4.8
Blatella germanica (not specifed)	German cockroach	Whole raw, not fasted	71.2	78.8	9.6a	4.3
Blatta lateralis (nymphs)	Turkestan cockroach	Whole raw, fasted	69.1	19	2.2	1.2

(Continued)

TABLE 5.4 (Continued)
Proximate analysis data (moisture, protein, fat, ash and fibre) for selected insect species and common high protein commodities

Food Insects	Common Name	Preparation	Moisture (%)	Protein (Crude Measured as N × 6.25)	Fat (% Crude Fat)	Fibre (a, Acid Detergent Fibre; b, Crude Fibre)	Ash
Brachytrupes sp.	Cricket	Fresh: blanched, inedible parts removed	73.3	47.9	21.3	13.5b	9.4
Cyrtacanthacris tatarica	—	Fresh: blanched, inedible parts removed	76.7	61.4	14.2	17.2b	4.7
Gryllotalpa africana	Mole cricket	Fresh: blanched, inedible parts removed	71.2	53.5	21.9	9.7b	9.4
Oxya verox	—	Whole raw, dried	29.8	64.2	2.4	—	3.4
Oxya yezoensis	—	Whole raw, not fasted	65.9	74.7	5.7	—	6.5
Sphenarium histrio (nymphs and adults)	Grasshoppers	Whole raw, not fasted	77.0	4.0	—	12.0b	2.0
Zonocerus sp.	Grasshoppers	Whole raw, not fasted	62.7	71.8	10.2	6.4b	3.2
Sphenarium purpurascens Ch	Grasshoppers	—	—	75.9	6.02	7.1	4.8
Taeniopoda eques B	Horse lubber grasshopper	—	—	71.1	5.9	10.6	9.6
Melanoplus femurrubrum D	Red-legged grasshopper	—	—	74.7	5.2	10.0	6.7

Schistocerca	Bird grasshoppers	—	—	62.5	10.1	7.0
Isoptera						
Cortaritermes silvestri (worker)	South American termites	Whole raw, not fasted	77.8	48.6	6.9	—	8.5
Macrotermes bellicosus (alate)	African termites	Dewinged, raw	6.0	34.8	46.1	—	10.2
Macrotermes subhyalinus (alate)	African termites	Dewinged, fried in oil	0.93	8.8	46.5	—	6.6
Nasutitermes corniger (soldier)	Central American tree termite	Whole raw, not fasted	69.6	58.0	11.2	34.8a	3.7
Nasutitermes corniger (worker)	Central American tree termite	Whole raw, not fasted	75.3	66.7	2.2	27.1a	4.6
Procornitermes araujoi (worker)	—	Whole raw, not fasted	78.1	33.9	16.1	—	3.5
Syntermes ditus (worker)	—	Whole raw, not fasted	79.7	43.2	3.4	—	17.1
Hymenoptera						
Apis mellifera (adult female)	European honeybee	Whole raw, not fasted	65.7	60.0	10.6	—	17.4
Apis mellifera (adult male)	European honeybee	Whole raw, not fasted	72.1	64.4	10.5	—	17.8
Apis mellifera (larva)	European honeybee	Whole raw, not fasted	76.8	40.5	20.3	1.3a	3.4
Atta mexicana (reproductive adult)	Leaf-cutter ant	Whole raw, not fasted	46.0	39.0	—	11.0b	4.0

(Continued)

TABLE 5.4 (Continued)
Proximate analysis data (moisture, protein, fat, ash and fibre) for selected insect species and common high protein commodities

Food Insects	Common Name	Preparation	Moisture (%)	Protein (Crude Measured as N × 6.25)	Fat (% Crude Fat)	Fibre (a, Acid Detergent Fibre; b, Crude Fibre)	Ash
Olecophylla smaragdina	Weaver ant	Fresh: blanched, inedible parts removed	74.0	53.5	13.5	6.9b	6.5
Oecophylla virescens	Green tree ant/ weaver ant	Inedible parts removed	78.32	41.0	26.7	–	6.0
Polybia sp. (adult)	Wasp	Whole raw, not fasted	63.0	13.0	–	15.0b	6.0
Trigon sp.	–	–	–	28	41	–	–
Parachartegus apicallis	–	–	–	55	–	–	–
Brachygastra azteca	Paper wasp	–	–	63	24	–	–
Brachygastra mellifica	Mexican honey wasp	–	–	53	20	–	–
Vespula squamosa	Southern yellow jacket	–	–	63	22	–	–
Polistes instabilis	Paper wasp	–	–	31	62	–	–
Diptera							
Copestylum anna & C. haggi (larva)	–	Whole raw, not fasted	37.0	31.0	–	15.0b	8.0
Drosophila melanogaster (adult)	Common fruit fly	Whole raw, not fasted	67.1	56.3	17.9	–	5.2

Insect-Derived Protein as Food and Feed

Hermetia illucens (larva)	Black soldier fly	Dried, ground, not fasted	3.8	47.0	32.6	6.7b	8.6
Musca autumnalis (pupa)	Face fly/ autumn house fly	Dried, ground, not fasted	51.7	11.4	28.9	–	–
Musca domestica (pupa)	Common house fly	Dried, ground, not fasted	61.4	9.3	11.9	–	–
Hemiptera							
Edessa petersii (nymphs and adults)	–	Whole raw, not fasted	37.0	42.0	–	18.0b	2.0
Euchistus egglestoni (nymphs and adults)	–	Whole raw, not fasted	35.0	45.0	–	19.0b	1.0
Pachilis gigas (nymphs and adults)	–	Whole raw, not fasted	64.0	22.5	–	7.5b	3.5
Hoplophorion monograma (nymphs and adults)	Treehopper	Whole raw, not fasted	64.0	14.0	–	18.0b	3.0
Umbonia reclinata (nymphs and adults)	–	Whole raw, not fasted	29.0	33.0	–	13.0b	11.0
Callipogon barbatus	–	–	–	41	34	–	–
Commonly consumed protein source							
Beef	–	Ground/raw	65.81	17.37	17.07	0	0.86
Pork	–	Ground/raw	64.46	15.41	17.18	0	0.79
Chicken	–	Ground/raw	73.24	17.44	8.1	0	1.17
Egg	–	Whole/raw	76.15	12.56	9.51	0	1.06

(*Continued*)

TABLE 5.4 (Continued)
Proximate analysis data (moisture, protein, fat, ash and fibre) for selected insect species and common high protein commodities

Food Insects	Common Name	Preparation	Moisture (%)	Protein (Crude Measured as N × 6.25)	Fat (% Crude Fat)	Fibre (a, Acid Detergent Fibre; b, Crude Fibre)	Ash
Salmon	–	Wild/raw	68.5	19.84	6.34	0	2.54
Milk	–	Dry/whole	2.47	26.32	26.71	0	6.08
Milk	–	Fluid/whole	87.69	3.28	3.66	0	0.72

Adapted from Williams, J. P., Williams, J. R., Kirabo, A., Chester, D., & Peterson, M. (2016). Nutrient content and health benefits of insects. In *Insects as Sustainable Food Ingredients* (pp. 61–84), with permission from Elsevier (License Number 4822981315653).

these important minerals are widespread among people in developing countries, especially in children and women of reproductive age, since their predominant diets consist primarily of cereals and legumes, but which are lacking in animal products. It has been found that 100 g of cooked caterpillars could provide the daily requirements of iron, copper, zinc, vitamins B_1 and B_2 (Shockley & Dossey, 2013). BSF larvae have 71 times the calcium and twice the magnesium and zinc contents of beef as well as significant amounts of vitamins B_{12}, B_1 and B_2, making them a solution for deficiency problems found in many developing counties (Akhtar & Isman, 2018). Malnutrition affects 178–195 million children worldwide with moderately acute to severely acute malnutrition. In developing countries, families with low-income suffer malnutrition primarily due to deficiency in protein and insufficient caloric intake. Many scientists believe these gaps could be filled by some insects that have good quality protein, fat and other nutrients (Shockley & Dossey, 2013). In Kenya, where many children are at risk of undernutrition, house crickets (*A. domesticus*) have been used to formulate biscuits for schoolchildren aged 5–10 years (Homann et al., 2017). House crickets have high contents of protein rich in the nine EAAs, unsaturated fatty acids, vitamin B_{12}, iron and zinc. Acceptability and nutritional composition of biscuits containing 10% cricket powder were compared with whole milk powder biscuits. The cricket biscuit was nutritionally comparable to the milk biscuit, but it had higher levels of iron, zinc, and iodine in addition to its acceptability. The authors proposed using the fortified biscuit as an alternative to milk biscuits in school feeding programs for the prevention of malnutrition. Insects have been consumed in different ways. Traditionally, they are eaten raw or prepared in steamed, boiled, baked, deep-fried, sun-dried and smoked formats (Van Huis, 2017). Nowadays, they are being processed into other forms to disguise them as a means to convince reluctant people in some cultures to eat them (Akhtar & Isman, 2018). Powdered/ground form is an ideal form for insect usage where it can be easily incorporated into the formulation of numerous consumer items (Shockley & Dossey, 2013). Although primary insect preparation methods for human consumption, like cooking, roasting, frying and searing, have been using in places where the malnutrition and poverty rates are high, these processes damage the nutritious materials and remove good quality fat that is naturally available in the insects. Thus, processing methods need to be improved to retain the nutritional status of insects (Shockley & Dossey, 2013).

5.11 SAFETY ISSUES WITH INSECTS AS SOURCE OF PROTEIN

Microbiological and chemical hazards of edible insects in certain concentrations which can be harmful for human health arise from different factors. These hazardous substances may come from contaminated feed which can include natural toxins, mycotoxins, heavy metals, veterinary resides (antibiotics), pesticides and pathogens. Also, insects themselves may have potential hazards in the form of contaminants, allergens, pathogens, and pesticides. The existence of these safety hazards depends on the species of insect, their feed and life environment, and applied production methods. Although studies on food safety of cultivated insects in the EU are very limited, non-European insects have been investigated more widely (van der Spiegel et al., 2013). Considering the safety of edible insects as a food source, in one study in Belgium, the accumulation level of different hazardous chemicals, including organic contaminants (i.e., flame retardants, PCBs, DDT, dioxin compounds, and pesticides) and metals (As, Cd, Co, Cr, Cu, Ni, Pd, Sn and Zn) in several species of insects (larvae of greater wax moth, adults of the migratory locust, larvae of the mealworm beetle, and larvae of buffalo worm) and four insect-based food products (bug balls of buffalo and locust, cricket croquettes and bug burger of buffalo worm), were investigated. The results of this study indicated that the concentration of these chemicals in insects and their products was low, e.g. in comparison with commonly eaten animal products, such as fish, meat and eggs. It also supported the idea that these insect food products can possibly substitute for more common sources of protein products (Poma et al., 2017).

In addition to chemical contaminants, microbial contaminants in fresh insects and their products is another hazard for human consumption. High microbial counts due to food spoilage and pathogenic microorganisms have been reported in some fresh insects, so appropriate processing steps and storage conditions are needed to reduce these sources of contamination (Nongonierma & FitzGerald, 2017). The microbial contents of fresh and processed (roasted and boiled) mealworm (*T. molitor*) and crickets (*A. domesticus* and *Brachytrupus* sp.) stored under refrigerated (5–7 °C) and ambient (28–30°C) conditions were analysed. Enterobacteriaceae and spore-formation were present in raw insects, while boiling for 5 min was sufficient to kill Enterobacteriacea but not spore-forming bacteria. Refrigeration has also been suggested to preserve boiled insects. In addition to refrigeration, acidification/drying have been considered promising ways to provide for the safety of insect products and to extend their shelf life (Klunder et al., 2012). In an effort to surreptitiously add insects to popular food products and to confirm their safety during production and storage, minced meat-like products from mealworm larvae (*T. molitor* and *A. diaperinus*) were produced. The results showed that the selected production methods and storage conditions had a significant impact on the safety of the final products and their shelf life. Steaming and frying of insects could reduce microbial loads in comparison with fresh insects, which contained high levels of spoilage and pathogenic microorganisms. More importantly, employing a modified atmosphere (60% CO_2/40% N_2) extended the shelf life of the products by 14 days and 28 days for the lesser and yellow mealworm, respectively, by keeping microbial numbers low (Stoops et al., 2017).

The safety of insect-obtained peptides and hydrolysates also has been investigated in several *in vitro* studies. In these experiments, the toxicity of yellow mealworm powder, silkworm pupae proteins, and silkworm pupae hydrolysates were investigated, and no toxicity and death were reported after feeding experimental animals (mice and rats) these insect extracts. However, one experiment revealed a cytotoxic effect of raw *S. gregaria*; however, boiled and cooked samples did not show the same effect. So, thermal treatments can be considered an effective way to negate the toxicity of insects and their extracts (Nongonierma & FitzGerald, 2017).

Allergenicity is another risk inherent to the consumption of some edible insects, similar to shellfish and crustaceans. Different food processing methods have been reported to be effective in decreasing the allergenicity of insect proteins. Various heating methods, including boiling, steaming, roasting, blanching and autoclaving, are most commonly used to denature the allergenic proteins. Other methods, including extrusion, fermentation using multiple mold strains, acid hydrolysis, acidification with probiotic lactic acid bacteria and enzymes, electron beam irradiation, γ-irradiation, Ultraviolet-C exposure, ultrasound treatment, high-pressure processing, pulsed ultraviolet light and ultrafiltration, which have been reported to be effective in reducing or eliminating allergens in plants and crustaceans, can also be effective in insects. A combination of these technologies is preferred for improved efficiency (Sun-Waterhouse et al., 2016). In a study in the Netherlands, the influence of three types of processing (boiling, frying, lyophilizing) and *in vitro* digestion on allergic cross-reactivity of three edible mealworm species (*T. molitor, Zophobas atratus* and *A. diaperinus*) was investigated, and the results revealed that IgE and HDM allergic patients showed cross-reactivity allergenicity to mealworms. Although heat processing diminished the risk, it could not eliminate it. Therefore, this research suggested that other processing techniques be used to reduce the allergic effect of proteins in mealworms (van Broekhoven et al., 2016).

It is compulsory to establish proportional international and national standards and legal frameworks for the production and marketing of edible insects on an industrial scale. For this purpose, two technological challenges must be overcome: First, finding methods and processing techniques which are applicable for turning insects into healthy, safe, and tasty food products; and second, producing enough insects cheaply, efficiently and sustainably to meet market demand; in particular, when they are intended to be utilized as an alternative to vertebrate livestock (Van Huis, 2017). Regarding one of the European regulations, as all insect-based products have been categorized as 'Novel Food' and based on this fact that breeding and marketing of insects intended for human utilization do not have particular regulations in place in Europe, some countries such as Belgium and the Netherlands, are producing and developing insect-based foods, which are present in the markets (Poma et al., 2017). Outside the EU, some companies such as Enterra Feed from Canada and AgriProtein from South Africa, have introduced their insect products to the local markets but not to the EU and US markets, due to legal prohibitions. These products include whole dried BSF larvae, dried protein powder, larval oil and fertilizer (Stamer, 2015). Consumer acceptance insects in animal feed seem to be increasing. But, EU legislation has strictly banned using animal products, such as insect meal, especially when the insects are fed on discarded food, for livestock feeding and also for other animals (Stamer, 2015). Since societies will need to change their diets in the near future, insects can be a suitable and favoured candidate for widespread use in food and feed ingredients, provided that related problems are solved. Appropriate regulations must be established with the help of government, agricultural, and regulatory agencies as well as with academics, industry partners and other practitioners in the fields of food and animal feeds. These must be enacted to establish procedures, recipes and methods to assure the safe and efficient usage of insects in all food systems (Shockley & Dossey, 2013; Van Huis, 2017).

5.12 CHALLENGES ASSOCIATED WITH THE CONSUMPTION OF INSECTS AS HUMAN FOOD

Although the consumption of insects in some developing countries is a common practice, in the Western countries of North America and Europe, and in regions where Western culture dominates, it has low popularity and acceptance (Akhtar & Isman, 2018; Stamer, 2015). The main obstacles for the consumption of insects as human food in these regions are legal prohibition, the 'Yuck' factor where consumers detest the idea of consuming insects, and lack of recognition of the

FIGURE 5.5 Cricket crackers (snacks) with different flavors containing 15% cricket powder (*Acheta domesticus*) having 20% protein content produced by Cricke Ltd company, adapted from https://crickefood.com.

beneficial aspects of insects as a future possible alternative food source (Van Huis, 2017). Moreover, cultural prejudice, safety concerns, and flavor are other barriers to consumer acceptance of insect-based products (Liu & Zhao, 2019).

Some strategies can be adapted to convince reluctant consumers, such as improving their awareness of the nutritional value and environmental benefits associated with insect consumption and with processing insects into familiar and popular products (Figure 5.5). This can be accomplished by food scientists and other scientists and officials making organoleptically acceptable food products that consumers will eventually purchase (Van Huis, 2017). For typical western societies, studies have illustrated an increased desire for the consumption of insects when they are used as an ingredient in processed foods (Hall et al., 2017). However, the biggest challenge is obtaining government approval for insect-based products for the human diet (Azzollini et al., 2018; Wang & Shelomi, 2017). Each insect product as a novel food requires solid evidence of its safety to human health. Therefore, microbiological, chemical and physical hazards analyses must be documented and receive approval from authorities before products can be placed on the market (Wang & Shelomi, 2017).

REFERENCES

Adámek, M., Mlček, J., Adámková, A., Borkovcová, M., Bednářová, M., Juríková, T., … Faměra, O. (2019). Is edible insect as a novel food digestible? *Potravinarstvo Slovak Journal of Food Sciences*, *13*(1), 470–476. doi:10.5219/1088

Adeniji, A. A. (2007). Effect of replacing groundnut cake with maggot meal in the diet of broilers. *International Journal of Poultry Science*, *6*(11), 822–825. doi:10.3923/ijps.2007.822.825

Adewolu, M. A., Ikenweiwe, N. B., & Mulero, S. M. (2010). Evaluation of an animal protein mixture as a replacement for fishmeal in practical diets for fingerlings of *Clarias gariepinus* (Burchell, 1822). *Israeli Journal of Aquaculture - Bamidgeh*, *62*(4), 237–244.

Agunbiade, J. A., Adeyemi, O. A., Ashiru, O. M., Awojobi, H. A., Taiwo, A. A., Oke, D. B., & Adekunmisi, A. A. (2007). Replacement of fish meal with maggot meal in cassava-based layers' diets. *Journal of Poultry Science*, *44*(3), 278–282. doi:10.2141/jpsa.44.278

Akhtar, Y., & Isman, M. B. (2018). Insects as an alternative protein source. In: *Proteins in Food Processing: Second Edition*, 263–288. doi:10.1016/B978-0-08-100722-8.00011-5

Alegbeleye, W. O., Obasa, S. O., Olude, O. O., Otubu, K., & Jimoh, W. (2012). Preliminary evaluation of the nutritive value of the variegated grasshopper (*Zonocerus variegatus* L.) for African catfish *Clarias gariepinus* (Burchell. 1822) fingerlings. *Aquaculture Research*, *43*(3), 412–420. doi:10.1111/j.1365-2109.2011.02844.x

Aniebo, A. O., Erondu, E. S., & Owen, O. J. (2009). Replacement of fish meal with maggot meal in African catfish (*Clarias gariepinus*) diets. *Revista Cientifica UDO Agricola*, *9*(3), 666–671.

Azzollini, D., Derossi, A., Fogliano, V., Lakemond, C. M. M., & Severini, C. (2018). Effects of formulation and process conditions on microstructure, texture and digestibility of extruded insect-riched snacks. *Innovative Food Science and Emerging Technologies*, *45*, 344–353. doi:10.1016/j.ifset.2017.11.017

Ballitoc, D. A., & Sun, S. (2013). Ground yellow mealworms (*Tenebrio molitor* L.) feed supplementation improves growth performance and carcass yield characteristics in broilers. *Open Science Repository Agriculture*, e23050425. doi:10.7392/openaccess.23050425

Bamgbose, A. M. (1999). Utilization of maggot-meal in cockerel diets. *Indian Journal of Animal Sciences*, *69*(12), 1056–1058.

Bayadina, G. V., & Inkina, Z. G. (1980). Effect of prolonged use of house-fly larvae in the diet of sows and their offspring, on the fattening and meat quality of the young. *Nauchnye Trudy Novosibirskogo Sel'skokhozyaistvennogo Instituta*, *134*, 52–59.

Belghit, I., Liland, N. S., Gjesdal, P., Biancarosa, I., Menchetti, E., Li, Y., … Lock, E. J. (2019). Black soldier fly larvae meal can replace fish meal in diets of sea-water phase Atlantic salmon (*Salmo salar*). *Aquaculture*, *503*, 609–619. doi:10.1016/j.aquaculture.2018.12.032

Boland, M. J., Rae, A. N., Vereijken, J. M., Meuwissen, M. P. M., Fischer, A. R. H., van Boekel, M. A. J. S., … Hendriks, W. H. (2013). The future supply of animal-derived protein for human consumption. *Trends in Food Science and Technology*, *29*(1), 62–73. doi:10.1016/j.tifs.2012.07.002

Bondari, K., & Sheppard, D. C. (1981). Soldier fly larvae as feed in commercial fish production. *Aquaculture*, *24*(C), 103–109. doi:10.1016/0044-8486(81)90047-8

Bondari, K., & Sheppard, D. C. (1987). Soldier fly, *Hermetia illucens* L., larvae as feed for channel catfish, *Ictalurus punctatus* (Rafinesque), and blue tilapia, *Oreochromis aureus* (Steindachner). *Aquaculture Research*, *18*(3), 209–220. doi:10.1111/j.1365-2109.1987.tb00141.x

Bußler, S., Rumpold, B. A., Jander, E., Rawel, H. M., & Schlüter, O. K. (2016). Recovery and techno-functionality of flours and proteins from two edible insect species: Meal worm (*Tenebrio molitor*) and black soldier fly (*Hermetia illucens*) larvae. *Heliyon*, *2*(12). doi:10.1016/j.heliyon.2016.e00218

Caligiani, A., Marseglia, A., Leni, G., Baldassarre, S., Maistrello, L., Dossena, A., & Sforza, S. (2018). Composition of black soldier fly prepupae and systematic approaches for extraction and fractionation of proteins, lipids and chitin. *Food Research International*, *105*, 812–820. doi:10.1016/j.foodres.2017.12.012

Chatsuwan, N., Nalinanon, S., Puechkamut, Y., Lamsal, B. P., & Pinsirodom, P. (2018). Characteristics, functional properties, and antioxidant activities of water-soluble proteins extracted from grasshoppers, *Patanga succincta* and *Chondracris roseapbrunner*. *Journal of Chemistry*, *2018*. doi:10.1155/2018/6528312

Choi, W. H., Yun, J. H., Chu, J. P., & Chu, K. B. (2012). Antibacterial effect of extracts of *Hermetia illucens* (Diptera: Stratiomyidae) larvae against gram-negative bacteria. *Entomological Research*, *42*(5), 219–226. doi:10.1111/j.1748-5967.2012.00465.x

Churchward-Venne, T. A., Pinckaers, P. J. M., van Loon, J. J. A., & van Loon, L. J. C. (2017). Consideration of insects as a source of dietary protein for human consumption. *Nutrition Reviews*, *75*(12), 1035–1045. doi:10.1093/nutrit/nux057

Coll, J. F. C., de Crespi, M. P. A. L., Itagiba, M. d. G. O. R., de Sousa, J. C. D., Gomes, A. V. d. C., & Donatti, F. C. (1992). Use of chrysalis meal of the silkworm (*Bombyx mori*) as a protein source in the feeding of pigs during the growing and finishing periods. *Uso Da Farinha de Crisalida Do Bicho-Da-Seda (Bombyx Mori L.) Como Fonte de Proteina Na Alimentacao de Suinos Em Crescimento-Terminacao*, *21*(3), 378–384.

Collavo, A. (2016). *Ecological Implications of Minilivestock. Potential of Insects, Rodents, Frogs and Snails*, Enfield, USA: Science Publishers.

Cullere, M., Tasoniero, G., Giaccone, V., Miotti-Scapin, R., Claeys, E., De Smet, S., & Dalle Zotte, A. (2016). Black soldier fly as dietary protein source for broiler quails: Apparent digestibility, excreta microbial load, feed choice, performance, carcass and meat traits. *Animal*, *10*(12), 1923–1930. doi:10.1017/S1751731116001270

Dang, X. L., Wang, Y. S., Huang, Y. D., Yu, X. Q., & Zhang, W. Q. (2010). Purification and characterization of an antimicrobial peptide, insect defensin, from immunized house fly (Diptera: Muscidae). *Journal of Medical Entomology*, *47*(6), 1141–1145. doi:10.1603/me10016

da Rosa Machado, C., & Thys, R. C. S. (2019). Cricket powder (*Gryllus assimilis*) as a new alternative protein source for gluten-free breads. *Innovative Food Science and Emerging Technologies*, *56*, 102180. doi:10.1016/j.ifset.2019.102180

de Castro, R. J. S., Ohara, A., Aguilar, J. G. d. S., & Domingues, M. A. F. (2018). Nutritional, functional and biological properties of insect proteins: Processes for obtaining, consumption and future challenges. *Trends in Food Science and Technology*, *76*, 82–89. doi:10.1016/j.tifs.2018.04.006

DeFoliart, G. R., Finke, M. D., & Sunde, M. L. (1982). Potential value of the mormon cricket (Orthoptera: Tettigoniidae) harvested as a high-protein feed for poultry. *Journal of Economic Entomology*, *75*(5), 848–852. doi:10.1093/jee/75.5.848

Dossey, A. T., Tatum, J. T., & McGill, W. L. (2016). Modern insect-based food industry: Current status, insect processing technology, and recommendations moving forward. In: *Insects as Sustainable Food Ingredients*, 113–152. doi:10.1016/b978-0-12-802856-8.00005-3

Duda, A., Adamczak, J., Chelminska, P., Juszkiewicz, J., & Kowalczewski, P. (2019). Quality and nutritional/textural properties of durum wheat pasta enriched with cricket powder. *Foods*, *8*(2), 1–10. doi:10.3390/foods8020046

Ebenso, I., & Udo, M. (2004). Effect of live maggot on growth of the nile perch, *Oreochromis niloticus* (cichlidae) in South Eastern Nigeria. *Global Journal of Agricultural Sciences*, *2*(2), 72–73. doi:10.4314/gjass.v2i2.2208

Finke, M. D., Sunde, M. L., & Defoliart, G. R. (1985). An evaluation of the protein quality of mormon crickets (*Anabrus simplex* Haldeman) when used as a high protein feedstuff for poultry. *Poultry Science*, *64*(4), 708–712. doi:10.3382/ps.0640708

Firmansyah, M., & Abduh, M. Y. (2019). Production of protein hydrolysate containing antioxidant activity from *Hermetia illucens*. *Heliyon*, *5*(6), e02005. doi:10.1016/j.heliyon.2019.e02005

Gasco, L., Henry, M., Piccolo, G., Marono, S., Gai, F., Renna, M., ... Chatzifotis, S. (2016). *Tenebrio molitor* meal in diets for European sea bass (*Dicentrarchus labrax* L.) juveniles: Growth performance, whole body composition and in vivo apparent digestibility. *Animal Feed Science and Technology* (220), 34–45. doi:10.1016/j.anifeedsci.2016.07.003

Gasco, L., Parisi, G., Terova, G., & Gai, F. (2015). Mealworm (*Tenebrio molitor*) as a potential ingredient in practical diets for rainbow trout (*Oncorhynchus mykiss*). In: *1st International Conference "Insects to Feed the World"*. Vantomme, P., Munke, C., & van Huis, A. (Eds). Ede-Wageningen, The Netherlands: Wageningen University. 2–3 September. https://www.researchgate.net/publication/288267673

Ghosh, S., Haldar, P., Kumar Mandal, D., & Dipak Kumar Mandal, C. (2016). Evaluation of nutrient quality of a short horned grasshopper, *Oxya hyla hyla* Serville (Orthoptera: Acrididae) in search of new protein source. *Journal of Entomology and Zoology Studies*, *4*(1), 193–197.

Hall, F. G., Jones, O. G., O'Haire, M. E., & Liceaga, A. M. (2017). Functional properties of tropical banded cricket (*Gryllodes sigillatus*) protein hydrolysates. *Food Chemistry*, *224*, 414–422. doi:10.1016/j.foodchem.2016.11.138

Halloran, A., Flore, R., Vantomme, P., & Roos, N. (2018). Edible insects in sustainable food systems. In: *Edible Insects in Sustainable Food Systems*, 1–479. doi:10.1007/978-3-319-74011-9

Hemsted, W. R. T. (1947). Locusts as a protein supplement for pigs. *The East African Agricultural Journal*, *12*(4), 225–226. doi:10.1080/03670074.1947.11664563

Homann, A. M., Ayieko, M. A., Konyole, S. O., & Roos, N. (2017). Acceptability of biscuits containing 10% cricket (*Acheta domesticus*) compared to milk biscuits among 5-10-year-old Kenyan schoolchildren. *Journal of Insects as Food and Feed*, *3*(2), 95–103. doi:10.3920/JIFF2016.0054

Hossain, M. A., Nahar, N., & Kamal, M. (1997). Nutrient digestibility coefficients of some plant and animal proteins for rohu (*Labeo rohita*). *Aquaculture*, *151*(1–4), 37–45. doi:10.1016/S0044-8486(96)01481-0

Hwangbo, J., Hong, E. C., Jang, A., Kang, H. K., Oh, J. S., Kim, B. W., & Park, B. S. (2009). Utilization of house fly-maggots, a feed supplement in the production of broiler chickens. *Journal of Environmental Biology*, *30*(4), 609–614.

Jintasatapomr, O. (2012). Production performance of broiler ghickens fed with silkworm pupa (*Bombyx mori*). *Journal of Agricultural Science and Technology A*, *2*, 7–9.

Jongema, Y. (2017). World list of edible insects. *Wageningen University*, 1–100. https://www.wur.nl/upload_mm/8/a/6/0fdfc700–3929-4a74-8b69-f02fd35a1696_Worldwide list of edible insects 2017.pdf

Józefiak, A., & Engberg, R. M. (2017). Insect proteins as a potential source of antimicrobial peptides in livestock production: A review. *Journal of Animal and Feed Sciences*, *26*(2), 87–99. doi:10.22358/jafs/69998/2017

Józefiak, D., Józefiak, A., Kierończyk, B., Rawski, M., Świątkiewicz, S., Długosz, J., & Engberg, R. M. (2016). Insects - a natural nutrient source for poultry - a review. *Annals of Animal Science*, *16*(2), 297–313. doi:10.1515/aoas-2016-0010

Khatun, R., Azmal, S. A., Sarker, M. S. K., Rashid, M. A., Hussain, M. A., & Miah, M. Y. (2005). Effect of silkworm pupae on the growth and egg production performance of Rhode Island Red (RIR) pure line. *International Journal of Poultry Science*, *4*(9), 718–720. doi:10.3923/ijps.2005.718.720

Kim, H. W., Setyabrata, D., Lee, Y. J., Jones, O. G., & Kim, Y. H. B. (2016). Pre-treated mealworm larvae and silkworm pupae as a novel protein ingredient in emulsion sausages. *Innovative Food Science and Emerging Technologies*, *38*, 116–123. doi:10.1016/j.ifset.2016.09.023

Klunder, H. C., Wolkers-Rooijackers, J., Korpela, J. M., & Nout, M. J. R. (2012). Microbiological aspectsof processing and storage of edible insects. *Food Control*, *26*, 628–631.

Kouřimská, L., & Adámková, A. (2016). Nutritional and sensory quality of edible insects. *NFS Journal*, *4*, 22–26. doi:10.1016/j.nfs.2016.07.001

Kroeckel, S., Harjes, A. G. E., Roth, I., Katz, H., Wuertz, S., Susenbeth, A., & Schulz, C. (2012). When a turbot catches a fly: Evaluation of a pre-pupae meal of the black soldier fly (*Hermetia illucens*) as fish meal substitute - growth performance and chitin degradation in juvenile turbot (*Psetta maxima*). *Aquaculture*, *364–365*, 345–352. doi:10.1016/j.aquaculture.2012.08.041

Lacroix, I. M. E., Dávalos Terán, I., Fogliano, V., & Wichers, H. J. (2019). Investigation into the potential of commercially available lesser mealworm (*A. diaperinus*) protein to serve as sources of peptides with DPP-IV inhibitory activity. *International Journal of Food Science and Technology*, *54*(3), 696–704. doi:10.1111/ijfs.13982

Laroche, M., Perreault, V., Marciniak, A., Gravel, A., Chamberland, J., & Doyen, A. (2019). Comparison of conventional and sustainable lipid extraction methods for the production of oil and protein isolate from edible insect meal. *Foods, 8*(11), 572. doi:10.3390/foods8110572

Liu, C., & Zhao, J. (2019). Insects as a novel food. In: *Encyclopedia of Food Chemistry*, 428–436. doi:10.1016/b978-0-08-100596-5.21782-4

Longvah, T., Mangthya, K., & Ramulu, P. (2011). Author's personal copy nutrient composition and protein quality evaluation of eri silkworm (*Samia ricinii*) prepupae and pupae. *Food Chemistry, 128*, 400–403. doi:10.1016/j.foodchem.2011.03.041

Madu, C. T., & Ufodike, E. B. C. (2003). Growth and survival of catfish (*Clarias anguillaris*) juveniles fed live tilapia and maggot as unconventional diets. *Journal of Aquatic Sciences, 18*(1), 47–52. doi:10.4314/jas.v18i1.19942

Makkar, H. P. S., Tran, G., Heuzé, V., & Ankers, P. (2014). State-of-the-art on use of insects as animal feed. *Animal Feed Science and Technology, 197*, 1–33. doi:10.1016/j.anifeedsci.2014.07.008

Manditsera, F. A., Luning, P. A., Fogliano, V., & Lakemond, C. M. M. (2019). Effect of domestic cooking methods on protein digestibility and mineral bioaccessibility of wild harvested adult edible insects. *Food Research International, 121*, 404–411. doi:10.1016/j.foodres.2019.03.052

Medhi, D., Nath, N. C., Gohain, A. K., & Bhuyan, R. (2009). Effect of silk worm pupae meal on carcass characteristics and composition of meat in pigs. *Indian Veterinary Journal, 86*(8), 816–818.

Mintah, B. K., He, R., Dabbour, M., Golly, M. K., Agyekum, A. A., & Ma, H. (2019a). Effect of sonication pretreatment parameters and their optimization on the antioxidant activity of *Hermitia illucens* larvae meal protein hydrolysates. *Journal of Food Processing and Preservation, 43*(9), 1–12. doi:10.1111/jfpp.14093

Mintah, B. K., He, R., Dabbour, M., Xiang, J., Agyekum, A. A., & Ma, H. (2019b). Techno-functional attribute and antioxidative capacity of edible insect protein preparations and hydrolysates thereof: Effect of multiple mode sonochemical action. *Ultrasonics Sonochemistry, 58*, 104676. doi:10.1016/j.ultsonch.2019.104676

Mishyna, M., Martinez, J. J. I., Chen, J., & Benjamin, O. (2019a). Extraction, characterization and functional properties of soluble proteins from edible grasshopper (*Schistocerca gregaria*) and honey bee (*Apis mellifera*). *Food Research International, 116*, 697–706. doi:10.1016/j.foodres.2018.08.098

Mishyna, M., Martinez, J. J. I., Chen, J., Davidovich-Pinhas, M., & Benjamin, O. (2019b). Heat-induced aggregation and gelation of proteins from edible honey bee brood (*Apis mellifera*) as a function of temperature and pH. *Food Hydrocolloids, 91*, 117–126. doi:10.1016/j.foodhyd.2019.01.017

Moore, D. (2018). Insects as food and feed. *Food Science and Technology (London), 32*(1), 22–25.

Nandeesha, M. C., Srikanth, G. K., Keshavanath, P., Varghese, T. J., Basavaraja, N., & Das, S. K. (1990). Effects of non-defatted silkworm-pupae in diets on the growth of common carp, *Cyprinus carpio*. *Biological Wastes, 33*(1), 17–23. doi:10.1016/0269-7483(90)90118-C

Newton, G. L., Booram, C. V., Barker, R. W., & Hale, O. M. (1977). Dried *Hermetia Illucens* larvae meal as a supplement for swine. *Journal of Animal Science, 44*(3), 395–400. doi:10.2527/jas1977.443395x

Newton, G. L., Sheppard, D. C., Watson, D. W., Burtle, G. J., Dove, C. R., Tomberlin, J. K., & Thelen, E. E. (2005). The black soldier fly, *Hermetia Illucens*, as a manure management/resource recovery tool. *Symposium on the State of the Science of Animal Manure and Waste Management*, 0–5. http://www.cals.ncsu.edu/waste_mgt/natlcenter/sanantonio/proceedings.htm

Ng, W. K. (2001). Potential of mealworm (*Tenebrio molifor*) as an alternative protein source in practical diets for African catfish, *Clarias gariepinus*. *Aquaculture Research, 32*(Suppl 1), 273–280. doi:10.1046/j.1355-557x.2001.00024.x

Nongonierma, A. B., & FitzGerald, R. J. (2017). Unlocking the biological potential of proteins from edible insects through enzymatic hydrolysis: A review. *Innovative Food Science and Emerging Technologies, 43*, 239–252. doi:10.1016/j.ifset.2017.08.014

Osimani, A., Milanović, V., Cardinali, F., Roncolini, A., Garofalo, C., Clementi, F., … Aquilanti, L. (2018). Bread enriched with cricket powder (*Acheta domesticus*): A technological, microbiological and nutritional evaluation. *Innovative Food Science and Emerging Technologies, 48*, 150–163. doi:10.1016/j.ifset.2018.06.007

Park, S. I., Chang, B. S., & Yoe, S. M. (2014). Detection of antimicrobial substances from larvae of the black soldier fly, *Hermetia illucens* (Diptera: Stratiomyidae). *Entomological Research, 44*(2), 58–64. doi:10.1111/1748-5967.12050

Park, S. I., Kim, J. W., & Yoe, S. M. (2015). Purification and characterization of a novel antibacterial peptide from black soldier fly (*Hermetia illucens*) larvae. *Developmental and Comparative Immunology, 52*(1), 98–106. 10.1016/j.dci.2015.04.018

Pauter, P., Różańska, M., Wiza, P., Dworczak, S., Grobelna, N., Sarbak, P., & Kowalczewski, P. (2018). Effects of the replacement of wheat flour with cricket powder on the characteristics of muffins. *Acta Scientiarum Polonorum, Technologia Alimentaria, 17*(3), 227–233. doi:10.17306/J.AFS.0570

Piccolo, G., Marono, S., Gasco, L., Iannaccone, F., Bovera, F., & Nizza, A. (2014). Use of *Tenebrio molitor* larvae meal in diets for Gilthead seabream *Sparus aurata* juveniles. *1st International Conference Insects to Feed the World.*

Poma, G., Cuykx, M., Amato, E., Calaprice, C., Focant, J. F., & Adrian Covaci, A. (2017). Evaluation of hazardous chemicals in edible insects and insect-based food intended for human consumption. *Food and Chemical Toxicology, 100*, 70–79.

Pretorius, Q. (2011). The evaluation of larvae of *Musca domestica* (common house fly) as protein source for broiler production. *Master Thesis, Stellenbosch University*, 95.

Purschke, B., Meinlschmidt, P., Horn, C., Rieder, O., & Jäger, H. (2018a). Improvement of techno-functional properties of edible insect protein from migratory locust by enzymatic hydrolysis. *European Food Research and Technology, 244*(6), 999–1013. doi:10.1007/s00217-017-3017-9

Purschke, B., Mendez Sanchez, Y. D., & Jäger, H. (2018b). Centrifugal fractionation of mealworm larvae (*Tenebrio molitor*, L.) for protein recovery and concentration. *LWT - Food Science and Technology, 89*, 224–228. doi:10.1016/j.lwt.2017.10.057

Purschke, B., Tanzmeister, H., Meinlschmidt, P., Baumgartner, S., Lauter, K., & Jäger, H. (2018c). Recovery of soluble proteins from migratory locust (*Locusta migratoria*) and characterisation of their compositional and techno-functional properties. *Food Research International, 106*, 271–279. doi:10.1016/j.foodres.2017.12.067

Ramos-Elorduy, J., González, E. A., Hernández, A. R., & Pino, J. M. (2009). Use of *Tenebrio molitor* (Coleoptera: Tenebrionidae) to recycle organic wastes and as feed for broiler chickens. *Journal of Economic Entomology, 95*(1), 214–220. doi:10.1603/0022-0493-95.1.214

Riddick, E. W. (2013). Insect protein as a partial replacement for fishmeal in the diets of juvenile fish and crustaceans. In: *Mass Production of Beneficial Organisms: Invertebrates and Entomopathogens*, 565–582. doi:10.1016/B978-0-12-391453-8.00016-9

Rumpold, B. A., & Schlüter, O. (2015). Insect-based protein sources and their potential for human consumption: Nutritional composition and processing. *Animal Frontiers, 5*(2), 20–24. doi:10.2527/af.2015-0015

Rumpold, B. A., & Schlüter, O. K. (2013). Potential and challenges of insects as an innovative source for food and feed production. *Innovative Food Science and Emerging Technologies, 17*, 1–11. doi:10.1016/j.ifset.2012.11.005

Sánchez-Muros, M. J., Barroso, F. G., & de Haro, C. (2016). Brief summary of insect usage as an industrial animal feed/feed ingredient. In: *Insects as Sustainable Food Ingredients*, 273–309. doi:10.1016/b978-0-12-802856-8.00010-7

Scholliers, J., Steen, L., Glorieux, S., Van de Walle, D., Dewettinck, K., & Fraeye, I. (2019). The effect of temperature on structure formation in three insect batters. *Food Research International, 122*, 411–418. doi:10.1016/j.foodres.2019.04.033

Sealey, W. M., Gaylord, T. G., Barrows, F. T., Tomberlin, J. K., McGuire, M. A., Ross, C., & St-Hilaire, S. (2011). Sensory analysis of rainbow trout, *Oncorhynchus mykiss*, fed enriched black soldier fly prepupae, *Hermetia illucens*. *Journal of the World Aquaculture Society, 42*(1), 34–45. doi:10.1111/j.1749-7345.2010.00441.x

Shakil Rana, K. M., Salam, M. A., Hashem, S., & Ariful Islam, M. (2015). Development of black soldier fly larvae production technique as an alternate fish feed. *International Journal of Research in Fisheries and Aquaculture, 5*(1), 41–47.

Sheikh, I. U., Sapcota, D., & Sarma, S. (2006). Effect of dietary muga silkworm pupae meal on the blood biochemistry in broilers. *Indian Veterinary Journal, 83*(3), 336–337.

Shike, D. (2013). Beef cattle feed efficiency. *Driftless Region Beef Conference 2013. University of Illinois at Urbana-Champaign.* https://lib.dr.iastate.edu/cgi/viewcontent.cgi?article=1027&context=driftlessconference

Shockley, M., & Dossey, A. T. (2013). Insects for human consumption. In: *Mass Production of Beneficial Organisms: Invertebrates and Entomopathogens*, 617–652. doi:10.1016/B978-0-12-391453-8.00018-2

Shyama, S., & Keshavanath, P. (1993). Growth response of Tor khudree to silkworm pupa incorporated diets. *Biarritz (France)* (61), 779–783.

Spranghers, T., Ottoboni, M., Klootwijk, C., Ovyn, A., Deboosere, S., De Meulenaer, B., … De Smet, S. (2017). Nutritional composition of black soldier fly (*Hermetia illucens*) prepupae reared on different organic waste substrates. *Journal of the Science of Food and Agriculture, 97*(8), 2594–2600. doi:10.1002/jsfa.8081

Stamer, A. (2015). Insect proteins—A new source for animal feed. *EMBO Reports*, *16*(6), 676–680. doi: 10.15252/embr.201540528

Stoops, J., Vandeweyer, D., Crauwels, S., Verreth, C., Boeckx, H. , Van Der Borght, M., Claes, J. (2017). Minced meat-like products from mealworm larvae (Tenebrio molitor and Alphitobius diaperinus): microbial dynamics during production and storage. *Innovative Food Science and Emerging Technologies*, *41*, 1–9.

Sun, T., Long, R. J., & Liu, Z. Y. (2013). The effect of a diet containing grasshoppers and access to free-range on carcase and meat physicochemical and sensory characteristics in broilers. *British Poultry Science*, *54*(1), 130–137. doi: 10.1080/00071668.2012.756575

Sun, T., Long, R. J., Liu, Z. Y., Ding, W. R., & Zhang, Y. (2012). Aspects of lipid oxidation of meat from free-range broilers consuming a diet containing grasshoppers on alpine steppe of the Tibetan Plateau. *Poultry Science*, *91*(1), 224–231. doi: 10.3382/ps.2011-01598

Sun-Waterhouse, D., Waterhouse, G. I. N., You, L., Zhang, J., Liu, Y., Ma, L., ... Dong, Y. (2016). Transforming insect biomass into consumer wellness foods: A review. *Food Research International*, *89*, 129–151. doi: 10.1016/j.foodres.2016.10.001

Tran, G., Heuzé, V., & Makkar, H. P. S. (2015). Insects in fish diets. *Animal Frontiers*, *5*(2), 37–44. doi: 10.2527/af.2015-0018

Trivedy, K., Kumar, S. N., Mondal, M., & Bhat, C. A. K. (2008). Protein banding pattern and major amino acid component in de-oiled pupal powder of silkworm, *Bombyx mori* Linn. *Journal of Entomology*, *5*(1), 10–16. doi: 10.3923/je.2008.10.16

Ueckert, D. N., Yang, S. P., & Albin, R. C. (1972). Biological value of rangeland grasshoppers as a protein concentrate. *Journal of Economic Entomology*, *65*(5), 1286–1288. doi: 10.1093/jee/65.5.1286

van Broekhoven, S., Bastiaan-Net, S., de Jong, N.W., & Wichers, H. J. (2016). Influence of processing and in vitro digestion on the allergic cross-reactivity of three mealworm species. *Food Chemistry*, *196*, 1075–1083. 10.1016/j.foodchem.2015.10.033.

van der Spiegel, M., Noordam, M. Y., & van der Fels-Klerx, H. J. (2013). Safety of novel protein sources (insects, microalgae, seaweed, duckweed, and rapeseed) and legislative aspects for their application in food and feed production. *Comprehensive Reviews in Food Science and Food Safety*, *12*(6), 662–678. doi: 10.1111/1541-4337.12032

Vangsoe, M. T., Thogersen, R., Bertram, H. C., Heckmann, L. H. L., & Hansen, M. (2018). Ingestion of insect protein isolate enhances blood amino acid concentrations similar to soy protein in a human trial. *Nutrients*, *10*(10), 1357. doi: 10.3390/nu10101357

Van Huis, A. (2017). New sources of animal proteins: Edible insects. In: *New Aspects of Meat Quality: From Genes to Ethics*, 443–461. doi: 10.1016/B978-0-08-100593-4.00018-7

van Huis, A., & Oonincx, D. G. A. B. (2017). The environmental sustainability of insects as food and feed. A review. *Agronomy for Sustainable Development*, *37*(5), 43. doi: 10.1007/s13593-017-0452-8

Van Huis, A., Van Itterbeeck, J., Klunder, H., Mertens, E., Halloran, A., Muir, G., & Vantomme, P. (2013). Edible insects. Future prospects for food and feed security. In: *Food and Agriculture Organization of the United Nations, FAO Forestry*, Vol. 171, 1–201.

Veldkamp, T., & Bosch, G. (2015). Insects: A protein-rich feed ingredient in pig and poultry diets. *Animal Frontiers*, *5*(2), 45–50. doi: 10.2527/af.2015-0019

Veldkamp, T., van Duinkerken, G., van Huis, A., Ottevanger, E., Bosch, G., & van Boekel, T. (2012). Insects as a sustainable feed ingredient in pig and poultry diets: a feasibility study = Insecten als duurzame diervoedergrondstof in varkens- en pluimveevoeders: een haalbaarheidsstudie. *Food Chemistry*, *50*, 192–195.

Vijayakumar Swamy, H. V., & Devaraj, K. V. (1995). Effect of plant and animal meal based diets on conversion rates, nutrient digestion and nutrient accretion by Indian major carp fry *Catla catla* (Ham.). *Journal of Animal Morphology and Physiology*, *42*(1–2), 27–32.

Virk, R. S., Lodhi, G. N., & Ichhponani, J. S. (1980). Deoiled silk worm pupae meal as a substitute for fish meal in White Leghorn laying ration. *Indian Journal of Poultry Science*, *15*(3), 149–154.

Wanasithchaiwat, V., & Saesakul, M. (1989). Effects of fly larval meal grown on pig manure as a source of protein in early weaned pig diets. *Thurakit Ahan Sat (Thailand)*, *6*, 25–31.

Wang, D., Bai, Y. Y., Li, J. H., & Zhang, C. X. (2004). Nutritional value of the field cricket (*Gryllus testaceus* walker). *Insect Science*, *11*(4), 275–283. doi: 10.1111/j.1744-7917.2004.tb00424.x

Wang, D., Shao, W. Z., Chuan, X. Z., Yao, Y. B., Shi, H. A., & Ying, N. X. (2005). Evaluation on nutritional value of field crickets as a poultry feedstuff. *Asian-Australasian Journal of Animal Sciences*, *18*(5), 667–670. doi: 10.5713/ajas.2005.667

Wang, W., Wang, N., Liu, C., & Jin, J. (2017). Effect of silkworm pupae peptide on the fermentation and quality of yogurt. *Journal of Food Processing and Preservation*, *41*(3), 1–7. doi:10.1111/jfpp.12893

Wang, Y.-S., & Shelomi, M. (2017). Review of black soldier fly (*Hermetia illucens*) as animal feed and human food. *Foods*, *6*(10), 91. doi:10.3390/foods6100091

Williams, J. P., Williams, J. R., Kirabo, A., Chester, D., & Peterson, M. (2016). Nutrient content and health benefits of insects. In: *Insects as Sustainable Food Ingredients (Production, Processing and Food Applications)*, 61–84. doi:10.1016/b978-0-12-802856-8.00003-x

Yi, L., Lakemond, C. M. M., Sagis, L. M. C., Eisner-Schadler, V., Van Huis, A., & Boekel, M. A. J. S. V. (2013). Extraction and characterisation of protein fractions from five insect species. *Food Chemistry*, *141*(4), 3341–3348. doi:10.1016/j.foodchem.2013.05.115

Yi, L., Van Boekel, M. A. J. S., Boeren, S., & Lakemond, C. M. M. (2016). Protein identification and in vitro digestion of fractions from *Tenebrio molitor*. *European Food Research and Technology*, *242*(8), 1285–1297. doi:10.1007/s00217-015-2632-6

Yoon, S., Wong, N. A. K., Chae, M., & Auh, J. H. (2019). Comparative characterization of protein hydrolysates from three edible insects: Mealworm larvae, adult crickets, and silkworm pupae. *Foods*, *8*(11), 563. doi:10.3390/foods8110563

Zhang, J. B., Zheng, L. Y., Jin, P., Zhang, D. N., & Yu, Z. N. (2014). Fishmeal substituted by production of chicken manure conversion with microorganisms and black soldier fly. *Insects to Feed the World, The Netherlands*, 14–17.

Zhou, J., & Han, D. (2006). Safety evaluation of protein of silkworm (Antheraea pernyi) pupae. *Food and Chemical Toxicology*, *44*(7), 1123–1130. 10.1016/j.fct.2006.01.009

Zielińska, E., Baraniak, B., & Karaś, M. (2017a). Antioxidant and anti-inflammatory activities of hydrolysates and peptide fractions obtained by enzymatic hydrolysis of selected heat-treated edible insects. *Nutrients*, *9*(9), 1–14. doi:10.3390/nu9090970

Zielińska, E., Karaś, M., & Jakubczyk, A. (2017b). Antioxidant activity of predigested protein obtained from a range of farmed edible insects. *International Journal of Food Science and Technology*, *52*(2), 306–312. doi:10.1111/ijfs.13282

6 Snails

*Alaa El-Din Bekhit[1], Jinlin Shi[2], Zhijing Ye[3],
Isam A. Mohamed Ahmed[4], Fahad Y. Al-Juhaimi[4],
William W. Riley[5], and Ravi Gooneratne[2]*

[1]Department of Food Science, University of Otago, Dunedin, New Zealand
[2]Faculty of Agriculture & Life Sciences, Lincoln University, Canterbury, New Zealand
[3]Eastern Institute of Technology, Hawke's Bay, New Zealand
[4]Department of Food Science and Nutrition, College of Food and Agricultural Sciences, King Saud University, Riyadh, Kingdom of Saudi Arabia
[5]International School, Jinan University, Guangzhou, China

CONTENTS

6.1	Introduction	133
	6.1.1 Marine Snails	134
	6.1.1.1 Turbinidae Family	134
	6.1.2 Terrestrial Snails	137
6.2	Nutritional Aspects of Snail Meat	138
	6.2.1 Proximate Composition	138
	6.2.1.1 Land Snails	138
	6.2.1.2 Comparison with Commercial Meats	141
	6.2.2 Amino Acid Composition	145
	6.2.3 Fatty Acid Composition	147
	6.2.4 Other Nutritionally Important Components	155
	6.2.4.1 Cholesterol	155
	6.2.4.2 Vitamin E	155
6.3	Minerals and Potential Toxic Compounds in Snail	156
	6.3.1 Minerals	156
	6.3.2 Organochlorine Pesticides (OCPs)	161
6.4	Health Risks	162
6.5	Health Aspects	163
6.6	Conclusions	164
	Acknowledgement	164
	References	164

6.1 INTRODUCTION

Snails belong to the class Gastropoda within the phylum Mollusca, which is the second largest phylum in the kingdom Animalia. It has been estimated that there are approximately 43,000 snail species in the world with about 60% of that figure being terrestrial snails (http://molluscs.at/gastropoda/index.html?/gastropoda/main.html). Snails are distributed all over the globe and are found in aquatic (marine and fresh waters) and terrestrial ecosystems. They have been a food source for humans, birds and animals for the entirety of their existence. This chapter discusses the nutritional and health aspects of marine and terrestrial snails with the aim to examine their potential as a good food source with high-quality protein.

6.1.1 Marine Snails

The marine grouping of class Gastropoda contains a large number of univalves, such as the valuable abalones (Backlip abalone, Black abalone, Green abalone, Red abalone and white abalone). The main three abalone species in New Zealand are *Haliotis virginea, Haliotis iris*, and *Haliotis australis*, collectively known as Pāua. Different species are found in other countries, such as *Haliotis midae* in South Africa, *Haliotis discus hannai* in Japan and China, *Haliotis laevigata* in Australia, and *Haliotis rufencens* in several locations (British Columbia, Canada, Baja California, Mexico and Chile). Production from natural harvested grounds in 2017 was one third what used to be obtained in the 1970s (declined from 20,000 metric tonnes to 6,500 metric tonnes) whereas the production from farmed abalone increased a negligible amount to more than 160,000 metric tonnes (Cook, 2019). Abalone is regarded as the most expensive gastropod, and it is a slow-growing animal. It is unlikely this expensive marine snail will be used as a mainstream source of protein, but the potential for other species (Table 6.1) is very promising. There are several rock snails (such as *Chorus giganteus, Concholepas concholepas, Turbo bruneus, Turbo cornutus, T. intercostalis, Tectus niloticus, Turbo militaris, Lunella torquata* and *L. undulata*) that have been reported to be consumed around the world. In New Zealand, various marine snails are found, such as *Turbo smaragdus, Nerita atramentosa, Melagraphia aethiops, Cookia sulcala, Trochus viridus,* and *Cantharidus purpureus*, that are considered edible.

Other species under the same category of univalves include true limpets (such as *Cellana exarate, C. sandwicensis, Patella caerulea, P. ferruginea, P. rustica, P. ulyssiponensis* and *P. vulgate*), winkles (such as *Austrolittorina antipodum* and *Littorina sitkana*), conchs (such as *Lobatus gigas* and *Laevistrombus canarium*), and whelks (*Haustrum albomarginatum, Buccinulum linea, Cominella glandiformis,* and *Cominella adspersa*). Many of these species (Figures 6.1 and 6.2) graze on algae and seaweed and they inhabit estuaries, harbours and rocky shores. Marine gastropods contribute to a small percentage (2%) of the world marine catch (Ab Lah et al., 2017).

6.1.1.1 Turbinidae Family

The family *Turbinidae* have a spirally growing, externally calcified, rigid operculum that completely fills the aperture of the shell when the soft parts are withdrawn (Vermeij & Williams, 2007). The operculum has an important protective function (Vermeij & Williams, 2007). The global catch of turban snails was 17,000 tonnes in 2000, but it declined to 8,500 tonnes in 2012 (Ab Lah, 2017). In Australia, the commercial catch is regulated under a quota system, and licences with 4 to 6 tonnes reported in New South Wales are caught annually (NSW, 2015). Such information from other regions is not easily accessible.

Cookia sulcata is an important example of this family and thus, it will be discussed in some detail. *C. sulcate* is a marine snail that belongs to the phylum Mollusca. The genus *Cookia* is found within the class Gastropoda, within the family *Turbinidae* and subfamily *Astraeiane* (Minson, 1972; Powell, 1979). The common name of this snail is Cook's Turban because it was collected by scientists sailing with Captain Cook. The family *Turbinidae* includes other snails, such as *Modelia granosa* and *Astraea heliotropium*, which are commonly known as granose turban and circular saw, respectively (Crowe, 1999; Morley, 2004; Penniket, 1982). A famous member in the same family, *Turbo smaragdus,* is called cat's eye and is often gathered for food by the Maori in New Zealand (Crowe, 1999).

Cookia sulcata is found in many parts of New Zealand (North, South, Stewart and Chatham Islands). *C. sulcata* lives along ledges or among seaweed, and it is frequently found under rocks or along the beaches on the open coast at low tide (Morley, 2004). This snail feeds on algae and

TABLE 6.1
Marine edible snails

Region/Country	Species
Asia	*Astralium calcar* (Linnaeus, 1758)
Indonesia, New Guinea	*Turbo (M.) 'bruneus'* (Röding, 1798)
	T. (M.) chrysostomus (Linnaeus, 1758)
	Lunella (Lunella) cinerea (Born, 1778)
Japan	*Astralium haematragum* (Menke, 1829)
	Bolma millegranosa
	B. modesta (Reeve, 1843)
	Guildfordia triumphans (Philippi, 1841)
	Lunella (Lunella) coreensis (Re´cluz, 1853)
	Pomaulax japonicus (Dunker, 1844)
	T. (Batillus) cornutus (Lightfoot, 1786)
Palau	*A. rhodostomum* (Lamarck, 1822)
India	*A. semicostatum* (Kiener, 1850)
East Asia	*L. (L.) granulata* (Gmelin, 1791)
	T. (M.) sparverius (Gmelin, 1791)
Africa	
Kenya, Madagascar	*Lunella (L.) coronata* (Gmelin, 1791)
Madagascar, Red Sea	*T. (s.l.) radiatus* (Gmelin, 1791)
South Africa	*T. (S.) sarmaticus* (Linnaeus, 1758)
	T. (Sarmaticus) cidaris (Gmelin, 1791)
Australasia	
New Guinea	*T. (M.) crassus* (Wood, 1828)
Western Pacific	*Turbo (Turbo) petholatus* (Linnaeus, 1758)
	T. (Lunatica) marmoratus (Linnaeus, 1758)
Guam	*T. (Marmarostoma) argyrostomus* (Linnaeus, 1758)
Mariana Islands	*A. rhodostomum* (Lamarck, 1822) sp. 1
New Caledonia	*A. cf. stellare* (Gmelin, 1791)
Northern Australia	*T. (M.) perspeciosus* (Iredale, 1929)
Southern Australia	*Micrastraea kesteveni* (Iredale, 1924)
Western Australia	*Astralium tentorium* (Thiele, 1930)
	Turbo (Turbo) jourdani (Kiener, 1839)
New South Wales	*L. (Ninella) torquata* (Gmelin, 1791)
	L. (Subninella) undulata (Lightfoot, 1786)
New Zealand	*Astraea heliotropium* (Martyn, 1784)
	Cookia sulcata (Lightfoot, 1786)
	L. (s.l.) smaragdus (Martyn, 1784)
	Modelia granosa (Martyn, 1784)
Mediterranean	*Bolma rugosa* (Linnaeus, 1758)
The Americas	
Baja California	*Lithopoma (Uvanilla) olivaceum* (Wood, 1828)
	L. (U.) unguis (Wood, 1828)
	Pomaulax gibberosa (Dillwyn, 1817)
	Turbo (Callopoma) fluctuosus (Wood, 1828)
Florida, Bermuda	*Lithopoma (Lithopoma) americanum* (Gmelin, 1791)
Florida, Puerto Rico	*Turbo (Senectus) castanea* (Gmelin, 1791)
Hawaii	*T. (M.) sandwicensis* (Pease, 1861)

(Continued)

TABLE 6.1 (Continued)
Marine edible snails

Region/Country	Species
Central Pacific	*T. (M.) setosus* (Gmelin, 1791)
Chile	*Prisogaster elevatus* (Souleyet, 1852)
	P. niger (Wood, 1828)
Panama	*Lithopoma (Uvanilla) buschii* (Philippi, 1848)
Clarion Island	*Turbo (Callopoma) funiculosus* (Kiener, 1847)
Panama	*T. (C.) saxosus* (Wood, 1828)
Mexico	*T. (Senectus) squamiger* (Reeve, 1843)
Caribbean	*L. (L.) caelatum* (Gmelin, 1791)
	L. (L.) phoebium (Ro¨ding, 1798)
	L. (L.) tectum (Lightfoot, 1786)
	L. (L.) tuber (Linnaeus, 1767)

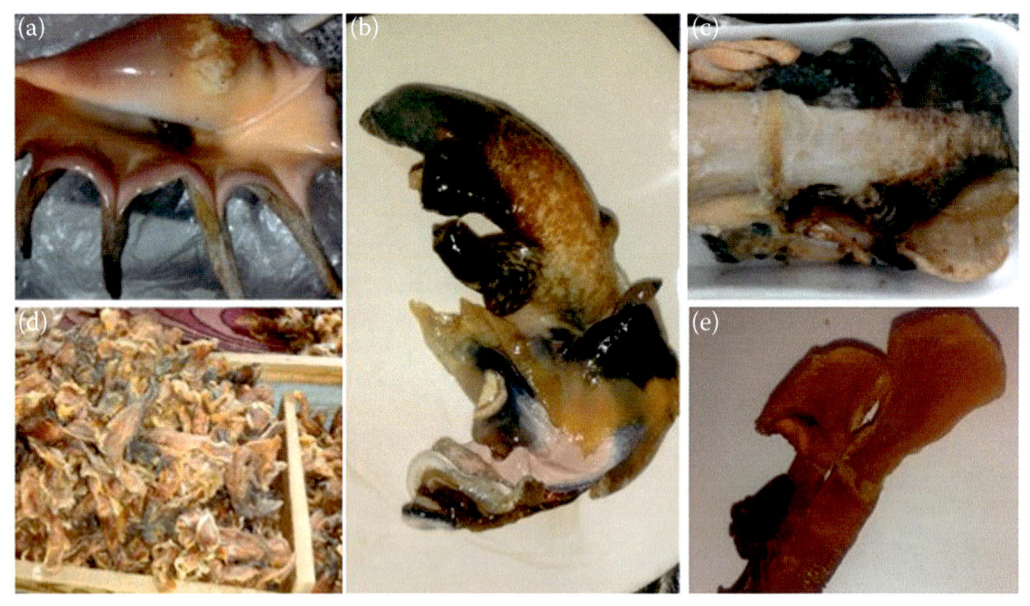

FIGURE 6.1 Spider conch (*Lambis lambis*) products. Live snail (a), fresh meat (b), frozen (c) and dried meat (d and e) are sold in Egyptian markets. Pictures are kindly provided by Professor Hesham F. Amin (Department of Fish Processing and Technology, Faculty of Fish Resources, Suez University, Suez, Egypt).

seaweed (Crowe, 1999; Morton et al., 1968). The size of an adult snail varies from about 65 to 80 mm in height and 65–90 mm in width (Powell, 1979). *C. sulcata* has a shell that is heavy, solid and strong, helping it to survive being ripped from the rocks by crashing waves and tossed around by the tide (Crowe, 1999). The shell is spirally coiled, forming a protoconch with up to four whorls, and it has a rounded to sub-angulated periphery with a strong and arcuated shell surface which varies with the rounding (Minson, 1972; Powell, 1979). The spiral structure inclines forward and is overridden by sharp spiral cords. The whole shell is crossed by fine lamellose growth striae (Minson, 1972; Powell, 1979). These fine striae are rarely visible on mature shells, as layers of calcified material form a coating up to about 6 mm thick on the top and sides of the shell (Minson,

FIGURE 6.2 Examples of edible marine snails. *Cookia sulcata* (a) and *Lunella smaragdus* (known in New Zealand as Cat's eye snail (b). Marine snails from Chinese wet market (c) (pictures provided by Dr. Zhijing Ye, Eastern Institute of Technology, New Zealand).

1972; Powell, 1979). The spire of shell is often encrusted with white, calcareous algae (Morley, 2004) which turn into a red colour as the snail grows. The surface of the shell is often worn off, showing the silver layer underneath (Crowe, 1999). The interior is white and can be sealed off by an operculum (Morley, 2004). The large oval shelly operculum is an oblong plate with several spiral ridges.

In New Zealand, Maori people consume the meat and use the shells to make tiny detailed woodcarvings and fish-hooks (Crowe, 1999). The shells of this snail have a commercial value, as they are polished and carved into exquisite spoons or mounted in gold or silver, set with jewels, and treasured as ceremonial goblets.

The whole body of the *C. sulcate*, after removal from the shell, consists of the viscera, a head, a foot and a muscle. The edible tissues of *C. sulcata* are the foot, muscle and some parts of the visceral hump. The visceral hump components (usually found further inside the shell) are white with some tinges of green. The foot is partly black and partly dark green in colour. Other important snails are spotted Babylon (*Babylonia areolata*) that is cultured in Thailand (Chotimarkorn et al., 2010) and the fresh water snail (*Pila ampullacea*) that is found in several aquatic systems and rice fields of many Asian countries (Broto et al., 2020). This latter snail appears to be a useful source of nutrients, and it contains 57.8% and 14.6% of protein and lipid, respectively.

6.1.2 Terrestrial Snails

There is a large number of wild and farmed land snails that have been used for food. The majority of farmed snails (e.g., the garden snail *Helix aspersa*, the Burgundy snail/Roman or escargot snail *Helix pomatia*, the giant African snails *Archatina fulica* and *Archachatina marginate*) belong to the family Achatinidae or Helicidae. Adeyeye and Afolabi (2004) stated that snails play several important functions as they are an important food source for many organisms due to their wide distribution in many ecosystems, and they could potentially be farmed for commercial uses, they are useful biomonitors of environmental pollution, and they could be used as a model for research investigations.

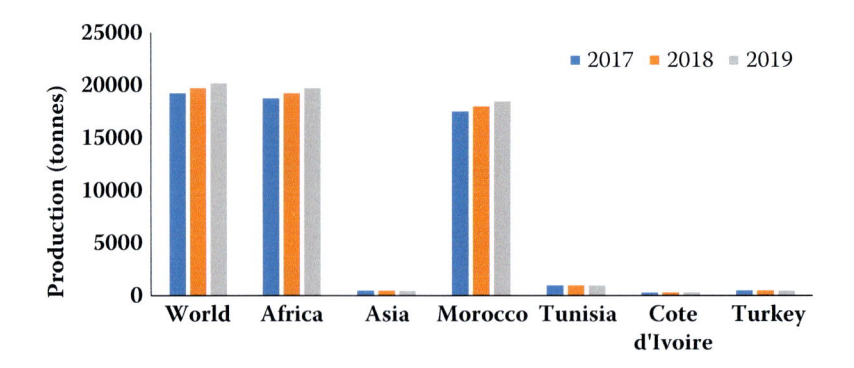

FIGURE 6.3 Production of land snails and major producing countries.

Also, they have health and agricultural significance due to their being host to several intermediates that cause diseases in humans and animals as well as the snails being able to damage crops. The consumption of land snails is common in several European, Asian, South America and African countries. The most notable are in West Africa (especially Morocco and Nigeria) and western Europe (France, Poland, Germany and Portugal). Heliciculture (farming of land snails) has been considered as a practical solution to obtaining high protein food in Morocco, Brazil and Nigeria (Adeyeye & Afolabi, 2004; Milinsk et al., 2006), and Morocco is responsible for >80% of world land snail production (Figure 6.3), mainly the escargot snail, whereas Nigeria produces giant African snails (Figure 6.4). The average weights of *A. marginate, A. archatina* and *Limicolaria* sp. are 302, 14.3 and 5.4 g, respectively (Adeyeye, 1996). Their edible portions are 49.2, 60.2 and 55.5%, respectively, and they have 20.8, 14.5 and 17.5% protein, respectively (Adeyeye & Afolabi, 2004).

6.2 NUTRITIONAL ASPECTS OF SNAIL MEAT

Snails are the largest group of molluscs. Mollusc is the largest animal group after the arthropods (Powell, 1979). The mollusc include univalve organisms such as snails and slugs; bivalves such as mussels, oysters and cockles, and cephalopods, such as octopus, squid and cuttlefish (Copper & Knower, 1991). Some molluscs are used as human food, among which oysters, mussels and some snails are the most popular (Miletic et al., 1991). Humans have consumed snails as food for thousands of years, and edible snails have had a place on the menu in many European countries, especially France, where snails are consumed in the greatest quantities (Milinsk et al., 2003). Similarly, many Asian countries harvest snails for food and are considered a delicacy in Korea and Japan (King & Bruce, 1949; Qun et al., 2004; Xia et al., 2007). Commercial production of edible snails has been considered for years, especially in China, where snail production was developed due to favourable weather and environmental conditions (Xia et al., 2007). It has been reported that turban snails are among the most edible gastropods due to their high nutritional value (Yearsley et al., 1999). They are considered a good source of PUFAs, essential amino acids, taurine, and trace elements (Ab Lah et al., 2017; Mason et al., 2014).

In the following section, a summary of the chemical composition of land and marine snails is presented, and the relative composition of snail meat compared with other marine molluscs and common commercial meats is discussed.

6.2.1 PROXIMATE COMPOSITION

6.2.1.1 Land Snails

Land snails are collected or farmed at a commercial scale, and considerable literature on basic information of their composition is available (Table 6.2). The snail species *Helix* spp.,

FIGURE 6.4 Giant African snails *Archtina fulica* and *Archachatina marginate* are major species farmed in West Africa.

TABLE 6.2
Proximate Composition of Land Snails

Species	Moisture	Protein FW	Protein DW	Lipids FW	Lipids DW	Ash FW	Ash DW	Carbohydrate FW	Carbohydrate DW	References
Archachatina sp.	74.3–78.0	20.3–20.8	–	1.2–1.4	–	1.4	–	<0.4	–	Adeyeye (1996), Fagbuaro et al. (2006)
Archachatina sp.	–	–	39.7–43.3	–	–	–	0.5–0.6	–	–	Hamzat et al. (2002)
Helix. Sp.	72.8–87.6	–	7.3–18.4	–	0.4–2.7	–	0.7–2.7	–	0.4–1.7	Adeyeye (1996), Gomot (1998), Milinsk et al. (2003; 2006b), Wiesre and Schuster (1975)
Helix. Sp.	–	–	51.4–72.5	–	3.1–10.8	–	8.8–13.4	–	–	Gomot (1998)
Achatina sp.	77.5–89.2	9.9–19.3	–	1.4–4.2	–	1.3–2.1	–	0.4–4.4	–	Adeyeye (1996), Fagbuaro et al. (2006), Watt and Merrill (1975)
Limicolaria sp.	71.2–78.7	17.5–18.7	–	1.2–4.3	–	1.1–1.4	–	0.2	–	Claeys and Demeyer (1986)
Limicolaria sp.	–	–	51.4	–	9.	–	11.8	–	27.1	Udoh et al. (1995)
Helix promatia Helix nemoralis	81.9 / 82.7	–	70.6 / 71.8	–	6.7 / 8.0	–	4.4 / 4.5	–	–	Miletic et al. (1991)
Archachatina marginata ovum	76.6–80.8	20.6	84.4	1.4	4.5	1.4	4.0	0.01	0.5	Eneji et al. (2008), Fagbuaro et al. (2006)
Archachatina marginata saturalis	76.7–80.3	20.3	81	1.2	4.0	1.4	4.5	0.4	1.0	
Limicolaria species	78.6–78.7	18.7	71.8	1.2	3.8	1.4	7.0	0.2	1.0	
Achatina achatina	77.5	19.3	–	1.4	–	1.4	–	0.01	–	Fagbuaro et al. (2006)
Cornu aspersum	–	–	57.9–66.0	–	0.8–5.4	–	1.6–1.9	–	–	Çelik et al. (2020)

Archachatina, spp. and *Achatina* spp. have been most thoroughly studied. Snail meat is high in protein, with a range of 8–20% (fresh weight basis), which equates to 60–70% on a dry weight basis, depending on the snail type (Adeyeye, 1996; Çelik et al., 2020; Diarra, 2015; Fagbuaro et al., 2006; Gomot, 1998; Hamzat et al., 2002; Milinsk et al., 2003; 2006b). In contrast, snail meat is low in fat. Usually, the fat content in snail meat is between 0.5% and 5% on a fresh weight basis, which equates to 3–20% of a dry weight basis. The most dominant component in snail meat is the moisture, which ranges between 70–85% of the fresh meat weight (Çelik et al., 2020; Diarra, 2015; Gomot, 1998; Udoh et al., 1995). The ash content has been reported to be low as well. For example, study results have shown that the ash content of snails is in the approximate range of 0.5–2.7% (fresh weight basis), which equates to 2–13.4% on a dry weight basis (Table 6.2). The carbohydrate content has not been extensively reported in research studies, but based on available data, it can be estimated to be in the range of 0.2–4.4% (fresh weight basis) (Çelik et al., 2020; Diarra, 2015; Hamzat et al., 2002; Milinsk et al., 2003; 2006b; Udoh et al., 1995).

6.2.1.1.1 Marine Snails

A large number of studies have been carried out to investigate the composition of marine snails (Table 6.3). Although marine species differ from land snails in terms of diet and living environment, the proximate composition of marine snails is not vastly different from land snails. The protein and lipid contents are slightly lower than land snails, 8–16% and 1.4–8% of fresh weight, respectively, whereas the moisture content is similar (approximately 80% of fresh weight). The ash and carbohydrate contents in marine snails vary widely, ranging from 1.7–9.0% and 2.9–10% on a wet weight basis (Table 6.3).

Several factors contribute to the variability in the proximate composition of snail meat. Variability due to snail species, size (age), sampling position (location) and season has been reported to lead to large differences in the meat proximate composition among different land-snail species (Ansell, 1972; Ansell & Trevallion, 1967; Blackmore, 1969; Mason et al., 2014; McLachlan & Lombard, 1980; Miletic et al., 1991). In commonality with snails, the proximate composition of other marine molluscs, such as mussels and oysters, varies widely and is species-specific (Table 6.3).

6.2.1.2 Comparison with Commercial Meats

The average proximate compositions of mutton, beef, lamb, pork, chicken and goat meat are highly variable, with a range of 1.8–23.9% for protein, 1.1–4.2% for fat, 44.4–78.6% for moisture and 0.6–3.2% for ash (Table 6.4). Moisture is the most predominant component in both domestic animals' meats and molluscs, and molluscs contain higher levels of moisture than do land-based animals. Poultry, pork, beef and lamb production, which are considered the major sources of meat protein for humans, currently face challenging conditions due to persistent drought, diseases, natural disasters, high cost of feed, and low productivity of local breeds, and this is most evident in some developing countries (Fagbuaro et al., 2006). At the same time, the human population continues to grow. This has led to greater pressure on existing animal protein sources. Hence, interest in snails as food has increased in recent years. The higher end of the scale for protein content in domestic animal meat is similar to land snails, and is slightly higher than marine snails and other molluscs. Therefore, in the terms of protein quantity, snails potentially can be used as alternative protein sources to address the shortage of land-based animal meat products.

Domestic meat products generally have high fat contents. Also, the fat in many domestic meats contains a high percentage of saturated fatty acids which are associated with several pathological conditions, such as elevated blood cholesterol levels and vascular coronary heart diseases. In contrast, snails (both land and marine) and other marine molluscs have much lower fat levels than do land-based animal meat. Also, snail fats contain a high proportion of monounsaturated fatty acids and long-chain fatty acids.

TABLE 6.3
Proximate Composition of Marine Snails and Common Marine Molluscs

Species	Moisture	Protein FW	Protein DW	Lipids FW	Lipids DW	Ash FW	Ash DW	Carbohydrate FW	Carbohydrate DW	References
Trobo sarmaticus	ND		62.7–74.8		3.2–6.7		4.7–7.6		15.9–23.1	McLachlan and Lombard (1980)
Monodonta turbinata	82.8		51.2		2.9		–		–	Miletic et al. (1991)
Hinia reticulata	72.7	22.0	–	1.5	–	1.7	–	–		Felici et al. (2020)
Nassarius mutabilis	73.3	21.1	–	1.8	–	1.7	–	–		
Lanistes varicus#	75.8		70.0		1.8		8.0		1.3	Eneji et al. (2008)
Nucella lapillus	73.7		82.3		8.5		8.0		1.5	
Monodonta turbinata	82.8		51.2		2.9		N/A		N/A	Miletic et al. (1991)
Lunella torquata	68.5	18.0		8.5		2.1		2.9		Ab Lah (2017)
Lunella undulata	70.8	18.5		5.2		2.0		3.5		
Turbo militaris	73.1	16.2		5.6		2.1		3.0		
Tegula brunneus	–	–	53–56	–	1–3	–	–	6–9	–	Ramesh and Ravichandran (2008)
Cookia sulcata	77.7	17.5	78.8	1.0	4.0	2.1	9.3	–	–	Mason et al. (2014)
Haliotis varia	70–76	–	66–76	–	3–7	–	6–8	1–11	–	Najmudeen (2007)
Haliotis discus	77.4	15	–	–	–	–	1.3	–	–	Bae et al. (2011)
Haliotis discus hannai	78	12.4	–	–	–	–	1.8	–	–	
Thais haemastoma	–	–	60–80	–	4–5	–	–	5–10	–	Belisle and Stickle (1978)
Hexaplex trunculus	68–73	–	10–17	–	17–23	–	–	–	2–6	Vasconcelos et al. (2009)
Babylonia spirata	–	–	54	–	9	–	–	–	17	Periyasamy et al. (2011)
Babylonia spirata	48–52	–	45–50	–	5–6	–	–	6–7	–	Shanmugam et al. (2006)
Rapana vanosa	63–71	–	60–66	–	1.5–2.5	–	9–10	–	24–28	Celik et al. (2014)
Babylonia spirata	73	–	36	–	1.5	–	1	–	14	Marget et al. (2013)
Babylonia zeylanica	82	–	43	–	6.2	–	1	–	20	Marget et al. (2013)
Dicathais orbita	70–80	2.5–4.0	–	7–10	–	2–4.5	–	–	–	Woodcock and Benkendorff (2008)
Littorina littorea	79.9	1.4	–	8.3	–	2.2	–	–	–	Zlatanos et al. (2009)
Patella coerulea	78	2.6	–	9.2	–	2.4	–	–	–	Zlatanos et al. (2009)
Hemifuses	65–70	–	30–45	–	9–11	–	–	3–9	–	Sekar et al. (2012)

Of some common marine molluscs consumed as food

Perna canaliculus	78.2–80.9	11.9–13.9	–	2.1–2.2	–	1.7–2.2	–	3.4	Vlieg (1988), Hughes et al. (1980)
Atrina zelandica	81.0	14.8	–	0.5	–	1.3	–	2.4	Vlieg (1988)
Ostra edulis	79.4	12.9	–	3.0	–	1.6	–	3.1	Vlieg (1988), Karakoltsidis et al. (1995)
Pecten novaezelandiae	78.7–82.4	14.3–15.4	–	0.7–1.3	–	1.6–1.9	–	2.7	Vlieg (1988), Hughes et al. (1980)
Mutilus galloprovinciallis	82.0–87.0	8.0–13.0	42.4–56.2	1.0–2.0	5.8–13.4	0.7–2.0	11.0–21.0	2.0–5.0	Orban et al. (2002), Karakoltsidis et al. (1995)
Ostra edulis	82.0–88.0	11.0–15.0	–	0.2–1.0	–	1.0–1.6	–	2.0–3.0	Vlieg (1988), Karakoltsidis et al. (1995)
Patella vulgate	75.0–84.0	ND	–	10.5	53.3	–	8.6–34.7	N/A	Blackmore (1969)
Tellina tenuis	71.0–83.0	7.9	10.9	3.9	12.8	–	5.8–27.7	6.4	Ansell and Trevallion (1967)
Venus verrucosa	79.7	–	44.3	9.6	–	–	8.1	–	Miletic et al. (1991)

= fresh water

TABLE 6.4
Proximate Composition of Raw Meat from Common Domestic Animals

Species	Proximate Composition (% fresh weight)				References
	Protein	Lipids	Moisture	Ash	Carbohydrate	

Species	Protein	Lipids	Moisture	Ash	Carbohydrate	References
Goat	19.8–24.0	2.9–16.1	68.3–78.7	0.9–1.7	N/A	Lee et al. (2008), Paleari et al. (2008)
Beef	22.5–24.0	1.1–6.9	44.4–74.9	1.2–1.4	N/A	Crosland et al. (1995), Seggern et al. (2005), Smith and Williamson (1986)
Chicken	20.4–22.7	2.8–9.2	69.7–74.3	0.3–1.3	N/A	Al-Najdawi and Abdullah (2002), Crosland et al. (1995)
Pork	15.0–23.1	1.7–22.1	59.2–73.9	1.0–3.2	N/A	Cheng and Sun (2007), Crosland et al. (1995)
Lamb	2.5–23.4	2.5–26.4	55.4–76.9	0.8–1.2	N/A	Badiani et al. (1998), Crosland et al. (1995), Kosulwat et al. (2003), Lee et al. (2008)

6.2.2 Amino Acid Composition

Proteins, which make up many essential components in living cells, are formed from twenty amino acids (Nollet, 2004). Once proteins are ingested, amino acids are released and absorbed by the body. Protein quality depends on their amino acid content and digestibility. Amino acids are generally supplied in food and/or may be synthesized through different metabolic pathways from other amino acids inside the organism. Essential amino acids cannot be synthesized in sufficient quantities in the organism and must be supplied in adequate amounts in the diet for optimal functioning of the organism. In addition, some amino acids are essential at certain ages, such as during infancy and/or pregnancy (Nollet, 2004). Therefore, the quality as well as the quantity of protein is equally important for any food. A simple method to determine amino acid composition and compare it to a reference protein is referred to as amino acid scoring, which is an evaluation of protein quality (Whitney & Rolfes, 2005). Whole egg protein, which is one of the most complete and digestible proteins, has been used as a standard or reference protein for measuring protein quality since the early 1970s. Egg protein is assigned a value of 100, and the quality of other food proteins is compared with the egg. The limiting amino acid is the one which is present in the least amount compared with its counterpart in the egg. In addition, a new standard for the reference protein, the daily essential amino acid requirements for human, has been established by the Food and Agricultural Organisation of the United Nations (FAO) and the World Health Organization (WHO) (FAO/WHO/UNU, 1981). Both whole egg protein and the daily essential amino acid requirements were used as standards for protein quality measurements in this study.

Given the nutritional importance of amino acids, considerable information on the amino acid profiles of land and marine snails, as well as some marine molluscs and common meats, are already available (Table 6.5). Aspartic acid (asp) and glutamic acid (glu) are the major amino acids in marine molluscs, land snails and meats (beef, pork and lamb). Marine molluscs contain higher levels of alanine (ala) and glycine (gly) compared with land snails and common meats. Molluscs (including land snails) and meats have similar amounts of lysine and leucine (Table 6.5). Marine molluscs and meats from domesticated animals exhibit high levels of total amino acid compared with land snails. Total essential amino acids in marine molluscs were similar to those in common meats (*circa* 40%), but they were 5–10% higher than in land snails (Table 6.5). In terms of protein quality, both molluscs (marine and land snails) and meats (beef, pork and lamb) have lower protein quality compared with egg protein because of the higher proportion of essential amino acids in eggs. Lysine (lys) is the predominant essential amino acid in marine molluscs, while histidine (his) is the most important essential amino acid in both land snails and meats. Methionine (met) and cysteine (cys) are the limiting amino acids in marine molluscs, land snails and meats (Table 6.6). Essential amino acids in marine molluscs, land snails and common meats generally meet the daily requirement for humans with the exception of the tryptophan requirements in infants and pre-schoolers (Table 6.6). Therefore, snails (both land and marine) can be used as a reliable protein source. It has been reported that farmed freshwater snails *Pomacea canaliculata* (Ampullariidae) meet the recommended levels of all essential amino acids except for methionine (Ghosh et al., 2017).

Mason et al. (2014) assessed the protein quality of *C. sulcata* based on the amino acids profile recommended by FAO/WHO/UNU (1981). The authors stated that a 100 g serving of snail meat would provide at least a quarter of the daily requirement of the essential amino acids for a 75 kg person, with the exception of methionine. It was noted that the sulphur-containing amino acids methionine and cysteine were the limiting amino acids with an amino acid score of 23%. The *C. sulcata* meat is particularly rich in threonine, tyrosine, phenylalanine, lysine and leucine, as well as lysine and tryptophan, and thus it will complement cereal-based diets that are usually deficient in lysine. In the same study, the authors found that *C. sulcata* meat had a high concentration of taurine ($\cong$ 9.5% of the protein content). Taurine is not a protein-building amino acid, but it plays an important role in several biological processes, such as the removal of cholesterol and lipid digestion and

TABLE 6.5
Amino Acid Profiles (g/100 g Protein) of Some Marine Molluscs.

AA	Marine Molluscs								Land Snail					Common Meats		
	Monodonta lineata	Gibbula umbilicalis	Gibbula pennanti	Gibbula cineraria	Mya arenaria	Cardium edule	Tapes decussatus	Perna canaliculus#	Limicolaria aurora	Archatina archatina	Archachatina marginata	Helix pomatia	Achatina spp.	Beef	Pork	Lamb
Asp	10.5	8.0	9.1	11.6	9.3	N/A	N/A	1.3	7.6–7.8	6.9	7.3	6.2	N/A	8.8	8.9	8.5
Glu	10.7	10.9	10.8	10.1	13.0	N/A	N/A	1.7	10.1–13.5	11.1	11.4	9.8	N/A	14.4	14.5	14.4
Ser	4.9	5.9	6.2	5.5	4.3	N/A	N/A	0.7	4.0–4.1	3.2	3.3	3.5	N/A	3.8	4.0	3.9
His*	2.3	2.5	2.6	2.2	1.8	1.6	1.6	0.2	3.6–3.7	3.0	4.7	2.2	0.96	2.9	3.2	2.7
Gly	8.5	10.4	10.5	10.0	6.9	N/A	N/A	1.1	5.1–6.5	5.2	4.6	1.8	N/A	7.1	6.1	6.7
Thr*	5.3	5.0	5.4	5.8	4.4	4.5	3.2	0.5	1.8–3.9	2.2	2.8	1.3	N/A	4.0	5.1	4.9
Arg	5.7	5.5	5.9	6.0	7.0	5.6	4.0	1.0	0.3	6.3	6.0	4.5	6.46	6.6	6.4	6.9
Ala	8.1	7.4	7.9	8.6	6.8	ND	ND	0.6	4.0–6.9	2.4	5.2	1.9	N/A	6.4	6.3	6.3
Tyr	2.8	3.0	3.1	2.9	3.2	1.1	ND	0.4	2.6–5.9	2.5	2.9	5.4	N/A	3.2	3.0	3.2
Val*	5.8	5.3	5.9	6.1	4.2	4.5	3.2	0.5	4.1–7.6	3.3	7.1	6.1	2.97	5.7	5.0	5.0
Phe*	4.0	3.5	3.8	3.7	3.3	4.4	3.2	0.4	4.4–6.7	3.8	4.7	2.3	2.58	4.0	4.1	3.9
Ile*	4.9	4.4	5.3	4.7	4.5	4.5	5.4	0.5	5.2–7.3	4.5	3.9	2.2	3.15	5.1	4.9	4.8
Lys*	8.5	8.9	6.1	7.1	7.7	11.2	8.0	1.0	7.2–8.3	6.1	5.7	4.7	5.97	8.4	7.8	7.6
Leu*	7.6	8.5	7.3	6.5	6.5	9.0	8.2	0.8	6.9–11.5	5.6	8.1	4.9	3.43	8.4	7.5	7.4
Pro	6.3	7.3	3.8	3.9	3.4	N/A	N/A	0.5	4.0–5.6	3.0	3.6	2.4	N/A	5.4	4.6	4.8
Cys	1.8	1.2	2.7	1.3	ND	ND	ND	0.1	0.5–2.0	0.9	1.1	N/A	N/A	1.4	1.3	1.3
Met*	2.3	2.4	3.3	2.8	2.4	2.2	2.3	0.3	1.8–2.3	1.4	2.0	5.6[a]	0.7	2.3	2.5	2.3
Trp*	N/A	N/A	N/A	N/A	1.2	1.2	1.1	N/A	ND	ND	ND	ND	ND	1.1	1.3	1.3
TAA	100.0	100.0	99.7	98.8	89.9	49.8	40.2	11.6	73.2–103.9	71.4	84.4	59.2	26.2	99.0	96.5	95.9
TEAA	49.2	50.9	50.2	48.9	42.9	43.1	36.2	5.3	35.0–51.3	29.9	39.0	23.7	19.8	41.9	41.4	39.9
TEAA/TAA	0.49	0.51	0.50	0.49	0.48	0.87	0.90	0.46	0.48–0.49	0.42	0.46	0.40	0.75	0.42	0.43	0.42
References	Daguzan (1983), Harvey (1970), Hughes et al. (1980), Mead and Kemmerer (1953), Miletic et al. (1991)								Adeyeye (1996), Mead and Kemmerer (1953), Crosland et al. (1995), Udoh et al. (1995)					Gibson et al. (1993), Pearson and Dutson (1990)		

g/100 g fresh weight; AA = Amino acid; TAA = total amino acids; TEAA = total essential amino acids; ND = not detected; * = essential amino acid; TEAA/TAA = total essential amino acids/total amino acids

TABLE 6.6
Daily Essential Amino Acids Requirement for Human

AA	Daily Requirement g/100 g Protein			Egg Protein	AA Score (%)		
	Infant[1]	School-Child[2]	Adult[3]		Marine Molluscs	Land Snails	Meats
His	1.4	/	/	2.3	90.7	167.4	127.5
Ile	3.5	3.7	1.8	5.4	89.5	96.8	91.4
Leu	8.0	5.6	2.5	8.6	89.0	93.3	90.3
Lys	5.2	7.5	2.2	7.0	117.4	97.5	113.3
Met + Cys	2.9	3.4	2.4	5.7	61.9	42.5	64.9
Phe + Tyr	6.3	3.4	2.5	9.3	64.5	95.4	76.7
Thr	4.4	4.4	1.3	4.7	102.1	56.9	99.3
Trp	0.85	0.46	0.65	1.7	68.6	N/A	72.5
Val	4.7	4.1	1.8	6.6	75.8	83.7	79.3
References	FAO/WHO/UNU (1981)			Whitney and Rolfes (2005)	Equated values from Table 6.4		

/ = There is no evidence for or against a His requirement for children or adult; 1 = 2–6 months old; 2 = 10–12 years old; 3 = >18 years

fat adsorption (Wright et al., 1986). Furthermore, taurine protects against diabetes, is involved in pro-inflammatory cell homeostasis, it is antihypertensive, and it regulates growth and reproduction (Hultman et al., 2007; Markwell et al., 1995; Redmond et al., 1998; Toshiro et al., 1987).

6.2.3 FATTY ACID COMPOSITION

Over the years, fat has been recognized as an unhealthy component of the diet. Many forms of fat, which have a range of differing biological properties and physiological effects, have been identified and studied (Mills et al., 2005). Fatty acids (FA) may be saturated, monounsaturated or polyunsaturated (PUFAs), and these FA serve different functions in the human body. For example, short-chain fatty acids provide energy, and long-chain FA are part of the cell membrane structure (Berg et al., 2007). Unlike some PUFAs, saturated and monounsaturated FA are not necessary in the diet because they can be produced in the human body. Some PUFAs are considered essential because animals and humans cannot synthesize them in the body, and therefore they must obtain them from the diet (Caballero et al., 2003). The carbon furthest from the carboxyl group is known as the omega (n)-carbon, and the position of the first double bond from the methyl group is known as the omega (n)-x, where x is the carbon number on which the double bond occurs (Ruxton et al., 2005). According to this classification, two PUFAs, omega-3 and omega-6 (n3 and n6) fatty acids, are essential in the diet and so are very frequently reported in food.

Recently, n3, n6 and the ratio of n6 to n3 fatty acids have acquired a great deal of attention. Most interest has been on n3 fatty acids, which have a number of beneficial effects on human health and disease. Many studies have shown a beneficial role for n3 fatty acids in reducing the severity of atherogenesis, chronic heart disease, hypertension, inflammatory disease, and cancer (Mills et al., 2005; Mozaffarian et al., 2004; Rose & Connolly, 1999; Simopoulos, 1991; 1999). Linolenic acid (LA) and alpha-linolenic acid (ALA) are the parent compounds of the ω6 and ω3 fatty acids, respectively, for FA metabolism (Ruxton et al., 2005). LA can be converted to Gamma-linolenic acid (GLA), which can be elongated to dihomo-gamma-linolenic acid (DGLA) and then further desaturated to arachidonic acid (AA). In the case of n6 FA, ALA can be converted to eicosapentaenoic acid (EPA) by using the same enzyme as n3 FA. Omega 6 FA have different metabolic effects than n3. More potential factors lead to heart disease and inflammatory disease with n6 metabolism (Wakil, 1970). Since there are different effects of n3 and n6 fatty acids on metabolism, the ratio of n6 to n3 FA is important as well (Caballero et al., 2003).

Fatty acid content and profile in shellfish vary between and within species. The amount and the profile of FA in shellfish will depend on their feed, size (age), gender, reproductive status, geographic location and season (Orban et al., 2002; Pirini et al., 2007; Ventrella et al., 2008). The fatty acids found in the oil of various seafood-species differ from those in terrestrial animals in having a substantial portion of 20- or 22-carbon chains. These consist of 20- and 22-carbon monounsaturated fatty acids and very long-chain PUFAs (Katvi, 2005). In Tables 6.7 and 6.8, summaries of the fatty acid compositions of some common molluscs, including mussel, oyster, scallop, octopus, land snails, and marine snails are provided. Land snails have high concentrations of C16:0 (range from 6.7 to 13.6%) and C18:0 (range from 8.9 to 14.4%). The highest monounsaturated fatty acid is C18:1 (range from 10 to 31.1%). Considerable amounts of the polyunsaturated fatty acid C18:2n6 have also been observed (range from 11 to 34.3%) with the exception of low values reported for *Helix lucorum* by Göçer and Olgunoğlu (2018). Similarly, wide variation has been reported for C20:2 (range from 0.39 to 12.8%) which appeared to be dependent on the species with a high content in *H. pomatia, Haplotrema sportella,* and *Vespericola columbiana*, while low contents are found in *Cornu aspersum* and *H. lucorum* (Table 6.7). Overall, marine snails have a high saturated fatty acids (SFA) content (range from 38.6 to 47.1%) with C16:0 being the dominant SFA at a range of 10.1 to 29.1% (Table 6.8). The C18:0 and C18:1 content in marine snails is lower than those found in land snails. The total polyunsaturated fatty acid content varied widely among the various species (Table 6.8). Marine shellfish such as scallop and mussels as well as the Mollusca octopus were rich in eicosapentaenoic acid (EPA C20:5) and docosahexaenoic acid (DHA C22:6), which are n3 FA, whereas snails had the largest amount of linoleic acid (LA C18:2) and arachidonic acid (AA C20:4), which are n6 fatty acids. Hence, the composition of PUFAs in snails has more n6 than n3.

The effect of cooking and freezing on the fatty acid composition of *H. pomatia, C. aspersa maxima* and *C. aspersum aspersum* was reported by Szkucik et al. (2018). The concentrations of C14:0, C16:0, C17:0, C18:0, C20:0, C22:0, C24:0 and total SFA were increased at various levels by cooking and freezing (Table 6.9). All the monounsaturated fatty acids were decreased by cooking and freezing, with the exception of C18:1, C20:1 and C22:1. Cooking and freezing reduced the concentrations of all polyunsaturated fatty acids, the PUFA/SFA ratio, and total n-6 and n-3 fatty acids. Molluscs cannot synthesize the bioactive EPA, DHA and ARA fatty acids, and thus they must obtain them from their diet. The quality and quantity of their feed will be influenced by their position in the ecosystem, and feed is probably the main source of variation of PUFAs in the molluscan tissue. Turban snails are herbivores that specifically feed on macroalgae (Foster & Hodgson, 1998,) and thus few subtle differences in the macroalgal diet of these species exist when they are collected from the same location (Ab Lah, 2017). This has been documented for *H. aspersa maxima* where changing the protein and soybean oil in the diet changed the fatty acid composition of the snail meat (Milinsk et al., 2006). Other factors that affect the fatty acid composition include food availability, environmental conditions (temperature and salinity) and reproductive status (Milinsk et al., 2003; Özogul et al., 2005; Ab Lah, 2017). The biosynthesis of fatty acids appears to respond to mineral fortification. Kowalczyk-Pecka et al. (2017) reported on an interesting study designed to increase PUFAs content in the tissue of *H. pomatia* by the addition of micro-doses of Cu. The treated groups had higher C18:2 n-6, C18:3 n-3, C20:2, C20:4 n-6, C20:5 n-3, C22:4 n-6, and C22:5 n-3 as well as total PUFAs than did the control counterpart. Furthermore, a negative correlation (r was almost 1) was found between the concentration of added Cu and saturated fatty acids and the total SFA in the snails.

TABLE 6.7
Fatty acid compositions of land snails

Fatty acid	Helix pomatia	Szkucik et al. (2018) Cornu aspersa maxima	Cornu aspersum aspersum	Cornu aspersa maxima	Milinsk et al. (2006b) Helix sp.	Özogul et al. (2005) Haplotrema sportella	Zhu et al. (1994) Vespericola columbiana	Göçer and Olgunoğlu (2018) Helix lucorum L. 1758 from Adana	Helix lucorum L. 1758 from Sinop
C12:0	0.12–0.16	0.31–0.35	0.36–0.37		N/A	N/A	N/A	2.25	2.36
C13:0	0.39–0.43	0	0		N/A	N/A	N/A		
C14:0	0.47	0.34–0.35	0.33–0.35	0.43–0.66	7.1	9.6	8	0.7	0.44
C15:0	0.25	0.28–0.29	0.28–0.29		N/A	N/A	N/A		
C16:0	10.2–10.3	8.27–8.36	8.66–8.93	6.7–10.1	10.4	10.6	8.9	13.6	11.7
C17:0	1.11–1.13	0.21–0.23	0.27–0.28	0.68–0.78	N/A	N/A	N/A	1.27	1.06
C18:0	14.3–14.4	12.2–12.3	12.3–12.8	12.3–14.5				5.51	4.53
C20:0	0.63–0.65	1.33–1.34	1.22–1.29					2.21	3.39
C21:0								4.61	3.51
C22:0	6.50–6.69	5.34–5.63	5.49–5.6		N/A	N/A	N/A		
C23:00	0.21–0.22	0	0						
C24:00	0.62–0.63	0	0		N/A	N/A	N/A		
ΣSFA	34.8–35.2	28.3–28.7	29.4–29.5	22.2–26.3				32.02	28.8
C14:1	0.13–0.14	0.26–0.27	0.26–0.30		N/A	N/A	N/A	0.63	0.73
C15:1	0.15–0.18	0.22–0.25	0.23–0.25		N/A	N/A	N/A	0.62	0.87
C16:1	1.36–1.48	0.73–0.82	0.80–0.82	0.41–0.83	1.4	1.5	3.2		
C17:1	0.23–0.28	0.12–0.14	0.11–0.14		N/A	N/A	N/A	0.68	0.46
C18:1	13.7–13.8	20.4–26.6	19.6–25.8	17.4–21.6	14.2	11.9	10	29.7	31.1
C20:1	1.75–1.80	2.52–2.78	2.57–2.87	1.4–1.5	2.2	0.9	3.6	0.59	0.43
C22:1	0.03–0.04	0.01	0.01		N/A	N/A	N/A	2.09	2.68
C24:1	2.01–2.30	0	0		N/A	N/A	N/A	2.08	1.28
ΣMUFA	19.6–19.8	24.2–30.9	23.9–29.8	20.7–23.8	15.7	14.5	11	36.4	37.5
C18:2n6	17.9–18.0	27.4–32.4	27.4–34.3	19.4–24.5	1.8	3.2	4.3	4.31	3.55
C18:3n3	2.47–2.54	3.50–3.70	3.70–3.85	1.0–1.3	N/A	N/A	N/A		
C18:3n6	0.27–0.35	0.25–0.29	0.25–0.27		12.1	10.5	9.1	0.52	0.44
	12.3–12.8	0.46–0.58	0.39	1.6–2.5					

(*Continued*)

TABLE 6.7 (Continued)
Fatty acid compositions of land snails

Fatty acid	Helix pomatia	Szkucik et al. (2018) Cornu aspersa maxima	Cornu aspersum aspersum	Cornu aspersa maxima	Milinsk et al. (2006b) Helix sp.	Özogul et al. (2005) Haplotrema sportella	Zhu et al. (1994) Vespericola columbiana	Göçer and Olgunoğlu (2018) Helix lucorum L. 1758 from Adana	Helix lucorum L. 1758 from Sinop
C20:2 n11, n14									
C20:3 n3	0	0.26	0.22–0.24						
C20:3 n6, 9n	1.73–1.96	5.70–6.93	7.06–7.37	11.0–13.1	N/A	N/A	N/A	0.49[a]±0.05	0.6
C20:04	1.02–1.32	0.20–0.30	0	9.5–10.8	14.8	13.8	16.9		
C20:5 n3	2.46–2.90	0.15–1.53	0.14–1.25	1.6–2.0	2.8	1.5	5.5	1.55	0.2
C22:2					N/A	N/A	N/A	0.86	0.95
C22:4 n-6				3.6–4.5	4.8	5.3	4		
C22:5	0.22–0.26	0.19–0.25	0.53–0.55	1.1–1.6	1.3	1.7	2	1.83	1.81
C22:6 n-3 (DHA)									
ΣPUFA	38.8–39.7	39.8–44.6	41.3–46.7	49.9–57.1				9.56	7.55
PUFA/SFA	1.10–1.14	1.41–1.55	1.40–1.59	1.9–2.6				0.3	0.26
Σ n6	21.26–21.28	33.61–39.90	35.04–41.65	33.1–38.5	50.3	48.8	45.9	5.32	4.59
Σ n3	5.00–5.37	3.91–5.49	4.06–5.34	5.5–6.2	6.6	7.2	11.9	3.38	2.01
n6/n3	3.96–4.25	6.12–10.2	6.56–10.26	5.5–6.9	7.8	6.9	5.2	1.59	2.27

TABLE 6.8
Fatty acid compositions of aquatic snails and shellfish

	Ab Lah (2017)			Mason et al. (2014) *Cookia sulcata*		Miletic et al. (1991) *Monodonta turbinata*	Felici et al. (2020)		Miletic et al. (1991)		Karakoltsidis et al. (1995)	1	2	3
Fatty acid	*L. torquata*	*L. undulata*	*T. militaris*	Small	Large		*N. mutabilis*	*H. reticulata*	*Mytilus gallopr,* mussel	*Venus verucos* Fresh water clam	Octopus	Scallop	Mussel	Oyster
C14:0	0.55	0.96	0.13	2.3	2.3	2.3	6.9	6.84	3.9	2.8	3	0.8–3.8	1.5–7.0	1.2–5.3
C15:0	1.18	1.08	1.49	2.7	2.4		0.46	0.52			0.3	0.2–1.0	0.4–5.0	0.3–1.1
C16:0	23.0	21.6	22.1	27.3	22.6	17.9	29.1	27.7	18.1	20.7	27	10.2–26.3	10.1–25.5	17.6–20.8
C17:0	2.39	1.87	2.99	5.3	4.7	2.07	1.33	1.62	0	0	1	0.5–1.9	0.2–2.9	1.3–2.1
C18:0	5.68	6.59	5.45	8.1	9.6	12.22	8.98	9.45	4.82	6.45	10	3.4–8.1	3.7–10.8	0.9–7.9
C20:0				0.4	0.3	5.3	0.3	0.28	4.97	5.99	*	<0.5	<3.6	*
C22:0				0.5	0.4						N/A	<2.1	<0.1	N/A
C24:00	7.14	6.49	7.65								N/A		<0.8	N/A
ΣSFA	39.9	38.6	40.8	46.6	42.2		47.1	46.4						
C14:1				ND	ND	2.68	0.02	0.28	1.02	0.89	*	*	<6.4	<0.3
C15:1				ND	ND						<0.1	<0.2	<2.0	0.2–0.4
C16:1	3.24	2.41	3.00	0.7	0.9	5.41	6.93	7.04	10.68	10.02	2	1.1–5.5	2.7–12.6	1.6–8.7
C17:1				0.5	0.5		1.48	1.04			2	0.2–4.1	<2.1	0.4–1.5
C18:1	8.21	8.41	7.89	8.8	8	16.46	11.75	9.24	8.9	14.57	7	1.7–8.6	1.5–7.3	5.3–9.0
C20:1	2.77	3.56	2.86	2.1	1	0	2.51	2.57	2.84	0	3	1.1–3.8	1.0–5.4	3.4–8.2
C22:1	0.23	0.45	0.30	2.8	0.2						5	0.1–2.5	<6.0	0.3–1.8
C24:1				ND	ND						N/A	<0.3	<0.8	*
ΣMUFA	14.45	14.82	14.05	14.9	10.8		22.69	20.17						
C18:2n6	0.87	2.33	1.87	2.3	2.1	2.95	1.54	1.05	3.82	3.4	1	0.3–1.8	1.6–5.0	1.7–11.9
C18:3n3	1.60	2.82	2.92	0.5	1	1.85	3.01	3.08	2.38	0.61	*	<1.9	<2.5	<4.4
C18:3n6				1.5	0.2		0.27	0.16			N/A	<0.2	<4.6	0.1–1.1
C18:4 n3											*	0.4–5.2	<6.0	1.6–7.9
C20:2 n11, n14	0.06	0.21	0.13	0.6	2.7	0.55			0.94	1.91	N/A	0.2–0.8	0.5–3.3	0.2–0.8

(*Continued*)

TABLE 6.8 (Continued)
Fatty acid compositions of aquatic snails and shellfish

Fatty acid	Ab Lah (2017) L. torquata	Ab Lah (2017) L. undulata	Ab Lah (2017) T. militaris	Mason et al. (2014) Cookia sulcata Small	Mason et al. (2014) Cookia sulcata Large	Miletic et al. (1991) Monodonta turbinata	Felici et al. (2020) N. mutabilis	Felici et al. (2020) H. reticulata	Miletic et al. (1991) Mytilus gallopr, mussel	Miletic et al. (1991) Venus verucos Fresh water clam	Karakoltsidis et al. (1995) Octopus	Scallop [1]	Mussel [2]	Oyster [3]
C20:3 n3	0.16	0.43	0.27	ND	ND						N/A	<0.3	N/A	0.1–0.2
C20:3 n6, 9n				ND	ND		4.64	8.13			N/A	0.2–8.8	<5.8	1.3–3.5
C20:4	14.93	16.01	15.06	11.1	11.7		2.83	6.92			18	12.5–23.2	11.6–31.6	7.9–21.2
C20:5 n3	5.29	4.63	3.70	4.9	6		13.86	12.89			N/A	0.2–0.8	<2.9	0.1–1.1
C22:2	6.61	5.83	7.48	3	3.9						N/A	0.5–0.6	1.1	N/A
C22:3											*	0.5–3.7	<1.7	0.6–2.4
C22:4 n6														
C22:5	15.27	13.79	13.33	8.4	7.6		0.81	0.86			*	0.9–2.9	0.7–2.3	0.7–1.2
C22:6n-3 (DHA)	0.80	0.53	0.37	0.6	0.6		5.45	5			21	8.7–31.0	9.0–26.4	7.3–21.9
ΣPUFA	45.61	46.58	45.13	32.3	36.3	21.76	23.13	21.83	30.6	26.18				
Σ n6				14.2	15.8		0.20	0.37			1	2.1–12.4	2.1–9.4	2.4–16.5
Σ n3				14.9	15.4		4.98	2.68			39	30.6–54.7	25.5–46.8	15.9–46.9
n6/n3				0.91	1						0.025–0.41	0.06–0.26	0.01–0.22	0.09–0.4

* = trace (less than 0.1%)

[1] *Pectan novaezealandiae*; *Patinopecten yessoensis*; and *Pecten maximus* Hughes et al. (1980), Vlieg and Body (1988), Silina and Zhukova (2007), Pazos et al., (1997)

[2] *Mytilus galloprovinciallis*; *Perna canaliculus*; *Atrinata pectinata*; and *Perna perna* [Karakoltsidis et al. (1995), Ventrella et al. (2008), Hughes et al. (1980), Vlieg and Body (1988), Taylor and Savage, (2006), Vlieg and Body, (1988)]

[3] *Crassostrea gigas*; *Ostrea sinuate* [Dridi et al. (2007), Abdulkadir and Tsuchiya, (2008), Vlieg and Body (1988)]

TABLE 6.9
Fatty acid composition of land snails under different preparation conditions from Szkucik et al. (2018).

Fatty acid	Helix pomatia Raw	Helix pomatia Cooked	Helix pomatia Frozen	Cornu aspersa maxima Raw	Cornu aspersa maxima Cooked	Cornu aspersa maxima Frozen	Cornu aspersum aspersum Raw	Cornu aspersum aspersum Cooked	Cornu aspersum aspersum Frozen
12:0	0.12–0.16	0.17–0.19	0.18–0.20	0.31–0.35	0.39–0.43	0.41–0.45	0.360.37	0.41–0.42	0.42–0.43
13:0	0.39–0.43	0.52–0.55	0.55–0.58	0	0	0	0	0	0
14:0	0.47	0.52–0.54	0.54–0.56	0.34–0.35	0.38–0.40	0.38–0.43	0.33–0.35	0.37–0.41	0.38–0.44
15:0	0.25	0.30	0.31–0.32	0.28–0.29	0.32–0.33	0.33–0.34	0.28–0.29	0.34–0.35	0.35
16:0	10.16–10.28	11.24–11.39	11.32–11.45	8.27–8.36	10.13–10.26	10.31–10.34	8.66–8.93	10.17–10.22	10.50-10-51
17:0	1.11–1.13	1.14–1.15	1.15–1.16	0.21–0.23	0.25–0.26	0.28–0.29	0.27–0.28	0.33–0.36	0.36–0.38
18:0	14.31–14.37	15.51–15.64	15.84–15.87	12.18–12.23	13.74–13.83	13.66–13.91	12.28–12.89	13.77–13.87	13.94–13.96
20:0	0.63–0.65	0.72–0.75	0.81–0.84	1.33–1.34	1.40–1.42	1.48–1.52	1.22–1.29	1.29–1.34	1.38–1.40
22:0	6.50–6.69	6.92–6.99	7.58–7.62	5.34–5.63	6.00–6.03	6.55–6.61	5.49–5.6	6.00–6.12	6.52–6.53
23:0	0.21–0.22	0.24	0.24	0	0	0	0	0	0
24:0	0.62–0.63	0.66–0.67	0.67–0.68	0	0	0	0	0	0
ΣSFA	34.84–35.21	37.98–38.38	38.40–39.26	28.3228.72	32.69–32.88	33.49–33.80	29.35–29.54	32.87–32.90	33.92–33.93
14:1	0.13–0.14	0.09–0.11	0.08–0.12	0.26–0.27	0.20–0.22	0.20–0.21	0.26–0.30	0.18–0.24	0.19–0.20
15:1	0.15–0.18	0.12–0.14	0.13–0.15	0.22–0.25	0.15–0.16	0.15–0.16	0.23–0.25	0.16–0.17	0.15–0.16
16:1	1.36–1.48	1.03–1.11	1.02–1.13	0.73–0.82	0.51–0.71	0.51–0.65	0.80–0.82	0.50–0.69	0.54–0.63
17:1	0.23–0.28	0.20–0.21	0.19–0.23	0.12–0.14	0.08–0.10	0.08–0.10	0.11–0.14	0.08–0.09	0.07–0.08
18:1	13.65–13.83	15.57–15.63	15.69–15.70	20.36–26.64	23.47–30.79	23.50–30.80	19.56–25.81	23.18–28.74	23.4–29.02
20:1	1.75–1.80	2.75–2.84	2.81–2.85	2.52–2.78	3.45–3.63	3.43–3.67	2.57–2.87	3.62–3.73	3.61–3.96
22:1	0.03–0.04	0.05–0.06	0.06	0.01	0.02–0.03	0.02–0.03	0.01	0.02	0.02–0.03
24:1	2.01–2.30	0	0	0	0	0	0	0	0
ΣMUFA	19.55–19.83	19.91–20.00	20.06–20.16	24.22–30.91	24.78–31.48	27.88–35.59	23.89–29.83	24.25–33.55	28.13–33.72
18:2n6	17.87–17.95	16.59–16.95	16.47–16.69	27.42–32.42	24.55–30.42	25.51–30.43	27.40–34.34	25.12–31.84	25.02–31.71
18:3n3	2.47–2.54	1.40–1.57	1.41–1.42	3.50–3.70	1.82–2.89	1.45–2.70	3.70–3.85	2.22–2.86	2.21–2.44
18:3n6	0.27–0.35	0.22–0.27	0.21–0.24	0.25–0.29	0.15	0.12–0.14	0.25–0.27	0.17–0.18	0.15–0.18
20:2 n11, n14	12.30–12.77	10.97–11.59	10.66–11.76	0.46–0.58	0	0	0.39	0	0

(Continued)

TABLE 6.9 (Continued)
Fatty acid composition of land snails under different preparation conditions from Szkucik et al. (2018).

Fatty acid	Helix pomatia Raw	Helix pomatia Cooked	Helix pomatia Frozen	Cornu aspersa maxima Raw	Cornu aspersa maxima Cooked	Cornu aspersa maxima Frozen	Cornu aspersum aspersum Raw	Cornu aspersum aspersum Cooked	Cornu aspersum aspersum Frozen
29:3 n3	0	0	0	0.26	0	0	0.22–0.24	0	0
20:3 n6, 9n	1.73–1.96	1.51–1.60	1.50–1.58	5.70–6.93	3.37–6.12	3.22–6.00	7.06–7.37	5.34–5.81	5.24–5.48
20:4	1.02–1.32	0.32–0.50	0.29–0.52	0.20–0.30	0	0	0	0	0
20:5 n3	2.46–2.90	1.32–1.68	1.27–1.68	0.15–1.53	0.07–0.67	0.06–0.65	0.14–1.25	0.06–0.50	0.06–0.48
22:2	0.22–0.26	0.12–0.16	0.12–0.13	0.19–0.25	0	0	0.53–0.55	0	0
ΣPUFA	38.78–39.68	32.63–34.14	30.89–32.11	39.81–44.58	31.54–38.58	31.57–38.00	41.30–46.65	33.99–40.11	33.09–39.34
PUFA/SFA	1.10–1.14	0.85–0.90	0.80–0.82	1.41–1.55	0.96–1.18	0.93–1.13	1.40–1.59	1.03–1.22	0.98–1.16
Σ n6	21.26–21.28	18.13–18.90	17.95–18.61	33.61–39.90	25.37–30.64	26.30–30.61	35.04–41.65	25.79–32.08	25.65–31.95
Σ n3	5.00–5.37	2.72–3.25	2.72–3.25	3.91–5.49	1.89–3.47	1.89–3.47	4.06–5.34	2.28–3.36	2.28–3.36
n6/n3	3.96–4.25	5.82–6.67	5.73–6.60	6.12–10.2	7.31–16.21	7.58–16.20	6.56–10.26	7.68–14.07	7.63–14.01

6.2.4 OTHER NUTRITIONALLY IMPORTANT COMPONENTS

6.2.4.1 Cholesterol

Cholesterol belongs to the sterol group of fats. Cholesterol is vital for several biological functions in the body, such as being an important constituent of cell membranes and influencing membrane fluidity and solute permeability. Cholesterol is also the precursor of steroid hormones, bile salts and vitamin D (Hames & Hooper, 2000). Although it plays a vital role in cell growth and development, the accumulation of cholesterol in certain tissues can lead to harmful effects. Increased concentration of cholesterol, particularly low-density lipoprotein cholesterol, in the blood (hypercholesterolemia), has been found to be a major cause of coronary heart disease (Gould et al., 2007; Kosulwat et al., 2003). This can damage the arteries, and especially the coronary arteries that supply the heart. This can lead to accumulation of cholesterol-laden 'plaques' in vessel linings, a condition called atherosclerosis. When blood flow to the heart is impeded, the heart muscle becomes starved of oxygen, causing chest pain. If a blood clot completely obstructs a coronary artery affected by atherosclerosis, a heart attack may occurs, which can lead to death (Orakzai et al., 2009). Furthermore, a high blood cholesterol level is correlated with increased risks of diabetes, stroke and hypertension (Gould et al., 2007; Law et al., 2003; MRC/BHF, 2003; Sever et al., 2003). Cholesterol is oxidized under certain conditions, such as thermal treatment, photocatalysis, or enzymatic oxidation. The oxidation process produces several hydroperoxide isomers which have been linked to several human diseases, such as atherogenesis, cytotoxicity, mutagenesis, and carcinogenesis (Guardiola et al., 2002).

Many clinical trials have provided evidence that lower blood cholesterol levels can reduce the incidence of heart attack (Gould et al., 2007). Hence, it is useful to identify and limit the consumption of foods that are rich in cholesterol. Cholesterol is the major sterol in gastropods (Table 6.10). Idler and Wiseman (1971) investigated the sterols in seven marine snails and found that more than 85% of the sterols were in the form of cholesterol in six of the snail species, while in for the remaining species, about 56% of the sterols were present as cholesterol. Three land snails have been studied by Zhu et al., (1994) where they found that more than 87% of the sterols were cholesterol with an average of 100 mg cholesterol/100 g fresh weight. Other marine molluscs, like oyster, scallop and clam, had a higher cholesterol content than did land snails (about 150–200 mg/100 g fresh weight).

6.2.4.2 Vitamin E

Vitamin E was discovered and labelled 'factor X' by Evans & Bishop (1922) while investigating dietary factors that are essential for reproduction in rats. Later in 1924, their experiment was repeated, and the substance was named vitamin E (Sure, 1924). Vitamin E is insoluble in water but readily soluble in non-polar solvents (Combs, 2008). Vitamin E is the collective name for a set of eight related tocopherols and tocotrienols, the α-, β-, γ-, and δ-tocopherols, and the α-, β-, γ-, and δ-tocotrienols, with α-tocopherol being the most abundant and important member (Figure 6.5). The vitamin E members are designated as α-, β-, γ-, and δ- according to the number and position of the constituent methyl groups on the chromanol ring of the tocopherols and tocotrienols (Ball, 2004). The tocotrienols have three double bonds in the phytyl side chain, whereas the tocopherols contain a trimethyltridecyl tail with three chiral centres which naturally occur in the *RRR* configuration (Zingg, 2007). A natural vitamin E, which is coined marine-derived tocopherol (MDT), was found in some marine organisms (Figure 6.5), with a single unsaturated bond at the end of the side chain, and this is thought to be responsible for cold-water adaptation (Zingg, 2007). However, its presence in snails is yet to be confirmed.

Vitamin E is rich in plant products, and especially in plant oils such as sunflower and soybean oils, with lesser amounts being present in animal tissues (Combs, 2008). Vitamin E has significant antioxidant activity (Rietjens et al., 2002). Vitamin E is the major antioxidant in the lipid environment, protecting against lipid oxidation, and the mechanism action has been described by

TABLE 6.10
Cholesterol Contents of Snails and Some Marine Molluscs

Species		Cholesterol Content		References
		mg/100 g FW	% total sterol	
Land Snails	*Helix* sp	86.6	87.2	Zhu et al. (1994),
	Haplotrema sportella	118.4	91.0	Miletic et al. (1991)
	Vespericola columbiana	116.0	86.0	
	Helix pomatia		94.8	
	Helix nemoralis		96.6	
Marine snails	*Lunatia groenlandica*	98.0	N/A 97.1	Idler and Wiseman (1971),
	Littorina littorea	56.0		Miletic et al. (1991)
	Urosalpinx cinerea	98.5		
	Buccinum undatum	94.4		
	Neptunea decemcostrata	93.5		
	Busycon canaliculatum	85.5		
	Melampus lineatus	85.1		
	Monodonta turbinata			
Clam		218.0	42.5	Kritchevsky et al. (1967),
		190.0	36.7	Lin et al. (1982)
Oyster		150.0	41.4	
		140.0	57.4	
Crab		175.0	25.7	
Scallop		N/A	34.1–68.0	Idler and Wiseman (1971)

FW = fresh weight

Rietjens et al. (2002). Vitamin E may help against the ageing process and in immune responses, and it may counteract atherosclerosis (Azzi & Stocker, 2000).

Since a large portion of unsaturated FA exists in marine snails, especially the long-chain FA and essential FA, the potential for vitamin E in marine snails to protect these FA from oxidation is higher than it is inland snails. α-tocopherol is the only tocopherol that was found in *C. sulcate,* and its content is dependent on snail size, with large snails containing significantly higher α-tocopherol levels than small snails (3.7 and 2.2 mg vitamin E/100 g FW, respectively). Whelk, periwinkle and limpet have 18, 40 and 150 μg of α-tocopherol per g fresh weight, respectively (Brjekkan et al., 1963). The flesh flour of the garden snail (*Limicolaria flammea*) had a much lower α-tocopherol content (18.12 μg/100 g) (Envin et al., 2018).

6.3 MINERALS AND POTENTIAL TOXIC COMPOUNDS IN SNAIL

6.3.1 Minerals

Minerals are the elements that are found in minute amounts in living organisms, but they can cause detrimental effects if the concentrations are higher or lower than the physiological basal concentration. Minerals are considered essential for normal growth and development of biological systems (Pais & Jones, 2000). A classification which was suggested by Feiden (1984) placed elements into various categories based on the amounts or each found in tissue rather than by assigning them a specific essential function (Table 6.11). Based on that definition, minerals can be categorized as structural elements [e.g., phosphorous (P)], essential trace elements [the most

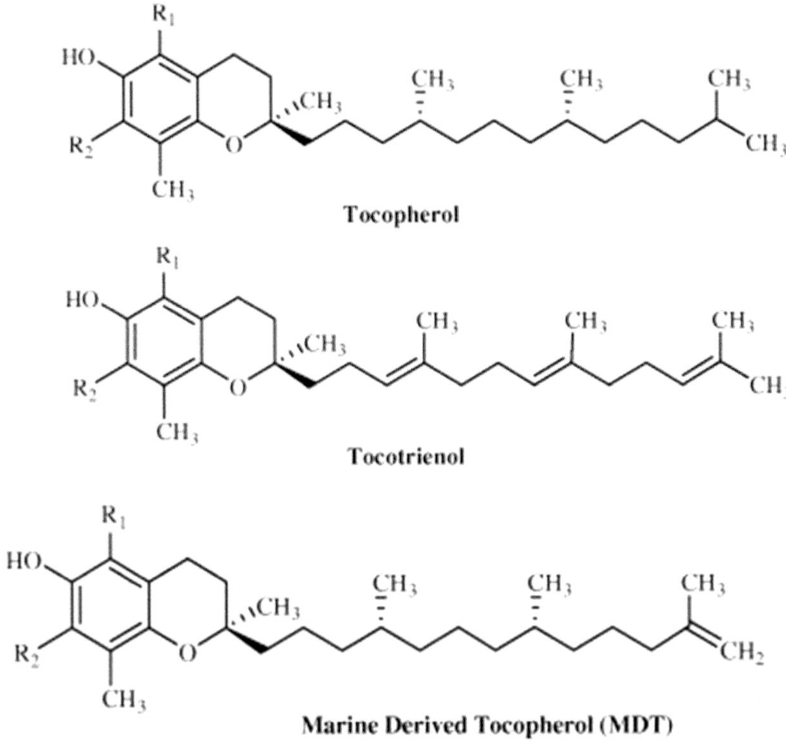

FIGURE 6.5 Vitamin E analogues (Zingg, 2007).

TABLE 6.11
Classification of Minerals (Feiden, 1984)

	Classification		Elements
Bulk structural elements			C, H, O, P, S
Essential elements	Macroelements		Ca, Cl, K, Na
	Microelements (Trace elements)		Cu, Fe, Zn
Toxic elements	Ultratrace elements	Non-metals	As, B, F, I, Se
		Metals	Cd, Cr, Co, Pb, Mn, Mo, Ni, Sn, V

important being iron (Fe), copper (Cu), and zinc (Zn)], and toxicity [e.g. lead (Pb), arsenic (As), cadmium (Cd), mercury (Hg)].

The essential elements include macro-elements and microelements, and these are required to support adequate growth, reproduction, and health throughout the life cycle, when all other nutrients are optimal (McDowell, 2003). The non-toxic elements have four broad functions: structural, physiological, catalytic, and hormonal or regulatory. The most obvious function of trace elements is to provide structural support. For example, Ca, P, Mg, F and Si contribute to mechanical stability in bones and teeth. Moreover, P and S are essential compounds in muscle proteins, which are the structural components of body tissues. Furthermore, Zn and P can also contribute to the structural stability of the molecules and membranes, which they are part of (McDowell, 2003).

Toxic elements, which are also referred to as heavy metals, have high atomic weights (Pais & Jones, 2000). Some of these are extremely toxic, and they are non-biodegradable, meaning they accumulate in the environment over time and can be absorbed by plants or animal tissues. After absorption, heavy metals tend to bind to biomolecules, such as proteins and nucleic acids, thus impairing their function (Yu, 2005). The toxic effects of heavy metals, which include growth rate depression, heavy-metal induced diseases, and compromised immune function, have been studied in detail (Ooik et al., 2008; Pattee et al., 2003; Yu, 2005). Heavy metals in aquatic systems originate from numerous sources, both natural (e.g., weathering of rocks, atmospheric deposition) and due to anthropogenic activities (e.g., storm-water runoff, industrial agricultural process and sewage discharges) (Florea & Büsselberg, 2006; Pattee et al., 2003). Aquatic organisms exposed to heavy metals suffer from decreased metabolic rates and decreased ability to siphon food, and the extent of toxic bioaccumulation of metals depends on the bioavailability of the metals to the organisms (Pattee et al., 2003; Waldichuk, 1985). However, different species of marine organisms have different rates of metal bioaccumulation, and the sites of accumulation within the organism may also differ from one species to another (Waldichuk, 1985).

Research on the trace elements of molluscs, including land snails and marine shellfishes, are summarized in Tables 6.12 and 6.13, respectively. The marine shellfish have a higher amount of both macro- and trace elements than do land snails, except for Ca. Calcium concentrations were higher (*circa* 260 mg/100 g) in land snails (varying from 22 in *Limicolaria* sp. to 726 mg/100 g in *Helix pomatia*) compared with marine shellfish (Adeyeye, 1996; Özogul et al., 2005). However, the predominant element in marine shellfish was sulphur (S) with a mean value of more than 300 mg/100 g (Vlieg et al., 1991). The concentrations of Na, K and P in land snails were within a narrow range from 100–120 mg/100 g. Similar concentrations were found in marine shellfish. In addition, the Mg content in both land snails and marine shellfish were similar, with mean values of 44 mg/100 g and 50 mg/100 g, respectively. Diet and environmental effects are very important in dictating the accumulation of minerals. The Se content in *H. pomatia* reflected their origin from Poland (low in Se) or Moldavia, Ukraine, and Russia (high in Se), and similar observations were documented for Cu and Zn in three snail species (*Helix pomatia*, *Helix aspersa* and *Arion rufus*) harvested in northern Italy (Drozd et al., 2017). Heavy metal concentrations differed among species and even within the same species of marine shellfish. Information on heavy metals in land snails is limited, as most of the interest was directed towards nutritional aspects of the snails. However, it appears that the contents are not different from those reported for other marine species (Table 6.14). Generally speaking, marine molluscs have higher Zn contents than fish and other muscle foods (Bilandzic et al., 2014). Turban snails are rich sources of S, K and Na (Ab Lah, 2017; Mason et al., 2014), and this trend was consistent across several studies of land snails (Özogual et al., 2005).

For quite some time, assessment of heavy metal contamination in aquatic environments has been based on four methods of analysis, namely the analysis of water, sediment, biological material or a combination of all three (Milne, 1998). However, all of these analyses contain weaknesses. Metal concentrations are often quite low in water, which makes quantification both difficult and expensive. Furthermore, metal concentrations in sediments can be affected by a number of factors, including sediment particle size, organic carbon content, and high spatial variability. Hence, in recent years, aquatic organisms have been used as a bio-monitor of heavy metal contamination in coastal environments (Morrisey et al., 1994; Phillips, 1977; Waldichuk, 1985). Aquatic organisms like shellfish are sedentary and cannot move from an environment that is becoming increasingly toxic from the heavy metals deposition (Kennedy, 1986; Smith & Williamson, 1986). Since *C. sulcata* is a common shellfish in New Zealand and has the advantage of being a stationary animal, we believe it can potentially be used as a bio-monitor for heavy metal contamination. Bioaccumulation of toxic metals in algivorous turbinids should be lower than in bivalves, cephalopods or carnivorous gastropods due to a natural bioaccumulation hierarchy. However, the life span of some species may be important, and the degree of variation between seasons and localities will influence the overall content of these metals.

TABLE 6.12
Essential and Toxic Element Contents of Land Snails

	Limicolaria sp.		Archachatina marginata	Archacha sp.			Helix sp.	Helix pomatia	Limicolaria sp.	Achatina fulica	Achatina achatina	Archachatina Marginata	Archachatina marginata ovum	Archachatina marginata saturalis	Limicolaria Sp.
	Udoh et al. (1995)	Adeyeye (1996)	Fagbuaro et al. (2006)	Adeyeye (1996)	Adeyeye (1996)	Fagbuaro et al. (2006)	Gomot (1998)	Özogul et al. (2005)	Babalola and Akinsoyinu (2009)				Eneji et al. (2008)		
Na	178*	54	65	196	182	53	61	N/A	91						
K	533*	73	198	44	50	210	194	N/A	82						
Ca	401*	22	209	212	189	208	205	319	726	36.2	66.3	106.3	126.4	180.7	179.1	172.8
Mg	771*	19	46	46	38	45	46	60	54	5.28	15.1	19.3	25.0	29.2	28.5	27.33*
P	636*	183	154	1	216	123	131	91	105	8.98	14.8	19.0	22.9	59.2	51.5	59.79*
S	N/A	N/A	4.0	N/A	N/A	2	3	N/A	N/A						
Fe	ND*	4.7	9.5	9.3	5	9.4	9.4	1.3	1.7	0.72	1.30	1.88	2.29	6.79	8.25	9.00
Cu	N/A	0.2	ND	0.6	0.6	ND	ND	3.2	N/A	0.29	0.58	0.77	1.03			
Zn	259.0*	1.2	1.5	1.4	1.9	1.7	1.8	1.1	1.4					1.19	1.18	1.14
Mn	N/A	0.6	0.4	0.4	0.4	0.4	0.4	N/A	0.2						
Al	N/A	N/A	N/A	N/A	N/A	N/A	N/A	N/A	N/A						
As	N/A	N/A	N/A	N/A	N/A	N/A	N/A	N/A	N/A						
Cd	N/A	ND	ND	ND	ND	ND	ND	N/A	N/A						
Co	N/A	ND	ND	ND	ND	ND	ND	N/A	N/A						
Cr	N/A	N/A	N/A	N/A	N/A	N/A	N/A	N/A	N/A						
Ni	ND*	N/A	N/A	ND	ND	ND	ND	N/A	N/A						
Pb			N/A	N/A	N/A	ND	ND	N/A	N/A						

Na, K, Ca, Mg, P, S, Fe, Cu, Zn and Mn are expressed as mg/100 g fresh weight
Al, As, Cd, Co, Cr, Ni and Pb are expressed as µg/100 g fresh weight
ND = not detected; * = mg/100 g dry weight basis; N/A = not reported

TABLE 6.13
Essential and Toxic Element Contents of Aquatic Snails

	Marine							Fresh water			
	Ab Lah (2017)			Mason et al. (2014)		Felici et al. (2020)		Ghosh et al. (2017)	Broto et al 2020	Eneji et al. (2008)	
				Cookia sulcata							
Elements	L. torquata	L. undulata	T. militaris	Small	Large	N. mutabilia	H. reticulata	Pomacea canaliculata	Pila ampullacea	Lanistes varicus	Nucella lapillus
Macroelements (mg/g FW)											
Na	3.01	2.7	4.0	4.0	4.1			0.09*	0.04*		
K	3.05	3.33	2.73	3.0	2.8	290	310	0.36*	71.13*	69.4	72.4
Ca	2.39	0.44	0.61	1.4	0.7	32	33	5.2*	129.18*	152.7	181.5
Mg	0.69	0.65	0.77	3.3	3.1	51	54	0.06*	31.19*	30.6	31.7
P	1.53	1.64	1.22	1.1	0.9			0.55*	60.52*	62.5	60.2
S	11.22	12.32	8.37	6.0	5.5						
Microelements (mg/kg FW)											
Fe	32.42	41.1	19.32	58.1	74.1	3.1	4.4	0.05*	10.9*	10.1	11.1
Zn	14.01	15.2	12.21	32.2	38.2	1.7	1.5	0.01*	1.31*	1.3	1.32
Cu	1.14	0.55	2.18	6.4	7.8			0.007*			
Mo	0.15	0.07	0.10								
Co	0.03	0.05	0.02								
Se	0.177	0.14	0.18			24	35				
Toxic elements (mg/kg FW)											
Mn	0.49	0.45	0.49	1.3	1.2			0.002*			
Al	8.73	11.12	0	14.8	15.9						
As	8.84	5.03	8.52	8.2	13.9						
Cd	0.06	0.05	0.04	0.1	0.2	0.03	0.04				
Cr	0.46	0.10	0.17	1.2	1.0	0.03	0.04				
Ni	0.05	0.06	0.14	0.02	0.05						
Pb	1.09	1.04	2.05	ND	ND	0.03	0.03				
Ag	0.15	0.17	0.04								
Hg	0.007	0.004	0.001								

* = mg/100 g dry weight basis

TABLE 6.14
Essential and Toxic Element Contents of Shellfish

	Mussel			Scallop				Oyster
Element	1	2	3	4	5	6	7	8
Na	N/A	N/A	211.0	429.0	319.0	149.0	N/A	N/A
K	328.0	N/A	320.0	236.0	315.0	348.0	N/A	N/A
Ca	88.0	N/A	11.0	134.0	43.0	31.0	N/A	N/A
Mg	44.0	N/A	41.0	58.0	55.0	50.0	N/A	N/A
P	N/A	N/A	138.0	179.0	279.0	258.0	N/A	N/A
S	N/A	N/A	324.0	310.0	N/A	N/A	N/A	N/A
Fe	10.9	7.7	0.6	4.2	14.3	9.4	1.9	5.5
Cu	1.1	0.2	1.2	9.3	0.2	0.1	0.2	7.9
Zn	4.6	3.4	1.3	1.9	1.5	2.0	2.3	84.4
Mn	0.8	0.2	16	148	0.9	4.6	0.8	0.3
Al	N/A	2.9	N/A	N/A	N/A	N/A	ND	13.4
As	N/A	29.7	297	336	N/A	N/A	8.8	9.1
Cd	2.0	0.7	41	34	N/A	N/A	2.8	ND
Co	0.2	0.1	N/A	N/A	N/A	N/A	2.3	0.2
Cr	10.0	ND	11	13	N/A	N/A	0.1	0.1
Ni	7.0	0.5	ND	ND	N/A	N/A	ND	0.5
Pb	1.0	1.1	N/A	N/A	N/A	N/A	0.3	24.9

References 1 from Karakoltsidis et al. (1995); 2, 7, 8 from Sidwell et al. (1978); 3, 4 from Vlieg et al. (1991); 5, 6 from Hughes et al. (1980)

Na, K, Ca, Mg, P, S, Fe, Cu, Zn and Mn are expressed as mg/100 g fresh weight
Al, As, Cd, Co, Cr, Ni, and Pb are expressed as µg/100 g fresh weight
NM = not determined; ND = not detected; * = on dry weight basis
1 = *Mediterranean*; 2 = *Mytilidae*; 3 = *Atrina zelandica*; 4 = *Perna canaliculu*; 5 = *Perna canaliculus*; 6 = *Pectan novaezealandiae*; 7 = *Pectinidae*; 8 = *Ostreida*

6.3.2 Organochlorine Pesticides (OCPs)

Pesticides refer to any chemicals intended to prevent, deter, destroy, or otherwise impair the ability of pests to compete with desired organisms (Yu, 2005). Depending on the target, pesticides can be classified as insecticides, herbicides, fungicides, rodenticides, algaecides, and nematodes. Organochlorine pesticides are effective against insects. DDT (2,2-bis [p-chlorophenyl]-1,1,1-trichloroethane or dichloro-diphenyl-trichloroethane), aldrin, chlordane, dieldrin, endrin, lindane (BHC), hexachlorobenzene (HCB) and heptachlor are some examples (Yu, 2005). Organochlorine pesticides, which are also called chlorinated hydrocarbons, are insecticides, and these were the first commercial organic insecticides to be developed, with DDT being the best-known example (Yu, 2005). DDT, which belongs to the family of organic halogen compounds, was prepared by the reaction of chloral with chlorobenzene in the presence of sulphuric acid, and it was first synthesized in 1874. It was initially used as an effective and cheap insecticide in 1939 for the control of disease-carrying insects, such as mosquitoes (Bearsd, 2006; Ross, 2005). During World War II, DDT was used by soldiers to control the body lice that spread typhus. Later, it was used worldwide, including in New Zealand, to combat a large number of pests, including gypsy moths, potato pests, corn earthworms, grass grubs and codlings (Yu, 2005). Organochlorine pesticides are fat-soluble and can enter the food chain through the absorption of fat and accumulation in food. For example, OCPs can enter aquatic systems a number of ways, including run-off from non-point sources, industrial discharge and sewerage wastewater and wet/dry deposition (Sarkar et al., 2008). Moreover, OCPs can be transferred globally through the atmosphere by 'chemical distillation' (Hong et al., 2008; Yang et al., 2008). This can be explained by the nature of OCPs, which are semi-volatile compounds. OCPs can evaporate and travel long distances from warmer areas to cooler regions following condensation, deposition and accumulation.

Organochlorine pesticides have been considered to be one of the most problematic chemicals due to their resistance to biodegradation, their persistence in the environment, and because they are bioaccumulated, and their adverse effects on wildlife and humans over the last few decades has been well-documented (Zhou et al., 2008). DDT can affect human health negatively. Thus, in the 1960s, DDT was limited or totally banned in industrialized countries since its environmental and hazardous impacts became evident (Zhou et al., 2008). DDT is stable to metabolic breakdown in the environment. However, it can degrade to DDE (ethyl 1,1-dichloro-2,2-bis(p-chlorophenyl) or DDD (ethane 1,1-dichloro-2,2-bis(p-chlorophenyl). Adverse impacts of DDT and its metabolites on human health include effects on the nervous system and interference with the endocrine and reproduction systems (Yu, 2005). DDT accumulation disrupts the body's normal hormonal system, and contamination is of great importance especially in pregnant women who can pass the chemicals to their infants via breast milk (WHO, 1972). Despite the global ban on DDT in the 1960s, DDT is persistent and has high lipophilicity, which means it is still present in the environment and tends to accumulate in adipose tissue of animals, including marine organisms, over long periods of time. As a result, fish and shellfish have been used as biological indicators of DDT contamination (Amaraneni & Pillala, 2001; Chen et al., 2002). It has been noted that the greatest risk of DDT was due to beach contaminated sediment near agricultural fields that had used DDT, which acted as long-term sinks for DDT and its metabolites, thus exposing marine organisms for decades (Yu, 2005). Many reports have shown that DDT and its metabolites could be directly toxic to marine organisms such as shellfish and fish at low concentrations (Kennish & Ruppel, 1998; Manirakiza et al., 2002; Solly & Harrison, 1972; Tavares et al., 1999). Mason et al. (2014) collected *C. sulcata* from a sampling area that was approximately 200 meters from a dairy farm, and they reported that maximum aldrin and dieldrin, BHC (except g-BHC), chlordane, the sum of DDT, DDE and DDD, and the sum of heptachlor, heptachlor epoxide and lindane concentrations were well below the residue limits of WHO (1972) of 0.1, 0.01, 0.05, 1.0, 0.1, 0.05, 1.0 (mg/kg), respectively. The total organochlorine concentration in *C. sulcata* was 100-fold below the maximum acceptable concentration.

6.4 HEALTH RISKS

Both land and marine snails are potential hosts of a wide range of parasites, especially those harvested from the wild. For example, the rat lungworm parasite (*Angiostrongylus cantonensis*) was found in the African giant snail (Iwanowicz et al., 2015), and the larvae of *Strongyloides stercoralis* was found at an overall prevalence of 54.04% in *Achatina achatina, Achatina fulica, Acharchatina marginata), Limicolaria aurora, L. flammea* and *Limicolariopsis* spp (Igbinosa et al. 2016). Certain snails were infected with *Alaria mesocercariae, Drocoelium dedriticum, Angiostrongylus cantonesis, Fasciola gigantica* and *Schistosoma mansoni* and thus these snails could be a possible parasite transmission pathway. A large number of studies have reported land snails (prevalence rate of 42%) as intermediate hosts for metacercariae (Gracenea & Gállego, 2017), which appear to increase with an increase in snail activity as a result of temperature, humidity, dormancy period and population density.

Allergic reactions are another major risk associated with molluscs. Several IgE binding proteins have been found in common whelk (*Buccinumun datum*), *Turbo cornutus*, *Haliotis midae* and *H. aspersa* that were resistant to heat but had moderate to substantial degradation in simulated gastric and intestinal digestion (Asturias et al., 2002; Bessot et al., 2010; Ishikawa et al., 1998; Lopata et al., 1997). Tropomyosin was found to be the allergen responsible for reactivity (Ruethers et al., 2018).

Several other health risks may arise, depending on the harvesting grounds. For example, the presence of tetramine, an odourless, tasteless, water-soluble toxin, in whelk tissue (range from 65 to 1280 µg/g tissue) was reported by Zhao et al. (1997). The presence of microplastics in *H. aperta*, *H. aspersa* and *H. pomatia* (51.8% of the samples were positive) (Panebianco et al., 2019). The occurrence of *Salmonella* spp. and *Listeria* spp. in raw and frozen (cooked) wild and farmed *Helix pomatia, Cornu aspersum aspersum* and *Cornu aspersum maxima* snail meat was investigated by Paszkiewicz et al. (2018). Salmonella was not detected in any sample (300 samples), whereas Listeria was found in 42% of the samples. Thermal treatment reduced the Listeria load, but it did not eliminate the risk.

Tetrodotoxin is a potent neurotoxin that causes paralysis in humans and animals with subsequent fatality in many instances. The toxin is believed to be produced by microorganisms and marine microalgae. The toxin is a major risk, as it is heat-stable, and cooking is believed to increase its toxicity (Boundy & Harwood, 2020). The occurrence of toxicity due to the consumption of marine snails have been reported in the following species; *Babylonia japonica, Nassarius siquijorensis, Charonia lampas, Tutufa lissostoma, Rapana rapiformis, Natica lineata, Polinices tumidus, Nassarius glans, Nassarius sinarum Nassarius variciferus, Charonia lampas lampas, Nassarius nitidus, Oliva hirasei, Oliva ornate, Oliva annulata* and *Phorcus lineatus* (Biessy et al., 2019). The major incidence occurred in China and Taiwan, as well as in Vietnam. The only snails found to contain the toxin in the Mediterranean were from Portugal, but this may be a reflection of lack of monitoring from other countries rather than localized occurrence.

6.5 HEALTH ASPECTS

Due to the high nutrition of snail meat, several studies investigated the physiological effects of consumption of snails in various forms. A study investigated the effects of crude extract of *Thais coronata* (rock snail) on haematological parameters in albino Wistar male rats (Archibong et al., 2014), and it was concluded that the use of the extract in addition (up to 52 mg protein/ kg) to a normal chow diet boosted the production of blood cells and could be a useful food supplement. The authors reported that 88.98 mg protein/kg was the LD50 for the rats.

The antibacterial activities of land snail secretion and the availability of some bioactive compounds, such as glycolic acid and allantoin, in the secretion have been known for some time (El Mubarak et al., 2013; Cilia & Fratini, 2018). Ulagesan and Kim (2018) investigated the antimicrobial activities of protein extracts of seven Indian freshwater and land snails viz *Achatina fulica* (Bowdich, 1822), *Cryptozona bistrialis* (Beck, 1837), *Pila globosa* (Swainson, 1822), *Pila virens* (Lamarck, 1822), *Bellamya dissimilis* (Mueller, 1774), *Bithynia (Digoniostoma) pulchella* (Benson, 1836), and *Melanoides tuberculata* (Muller, 1774) (Figure 6.6). A protein fraction obtained from *Cryptozona bistrialis* was capable of complete inhibition of a wide range of pathogenic bacteria (*Staphylococcus aureus, Micrococcus luteus, Pseudomonas aeruginosa, Proteus vulgaris, Serratia marcescens* and *Hafnia alvei*) and fungal (*Candida albicans, Aspergillus fumigatus, Penicillium chrysogenum* and *Mucor racemosus*). This is very promising with the emergence of antibiotic resistance bacteria. Several reports described antimicrobial activities against pathogenic strains to proteins and mucus components in *H. lucorum* (Dolashka et al., 2015), *Achatina fulica* (Alcantara Santana et al., 2012), *Hemifusus puglinus* (Sugesh et al., 2013), and *Pila virens* (Gayathri & Sanjeevi, 2014).

The production of protein hydrolysates from *Babylonia spirata* (Linnaeus, 1758) using trypsin resulted in peptides with high antimicrobial activity against *Staphylococcus aureus* and *Aspergillus fumigatus* (Kuppusamy & Ulagesan, 2016). Protein hydrolysates obtained from *H. aspersa* by Alcalase hydrolysis exhibited a comparable Angiotensin-I converting Enzyme (ACE-1; EC 3.4.15.1) inhibition activity to Captopril (standard drug) (Hayes & Mora, 2021).

FIGURE 6.6 Seven snail species investigated for their antimicrobial activities by Ulagesan and Kim (2018). (a) *Achatina fulica* (LM-550), (b) *Cryptozona bistrialis* (LM-551), (c) *Pila globose* (LM-552), (d) *Pila virens* (LM-553), (e) *Bellamya dissimilis* (LM-554), (f) *Bithynia (Digoniostoma) pulchella* (LM-555), and (g) *Melanoides tuberculate* (LM-556). The image is obtained from Ulagesan and Kim (2018) under the open access article under the terms and conditions of the Creative Commons Attribution (CC BY) license (http://creativecommons.org/licenses/by/4.0/).

Collectively, the above information supports positive aspects of snail nutrition, but as with any other food product, there needs to be implementation of health and safety controls to ensure proper food production that is fit for human consumption.

6.6 CONCLUSIONS

Snails are a very nutritious food source. They contain favourable amino acid and fatty acid profiles that are quite diverse among the various species and sources (aquatic and terrestrial). The majority of snails are sourced from the wild and this is will affect the available snail population. The decline in wild snail populations due to natural and human activities (deforestation for agricultural activities, pesticide use, competition for snails with animals/ birds, and natural disasters such as fires, floods and algae blooms) necessitates the consideration of Heliculture and marine snail aquaculture to boost production. The introduction of snails into food products may need requirement declarations since risks associated with allergenicity as well as religious restrictions from certain faiths, such as Islam and Judaism, may be induced.

ACKNOWLEDGEMENT

The authors extend their appreciation to the International Scientific Partnership Program ISPP at King Saud University for funding this research work through ISPP-16–73(2).

REFERENCES

Ab Lah, R. (2017). *Biochemical Composition of Turbinid Snails and Its Sensitivity to Ocean Climate Change*. PhD thesis, Southern Cross University, Lismore, NSW.

Ab Lah, R., Smith, J., Savins, D., Dowell, A., Bucher, D., & Benkendorff, K. (2017). Investigation of nutritional properties of three species of marine turban snails for human consumption. *Food Science & Nutrition*, 5(1), 14–30. doi: 10.1002/fsn3.360.

Abdulkadir, S., & Tsuchiya, M. (2008). One-step method for quantitative and qualitative analysis of fatty acids in marine animal samples. *Journal of Experimental Marine Biology and Ecology, 354,* 1–8.

Adeyeye, E. I. (1996). Waste yield, proximate and mineral composition of three different types of land snails found in Nigeria. *International Journal of Food Sciences and Nutrition, 47*(2), 111–116.

Adeyeye, E. I., & Afolabi, E. O. (2004). Amino acid composition of three different types of land snails consumed in Nigeria. *Food Chemistry, 85*(4), 535–539.

Alcantara Santana, W., Melo, C., Cardoso, J., Nely Pereira-Filho, R., Rabelo, A., Reis, F., & de Albuquerque, R. L. C. (2012). Assessment of antimicrobial activity and healing potential of mucous secretion of *Achatina fulica. International Journal of Morphology, 30,* 365–373.

Al-Najdawi, R., & Abdullah, B. (2002). Proximate composition, selected minerals, cholesterol content and lipid oxidation of mechanically and hand-deboned chickens from the Jordanian market. *Meat Science, 61*(3), 243–247.

Amaraneni, S. R., & Pillala, R. R. (2001). Concentrations of pesticide residues in tissues of fish from Kolleru Lake in India. *Environmental Toxicology, 16*(6), 550–556.

Ansell, A. D. (1972). Distribution, growth and seasonal changes in biochemical composition for the bivalve *Donax vittatus* (da Costa) from Kames Bay, Millport. *Journal of Experimental Marine Biology and Ecology, 10*(2), 137–150.

Ansell, A. D., & Trevallion, A. (1967). Studies on *Tellina tenuis da costa* I. Seasonal growth and biochemical cycle. *Journal of Experimental Marine Biology and Ecology, 1*(2), 220–235.

Archibong, A. N., Akwari, A. A., Ukweni, S. U., Ofem, O. E., Oka, V. O., & Eno, A. E. (2014). Edible seafood –*Thais coronata* (Rock Snail) extract boosts RBC, PCV, Hb, platelets, WBC and lymphocytes counts in rats. *Journal of Scientific Research & Reports, 3*(24) 3096–3105. doi:10.9734/JSRR/2014/12583

Asturias, J.A., Eraso, E., Arilla, M.C., Gomez-Bayon, N., Inacio, F., Martinez, A. (2002). Cloning, isolation, and IgE-binding properties of *Helix aspersa* (brown garden snail) tropomyosin. *International Archives of Allergy and Immunology, 128*(2), 90–96.

Azzi, A., & Stocker, A. (2000). Vitamin E: Non-antioxidant roles. *Progress in Lipid Research, 39*(3), 231–255.

Badiani, A., Nanni, N., Gatta, P. P., Bitossi, F., Tolomelli, B., & Manfredini, M. (1998). Nutrient content and retention in selected roasted cuts from 3-month-old ram lambs. *Food Chemistry, 61*(1–2), 89–100.

Babalola, O. O., & Akinsoyinu, A. O. (2009). Proximate composition and mineral profile of snail meat from different breeds and land snail in Nigeria.*Pakistan Journal of Nutrition,* 8, 1842–1844.

Bae, J.H., Yoon, S.H. & Lim, S.Y. (2011). A comparative of heavy metal contents and biochemical characteristics of Japanese (*Haliotis discus*) and Korean abalone (*Haliotis discus hannai*). *Food Science Biotechnology, 20*(1), 273–276.

Ball, G. F. M. (2004). *Vitamins: Their Role in the Human Body.* Oxford, UK: Blackwell Science.

Bearsd, J. (2006). DDT and human health. *Science of Total Environment, 335,* 78–89.

Belisle, B.W., & Stickle, W.B. (1978). Seasonal patterns in the biochemical constituents and body component indexes of the muricid gastropod, *Thais haemastoma. Biology Bulletin, 155,* 259–272.

Berg, J. M., Tymoczko, J. L., & Stryer, L. (2007). *Biochemistry.* Freeman Publishing Company, New York.

Bessot, J. C., Metz-Favre, C., Rame, J. M., De Blay, F., Pauli, G. 2010. Tropomyosin or not tropomyosin, what is the relevant allergen in house dust mite and snail cross allergies? *European Annals of Allergy and Clinical Immunology, 42*(1), 3–10.

Biessy, L., Boundy, M. J., Smith, K. F., Harwood, T., Ian Hawes, I., & Wood, S. A. (2019). Tetrodotoxin in marine bivalves and edible gastropods: A mini-review. *Chemosphere, 236,* 124404.

Bilandzic, N., Sedak, M., Dokic, M., Varenina, I., Kolanovoc, B. S., Bozic, D., Brstilo, M. & Simic, B. (2014). Determination of zinc concentrations in foods of animal origin, fish and shellfish from Croatia and assessment of their contribution to dietary intake. *Journal of Food Composition and Analysis, 35,* 61–66.

Blackmore, D. T. (1969). Studies of *Patella vulgata* L. II. Seasonal variation in biochemical composition. *Journal of Experimental Marine Biology and Ecology, 3*(3), 231–245.

Boundy, M. J., Harwood, D. T. (2020). Review of literature to help identify risks associated with tetrodotoxin in seafood, including bivalve molluscs. Prepared for MPI. Cawthron Report No. 2986A. https://www.mpi.govt.nz/dmsdocument/40775/direct#:~:text=TTX%20is%20heat%2Dstable%20and,cooking%20may%20increase%20its%20toxicity

Brjekkan, O. R., Lambertsen, G., & Yklestad, H. M. (1963). Alpha-tocopherol in some marine organisms and fish oils. Serie Teknologiske unders0kelser (Reports on Technological Research concerning Norwegian Fish Industry), Vol. IV No. 8, Published by the Director of Fisheries Government Vitamin Laboratory Norwegian Fisheries Research Institute Bergen, Norway.

Broto, R. T. D. W., Arifan, F., Setyati, W. A., Eldiarosa, K., & Zein, A. R. (2020). Crackers from freshwater snail (*Pila ampullacea*) waste as alternative nutritious food. *IOP Conference Series: Earth and Environmental Science, 448*, 012039. doi:10.1088/1755-1315/448/1/012039

Caballero, B., Trugo, L. C., & Finglas, P. M. (2003). *Encyclopaedia of Food Sciences and Nutrition*. Academic Press, New York.

Celik, M. Y., Culha, S. T., Culha, M., Yildiz, H., Acarli, S., Celik, I. & Celik, P. (2014). Comparative study on biochemical composition of some edible marine molluscs at Canakkale coasts, Turkey. *Indian Journal of Geo-Marine Science, 43*(4), 601–606.

Çelik, M. Y., Duman, M. B., Sariipek, M., Gören, G. U., Öztürk, D. K., Kocatepe, D., & Karayücel, S. (2020). Comparison of proximate and amino acid composition between farmed and wild land snails (*Cornu aspersum* Müller, 1774). *Journal of Aquatic Food Product Technology, 29*, 383–390, doi:10.1080/10498850.2020.1740850

Chen, W., Zhang, L., Xu, L., Wang, X., Hong, L., & Hong, H. (2002). Residue levels of HCHs, DDTs and PCBs in shellfish from coastal areas of east Xiamen Island and Minjiang Estuary, China. *Marine Pollution Bulletin, 45*(1–12), 385–390.

Cheng, Q., & Sun, D.-W. (2007). Effect of cooking bag and netting packaging on the quality of pork ham during water cooking. *Meat Science, 75*(2), 243–247.

Chotimarkorn, C., Silalai, N., & Chaitanawisuit, N. (2010). Post-mortem changes in farmed spotted Babylon Snail (*Babylonia areolata*) during iced storage. *Food Science and Technology International, 16*(3), 277–288.

Cilia, G., & Fratini, F. (2018). Antimicrobial properties of terrestrial snail and slug mucus. *Journal of Complementary and Integrative Medicine, 15*, 20170168. doi:10.1515/jcim-2017-0168

Claeys, E., & Demeyer, D. (1986). Nutritional quality of snails (*Helix aspersa*). Paper presented at the 32nd European Meeting of Meat Research Workers, Ghent, Belgium.

Combs, G. F. (2008). *Vitamins: Their Role in the Human Body*. Blackwell Science, Oxford, UK.

Cook, P. A. (2019). Worldwide Abalone production statistics. *Journal of Shellfish Research, 38*(2), 401–404. doi:10.2983/035.038.0222

Copper, J. E., & Knower, C. (1991). Snails and snail farming: An introduction for the veterinary profession. *Veterinary Record, 129*(21/28), 541–549.

Crosland, A. R., Patterson, R. L. S., Higman, R. C., Stewart, C. A., & Hargin, K. D. (1995). Investigation of methods to detect mechanically recovered meat in meat products – I: Chemical composition. *Meat Science, 40*(3), 289–302.

Crowe, A. (1999). *Which Seashell?: A Simple Guide to the Identification of New Zealand Seashells*. Penguin, Auckland, NZ.

Daguzan, J. (1983). Study of the nitrogen content and amino-acids composition of the tissues of some trochidae of the Brittany coast (Prosobranch Gastropod Molluscs). *Comparative Biochemistry and Physiology. Part A: Comparative Physiology, 74*(2), 323–325.

Diarra, S. S. (2015). Utilisation of snail meal as a protein supplement in poultry diets. *World's Poultry Science Journal, 71*, 547–554. doi:10.1017/S0043933915002159

Dolashka, P., Dolashki, A., Voelter, W., Van Beeumen, J., & Stevanovic, S. (2015). Antimicrobial activity of peptides from the hemolymph of *Helix lucorum* snails. *International Journal of Current Microbiology and Applied Sciences, 4*, 1061–1071.

Dridi, S., Romdhane, M. S., & M'hamed Elcafsi, M. (2007). Seasonal variation in weight and biochemical composition of the Pacific oyster, *Crassostrea gigas* in relation to the gametogenic cycle and environmental conditions of the Bizert lagoon, Tunisia. *Aquaculture, 263*, 238–248.

Drozd, L., Ziomek, M., Szkucik, K., Paszkiewicz, W., Maćkowiak-Dryka, M., Bełkot, Z., & Gondek, M. (2017). Selenium, copper, and zinc concentrations in the raw and processed meat of edible land snails harvested in Poland. *Journal of Veterinary Research, 61*(3), 293–298. doi:10.1515/jvetres-2017-0039

El Mubarak, M.A.S., Lamari, F.N., & Kontoyannis, C. (2013). Simultaneous determination of allantoin and glycolic acid in snail mucus and cosmetic creams with high performance liquid chromatography and ultraviolet detection. *Journal of Chromatography A, 1322*, 49–53.

Eneji, C. A., Ogogo, A. U., Emmanuel-Ikpeme, C. A., & Okon, O. E. (2008). Nutritional assessment of some Nigerian land and water snail species. *Ethiopian Journal of Environmental Studies and Management, 1*, 56–60.

Envin, A. J. B., Ekissi, G. S. E., Sea, B. T., & Kouame, P. L. (2018). Biochemical and nutritional composition of garden snail (*Limicolaria flammea*) flesh consumed in Côte d'Ivoire. *Journal of Basic and Applied Research, 4*(4), 63–70.

Evans, H. M., & Bishop, K. S. (1922). On the existence of a hitherto unrecognized dietary factor essential for reproduction. *Science, 56*, 650–651.

Fagbuaro, O., Oso, J. A., Edward, J. B., & Ogunleye, R. F. (2006). Nutritional status of four species of giant land snails in Nigeria. *Journal of Zhejiang University Science B, 7*(9), 686–689.

FAO/WHO/UNU. (1981). *Energy and Protein Requirement. Report of a Joint FAO/WHO/UNU Expert Consultation. Technicial Report Series No. 724.* World Health Organization, Geneva.

Feiden, E. (1984). *Biochemistry of the Essential Ultratrace Elements.* Plenum, New York.

Felici, A., Bilandžić, N., Magi, G. E., Iaffaldano, N., Fiordelmondo, E., Doti, G., & Roncarati, A. (2020). Evaluation of long sea snail *Hinia reticulata* (Gastropod) from the Middle Adriatic sea as a possible alternative for human consumption. *Foods, 9*, 905. doi:10.3390/foods9070905

Florea, A. M., & Büsselberg, D. (2006). Occurrence, use and potential toxic effects of metals and metal compounds. *Biometals, 19*(4), 419–427.

Foster, G. G., & Hodgson, A. N. (1998). Consumption and apparent dry matter digestibility of six intertidal macroalgae by *Turbo sarmaticus* (Mollusca: Vetigastropoda: Turbinidae). *Aquaculture, 167*(3–4), 211–227.

Gayathri, M., & Sanjeevi, S. B. (2014). Antipathogenic activity of freshwater Gastropod *Pila virens* (Lamarck, 1822) from Lower Grand Anaicut Reservoir, Tamilnadu. *International Journal of Pharmaceutical and Life Sciences, 5*, 3894–3898.

Ghosh, S., Jung, C., & Meyer-Rochow, V. B. (2017). Snail as mini-livestock: Nutritional potential of farmed *Pomacea canaliculata* (Ampullariidae). *Agriculture and Natural Resources, 51*, 504–511.

Gibson, J., West, J., & Diprose, B. (1993). *Composition of New Zealand Foods*, 4. New Zealand Institute for Crop & Food Research and Poultry Industry Association of New Zealand, Poultry Palmerston North and Auckland, New Zealand.

Göçer, M., & Olgunoğlu, I. A. (2018). Comparison of fatty acid profile of edible tissues of wild terrestrial snail (*Helix lucorum* L. 1758) collected in two province (Adana and Sinop). *Turkish Journal of Agriculture - Food Science and Technology, 6*(7), 877–880.

Gomot, A. (1998). Biochemical composition of *Helix* snails: Influence of genetic and physiological factors. *Journal of Molluscan Studies, 64*(2), 173–181.

Gould, A. L., Davies, G. M., Alemao, E., Yin, D. D., & Cook, J. R. (2007). Cholesterol reduction yields clinical benefits: Meta-analysis including recent trials. *Clinical Therapeutics, 29*(5), 778–794.

Gracenea, M., & Laia Gállego, L. (2017). Brachyaimiasis: Brachylaima spp. (Digenea: Bracchylaimidae) Metacerariae parasitizing the edible snail *Cornu aspersum* (Heicidae) in Spanish public marketplaces and health-associated risk factors. *Journal of Parasitology, 103*, 440–450.

Guardiola, F., Dutta, P. C., Codony, R., & Savage, G. P. (2002). *Cholesterol and Phytosterol Oxidation Products: Analysis, Occurrence, and Biological Effects.* AOCS Press, Rockville, MD, USA.

Hames, B. D., & Hooper, N. M. (2000). *Biochemistry*, 2nd Edition. Garland Science, Oxon, UK.

Hamzat, R. A., Jaiyeola, C. O., & Longe, O. G. (2002). Nutritional qualities of snails (*Archachatina marginata*) fed solely with fresh kola testa. *Nutrition and Food Science, 32*(4), 134–136.

Harvey, D. (1970). *Tables of the Amino Acids in Foods and Feeding Stuffs*, 2nd Edition. Commonwealth Agricultural Bureaux, Farnum Royal, Bucks, England.

Hayes, M., & Mora, L. (2021). Alternative proteins as a source of bioactive peptides: The edible snail and generation of hydrolysates containing peptides with bioactive potential for use as functional foods. *Foods, 10*, 276. doi:10.3390/foods10020276

Hong, S. H., Yim, U. H., Shim, W. J., Oh, J. R., Viet, P. H., & Park, P. S. (2008). Persistent organochlorine residues in estuarine and marine sediments from Ha Long Bay, Hai Phong Bay, and Ba Lat Estuary, Vietnam. *Chemosphere, 72*, 1193–1202.

Hughes, J. T., Czochanska, Z., Pickston, L., & Hove, E. L. (1980). The nutritional composition of some New Zealand marine fish and shellfish. *New Zealand Journal of Science, 23*, 43–51.

Hultman, K., Alexanderson, G., Manneras, L., Sandberg, M., Holmang, A., & Jansson, T. (2007). Maternal taurine supplementation in the late pregnant rat stimulates postnatal growth and induces obesity and insulin resistance in adult offspring. *Journal of Physiology, 579*(3), 822–833.

Idler, D. R., & Wiseman, P. (1971). Sterols of molluscs. *International Journal of Biochemistry, 2*(11), 516–528.

Igbinosa, I. B., Isaac, C., Adamu, H. O., &, Adeleke, G. (2016). Parasites of edible land snails in Edo State, Nigeria. *Helminthologia, 53*, 331–335.

Ishikawa, M., Ishida, M., Shimakura, K., Nagashima, Y., & Shiomi, K. (1998). Purification and IgE-binding epitopes of a major allergen in the gastropod *Turbo cornutus*. *Bioscience, Biotechnology, and Biochemistry, 62*(7), 1337–1343.

Iwanowicz, D. D., Sanders, L. R., Schill, W. B., Xayavong, M. V., J. da Silva, A., Qvarnstrom, Y., & Smith, T . (2015). Spread of the rat lungworm (Angiostrongylus cantonensis) in giant African land snails (Lissachatina fulica) in Florida, USA. *Journal of Wildlife Diseases*, 51(3), 749–753.

Karakoltsidis, P. A., Zotos, A., & Constantinides, S. M. (1995). Composition of the commercially important Mediterranean finfish, crustaceans, and molluscs. *Journal of Food Composition and Analysis*, 8(3), 258–273.

Katvi, S. R. (2005). *Investigating the Lipid Profiles of Common New Zealand Seafood*. Masters thesis, The University of Auckland, Auckland, New Zealand.

Kennedy, P. C. (1986). The use of molluscs for monitoring trace elements in the marine environment in New Zealand 1. The contribution of ingested sediment to the trace element concentrations in New Zealand molluscs. *New Zealand Journal of Marine and Freshwater Research*, 20, 627–640.

Kennish, M. J., & Ruppel, B. E. (1998). Organochlorine contamination in selected estuarine and coastal marine finfish and shellfish of New Jersey. *Water, Air and Soil pollution*, 101, 123–136.

King, F. H., & Bruce, J. P. (1949). *Farmers of Forty Centuries or Permanent Agriculture in China, Korea and Japan*. Cape Publishing Ltd, London, UK.

Kosulwat, S., Greenfield, H., & James, J. (2003). Lipid composition of Australian retail lamb cuts with differing carcass classification characteristics. *Meat Science*, 65(4), 1413–1420.

Kowalczyk-Pecka, D., Kowalczuk-Vasilev, E., & Peck, S. (2017). The effect of heterogeneous copper micro-supplementation on fatty acid profiles in the tissues of snails *Helix pomatia* (*Gastropoda Pulmonata*). *Ecological Indicators*, 76, 335–343.

Kritchevsky, D., Tepper, S. A., Ditullo, N. W., & Holmes, W. L. (1967). The sterols of seafood. *Journal of Food Science*, 32, 64–66.

Kuppusamy, A., & Ulagesan, S. (2016). Antimicrobial activity of protein hydrolysate from marine molluscs *Babylonia spirata* (Linnaeus, 1758). *Journal of Applied Pharmaceutical Science*, 6(07), 073–077. http://www.japsonline.com; doi:10.7324/JAPS.2016.60711

Law, M. R., Wald, N. J., & Rudnicka, A. R. (2003). Quantifying effect of statins on low density lipoprotein cholesterol, ischaemic heart disease, and stroke: systematic review and meta-analysis. *British Medical Journal*, 326, 1423–1429.

Lee, J. H., Kannan, G., Eega, K. R., Kouakou, B., & Getz, W. R. (2008). Nutritional and quality characteristics of meat from goats and lambs finished under identical dietary regime. *Small Ruminant Research*, 74(1–3), 255–259.

Lin, D. S., Ilias, A. M., Connor, W. E., Caldwell, R. S., Cory, H. T., & Daves, G. D. (1982). Composition and biosynthesis of sterols in selected marine phytoplankton. *Lipids*, 17(11), 818–824.

Lopata, A. L., Zinn, C., Potter, P. C. 1997. Characteristics of hypersensitivity reactions and identification of a unique 49 kd IgE-binding protein (Hal-m-1) in abalone (*Haliotis midae*). *Journal of Allergy and Clinical Immunology*, 100(5), 642–648.

Manirakiza, P., Covaci, A., Nizigiymana, L., Ntakimazi, G., & Schepens, P. (2002). Persistent chlorinated pesticides and polychlorinated biphenyls in selected fish species from Lake Tanganyika, Burundi, Africa. *Environmental Pollution*, 117(3), 447–455.

Marget, M. S., Santhiya, M., Mary, M. T. & Jansi, M. (2013). Comparative study on the biochemical compositions of four gastropods along the Kanyakumari Coast. *World Journal of Fish and Marine Sciences*, 5(6), 637–640.

Markwell, P. J., Mrcvs, B., & Earle, K. E. (1995). Taurine: An essential nutrient for the cat. A brief review of the biochemistry of its requirement and the clinical consequences of deficiency. *Nutrition Research*, 15(1), 53–58.

Mason, S. L., Shi, J., Bekhit, A. E. D., & Gooneratne, R. (2014). Nutritional and toxicological studies of New Zealand *Cookia sulcata*. *Journal of Food Composition and Analysis*, 36, 79–84.

McDowell, L. R. (2003). *Minerals in Animal and Human Nutrition*, 2nd edition. Elsevier Science, Gainesville, FL.

McLachlan, A., & Lombard, H. W. (1980). Seasonal variations in energy and biochemical components of an edible gastropod, *Turbo sarmaticus* (Turbinidae). *Aquaculture*, 19(2), 117–125.

Mead, A. R., & Kemmerer, A. R. (1953). Amino acid content of dehydrated giant African snails (*Achatina fulica* Bowdich). *Science*, 117, 138–139.

Miletic, I., Miric, M., Lalic, Z., & Sobajic, S. (1991). Composition of lipids and proteins of several species of molluscs, marine and terrestrial, from the Adriatic Sea and Serbia. *Food Chemistry*, 41(3), 303–308.

Milinsk, M. C., das Gracas Padre, R., Hayashi, C., de Souza, N. E., & Matsushita, M. (2003). Influence of diets enriched with different vegetable oils on the fatty acid profiles of snail *Helix aspersa maxima*. *Food Chemistry*, 82(4), 553–558.

Milinsk, M. C., Padre, R. D. G., Hayashi, C., de Oliveira, C. C., Visentainer, J. V., de Souza, N. E., & Matsushita, M. (2006a). Effects of diets enriched with different vegetable oils on the fatty acids profiles of snail *Helix aspersa maxima*. *Food Chemistry*, *82*, 553–558.

Milinsk, M. C., Padre, R. D. G., Hayashi, C., de Oliveira, C. C., Visentainer, J. V., de Souza, N. E., & Matsushita, M. (2006b). Effects of feed protein and lipid contents on fatty acid profile of snail (*Helix aspersa maxima*) meat. *Journal of Food Composition and Analysis*, *19*(2–3), 212–216.

Mills, S. C., Windsor, A. C., & Knight, S. C. (2005). The potential interactions between polyunsaturated fatty acids and colonic inflammatory processes. *Clinical & Experimental Immunology*, *142*(2), 216–228.

Milne, J. R. (1998). *Shellfish as Biomonitors of Heavy Metal Contamination: Programme Design Considerations.* Unpublished. A thesis submitted in partial fulfilment of the requirements for the degree of Master of Applied Science in Resource Management at Lincoln University. Lincoln University, Christchurch, NZ.

Minson, J. E. (1972). *Polychaetes from the Shell of Cookia sulcata (Gmelin) at Kaikoura.* Honours Project. University of Canterbury, Christchurch, NZ.

Morley, M. S. (2004). *A Photographic Guide to Seashells of New Zealand.* New Holland Publishers Ltd, Auckland, NZ.

Morrisey, D. J., Stark, J. S., Howitt, L., & Underwood, A. J. (1994). Spatial variation in concentrations of heavy metals in marine sediments. *Marine and Freshwater Research*, *45*(2), 177–184.

Morton, J. E., Miller, M., & Slinn, D. J. (1968). *The New Zealand Seashore.* Collins Publishing Company, London, UK.

Mozaffarian, D., Psaty, B. M., Rimm, E. B., Lemaitre, R. N., Burke, G. L. L. M. F., Lefkowitz, D., & Siscovick, D. S. (2004). Fish intake and risk of incident atrial fibrillation. *Circulation*, *110*(4), 368–373.

MRC/BHF. (2003). Heart Protection Study of cholesterol-lowering with simvastatin in 5963 people with diabetes: a randomised placebo-controlled trial. *Lancet*, *361*(9374), 2005–2016.

Najmudeen, T.M. (2007). Variation in biochemical composition during gonad maturation of the tropical abalone *Haliotis varia* Linnaeus 1758 (Vetigastropoda: Haliotidae). *Marine Biology Research*, *3*, 454–461.

Nollet, L. M. L. (2004). *Handbook of Food Analysis*, 2nd Edition. Marcel Dekker, New York.

NSW (2015). Assessment of the NSW Sea Urchin and Turban Shell Fishery - Prepared for the Department of the Environment for the purpose of assessment under Part 13 and 13(A) of the Environment Protection and Biodiversity Conservation Act 1999. Published by the NSW Department of Primary Industries. https://www.environment.gov.au/system/files/pages/910b7922-a02d-4a43-a35b-9d0f0690069/files/assessment-sea-urban-turban-shell-2015.pdf

Ooik, T. V., Pausio, S., & Rantala, M. J. (2008). Direct effects of heavy metal pollution on the immune function of a geometrid moth, *Epirrita autumnata*. *Chemosphere*, *71*(10), 1840–1844.

Orakzai, S. H., Nasir, K., Blaha, M., Blumenthal, R. S., & Raggi, P. (2009). Non-HDL cholesterol is strongly associated with coronary artery calcification in asymptomatic individuals. *Atherosclerosis*, *202*(1), 289–295. doi:10.1016/j.atherosclerosis.2008.03.014

Orban, E., Di Lena, G., Nevigato, T., Casini, I., Marzetti, A., & Caproni, R. (2002). Seasonal changes in meat content, condition index and chemical composition of mussels (*Mytilus galloprovincialis*) cultured in two different Italian sites. *Food Chemistry*, *77*(1), 57–65.

Özogul, Y., Özogul, F., & Olgunogl, A. I. (2005). Fatty acid profile and mineral content of the wild snail (*Helix pomatia*) from the region of the south of Turkey. *European Food Research and Technology*, *221*, 547–549.

Pais, I., & Jones, J. B. (2000). *The Handbook of Trace Element.* St. Lucie Press, Boca Raton, FL.

Paleari, M. A., Moretti, V. M., Beretta, G., & Caprino, F. (2008). Chemical parameters, fatty acids and volatile compounds of salted and ripened goat thigh. *Small Ruminant Research*, *74*(1–3), 140–148.

Panebianco, A., Nalbone, L., Giarratana, F., & Ziino, G. (2019). First discoveries of microplastics in terrestrial snails. *Food Control*, *106*, 106722.

Paszkiewicz, W., Szkucik, K., Ziomek, M., Gondek, M., & Pyz-Łukasik, R. (2018). Occurrence of *Salmonella* spp. and *Listeria* spp. in snail meat. *Medycyna Weterynaryjna*, *74*, 110–113. doi:10.21521/mw.6074

Pattee, O. H., Fellows, V. L., & Bounds, D. L. (2003). Animal species endangerment: The role of environmental pollution. In: *Handbook of Ecotoxicology*, 2nd Edition. Hoffman, D. J., Rattner, B. A., Burton, G. A., & Cairns, J. (Eds). Washington, DC: Lewis Publishers.

Pazos, A. J., Román, G., Acosta, C. P., Sánchez, J. L., & Abad, M. (1997). Lipid classes and fatty acid composition in the female gonad of *Pecten maximus* in relation to reproductive cycle and environmental variables. *Comparative Biochemistry and Physiology Part B: Biochemistry and Molecular Biology*, *117*, 393–402.

Pearson, A. M., & Dutson, T. R. (1990). *Meat and Health*. Elsevier Applied Science, New York.

Penniket, J. R. (1982). *Common Seashells*. Reed Publishing Ltd, Wellington, NZ.

Periyasamy, N., Srinivasan, M., Devanathan, K., & Balakrishan, S. (2011). Nutritional value of gastropod *Babylonia spirata* (Linnaeus, 1758) from Thazhanguda, Southeast coast of India. *Asian Pacific Journal of Tropical Biomedicine*, *12*, 249–252.

Phillips, D. J. H. (1977). The use of biological indicator organisms to monitor trace metal pollution in marine and estuarine environments: A review. *Environmental Pollution*, *13*(4), 281–317.

Pirini, M., Manuzzi, M. P., Pagliarani, A., Trombetti, F., Anna Rosa Borgatti, A. R., & Ventrella, V. (2007). Changes in fatty acid composition of *Mytilus galloprovincialis* (Lmk) fed on microalgal and wheat germ diets. *Comparative Biochemistry and Physiology Part B: Biochemistry and Molecular Biology*, *147*, 616–626. doi:10.1016/j.cbpb.2007.04.003

Powell, A. W. B. (1979). *New Zealand Mollusca: Marine, Land, and Freshwater Shells*. Collins, Auckland, NZ.

Qun, F. Z., Gui, B. J., Zhong, Y. L., Li, L. N., Chun, G. Y., & Yong, W. N. (2004). Survey of butyltin compounds in 12 types of foods collected in China. *Food Additives and Contaminants*, *21*(12), 1162–1167.

Ramesh, R., & Ravichandran, S. (2008). Seasonal variation on the proximate composition of *Turbo brunneus*. *International Journal of Zoological Research*, *4*(1), 28–34.

Redmond, H. P., Frcsi, M., Stapleton, P. P., & Neary, P. P. (1998). Immunonutrition: Role of taurine. *Journal of Nutrition*, *14*, 599–604.

Rietjens, I. M. C. M., Boersma, M. G., Haan, L. D., Spenkelink, B., Awad, H. M., Cnubben, N. H. P., van Zanden, J. J., Woude, H. V. D., Alink, G. M., & Koeman, J. H. (2002). The pro-oxidant chemistry of the natural antioxidants vitamin C, vitamin E, carotenoids and flavonoids. *Environmental Toxicology and Pharmacology*, *11*(3-4), 321–333.

Rose, D. P., & Connolly, J. M. (1999). Omega-3 fatty acids as cancer chemopreventive agents. *Pharmacology & Therapeutics*, *83*(3), 217–244.

Ross, G. (2005). Risk and benefits of DDT. *Lancet*, *366*, 771–1772.

Ruethers, T., Taki, A. C., Elecia B., Johnston, E. B., Nugraha, R., Lea, T. T. K., Kali, T., McLean, T. R., Kamath, S. D., Lopata, A. L. (2018). Seafood allergy: A comprehensive review of fish and shellfish allergens. *Molecular Immunology*, *100*, 28–57.

Ruxton, C. H. S., Calder, P. C., Reed, S. C., & Simpson, M. J. A. (2005). The impact of long-chain n-3 polyunsaturated fatty acids on human health. *Nutrition Research Reviews*, *18*(1), 113–129.

Sarkar, S. K., Bhattacharya, B. D., Bhattacharya, A., Chatterjee, M., Alam, A., Satpathy, K. K., & Jonathan, M. P. (2008). Occurrence, distribution and possible sources of organochlorine pesticide residues in tropical coastal environment of India: An overview. *Environment International*, *34*, 1062–1071.

Seggern, D. D. V., Calkins, C. R., Johnson, D. D., Brickler, J. E., & Gwartney, B. L. (2005). Muscle profiling: Characterizing the muscles of the beef chuck and round. *Meat Science*, *71*(1), 39–51.

Sekar, V., Ravi, V., Rajsekaran, A. D. R., & Elaiyaraja, C. (2012). Nutritive profiles in different size groups and body parts of common whelk *Hemifuses pugilinus* (Born, 1778) from Pazhayar, Southeast Coast of India. *Journal of Animal and Feed Research*, *2*(2), 189–196.

Sever, P. S., Dahlof, B., Poulter, N. R., Wedel, H., Beevers, G., Caulfield, M., Collins, R., Kjeldsen, S. E., Kristinsson, A., McInnes, G. T., Mehlsen, J., Nieminen, M., O'Brien, E., & Ostergren, J. (2003). Prevention of coronary and stroke events with atorvastatin in hypertensive patients who have average or lower-than-average cholesterol concentrations, in the Anglo-Scandinavian Cardiac Outcomes Trial–Lipid Lowering Arm (ASCOT-LLA): A multicentre randomised controlled trial. *Lancet*, *361*(9364), 1149–1158.

Shanmugam, A., Bhuvanewari, T., Arumugam, M., Nazeer, R. A., & Sambasivam, S. (2006). Tissue chemistry of *Babylonia spirata* (Linnaeus). *Indian Journal of Fisheries*, *53*(1), 33–39.

Sidwell, V. D., Loomis, A. L., Lommis, K. J., Foncannon, P. R., & Buzzell, D. H. (1978). Composition of the edible portion of raw (fresh or frozen) crustaceans, finfish, and mollusks. 3 Microelements. *Marine Fisheries Review*, *40*(9), 1–20.

Silina, A. V., & Zhukova, N. V. (2007). Growth variability and feeding of scallop *Patinopecten yessoensis* on different bottom sediments: Evidence from fatty acid analysis. *Journal of Experimental Marine Biology and Ecology*, *348*(1), 46–59.

Simopoulos, A. P. (1991). Omega-3 fatty acids in health and disease and in growth and development. *American Journal of Clinical Nutrition*, *54*(3), 438–463.

Simopoulos, A. P. (1999). Essential fatty acids in health and chronic disease. *American Society for Clinical Nutrition*, *70*(3), 560s–569s.

Smith, D. G., & Williamson, R. B. (1986). *Heavy Metals in the New Zealand Aquatic Environment: A Review*. Ministry of Works and Development, Wellington, New Zealand.

Solly, S. R. B., & Harrison, D. L. (1972). DDT in some New Zealand marine and freshwater fauna. *New Zealand Journal of Marine and Freshwater Research*, 6(4), 456–462.

Sugesh, S., Mayavu, P., Ezhilarasan, P., Sivashankar, P., & Arivuselvan, N. (2013). Screening of antibacterial activities of marine gastropod *Hemifusus Pugilinus*. *Current Research Journal of Biological Sciences*, 5, 49–52.

Sure, B. (1924). Dietary requirement for reproduction. II. The existence of a specific vitamin for reproduction. *Journal of Biological Chemistry*, 58, 693–709.

Szkucik, K., Ziomek, M., Paszkiewicz, W., Drozd, L., Gondek, M., & Knysz, P. (2018). Fatty acid profile in fat obtained from edible part of land snails harvested in Poland. *Journal of Veterinary Research*, 62, 519–526. doi:10.2478/jvetres-2018-0074

Tavares, T. M., Beretta, M., & Costa, M. C. (1999). Ratio of DDT/DDE in the all Saints bay, Brazil and its use in environmental management. *Chemosphere*, 38(6), 1445–1452.

Taylor, A. G., & Savage, C. (2006). Fatty acid composition of New Zealand green-lipped mussels, *Perna canaliculus*: Implications for harvesting for n-3 extracts. *Aquaculture*, 261, 430–439.

Toshiro, F. M. D., Katsutuki, A. M. D., Hiroshi, N. M. D., & Yasushi, I. (1987). Effects of increased adrenomedullary activity and taurine in young patients with borderline hypertension. *Circulations*, 75(3), 1987–1989.

Udoh, A. P., Akpanyung, E. O., & Igiran, I. E. (1995). Nutrients and anti-nutrients in small snails (*Limicolaria aurora*). *Food Chemistry*, 53(3), 239–241.

Ulagesan, S., & Kim, H.-J. (2018). Antibacterial and antifungal activities of proteins extracted from seven different snails. *Applied Science*, 8, 1362. doi:10.3390/app8081362

Vasconcelos, P., Gasper, M. B., Castro, M. & Nunes, M. L. (2009). Influence of growth and reproductive cycle on the meat yield and proximate composition of *Hexaplex trunculus* (Gastropoda: Muricidae). *Journal of Marine Biological Association of the United Kingdom*, 89(6), 1223–1231.

Ventrella, V., Pirini, M., Pagliarani, A., Trombetti, F., Manuzzi, M. P., & Anna Rosa Borgatti, A. R. (2008). Effect of temporal and geographical factors on fatty acid composition of *M. galloprovincialis* from the Adriatic sea. *Comparative Biochemistry & Physiology, Part B. Biochemistry and Molecular Biology*, 149(2), 241–250. doi:10.1016/j.cbpb.2007.09.012

Vermeij, G. J., & Williams, S. T. (2007). Predation and the geography of opercular thickness in turbinid gastropods. *Journal of Molluscan Studies*, 73(1), 67–73.

Vlieg, P. (1988). *Proximate Composition of New Zealand Marine Finfish and Shellfish*. Biotechnology Division, Department of Scientific and Industrial Research, Palmerston North, NZ.

Vlieg, P., & Body, D. R. (1988) Lipid contents and fatty acid composition of some New Zealand freshwater finfish and marine finfish, shellfish, and roes. *New Zealand Journal of Marine and Freshwater Research*, 22, 151–162. doi: 10.1080/00288330.1988.9516287

Vlieg, P., Lee, J., & Grace, N. D. (1991). Elemental concentration of marine and freshwater finfish, and shellfish from New Zealand waters. *Journal of Food Composition and Analysis*, 4(2), 136–147.

Wakil, S. J. (1970). *Lipid Metabolism*. Academic Press, New York.

Waldichuk, M. (1985). Biological availability of metals to marine organisms. *Marine Pollution Bulletin*, 16(1), 7–11.

Watt, B. K., & Merrill, A. L. (1975). Composition of Foods. Agriculture Handbook 8. Department of Agriculture, Washington, DC.

Whitney, E., & Rolfes, S. R. (2005). *Understanding Nutrition*. Wadsworth, Belmont.

WHO. (1972). *Health Hazards of the Human Environment*. World Health Organization, Rome.

WHO. (1990). *Diet, Nutrition and the Prevention of Chronic Diseases*. Technical Report Series, 797, Geneva.

Wiesre, W., & Schuster, M. (1975). The relationship between water content, activity and free amino acids in *Helix pomana* L. *Journal of Comparative Physiology*, 98, 169–181.

Woodcock, S.H. & Benkendorff, K. (2008). The impact of diet on the growth and proximate composition of juvenile whelks, *Dicathais orbita* (Gastropoda: Mollusca). *Aquaculture*, 276(1–4), 162–170.

Wright, C. E., Tallan, H. H., & Lin, Y. Y. (1986). Taurine: Biological update. *Annual Review of Biochemistry*, 55, 427–453.

Xia, S. H., Wang, Z., & Xu, S. Y. (2007). Characteristics of *Bellamya purificata* snail foot protein and enzymatic hydrolysates. *Food Chemistry*, 101(3), 1188–1196.

Yang, R., Yao, T., Xu, B., Jiang, G., & Zheng, X. (2008). Distribution of organochlorine pesticides (OCPs) in conifer needles in the southeast Tibetan Plateau. *Environmental Pollution*, 153(1), 92–100.

Yearsley, G. K., Last, P. R. & Ward, R.D. (1999). *Australian Seafood Handbook: An Identification Guide to Domestic Species*. CSIRO Division of Marine Research, Hobart. http://hdl.handle.net/102.100.100/214252?index=1

Yu, M. H. (2005). *Environmental Toxicology: Biological and Health Effects of Pollutants*, 2nd Edition. CRC Press, Boca Raton, FL.

Zhao, J.-Y., Thibaut, P., Tazawa, T., & Quilliam, M. A. (1997). Analysis of tetramine in sea snails by capillary electrophoresis-tandem mass spectrometry. *Journal of Chromatography A*, *781*, 555–564.

Zhou, R., Zhu, L., & Kong, Q. (2008). Levels and distribution of organochlorine pesticides in shellfish from Qiantang River, China. *Journal of Hazardous Materials*, *152*(3), 1192–1200.

Zhu, N., Dai, X. N., Lin, D. S., & Connor, W. E. (1994). The lipids of slugs and snails: evolution, diet and biosynthesis. *Lipids*, *29*(2), 869–875.

Zingg, J.-M. (2007). Vitamin E: An overview of major research directions. *Molecular Aspects of Medicine*, *28*(5-6), 400–422.

Zlatanos, S., Laskaridis, K. & Sagredos, A. (2009). Determination of proximate composition, fatty acid content and amino acid profile of five lesser-common sea organisms from the Mediterranean Sea. *International Journal of Food Science and Technology*, *44*, 1590–1594.

7 Keratin as an Alternative Protein in Food and Nutrition

Thirawat Tantamacharik[1], Alan Carne[2], Amin Shavandi[3], and Alaa El-Din Ahmed Bekhit[1]

[1]Department of Food Science, University of Otago, Dunedin, New Zealand
[2]Department of Biochemistry, University of Otago, Dunedin, New Zealand
[3]BTL, École interfacultaire de Bioingénieurs, Université Libre de Bruxelles, 1050 Brussels, Belgium

CONTENTS

7.1	Introduction	174
7.2	Structure and Chemical Composition of Keratins	176
7.3	Keratin Amino Acid Composition	178
7.4	Methods for Keratin Extraction and Degradation	179
	7.4.1 Alkaline Hydrolysis Methods	181
	7.4.2 Oxidation Methods	183
	7.4.3 Reduction Methods	183
	7.4.4 Sulphitolysis Methods	184
	7.4.5 Ionic Liquid Dissolution Methods	185
	7.4.6 Steam Flash Explosion Methods	187
	7.4.7 Microwave-Assisted Methods	188
7.5	Microbial and Enzymatic Methods for the Degradation and Hydrolysis of Keratins	188
	7.5.1 Keratinolytic Microorganisms	189
	7.5.1.1 Keratinolytic Fungi	193
	7.5.1.2 Keratinolytic Bacteria	193
	7.5.1.3 Keratinolytic Actinomycetes	193
	7.5.2 Keratinases	193
	7.5.2.1 Catalytic Mechanisms of Keratinases	194
	7.5.3 Production of Keratinases by Keratinolytic Microorganisms	195
	7.5.4 Applications of Keratinases	196
7.6	Applications of Use of Extracted Keratins and Keratin Hydrolysates in Food and Nutrition	196
7.7	Keratin Hydrolysates in Food and Nutrition	198
	7.7.1 Keratin-Derived Bioactive Peptides	200
	7.7.1.1 Antioxidant Peptides	200
	7.7.1.2 Antihypertension or Angiotensin I-Converting Enzyme (ACE) Inhibitory Peptides	201
	7.7.1.3 Antidiabetic or Dipeptidyl Peptidase-IV (DPP-IV) Inhibitory Peptides	201
	7.7.2 Keratins in Food Packaging	201
	7.7.2.1 Use of Keratin in Microencapsulates and Edible Coatings	202

7.8 Safety Considerations 202
7.9 Consumer Issues 204
7.10 Conclusions and Future Outlooks 204
References 205

7.1 INTRODUCTION

Global growth in the human population is anticipated to increase demand for food and, as a result, exacerbate the risk of a shortage in protein availability (Food Security Information Network, 2019). Current agricultural activities around the world are challenged by national conflicts, insecurity, limited geographical space, and global warming, which contributes to climate disasters, such as severe flooding, drought, and erratic rains, all of which contribute to food insecurity in many regions of the World. Food shortage can lead to acute and chronic malnutrition as well as an increase in the risk of disease development. In 2018, it was estimated that more than 113 million people had experienced severe hunger across 53 countries and were urgently in need of essential food and medical treatments (IPC/CH Phase 3 or above) (Food Security Information Network, 2019). Several populated countries suffer from severe food crises (IPC/CH Phase 4), including Afghanistan, Congo, Ethiopia, Northern Nigeria, Sudan, South Sudan, Syria, Yemen and others (Food Security Information Network, 2019). This has motivated nutritionists, food scientists, local government and international agencies to escalate the search for alternative sources of food, and in particular, foods that contain substantial amounts of quality protein.

Livestock and poultry are major sources of muscle food rich in protein. In addition to meat, livestock and poultry generate large amounts of processing by-products that present an opportunity for enhanced utilization. For the components that require disposal, the challenge is to minimize the environmental impact. A schematic showing different by-products produced by industrial processing of livestock and poultry is shown in Figure 7.1.

Keratin-containing materials contribute a substantial quantity of poultry and livestock processing by-products. Keratin has a high protein content with several essential amino acids that can be harnessed and utilized in food, nutrition biomedical and biotechnological applications. In 2016, 30 billion tonnes of keratin-containing by-products were generated annually worldwide (Holkar et al., 2018). Keratin is a fibrous scleroprotein that represents a major component of excrescence tissues such as wool (95% protein) (Holkar et al., 2018; Yamauchi & Khoda, 1997), feathers (90% protein) (Gessesse et al., 2003; Korniłłowicz-Kowalska & Bohacz, 2011; Shavandi et al., 2017), hair, nails, horns, hooves, beaks and other integuments such as skin (~80% protein) (Holkar et al., 2018; Rogers, 1985). The major component in keratin-containing materials is protein, and the remaining components are non-protein nitrogen, fat and minerals (Korniłłowicz-Kowalska & Bohacz, 2011). Generally, the composition of keratin from various sources is influenced by structural configuration, physiological function and the diet of the animals (Shavandi et al., 2017).

Among these by-products, chicken feathers are the major keratin-containing component (several million tonnes) generated from poultry slaughterhouses around the globe. World poultry production was estimated by the Food Agriculture Organization of the United Nations (2019) to be 32 billion head, including chicken, duck, turkey, goose and guinea fowl. Chicken is the leading poultry farmed, contributing 90.7% of poultry production (Food Agriculture Organization of the United Nations, 2019). The average weight range of a mature chicken (at 42 days old) is reported to be approximately 1.48–2.5 kg, of which feathers constitute about 5–7% of the total weight (Gessesse et al., 2003). A conservative estimate of an average weight of a poultry bird is 1.5 kg and of this, 5% of the weight is contributed by the feathers, and the most conservative estimate of feathers generated annually worldwide is reported to be 2.4 million tonnes (Rahayu & Bata, 2015). However, a higher estimate of 65 million tonnes has been suggested (Shavandi et al., 2017). A small fraction of this natural resource is used as insulation filler, adornment, fertilizers and feed. Dumping of feathers in landfill has become a common practice, due to lack of established economic utilization. It has been considered acceptable, as feathers can be

Keratin as an Alternative Protein 175

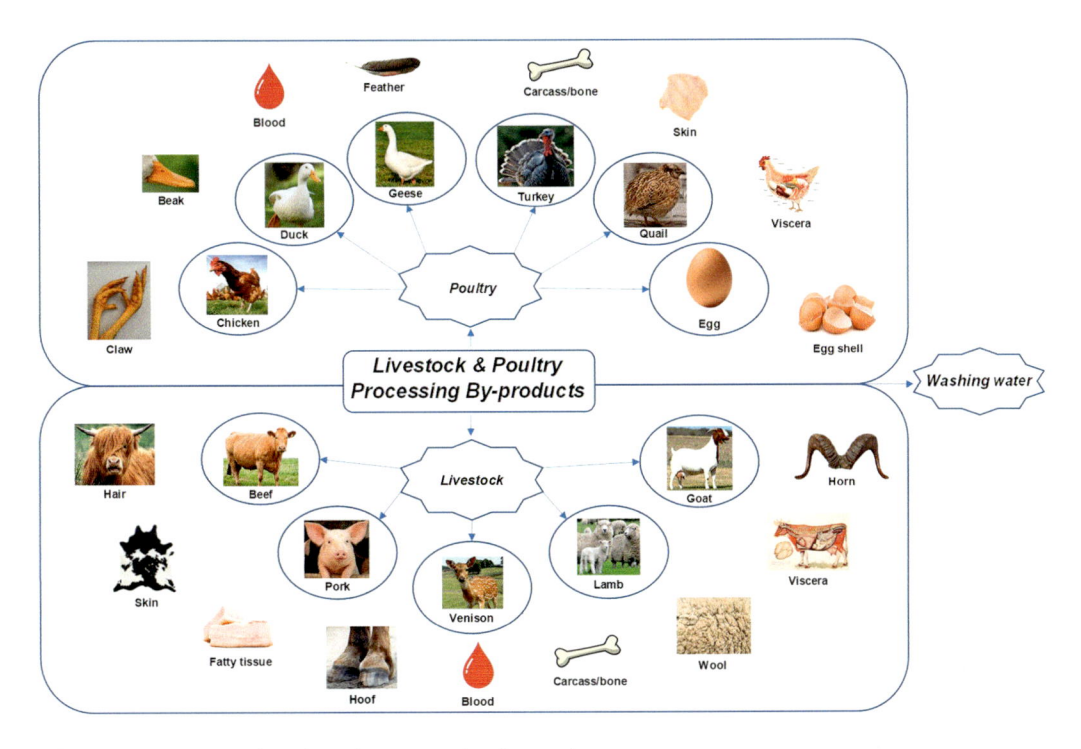

FIGURE 7.1 Livestock and poultry processing by-products.

degraded over time by soil-born organisms. However, environmental issues, such as generation of landfill leachate and pollution, can occur (Ji et al., 2014). Several studies have investigated the use of keratin in edible products, or in applications such as bio-composite scaffolds in human and animal medicine (Wu et al., 2017), generation of keratin hydrolysates, production of microparticles exhibiting angiotensin I converting enzyme (ACE) inhibitory activity (Fontoura et al., 2014; Karamać et al., 2005), hydrolysates exhibiting antioxidant activity (Fakhfakh et al., 2011; Fontoura et al., 2014; Lai et al., 2018; Ohba et al., 2003; Sharma et al., 2017), anticancer properties (Sharma et al., 2017) dipeptidyl peptidase IV (DPP-IV) inhibitory activity (Fontoura et al., 2014), antifungal (Gousterova et al., 2011), and antibacterial activities (Sundaram et al., 2015). Poultry feather hydrolysates have been reported for the production of amino acids, such as L-cysteine, as keratins has a high cysteine content (Ji et al., 2014), that is used in food supplements and baked products. L-cysteine has been reported to be produced in China from human hair (Winterman, 2010). However, the production of L-cysteine from keratin involves the use of strong acids and can result in pollution (Ji et al., 2014). Similarly, wool and hair from various sources have been investigated for the production of multiple bioactivities (Damps et al., 2017; Lai et al., 2018). The annual world wool production has been estimated to be 2.5 million tonnes, with Australia, China, New Zealand, Iran and Argentina being the major wool producing countries (Shavandi et al., 2017). The drop in wool prices, and export value in recent years (Cook, 2017) and the availability of coarse low-value phenotypes as well as generation of significant amounts of wool slips (small wool patches produced in slaughterhouses) have led to increased consideration of strategic diversification of uses for these materials.

The current use of keratin-containing materials has traditionally involved utilization in value-added products such as clothing, insulation, cushion filling, animal feed, fertilizers, biodegradable surfactants and adhesives. Pure or semi-purified keratin has also been exploited for various unconventional applications such as the production of composite materials (Sun et al., 2017; Zhang et al., 2016), textile finishing (Lee et al., 2019; Reddy et al., 2014), cosmetics (Mokrejs et al., 2017), water purification (Figoli et al., 2019) and numerous medical applications, particularly in tissue engineering and regeneration (Shavandi et al., 2017). However, the possibility of utilization

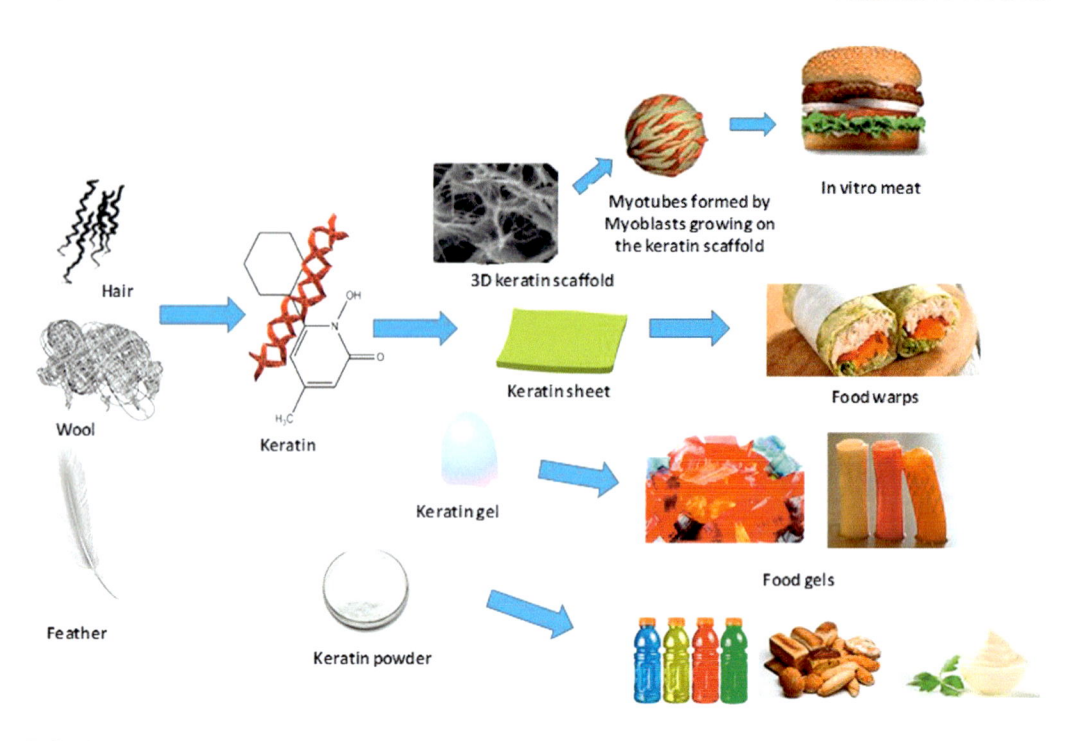

FIGURE 7.2 Futuristic vision for utilization of keratin in food applications.

of keratin as a rich protein source for inclusion in human food and nutrition has not been explored fully. Few studies having been carried out to investigate the nutritional aspects of keratin, and only a few animals and human feeding studies have been undertaken. Considering their ready availability, and hence the moderate cost of keratin-containing raw materials, and the nutritional profile of keratin consisting of up to 17 amino acids depending on keratin source, keratin-containing materials have considerable potential as an alternative protein source for food and nutrition applications. The insoluble nature of native keratin and its resistance to enzymatic digestion by animal, plant and many known microbial proteases, as well as the lack of some essential amino acids in some keratin sources, has led to low interest in keratin as a food supplement. A futuristic vision for the use of keratin-containing materials in food applications is presented in Figure 7.2.

7.2 STRUCTURE AND CHEMICAL COMPOSITION OF KERATINS

At least 17 different types of keratins are known, based on physicochemical properties, structure, and the integumental cells forming them (Holkar et al., 2018). Keratin is a cystine-rich protein that also contains substantial amounts of glycine, proline and serine, but it is low in lysine, histidine and methionine, and it lacks tryptophan (Korniłowicz-Kowalska & Bohacz, 2011; Shavandi et al., 2017). Keratins are resistant to chemical, physical and enzymatic degradation. The typically rigid physical property of keratin-containing structures is due to their high cysteine content and disulphide bonding, which involves covalent links between two adjacent cysteine residues, as well as keratin amino acid polymers forming hydrogen bonds and hydrophobic and ionic interactions (Shavandi et al., 2017). These inter- and intra-polypeptide interactions allow keratins to exhibit their strong tightly packed protein chain structure and low solubility in various solvents, including water, weak acids, alkaline reagents and organic solvents, and resistance to proteases, such as pepsin or trypsin.

An illustration of keratin molecular structure is provided in Figure 7.3. The arrangement of keratin in various materials, including filaments, exists in different forms as a result of different post-translational modifications involving disulphide bonds, glycosylation, and phosphorylation (Lange

Keratin as an Alternative Protein

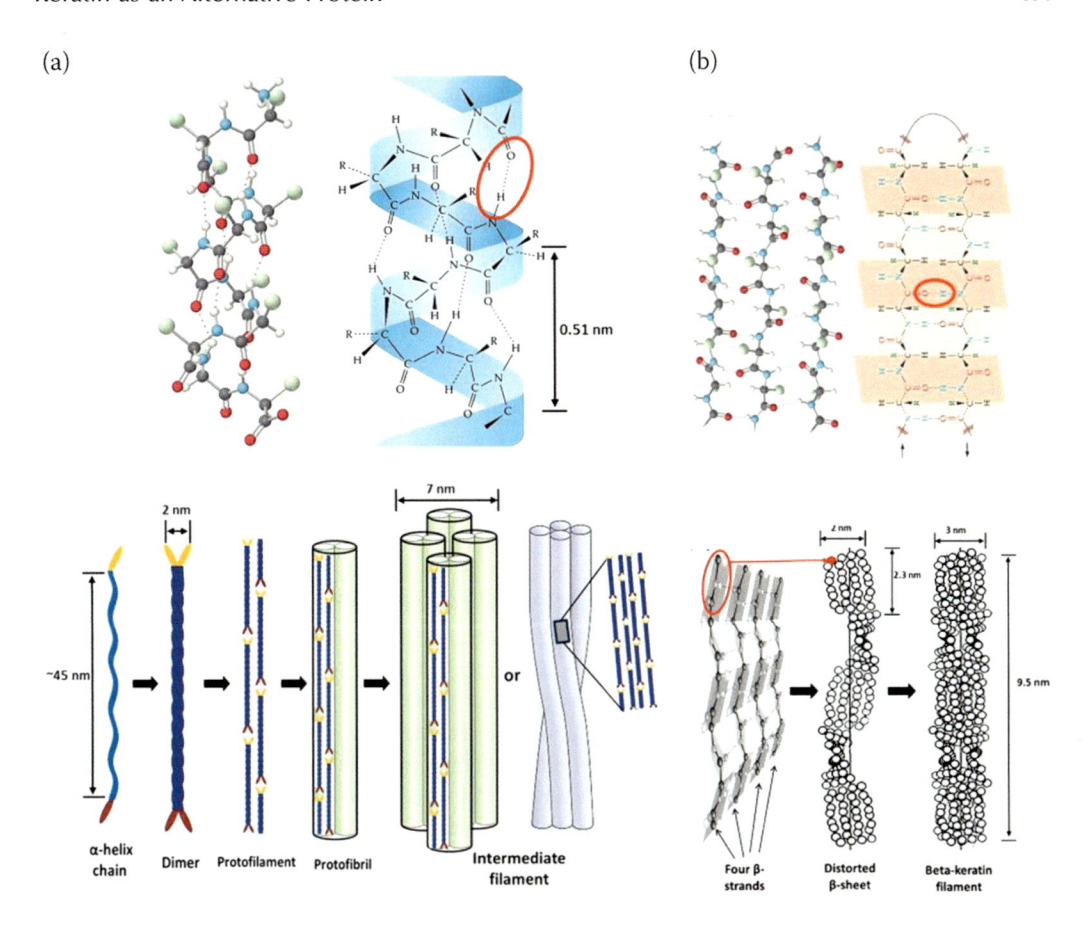

FIGURE 7.3 Intermediate filament structure of α-keratin (a) and β-keratin (b) in the ball-and-stick model and configuration of the polypeptide chain. The α-helix chains twist to form the dimers that constitute the protofilament. Four protofilaments assemble to form an intermediate filament. In the beta-keratin, a polypeptide chain folds to form four β-strands that twist to form the distorted β-sheet. The β-keratin filament is formed by two sheets assembly. (Reprinted from Progress in Materials Science, 76, Wang et al. (2016) 229–318, Copyright 2016, with permission from Elsevier (License Number 4771600199347).

et al., 2016). Structurally, keratins exist in two forms, α-keratins (mostly found in wool, hair, hooves and skin), and β-keratins (mostly found in feathers, beaks, claws and fish scales) (Shavandi et al., 2017). The α-keratins are made up of coils of α-helical polypeptides assembled into intermediate filaments; while β-keratins are made of β-pleated sheets of keratin molecules assembled into supramolecular bundles that form keratin fibrils (Figure 7.3). These keratin-containing materials contain both α- and β-keratins in various proportions and configurations. For example, feathers are made up of amorphous keratins (41–67%) and β-keratins (33–38%); while wool and hair consist mainly of bristle α-keratins (50%), and other keratin-associated or matrix proteins (20–30%), that exist in the amorphous area between intermediate filaments, and the remaining portion is made up of β-keratins (Lange et al., 2016). The β-keratins are susceptible to keratinase hydrolysis due to their low content disulphide bonds and more open structure. The degree of softness or hardness of various keratin structures dictates the protein flexibility and susceptibility to degradation. This property is dictated by their sulphur-containing amino acid content in the polypeptide and the number of disulphide bonds. Soft keratins (a major keratin component in the core of hair and fur fibres, and in the outer layers of epidermal tissues or stratum corneum) were found to contain approximately 2% sulphur-containing amino acids and 50–75% moisture. In contrast, hard keratins (the major keratin component in beaks, claws, hooves, horns, and nails) contain between 4 and 8% sulphur-containing amino acids (Shavandi et al., 2017).

Three different parts of a keratin polymer play a central role in the polypeptide configuration; the N-terminal, central helical region and tail domain (Vidmar & Vodovnik, 2018). The C-terminal and N-terminal domains contain β-turns with a negative and a positive net charge globular structure, respectively. These termini contain between 50 to 100 amino acids (Vidmar & Vodovnik, 2018). The central helical domains (made up of approximately 310 amino acids) are divided into four α-helical sub-domains, which differ in length and amino acid content (Parry et al., 2001). These sub-domains are separated by non-helical β-turns (linker regions). The disulphide bonds, hydrogen bonds and hydrophobic interactions between these domains and subdomains are formed on the adjacent acidic and basic keratin molecules that are orientated parallel to each other, creating protein quaternary structures such as heterodimers, tetramers (2 nm protofilament), octamer (4.5 nm protofibril made up of two protofilaments), and 20 nm diameter unit-length filaments (ULFs) comprised of four protofibril bundles, and finally assembly into keratin filaments and various higher-order keratin-based material forms (Vidmar & Vodovnik, 2018).

7.3 KERATIN AMINO ACID COMPOSITION

Keratins contain high levels of cysteine, glycine, proline, serine, and various acidic amino acids such as glutamic acid, but they provide a low content of methionine, histidine and lysine (Korniłowicz-Kowalska & Bohacz, 2011; Shavandi et al., 2017). Tryptophan is at undetectable levels in wool and hair keratins, but present at a low level in feather keratin. The high content of cysteine uniquely identifies keratins from other structural proteins such as collagen and elastin. As mentioned previously, the sulphur-containing amino acid cysteine is essential for the formation of disulphide bonds in keratin that has a structural effect on the properties of keratin. The high content of cysteine in keratin is an advantage for its use in food formulation where a better balance of the amino acids profile could be achieved by incorporating keratin with protein from other ingredients.

The composition of amino acids may vary depending on the method used for wool hydrolysis (e.g., hot water, acids, alkaline or enzymes, Table 7.1). Wool hydrolysates obtained from superheated water at 140 °C were similar to that of original wool except for higher cysteine (300%) and methionine (148.1%) contents (Bhavsar et al., 2017). At higher temperatures (170 °C), higher alanine, glutamic acid, glycine, lysine were found in addition to the cysteine. The use of alkaline hydrolysis produces higher released amino acid contents (Table 7.2), particularly cysteine. However, there were no trends for the temperature, or the concentration of the alkali used. The acid hydrolysis process results in much lower levels of released amino acids compared to superheated water and alkaline hydrolysis. Almost all the amino acid contents are reduced by acid hydrolysis except for tyrosine and arginine. A critical advantage of acid hydrolysis is the lack of lanthionine formation, whereas a very high content of lanthionine is produced by superheated water and alkaline processing. One of the major issues related to the use of superheated water and alkaline hydrolysis is the production of large amounts of lanthionine (Table 7.3), which has a great impact on health, and subsequently the use of the hydrolysed keratin in food applications. The presence of lanthionine gives rise to unwanted nutritional effects such as a reduction in protein digestibility and availability of (essential) amino acids as well as possible toxic side effects (Baker, 2006; Friedman, 1999).

Cysteine is an important amino acid that is involved in vital cellular roles such as catalysis, tracking, and mediating the oxidative stress response (Combs & DeNicola, 2019) that maintain cell homeostasis (Figure 7.4). Nutritionally, cysteine is considered as a 'semi-essential amino acid' since methionine, an essential amino acid can provide the sulphur required for the synthesis of cysteine. The average adult daily requirement for methionine and cysteine is about 15 mg kg^{-1}, and the recommended daily allowance is 19 mg kg^{-1} (Stipanuk, 2004). The susceptibility of the nucleophilic thiol (–SH) group in cysteine to oxidation is due to the large atomic radius of the sulphur atom and the low dissociation energy of the thiol S–H bond. Disulphide bridges play essential roles in stabilizing the protein conformation.

Cysteine is also an essential component in several biological systems. For example, cysteine is the limiting amino acid for the synthesis of the endogenous antioxidant glutathione, a critical physiological

TABLE 7.1
Amino acid composition (mol%) of wool, hair and feather

Amino Acid	Wool[1,2,3,4]	Hair[2]	Feather[5,6]
Alanine	5.5–5.8	4.4	3.6–8.7
Arginine	3.3–6.6	6.4	3.8–5.4
Aspartic acid	6.0–6.5	5	4.7–5.6
Glutamic acid	11.1–12.2	13	6.9–7.7
Glycine	8.8–9.4	5.7	7.7–13.7
Half-cystine	10.7–11.4	17.4	6.2–7.8
Histidine	0.8–0.9	0.9	tra.–0.2
Isoleucine	3.0–3.5	2.6	3.2–4.3
Leucine	7.3–8.1	6.1	7.0–8.3
Lysine	3.0	2.5	0.6
Methionine	0.5–0.59	0.6	0.1–1.3
Phenylalanine	2.5–2.9	1.6	3.1–4.2
Proline	6.0–7.1	8	8.7–9.8
Serine	9.6–10.9	11.4	9.3–14.1
Threonine	6.1–6.4	7.1	3.5–4.1
Tyrosine	3.5–4.3	2.1	1.4–1.95
Valine	5.6–6.4	5.4	6.94–7.8
Tryptophan	-	-	0.7

Notes
1. Thompson and O'donnell (1962)
2. Gillespie and Marshall (1989)
3. Cardamone (2010)
4. Fraser et al. (1972)
5. Harrap and Woods (1964)
6. Moore et al. (2006)

antioxidant that plays a significant function in combating cellular oxidative stress. Glutathione consists of three amino acids (glycine, glutamate, and cysteine) and the oxidation of the nucleophilic thiol (–SH) group is vital in scavenging cellular reactive species and maintaining homeostasis. Cysteine is also required for the synthesis of taurine (2-aminoethane-sulfonic acid), an amino acid that plays important physiological roles, including acting as an osmolyte, ion channel regulator, intracellular calcium regulator, antioxidant, anti-inflammatory, antiproliferative, and in anti-endoplasmic reticulum stress activities (De Luca, Pierno, & Camerino, 2015). Also, cysteine is a co-factor for some enzymes such as aconitase (EC 4.2.1.3 – aconitate hydratase). This protein is involved in a wide range of physiological activities (for details, please see https://www.brenda-enzymes.org/enzyme.php?ecno=4.2.1.3&organism%5B%5D=Homo+sapiens&showtm=0&UniProtAcc=Q99798&onlyTable=Disease), and acts as a substrate for the cystathionine-β-synthase (EC 4.2.1.22) in the central nervous system, and has been shown to attenuate early brain injury in rats subjected to brain damage, and has a neuroprotective function (Li et al., 2017).

7.4 METHODS FOR KERATIN EXTRACTION AND DEGRADATION

Various chemical, physical, enzymatic and microbial methods for utilization, extraction, and degradation of keratin have been reviewed comprehensively, and the below information on keratin extraction provides an updated summary based on those reviews, with additional details (Holkar et al., 2018; Shavandi et al., 2017). The basic principles of keratin extraction and degradation

TABLE 7.2
Percent increase in amino acids (%) of wool hydrolysates compared with wool. The hydrolysates were obtained using superheated, alkaline, and acid treatments at different temperatures (Bhavsar et al., 2017; Deb-Choudhury et al., 2018)

	Superheated		Alkaline Treatment												Acid treatment
	140 °C	170 °C	5% CaO 140 °C	10% CaO 140 °C	15% CaO 140 °C	5% KOH 140 °C	10% KOH 140 °C	15% KOH 140 °C	5% CaO 170 °C	10% CaO 170 °C	15% CaO 170 °C	5% KOH 170 °C	10% KOH 170 °C	15% KOH 170 °C	11 N HCl
Alanine	105.7	146.2	123.8	163.8	170.0	128.4	151.6	157.6	163.0	150.8	165.8	144.0	156.6	157.2	97.6
Arginine	105.1	81.1	115.5	78.6	57.8	96.1	80.8	74.1	52.0	90.9	41.7	95.2	78.1	54.1	106.7
Aspartic acid	100.3	70.5	80.8	143.2	158.8	125.8	142.9	148.3	129.6	127.5	128.3	71.2	72.9	120.8	95.9
Cysteine	300.0	331.3	56.3	1100.0	787.5	531.3	318.8	787.5	456.3	862.5	550.0	443.8	468.8	593.8	43.6
Glutamic acid	103.6	154.8	62.2	160.3	187.1	136.0	147.7	164.9	167.4	91.7	181.4	134.4	138.5	175.0	93.1
Glycine	107.2	123.5	140.3	110.1	92.3	113.5	126.8	123.0	132.3	145.8	99.9	170.0	176.4	130.9	124.4
Histidine	116.7	83.9	148.2	156.5	120.8	56.0	20.2	63.1	119.0	153.6	94.6	117.3	114.3	115.5	122.2
Isoleucine	103.2	112.2	98.7	140.5	144.5	114.1	122.5	138.6	142.9	75.2	162.0	126.8	144.1	150.3	100.0
Leucine	105.0	109.1	59.6	156.7	159.7	117.7	133.7	155.4	163.6	195.9	174.8	136.4	154.6	165.6	101.2
Lysine	93.6	184.4	11.4	140.1	167.1	129.8	136.1	139.0	169.7	13.7	158.3	169.7	188.0	180.6	63.2
Methionine	148.1	114.8	2711.1	187.0	250.0	161.1	190.7	200.0	305.6	2650.0	346.3	205.6	277.8	285.2	100.0
Phenylalanine	119.4	67.6	364.4	112.8	96.6	92.1	97.1	113.5	118.9	379.1	111.0	109.9	129.3	103.6	102.9
Proline	99.4	97.8	124.7	67.1	57.4	90.2	82.3	65.0	64.5	90.2	62.3	87.6	84.0	66.4	112.7
Serine	101.2	76.0	113.2	11.1	4.4	85.2	49.3	14.5	13.6	35.7	7.6	49.8	22.5	6.4	102.6
Threonine	100.2	84.8	124.1	17.7	3.7	81.0	36.4	14.5	16.0	27.5	13.7	56.6	25.6	6.0	96.9
Tyrosine	64.8	75.8	121.4	105.4	86.4	60.1	90.9	106.1	96.2	21.1	103.3	113.1	116.4	103.0	130.0
Valine	101.6	117.5	23.5	121.2	122.9	107.7	112.5	120.8	123.3	36.7	137.6	118.6	128.7	130.6	118.9
Lanthionine	725.0	1354.2	1941.7	708.3	354.2	1679.2	1479.2	629.2	237.5	1204.2	150.0	279.2	141.7	120.8	ND
1/2 Cystine	74.9	5.7	0.1	2.9	2.3	7.9	5.3	3.1	1.4	0.1	1.0	1.4	0.4	1.0	-

Highlighted cells indicate high content of amino acid detected after extraction treatment.
Acid treatment: 4 h HCl digestion, followed by further hydrolysis by HCl exposure for 24 h; ND: not detected.

TABLE 7.3
Oxidation parameters reported for the keratin solubilization. Reproduced from Shavandi et al. (2017) with permission from the Royal Society of Chemistry

Material	Processing Parameters	Properties of the Hydrolysed Product
Wool	30 h 2% peracetic acid	Sulfonic acid formation
Wool	5 min 2% peracetic acid	Cystine monoxide and dioxide residues
Wool	24% peracetic acid–10% H_2O_2	Sulfonate and cystine monoxide
Wool	H_2O_2 3.5N, pH 11.5, 9.5, 4.5	Formation of either sulfonate or sulfonic acid groups the highest oxidation at pH 11.5 no oxidation at pH 4.5
Wool	2% peracetic acid for 10 h at 37 °C on a 150-rpm orbital shaker.	
Wool	24 h at 250 with 100 ml of 1.6% (w/v) peracetic acid,	
Wool	performic acid [100-volume H_2O_2/98% formic acid (1:39, v/v)] for 18 h at 4 °C.	Peracetic acid oxidizes the disulfite bond (-S-S-) of cystine dimeric amino acid into two cysteic acids containing the sulfonic acid (eSO$_3$H) functional group >99% protein
Hair	2% peracetic acid, boiled for 2,	
Hair	30 grams of hair with 500 mL of 32% peracetic acid at 4 °C for 24 h.	Partially oxidize the naturally occurring disulfite linkages to produce a protein with cysteic acid (—CH$_2$SO$_3$H) residues, and remaining disulfite linkages.
Wool	or 50% aqueous on-propanol for 4 h at 70 °C	Rich in glycine, tyrosine, phenylalanine, and serine, moderately rich in half-cystine, and low in lysine, histidine, methionine, and isoleucine the molecular weight of approximately 6000–10000.
Wool	98–100% formic acid at 20 °C for 1 h	Rich in glycine, tyrosine, phenylalanine, and serine with a large amount of glutamic acid and virtually no half-cystine molecular weight of approximately 6000–10000.

involve the cleavage of disulphide bonds and partial disruption of the keratin structure. Most such techniques are chemical-based methods, such as alkali hydrolysis, oxidation, reduction including the Shindai method, dissolution by sulphitolysis, and dissolution by use of ionic liquids. Other techniques include the physical practice of steam flash explosion (SFE) and unique approaches involving microbial and enzymatic keratinolysis. These techniques are shown in Figure 7.5. However, many of these techniques are costly (high energy consuming and require the use of expensive chemicals, as well as processing apparatus setup), are time-consuming, and may cause detrimental damage to the environment as well as to the keratin-backbone. Besides, the different techniques also generate extracted keratin products with different physicochemical and functional properties. Therefore, choosing a suitable extraction technique for keratin depends on the desired physicochemical properties for the downstream application. These methods and various chemicals such as protein denaturant, and surfactants can often be combined to achieve desirable yields of extraction as a result of increased hydrophilicity, structural accessibility and product stabilization (Jiang-Tao et al., 2015; Shavandi et al., 2017).

7.4.1 Alkaline Hydrolysis Methods

Keratin extraction by alkaline hydrolysis involves the application of various amounts of alkaline chemicals such as sodium hydroxide (NaOH), potassium hydroxide (KOH), calcium oxide (CaO), and Schweitzer's reagent, a complex tetraammine copper(II) hydroxide, $Cu(NH_3)_4(H_2O)_2](OH)_2$,

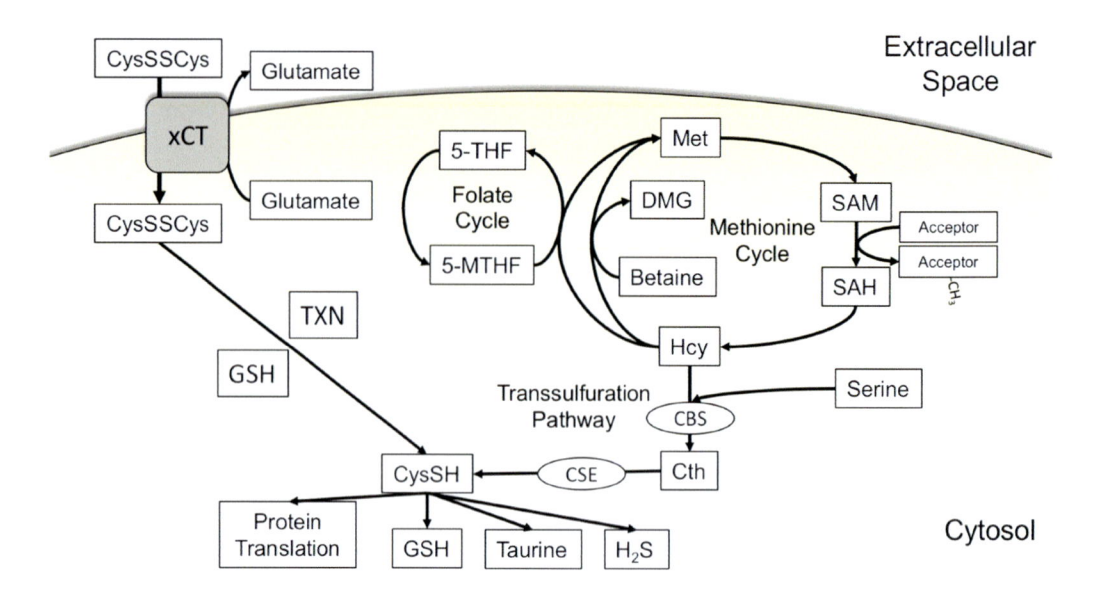

FIGURE 7.4 Schematic diagram of extracellular cystine uptake mechanisms through glutamate/cystine xCT antiporter and acquisition of cysteine from cystine via the transsulfuration (Combs & DeNicola, 2019). CBS: cystathionine β-synthase; Cth: cystathionine; CSE: cystathionine γ-lyase; CysSSCys: cystines; CysSH: cysteine; DMG: dimethylglycine; GSH: glutathione; Hcy: homocysteine; Met: methionine; SAH: Sadenosylhomocysteine; SAM: S-adenosylm TXN: thioredoxin; xCT: glutamate/cystine xCT antiporter; 5-MTHF: 5-tetramethylhydrofolate; 5-THF: 5-tetrahydrofolate. This article is an open-access article distributed under the terms and conditions of the Creative Commons Attribution (CC BY) license (http://creativecommons.org/licenses/by/4.0/).

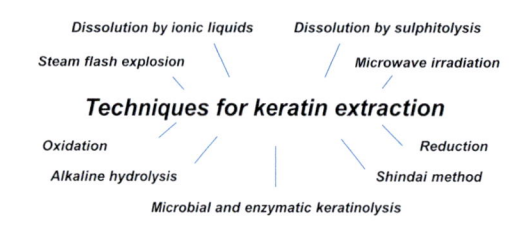

FIGURE 7.5 Available methods for keratin extraction.

and treatment at temperatures between 80 and 170 °C, to solubilize keratin by dissociating hydrogen from sulphate (R–O–SO$_3$H) and carboxylic groups (R–COOH) on keratin molecules. The yield of solubilized keratin proportionally increases with the concentration of the alkali used, up to 15% alkali concentration. Alkali treatment concentration above 15% has been reported to increase wool fibre strength and reduce the yield of solubilized wool (Shavandi et al., 2017). The use of sodium sulphide as a catalyst in NaOH alkaline treatment can improve the solubilization process. Solubilized keratin obtained from feather and wool using alkaline treatment has been found to vary, with the amount of cysteine being 7% from feather and 11–17% in wool, and the feather solubilized material had a higher hydrophobic content (Shavandi et al., 2017).

The major drawbacks of this technique for commercialization are (1) the high amount of alkali needed, (2) a large amount of acid is required for neutralization and precipitation of the final keratin product, (3) substantial damage to the backbone of the proteins occurs, and (4) an undesirable sulphide odour is generated.

As mentioned above, the keratin structure and amino acid composition can be drastically affected by the extraction method. Various amounts of the alkaline chemical have been used in reported studies that result in varying levels of the breakdown of wool and feather structure. Tsuda and Nomura (2014) used 10 g/L solution of NaOH with a heating step (120 °C for 10 minutes) to hydrolyse wool and feather. A preserved intact keratin secondary structure was obtained, but a significant reduction in cysteine was found. The use of 5% CaO resulted in more than 40% cysteine loss at 140°C but not at 170°C (Table 7.2). Conversely, higher CaO concentrations and KOH at ≥5% at both temperatures (140 and 170°C) resulted in higher cysteine content. The results show that the type and concentration of alkali used, and the treatment temperature, can affect the cysteine content of the solubilized keratin. In parallel to the increase in cysteine content during alkaline hydrolysis, lanthionine formation also increases (Table 7.2). It appears that increasing both the concentration of alkali and the temperature used in the process decreases the content of lanthionine formation. Treatment of feather with Schweitzer's reagent resulted in no lanthionine formation during the process (Nagai & Nishikawa, 1970), but the hydrolysed keratin contained copper-protein complexes and hence produced toxicological considerations.

7.4.2 Oxidation Methods

Oxidation methods involve the use of oxidizing agents such as formic acid (HCOOH), peracetic acid (PAA, CH_3COOOH) or performic acid (PFA, CH_2O_3), hydrogen peroxide (H_2O_2), sodium hypochlorite (NaClO), and potassium permanganate ($KMnO_4$), to oxidize the disulphide linkages of keratin (Table 7.3). These chemicals convert keratin into protein fragments with the cysteine end containing a hydrophilic pendant sulphonate group that can complex with water forming a sulphonic acid group (R-SO_3H). This is then followed by solubilization by treatment with ammonia, followed by acid precipitation using hydrochloric acid (HCl) to obtain the final product.

Early work by Earland and Knight (1955) and Buchanan (1977) used 2% peracetic acid and 2% performic acid, respectively, to hydrolyse wool for 30 hours followed by a mild ammonia (0.2 N) treatment and finally a precipitation step using HCl. The majority of the α-keratin was solubilized, but some insoluble residue forming a jelly-like structure was obtained, which was believed to be mainly β-keratin.

These oxidation treatments are time-consuming processes. Besides, nutritional loss due to oxidation of various amino acids such as tryptophan, methionine, serine, threonine, tyrosine, histidine, phenylalanine and, to some extent cysteine, is also a disadvantage.

7.4.3 Reduction Methods

Reduction methods involve thiol-containing reducing agents such as 2-mercaptoethanol (2-ME), dithiothreitol (DTT), sodium sulphide (Na_2S), toluenethiol or methylbenzene, sodium or potassium thioglycolate, thioglycolic acid and other thiol-containing reagents, to cleave the cystine-disulphide bonds in keratin (Table 7.4). Cysteine, although it contains a thiol functional group, does not have strong reducing capability. It thus cannot be used as the sole reducing agent to dissociate the disulphide bonds of keratin-containing materials. However, it can be coupled with other reducing agents to enhance the yield during keratin extraction. Another improved reduction technique is known as the 'Shindai method' which is a modified version of the Yamauchi method developed in Shinshu University, Japan. This method uses a solution containing 25 mM Tris-HCl, 2.6 M thiourea, 5 M urea and 5% 2-mercaptoethanol as a reducing solution (Nakamura et al., 2002; Yamauchi et al., 1996). However, the disadvantages of these reduction methods are (1) expensive cost of reducing agents, (2) generation of unpleasant odour, and (3) high toxicity of the reagent to the environment and the users.

Several researchers have demonstrated that the reduction process is effective at pH 6 or higher (Goddard & Michaelis, 1935; Shavandi et al., 2017). The use of low pH (pH = 2), reducing conditions and heating at 50-60 °C was later reported to extract keratin (Savige, 1960). Recent work by Deb-Choudhury et al. (2018) used 11 N HCl to generate keratin hydrolysates. Despite the relatively high protein content (47%) obtained using this method, the authors observed an

TABLE 7.4
Characteristics of some of the keratin extraction conditions using reduction methods. Reproduced from Shavandi et al. (2017) with permission from the Royal Society of Chemistry

Thiol	Conditions			Temperature and Time	%Yield
	Urea (M)	Surfactant/Buffering	pH		
MEC (5% v/v)	7	2% SDS (w/v)	neutral	50 °C for 24 h	60
MEC (5% v/v)	7	No SDS	neutral	50 °C for 24 h	45
Thiourea (2.5 M), 5 % thioglycolic acid	5	25 mM Tris- HCl	9.5	50 °C for 3 d	
Thioglycolic acid (0.2M)	6		10.5	40 °C, for 3 h	85
Thioglycolic acid (0.2M)	6-10		11	40 °C for 2 h	91
MEC (0.6 M)	8	1M Tris/0.25 M EDTA	11	20 °C for 16 h	73
MEC (4 M)	-		5	20 °C for 24 h	75
MEC (0.14 M)	8		10.5	20 °C for 3 h	80
MEC (1.4 M)	6	1.4 g SDS3 mM EDTA, (0.2 M) KCl–NaOHNaHCO$_3$, Tris	9	40 °C for 1 h	72
MEC (1.4 M)	6	NO SDS3 mM EDTA, (0.2 M) KCl–NaOH NaHCO$_3$, Tris	9	40 °C for 1 h	77
MEC (125 mM)	8	3 mM EDTA, 200 mM Tris,	9.0	40 °C, 30 min	75
Thiourea (2.4 M)	15	15% DTT, 25 mM Tris	8.5	50 °C for 2 d	67
2-ME (5%)	8	25 mM Tris–HCl	9.5	50 °C for 1-3 d	27

MEC = mercaptoethanol

increased amount of lanthionine formation during the process, and its formation rate was directly related to processing temperature (Zahn et al., 1960).

The majority of reducing agents used for keratin solubilization are alkaline thiols that involve the use of high pH and temperature. This has consequently led to the formation of lanthionine and degradation of protein structure. To facilitate the reduction process, high urea concentrations up to 8 M, weaken hydrophobic bonds and cause the polypeptide structure to swell. Urea, 2-mercaptoethanol and sodium dodecyl sulphate (SDS) are commonly used in reduction methods to accelerate the solubilization process and reduce the oxidation of cysteine.

Experimentation with cysteine as a safe and environmentally friendly reducing agent (Xu et al., 2014) led to controlled production of solubilized keratin that is suitable for making of electrospun materials and 3D structures that could be useful for *in vitro* meat production applications.

7.4.4 Sulphitolysis Methods

Due to the associated drawbacks of the reduction technique, dissolution by sulphitolysis was designed as an alternative method to extract keratin (Table 7.5) by using sodium sulphite (Na$_2$SO$_3$), sodium bisulphite (NaHSO$_3$) or sodium disulphite (Na$_2$S$_2$O$_5$) to cleave the disulphide linkages (sulphitolysis) to form both cysteine with a thiol functional group (R-S-H), and cysteine with a sulfonate functional group (R-S-S-O$_3$H or R-S-S-O$_3$Na). The reaction is achieved faster when the sulphite compound used is in the form of sodium sulphite; as well as when the pH is raised to 9.0 to increase the concentration of sulphite (SO$_3^{2-}$) (Maclaren & Milligan, 1981; Shavandi et al., 2017). At different pH, these sulphites exist in various forms. For example, under

TABLE 7.5
Characteristics of some of the keratin extraction conditions using sulfitolysis methods. Reproduced from Shavandi et al. (2017) with permission from the Royal Society of Chemistry

Material	Chemical Used	Condition		Remark
Feather	Na$_2$S (10 g/L)	130 RPM 30 °C	Flush with N$_2$ gas	Keratin yield of 62% after 24 h.
Feather	Na$_2$S (10 g/L) + SDS 10 g/L + Urea 9 M	130 RPM 30 °C	Flush with N$_2$ gas	Addition of urea and SDS enhanced the yield
Feather	7 g in 250 ml, urea 8 M, 0.6 g SDS per g of feather /0-0.5 M Na$_2$S	65 °C for 7 h pH 6.5	-	87.6% at 0.2 M Na$_2$S solution pH adjusted to 6.5
Wool	150 g in 1.5 L, urea 8 M, 75 g SDS, 150 g sodium disulfite	100 °C for 30 min	-	
Wool	5 g in 100 ml, urea 8 M, sodium metabisulfite (0.5 M),	Shaking 2 h for 65 °C.	-	pH adjusted to 6.5 using 5 M NaOH, extraction yield of 38%
Wool	0.5 mol/L LiBr, 0.1 mol/L, SDS 0.02 mol/L	90 °C for 4 h, pH=12	-	94% wool dissolution rate (WDR) and 50.2% keratin extraction rate (KER)
Wool	1 g in 10 ml, 0.125 mol/l Na$_2$S$_2$O$_5$, 0.05 mol/l SDS, 2.0 mol/l urea	30–100 °C 15-45 min	-	Dissolution yield of 48.6% Regeneration yield 76.7%
Wool	5 g/100 mL: urea (8M), sodium metabisulfite (0.5 M) (SDS, 0.1 M),	65 °C overnight.	-	-

acidic pH, HSO$_3^-$ predominates, while with a pH of higher than 7.0 SO$_3^{2-}$ is dominant (Shavandi et al., 2017). However, it is not advisable to increase the pH above 9.0 as the rate of sulphitolysis is reduced as a result of the repulsion forces of carboxylic anions on the sulphite ions. Also, cysteine sulphitolysis is reversible and does not lead to complete sulphitolysis under these conditions (Shavandi et al., 2017). To assist the completion of sulphitolysis, the elevation of temperature and the addition of a protein denaturant such as SDS and urea can be incorporated. This method is relatively cheap compared to reduction methods, but it was found to have impacted only on the cystine crosslinks while the long chain of keratin remains intact. However, this technique can be coupled with an enzymatic method to assist enzymatic hydrolysis and the generation of soluble keratin hydrolysates.

7.4.5 Ionic Liquid Dissolution Methods

Dissolution by ionic liquid is an environment-friendly method that involves the use of hot salts liquid (< 100°C) containing a mixture of molten organic cation and various organic and inorganic

TABLE 7.6
Characteristics of some of the keratin extraction conditions using ionic liquid methods. Reproduced from Shavandi et al. (2017) with permission from The Royal Society of Chemistry

Material	Ionic liquids and additives	Temperature (°C)	Solid: liquid ratio	Time	Solubility (wt.%)	Yield of keratin
Feather	[Amim]Cl + 10 wt.% Na$_2$SO$_3$	90	1:20	1h	4.8%	-
Feather	[Bmim]Cl +10 wt.% Na$_2$SO$_3$	90	1:20	1h	4.8%	-
Feather	[Bmim]Br +10 wt.% Na$_2$SO$_3$	90	1:20	1h	4.2%	-
Feather	[Bmim]NO$_3$ +10wt.% Na$_2$SO$_3$	90	1:20	1h	4.2%	-
Feather	[Hmim]CF$_3$SO$_3$ +10 wt.% Na$_2$SO$_3$	90	1:20	1h	0.2%	-
Feather	[Bmim]HSO$_4$ +10 wt.% Na$_2$SO$_3$	90	1:20	1h	4.1%	-
Wool	[Bmim]Br	130	-	10h	2%	-
Wool	[Bmim]Cl	100	-	10h	4%	-
Wool	[Bmim]Cl	130	-	10h	11%	-
Wool	[Amim]Cl	130	-	10h	8%	-
Wool	[Bmim] BF$_4$	130	-	24h	insoluble	-
Wool	[Bmim] PF$_6$	130	-	24h	insoluble	-
Wool	[Amim]Cl	130	-	640 min	21%	-
Wool	[Bmim]Cl	130	-	535 min	15%	-
Wool	[Bmim]Cl	120	1:6	30 min	-	57%
Wool	[Bmim]Cl	150	1:6	30 min	-	35%
Wool	[Bmim]Cl	180	1:6	30 min	-	18%
Feather	[Bmim]Cl	130	1:2	10h	50%	60%
Feather	[Amim]Cl	130	1:2	10h	50%	60%
Feather	cholin thioglycolate	130	1:2	10h	45%	55%
Feather	[Bmim]Cl	100	-	48h	23%	-
Wool	[Amim][dca]	130	-	-	23%	-
Wool	[Bmim]Cl	130	-	-	12%	-
Wool	[Amim]Cl	130	-	-	10%	-
Wool	cholin thioglycolate	130	-	-	11%	-
Feather	[HOEMIm][NTf2] + 1.0 g NaHSO$_3$	80	1:45	4h	-	21.75%

anions (Table 7.6). Examples of ionic liquids include choline thioglycolate and salts containing cations, such as 1-allyl-3-methylimidazolium or (Amim)⁻, 1-butyl-3-methyl-imidazolium or (Bmim)⁻, 1-hexyl-3-methylimidazolium or (Hmim)⁻ with anions such as -Cl, -Br, NO$_3$, -CF$_3$SO$_3$, -HSO$_4$, -BF$_4$, -PF$_6$ and dicyanamide (dca) forms, and 1-(2-hydroxyethyl)-3- methylimidazolium – bis(trifluoromethylsulphonyl)imide (HOEMIm)(NTf2). However, the extraction process is often performed at elevated temperatures between 80–180 °C with the highest extraction yield found at 120 °C. The mechanism of keratin extraction and dissolution using this technique is hypothesized to start with the disruption of the surface lipid layer on the keratin-containing material (Ghosh et al., 2014). The major constituents of this layer are 18-methyleicosanoic acids which are linked to

TABLE 7.7
The effect of different temperatures on physicochemical properties of the keratin fibre

Material	Pressure	Temperature (°C)	Time (min)	Sample Properties
Steam explosion				
Wool	0.2–0.8 MPa	-	-	Scales on the fibre surface were damaged, sample moisture regains, mechanical properties and dissolving ability in caustic solution decreased as the explosion pressure increased
Wool	0.2–0.6 MPa	164.2	2–8	Up to 80% digestion yield, 50% reduction in cystine content
Wool	-	220	10	The decrease of disulfite bonds, 62.36% of dry solid, 18.66% of proteins dissolved in the supernatant, 1.12% of sediment, the presence of wool structure in treated sample
Feathers	0–2.0 MPa	50	<3	93.2% pepsin digestibility wool structure disrupted completely in treated sample
Feathers	1.4–2.0 MPa	60	0.5–5	Extraction rate of feathers of 65.78% and a yield of keratin of 42.78%
Feathers	0.5–2.5 MPa	-	1	91% digestibility
Feathers	2.2 MPa	220	120	Arginine diminishes
Microwave irradiation				
Wool	Microwave irradiation	150-180	Up to 60	60% extraction yield
Wool	Microwave superheated water	180	30	31% extraction yield
Feathers	Microwave 1200W	160-200	20	71.83% yield

the inner cysteine-rich protein layer by thioester bonds (Shavandi et al., 2017). Under high temperature, these thioesters are disrupted by anions, while the above organic cations disrupt the hydrogen bonds (Feng & Chen, 2008; Zhang et al., 2005). The chloride form was found to possess the most potent nucleophilic activity on keratin hydrogen bonds. Several studies have also used sulphitolysis agents such as Na_2SO_3 and $NaHSO_3$ to facilitate the breakdown of disulphide bonds coupled with ionic liquids which are potent polar molecules that can disrupt hydrogen bonds. This method was recognized as one of the environmentally friendly ways to extract keratin, as the ionic salts are non-volatile substances, stable under high temperature, and non-flammable (Dupont et al., 2002; Shavandi et al., 2017; Ueki, 2014; Wang et al., 2014). The disadvantages of this method are that (1) the process is required to be performed under precise temperature control with nitrogen to prevent combustion of keratin substances, (2) only small amounts of the raw materials can be added, and (3) the final extracted keratin products are relatively hydrophobic.

7.4.6 STEAM FLASH EXPLOSION METHODS

Steam flash explosion (SFE) utilizes thermal energy and rapid depressurization to break the disulphide bonds in keratin, causing tearing and dissociation of the keratin-containing materials (Table 7.7). SFE consist of two processing phases: (1) thermal-pre-treatment, and (2) explosion. Thermal pre-treatment involves high pressure steaming at up to 220 °C and 2 MPa for a short period allowing the hot stream to penetrate the keratin material. The explosion phase is a physical expansion of the keratin structure that occurs because of rapid depressurization and explosion and is as fast as 87.5 milliseconds. Although this technique is perceived as a green method, chemicals such as urea and alkali at a high pH are generally required to increase the extraction yield and improve the hydrophilicity of the extracted keratins. To achieve adequately high processing temperature and pressure, expensive specialized processing apparatus is required.

7.4.7 Microwave-Assisted Methods

This technique involves the application of microwave irradiation on the keratin-containing material solution at 150–570 W for up to 7 minutes and at a temperature of between (50-180°C). The mechanism involved with microwave extraction of keratin remains unclear. It was found that microwave treatment causes a homogeneous distribution of heat through keratin-containing materials, and lower processing temperature and time are required compared to SFE, due to the reduced activation energy needed for keratin extraction by the method (Chen et al., 2015; Shavandi et al., 2017). However, this technique was found to have a lower extraction yield of only up to 60% (Shavandi et al., 2017; Zoccola et al., 2012).

7.5 MICROBIAL AND ENZYMATIC METHODS FOR THE DEGRADATION AND HYDROLYSIS OF KERATINS

Keratinolytic microorganisms and their keratinases offer a unique strategy to utilize keratin-containing wastes by generating keratin hydrolysates that can be incorporated in various value-added products. Due to the quality nutritional profile of keratin-containing materials, they also represent a cheap source of nutrients for microbial growth and the production of valuable products such as microbial secreted enzymes, microbial biomass, and keratin protein hydrolysates. These methods are considered more ecologically friendly and can be performed with less chemical requirements and under relatively milder conditions compared to the physical and chemical processes of keratin extraction discussed above. As also discussed above, many of those methods cause detrimental damage to the protein backbone, leading to the modification of several amino acids (tryptophan, methionine, partially cysteine, serine, threonine, tyrosine, histidine and phenylalanine), and formation of non-nutritive amino acids (lysinoalanine and lanthionine) (Eslahi et al., 2013; Simmonds, 1955; Suzuki et al., 2006; Toennies & Homiller, 1942; Weiss et al., 2018). Enzyme-based keratin extraction methods also preserve the biological and functional properties of partially hydrolysed products. However, unlike the methods mentioned above, microbial and enzymatic methods generally to date are reported to not be able to extract all the keratin. This is because the keratin-containing material's higher-order structure can involve parts of the keratin structure not being accessible to proteases. However, many keratin peptides that are extracted possess various bioactivities and functionality that are of value in food, medical, and biotechnological applications.

Although keratin-containing materials have evolved to be somewhat resistant to degradation, they are recycled and utilized in the environment, and the hydrolysed keratin components are used for growth and survival by some microorganisms that can secrete proteases that can hydrolyse keratin (i.e., keratinases), and these microorganisms are referred to as 'keratinolytic microorganisms'.

Degradation and hydrolysis of keratin are facilitated by elevated temperatures and alkali pH (Brandelli et al., 2010; Wang et al., 2015). Thus, it is becoming of increasing interest to search for thermo-alkalophilic keratinolytic microorganisms and their keratinases. Keratinases employed to hydrolyse keratin industrially should preferably be thermo-alkalophilic hydrolases to enable faster keratinolysis and lower risk of microbial contamination. In addition, mesophilic keratinases are also of interest for use in various applications.

7.5.1 KERATINOLYTIC MICROORGANISMS

Numerous keratinolytic microorganisms belonging to archaea, bacteria and eukaryotes have been discovered. These microbes have been isolated from a wide range of environments from aerobic and anaerobic niches such as Antarctic soils (Gushterova et al., 2005), penguin feathers (Pereira et al., 2014), geothermal vents, hot springs, solfataras and volcanic areas (Cavello et al., 2018; Kublanov et al., 2009), but predominantly they are found and isolated from soils or environments rich in keratinous materials as shown in Table 7.8. Although some of these keratinolytic microbes were isolated from extreme environments, some of their produced keratinases may operate well under both mesophilic and extreme conditions. For example, two strains of keratinolytic actinomycete isolated from Antarctic, *Streptomyces flavis* 2BG and *Microbispora aerata* IMBAS-11A, were found to be both mesophilic and thermophilic, respectively (Brandelli et al., 2010; Gushterova et al., 2005). A list of some keratinolytic microorganisms is provided in Table 7.8. Furthermore, these keratinolytic microorganisms can be immobilized on a solid matrix and used in solid-state fermentation. For example, *Bacillus halodurans* PPKS-2 has been immobilized on alginate beads, which were found to be effective for continuous degradation of keratin-containing materials and keratinase production without the requirement to remove or deactivate the microorganisms in the final products (Prakash et al., 2010).

However, these microorganisms have been separated into two classes of keratinolytic microorganisms: (1) 'true keratinolytic' and (2) 'potential keratinolytic' microorganisms. True keratinolytics are those microbes with the capability to solubilize and degrade hard keratin fully. While potential keratinolytic microbes produce proteases that can potentially hydrolyse keratin, the rate of keratin solubilization by true keratinolytic microorganisms varies between species. It may require different growth conditions and nutrient requirements to achieve hydrolytic capability.

Microbial keratinolysis does not rely solely on the keratinases to breakdown keratin-containing materials. Keratinolytic microorganisms also have a sulphitolysis capability for degrading keratin-containing materials involving a cell-bound redox system. This involves production and release of thiol-containing compounds such as sulphite and thiosulphate by the sulphite efflux pump and cysteine dioxygenase, production of membrane-, and extra- and/or intra-cellular disulphide reductases (Brandelli et al., 2010; Fang et al., 2013a; Korniłłowicz-Kowalska & Bohacz, 2011; Lange et al., 2016; Ramnani et al., 2005; Shavandi et al., 2017; Yamamura et al., 2002). Keratinolytic microorganisms were also found to produce and secrete more than one protease, including keratinases, which are believed to work synergistically to degrade keratin-containing materials. Also, direct contact between keratinolytic microorganisms and keratin-containing materials has been shown to enhance the degradation of keratin. Keratinolytic fungi can also physically break down keratin-containing materials through mycelial penetration induced by mechanical pressure (Brandelli et al., 2010; Moreira et al., 2007). Not only that, the lytic polysaccharide mono-oxygenases (LPMOs) in fungi have also been found to assist in degradation of keratin-containing materials. LPMOs were found to disrupt the glycosylated bonds between threonine and serine and N-aceytylglucosamine on keratin filaments leading to the changes in the steric conformation of the keratin monomer and head, and loosening of the structure (Lange et al., 2016). A detailed diagram showing the overview of microbial degradation of keratin-containing material mechanisms can be found in Lange et al. (2016).

Lastly, some keratinolytic microorganisms are regarded as safe, while others are potential pathogens. However, some of the keratinolytic microorganisms that were regarded as non-pathogenic were also found to be antibiotic-resistant microorganisms such as *Serratia* spp. (Livrelli et al., 1996; Simsek, 2019). Therefore, it is important to carefully screen and select keratinolytic microorganisms that are intended to be used in research and industrial applications.

TABLE 7.8
Some examples of keratinolytic microorganisms

Microorganisms	Source	Molecular Weight	Optimal Activity	Substrates Used in Protease Assay	Effects of Metal Ions	Degradation of Keratin-Containing Materials	References
Alcaligenes sp. AQ05-001	Feather dumping site soil	-	-	Azokeratin	-	-	(Yusuf et al., 2016)
Actinomadura keratinilytica Cpt29	Poultry compost	29.23 kDa	70 °C pH 10	Keratin azure	Activity and thermostability enhanced by 5 mM Mn^{2+}	Microbial fermentation and enzymatic degradation	(Habbeche et al., 2014)
Amycolatopsis sp. strain MBRL 40	Limestone habitat	-	-	Keratin azure and ground feather	-	Enzymatic degradation	(Ningthoujam et al., 2016; Ramakrishna Reddy et al., 2017)
Aphanoasus keratinophilus	Lignocellulosic waste & chicken feathers	-	37 °C pH 7.8	Casein and chicken feather	-	Microbial fermentation of chicken feather	(Bohacz & Korniłłowicz-Kowalska, 2019)
Bacillus amyloliquefaciens S13	Marine brown algae (*Zonaria tournefortii*) from Mediterranean coast of Algeria east of Tipaza	KERZT-A: 47 kDaKERZT-B: 28 kDa	50C, at pH 6.560 °C at pH 8.0	Hammerstein casein Keratin azure	Activity enhances by Ca^{2+}, Mn^{2+}, Mg^{2+}, and Zn^{2+}, Activity inhibits by Ni^{2+}, Cd^{2+}, and Hg^{2+}.	Enzymatic degradation of chicken & duck feather	(Hamiche et al., 2019)
B. cereus B5esz	-	-	-	Pig bristle	-	Microbial fermentation and enzymatic degradation with addition of 10-100 mM sulphite of bristles	(Laba et al., 2015)
B. halodurans JB 99	Sugarcane molasses	29 kDa	70 °C pH 11.0	CaseinKeratin	Activity enhances by Ca^{2+}, Ba^{2+}, Mg^{2+} Activity inhibited by Zn^{2+}	Enzymatic degradation of chicken feathers with reduction by 0.1% (v/v) β-mercaptoethanol	(Shrinivas & Naik, 2011)
B. licheniformis ALW1	Keratinous wastes (feather, leather and wool)	-	65 °C pH 8.0	Soluble keratin	-	Microbial fermentation and enzymatic degradation of feather.	(Abdel-Fattah et al., 2018)
B. licheniformis RG1	-	-	-	Feather and casein		Microbial fermentation and enzymatic degradation of feather	(Ramakrishna Reddy et al., 2017; Ramnani et al., 2005)

Keratin as an Alternative Protein 191

B. pumilus A1	Slaughterhouse polluted water	-	55–60 °C pH 8.5–9.0	Casein and Keratin respectively	Activity is enhanced by 5 mM Ca^{2+} and Na^+. Activity is inhibited by, Cu^{2+}, Mn^{2+} and Hg^{2+}	Microbial fermentation	(Fakhfakh-Zouari et al., 2010; Ramakrishna Reddy et al., 2017)
B. pumilus NRC21	Natural composting wastes from chicken farm soil and feather	30 kDa	45–50 °C pH 7.5–8.5	Keratin azure and azocasein	Activity and thermostability are stimulated and enhanced by up to 5 mM Na^+, K^+, and Mg^{2+}. Activity inhibited by Mn^{2+}, Ni^{2+}, Co^{2+}, Zn^{2+} and Cu^{2+}	Enzymatic degradation of ground feather.	(Tork et al., 2016)
B. pumilus GRK	Feather dumping site soil	-	-	Soluble keratin	Activity enhanced by Ca^{+2} and Mg^2 Activity inhibited by Hg^+	Microbial fermentation of chicken feather	(Ramakrishna Reddy et al., 2017)
B. thruingiensis AD-12	Soil	39 kDa	30 °C pH 7.0	Wool keratin	Activity is stimulated by Mn^{2+}, and Li^+	-	(Gegeckas et al., 2014)
B. subtilis DP1	Poultry farm soil	97.4 kDa	37 °C pH 10.0	Soluble keratinGrounded feather	Activity enhanced by up to 5mM Ca^{2+} and Mg^{2+} Activity inhibited by Zn^{2+} and Mn^{2+}	Microbial fermentationEnzymatic Dehairing effect	(Sanghvi et al., 2016)
B. subtilis NRC3	Natural composting wastes from chicken farm soil and feather	32 kDa	40–50 °C pH 7.5–8.0	Keratin azure, and azocasein	Activity stimulated by up to 5 mM Na^+, K^+, Mg^{2+}, Ba^{2+}, and Ca^{2+}. Activity inhibited by Mn^{2+}, Ni^{2+}, Co^{2+}, Zn^{2+} and Cu^{2+}	-	(Tork et al., 2013)
Bacillus subtilis SCK6	Saline alkali soil	40.08 kDa	50 °C pH 6.5	Casein	Activity slightly enhanced by up to 5 mM Li^+ and K^+. Activity slightly inhibited slightly by other ions at 5 mM concentration	Enzymatic dehairing effect.	(Tian et al., 2019)
Caldicoprobacter algeriensis	Terrestrial hot spring water in Guelma, Algeria	33.2 kDa	50 °C pH 7.0	Keratin azure	Activity enhances by Ca^{2+}, Mg^{2+}, and Mn^{2+} Activity inhibits by Ni^{2+}, Hg^{2+} and Cd^{2+}.	-	(Bouacem et al., 2016)
Lysobacter sp. A03	Penguin feathers	20-110 kDa	15–20 °C pH 8.5	Azokeratin	-	Microbial fermentation of feather meal	(Pereira et al., 2014)

(Continued)

TABLE 7.8 (Continued)
Some examples of keratinolytic microorganisms

Microorganisms	Source	Molecular Weight	Optimal Activity	Substrates Used in Protease Assay	Effects of Metal Ions	Degradation of Keratin-Containing Materials	References
Microbacterium sp. Kr10	Decomposing chicken feathers	42 kDa	50 °C pH 7.5	Azocasein	Activity stimulated by up to 5 mM Mg^{2+} and Zn^{2+} Activity was strongly inhibited by Hg^{2+} and Cu^{2+}, and partially inhibited by Sn^{2+}	Enzymatic hydrolysis of ground feather in sodium mercaptoacetate solution	(Thys & Brandelli, 2006)
Pseudomonas sp. LM19	Feather dumping site soil	-	-	Azokeratin and feather	-	Microbial fermentation of ground feather	(Mohamad et al., 2017)
Paenibacillus woosongensis TKB2	Feather dumping site soil	-	-	Keratin	-	-	(Paul et al., 2013)
Purpureocillium lilacinum LPS # 876	Soil	37 kDa	40 °C pH 8.0-8.75	Azocasein	Activity inhibited by K^+, Ca^{2+}, Mg^{2+}, Zn^{2+}, Hg^{2+}	-	(Cavello et al., 2013)
Serratia marcescens P3	Brazilian Atlantic forest soil	53 kDa	40-45 °C, pH 6.5	Azokeratin	Activity stimulated by Zn^{2+} and Ca^{2+}	-	(Bach et al., 2012)
Streptocyces auerofaciens K13	Livestock farm soil	46 kDa	75 °C pH 12.0	Keratin	Activity enhanced by K^+, Cu^{2+}, Mn^{2+}, Ca^{2+}, Li^+, and Sr^{2+}	-	(Gong et al., 2015)
Trichoderma harzianum isolate HZN12	Poultry farm soil	-	-	Keratin azure	-	Dehairing effect	(Bagewadi et al., 2018)
Xanthomonas sp. P5	Rhizospheric soil from roots of various plants	-	-	Soluble keratin	-	Microbial fermentation of feather	(Jeong et al., 2010)

7.5.1.1 Keratinolytic Fungi

Keratinolytic fungi are classed based on their pathogenicity. The keratinolytic dermatophytic fungi include *Chrysosporium*, *Microsporum* and *Trichophyton* genera; while the keratinolytic nondermatophytic fungi include *Acremonium, Alternaria, Aspergillus, Beauveria, Curvularia, Doratomyces, Myrothecium, Paecilomyces, Penicillium, Purpureocillium lilacinum* LPS # 876, *Trichoderma, Scopulariopsis* (Bohacz & Korniłłowicz-Kowalska, 2019; Brandelli et al., 2010; Cavello et al., 2013; Shavandi et al., 2017). Although the keratinolytic dermatophytic fungi possess various biotechnological potentials, their pathogenicity excludes them from use in commercial applications.

7.5.1.2 Keratinolytic Bacteria

Of all microbes, bacteria are the most extensively studied keratinolytic microorganisms. This is because most bacteria generally grow faster under their optimal growth conditions and nutrient requirements. *Bacillus* genus is the major producer of bacterial keratinases. Among them, *Bacillus licheniformis* PWD-1 and its produced keratinase are the most extensively studied. Other keratinolytic *Bacillus* species include *B. aerius* (Bhari et al., 2018), *B. amyloliquefaciens* (Hamiche et al., 2019), *B. cereus* (Chen et al., 2011; Laba et al., 2015), *B. halodurans* (Shrinivas & Naik, 2011), *B. subtilis* (Sanghvi et al., 2016; Tork et al., 2013), *B. pumilus* (Fakhfakh-Zouari et al., 2010; Ramakrishna Reddy et al., 2017; Tork et al., 2016), and *B. pseudofirmus* (Kojima et al., 2006), *B. thuringienesis* (Gegeckas et al., 2014) also produce keratinases. However, only some strains of these *Bacillus* species are considered keratinolytic, while some are also alkalophilic and thermophilic. Not only that, different strains from the same species were also found to produce different keratinases, as shown in Table 7.8.

Some thermophilic bacteria have been found to possess keratinolytic activity. However, only a few of them are considered cultivatable. These thermophilic and thermotolerant keratinolytic bacteria include *Clostridium sporogenes* (Ionata et al., 2008), *Fervidobacterium* spp. such as *F. pennavorans* (Mehta et al., 2016) and *F. islandicum* (Lee et al., 2015), *Meiothermus ruber* H328 (Kataoka et al., 2014), *Thermoanaerobacter* spp. (Kublanov et al., 2009; Riessen & Antranikian, 2001), and *Thermoactinomyces* spp. (Wang et al., 2015). Examples of alkaliphilic keratinolytic bacteria include *B. halodurans* JB 99 and PPKS-2 (Prakash et al., 2010; Shrinivas & Naik, 2011), *B. pseudofirmus* FA30-01 (Kojima et al., 2006), *B. pumilus* GRK (Ramakrishna Reddy et al., 2017), *B. subtilis* DP1 (Sanghvi et al., 2016), *Brevibacillus* spp. AS-S10-II (Rai & Mukherjee, 2011), *Nesterenkonia* spp. AL20 (Bakhtiar et al., 2005), and *Nocardiopsis* sp. TOA-1 (Mitsuiki et al., 2002). Other keratinolytic microorganisms include *Chryseobacterium* spp. (Chaudhari et al., 2013; Lv et al., 2010; Park et al., 2015), *Lysobacter* spp. (Pereira et al., 2014), *Serratia* spp. (Fuke et al., 2018; Khardenavis et al., 2009), and *Stenotrophomonas* spp. (Fang et al., 2013a; 2013b).

7.5.1.3 Keratinolytic Actinomycetes

Many keratinolytic actinomycetes have been found, while *Streptomyces* spp. were found to be the most predominant keratinolytic actinomycetes. For example, thermophilic keratinolytic actinomycetes include *Actinomadura keratinilytica* Cpt29 (Habbeche et al., 2014), *Microbispora aerata* IMBAS-11A (Gushterova et al., 2005), *Streptomyces* spp. such as, *S. gulbarguensis* (Syed et al., 2009), *S. thermoviolaceus*, and *S. thermonitrificans* (Brandelli et al., 2010); while, mesophilic actinomycetes include *S.* sp. MS-2 (Mabrouk, 2008) *S. albidoflavus* K1-02, *S. flavis*, *S. graminofaciens*, *S. pactum* DSM 40530 (Brandelli et al., 2010). And, thermophilic and alkalophilic actinomycetes include *S. aureofaciens* K13 (Gong et al., 2015).

7.5.2 KERATINASES

In a similar way to using microbial degradation methods, enzymatic methods can also be applied to hydrolyse keratin-containing materials, but with a more precise and controlled effect. Keratinolytic microorganisms have been found to produce more than one keratinase and other proteases, as well as having other characteristics which work synergistically to breakdown keratin-containing compounds. Due to complex multi-action of various biochemical factors, obtaining reproducible products can often be a challenge. In addition, different keratinases also have different catalytic properties, including different hydrolytic specificity and conditions for optimal activity. Hence, it is possible to choose one or more keratinases and/or proteases, for hydrolysis of keratin-containing materials to produce hydrolysates with desirable structural (amino acids sequence and protein conformation) and functional properties, which will later be discussed in Sections 1.5.1. However, the cost of enzymes may increase production costs, and they are often single-use materials. However, immobilization of enzymes can often improve the enzyme stability and shelf-life by preventing autolysis and provide protection against the environment, such as temperature and pH, and facilitate recovery (Konwarh et al., 2009). However, the disadvantages of immobilized enzymes are that the enzyme-substrate interaction can often be limited, even with the inclusion of suitable spacer chemistry on the immobilization material, and thus result in a lower extraction yield. Examples of immobilization systems for keratinases include poly(ethylene glycol)-supported Fe_3O_4 superparamagnetic nanoparticles for tannery dehairing (Konwarh et al., 2009), pectin PVA cryogel patches used in antimicrobial treatment (Martinez et al., 2013), and keratinases immobilized on modified bagasse cellulose have been applied to treated wastewater (Zhang et al., 2019).

Most of the documented keratinases from various actinomycetes, bacteria and fungi are predominantly secreted from the cells. This is because keratin-containing substances are often large and insoluble in water. Thus, the microorganisms must secrete keratinases into the environment to breakdown keratinous compounds into smaller size peptides which are usually soluble in water, and then they can be transported across the cell membrane. Keratinases exist in heterogeneous multimeric forms with molecular weights ranging from 18 to 500 kDa (Kataoka et al., 2014), but most are less than 50 kDa and in the form of monomers (Brandelli et al., 2010). The larger keratinases are often produced by thermophilic microorganisms, and they are often metalloproteases, as shown in Table 7.8.

7.5.2.1 Catalytic Mechanisms of Keratinases

Most keratinases are endo-proteases possessing a broad spectrum of activity capable of hydrolysing both soluble and insoluble proteins. Keratinases were found to have a wide range of optimal activity generally between 15–85 °C and pH 6.5–12.5, but predominantly between 40–60 °C and pH 7.5–10.0 (Table 7.8). However, some keratinases were found to have optimal activity at temperatures up to 100 °C and under slightly acidic to extreme alkali conditions (Brandelli et al., 2010). Keratinases are related to the serine-type subtilisin-like protease family (S8 family) (Lange et al., 2016). However, it remains unclear as to which subtilisin-related features are linked to the mechanisms of keratin hydrolysis, as not all subtilisin-related proteases are capable of degrading keratins. Most keratinase proteomic sequence analyses are compared based on the similarity of sequence to *B. licheniformis* KerA keratinase (Lin et al., 1992). Besides, these keratinases have been tested with specific substrates and inhibitors and were found that most of them are either serine proteases or metalloproteases with the target site of hydrolysis at aromatic and hydrophobic amino acids at the P1 position of the keratins (Brandelli et al., 2010).

The amino acid composition of keratins (constituted of 50–60% of hydrophobic and aromatic amino acids) and the type of amino acids residing next to the cleaved bond at P1 also affects the keratinase site of cleavage (Brandelli et al., 2010). Besides, many keratinases were found to possess an extended active site which allows them to bind complex multi-protein assemblies such as keratin, as a substrate, via electrostatic interactions (Brandelli et al., 2010).

The activity of keratinases is often enhanced by the presence of Na^+, K^+, Ca^{2+}, Mg^{2+}, and Mn^{2+} (Table 7.8), resulting in enzyme-substrate complex stabilization and improved thermostability. Conversely, transition and heavy metals (especially Cu^{2+}, Ag^+, Hg^{2+}, Pb^{2+}, Cd^{2+}, Ni^{2+}, and Fe^{2+}) have been found to inhibit keratinase activity (Table 7.8). Furthermore, the activity of many keratinases is generally enhanced in the presence of reducing or sulphitolysis agents, which reduce the disulphide bonds and improve the access of the keratinases to the reduced keratin substrate. Most keratinases are unable to hydrolyse keratin in the presence of cysteine disulphide linkages efficiently.

The enhanced resistance of keratinases in the presence of reducing conditions is achieved by the introduction of prolines in the keratinases autolytic sites by rigidifying the autolysis loop (Liang et al., 2010). This also leads to thermostabilizing the keratinases.

In addition, Kataoka et al. (2014) found large molecular size (>500 kDa) keratinases from *Meiothermus ruber* H328 assembled and existed in the form of membrane-associated proteins extruding out of the outer cell membrane. This keratinases complex may be lipophilic and provide tolerance against various denaturants such as 30% (w/v) SDS, and 40% (v/v) organic solvents (acetone, acetonitrile, chloroform ethanol, and methanol).

Although the mechanism of enzymatic keratinolysis is fully understood, it is hypothesized that microbial and enzymatic keratinolysis is achieved by a combination of sulphitolysis and hydrolytic proteolysis. Sulphitolysis is the process of cleaving or reducing disulphide bonds into cysteine and S-sulfocysteine by keratinolytic microorganisms, or by the addition of sulphite reducing agents. Other mechanisms of sulphitolysis by keratinolytic microorganisms were mentioned in Section 1.4.1. After the disulphide bonds in keratin are reduced, the protein structure of the partially denatured keratin becomes exposed and more accessible for hydrolysis by keratinases.

7.5.3 Production of Keratinases by Keratinolytic Microorganisms

The production of keratinases can be achieved with both submerged cultivations and with solid-state or immobilized fermentation. Apart from the cultivation temperature, pH, and aeration, the nutrient requirement also can have a significant effect on keratinase production. The impact of different nutrient requirements on keratinase production by different species and strains of keratinolytic microorganisms is highly variable (Table 7.8). The maximum keratinase yields are generally obtained in late log and/or stationary growth phases of microorganisms, depending on the species and strain (Wang et al., 2015).

The production of keratinases is usually induced by the presence of keratin-containing materials in the cultivation medium. However, it was found that the incorporation of keratin-containing materials alone in the media can result in reduced production of keratinases by the microorganism, due to limitations in available nitrogen. For keratinolytic microorganisms to survive in a limited nutrient environment, they must produce and secrete keratinases in order to obtain nutrients from keratinous substrates. Other non-keratin-containing substrates have also been found to induce the production of keratinases, such as casein, cheese whey, gelatin soy flour, shrimp shell powder, skim milk (Brandelli et al., 2010). It was found that these non-keratin-containing compounds are also large macronutrients that are not readily absorbable into the cells, which may trigger keratinases and other enzyme production (Tiwary & Gupta, 2010).

The supplementation of keratin-containing media with different carbohydrates, such as glucose, sucrose, bagasse, molasses and starch, as well as additional nitrogen sources, including yeast extract, peptone, tryptone, urea, ammonium chloride and sodium nitrate, have also been found to often enhance keratinase production in certain keratinolytic microorganisms (Brandelli et al., 2010). This is because these easy-to-digest or readily absorbable compounds can boost and provide an adequate level of energy for keratinolytic microorganisms to increase the rate of keratinase production. However, it was found that different nutrient concentrations also have different effects, either enhancing or suppressing the level of keratinase production. This supplementary carbon, inorganic and/or organic nitrogen sources must be at a low level as they may lead to catabolite repression, which may suppress the level of keratinase production in keratinolytic microorganisms (Table 7.8). On the other hand, an excess amount of nutrients can cause the environment to be stressful for the microbes, such as increasing osmotic pressure, lowering water activity, changing the environmental ionic strength, which alters the ionized state of various biological compounds, and increasing the viscosity of the media, which may limit compound migration rate and reduce the oxygen level (Abdel-Fattah et al., 2018).

Many keratinolytic microorganisms, including opportunistic pathogens, have undergone genetic mutations, recombination and cloning to enhance the level of keratinase production, increase the ability to breakdown keratin-containing materials, and improve safety assurance. Cloning a gene encoding keratinase into another microorganism can be an alternative way to increase the production of keratinases, and the new host microorganism may be easier to cultivate under mesophilic conditions, have cheaper production cost, and be safer for users. The expression of a keratinase gene such as the *B. licheniformis* gene encoding the kerA keratinase was found to be enhanced when the microbe detected the presence of keratin-containing materials as the sole carbon and nitrogen source in their surroundings (Lin et al., 1995). This kerA gene has been integrated into the *E. coli* and *B. subtilis* genomes, but was found to produce a lower level of kerA keratinase compared to the wild strain (Brandelli et al., 2010). To enhance the level of keratinase production, multiple copies of the kerA gene were incorporated into the microbial host chromosome (Brandelli et al., 2010).

7.5.4 Applications of Keratinases

Keratinases have been applied to many food products to improve the nutritional value of food production by increasing food digestibility as well as cause plastein reactions, decontaminate, and generate bioactive peptides, soluble proteins and amino acids. Keratinases have been added to animal diets as feed additives to improve their nutritional value and dietary digestibility. In addition, animal feed supplemented with keratinase preparations were found to positively promote animal growth, meat yield, and the development of the intestinal microflora (Brandelli et al., 2010; Odetallah et al., 2003; Wang et al., 2008). These keratinases can also be applied to further decontaminate food and animal feed by hydrolysing disease-causing prion proteins (Brandelli et al., 2010; Sharma & Gupta, 2012). They may also be used to modify the functional properties of the proteins, such as the emulsification (Ewert et al., 2019), gelation (Lamsal et al., 2007), and solubility (Veselá & Friedrich, 2009) of the food by limited proteolysis.

Other applications of keratinases include inclusion in biomedical and pharmaceutical products as dermatological treatments (Gupta et al., 2017), hydrolysis of disease causative prions (Sharma & Gupta, 2012), drug delivery (Martinez et al., 2013; Mohorčič et al., 2007), biotechnology as detergents (Paul et al., 2014; Ramakrishna Reddy et al., 2017), cosmetics (Sanghvi et al., 2016; Villa et al., 2013), fertilizer production (Brandelli et al., 2015; Rai & Mukherjee, 2015), solid and liquid waste treatment (Verma et al., 2017), dehairing (Gumilar et al., 2017; Tian et al., 2019a; 2019b), insect control (Poopathi et al., 2014) and the production and modification of biopolymers and biogas (Brandelli et al., 2010; 2015). The full list of potential applications of keratinases is shown in Figure 7.6.

7.6 APPLICATIONS OF USE OF EXTRACTED KERATINS AND KERATIN HYDROLYSATES IN FOOD AND NUTRITION

Modified keratins have been regarded as safe and implemented in biomedical areas, such as cell transplantation, tissue engineering, and wound healing, which allows cell diffusion and seeding, and with implantable or topical drug delivery biomaterials, and reconstruction of tissues (Cardamone, 2010; Shavandi et al., 2017; Zhao et al., 2015). The low antigenicity of keratin (Li et al., 2013) indicates that keratins may be safe for utilization in food and supplements for both human and animal consumption. Also, keratin could be used to provide intermediate strength to scaffolds that could be used for *in vitro* meat production (Wu et al., 2017). The concept of using wool as a nutritional protein source was investigated by Shorland and co-workers (Shorland &

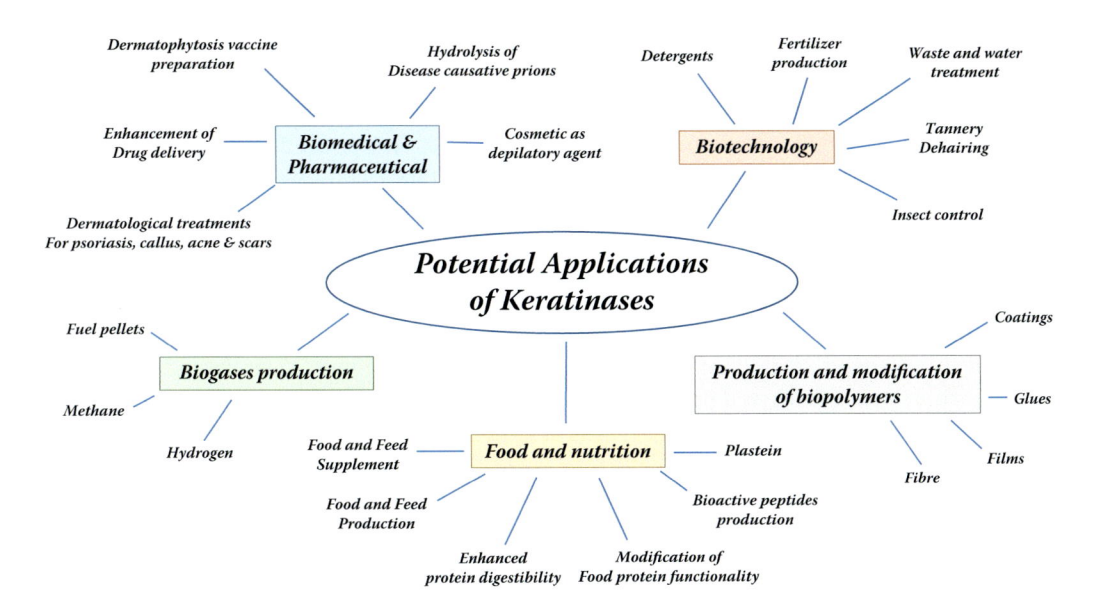

FIGURE 7.6 Potential applications of keratinases.

Bentley, 1968; Shorland & Gray, 1970; Shorland & Matthews, 1968). Earlier studies that used ground wool or wool protein extracted by the reduction method (sodium sulphite followed by acetic acid precipitation) were unsuccessful, as their use in an adult rat diet was rejected by the animals (Shorland & Matthews, 1968). The authors reported the production of acceptable food-grade wool protein after chemical or enzymatic solubilization of wool that was used in a range of baked products to substitute for flour by up to 35%. Sensory evaluation of the products produced with the hydrolysed wool protein was not different from that of control baked products (Shorland & Matthews, 1968; Shorland & Gray, 1970). However, neither chemically nor enzymatically obtained wool protein were successful in supporting the growth of weanling rats (Shorland & Gray, 1970). The use of wool protein and tripe protein in equal parts in a rat diet at 15% was found to be non-toxic and supported the growth of the rats with a 29% body weight gain in 10 days.

This led to the perception of supplementation of the missing amino acids (histidine and lysine) that resulted in nutritionally adequate protein. The protein was obtained using sodium sulphide and sodium hyposulfite reduction, followed by acid precipitation at pH 5.0 with acetic acid and washing steps with hot water (60 °C) and ethanol. The amino acid profile of wool protein extracts has lower histidine, lysine, methionine and tryptophan content than what is recommended by the World Health Organization, the Food and Agriculture Organization of the United Nations, and the United Nations University (WHO/FAO/UNU) essential amino acid contents for healthy individuals (Food and Agriculture Organization of the United Nations, World Health Organization, & United Nations University, 2007). The deficiency levels appear to be similar when wool protein is extracted by either reduction or acid hydrolysis (Tables 7.2 and 7.4), except for a higher lysine content in the reduction method and a higher histidine content in the acid extracted protein). A clear difference, however, is the higher cysteine content in the reduction method that was >2-fold higher than with the acid extraction. Supplementation with histidine and methionine or lysine improved the daily weight gain, and no weight gain was observed in rats on un-supplemented diets that were fed a diet containing 10% wool protein (Shorland & Gray, 1970). Also, cats consuming a diet supplemented with 2% wool protein with the diet having a similar amino acid profile to that of a control diet and a special cat diet, except for higher cysteine content, had similar growth to that with the control and the special diet (Deb-Choudhury et al., 2018). The results from these trials, however, are limited in the number of experimental units used (2–6 rats and 8 cats). Overall, these results support the potential use of wool protein at low levels (2–10%) in diets, without any detrimental issues in terms of acceptability or growth performance in animal models. According to Shorland and Gray (1970), methionine appears to be the most important amino acid that needs to be supplemented. The incorporation of wool in any food formulation would allow greater flexibility in terms of potential mixing of various ingredients to achieve a suitable amino acid balance.

As mentioned earlier, keratins were found to be resistant to digestion by common digestive enzymes. Thus, pre-hydrolysis of keratin using either keratinolytic microorganisms or keratinases is a possible solution to increase their digestibility and improve their nutritional value and functional properties.

A full list of keratin hydrolysate applications is displayed in Figure 7.7. In food and nutrition, keratin hydrolysates and derived peptides have been applied in animal feed (Brandelli et al., 2010; Korniłłowicz-Kowalska & Bohacz, 2011), packaging technology in the form of films, foils and encapsulates (Mokrejs et al., 2011), as well as generation of bioactive peptides exhibiting antioxidant activity (Fakhfakh et al., 2011; Fontoura et al., 2014; 2019; Ohba et al., 2003; Wan et al., 2016), antihypertension or suppression of high blood pressure (ACE-inhibitory) (Fontoura et al., 2014; Ohba et al., 2003; Sinkiewicz et al., 2018), and antidiabetic or suppression of accumulated blood sugar (DPP-IV inhibitory peptides) properties (Fontoura et al., 2014; Sinkiewicz et al., 2018). Other applications include using hydrolysed keratin as a crop fertilizer (Popko et al., 2015), or for biogas/biofuel production (Patinvoh et al., 2016).

7.7 KERATIN HYDROLYSATES IN FOOD AND NUTRITION

Wool keratin hydrolysates and polypeptides have been verified to have low antigenicity and oral toxicity, based on no negative impacts on the cell viability, blood chemistry, haematology, feed consumption and body weight tested, both *in vitro* and *in vivo* (Li et al., 2013). Due to the high-protein content, keratin-containing by-products, especially feathers, are largely converted into animal feed as a feather meal. The methods that have been applied to convert keratin-containing materials into soluble protein, and to increase their digestibility, include ammonolysis, acidic and

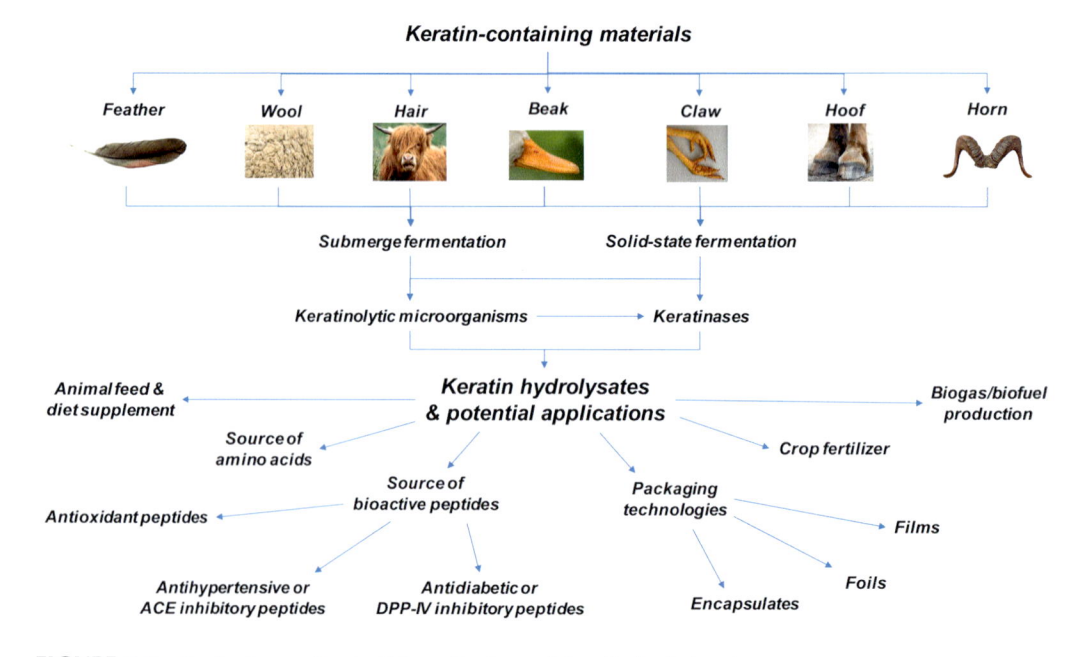

FIGURE 7.7 Production and potential applications of keratin hydrolysates.

alkaline hydrolysis and physicochemical methods involving thermal treatment of keratin-containing materials with organic solvents such as dimethylformamide (DMF) and dimethyl sulfoxide (DMSO) (Korniłłowicz-Kowalska & Bohacz, 2011). The taste of the extracted keratin was found to be similar to that of fresh cottage cheese with a protein composition similar to that of cottonseed and soybean (Korniłłowicz-Kowalska & Bohacz, 2011). Because of these acceptable sensory properties obtained with extracted keratin, it can potentially be utilized in human food and for nutritional supplement purposes. However, although these meals contain a high content of protein and minerals, they are deficient in arginine, lysine, methionine, threonine, histidine, and also cysteine, depending on the technique used (Korniłłowicz-Kowalska & Bohacz, 2011). Although keratin generally contains a high level of cysteine and/or cystine, this amino acid is often degraded during thermal and chemical treatments (Weiss et al., 2018). Not only that, but by applying these techniques to obtain keratin for animal diets, often it is expensive and requires considerable energy for heat processing and various chemicals, k which could impact the environment. However, these issues can be overcome using microbial and enzymatic keratinolysis techniques.

On the other hand, enzymatic hydrolysis has been applied to improve the nutritional value of keratin and was found to have minimal impact on the keratin backbone (Grazziotin et al., 2006). Both mesophilic and thermophilic keratinolytic microorganisms and their keratinases have been applied to obtain feather lysate, with a nutritional profile similar to that of soya protein, and rich in soluble proteins containing essential amino acids such as isoleucine, lysine, leucine, threonine and valine, although having a lower level of proline and serine (Korniłłowicz-Kowalska & Bohacz, 2011; Vasileva-Tonkova et al., 2009). Microbial and enzymatic hydrolysis methods can also be applied, coupled with the above methods, with a lower level of chemicals or alkali treatments to further improve the digestibility.

The lack of the above-mentioned essential amino acids can be addressed using plastein reactions, which can enhance the nutritional value of protein hydrolysates and improve their functional food properties (Brandelli et al., 2015; Gong et al., 2014; Synowiecki et al., 1996). The exact role of the protease in plastein remains unclear. It has been hypothesized that plasteins are formed because of condensation leading to peptide elongation as well as aggregation and an increase in molecular weight. These reactions are also believed to be related to the hydrophobic interaction between constituent hydrophobic amino acids on peptides (Gong et al., 2014). As keratin is made up of 50–60% hydrophobic amino acids (Sinkiewicz et al., 2018), it is thought that this favours keratin hydrolysates forming plasteins. Plasteins can form from peptides of all sizes, but generally, formation is more favourable with smaller peptides (Gong et al., 2014). However, scientists have applied this technique to improve the biological functionality and amino acid composition, through supplementation of lysine and other essential amino acids, such as methionine, cysteine, tryptophan, glutamic acid and threonine to the keratin hydrolysates (Dalev et al., 1997; Gong et al., 2014). However, under certain circumstances, the disadvantage of plastein aggregation, and structural alteration caused by transpeptidation and peptidyl condensation, may either mask or induce the biological activities of the keratin hydrolysates described in the following Section 1.5.1. One research article was found involving plastein to supplement a keratin hydrolysate with lysine, that reported improved nutritional value (Dalev et al., 1997). With more research on keratin hydrolysate plastein modification, the functional and biological activities of keratin hydrolysates could be further enhanced to incorporate other biological activity.

Chicken feathers were used to produce a keratin hydrolysate using alkaline hydrolysis (at 155 °C for 2 hours at pH 9.5) and a *Bacillus licheniformis* protease, resulted in the formation of potent meat flavour compounds (3-methylbutanal, 4-decadienal, γ-dodecalactone, 2-methyl-3-furanthiol, 2-ethyl-3, 5-dimethylpyrazine, 3-hydroxy-4,5-dimethyl-2(5H)-furanone, bis(2-methyl-3-furyl) disulphide, 2-methylthiophene and 2-thiophenecarboxladehyde) (Opeyemi, 2013). This suggested a potential use of keratin hydrolysates in flavour compound formation. The main advantage of this approach is that potentially only small amounts would need to be used for flavouring food products, but an evaluation of the toxic effects of such products still needs to be assessed.

In addition, consumer acceptability of food is greatly influenced by the sensory properties of food, including taste. Some lower molecular weight protein hydrolysates rich in hydrophobic amino acids, such as leucine, isoleucine, proline, phenylalanine, tryptophan and tyrosine were found to have a bitter taste (Saha & Hayashi, 2001). Previously, it has been shown that protein hydrolysate debittering can be achieved by methods such as protein precipitation, chromatography, activated carbon treatment, and alcohol extraction that is primarily aimed at the removal of hydrophobic and smaller peptides (Gong et al., 2014). However, these small hydrophobic peptides still contain amino acids and possess various biological activities which are health-promoting. Potentially, the use of the plastein reaction can debitter keratin hydrolysates rich in hydrophobic amino acids by increasing the size of the peptide molecules. In addition, plastein gelling enhancing the thixotropic properties can also be used to improve the texture and other sensory properties of food, and supplements containing keratin hydrolysates. Nevertheless, use of the plastein reaction in keratin hydrolysates has the potential to enhance keratin hydrolysates as a functional food, without the loss of structural properties. Although the plastein reaction can be applied to keratin hydrolysates to improve their nutritional value and their food functionality, their associated production cost is the primary limiting factor for industrial application. However, with more research and a better understanding of the mechanism of plastein formation, it may be possible to develop plastein methods with lower production cost for enhanced hydrolysate properties.

7.7.1 KERATIN-DERIVED BIOACTIVE PEPTIDES

As mentioned above, keratins contain 50–60% hydrophobic and aromatic amino acids (Sinkiewicz et al., 2018). During keratin hydrolysis, these amino acids within the keratin structure become exposed, and it is believed that these amino acids primarily contribute to the bioactivities described below.

7.7.1.1 Antioxidant Peptides

Some keratin hydrolysates and peptides have been found to possess antioxidant activity and to prevent free-radical formation (Fakhfakh et al., 2011; Fontoura et al., 2014; 2019; Ohba et al., 2003; Wan et al., 2016). With regards to peptide amino acid composition, the antioxidant properties are hypothesized to be caused by the high level of cysteine, which contains a thiol functional group (R-SH) that acts as a reducing agent or hydrogen donor to the free radicals. In addition, arginine and some hydrophobic amino acids can donate a hydrogen ion (Wan et al., 2016), and phenylalanine, proline and glycine can donate hydrogen atoms to the free radicals or quenched unpaired electrons, while isoleucine, leucine and valine can interact with acyl groups (R-C=O) (Zou et al., 2016).

Fontoura et al. (2019) identified a keratin-derived antioxidant peptide (LPGPILSSFPQ) that was generated by cultivation of *Chryseobacterium* sp. kr6 in feather containing media and was found to possess 2,2'-azino-bis-3-ethylbenzothiazoline-6-sulfonic acid (ABTS) radical scavenging activity and to have total reactive antioxidant potential (TRAP). However, it was found that the peptide did not display Fe^{2+} chelating activity, but it was able to reduce Fe^{3+}. This indicates that the primary antioxidant properties are due to the ability of the peptide to scavenge hydroxyl radicals, transfer electrons and donate hydrogen atoms. In terms of amino acid composition, the peptide contains glycine and proline, which are believed to contribute to antioxidant properties. Wan et al. (2016) identified an antioxidant peptide (SNLCRPCG) that was obtained from the cultivation of *B. subtilis* S1-4 in chopped feather fragments. The peptide was found to possess 2,2,-diphenyl-1-picrylhydrazyl (DPPH) (IC_{50} = 0.39 mg mL^{-1}) and ABTS radical scavenging activity (IC_{50} = 0.35 mg mL^{-1}), Fe^{2+} chelating activity (IC_{50} = 1.85 mg mL^{-1}), and Fe^{3+} reduction to Fe^{2+} activity. The authors stated that the antioxidant properties of their peptide are due to the ability of cysteine, glycine, proline and arginine to donate protons.

7.7.1.2 Antihypertension or Angiotensin I-Converting Enzyme (ACE) Inhibitory Peptides

Angiotensin-converting enzyme (ACE) is an enzyme that regulates physiological blood pressure by converting angiotensin I into the vasoconstrictor angiotensin II, as well as degrading the vasodilator bradykinin. Patients suffering from cardiovascular disease can use ACE inhibitor to lower their blood pressure. ACE inhibitor binding to the ACE enzyme is reported to be enhanced by the presence of proline and hydroxylproline (Sinkiewicz et al., 2018) and by hydrophobic amino acids located in the C-terminal sequence of the peptide (Fontoura et al., 2014).

Fontoura et al. (2014) demonstrated that feather hydrolysates were capable of inhibiting ACE up to 65%, to a level similar to that of milk protein hydrolysates and soybean hydrolysates. However, a study by Ohba et al. (2003) showed that hydrolysates from horn and hoof showed a relatively low ACE-inhibitory effect.

7.7.1.3 Antidiabetic or Dipeptidyl Peptidase-IV (DPP-IV) Inhibitory Peptides

Diabetes mellitus (DM) is a chronic, life-threatening disease that results in poor control of blood sugar (glucose). Until to date, no cure for both types of DM has been found, but treatment can be done to control the level of sugar in the blood. One of the treatments is to inhibit the action of the dipeptidyl peptidase-IV enzyme (DPP-IV). DPP-IV is a protease that deactivates gastric inhibitory polypeptide (GIP) and glucagon-like peptide 1 (GLP-1) which are incretin hormones that assist in regulating the blood sugar level by stimulating the secretion of glucose-induced insulin. By inactivating DDP-IV, the degradation rate of these two incretin hormones is reduced, resulting in the lowering of blood glucose levels. Fontoura et al. (2014) demonstrated that feather hydrolysates were capable of inhibiting DPP-IV by up to 44%. However, the information on the correlation between the amino acid sequences of the keratin hydrolysates and DPP-IV inhibitory properties has not been fully evaluated.

7.7.2 KERATINS IN FOOD PACKAGING

With regards to the emerging global awareness of the environmental impact of plastics, the search for alternatives to single-use plastics, including food packaging and the challenges in their recyclability, is of increasing interest. Keratins have considerable potential for use in applications requiring robust, impermeable and biodegradable food packaging materials. Extracted feather and wool keratins (Mokrejs et al., 2011) have been incorporated with various biopolymers, such as dialdehyde starch (Dou et al., 2015) from wheat or corn, polyhydroxyalkanoates (PHAs) (Pardo-Ibáñez et al., 2014), ethylene glycol diglycidyl ether (EGDE) and glycerol diglycidyl ether (GDE) (Garavand et al., 2017), polyvinyl alcohol (PVA) (Dou et al., 2014) and methylcellulose (Liebeck et al., 2017) for food packaging. Before keratin can be utilized in food packaging, it needs to be extracted in the form of a monomeric reduced keratin polymer. This can be achieved by disrupting the intermolecular disulphide bonds and other intermolecular interactions within the keratin fibre. The methods for obtaining such extracted keratin (Sections 7.3, 7.4.1, and 7.5.1) have been highly variable between studies, depending on the keratinous substrates, the target structural properties, and the application of end products. Aqueous solutions containing solubilized reduced keratin can be cast with the above-mentioned biopolymers and cross-linked to form a semi-crystalline structure and allow disulphide bonds to form (Baldwin et al., 2011). The advantages of utilizing keratin in food packaging are that they have low antigenicity (Li et al., 2013), they are biodegradable, relatively hydrophobic and impermeable to most organic solvents, are mechanically strong, biocompatible, and their flexibility can be modified. However, there is limited information available on the use of keratin hydrolysates in food packaging. Mokrejs et al. (2011) suggested that keratin hydrolysates could potentially be applied in packaging technology by using controlled partial hydrolysis to modify and improve the physicochemical properties of the keratin hydrolysates for different packaging purposes. Keratin hydrolysates typically have a much smaller molecule size range compared to that of extracted keratin using methods listed in Section 1.3. It has been suggested that keratin hydrolysates may have potential applications more suitable for microencapsulation purposes.

7.7.2.1 Use of Keratin in Microencapsulates and Edible Coatings

Microencapsulation is of considerable interest in the food industry as there is potential for the protection and controlled release for sensitive nutrients, drugs, colouring dyes, flavours and various other food compounds which may not be immiscible in the food matrix, and for prolonging shelf-life. Extracted oxidized wool keratins have been incorporated into microcapsules (Rajabinejad et al., 2018; Yamauchi & Khoda, 1997) by a sonication method. The formation of microencapsulation can be achieved through (1) physical processes such as solvent evaporation, lyophilization, spray drying, and the use of supercritical fluids, (2) chemical-based methods, such as molecular inclusion complexation and interfacial polymerization, and lastly (3) physicochemical techniques, such as ionic gelation, coacervation, and liposome formation (Ozkan et al., 2019). Apart from the protection and preservation of food compounds, microencapsulation was also found to be capable of masking undesirable sensory properties such as taste, colour and aroma of supplemented nutrient and food compounds. In addition, Baldwin et al. (2011) reported that keratin microencapsulated vessels are more capable of encapsulated hydrophobic compounds such as dyes and glycerides compared to other encapsulates prepared from common proteins such as egg yolk, soy protein, bovine serum albumin (BSA), and α-lactalbumin. The superior barrier properties and membrane fabrication are achieved because of the reformation of disulphide bonds between the cysteine residues of the reduced keratin molecules.

Only limited information on the application of keratin hydrolysates in microencapsulation is available, and more research on the use of hydrolysed keratin in encapsulation technology is required (Mokrejs et al., 2011).

7.8 SAFETY CONSIDERATIONS

Keratin protein presents a great opportunity as a novel protein source, as it has several environmental and commercial advantages. However, there are unaddressed concerns in terms of safety in medical products and consideration of related environmental pollutants. Depending on the farming systems used, there might be a wide range of pesticides, permitted veterinary medicines, such as regular vaccination, treatments for sun exposure and insects that leave some residues in wool which could end up in the extracted keratin. Furthermore, the same environmental pollution issues found in meat products will be found in keratin. The life span of chicken under current commercial production systems (45 days) and annual wool shearing of sheep, it expected the accumulation of such contaminants might be at a lower level compared with meat.

Keratin extraction and processing can lead to the formation of lanthionine and lysinoalanine, during extraction using high temperatures and alkaline treatments (Table 7.9). A comprehensive review on the occurrence, chemistry, microbiology and formation of these compounds has been reported by Friedman (1999). These compounds may influence nutritional value and have biological and health implications. Lanthionine and lysinoalanine are found in some peptides and proteins that exert antimicrobial activity (cinnamycin, duramycin, epidermin, nisin, and subtilin), that are termed lantibiotics and are also naturally found in body compartments such as aorta, bone, collagen, dentin, and eye cataract, and their presence is suggested to be related to the aging process (Friedman, 1999). The critical biological effects reported for these compounds are;

1. Lysinoalanine has a strong metal-binding capacity and thus can influence the bioavailability of minerals such as copper, nickel and zinc.
2. Lysinoalanine causes nephrocytomegaly, that can induce enlargement of kidney cell nuclei, which has been studied in rodents but not in primates (Friedman, 1999).

TABLE 7.9
Amino acid composition of wool extracts obtained from reduction (Shorland & Gray, 1970) and acid hydrolysis (Deb-Choudhury, 2018) methods compared to common commercial proteins (% protein)

Amino Acids	Food and Agriculture Organization of the United Nations, World Health Organization, & United Nations University, 2007	Liu et al. (2019) Casein Protein	Liu et al. (2019) Whey Protein	Liu et al. (2019) Soy Protein	Liu et al. (2019) Pea Protein	Shorland and Gray (1970) Wool Keratin	Deb-Choudhury et al. (2018) Wool Hydrolysate	(Houltham et al., 2014) Keratin	(Houltham et al., 2014) Casein
Histidine	1.5	3.1	1.6	2.5	2.4	0.91	1.1	0.5	2.8
Isoleucine	3	5.9	7.4	4.9	4.4	3.76	3.8	5.3	5.5
Leucine	5.9	10.2	12.1	5.6	7.6	8.38	8.5	8.3	9.2
Lysine	4.5	8.5	10.9	5.6	6.7	3.76	2.4	1.2	7.4
Methionine	1.6	2.9	2.5	1.4	0.9	0.57	0.6	0.4	2.5
Phenylalanine	2.8	5.5	3.8	5.5	5.7	3.52	3.6	4.6	4.9
Threonine	2.3	4.6	8.8	3.9	3.8	6.40	6.2	4.9	1.1
Tryptophan	0.6	1.4	1.7	1.3	0.9	-	-	-	1.2
Valine	3.9	7.6	6.9	5.1	4.9	5.32	6.3	8.8	6.5
Alanine	6.9	3.2	5.5	4.5	5.4	4.14	4.0	4.2	2.7
Arginine	7.1	3.7	2.7	7.8	8.4	10.42	11.1	7.0	3.7
Aspartic acid	6.9	7.5	12.2	11.8	11.9	7.25	7.0	7.6	6.9
Cysteine	0.6	0.4	2.7	1.2	1.0	11.86	5.1	0.4$	0.3
Glutamic acid	12.1	22.7	21.5	20.5	16.4	16.04	14.9	11.8	23.2
Glycine	7.7	1.9	2.3	4.4	4	4.10	5.1	6.3	2.4
Proline	8.2	10.5	6.1	4.9	4.4	6.34	7.1	10	10.7
Serine	4.2	6.5	6.7	5.2	5.4	7.71	7.9	10.6	4.4
Tyrosine	4	5.9	3.7	3.9	4	4.00	5.2	2.1	5.7
NH$_4$						1.32			

$: in addition to 6.15 % cysteic acid

In Table 7.2, there seems to be a correlation of lower lanthionine content in extracted keratin with an increase in alkaline extraction solution concentration. Several compounds have been reported to reduce the formation of lysinoalanine and lanthionine, such as sodium sulphite that eliminated the formation lanthionine, reduced the formation of lysinoalanine by 58% and improved the retention of lysine by 17% (Friedman, 1999). Other compounds that can control the formation of lanthionine and lysinoalanine are SH-containing amino acids, ammonia, ascorbic acid, citric acid, malic acid, and glucose and acylation of amine groups of lysine (Friedman, 1999).

Recent studies on lanthionine derivatives have suggested that a synthetic compound lanthionine ketimine ethyl ester (LKE), which is a derivative of anthionine ketamine, a naturally occurring compound in brain and the central nervous system, was found to have direct neuroprotective and neurotrophic effects in SH-SY5Y human neuronal cells, in primary mouse cerebellar granule neurons, and a mouse model of multiple sclerosis (MS) (Koehler et al., 2018; Marangoni et al., 2018). Furthermore, LAN-stabilized angiotensin-(1–7) was found to have a therapeutic effect in diabetes mouse models (Kuipers et al., 2019).

7.9 CONSUMER ISSUES

Information regarding the use of keratin in human trials is sparse. Unpublished results from collaborative studies between the University of Otago and Massey University, New Zealand (https://www.stuff.co.nz/national/health/84192576/keratinderived-protein-tested-in-type-2-diabetes-in-11m-research) using muffins containing 10% wool protein indicated that they were acceptable for 1 month and that other baked products were acceptable containing 15% wool protein in sensory trials (non-peer-reviewed data). Furthermore, keratin protein supplementation in the form of drink powder or bar form was investigated in a blind, randomized, cross-over experiment using 17 adult males (Houltham et al., 2014). The keratin dose was provided to the subjects at the rate of 10 g per day for 3 days, followed by 20 g per day for 3 days, and then 30 g per day for 3 days, and finally at 40 g per days for another 5 days). The authors concluded that the keratin protein supplementation did not cause any acute gastrointestinal disturbances, except for increased flatulence, compared to a casein supplementation. This finding creates the opportunity for further research relating to the proposed health and/or ergogenic benefits of keratin protein ingestion for athletes and the general population. A survey carried out in the United States among sports fans, especially those interested in bodybuilding, indicated that the use of keratin in place of casein and whey proteins was considered acceptable and cost less (unpublished results Prof. George Dias, Anatomy Department, Medical School, University of Otago, New Zealand). In terms of religious views or restrictions on the use of keratin, there is apparently no clear probation regarding this in many faiths, to the best of the authors' knowledge. The use of wool for garments and clothing is practice by all religions and there are no exceptions for this to the authors' knowledge. Keratin is present in many parts of animals and birds such as skin hair, fur, nails, claws, and other organs that are permitted in various religions, permitting meat consumption.

7.10 CONCLUSIONS AND FUTURE OUTLOOKS

There is no doubt that keratin has great potential in various food and pharmaceutical applications. Due to its relative high abundancy in many food-processing by-products, keratin-containing materials may be a useful protein alternative to meet required future protein needs that could arise for economic, environmental, or ethical reasons. Various keratin extracts and hydrolysates have been verified as safe for human and animal consumption in several model systems. Several techniques for keratin extraction and hydrolysis have been discussed above. Choosing a suitable keratin extraction technique is important, as the described methods can give rise to keratin extracts and hydrolysates with different physicochemical, sensory, and biological properties. It is very important to determine the formation of lanthionine and lysinoalanine and the cytotoxic or biological activity of the generated keratin. Although some keratin extracts and hydrolysates may be rich or deficient in certain amino acids, their amino acids composition could be balanced by amino supplementation. The utilization of plastein reactions can potentially be applied to mask undesirable sensory properties and to improve biological activities and amino acids profiles. Apart from nutritional applications, keratin can also be used in food packaging and as a scaffold for *in vitro* meat production to provide intermediate strength. Microencapsulation and edible coating applications have also been reported. Increasing concerns regarding animal welfare, climate change and increased need for alternative proteins support consideration of keratin as a potential ethical and sustainable source need to be explored.

REFERENCES

Abdel-Fattah, A. M., El-Gamal, M. S., Ismail, S. A., Emran, M. A., & Hashem, A. M. (2018). Biodegradation of feather waste by keratinase produced from newly isolated *Bacillus licheniformis* ALW1. *Journal of Genetic Engineering and Biotechnology*, 16(2), 311–318. Retrieved from http://www.sciencedirect.com/science/article/pii/S1687157X18300544

Bach, E., Sant'Anna, V., Daroit, D. J., Corrêa, A. P. F., Segalin, J., & Brandelli, A. (2012). Production, one-step purification, and characterization of a keratinolytic protease from Serratia marcescens P3. *Process Biochemistry*, 47(12), 2455–2462. Retrieved from http://www.sciencedirect.com/science/article/pii/S1359511312003765

Bagewadi, Z. K., Mulla, S. I., & Ninnekar, H. Z. (2018). Response surface methodology based optimization of keratinase production from *Trichoderma harzianum* isolate HZN12 using chicken feather waste and its application in dehairing of hide. *Journal of Environmental Chemical Engineering*, 6(4), 4828–4839. Retrieved from http://www.sciencedirect.com/science/article/pii/S2213343718303828

Baker, D. H. (2006). Comparative species utilization and toxicity of sulfur amino acids. *The Journal of Nutrition*, 136(6), 1670S–1675S. doi:10.1093/jn/136.6.1670S

Bakhtiar, S., Estiveira, R. J., & Hatti-Kaul, R. (2005). Substrate specificity of alkaline protease from alkaliphilic feather-degrading Nesterenkonia sp. AL20. *Enzyme and Microbial Technology*, 37(5), 534–540. doi:10.1016/j.enzmictec.2005.04.003

Baldwin, E. A., Hagenmaier, R., & Bai, J. (2011). *Edible Coatings and Films to Improve Food Quality*, 2nd Edition. Boca Raton, FL, United States, CRC Press.

Bhari, R., Kaur, M., Singh, R. S., Pandey, A., & Larroche, C. (2018). Bioconversion of chicken feathers by *Bacillus aerius* NSMk2: A potential approach in poultry waste management. *Bioresource Technology Reports*, 3, 224–230. Retrieved from http://www.sciencedirect.com/science/article/pii/S2589014X1830063X

Bhavsar, P., Zoccola, M., Patrucco, A., Montarsolo, A., Rovero, G., & Tonin, C. (2017). Comparative study on the effects of superheated water and high temperature alkaline hydrolysis on wool keratin. *Textile Research Journal*, 87(14), 1696–1705.

Bohacz, J., & Korniłowicz-Kowalska, T. (2019). Fungal diversity and keratinolytic activity of fungi from lignocellulosic composts with chicken feathers. *Process Biochemistry*, 80, 119–128. Retrieved from http://www.sciencedirect.com/science/article/pii/S135951131831599X

Bouacem, K., Bouanane-Darenfed, A., Zaraî Jaouadi, N., Joseph, M., Hacene, H., Ollivier, B., ... Jaouadi, B. (2016). Novel serine keratinase from *Caldicoprobacter algeriensis* exhibiting outstanding hide dehairing abilities. *International Journal of Biological Macromolecules*, 86, 321–328. Retrieved from http://www.sciencedirect.com/science/article/pii/S0141813016300757

Brandelli, A., Daroit, D. J., & Riffel, A. (2010). Biochemical features of microbial keratinases and their production and applications. *Applied Microbiology and Biotechnology*, 85(6), 1735–1750. doi:10.1007/s00253-009-2398-5

Brandelli, A., Sala, L., & Kalil, S. J. (2015). Microbial enzymes for bioconversion of poultry waste into added-value products. *Food Research International*, 73, 3–12.

Buchanan, J. H. (1977). A cystine-rich protein fraction from oxidized α-keratin. *Biochemical Journal*, 167(2), 489–491.

Cardamone, J. M. (2010). Investigating the microstructure of keratin extracted from wool: Peptide sequence (MALDI-TOF/TOF) and protein conformation (FTIR). *Journal of Molecular Structure*, 969(1-3), 97–105.

Cavello, I., Hours, R., Rojas, N., & Cavalitto, S. (2013). Purification and characterization of a keratinolytic serine protease from *Purpureocillium lilacinum* LPS # 876. *Process Biochemistry*, 48(5), 972–978. Retrieved from http://www.sciencedirect.com/science/article/pii/S1359511313001426

Cavello, I., Urbieta, M., Segretin, A., Giaveno, A., Cavalitto, S., & Donati, E. (2018). Assessment of Keratinase and other hydrolytic enzymes in thermophilic bacteria isolated from geothermal areas in Patagonia Argentina. *Geomicrobiology Journal*, 35(2), 156–165.

Chaudhari, P. N., Chincholkar, S. B., & Chaudhari, B. L. (2013). Biodegradation of feather keratin with a PEGylated protease of *Chryseobacterium gleum*. *Process Biochemistry*, 48(12), 1952–1963.

Chen, J., Ding, S., Ji, Y., Ding, J., Yang, X., Zou, M., & Li, Z. (2015). Microwave-enhanced hydrolysis of poultry feather to produce amino acid. *Chemical Engineering and Processing: Process Intensification*, 87, 104–109. Retrieved from http://www.sciencedirect.com/science/article/pii/S0255270114002542

Chen, K., Huang, J., Chung, C., Kuo, W., & Chen, M. (2011). Identification and characterization of H10 enzymes isolated from *Bacillus cereus* H10 with keratinolytic and proteolytic activities. *World Journal of Microbiology and Biotechnology*, 27(2), 349–358.

Combs, J. A., & DeNicola, G. M. (2019). The non-essential amino acid cysteine becomes essential for tumor proliferation and survival. *Cancers, 11*(5), 678. Retrieved from https://www.mdpi.com/2072-6694/11/5/678

Cook, A. (2017). Wool export value drops 25% coming into 2017. Retrieved from https://www.radionz.co.nz/news/business/325941/wool-export-value-drops-25-percent-coming-into-2017

Dalev, P., Ivanov, I., & Liubomirova, A. (1997). Enzymic modification of feather keratin hydrolysates with lysine aimed at increasing the biological value. *Journal of the Science of Food and Agriculture, 73*(2), 242–244. Retrieved from 10.1002/(SICI)1097-0010(199702)73:2<242::AID-JSFA712>3.0.CO;2-3

Damps, T., Laskowska, A. K., Kowalkowski, T., Prokopowicz, M., Puszko, A. K., Sosnowski, P., ... Borkowska, J. K. (2017). The effect of wool hydrolysates on squamous cell carcinoma cells in vitro. Possible implications for cancer treatment. *PloS One, 12*(8).

Deb-Choudhury, S., Bermingham, E. N., Young, W., Barnett, M. P. G., Knowles, S. O., Harland, D., ... Dyer, J. M. (2018). The effects of a wool hydrolysate on short-chain fatty acid production and fecal microbial composition in the domestic cat (*Felis catus*). *Food & Function, 9*(8), 4107–4121.

De Luca, A., Pierno, S., & Camerino, D. C. (2015). Taurine: The appeal of a safe amino acid for skeletal muscle disorders. *Journal of Translational Medicine, 13*(1), 243-243.

Dou, Y., Huang, X., Zhang, B., He, M., Yin, G., & Cui, Y. (2015). Preparation and characterization of a dialdehyde starch crosslinked feather keratin film for food packaging application. *RSC Advances, 5*(34), 27168–27174.

Dou, Y., Zhang, B., He, M., Yin, G., & Cui, Y. (2014). Preparation and physicochemical properties of dialdehyde starch crosslinked feather keratin/PVA composite films. *Journal of Macromolecular Science, Part A, 51*(12), 1009–1015.

Dupont, J., de Souza, R. F., & Suarez, P. A. (2002). Ionic liquid (molten salt) phase organometallic catalysis. *Chemical Reviews, 102*(10), 3667–3692.

Earland, C., & Knight, C. (1955). Studies on the structure of keratin: I. The analysis of fractions isolated from wool oxidized with peracetic acid. *Biochimica et Biophysica Acta, 17*, 457–461.

Eslahi, N., Dadashian, F., & Nejad, N. H. (2013). An investigation on keratin extraction from wool and feather waste by enzymatic hydrolysis. *Preparative Biochemistry and Biotechnology, 43*(7), 624–648.

Ewert, J., Luz, A., Volk, V., Stressler, T., & Fischer, L. (2019). Enzymatic production of emulsifying whey protein hydrolysates without the need of heat inactivation. *Journal of the Science of Food and Agriculture, 99*(7), 3443.

Fakhfakh, N., Ktari, N., Haddar, A., Mnif, I. H., Dahmen, I., & Nasri, M. (2011). Total solubilisation of the chicken feathers by fermentation with a keratinolytic bacterium, *Bacillus pumilus* A1, and the production of protein hydrolysate with high antioxidative activity. *Process Biochemistry, 46*(9), 1731–1737.

Fakhfakh-Zouari, N., Haddar, A., Hmidet, N., Frikha, F., & Nasri, M. (2010). Application of statistical experimental design for optimization of keratinases production by *Bacillus pumilus* A1 grown on chicken feather and some biochemical properties. *Process Biochemistry, 45*(5), 617–626. Retrieved from http://www.sciencedirect.com/science/article/pii/S1359511309003894

Fang, Z., Zhang, J., Liu, B., Du, G., & Chen, J. (2013a). Biochemical characterization of three keratinolytic enzymes from *Stenotrophomonas maltophilia* BBE11-1 for biodegrading keratin wastes. *International Biodeterioration & Biodegradation, 82*, 166–172.

Fang, Z., Zhang, J., Liu, B., Du, G., & Chen, J. (2013b). Biodegradation of wool waste and keratinase production in scale-up fermenter with different strategies by *Stenotrophomonas maltophilia* BBE11-1. *Bioresource Technology, 140*, 286–291.

Feng, L., & Chen, Z.-l. (2008). Research progress on dissolution and functional modification of cellulose in ionic liquids. *Journal of Molecular Liquids, 142*(1-3), 1–5.

Figoli, A., Ursino, C., Ramirez, D. O. S., Carletto, R. A., Tonetti, C., Varesano, A., ... Vineis, C. (2019). Fabrication of electrospun keratin nanofiber membranes for air and water treatment. *Polymer Engineering and Science, 59*(7), 1472. doi:10.1002/pen.25146

Fontoura, R., Daroit, D. J., Correa, A. P., Meira, S. M., Mosquera, M., & Brandelli, A. (2014). Production of feather hydrolysates with antioxidant, angiotensin-I converting enzyme-and dipeptidyl peptidase-IV-inhibitory activities. *New Biotechnology, 31*(5), 506–513.

Fontoura, R., Daroit, D. J., Corrêa, A. P. F., Moresco, K. S., Santi, L., Beys-da-Silva, W. O., ... Brandelli, A. (2019). Characterization of a novel antioxidant peptide from feather keratin hydrolysates. *New Biotechnology, 49*, 71–76. Retrieved from http://www.sciencedirect.com/science/article/pii/S1871678418301547

Food and Agriculture Organization of the United Nations, World Health Organization, & United Nations University. (2007). Protein and amino acid requirements in human nutrition: Report of a joint FAO/WHO/UNU expert consultation. Retrieved from http://www.who.int/iris/handle/10665/43411

Food Agriculture Organization of the United Nations. (2019). FAOSTAT - Live animals. Retrieved from http://www.fao.org/faostat/en/#data/QA

Food Security Information Network. (2019). Global report on food crises 2019. Retrieved from http://www.fao.org/resilience/resources/resources-detail/en/c/1187704//

Fraser, R. D. B., MacRae, T. P., Rogers, G. E. (1972). Keratins: Their composition, structure, and biosynthesis. Volume 845 of American lectures series, Bannerstone Division Thomas Publishing, HOMAS. https://books.google.co.nz/books?id=SMCJEPLy-XAC

Friedman, M. (1999). Chemistry, biochemistry, nutrition, and microbiology of lysinoalanine, lanthionine, and histidinoalanine in food and other proteins. *Journal of Agricultural and Food Chemistry, 47*(4), 1295–1319.

Fuke, P., Gujar, V., & Khardenavis, A. (2018). Genome annotation and validation of keratin-hydrolyzing proteolytic enzymes from *Serratia marcescens* EGD-HP20. *Applied Biochemistry and Biotechnology, 184*(3), 970–986.

Garavand, F., Rouhi, M., Razavi, S. H., Cacciotti, I., & Mohammadi, R. (2017). Improving the integrity of natural biopolymer films used in food packaging by crosslinking approach: A review. *International Journal of Biological Macromolecules, 104*, 687–707. Retrieved from http://www.sciencedirect.com/science/article/pii/S0141813017309509

Gegeckas, A., Gudiukaitė, R., & Citavicius, D. (2014). Keratinolytic proteinase from *Bacillus thuringiensis* AD-12. *International Journal of Biological Macromolecules, 69*, 46–51. Retrieved from http://www.sciencedirect.com/science/article/pii/S0141813014003201

Gessesse, A., Hatti-Kaul, R., Gashe, B. A., & Mattiasson, B. (2003). Novel alkaline proteases from alkaliphilic bacteria grown on chicken feather. *Enzyme and Microbial Technology, 32*(5), 519–524. Retrieved from http://www.sciencedirect.com/science/article/pii/S0141022902003241

Ghosh, A., Clerens, S., Deb-Choudhury, S., & Dyer, J. M. (2014). Thermal effects of ionic liquid dissolution on the structures and properties of regenerated wool keratin. *Polymer Degradation and Stability, 108*, 108–115. Retrieved from http://www.sciencedirect.com/science/article/pii/S0141391014002444

Gillespie, J. M., & Marshall, R. C. (1989). Effect of mutations on the proteins of wool and hair. In: *The Biology of Wool and Hair.* Rogers, G. E., Reis, P. J., Ward, K. A., & Marshall, R. C. (Eds). Dordrecht: Springer Netherlands, 257–273.

Goddard, D. R., & Michaelis, L. (1935). Derivatives of keratin. *Journal of Biological Chemistry, 112*(1), 361–371.

Gong, J., Wang, Y., Zhang, D., Zhang, R., Su, C., Li, H., ... Shi, J. (2015). Biochemical characterization of an extreme alkaline and surfactant-stable keratinase derived from a newly isolated actinomycete *Streptomyces aureofaciens* K13. *RSC Advances, 5*(31), 24691–24699.

Gong, M., Mohan, A., Gibson, A., & Udenigwe, C. C. (2014). Mechanisms of plastein formation, and prospective food and nutraceutical applications of the peptide aggregates. *Biotechnology Reports (Amsterdam, Netherlands), 5*, 63–69. Retrieved from https://www.ncbi.nlm.nih.gov/pubmed/28626684

Gousterova, A., Nustorova, M., Paskaleva, D., Naydenov, M., Neshev, G., & Vasileva-Tonkova, E. (2011). Assessment of feather hydrolysate from *Thermophilic Actinomycetes* for soil amendment and biological control application. *International Journal of Environmental Research, 5*(4), 1065–1070. Retrieved from https://ijer.ut.ac.ir/article_464_c85e86d94afc22159ddd9b3b9bb09c77.pdf

Grazziotin, A., Pimentel, F. A., de Jong, E. V., & Brandelli, A. (2006). Nutritional improvement of feather protein by treatment with microbial keratinase. *Animal Feed Science and Technology, 126*(1), 135–144.

Gumilar, J., Pertiwiningrum, A., Nakagawa, T., & Triatmojo, S. (2017). A novel extracellular keratinase from *Exiguobacterium* sp. Dg1: Enzyme production and dehairing application. *Revista de Pielarie Incaltaminte, 17*(4), 209–216.

Gupta, S., Tewatia, P., Misri, J., & Singh, R. (2017). Molecular modeling of cloned *Bacillus subtilis* keratinase and its insinuation in Psoriasis treatment using docking studies. *Indian Journal of Microbiology, 57*(4), 485–491.

Gushterova, A., Vasileva-Tonkova, E., Dimova, E., Nedkov, P., & Haertlé, T. (2005). Keratinase production by newly isolated antarctic actinomycete Strains. *World Journal of Microbiology and Biotechnology, 21*(6-7), 831–834.

https://www.ncbi.nlm.nih.gov/pmc/articles/PMC5466193/

Habbeche, A., Saoudi, B., Jaouadi, B., Haberra, S., Kerouaz, B., Boudelaa, M., ... Ladjama, A. (2014). Purification and biochemical characterization of a detergent-stable keratinase from a newly thermophilic actinomycete *Actinomadura keratinilytica* strain Cpt29 isolated from poultry compost. *Journal of Bioscience and Bioengineering, 117*(4), 413–421.

Hamiche, S., Mechri, S., Khelouia, L., Annane, R., El Hattab, M., Badis, A., & Jaouadi, B. (2019). Purification and biochemical characterization of two keratinases from *Bacillus amyloliquefaciens* S13 isolated from marine brown alga *Zonaria tournefortii* with potential keratin-biodegradation and hide-unhairing activities. *International Journal of Biological Macromolecules*, *122*, 758–769. Retrieved from http://www.sciencedirect.com/science/article/pii/S0141813018342430

Harrap, B. S., & Woods, E. F. (1964). Soluble derivatives of feather keratin. 1. Isolation, fractionation and amino acid composition. *The Biochemical Journal*, *92*(1), 8–18. doi:10.1042/bj0920008

Holkar, C. R., Jain, S. S., Jadhav, A. J., & Pinjari, D. V. (2018). Valorization of keratin based waste. *Process Safety and Environmental Protection*, *115*, 85–98.

Houltham, S., Starck, C., & Stannard, S. (2014). Two week keratin-based protein supplementation is comparable in gastrointestinal handling to a milk-based equivalent. *Journal of Human Nutrition & Food Science*, *2*, 1040.

Ionata, E., Canganella, F., Bianconi, G., Benno, Y., Sakamoto, M., Capasso, A., ... La Cara, F. (2008). A novel keratinase from *Clostridium sporogenes* bv. pennavorans bv. nov., a thermotolerant organism isolated from solfataric muds. *Microbiological Research*, *163*(1), 105–112. Retrieved from http://www.sciencedirect.com/science/article/pii/S0944501306000917

Jeong, J., Park, K., Oh, D., Hwang, D., Kim, H., Lee, C., & Son, H. (2010). Keratinolytic enzyme-mediated biodegradation of recalcitrant feather by a newly isolated Xanthomonas sp. P5. *Polymer Degradation and Stability*, *95*(10), 1969–1977. Retrieved from http://www.sciencedirect.com/science/article/pii/S0141391010003149

Ji, Y., Chen, J., Lv, J., Li, Z., Xing, L., & Ding, S. (2014). Extraction of keratin with ionic liquids from poultry feather. *Separation and Purification Technology*, *132*, 577–583. Retrieved from http://www.sciencedirect.com/science/article/pii/S138358661400344X

Jiang-Tao, X., Ping, Z., Lin, Z., Shu-ying, S., Zhao-hong, D., & Yi, Z. (2015). Study of keratin extraction from human hair. *Wool Textile Journal*, *43*(5).

Karamać, M., Flaczyk, E., Janitha, P., Wanasundara, P., & Amarowicz, R. (2005). Angiotensin I-converting enzyme (ACE) inhibitory activity of hydrolysates obtained from muscle food industry by-products – A short report. *Polish Journal of Food and Nutrition Sciences*, *14*, 133–137.

Kataoka, M., Yamaoka, A., Kawasaki, K., Shigeri, Y., & Watanabe, K. (2014). Extraordinary denaturant tolerance of keratinolytic protease complex assemblies produced by *Meiothermus ruber* H328. *Applied Microbiology and Biotechnology*, *98*(7), 2973–2980.

Khardenavis, A. A., Kapley, A., & Purohit, H. J. (2009). Processing of poultry feathers by alkaline keratin hydrolyzing enzyme from *Serratia* sp. HPC 1383. *Waste Management*, *29*(4), 1409–1415.

Koehler, D., Shah, Z. A., Hensley, K., & Williams, F. E. (2018). Lanthionine ketimine-5-ethyl ester provides neuroprotection in a zebrafish model of okadaic acid-induced Alzheimer's disease. *Neurochemistry International*, *115*, 61–68. doi:10.1016/j.neuint.2018.02.002

Kojima, M., Kanai, M., Tominaga, M., Kitazume, S., Inoue, A., & Horikoshi, K. (2006). Isolation and characterization of a feather-degrading enzyme from *Bacillus pseudofirmus* FA30-01. *Extremophiles*, *10*(3), 229–235.

Konwarh, R., Karak, N., Rai, S. K., & Mukherjee, A. K. (2009). Polymer-assisted iron oxide magnetic nanoparticle immobilized keratinase. *Nanotechnology*, *20*(22), 225107.

Korniłłowicz-Kowalska, T., & Bohacz, J. (2011). Biodegradation of keratin waste: Theory and practical aspects. *Waste Management*, *31*(8), 1689–1701. doi:10.1016/j.wasman.2011.03.024

Kublanov, I., Tsiroulnikov, K., Kaliberda, E., Rumsh, L., Haertlé, T., & Bonch-Osmolovskaya, E. (2009). Keratinase of an anaerobic thermophilic bacterium *Thermoanaerobacter* sp. strain 1004-09 isolated from a hot spring in the Baikal rift zone. *Microbiology*, *78*(1), 67–75.

Kuipers, A., Moll, G. N., Wagner, E., & Franklin, R. (2019). Efficacy of lanthionine-stabilized angiotensin-(1-7) in type I and type II diabetes mouse models. *Peptides*, *112*, 78–84. Retrieved from http://www.sciencedirect.com/science/article/pii/S0196978118301906

Laba, W., Kopec, W., ChorAa, Kancelista, A., Piegza, M., & Malik, K. (2015). Biodegradation of pretreated pig bristles by *Bacillus cereus* B5esz. *International Biodeterioration & Biodegradation*, *100*, 116–123.

Lai, H. Y., Wang, S., Singh, V., Nguyen, L. T. H., & Ng, K. W. (2018). Evaluating the antioxidant effects of human hair protein extracts. *Journal of Biomaterials Science, Polymer Edition*, *29*(7-9), 1081–1093.

Lamsal, B. P., Jung, S., & Johnson, L. A. (2007). Rheological properties of soy protein hydrolysates obtained from limited enzymatic hydrolysis. *LWT – Food Science and Technology*, *40*(7), 1215–1223.

Lange, L., Huang, Y., & Busk, P. (2016). Microbial decomposition of keratin in nature—a new hypothesis of industrial relevance. *Applied Microbiology and Biotechnology*, *100*(5), 2083–2096.

Lee, K. S., Park, Y. J., Shim, J., Chung, H.-S., Yim, S.-Y., Hwang, J. Y., ... Son, D. I. (2019). ZnO@graphene QDs with tuned surface functionalities formed on eco-friendly keratin nanofiber textile for transparent and flexible ultraviolet photodetectors. *Organic Electronics*, 105489. doi:10.1016/j.orgel.2019.105489

Lee, Y., Dhanasingh, I., Ahn, J., Jin, H., Choi, J., Lee, S., & Lee, D. (2015). Biochemical and structural characterization of a keratin-degrading M32 carboxypeptidase from *Fervidobacterium islandicum* AW-1. *Biochemical and Biophysical Research Communications*, 468(4), 927–933.

Li, J., Li, Y., Zhang, Y., Liu, X., Zhao, Z., Zhang, J., ... Zhou, D. (2013). Toxicity study of isolated polypeptide from wool hydrolysate. *Food and Chemical Toxicology*, 57, 338.

Li, T., Wang, L., Hu, Q., Liu, S., Bai, X., Xie, Y., ... Wang, Z. (2017). Neuroprotective roles of l-cysteine in attenuating early brain injury and improving synaptic density the CBS/HS pathway following subarachnoid hemorrhage in rats. *Frontiers in Neurology*, 8, 176.

Liang, X., Bian, Y., Tang, X.-F., Xiao, G., & Tang, B. (2010). Enhancement of keratinolytic activity of a thermophilic subtilase by improving its autolysis resistance and thermostability under reducing conditions. *Applied Microbiology and Biotechnology*, 87(3), 999–1006.

Liebeck, M. B., Hidalgo, N., Roth, G., Popescu, C., & Böker, A. (2017). Synthesis and characterization of methyl cellulose/keratin hydrolysate composite membranes. *Polymers*, 9, 91. doi:10.3390/polym9030091

Lin, X., Kelemen, D. W., Miller, E. S., & Shih, J. C. (1995). Nucleotide sequence and expression of kerA, the gene encoding a keratinolytic protease of *Bacillus licheniformis* PWD-1. *Applied and Environmental Microbiology*, 61(4), 1469.

Lin, X., Lee, C.-G., Casale, E. S., & Shih, J. C. H. (1992). Purification and characterization of a keratinase from a feather-degrading *Bacillus licheniformis* strain. *Applied and Environmental Microbiology*, 58(10), 3271.

Liu, J., Klebach, M., Visser, M., & Hofman, Z. (2019). Amino acid availability of a dairy and vegetable protein blend compared to single casein, whey, soy, and pea proteins: A double-blind, cross-over trial. *Nutrients*, 11(11), 2613. Retrieved from https://www.mdpi.com/2072-6643/11/11/2613

Livrelli, V., De Champs, C., Di Martino, P., Darfeuille-Michaud, A., Forestier, C., & Joly, B. (1996). Adhesive properties and antibiotic resistance of *Klebsiella, Enterobacter*, and *Serratia* clinical isolates involved in nosocomial infections. *Journal of Clinical Microbiology*, 34(8), 1963. Retrieved from http://jcm.asm.org/content/34/8/1963.abstract

Lv, L., Sim, M., Li, Y., Min, J., Feng, W., Guan, W., & Li, Y. (2010). Production, characterization and application of a keratinase from *Chryseobacterium L99* sp. nov. *Process Biochemistry*, 45(8), 1236–1244.

Mabrouk, M. (2008). Feather degradation by a new keratinolytic *Streptomyces* sp. MS-2. *World Journal of Microbiology and Biotechnology*, 24(10), 2331–2338. doi:10.1007/s11274-008-9748-9

Maclaren, J. A., & Milligan, B. (1981). *Wool Science. The Chemical Reactivity of the Wool Fibre*. Alexandria NSW, Australia, Science Press.

Marangoni, N., Kowal, K., Deliu, Z., Hensley, K., & Feinstein, D. L. (2018). Neuroprotective and neurotrophic effects of Lanthionine Ketimine Ester. *Neuroscience Letters*, 664, 28–33. Retrieved from http://www.sciencedirect.com/science/article/pii/S0304394017309163

Martinez, Y. N., Cavello, I., Hours, R., Cavalitto, S., & Castro, G. R. (2013). Immobilized keratinase and enrofloxacin loaded on pectin PVA cryogel patches for antimicrobial treatment. *Bioresource Technology*, 145, 280–284.

Mehta, R., Singhal, P., Singh, H., Damle, D., & Sharma, A. K. (2016). Insight into thermophiles and their wide-spectrum applications. *3 Biotech*, 6(1), 81, doi: 10.1007/s13205-016-0368-z.

Mitsuiki, S., Sakai, M., Moriyama, Y., Goto, M., & Furukawa, K. (2002). Purification and some properties of a keratinolytic enzyme from an alkaliphilic *Nocardiopsis* sp. TOA-1. *Bioscience, Biotechnology, and Biochemistry*, 66(1), 164–167. doi:10.1271/bbb.66.164

Mohamad, N., Phang, L.-Y., & Abd-Aziz, S. (2017). Optimization of metallo-keratinase production by *Pseudomonas sp.* LM19 as a potential enzyme for feather waste conversion. *Biocatalysis and Biotransformation*, 35(1), 41–50.

Mohorčič, M., Torkar, A., Friedrich, J., Kristl, J., & Murdan, S. (2007). An investigation into keratinolytic enzymes to enhance ungual drug delivery. *International Journal of Pharmaceutics*, 332(1), 196–201. Retrieved from http://www.sciencedirect.com/science/article/pii/S0378517306007976

Mokrejs, P., Hutta, M., Pavlackova, J., Egner, P., & Benicek, L. (2017). The cosmetic and dermatological potential of keratin hydrolysate. *Journal of Cosmetic Dermatology*, 16(4), e21–e27. doi:10.1111/jocd.12319

Mokrejs, P., Svoboda, P., Hrncirik, J., Janacova, D., & Vasek, V. (2011). Processing poultry feathers into keratin hydrolysate through alkaline-enzymatic hydrolysis. *Waste Management & Research*, *29*(3), 260–267.

Moore, G. R. P., Martelli, S. M., Gandolfo, C. A., Pires, A. T. N., & Laurindo, J. B. (2006). Queratina de penas de frango: Extração, caracterização e obtenção de filmes. *Food Science and Technology*, *26*(2), 421–427.

Moreira, F. G., de Souza, C. G. M., Costa, M. A. F., Reis, S., & Peralta, R. M. (2007). Degradation of keratinous materials by the plant pathogenic fungus *Myrothecium verrucaria*. *Mycopathologia*, *163*(3), 153–160. Retrieved from 10.1007/s11046-007-0096-3

Nagai, Y., & Nishikawa, T. (1970). Solubilization of chicken feather keratin by ammonium copper hydroxide (Schweitzer's reagent). *Agricultural and Biological Chemistry*, *34*(4), 575–584.

Nakamura, A., Arimoto, M., Takeuchi, K., & Fujii, T. (2002). A rapid extraction procedure of human hair proteins and identification of phosphorylated species. *Biological and Pharmaceutical Bulletin*, *25*(5), 569–572.

Ningthoujam, D., Devi, L. J., Devi, P. J., Kshetri, P., Tamreihao, K., Mukherjee, S., ... Betterson, N. (2016). Optimization of keratinase production by Amycolatopsis sp strain MBRL 40 from a limestone habitat. *Journal of Bioprocessing & Biotechniques*, *40*, 2.

Odetallah, N. H., Wang, J. J., Garlich, J. D., & Shih, J. C. (2003). Keratinase in starter diets improves growth of broiler chicks. *Poultry Science*, *82*(4), 664–670. Retrieved from 10.1093/ps/82.4.664

Ohba, R., Deguchi, T., Kishikawa, M., Arsyad, F., Morimura, S., & Kida, K. (2003). Physiological functions of enzymatic hydrolysates of collagen or keratin contained in livestock and fish waste. *Food Science and Technology Research*, *9*(1), 91–93.

Opeyemi, L. A. (2013). *Generation of meaty flavoring using chicken feather keratin hydrolysate-glucose interaction model*. MSc. thesis, Universiti Putra Malaysia.

Ozkan, G., Franco, P., De Marco, I., Xiao, J., & Capanoglu, E. (2019). A review of microencapsulation methods for food antioxidants: Principles, advantages, drawbacks and applications. *Food Chemistry*, *272*, 494–506. Retrieved from http://www.sciencedirect.com/science/article/pii/S0308814618313669

Pardo-Ibáñez, P., Lopez-Rubio, A., Martínez-Sanz, M., Cabedo, L., & Lagaron, J. M. (2014). Keratin–polyhydroxyalkanoate melt-compounded composites with improved barrier properties of interest in food packaging applications. *Journal of Applied Polymer Science*, *131*(4). Retrieved from 10.1002/app.39947

Park, G., Hong, S., Jung, B., Khan, A., Park, Y., Park, C., ... Shin, J. (2015). Complete genome sequence of a keratin-degrading bacterium *Chryseobacterium gallinarum* strain DSM 27622T isolated from chicken. *Journal of Biotechnology*, *211*, 66–67.

Parry, D. A., Marekov, L. N., & Steinert, P. M. (2001). Subfilamentous protofibril structures in fibrous proteins: Cross-linking evidence for protofibrils in intermediate filaments. *The Journal of Biological Chemistry*, *276*(42), 39253–39258.

Patinvoh, R., Feuk-Lagerstedt, E., Lundin, M., Sárvári Horváth, I., & Taherzadeh, M. (2016). Biological pretreatment of chicken feather and biogas production from total broth. *Applied Biochemistry and Biotechnology*, *180*(7), 1401–1415.

Paul, T., Das, A., Mandal, A., Halder, S. K., Jana, A., Maity, C., ... Mondal, K. C. (2014). An efficient cloth cleaning properties of a crude keratinase combined with detergent: Towards industrial viewpoint. *Journal of Cleaner Production*, *66*, 672–684. doi:10.1016/j.jclepro.2013.10.054

Paul, T., Halder, S. K., Das, A., Bera, S., Maity, C., Mandal, A., ... Mondal, K. C. (2013). Exploitation of chicken feather waste as a plant growth promoting agent using keratinase producing novel isolate *Paenibacillus woosongensis* TKB2. *Biocatalysis and Agricultural Biotechnology*, *2*(1), 50–57. Retrieved from http://www.sciencedirect.com/science/article/pii/S1878818112001302

Pereira, J. Q., Lopes, F. C., Petry, M. V., Medina, L. F. D. C., & Brandelli, A. (2014). Isolation of three novel Antarctic psychrotolerant feather-degrading bacteria and partial purification of keratinolytic enzyme from Lysobacter sp. A03. *International Biodeterioration & Biodegradation*, *88*, 1–7. Retrieved from http://www.sciencedirect.com/science/article/pii/S096483051300423X

Poopathi, S., Thirugnanasambantham, K., Mani, C., Lakshmi, P., & Ragul, K. (2014). Purification and characterization of keratinase from feather degrading bacterium useful for mosquito control – A new report. *Tropical Biomedicine*, *31*(1), 97–109.

Popko, M., Wilk, R., Górecka, H., Chojnacka, K., & Górecki, H. (2015). Assessment of new NKSMg fertilizer based on protein hydrolysate of keratin in pot experiments. *Polish Journal of Environmental Studies*, *24*(4), 1765–1772.

Prakash, P., Jayalakshmi, S. K., & Sreeramulu, K. (2010). Production of keratinase by free and immobilized cells of *Bacillus halodurans* strain PPKS-2: Partial characterization and its application in feather degradation and dehairing of the Goat skin. *Applied Biochemistry and Biotechnology, 160*(7), 1909–1920. Retrieved from 10.1007/s12010-009-8702-0

Rahayu, S., & Bata, M. (2015). Quality of chicken feather processed in different conditions. *Animal Production, 16*(3), 170–175.

Rai, S. K., & Mukherjee, A. K. (2011). Optimization of production of an oxidant and detergent-stable alkaline β-keratinase from *Brevibacillus* sp. strain AS-S10-II: Application of enzyme in laundry detergent formulations and in leather industry. *Biochemical Engineering Journal, 54*(1), 47–56.

Rai, S. K., & Mukherjee, A. K. (2015). Optimization for production of liquid nitrogen fertilizer from the degradation of chicken feather by iron-oxide (Fe3O4) magnetic nanoparticles coupled β-keratinase. *Biocatalysis and Agricultural Biotechnology, 4*(4), 632–644. Retrieved from http://www.sciencedirect.com/science/article/pii/S1878818115000833

Rajabinejad, H., Patrucco, A., Caringella, R., Montarsolo, A., Zoccola, M., & Pozzo, P. D. (2018). Preparation of keratin-based microcapsules for encapsulation of hydrophilic molecules. *Ultrasonics Sonochemistry, 40*, 527–532. Retrieved from http://www.sciencedirect.com/science/article/pii/S1350417717303437

Ramakrishna Reddy, M., Sathi Reddy, K., Ranjita Chouhan, Y., Bee, H., & Reddy, G. (2017). Effective feather degradation and keratinase production by *Bacillus pumilus* GRK for its application as biodetergent additive. *Bioresource Technology, 243*, 254–263.

Ramnani, P., Singh, R., & Gupta, R. (2005). Keratinolytic potential of Bacillus licheniformis RG1: structural and biochemical mechanism of feather degradation. *Canadian Journal of Microbiology, 51*(3), 191–196.

Reddy, N., Chen, L., Zhang, Y., & Yang, Y. (2014). Reducing environmental pollution of the textile industry using keratin as alternative sizing agent to poly(vinyl alcohol). *Journal of Cleaner Production, 65*, 561–567. doi:10.1016/j.jclepro.2013.09.046

Riessen, S., & Antranikian, G. (2001). Isolation of *Thermoanaerobacter keratinophilus* sp. nov., a novel thermophilic, anaerobic bacterium with keratinolytic activity. *Extremophiles, 5*(6), 399–408.

Rogers, G. E. (1985). Genes for hair and avian keratins. *Annals of the New York Academy of Sciences, 455*(1), 403–425.

Saha, B. C., & Hayashi, K. (2001). Debittering of protein hydrolyzates. *Biotechnology Advances, 19*(5), 355–370. Retrieved from http://www.sciencedirect.com/science/article/pii/S0734975001000702

Sanghvi, G., Patel, H., Vaishnav, D., Oza, T., Dave, G., Kunjadia, P., & Sheth, N. (2016). A novel alkaline keratinase from *Bacillus subtilis* DP1 with potential utility in cosmetic formulation. *International Journal of Biological Macromolecules, 87*, 256–262. Retrieved from http://www.sciencedirect.com/science/article/pii/S0141813016301982

Savige, W. E. (1960). The dispersion of wool protein by thiols in acid solution. *Textile Research Journal, 30*(1), 1–10. Retrieved from https://journals.sagepub.com/doi/abs/10.1177/004051756003000101

Sharma, R., & Gupta, R. (2012). Coupled action of γ-glutamyl transpeptidase-glutathione and keratinase effectively degrades feather keratin and surrogate prion protein, Sup 35NM. *Bioresource Technology, 120*, 314–317. doi:10.1016/j.biortech.2012.06.038

Sharma, S., Gupta, A., Chik, S. M. S. T., Kee, C. G., Mistry, B. M., Kim, D. H., & Sharma, G. (2017). Characterization of keratin microparticles from feather biomass with potent antioxidant and anticancer activities. *International Journal of Biological Macromolecules, 104*(Pt A), 189–196.

Shavandi, A., Silva, T. H., Bekhit, A. A., & Bekhit, A. E.-D. A. (2017). Keratin: Dissolution, extraction and biomedical application. *Biomaterials Science, 5*(9), 1699–1735.

Shorland, F., & Matthews, J. (1968). A preliminary investigation of the food value of wool. *New Zealand Journal of Science, 11*, 131–136.

Shorland, F. B., & Bentley, K. W. (1968). Note on edible wool products. *New Zealand Journal of Science, 11*, 16.

Shorland, F. B., & Gray, J. M. (1970). The preparation of nutritious protein from wool. *British Journal of Nutrition, 24*(3), 717–725.

Shrinivas, D., & Naik, G. R. (2011). Characterization of alkaline thermostable keratinolytic protease from thermoalkalophilic *Bacillus halodurans* JB 99 exhibiting dehairing activity. *International Biodeterioration & Biodegradation, 65*(1), 29–35. Retrieved from http://www.sciencedirect.com/science/article/pii/S0964830510001034

Simmonds, D. (1955). The amino acid composition of keratins II. The amino acid composition of a keratin derivative extracted from wool with alkaline thioglycollate solution. *Australian Journal of Biological Sciences*, *8*(1), 114–121.

Simsek, M. (2019). Determination of the antibiotic resistance rates of isolates obtained from various clinical specimens. *Nigerian Journal of Clinical Practice*, *22*(1), 125. doi:10.4103/njcp.njcp_362_18

Sinkiewicz, I., Staroszczyk, H., & Śliwińska, A. (2018). Solubilization of keratins and functional properties of their isolates and hydrolysates. *Journal of Food Biochemistry*, *42*(2), e12494. Retrieved from 10.1111/jfbc.12494

Stipanuk, M. H. (2004). Sulfur amino acid metabolism: pathways for production and removal of homocysteine and cysteine. *Annual Review of Nutrition*, *24*, 539–577.

Sun, Z., Yi, Z., Zhang, H., Ma, X., Su, W., Sun, X., & Li, X. (2017). Bio-responsive alginate-keratin composite nanogels with enhanced drug loading efficiency for cancer therapy. *Carbohydrate Polymers*, *175*, 159–169. doi:10.1016/j.carbpol.2017.07.078

Sundaram, M., Legadevi, R., Banu, N. A., Gayathri, V., & Palanisammy, A. (2015). A study on anti bacterial activity of keratin nanoparticles from chicken feather waste against *Staphylococcus aureus* (Bovine mastitis bacteria) and its antioxidant activity. *European Journal of Biotechnology and Bioscience*, *3*, 1–5.

Suzuki, Y., Tsujimoto, Y., Matsui, H., & Watanabe, K. (2006). Decomposition of extremely hard-to-degrade animal proteins by thermophilic bacteria. *Journal of Bioscience and Bioengineering*, *102*(2), 73–81.

Syed, D. G., Lee, J. C., Li, W.-J., Kim, C.-J., & Agasar, D. (2009). Production, characterization and application of keratinase from *Streptomyces gulbargensis*. *Bioresource Technology*, *100*(5), 1868–1871.

Synowiecki, J., Jagietka, R., & Shahidi, F. (1996). Preparation of hydrolysates from bovine red blood cells and their debittering following plastein reaction. *Food Chemistry*, *57*(3), 435–439. Retrieved from http://www.sciencedirect.com/science/article/pii/S0308814696000052

Thompson, E., & O'donnell, I. (1962). Studies on reduced wool I. The extent of reduction of wool with increasing concentrations of thiol, and the extraction of proteins from reduced and alkylated wool. *Australian Journal of Biological Sciences*, *15*(4), 757–768. Retrieved from https://www.publish.csiro.au/paper/BI9620757

Thys, R., & Brandelli, A. (2006). Purification and properties of a keratinolytic metalloprotease from *Microbacterium* sp. *Journal of Applied Microbiology*, *101*(6), 1259–1268.

Tian, J., Long, X., Tian, Y., & Shi, B. (2019a). Eco-friendly enzymatic dehairing of goatskins utilizing a metalloprotease high-effectively expressed by *Bacillus subtilis* SCK6. *Journal of Cleaner Production*, *212*, 647–654. Retrieved from http://www.sciencedirect.com/science/article/pii/S0959652618337934

Tian, J., Xu, Z., Long, X., Tian, Y., & Shi, B. (2019b). High-expression keratinase by *Bacillus subtilis* SCK6 for enzymatic dehairing of goatskins. *International Journal of Biological Macromolecules*, *135*, 119–126.

Tiwary, E., & Gupta, R. (2010). Medium optimization for a novel 58kDa dimeric keratinase from *Bacillus licheniformis* ER-15: Biochemical characterization and application in feather degradation and dehairing of hides. *Bioresource Technology*, *101*(15), 6103–6110. Retrieved from http://www.sciencedirect.com/science/article/pii/S0960852410004013

Toennies, G., & Homiller, R. P. (1942). The oxidation of amino acids by hydrogen peroxide in formic acid. *Journal of the American Chemical Society*, *64*(12), 3054–3056.

Tork, S. E., Shahein, Y. E., El-Hakim, A. E., Abdel-Aty, A. M., & Aly, M. M. (2013). Production and characterization of thermostable metallo-keratinase from newly isolated *Bacillus subtilis* NRC 3. *International Journal of Biological Macromolecules*, *55*, 169–175.

Tork, S. E., Shahein, Y. E., El-Hakim, A. E., Abdel-Aty, A. M., & Aly, M. M. (2016). Purification and partial characterization of serine-metallokeratinase from a newly isolated *Bacillus pumilus* NRC21. *International Journal of Biological Macromolecules*, *86*, 189–196.

Tsuda, Y., & Nomura, Y. (2014). Properties of alkaline-hydrolyzed waterfowl feather keratin. *Animal Science Journal*, *85*(2), 180–185.

Ueki, T. (2014). Stimuli-responsive polymers in ionic liquids. *Polymer Journal*, *46*(10), 646.

Vasileva-Tonkova, E., Gousterova, A., & Neshev, G. (2009). Ecologically safe method for improved feather wastes biodegradation. *International Biodeterioration & Biodegradation*, *63*(8), 1008–1012.

Verma, A., Singh, H., Anwar, S., Chattopadhyay, A., Tiwari, K. K., Kaur, S., & Dhilon, G. S. (2017). Microbial keratinases: Industrial enzymes with waste management potential. *Critical Reviews in Biotechnology*, *37*(4), 476–491. Retrieved from 10.1080/07388551.2016.1185388

Veselá, M., & Friedrich, J. (2009). Amino acid and soluble protein cocktail from waste keratin hydrolysed by a fungal keratinase of *Paecilomyces marquandii*. *Biotechnology and Bioprocess Engineering: BBE*, *14*(1), 84–90.

Vidmar, B., & Vodovnik, M. (2018). Microbial keratinases: Enzymes with promising biotechnological applications. *Food Technology and Biotechnology*, *56*(3), 312–328.

Villa, A. L. V., Aragão, M. R. S., Dos Santos, E. P., Mazotto, A. M., Zingali, R. B., de Souza, E. P., & Vermelho, A. B. (2013). Feather keratin hydrolysates obtained from microbial keratinases: Effect on hair fiber. *BMC Biotechnology*, *13*, 15-15. doi:10.1186/1472-6750-13-15

Wan, M.-Y., Dong, G., Yang, B.-Q., & Feng, H. (2016). Identification and characterization of a novel antioxidant peptide from feather keratin hydrolysate. *Biotechnology Letters*, *38*(4), 643–649.

Wang, B., Yang, W., McKittrick, J., & Meyers, M. A. (2016). Keratin: Structure, mechanical properties, occurrence in biological organisms, and efforts at bioinspiration. *Progress in Materials Science*, *76*, 229–318. Retrieved from http://www.sciencedirect.com/science/article/pii/S0079642515000596

Wang, H., Guo, Y., & Shih, J. C. H. (2008). Effects of dietary supplementation of keratinase on growth performance, nitrogen retention and intestinal morphology of broiler chickens fed diets with soybean and cottonseed meals. *Animal Feed Science and Technology*, *140*(3), 376–384. Retrieved from http://www.sciencedirect.com/science/article/pii/S0377840107001289

Wang, H., Gurau, G., & Rogers, R. D. (2014). Dissolution of biomass using ionic liquids. In: *Structures and Interactions of Ionic Liquids*, Berlin/Heidelberg, Germany, Springer, 79–105.

Wang, L., Cheng, G., Ren, Y., Dai, Z., Zhao, Z.-S., Liu, F., ... Tang, B. (2015). Degradation of intact chicken feathers by *Thermoactinomyces* sp. CDF and characterization of its keratinolytic protease. *Applied Microbiology and Biotechnology*, *99*(9), 3949–3959. Retrieved from 10.1007/s00253-014-6207-4

Weiss, I. M., Muth, C., Drumm, R., & Kirchner, H. O. K. (2018). Thermal decomposition of the amino acids glycine, cysteine, aspartic acid, asparagine, glutamic acid, glutamine, arginine and histidine. *BMC Biophysics*, *11*, 2-2. doi:10.1186/s13628-018-0042-4

Winterman, D. (2010). From food to fashion, the thriving market in human hair. Retrieved from http://news.bbc.co.uk/2/hi/uk_news/magazine/8753698.stm

Wu, X., Liu, Y., Liu, A., & Wang, W. (2017). Improved thermal-stability and mechanical properties of type I collagen by crosslinking with casein, keratin and soy protein isolate using transglutaminase. *International Journal of Biological Macromolecules*, *98*, 292–301. Retrieved from http://www.sciencedirect.com/science/article/pii/S0141813016327684

Xu, H., Ma, Z., & Yang, Y. (2014). Dissolution and regeneration of wool via controlled disintegration and disentanglement of highly crosslinked keratin. *Journal of Materials Science*, *49*(21), 7513–7521. Retrieved from 10.1007/s10853-014-8457-z

Yamamura, S., Morita, Y., Hasan, Q., Yokoyama, K., & Tamiya, E. (2002). Keratin degradation: A cooperative action of two enzymes from Stenotrophomonas sp. *Biochemical and Biophysical Research Communications*, *294*(5), 1138–1143. Retrieved from http://www.sciencedirect.com/science/article/pii/S0006291X02005806

Yamauchi, K., & Khoda, A. (1997). Novel proteinous microcapsules from wool keratins. *Colloids and Surfaces B: Biointerfaces*, *9*(1-2), 117–119.

Yamauchi, K., Yamauchi, A., Kusunoki, T., Kohda, A., & Konishi, Y. (1996). Preparation of stable aqueous solution of keratins, and physiochemical and biodegradational properties of films. *Journal of Biomedical Materials Research: An Official Journal of The Society for Biomaterials and The Japanese Society for Biomaterials*, *31*(4), 439–444.

Yusuf, I., Ahmad, S. A., Phang, L. Y., Syed, M. A., Shamaan, N. A., Abdul Khalil, K., ... Shukor, M. Y. (2016). Keratinase production and biodegradation of polluted secondary chicken feather wastes by a newly isolated multi heavy metal tolerant bacterium-*Alcaligenes* sp. AQ05-001. *Journal of Environmental Management*, *183*, 182–195. Retrieved from http://www.sciencedirect.com/science/article/pii/S030147971630603X

Zahn, H., Kunitz, F. W., & Hildebrand, D. (1960). The role of SH groups in wool. *Journal of the Textile Institute Transactions*, *51*(12), T740–T755. Retrieved from 10.1080/19447026008662513

Zhang, H., Wang, J., Ma, H., Zhou, Y., Ma, X., Liu, J., ... Yu, N. (2016). Bilayered PLGA/wool keratin composite membranes support periodontal regeneration in Beagle dogs. *ACS Biomaterials Science & Engineering*, *2*(12), 2162–2175. doi:10.1021/acsbiomaterials.6b00357

Zhang, H., Wu, J., Zhang, J., & He, J. (2005). 1-Allyl-3-methylimidazolium chloride room temperature ionic liquid: A new and powerful nonderivatizing solvent for cellulose. *Macromolecules*, *38*(20), 8272–8277.

Zhang, Z., Li, D., & Zhang, X. (2019). Enzymatic decolorization of melanoidins from molasses wastewater by immobilized keratinase. *Bioresource Technology*, *280*, 165–172.

Zhao, X., Lui, Y. S., Choo, C. K. C., Sow, W., Huang, C. L., Ng, K. W., ... Loo, J. S. C. (2015). Calcium phosphate coated Keratin–PCL scaffolds for potential bone tissue regeneration. *Materials Science and Engineering: C*, *49*, 746–753. Retrieved from http://www.sciencedirect.com/science/article/pii/S0928493115000946

Zoccola, M., Aluigi, A., Patrucco, A., Vineis, C., Forlini, F., Locatelli, P., ... Tonin, C. (2012). Microwave-assisted chemical-free hydrolysis of wool keratin. *Textile Research Journal*, *82*(19), 2006–2018. Retrieved from 10.1177/0040517512452948

Zou, T.-B., He, T.-P., Li, H.-B., Tang, H.-W., & Xia, E.-Q. (2016). The structure-activity relationship of the antioxidant peptides from natural proteins. *Molecules*, *21*(1).

8 Non-Traditional Meat Sources, Production, Nutritional and Health Aspects, Consideration of Safety Aspects and Religious Views

Isam A. Mohamed Ahmed[1], Fahad Y. Al-Juhaimi[1], Zuhaib F. Bhat[2], Alan Carne[3], and Alaa El-Din Bekhit[4]

[1] Department of Food Science and Nutrition, College of Food and Agricultural Sciences, King Saud University, Riyadh, Kingdom of Saudi Arabia
[2] Livestock Products Technology, SKUAST-Jammu, India
[3] Department of Biochemistry, University of Otago, Dunedin, New Zealand
[4] Department of Food Science, University of Otago, Dunedin, New Zealand

CONTENTS

8.1	Introduction	216
8.2	Production of Non-traditional Meats	217
8.3	Nutritional Composition of Non-traditional Meats	220
	8.3.1 Camelids	220
8.4	Non-traditional Meat from Bison, Buffalo, Yak and Eland	241
	8.4.1 Bison	241
	8.4.2 Buffalo and Yak	241
	8.4.3 Eland	241
8.5	Non-traditional Meat from Donkey, Horse and Mule	241
	8.5.1 Donkey	241
	8.5.2 Horse	242
8.6	Non-traditional Meat from Game Animals	242
	8.6.1 Deer	242
8.7	Non-traditional Meat from Rodents	243
	8.7.1 Cane Rat	243
	8.7.2 Nutria	243
	8.7.3 Guinea Pig	244
	8.7.4 Chinchilla	244
	8.7.5 Capybara	245
8.8	Non-traditional Meat from Reptiles	245
	8.8.1 Crocodile	245

DOI: 10.1201/9780429299834-8

        8.8.2   Caiman 246
   8.9   Non-traditional Meat from Other Animals...247
        8.9.1   Rabbit...247
   8.10 Safety Issue Considerations of Non-conventional Meats 247
   8.11 Religious Issues Associated with Meat Obtained from Non-traditional Sources............248
   8.12 Conclusions and Future Perspectives 251
   Acknowledgement 252
   References..252

8.1   INTRODUCTION

Meat is one of the most important and nutritious food products that is obtained from the muscles of a diverse range of animals (Pereira & Vicente, 2013). Meat consumption has a long history, as archaeological evidence exists of butchery marks on surfaces and stone tools, that indicate that hominins incorporated animal meat and bone marrow in their diet around at least 2.6 million years ago (Pobiner, 2013). The evolution in hominids of a large brain that requires food sources containing intensive nutrients and energy is likely one of the reasons why hominids consumed meat (Leonard et al., 2007). Since that time and until developing hunting skills around 500,000 years ago, the hominins are thought to have scavenged meat from the kills of larger animals (Cawthorn & Hoffman, 2014). Subsequent domestication of animals and the establishment of animal husbandry practices led to the generation of abundant and consistent meat sources, along with increase in human population growth (Cawthorn & Hoffman, 2014; Diamond, 2002). Nowadays, the world population exceeds 7.5 billion people (FAOSTAT, 2018) which has increased the demand for animal meat from both 'traditional' and 'non-traditional' sources. By 'traditional' it is meant in the sense of animals that became domesticated and then subsequently have been subjected to mass production farming practices essentially worldwide, as opposed to other animals (that are being referred to as 'non-traditional' meat animals) that have essentially remained as feral existing species, or in some cases have been farmed to varying, but somewhat limited extents, and that exist often in limited regions of the World. In addition to developed countries, developing countries also face high demand for animal proteins in the diet due to increasing population, leading to increased urbanization, and often improvement in income (Thornton, 2010). Therefore, the global meat industry is facing considerable challenges with the production of sufficient, sustainable, and safe meat to fulfil consumer needs. While meat sources considered both traditional and non-traditional have been used for human consumption for centuries, it is only in more recent times that there has been increasing mass production of the considered traditional meats, from animals such as pigs, cattle, sheep and chickens (Leroy & De Smet, 2019). However, increasing production of these traditional meat sources will be affected by global warming and limitations of natural resources, including water, forage, and farmland, resulting in shortages to feed the increasing world population (Hoffman & Cawthorn, 2013). To overcome such limitations, utilization of non-traditional meat sources is becoming increasingly attractive. The animals used for non-traditional meat sources are quite diverse (*e.g.*, ass, camel, goat, horse, llama, alpaca, kangaroo, rabbit, deer, game, frog, dog, duck, goose, quail, rodents, etc), along with the quality, quantity and safety, as well as the production regions (Suman & McMillin, 2014). The consumption of non-traditional meat depends on many factors that are influenced by such aspects as culture, religion and consumer preferences and perceptions (Joy, 2010). However, non-traditional meats have the potential to provide multiple choices, different flavour and composition, and enhance security of protein supply for meat consumers across the globe. Despite international recognition and export of some non-traditional meats, non-traditional meats have received less attention compared to traditional meats (Suman & McMillin, 2014). This chapter summarizes the production, nutritional quality, safety, and religious and cultural aspects of non-traditional meat.

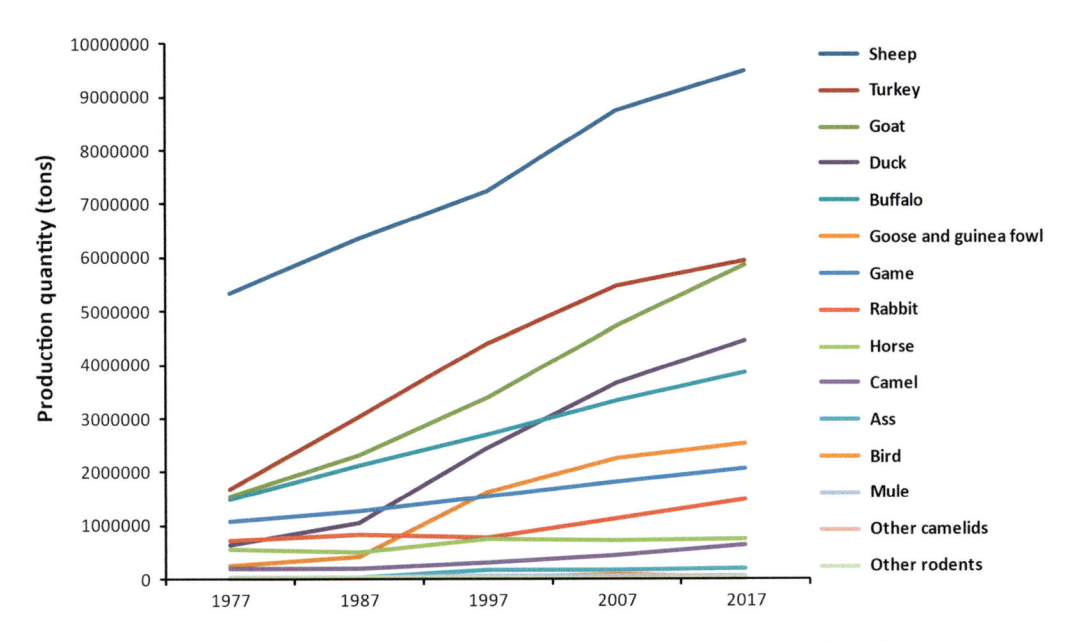

FIGURE 8.1 World production of non-traditional meats compared to sheep as a traditional meat source over the last 40 years (FAOSTAT, 2020).

8.2 PRODUCTION OF NON-TRADITIONAL MEATS

The human population has increased substantially from 2.6 billion people in 1950 to 7.7 billion in 2020 and is predicted to increase to 9.7 billion persons over the next 30 years (United Nations, 2020). Parallel to this, an increase in meat production and consumption have been observed. This increase is driven by a combination of improvement of the income of people in developing countries, resulting in diets shifting from grain-based to meat-based (Gordon, 2018). This will continue to outstrip demand for meat from traditional sources, creating increased interest in utilizing meat from other non-traditional sources. Hence the production of non-traditional meats has been greatly increased over the past 50 years (Figure 8.1). Turkey, goat, duck, and buffalo have represented the major sources of non-traditional meats used to date, along with production of meat from other sources, as indicated in Table 8.1.

Production of sheep meat increased from 5.3 million tons in 1977 to 9.5 million tons in 2017 and most of the production was in Asia and Africa (FAOSTAT, 2020). Increase in sheep meat production could be in part attributed to the ability of sheep to survive under a variety of climatic conditions (Zygoyiannis, 2006). In addition, sheep meats have high nutritional value and unique sensory attributes such as tenderness and tastiness that appeals to consumers, resulting in increasing global demand (Knapik et al., 2017). Turkey meat production increased from 1.7 million tons in 1977 to 5.9 million tons in 2017 (FAOSTAT, 2020). Turkey meat is the second-highest produced poultry meat after chicken (Oz & Yuzer, 2017). Turkey meat is a healthy good quality source of protein, which is in demand and has resulted in increasing production (Ferreira et al., 2000; Lesiów & Xiong, 2004). Turkey meat has a high content of sodium, potassium, copper, iron, and zinc, low level of cholesterol, total lipids and saturated fatty acids, and has good acceptability due to its neutral taste and smooth texture (Baggio et al., 2005; Ferreira et al., 2000; Gok & Bor, 2016). Production of goat meat has greatly increased from 1.55 million tons in 1977 to 5.9 million tons in 2017 (FAOSTAT, 2020). Goat meat production and consumption occurs mainly in developing countries and has been less popular in developed countries (Webb, 2014). Compared to other red meats, goat meat is lean and has lower total saturated fatty acids, and cholesterol content

TABLE 8.1
World production of non-traditional meats compared to sheep as a traditional meat source (FAOSTAT, 2020)

Meat sources	Production quantity (tons)
Sheep	9498356
Turkey	5948197
Goat	5853336
Duck	4460226
Buffalo	3838647
Goose and guinea fowl	2522202
Game	2076896
Rabbit	1482441
Horse	732719
Camel	630210
Ass	177233
Mule	46134
Other camelids	29622
Birds	20520
Other rodents	18711

and consequently the recognition and popularity of goat meat as a healthy food has greatly increased in recent years (Ivanovic et al., 2016; Mazhangara et al., 2019). In addition, other factors such as the culture of communities, civilization, adaptability to harsh environment, and lower price of goat meat are also affecting the popularity of goat meat (Webb et al., 2005). Duck meat production increased from 0.6 million tons in 1977 to 4.5 million tons in 2017 (FAOSTAT, 2020). Duck meats are mainly produced in Asia, with China being the top producer, exporter and consumer of duck meat (FAOSTAT, 2020). The adaptability of ducks to various environmental conditions and their relatively low susceptibility to various diseases are reasons for increased production of duck meat (Adzitey & Adzitey, 2011). Several duck species are used for meat production in different regions such as Pekin in the United States, and Muscovy, Mallard and Moulard-mule in Europe and Asia. In addition, breeding has led to improved duck species having faster growth rates and better meat quality (Adzitey & Adzitey, 2011). Buffalo meat production increased from 1.5 million tons in 1977 to 3.8 million tons in 2017 (FAOSTAT, 2020). The two major subspecies of buffalo are water buffalo (*Bubalus arnee bubalis*) and swamp buffalo (*Bubalus arnee carabanesis*), and they are primarily raised for milk production (Juárez et al., 2019). In addition to dairying, water buffalo are also used for meat production and are considered as a relatively cheap source of animal protein compared to other meats such as beef and pork (Banjade et al., 2017; Nanda & Nakao 2003).

Another group of smaller animal non-traditional meat source include goose, guinea fowl and other game, and rabbit, from which a total of 6 million tons of meat was produced in 2017 (FAOSTAT, 2020). The production of goose and guinea fowl increased from 2.55 million tons in 1977 to 4.1 million tons in 1987, and although production was reduced to 1.6 million tons in 1997, production increased to 2.2 and 2.5 million tons in 2007 and 2017, respectively (FAOSTAT, 2020). China is the main producer of goose and guinea fowl meat (FAOSTAT, 2020). As one of the first domesticated poultry animals, goose meat is considered as an important protein source by peoples in many developing countries (Geldenhuys et al., 2015; Oz et al., 2016). Although in many parts of the globe, guinea fowl meat is produced primarily by smallholders, especially in tropical environments, it is however increasing considered to be a viable and profitable enterprise and deserving of commercialization (Nahashon et al., 2006). Guinea fowl are less susceptible to many poultry diseases and are considered a cheap source of meat compared to chicken (Mareko et al., 2006; Saina et al., 2005). Guinea fowl meat has high nutritional quality and limited cultural consumption barriers (Adeyinka et al., 2007; Saina et al., 2005), and meat is lean and contains less fat and hence is considered desirable by a health-conscious population (Madzimure et al., 2011). Game meat production increased from 1.1 million tons in 1977 to 2.1 million tons in 2017 and half of the world production of game meat occurs in Africa (FAOSTAT, 2020). Game meat is a suitable alternative to beef, pork, lamb and chicken meats as it has good nutritional, sensory and health attributes (Hoffman, 2008; Morales et al., 2018; Strazdina et al., 2011), however, game meat consumption varies among populations (Morales et al., 2018). Low consumption of game meat by some populations can be due to various reasons, such as high price, limited access to the product, lack of information about the product, unattractiveness due to the blood-red appearance of the meat, and low hygienic quality (Morales et al., 2018; Taylor et al., 2014). Whereas in some areas of the world game meat is available and is appreciated as a healthy alternative to domestic animal meat, thereby increasing demand for the product (Lehel et al., 2016; Sales & Kotrba, 2013). Rabbit meat production increased from 0.7 million tons in 1977 to 1.5 million tons in 2017 and about three quarters of all rabbit meat is produced in Asia (FAOSTAT, 2020). China is the main producer of rabbit meat (FAOSTAT, 2020) where it has been consumed on a regular basis for a long time due to its recognized high nutritional, health and sensory qualities (Li et al., 2018). Rabbit meat contains a high content of polyunsaturated fatty acids, proteins, and essential amino acids, as well as a low fat, sodium, and cholesterol contents (Dalle Zotte & Szendrő, 2011; Li et al., 2018). Rabbits are considered as attractive for meat production due to their short life cycle and gestation period, they are highly prolific, have good feed conversion to meat efficiency, and have less competition for consuming foods suitable for humans (Cullere & Dalle Zotte, 2018).

Production of meat from horse, camel and ass, together was about 1.54 million tons of meat, whereas meat production from mule, birds, other camelids and other rodents, together was about 115 thousand tons of meat in 2017 (FAOSTAT, 2020). Horse meat production increased from 0.55 million tons in 1977 to 0.73 million tons in 2017 and about three-quarters of the world horse meat is produced in Asia and Americas (FAOSTAT, 2020). China, followed by Kazakhstan are the top world producer of horse meat, producing about 40% of the total global horse meat (FAOSTAT, 2020). Horses were domesticated relatively early (5000 BC) compared to some animals and thereafter they are used for various purposes, including as working animals, for recreation, and as a meat source (Belaunzaran et al., 2017). Horse meat plays a central role in the preparation of traditional foods in many European, South American, and Asian countries, and it used as the main meat in Tonga and some central Asian countries (Lorenzo et al., 2019). The consumption of horse meat has been limited in some populations due to cultural, social, and religious beliefs, however, the production and consumption of horse meat is increasing in part due to its recognized nutritional value (Belaunzaran et al., 2017). Camel meat production increased from 0.2 million tons in 1977 to 0.6 million tons in 2017 (FAOSTAT, 2020), with about two-thirds of the total camel meat produced in Africa, followed by Asia (FAOSTAT, 2020). Sudan is the main producer of camel meat-producing about one third of the global production (FAOSTAT, 2020). Although camels are used for various transport and work purposes, in many countries, camels are considered to be increasingly economically important, in that they can live in harsh environments and provide substantial amounts of cheap and high-quality meat that can fulfil the increasing need for animal protein for the human population (Kadim et al., 2009). Camel meat contains a relatively high proportion of polyunsaturated fatty acids, less fat, and a low cholesterol content compared to other red meats (Al-Owaimer et al., 2014; Kadim et al., 2008). Donkey (Ass) meat production increased from 28690 tons in 1977 to 177233 tons in 2017 and China contributed about 88% of the global production, with the rest produced in some African and European countries (FAOSTAT, 2020).

Young male donkey is considered to be a cheap source of nutritionally good quality meat for human consumption (Polidori et al., 2008), while the meat of older animals is less tender and hence considered not desirable by many consumers (Polidori et al., 2009). Mule meat production increased from 13790 tons in 1977 to 46134 tons in 2017 (FAOSTAT, 2020). Meat of various other birds increased from 7839 tons in 1977 to 20520 tons in 2017 (FAOSTAT, 2020). Globally, several species of domestic and game birds such as pheasant and quail are used for meat production and their meat is characterized by low fat and high-quality protein (Neethling et al., 2016). The quality of bird meat depends on several factors such as genotype, diet and raring conditions of the bird (López-Pedrouso et al., 2019). Increased production of bird meat in recent times is likely due to cheapness, low susceptibility of birds to diseases, early sexual maturity, high adaptability, and better-quality farm production and processing, due to higher consumer perception of animal welfare (Cawthorn & Hoffman, 2014; Kilonzo-Nthenge et al., 2008; Nuno et al., 2018). Meat production from other camelids is increased from 15970 tons in 1977 to 29622 in 2017, whereas meat production from rodents reduced from 21310 tons in 1977 to 18711 tons in 2017 (FAOSTAT, 2020). This is likely due to the increase in income of nations that used to consume rodents (such as Brasil and China) and shift in their meat preferences and purchase power. Llama and alpaca are the main camelids used for meat production in many South American countries and their meat is recognized as being highly nutritive and healthy (Fairfield, 2006; Mamani-Linares & Gallo, 2013). Rodents such as beaver, cavia, vicugna, and nutria have been used traditionally for meat production in many South American countries (Saadoun et al., 2014).

8.3 NUTRITIONAL COMPOSITION OF NON-TRADITIONAL MEATS

Meat is a highly nutritious food as it contains substantial quantities of important nutrients such as high biological value protein, essential vitamins (B2, B3, B6, B12, and D), essential minerals (iron, zinc, phosphorus, and selenium), omega-3 polyunsaturated fatty acids, bioactive compounds and antioxidants (Williams, 2007). In addition to the aforementioned nutritional components, meat from non-traditional sources is typically characterized by low cholesterol and saturated fatty acids and high n3 polyunsaturated fatty acids (Valencak & Gamsjager, 2014), which contributes to the nutritional and health qualities of these types of meat. However, several factors such as genotype, gender, species, age, climate, carcass type and meat cut, animal nutrition and rearing system can affect the chemical composition of non-traditional meat. The chemical composition of non-traditional meat varies considerably among the meat sources (Tables 8.2–8.16). Hereafter, the chemical composition of non-traditional meat from different sources will be discussed.

8.3.1 CAMELIDS

The camelids have been used for meat production for centuries, since domestication of camels. Among camelids, the chemical composition of camel meat is well reviewed in the literature (Bekhit & Farouk, 2013; Hoffman, 2008; Kadim et al., 2008; Kadim et al., 2014) and will thus not be discussed in this chapter. The other camelids used for meat production include Alpaca (*Vicugna pacos*), Llama (*Lama glama*), and Guanaco (*Lama guanicoe*). The approximate composition, cholesterol content, amino acids, and minerals of alpaca, llama, and guanaco meat are presented in Tables 8.2. Wide ranges of moisture, protein, fat, and ash contents were reported for alpaca and llama meats. The variation in the approximate composition of each meat is attributed to the differences in rearing systems, animal nutrition, age, gender, seasons, and meat cuts (Mamani-Linares & Gallo, 2013; Perez et al., 2000; Salvá et al., 2009; Smith et al., 2017). Alpaca and llama meats are considered as the major protein sources for Andean rural communities (Perez et al., 2000). The protein content of alpaca, llama, and guanaco meats is high while the intramuscular fat is low, indicating the high nutritional and health quality of these meats (Cristofanelli et al., 2004; Gonzalez et al., 2004). An increase in the age of alpaca from 18–36

TABLE 8.2
Amino acid composition (g/100 g DW) and mineral composition (mg/ 100 g FW) of other camelid non-traditional meats

Trait	Alpaca	Llama	Guanaco
Moisture	73.64–74.07	67.2–73.94	73.9
Protein	22.69–23.33	19.2–25.5	20.9
Fat	0.49–2.05	0.40–10.1	1.02
Ash	1.10–2.54	1.3–3.06	1.10
Cholesterol (mg/100 g)	51.14-	39.04–104.67	27.2
Essential amino acids			
His	–	3.52–4.50	–
Ileu	–	3.20–3.26	–
Leu	–	4.13–7.61	–
Lys	11.05	11.38–1.65	–
Met	2.19	2.59–7.59	–
Phe	–	3.15–3.33	–
Thr	–	4.94–8.43	–
Val	3.33	4.93–6.55	–
Non–essential amino acids			
Ala	7.30	3.41–9.99	–
Arg	6.90	4.44–6.94	–
Asp	12.06	3.37–9.79	–
Cys	–	0.97–5.43	–
Glu	16.61	2.97–14.93	–
Gly	5.97	4.54–9.28	–
Pro	3.27	7.95–9.11	–
Ser	4.76	3.83–4.16	–
Tyr	2.36	3.72–4.36	–
Minerals			
Ca	2.51–10.70	8.21–16.5	–
Cu	0.054–0.10	–	–
Fe	0.99–2.69	1.68–4.24	–
K	354.6–419.0	332.0–683.3	–
Mg	23.89–33.80	15.5–34.4	–
Mn	0.002–0.015	–	–
Na	33.03–88.40	68.3–146.5	–
P	224.03–295.00	285.1–534.5	–
Zn	1.50–4.44	3.01–6.11	–
References	Salvá et al., 2009; Smith et al., 2017; Cristofanelli et al., 2004	Polidori et al., 2007; Perez et al., 2000; Cristofanelli et al., 2004; Mamani-Linares & Gallo, 2014	Gonzalez et al., 2004

TABLE 8.3
Fatty acid composition (g/ 100 g oil) of other camelid non-traditional meats

Fatty acids	Alpaca	Llama	Guanaco
Saturated fatty acids (SFA)			
C 12:0	0.17–0.18	0.48–0.64	–
C 13:0	0.06–0.09	0.37–0.45	–
C 14:0	2.24–2.67	2.56–5.19	2.7–3.2
C 15:0	1.03–1.33	1.31–1.62	–
C 16:0	19.06–22.1	20.13–27.15	19.6–23.1
C 17:0	0.86–1.22	0.61–0.67	–
C 18:0	19.82–33.44	11.73–21.47	25.4 26.0
C 20:0	0.36–0.96	0.03	–
C 21:0	0.16	–	–
C 22:0	0.10–0.33	–	–
Mono–unsaturated fatty acids (MUSFA)			
C 14:1	0.04–0.07	2.25–2.71	–
C 15:1	0.07–0.10	0.44–0.50	–
C 16:1	1.64–3.16	6.75–7.08	–
C 17:1	0.37–0.41	0.54–.71	–
C 18:1n9	14.12–24.24	28.77–34.10	26.7–30.6
Poly–unsaturated fatty acids (PUSFA)			
C18:2ω6	2.58–6.02	2.20–6.99	8.9–9.3
C18:3ω3	1.10–1.75	0.53–1.73	3.5–4.5
C20:2ω6	0.07–0.16	0.22–0.38	
C20:3ω6	0.22	0.43–1.02	3.4–5.0
C20:4ω6	0.13–1.28	0.20–1.78	–
C20:5ω3	0.012–0.018	0.65	–
C22:5ω3	0.008–0.011	–	–
C22:6ω3	0.001–0.0014	0.48	–
Σ ω6	2.96–9.61	3.05–10.17	8.9–9.3
Σ ω3	1.193–1.793	1.66–2.86	3.5–4.5
Σ SFA	51.23–63.92	42.60–50.34	47.7–52.3
Σ USFA	36.08–48.77	38.20–56.50	39.1–44.4
ΣMUSFA	30.33–37.06	31.02–44.70	26.7–30.6
ΣPUSFA	5.75–11.71	7.18–11.80	12.4–13.8
SFA/USFA	1.31–1.42	0.89–1.12	1.18–1.22
SFA/MUSFA	1.69–1.72	1.13–1.37	1.71–1.79
SFA/PUSFA	5.46–8.91	4.27–5.93	3.79–3.85
PUSFA/SFA	0.19–0.26	0.17–0.23	0.45–0.46
ω6/ω3	2.48–5.36	1.84–3.56	2.07–2.54
References	Salvá et al., 2009; Smith et al., 2017	Coates & Ayerza, 2004; Polidori et al., 2007; Mamani-Linares & Gallo, 2014	Gonzalez et al., 2004

months showed increased intramuscular fat in *longissimus thoracis et lumborum* (LTL) and *biceps femoris* (BF) muscles (Smith et al., 2017). It has also been reported that meat of adult llama has less moisture and a higher fat content than that of younger animals (Perez et al., 2000). Cristofanelli et al. (2004) compared the chemical composition of LTL muscle of alpaca and llama and found insignificant differences between fat and protein contents, while ash content was

TABLE 8.4
Amino acid and mineral compositions (mg/ 100 g FW) of bison, buffalo and yak non-traditional meats

Trait	Bison	Buffalo	Yak
Moisture	72.18–75.40	66.46–79.00	74.87–76.80
Protein	21.08–22.72	18.70–24.39	19.28–22.58
Fat	0.77–4.58	0.90–7.33	1.31–10.86
Ash	1.03–2.09	0.33–1.61	0.93–1.00
Cholesterol (mg/ 100 g)	25.07–71.0	32.20–233.26	–
Essential amino acids	mmol/kg	g/100 g protein	g/100 g
His	–	3.07–3.59	0.88–2.88
Ileu	0.32–1.15	1.22–1.40	1.06–4.01
Leu	0.29–1.19	6.28–8.19	1.83–7.76
Lys	0.31–1.12	9.47–9.92	2.07–6.65
Met	–	4.43–4.59	0.54–1.43
Phe	0.21–0.93	4.17–4.28	1.02–4.04
Thr	–	3.68–3.82	1.03–3.79
Val	0.75–2.95	4.43–4.59	1.09–4.28
Try	0.09–0.22	–	–
Non–essential amino acids			
Ala	–	3.15–3.32	1.30–5.87
Arg	–	0.96–1.87	1.42–6.93
Asp	0.13–0.34	7.50–7.74	2.10–8.57
Cys	0.03–0.26	0.94–1.59	0.20–0.24
Glu	2.43–3.79	12.32–12.69	3.41–16.49
Gly	0.29–0.53	4.28–4.72	0.94–5.83
Pro	0.53–1.00	3.18–4.01	0.82–4.26
Ser	–	3.30	0.88–3.73
Tyr	0.26–1.23	2.91–3.46	0.78–3.22
Minerals			
Ca	3.23–10.90	2.43–21.99	1.26–1.99
Cu	0.13–0.16	0.09–9.46	0.11–0.15
Fe	2.61–3.15	2.28–5.99	2.20–3.22
K	322.0–345.0	288.52–369.46	328.33–348.33
Mg	23.3–24.8	8.46–25.34	24.93–26.77
Mn	0.01–0.02	0.01–0.02	0.015–0.017
Na	39.00–60.09	61.42–72.95	79.33–89.33
P	189.0–204.0	202.53–223.78	17.97–33.37
Zn	3.2–5.0	0.14–5.49	1.32–1.35
References	Marchello et al., 1998; Dhanda et al., 2002; Galbraith et al., 2006; Williamson et al., 2014; Łozicki et al., 2017	Ziauddin et al., 1994; Giuffrida-Mendoza et al., 2007; Tajik et al., 2010; Calabrò et al., 2014; Hassan et al., 2018; Li et al., 2018	Zi et al., 2004; Luo et al., 2006; Zhang et al., 2016

TABLE 8.5
Fatty acid composition (g/ 100 g oil) of bison, buffalo and yak non-traditional meats

Fatty acids	Bison	Buffalo	Yak
Saturated fatty acids (SFA)			
C 14:0	1.0–1.27	0.91–1.64	0.76–0.81
C 15:0	0.33–3.20	0.27–0.59	ND
C 16:0	14.9–18.9	20.04–23.30	18.87–22.65
C 17:0	0.86–1.41	0.97–1.71	0.31–0.36
C 18:0	14.0–19.0	19.80–29.10	25.43–26.93
C 20:0	0.31	0.13–1.02	0.30–0.33
C 22:0	0.93–2.90	0.17–0.21	–
C 24:0	–	0.15–0.21	–
Mono–unsaturated fatty acids (MUSFA)			
C 14:1	0.05–0.16	0.32–0.73	–
C 15:1	0.36	0.27	–
C 16:1	1.43–2.40	1.00–1.84	4.41–5.75
C 17:1	0.51	0.40–0.96	–
C 18:1n9	33.5–44.0	27.80–34.76	33.43–35.97
Poly–unsaturated fatty acids (PUSFA)			
C18:2ω6	7.10–11.90	3.32–9.13	5.34–5.69
C18:3ω3	0.40–2.90	0.16–0.94	–
C20:3ω3	0.26	0.24–0.53	–
C20:3ω6	0.09–0.38	0.26–0.80	–
C20:4ω6	3.17–3.72	0.38–3.19	1.15–2.97
C20:5ω3	1.15–4.99	0.04–0.29	0.22–0.30
C22:4ω6	0.16–0.23	0.18–0.46	–
C22:5ω3	0.76–1.72	0.10–0.69	–
C22:6ω3	0.25–0.41	0.20–0.24	0.40–0.49
Σ ω6	10.52–16.23	4.14–13.58	6.84–8.31
Σ ω3	2.82–10.28	0.74–2.69	0.72–0.77
Σ SFA	32.33–46.99	42.44–57.77	50.23–52.44
Σ USFA	49.10–73.56	34.67–54.83	46.80–49.42
ΣMUSFA	35.85–47.43	29.79–38.56	39.18–40.38
ΣPUSFA	13.25–26.13	4.88–16.27	7.61–9.03
SFA/USFA	0.64–0.66	1.05–1.22	1.06–1.07
SFA/MUSFA	0.90–0.99	1.42–1.50	1.28–1.29
SFA/PUSFA	1.80–2.44	3.55–8.70	5.80–6.60
PUSFA/SFA	0.41–0.56	0.11–0.28	0.15–0.17
ω6/ω3	1.58–3.73	5.05–5.59	9.38–12.36
References	Marchello et al., 1998; Galbraith et al., 2016; Łozicki et al., 2017	Juárez et al., 2010; Calabrò et al., 2014; Hassan et al., 2018;	Zhang et al., 2015

higher in llama muscles compared with alpaca muscles. Cholesterol levels of alpaca, llama, and guanaco meats were reported to be 51.14 mg/100 g, 39.04–56.29 mg/100 g, and 27.2 mg/100 g, respectively which is relatively low compared to that reported for the meat of various other animals (Cristofanelli et al., 2004). The cholesterol content of guanaco was found to be considerably lower than that of alpaca and llama, which could be due to variation in genotype,

TABLE 8.6
Amino acid and mineral compositions (mg/ 100 g) of horse and donkey non-traditional meats

Trait	Horse	Donkey
Moisture	65.06–84.23	70.10–77.80
Protein	12.50–25.98	19.54–23.70
Fat	0.15–12.14	1.76–3.71
Ash	0.58–4.03	1.01–1.33
Cholesterol (mg/100 g)	36.30–79.50	62.40–68.70
Essential amino acids		
His	0.71–1.14	0.74–0.93
Ileu	0.77–1.15	0.85–1.05
Leu	0.81–1.99	1.44–1.60
Lys	1.45–2.14	1.53–1.77
Met	0.13–0.74	0.51–0.74
Phe	0.76–1.04	0.76–0.92
Thr	0.77–1.16	0.86–0.96
Val	0.84–1.18	1.01–1.11
Try	–	0.19–0.33
Non-essential amino acids		
Ala	1.08–1.37	1.08–1.22
Arg	1.08–1.87	1.22–1.44
Asp	1.65–2.18	1.65–1.92
Cys	0.11–0.24	0.17–0.22
Glu	2.53–3.57	2.53–3.26
Gly	0.82–1.31	0.84–0.97
Pro	0.78–1.10	0.84–1.00
Ser	0.63–0.97	0.64–0.82
Tyr	0.48–0.77	0.84–0.70
Minerals		
Ca	3.64–11.50	7.95–8.65
Cu	0.13–2.47	0.19-
Fe	2.13–4.77	3.80–3.95
K	191.00–438.00	343.70–353.00
Mg	18.50–43.30	24.8
Mn	0.01–0.02	–
Na	36.80–83.60	48.75–52.50
P	185.00–335.00	212.90–227.00
Zn	1.65–5.45	3.17–3.67
References	Franco & Lorenzo, 2014; De Palo et al., 2016; Seong et al., 2016; Domínguez et al., 2018; Seong et al., 2019; Lorenzo et al., 2019	Polidori et al., 2008; Polidori et al., 2009; Polidori and Vincenzetti, 2013Polidori et al., 2015; De Palo et al., 2017.Salazar-Pressler et al., 2018

TABLE 8.7
Fatty acid composition (g/ 100 g oil) of horse, donkey and mule non-traditional meats

Fatty acids	Horse	donkey
Saturated fatty acids (SFA)		
C 14:0	1.33–4.57	2.27–4.51
C 15:0	0.15–3.06	0.36–0.61
C 16:0	22.08–31.16	22.08–29.77
C 17:0	0.29–1.37	0.34–1.44
C 18:0	3.56–7.47	6.83–15.53
C 20:0	0.06–0.11	0.28–1.12
C 22:0	0.01–0.04	–
C 24:0	0.05–0.06	–
Mono-unsaturated fatty acids (MUSFA)		
C 14:1	0.24–0.49	0.06–0.30
C 15:1	0.014–0.023	0.98–1.41
C 16:1	2.44–6.95	2.64–4.16
C 17:1	0.37–1.34	0.27–1.37
C 18:1n9	20.57–34.52	21.88–29.65
Poly-unsaturated fatty acids (PUSFA)		
C18:2ω6	10.69–24.85	16.61–22.60
C18:3ω6	0.02–0.14	–
C18:3ω3	1.88–3.51	2.83–4.32
C20:3ω3	0.17–2.55	0.02–0.27
C20:3ω6	0.18–0.52	0.18–1.45
C20:4ω6	0.10–3.84	1.65–2.28
C20:5ω3	0.01–0.97	0.15–0.20
C22:4ω6	0.03–0.09	–
C22:5ω3	0.80–1.81	–
C22:6ω3	0.16–0.48	–
Σ ω6	11.0–29.30	18.44–26.33
Σ ω3	3.02–19.32	3.00–4.79
Σ SFA	27.53–47.84	32.16–52.98
Σ USFA	37.49–82.08	44.44–63.69
ΣMUSFA	23.63–43.32	25.83–36.89
ΣPUSFA	13.86–38.76	18.61–26.80
SFA/USFA	0.58–0.73	0.72–0.83
SFA/MUSFA	1.10–1.17	1.25–1.44
SFA/PUSFA	1.23–1.99	1.73–1.98
PUSFA/SFA	0.50–0.81	0.51–0.58
ω6/ω3	1.52–3.64	5.50–6.15
References	Lanza et al., 2009; Juárez et al., 2009; Franco, & Lorenzo, 2014; Seong et al., 2016; Domínguez et al., 2015; Belaunzaran et al., 2017; Domínguez et al., 2018	Polidori et al., 2009; Polidori et al., 2015; De Palo et al., 2017;

TABLE 8.8
Amino acid composition (g/100 g) and mineral composition (mg/100 g) of game animal non-traditional meats

Trait	Blesbok	Springbok	Hartebeest	Kudu	Impala	Common duiker
Moisture	68.20–76.51	60.8–75.3	74.40–75.1	74.14–75.77	65.00–74.96	71.21–71.41
Protein	18.71–23.7	17.4–24.2	22.6–24.7	22.18–24.30	18.9–23.37	25.71–25.88
Fat	0.21–9.0	2.5–8.0	0.3–1.2	1.48–2.08	1.2–5.8	2.01–2.10
Ash	1.04–6.1	1.2–6.4	1.1–1.3	1.14–1.23	1.16–7.5	1.29
Cholesterol (mg/100 g)	49.74–54.56	54.45–59.34	44.8 – 59.9	71.42	52.54	–
Amino acids (g/100 g)						
His	0.76–2.34	0.49–0.53	1.0–1.6	0.86–0.93	1.68	0.66–0.67
Ileu	1.05–4.22	0.93–1.04	0.9–1.2	1.13–1.17	1.16	1.16–1.19
Leu	2.04–8.90	1.79–2.04	1.9–2.3	1.91–1.95	2.61	2.21–2.32
Lys	1.40–15.16	1.34–1.86	1.3–1.7	1.57–1.57	2.61	2.47–2.67
Met	0.62–2.63	0.56–0.62	0.6–0.7	0.60–0.61	0.79	0.66–0.67
Phe	0.77–3.14	0.62–0.69	0.7–0.9	0.73–0.75	1.01	1.02–1.04
Thr	1.49–6.43	1.31–1.48	1.3–1.7	1.27–1.30	1.77	1.08–1.10
Val	1.34–5.29	1.16–1.28	1.2–1.5	1.37–1.43	1.47	1.38–1.40
Try	–	–	–	–	–	–
Ala	2.29–9.44	2.08–2.24	2.1–2.5	1.98–2.06	3.27	1.53–1.58
Arg	1.14–5.05	1.07–1.17	1.1–1.4	1.16–1.18	1.49	1.58–1.67
Asp	2.27–10.88	2.31–2.54	1.8–2.5	2.15–2.23	3.26	–
Cys	0.18–0.87	0.16–0.18	0.2–0.2	0.13–0.13	0.23	–
Glu	2.93–11.20	2.47–2.74	2.7–3.4	3.08–3.14	4.55	–
Gly	1.61–6.89	1.43–1.71	1.5–1.8	1.65–1.72	2.42	–
Pro	1.22–4.80	1.01–1.09	1.2–1.3	1.10–1.12	1.47	–
Ser	1.48–6.98	1.44–1.60	1.3–1.7	1.13–1.16	1.72	0.85–0.86
Tyr	0.68–2.72	0.59–0.63	0.6–0.8	0.60–0.62	0.82	0.87–0.88

(Continued)

TABLE 8.8 (Continued)
Amino acid composition (g/100 g) and mineral composition (mg/100 g) of game animal non-traditional meats

Trait	Blesbok	Springbok	Hartebeest	Kudu	Impala	Common duiker
Minerals (mg/100 g)						
Ca	5.85–6.94	6.57–145.18	6.74–27.8	4.62–9.68	6.32–7.98	28.81–30.83
Cu	0.12–0.44	0.08–0.10	0.1–6.2	0.011–0.035	0.05–0.07	0.79–0.85
Fe	3.06–3.96	2.67–3.04	2.41–307.1	1.27–2.85	2.07–2.49	12.93–14.38
K	142.46–157.84	119.44–131.25	125.90–532.2	119.00–215.44	114.58–124.28	280.52–297.57
Mg	16.92–22.50	17.21–19.84	16.57–75.6	19.78–26.72	20.26–22.55	61.86–65.79
Mn	–	–	–	0.03–0.09	0.002–0.009	–
Na	14.47–17.04	12.84–14.81	13.03–726.3	7.40–10.05	10.18–10.95	36.97–46.48
P	129.37–154.89	122.92–159.78	117.81–511.1	159.99–173.00	148.64–152.42	476.75–4.89.40
Zn	1.23–3.02	1.16–1.79	1.38–62.1	1.07–2.80	1.16–1.81	4.87–7.25
References	Smit, 2004; Hoffman, 2008; Neethling et al., 2014; Costa et al., 2016	Van Zyl & Ferreira, 2004; Hoffman et al., 2007b; Costa et al., 2016	Smit, 2004; Hoffman et al., 2010	Hoffman et al., 2005; Mostert & Hoffman, 2007; Hoffman et al., 2009a & b; Costa et al., 2016	Van Zyl & Ferreira, 2004; Hoffman et al., 2009a & b; Costa et al., 2016	Hoffman, & Ferreira, 2004

Trait	Black wildebeest	Red deer	Roe deer	Fallow deer	Elk	Wild boar	Reedbuck
Moisture	74.77–78.10	76.90	71.40–74.4	73.3–76.2	73.50–75.70	70.50 – 74.60	72.59–72.76
Protein	19.40–23.43	21.70	22.82–25.70	20.4–23.1	22.00–22.60	18.77 – 25.87	23.68–24.51
Fat	1.26–1.80	0.60	1.0–2.12	0.24–3.4	1.09–2.40	0.83 – 3.13	2.43–2.94
Ash	1.10–1.38	1.11	0.98–1.11	1.1–1.5	0.88–1.40	0.71–2.79	1.22–1.23
Cholesterol (mg/100 g)	44.87–51.63	45.34–52.78	67.92	–	38.70–64.41	95.07–98.11	51.08–52.05
Amino acids							
His	0.60–0.72	0.76–0.81	0.10	–	0.24–0.74	0.21–0.70	0.75–0.78
Ileu	1.14–1.35	1.03–1.07	0.37	–	0.38–0.91	0.27–0.79	1.27–1.28
Leu	2.32–2.77	1.76–1.83	0.62	–	0.59–1.82	0.54–1.11	2.49–2.51
Lys	1.99–2.28	1.88–1.97	0.64	–	0.67–1.93	0.50–1.24	3.00–4.31

Met	0.68–0.75	0.23–0.25	0.17		0.18–0.58	0.84–0.84
Phe	0.50–1.00	0.90–0.94	0.35	—	0.30–0.87	0.91–0.97
Thr	1.71–2.05	0.94–0.96	0.42	—	0.40–0.97	1.84–1.88
Val	1.44–1.67	1.07–1.13	0.39	—	0.40–1.02	1.41–1.57
Try	—	—	0.11	—	0.11–0.79	0.82–0.86
Ala	2.55–2.74	1.17–1.20	0.45	—	0.49–1.24	2.66–2.72
Arg	1.39–1.60	1.69–1.74	0.52	—	0.43–1.34	1.50–1.52
Asp	2.85–3.04	1.88–1.96	0.75	—	0.67–1.97	2.91–2.97
Cys	0.20–0.25	—	—	—	0.24–0.25	0.23–0.24
Glu	3.18–3.53	3.15–3.28	1.33	—	1.49–3.39	3.62–3.72
Gly	1.88–2.12	0.77–0.78	0.35	—	0.32–0.93	2.07–2.07
Pro	1.34–1.39	0.78–0.79	0.27	—	0.26–0.97	1.41–1.47
Ser	1.82–2.14	0.78–0.83	0.27	—	0.86–1.21	1.96–1.98
Tyr	0.73–0.86	0.71–0.74	0.42	—	0.42–0.67	0.82–0.86
Minerals						
Ca	6.47–7.03	6.00	46.2–98.6	3.48–3.71	137.0	3.22–54.9
Cu	0.08–0.16	0.19–0.21	0.73–0.97	0.19–0.20	0.54	0.04–0.75
Fe	2.59–3.07	2.73–3.37	4.95–15.68	3.83–4.32	13.0	7.71–21.70
K	144.54–189.72	279.00–289.00	1272.0–1409.0	362.24–374.	1350.0	930.0–1478.0
Mg	18.15–22.04	30.00–38.00	84.4–86.2	25.94–27.30	96.0	7.31–91.0
Mn	—	0.018–0.022	0.20–0.26	0.02–0.021	0.17	0.06–0.14
Na	14.19–16.07	105.00–121.00	217.0–250.0	43.29–43.53	167.0	20.43–269.0
P	151.43–186.83	217.0–235.0	898.0–923.0	224.58–230.19	747.0	91.15–847.0
Zn	1.00–1.61	1.36–1.83	10.88–1.81	1.50–2.08	12.50	4.10–17.83
References	Van Schalkwyk, 2004; Hoffman et al., 2009	Lorenzo et al., 2019	Zomborszky et al., 1996; Cygan-Szczegielniak & Janicki, 2012; Strazdina et al., 2011 & 2013	Venguš̌t, & Venguš̌t, 2004; Fitzhenry 2016;Tesařová et al., 2018	Dhanda et al., 2003; Strazdina et al., 2011; Kim et al., 2016; Shelepov et al., 2019	Zomborszky et al., 1996; Brudnicki et al., 2012; Sales & Kotrba, 2013; Strazdina et al., 2014; Amici et al., 2015; Roślewska et al.,2016; "Tesařová et al., 2018; Kasprzyk et al., 2019	Hoffman et al., 2008b

TABLE 8.9
Fatty acid composition of game animal non-traditional meats

Fatty acids (% of total fatty acids)	Blesbok	Springbok	Hartebeest	Kudu	Impala	Zebra	Common duiker	Mouflon
Saturated fatty acids (SFA)								
C 14:0	–	–	–	0.12–0.83	0.32–0.58	0.33–1.41	0.64–0.75	0.93–2.63
C 16:0	15.31–18.19	13.34–15.06	16.05–19.16	11.85–14.85	15.04–22.47	21.27–27.36	0.86–1.32	16.10–20.87
C 18:0	25.20–26.71	23.92–27.02	27.60–44.61	16.83–21.59	20.36–22.25	7.77–18.58	18.39–19.68	15.78–16.42
C 20:0	0.28–0.33	0.28–0.40	0.38–0.67	0.18–0.38	0.10–0.14	0.06–0.17	0.77–0.81	0.12–0.14
C 22:0	0.28–0.31	0.24–0.26	0.27–0.65	–	0.09–0.19	0.49–3.21	0.06–0.08	0.10–0.16
C 24:0	0.44–0.58	0.39–0.63	0.53–1.14	–	0.14–0.19	–	0.05–0.06	–
Mono-unsaturated fatty acids (MUSFA)								
C 16:1	0.00	0.03–0.20	0.00	0.51–0.88	0.57–0.67	0.00–3.42	18.58–18.62	1.03–1.45
C 18:1n9	9.17–24.09	16.33–20.45	16.01–18.39	26.91–29.49	15.98–21.81	10.24–30.80	17.39–18.70	22.42–25.09
C 20:1n9	0.04–0.05	0.08–0.12	0.38	0.06–0.10	0.07–0.13	0.17–0.33	0.19–0.23	0.08–0.11
C 24:1n9	0.49	0.15–0.29	11.71	–	0.09–0.14	–	–	–
Poly-unsaturated fatty acids (PUSFA)								
C18:2ω6	15.83–18.63	18.77–21.62	13.91–16.42	21.99–24.59	16.16–22.74	11.91–29.95	19.79–19.91	13.50–19.31
C18:3ω6	0.03–0.29	0.09–0.15	0.16–0.32	0.15–0.34	0.13–0.20	0.37–0.81	0.12–0.13	0.05–0.06
C18:3ω3	3.22–4.20	3.33–3.49	4.00	1.70–2.34	3.59–5.09	4.60–20.06	4.19–5.24	2.02–3.02
C20:2ω6	0.03–0.04	0.22–0.28	0.08	0.12–0.15	0.13–0.18	–	0.29–0.39	0.08–0.09
C20:3ω3	–	–	–	–	0.06–0.09	0.04–0.59	0.19–0.64	0.03–0.08
C20:3ω6	0.77–1.85	0.20–0.24	1.40	0.52–1.25	0.69–0.96	0.39–3.06	0.14–2.94	0.30–0.37
C20:4ω6	6.94–10.96	7.63–9.30	6.96–7.63	6.38–7.75	5.87–7.87	0.45–0.85	6.47–7.83	6.24–8.42
C20:5ω3	1.75–3.05	1.89–2.70	2.11–2.85	2.50–3.17	2.41–3.44	0.24–1.53	1.88–2.10	1.30–1.49

C22:2ω6	—	—	—	—	0.08–0.14	—	0.01–0.09	—
C22:3ω3	—	—	—	—	—	—	0.14–0.14	—
C22:4ω6	0.20–0.41	0.21–0.37	0.28–41	—	0.22–0.43	—	0.13–0.31	0.18–0.29
C22:5ω3	1.29–2.93	2.19–2.71	2.31–2.89	0.07–0.25	2.02–2.82	0.54–2.48	0.69–1.14	1.68–2.14
C22:6ω3	0.39–0.41	0.94–1.26	0.34–0.53	0.60–1.48	0.56–1.00	0.16–1.20	0.84–1.09	0.44–0.47
Σ ω6	23.80–32.18	27.12–31.96	23.24–26.26	29.16–34.08	23.28–32.43	13.32–33.78	26.95–31.60	20.35–28.54
Σ ω3	6.65–10.59	8.35–10.16	8.76–10.27	4.87–7.24	9.51–10.51	9.20–22.57	7.93–10.35	5.47–7.20
Σ SFA	41.51–46.12	38.40–42.69	44.83–66.23	28.98–37.65	38.11–45.13	33.91–45.73	20.77–22.70	33.03–40.22
Σ USFA	40.15–67.40	53.01–62.63	60.10–67.01	61.51–71.79	50.59–64.60	42.37–81.37	71.04–79.50	49.35–62.39
ΣMUSFA	9.70–24.63	16.67–20.99	28.10–30.48	27.48–30.47	16.80–22.66	11.37–34.70	36.16–37.55	23.53–26.65
ΣPUSFA	30.45–42.77	36.34–41.64	32.00–36.53	34.03–41.32	33.79–41.94	31.40–46.67	34.88–41.95	25.82–35.74
SFA/USFA	0.68–1.03	0.68–0.72	0.76–0.99	0.47–0.52	0.70–0.75	0.56–0.80	0.28–0.29	0.64–0.67
SFA/MUSFA	1.87–4.28	2.03–2.30	1.60–2.17	1.05–1.24	1.99–2.27	1.32–2.98	0.57–0.60	1.40–1.51
SFA/PUSFA	1.36–1.58	1.03–1.06	1.40–1.81	0.85–0.91	1.08–1.13	0.98–1.08	0.54–0.60	1.13–1.28
PUSFA/SFA	0.63–0.73	0.96–1.18	0.55–0.71	1.10–1.17	0.89–0.93	0.85–1.21	1.68–1.85	0.78–0.89
ω6/ω3	3.04–3.58	2.83–3.44	2.56–2.65	4.71–5.99	2.43–3.08	0.74–3.67	3.05–3.40	3.72–3.96
References	Smit, 2004; Hoffman, 2008	Hoffman et al., 2007b, 2008; Costa et al., 2016	Smit 2004; Hoffman et al., 2010	Mostert, 2007; Mostert & Hoffman, 2007	Hoffman et al., 2005	Hoffman et al., 2016	Hoffman, & Ferreira, 2004	Ugarkovic´ & Ugarkovic´, 2013

TABLE 8.10
Amino acid composition (g/100 g) and mineral composition (mg/100 g) of rodent non-traditional meats

Trait	Beaver	Cane	Capybara	Guinea Pig	Chinchilla	Nutria	African Giant (rat)
Moisture	70.84–76.75	67.0–71.2	71.90–78.05	70.60–75.80	68.24–73.70	71.17–76.10	62.10–65.40
Protein	20.52–22.16	17.8–18.8	18.98–22.62	13.58–22.89	18.70–20.03	19.60–25.50	18.39–20.10
Fat	0.51–6.58	6.5–10.1	0.36–4.74	2.64–15.95	6.00–11.26	1.00–8.80	10.20–11.40
Ash	1.08–1.19	1.2–1.4	0.83–1.30	0.90–1.13	0.98–1.10	0.80–1.23	2.00–5.70
Cholesterol (mg/100 g)	49.00–72.00	—	17.70–52.10	45.33–61.88	—	29.00–72.70	72.2–140.7
Amino acids	(g/100 g meat)	(g/100 g meat)			mg/100 g protein		g/100 g protein
His	0.83–1.10	0.21	—	—	3.64	7.45–8.48	2.30–3.03
Ileu	0.89–1.30	0.32	—	—	7.90	9.08–10.20	3.60–4.20
Leu	1.52–1.65	0.72	—	—	4.80	16.20–17.60	6.94–7.65
Lys	1.64–1.85	0.52	—	—	8.67	17.40–19.10	6.03–6.96
Met	0.39–0.78	0.43	—	—	5.43	4.26–4.72	2.16–3.04
Phe	0.10–0.87	0.41	—	—	4.09	8.09–8.74	4.11–4.30
Thr	0.08–0.90	0.20	—	—	4.43	8.42–9.65	2.65–4.20
Val	0.91–0.94	0.62	—	—	5.11	10.30–11.20	5.02–5.60
Try	0.31–0.34	—	—	—	—	—	—
Ala	1.11–1.36	0.24	—	—	6.63	10.50–10.80	4.07–4.18
Arg	1.17–1.42	0.70	—	—	7.74	14.30–15.80	6.38–6.55
Asp	1.61–1.89	0.81	—	—	9.79	19.90–20.00	9.70–10.60
Cys	—	0.11	—	—	—	1.82–1.94	1.19–1.20
Glu	2.95–3.49	1.50	—	—	15.42	29.40–30.10	12.90–13.00
Gly	0.85–1.01	1.22	—	—	4.91	9.01–9.08	4.22–8.00
Pro	0.75–0.82	0.30	—	—	3.90	8.49–8.85	3.26–4.22
Ser	0.67–0.90	0.32	—	—	3.90	7.36–7.60	3.00–3.88
Tyr	0.61–0.70	0.30	—	—	3.67	6.17–6.95	3.02–3.65

Minerals (mg/100 g)

Ca	4.45–8.67	12.3	20.02–39.65	—	5.9	4.14–5.90	32.7–49.8
Cu	0.07–0.12	0.04–0.10	—	—	—	0.19–0.23	—
Fe	3.82–8.38	1.06–1.27	0.40–0.65	—	1.35	1.04–2.40	10.8–66.8
K	377.40–415.90	33.9	—	—	243.75	104.7–111.2	40.4–50.2
Mg	23.88 25.84	3.6	—	—	27.3	25.1–26.0	20.0–42.1
Mn	0.01–0.02	0.28–0.52	—	—	—	0.05–0.06	1.86
Na	34.59–60.93	193.2	—	—	32.65	60.0–232.4	30.0–44.9
P	—	1.05	190.68–215.29	—	119.1	—	22.8–61.3
Zn	2.86–6.13	0.17–0.74	—	—	—	2.36–3.87	3.16–21.4
References	Jankowska et al., 2005; Strazdina et al., 2015; Florek et al., 2017a & b; Domaradzki et al., 2019	Ajayi & Tewe, 1980; Van Zyl et al., 1999; Adeyeye & Jegede, 2010; Joyce et al., 2016	Oda et al. (2004); Girardi et al. (2015); Felix et al. (2014)	Higaonna et al. (2008); Tandzong et al. (2015); Sánchez-Macías et al. (2018); Dalle Zotte and Cullere (2019); Ordoñez et al., 2019	Fellenberg et al., 2016; Vinauskiene et al., 2019	Tulley et al. (2000); Saadoun et al. (2006); Głogowski & Panas (2009); Migdal et al. (2013); Cholewa et al. (2014); Januškevičius et al. (2015)	Oyarekua & Ketiku. 2010; Adeyeye & Aremu, 2011; Adeyeye & Falemu, 2012; Adeyeye & Adesina, 2018

TABLE 8.11
Fatty acid composition of rodent non-traditional meats

Fatty acids (% of total fatty acids)	Beaver	Cane	Capybara	Guinea Pig	Chinchilla	Nutria	Paca
Saturated fatty acids (SFA)							
C 14:0	0.34–1.43	tr	0.88–3.93	0.31–1.74	1.60–2.52	3.60–3.94	2.8
C 16:0	12.96–23.05	13.4–21.5	22.0–29.8	10.47–17.89	16.56–18.33	21.9–26.96	26.6
C 18:0	3.02–13.36	20.0–26.1	3.16–8.16	8.74–19.01	2.41–3.13	4.66–1.40	8.4
C 20:0	0.01–0.81	tr	–	0.09–0.22	0.03–0.5	0.03–0.10	–
C 22:0	0.08–0.49	tr	–	–	–	–	–
C 24:0	0.05–0.14	tr	–	0.96–1.02	–	–	–
Mono-unsaturated fatty acids (MUSFA)							
C 16:1	2.39–6.07	0.42–0.67	0.44–0.62	0.27–0.92	4.98–9.39	5.58–18.40	2.2
C 18:1n9	5.23–11.72	1.67–4.48	23.7–32.0	3.46–13.38	28.58–30.57	16.20–24.50	21.6
C 20:1n9	0.23–0.33	0.13	0.42–0.70	0.03–0.23	0.03–0.27	0.10–0.30	–
C 24:1n9	0.08–0.16	–	–	–	–	–	–
Poly-unsaturated fatty acids (PUSFA)							
C18:2ω6	18.56–20.26	12.4–12.8	18.79–28.60	16.62–32.28	29.44–36.23	12.60–21.70	13.3
C18:3ω6	0.02–0.09	0.18–0.33	–	0.13–0.26	0.04–0.11	0.06–0.09	–
C18:3ω3	3.27–21.87	0.15–0.26	2.00–5.08	6.06–21.24	3.34–4.88	2.21–4.80	12.3
C20:2ω6	0.43–0.59	–	–	0.01–0.70	0.24–0.24	0.09–0.30	–
C20:3ω3	0.19–0.41	–	–	0.32–1.63	–	–	9.9
C20:3ω6	0.18–0.51	tr	0.51	0.12–0.74	0.08–0.10	0.09–0.10	–
C20:4ω6	0.54–9.85	8.63–12.0	1.04–12.81	0.33–8.04	0.06–0.12	1.24–4.37	–
C20:5ω3	0.15–0.84	–	0.11–2.77	0.25–1.16	–	0.06–0.07	–
C22:2ω6	0.01–0.11	–	–	–	0.05	–	–
C22:3ω3	–	–	–	–	–	–	–
C22:4ω6	0.22–0.59	–	0.35–0.89	0.07–0.28	–	0.33–0.44	–
C22:5ω3	0.69–2.85	–	–	0.87–5.60	0.02	0.15–0.56	1.0
C22:6ω3	0.20–1.17	8.41–12.6	0.10–0.24	0.38–3.10	0.05–0.07	0.08–0.36	–
Σ ω6	19.96–32.00	35.8–37.0	20.69–42.81	17.28–42.30	29.91–36.73	14.41–26.73	13.3
Σ ω3	4.50–27.14	8.56–12.9	2.21–8.09	7.88–32.73	3.41–4.97	2.5–5.79	22.5
Σ SFA	16.46–39.28	39.5–41.5	26.04–41.89	19.61–38.86	20.60–24.48	30.19–42.40	36.3
Σ USFA	32.39–77.42	58.9–60.4	47.46–83.59	28.92–89.56	66.91–81.93	38.79–75.72	60.7
ΣMUSFA	7.93–18.28	10.5–14.0	24.56–33.32	3.76–14.53	33.59–40.23	21.88–43.20	24.6
ΣPUSFA	24.46–59.14	44.4–49.9	22.90–50.27	25.16–75.03	33.32–41.70	16.91–32.52	36.1
SFA/USFA	0.50–0.51	0.67–0.69	0.50–0.55	0.43–0.68	0.30–0.31	0.56–0.78	0.6
SFA/MUSFA	2.08–2.15	2.96–3.76	1.06–1.26	2.67–5.22	0.60–0.61	0.98–1.38	1.48
SFA/PUSFA	0.66–0.67	0.83–0.89	0.83–1.14	0.52–0.78	0.59–0.62	1.30–1.79	1.01
PUSFA/SFA	1.49–1.51	1.12–1.20	0.88–1.20	1.28–1.93	1.62–1.70	0.56–0.77	0.99
ω6/ω3	1.18–4.44	2.87–4.18	5.29–9.36	1.29–2.19	7.39–8.77	4.62–5.76	0.5
References	Strazdina et al., 2015; Florek et al., 2017a & b; Domaradzki et al., 2019; Razmaitė & Pileckas, 2019; Razmaitė et al., 2011 & 2019	Adeyeye et al., 2012	Oda et al. (2004); Girardi et al. (2005); Pinheiro, & Moreira, 2013	Kouakou et al. (2013); Mustafa et al. (2019).	Fellenberg et al., 2016; Vinauskiene et al., 2019	Saadoun et al. (2006); Głogowski et al. (2010); Migdal et al. (2013)	Betancourt & Jair Diaz, 2014

TABLE 8.12
Amino acid composition (g/100 g) and mineral composition (mg/100 g) of reptile non-traditional meats

Trait	Crocodile Nile crocodile	Crocodile Caiman yacare	Crocodile A. mississippiensis	Pelodiscus sinensis	Turtle Chelonia mydas	Chelydra serpentina	Tegu lizard	Lizard Dhub Lizard	Green iguana
	g/100 g	g/100 g	g/100 g	%	g/100 g	g/100g	g/100 g		g/100 g
Moisture	66.1–76.6	71.2–78.2	73.0–80.0	60.05–80.38	78.1–81.4	83.0	71.2–72.6	–	73.1–77.2
Protein	14.0–22.9	18.8–23.8	16.0–18.0	15.90–31.34	16.0–20.0	15.8	23.2–24.1	–	18.8–20.8
Fat	0.47–15.5	0.3–2.4	0.8–1.0	0.28–10.10	0.40–1.0	0.2	3.2–5.5	–	1.92–4.45
Ash	0.36–0.65	0.9–2.8	0.5–1.0	0.47–3.80	0.87–1.20	1.0	1.1–1.3	–	0.19–1.59
Cholesterol (mg/100 g)			65.0	–	50.0	–	14.2–24.8	–	–
Amino acids	g/kg meat	mg/100 g		mg/100 mg	g/100 g	% of DM		g/100 protein	mg/g N
His	2.15–6.10	4.98–10.33	–	0.97–3.65	1.86	1.55	–	2.16	199.0
Ileu	3.56–9.46	0.28–0.52	–	1.45–3.83	2.56	1.96	–	5.10	553.0
Leu	6.43–13.80	0.67–1.03	–	2.84–7.05	3.44	3.47	–	7.12	607.0
Lys	6.97–14.5	1.13–1.29	–	3.31–9.22	3.70	3.44	–	7.70	590.0
Met	2.06–7.12	0.02–0.07	–	0.65–1.78	2.09	1.24	–	2.27	163.0
Phe	2.91–6.57	0.55–1.08	–	2.54–4.45	1.17	2.04	–	3.14	705.0
Thr	3.29–7.95	0.99–146	–	2.25–4.37	1.60	2.49	–	3.47	468.0
Val	3.47–8.88	1.07–1.93	–	1.87–4.17	2.77	2.25	–	6.34	334.0
Try	–	0.23–0.39	–	–	–	0.50	–	1.00	–
Ala	4.53–9.88	11.03–20.36	–	4.53–8.28	–	–	–	5.40	–
Arg	6.30–10.20	2.11–3.52	–	5.04–7.75	2.80	3.37	–	5.70	349.0
Asp	12.00–18.50	0.60–0.95	–	5.05–8.02	–	–	–	7.78	–
Cys	1.82–2.88	–	–	0.46–0.82	–	–	–	1.50	–
Glu	19.40–28.90	2.70–6.00	–	8.47–13.84	–	–	–	11.12	–
Gly	4.05–11.90	12.01–37.87	–	3.79–20.91	–	–	–	3.50	–

(Continued)

TABLE 8.12 (Continued)
Amino acid composition (g/100 g) and mineral composition (mg/100 g) of reptile non-traditional meats

	Crocodile			Turtle			Lizard		
Trait	Nile crocodile	Caiman yacare	A. mississippiensis	Pelodiscus sinensis	Chelonia mydas	Chelydra serpentina	Tegu lizard	Dhub Lizard	Green iguana
Pro	4.24–6.93	1.94–8.83	–	3.15–11.56	–	–	–	3.20	–
Ser	2.82–6.33	1.50–2.11	–	3.37–4.40	–	–	–	–	–
Tyr	2.60–6.41	0.41–0.94	–	1.16–2.84	–	–	–	3.01	–
Minerals (mg/100 g)				ug/g	mg/100 g				mg/100 g
Ca	6.8		9.0	–	12.0–18.0	–	–	–	10.1–39.5
Cu	1.1		0.2	1.43–2.97	–	–	–	–	0.22
Fe	0.3		0.9	18.2–25.2	1.3–1.61	–	–	–	0.20–1.93
K	242.3		367.0	139.5–176.2	–	–	–	–	193.8–1323.0
Mg	18.5		27.0	–	–	–	–	–	7.9–28.2
Mn	1.8		0.08	–	–	–	–	–	0.05
Na	28.2		47.0	–	–	–	–	–	67.1–189.4
P	193.9		231.0	–	–	–	–	–	217.0
Zn	1.1		1.0	23.4–25.5	0.61–1.00	–	–	–	2.53
References	Hoffman et al., 2010; Swanepoel et a., 2000; Cernkova´ et al. 2015	Canto et al., 2014; Fernandes et al., 2017; Huang etal. 2018	Peplow et al., 1990; Ockerman & Basu, 2009;	Huang &Lin, 2004; Wu & Huang, 2008; Chen & Huang, 2015; Liang et al., 2018	Olmedo et al., 2004; Domínguez et al., 2019	Mayeaux, 1994; Domínguez et al., 2019	Caldironi & Manes, 2006	Abu–Tarboush et al., 1996	Saadoun, & Cabrera, 2008; Domínguez et al., 2019

TABLE 8.13
Fatty acid content of reptile non-traditional meats

	Crocodile			Turtle			Lizard		
Fatty acids	Nile crocodile	Caiman yacare	A. mississippiensis	Pelodiscus sinensis	Chelonia mydas	Chelydra serpentina	Tegu	Dhub	Green iguana
SFA	%	%	%	%	g/100 g	%	g/100 g	%	%
C 14:0	0.3–0.8	0.70–1.90	0.03–0.19	2.3–2.4		0.82–3.12	0.15	4.00–11.0	–
C 16:0	20.2–25.4	20.50–24.70	19.9–22.1	15.5–19.1		12.39–19.16	16.37–18.49	15.4–18.0	28.9
C 18:0	7.9–9.9	7.10–14.31	3.1–8.4	4.3–7.6		5.23–7.53	5.14–16.40	1.20–2.60	7.0
C 20:0	0.1–1.4	0.83–3.55	–	–	–	0.11–0.22	–	1.6	–
C 22:0	–	0.58–7.75	–	–		–	–	2.0	–
C 24:0	–	–	–	–	–	–	–	–	–
MUSFA									
C 16:1	3.1–5.9	1.36–5.90	4.4–7.7	6.5–20.8		3.82–5.63	1.81–8.10	5.10–11.40	6.2
C 18:1n9	27.3–43.5	17.24–30.59	33.2–44.1	23.8–43.7		12.64–28.62	33.20–42.77	5.70–12.00	34.0
C 20:1n9	–	2.10–2.69	0.9–2.8	0.5–1.8		0.92–2.30	0.22	4.50–10.40	–
C 24:1n9	–	–	0.01–0.14	–	–	–	–	–	–
PUSFA									
C18:2ω6	9.1–29.6	8.34–18.41	3.4–13.4	2.9–26.8		11.40–22.17	17.30–22.66	1.10–10.0	5.2
C18:3ω6	0.2	0.42–1.30	–	–	–	0.13–0.35	–	–	–
C18:3ω3	1.6	0.74–3.18	0.9–3.4	0.3–3.3		0.08–1.75	1.33–1.41	7.70–13.00	9.7
C20:2ω6	0.3	–	0.11–0.17	–		0.27–0.81	–	1.8	–
C20:3ω3	0.4	–	–	–	–	–	–	–	–
C20:3ω6	–	–	–	–		0.36–1.39	–	8.00	–
C20:4ω6	4.2	4.66–8.30	–	1.0–4.1		3.82–20.23	0.51–7.90	0.70	0.1
C20:5ω3	0.2–0.5	0.21–2.24	1.2–4.0	1.7–6.6	0.023	2.27–7.72	0.11–0.60	4.00	0.1
C22:2ω6	–	–	–	–	–	–	–	0.90	–
C22:3ω3	–	–	–	–	–	–	–	–	–

(Continued)

TABLE 8.13 (Continued)
Fatty acid content of reptile non-traditional meats

Fatty acids	Crocodile			Turtle			Lizard	
	Nile crocodile	Caiman yacare	A. mississippiensis	Pelodiscus sinensis	Chelonia mydas	Chelydra serpentina	Tegu	Dhub	Green iguana
C22:4ω6	–	0.77–4.25	–	–	–	–	0.21	–	–
C22:5ω3	0.3–0.5	1.00–2.19	–	–	–	2.80–3.88	0.07	–	–
C22:6ω3	0.9–1.1	0.24–8.76	4.3–11.1	3.7–8.1	0.033	4.34–9.39	0.02–0.09	1.80	–
Σ ω6	13.8–34.3	14.19–32.26	3.51–13.57	3.9–30.9	–	21.46–33.62	23.38–25.20	12.00–22.00	5.4
Σ ω3	3.4–4.1	2.19–16.37	6.4–18.5	5.7–18.0	–	12.66–21.02	1.53–2.10	12.70–13.20	10.1
Σ SFA	28.5–37.5	29.71–52.21	23.03–30.69	23.2–29.1	0.13	20.54–27.36	23.78–35.84	24.50–49.60	**36.9**
Σ USFA	47.6–87.8	37.08–87.71	46.32–86.81	40.4–115.2	–	72.64–79.47	61.62–79.41	50.40–75.50	61.4
ΣMUSFA	30.4–49.4	20.70–39.18	38.51–54.74	30.8–66.3	0.08	21.10–42.35	35.63–50.87	22.70–41.00	45.6
ΣPUSFA	17.2–38.4	16.38–48.63	7.81–32.07	9.6–48.9	0.17	19.87–38.79	25.99–28.54	27.70–34.50	15.8
SFA/USFA	0.42–0.60	0.60–0.80	0.35–0.50	0.25–0.57	–	0.28–0.34	0.39–0.45	0.49–0.66	0.60
SFA/MUSFA	0.76–0.94	1.33–1.44	056–0.60	0.44–0.75	–	0.65–0.97	0.67–0.71	1.08–1.21	0.81
SFA/PUSFA	0.98–1.66	1.07–1.81	0.96–2.95	0.60–2.42	–	0.71–1.03	0.91–1.26	0.88–1.44	2.35
PUSFA/SFA	0.6–1.02	0.55–0.93	0.34–1.04	1.74–3.96	1.31	0.97–1.42	0.79–1.09	0.70–1.13	0.42
ω6/ω3	4.06–8.37	1.97–6.80	0.55–0.73	0.68–1.72	–	1.50–2.34	15.3–17.20	0.94–1.67	0.53
References	Hoffman et al., 2010; Osthoff et al., 2010	Vicente Neto et al., 2010; Huang et al., 2018	Peplow et al., 1990	Huang et al., 2005; Domínguez et al., 2019	Olmedo et al., 2004; Domínguez et al., 2019	Mayeaux, 1994; Mayeaux et al., 1998	Caldironi & Manes, 2006; Domínguez et al., 2019	Mohamed, 2013	Domínguez et al., 2019

TABLE 8.14
Amino acid comoposition (g/100 g) and mineral composition (mg/ 100 g) of frog, kangaroo and rabbit non-traditional meats

Trait	*Rana ridibunda* g/100g meat	*Rana esculenta* g/100g	Kangaroo %	Rabbit g/100 g
Moisture	74.79–79.37	78.8–79.7	72.04–76.06	66.20–75.30
Protein	18.52–22.95	18.8–19.2	19.03 –23.20	18.10–24.21
Fat	0.74–0.93	0.62–1.2	0.53–2.60	0.60 –14.10
Ash	1.00–1.37	0.56–0.85	0.98 –1.40	1.21–1.80
Cholesterol (mg/100 g)	–	–	–	48.40–69.50
Amino acids	g/100 g meat	g/100 g protein	g/100 g	g/100 g protein
His	0.52–0.57	2.4–3.1	3.20	3.99–5.25
Ileu	0.82–0.97	3.4–4.0	5.70	4.90–5.75
Leu	0.87–1.45	6.1–7.1	8.20	8.44–9.93
Lys	1.34–1.72	5.4–6.9	7.5	9.21–10.32
Met	0.53–0.56	3.0–4.6	–	1.98–2.46
Phe	0.79–0.80	3.8–5.0	–	2.92–4.35
Thr	0.50–0.74	3.5–4.3	4.30	3.21–4.84
Val	0.85–0.94	4.0–4.8	–	5.35–6.26
Try	–	–	1.10	–
Ala	1.01–1.30	5.6–6.1	5.00	5.91–6.63
Arg	0.75–1.20	5.8–6.6	6.10	5.58–7.02
Asp	1.39–1.75	6.5–9.7	7.80	9.15–9.68
Cys	0.15–0.20	1.1	–	1.09–1.20
Glu	1.82–2.79	10.6–13.2	15.2	16.73–18.75
Gly	0.71–0.81	5.0–8.9	4.60	4.77–5.34
Pro	0.37–0.61	5.1–7.7	4.90	0.84–5.08
Ser	0.70–0.91	4.9–5.2	4.30	1.55–4.10
Tyr	0.62–0.69	2.4–4.0	–	2.54–5.34
Minerals (mg/100 g)				
Ca	22.49–24.00	7.7– 15.6	38.90–40.11	2.70–15.10
Cu	–	–	0.77–0.82	0.34–2.14
Fe	0.55–1.21	0.18–0.20	15.59–16.08	2.93–9.22
K	350.00–366.70	32.7–62.1	952.49–1218.53	342.0–450.0
Mg	17.00–23.00	6.6–8.9	96.25–105.68	22.0–33.0
Mn	–	–	0.23–0.24	0.13–0.51
Na	28.90–48.00	0.91–1.22	122.33–124.73	37.0–75.0
P	140.0–160.0	28.6–46.4	787.60–843.34	219.0–249.0
Zn	–		12.17–13.62	8.10–16.5
References	Cagiltay et al., 2014; Domínguez et al., 2019	Özogul et al., 2008; Çaklı et al., 2009; Domínguez et al., 2019	Georgiev et al., 2001; Shul'gin et al., 2015	Dalle Zotte, 2002; Hermida et al., 2006; Simonová et al., 2010; Bivolarski et al., 2011; Dalle Zotte, & Szendrő, 2011; Cardinali et al., 2015; Simonová et al., 2020

TABLE 8.15
Fatty acid composition of frog, kangaroo and rabbit non-traditional meats

Fatty acids (% of total fatty acids)	*Rana ridibunda*	*Rana esculenta*	Kangaroo	Rabbit
Saturated fatty acids (SFA)		mg/100 g meat	g/100 g	%
C 14:0	1.13–2.30	1.57–1.85	2.4	1.31–3.15
C 16:0	19.67–23.23	70.56–125.44	15.0–18.1	24.34–29.01
C 18:0	3.61–6.26	54.88–74.00	14.0–16.0	5.03–11.00
C 20:0	0.07–0.11	–	–	0.06–0.10
C 22:0	–	5.49–7.40	–	–
C 24:0	–	–	–	
Mono-unsaturated fatty acids (MUSFA)				
C 16:1	7.06–13.08	6.27–7.84	2.7–3.0	2.14–3.52
C 18:1n9	10.83–26.00	54.17–75.07	28.0–31.5	23.78–41.64
C 20:1n9	0.07–0.29	1.61–1.88	–	0.19–0.66
C 24:1n9	–	3.92–5.55	–	–
Poly-unsaturated fatty acids (PUSFA)				
C18:2ω6	6.44–16.70	38.05–81.54	4.4–22.7	9.76–20.13
C18:3ω6	0.13–0.27	–	–	–
C18:3ω3	2.32–3.37	15.68–18.50	1.9–7.0	0.24–3.14
C20:2ω6	0.10–0.22	5.49–5.55	–	–
C20:3ω3	4.71–7.72	1.48–1.84	–	0.05–0.11
C20:3ω6	0.44–0.51	–	–	0.32–0.44
C20:4ω6	0.16–0.22	70.56–92.50	5.3–9.0	1.64–3.19
C20:5ω3	3.96–6.05	31.36–37.00	0.7–2.7	0.10–0.46
C22:2ω6	0.1	–	–	–
C22:3ω3	–	–	–	–
C22:4ω6	–	–	–	–
C22:5ω3	–	–	1.2–3.4	0.13–0.78
C22:6ω3	2.77–6.67	36.85–81.40	0.5–1.9	0.03–0.57
Σ ω6	7.37–18.20	90.58–179.59	9.7–31.7	11.72–23.76
Σ ω3	13.76–23.81	85.37–138.74	4.3–15.0	0.55–5.06
Σ SFA	24.48–31.90	132.50–208.69	31.4–36.5	30.74–43.26
Σ USFA	39.09–81.38	241.92–408.67	44.7–81.2	38.38–74.64
ΣMUSFA	17.96–39.37	65.97–90.34	30.7–34.5	26.11–45.82
ΣPUSFA	21.13–42.01	175.95–318.33	14.0–46.7	12.27–28.82
SFA/USFA	0.39–0.63	0.51–0.55	0.45–0.70	0.58–0.80
SFA/MUSFA	0.81–1.36	2.01–2.31	0.78–1.02	0.94–1.18
SFA/PUSFA	0.76–1.16	0.66–0.75	0.78–2.24	1.50–2.51
PUSFA/SFA	0.86–1.32	1.33–1.53	0.45–1.28	0.40–0.67
ω6/ω3	0.54–0.76	1.06–1.29	2.11–2.85	4.70–21.31
References	Özogul et al., 2008; Domínguez et al., 2019	Cagiltay et al., 2014; Domínguez et al., 2019	Redgrave & Jeffery, 1981; Sinclair et al., 1997; Engelke et al., 2004	Dalle Zotte, 2002; Dal Bosco et al., 2012; Simonová et al., 2020

animal nutrition, climate conditions, but variation could also be due to muscle type and analysis methods (Gonzalez et al., 2004; Mamani-Linares & Gallo, 2013; Polidori et al., 2007). Amino acid composition provides useful information in relation to the nutritional value, and this has only been well reported for llama meat, with limited information for alpaca meat, and guanaco meat has not been analyzed (Mamani-Linares & Gallo, 2013; Salvá et al., 2009; Saadoun et al., 2014).

8.4 NON-TRADITIONAL MEAT FROM BISON, BUFFALO, YAK AND ELAND

8.4.1 BISON

The meat from bison has been reported to have a fatty acid profile favourable for nutrition and health, and a lower total fat and cholesterol content compared to beef (Cordain et al., 2002; McClenahan & Driskell, 2002; Rule et al., 2002). Meat from ruminants contributes a substantial amount of conjugated linoleic acid (CLA) to the human diet. Bison meat contains more CLA than common non-ruminant sources of meat such as chicken, pork, fish, and turkey (Chin et al., 1992; Turpeinen et al., 2002). Bison meat contains a higher ratio of PUFA/SFA and a nearly three- to four-fold higher amount of anti-inflammatory omega-3 PUFA, specifically alpha linolenic acid (Rule et al., 2002). In comparing the effects of both acute and chronic consumption of bison and beef on cardiovascular health risks in humans, McDaniel et al. (2013) reported that the consumption of bison meat was associated with lower atherogenic risk compared to beef and did not result in decreased vascular function or increased oxidative stress and inflammation. The authors concluded that bison meat provides a healthier red meat option.

8.4.2 BUFFALO AND YAK

Considered as a suitable alternative to beef due to its good nutritional characteristics, buffalo meat is rich in protein and essential amino acids and contains lower saturated fatty acids, intramuscular fat, cholesterol, and triglycerides (Li et al., 2018). Yak meat is also considered as another healthier alternative to beef in that it contains a higher content of unsaturated fatty acids, specifically omega 3, compared to saturated fatty acids and a favorable ratio of unsaturated to saturated fatty acids (UFS/SFA) (Wang et al., 2009; Wang et al., 2013).

8.4.3 ELAND

A large bovid species with cattle-like appearance, eland (*Taurotragus oryx*) has been recommended for domestication for its meat due to its favorable nutritional characteristics (Scherf, 2000). It is considered as a suitable alternative to beef due to its low intramuscular fat content (0.2%) and high proportions of essential fatty acids (Cordain et al., 2002).

8.5 NON-TRADITIONAL MEAT FROM DONKEY, HORSE AND MULE

8.5.1 DONKEY

Polidori et al. (2008) studied the nutritional characteristics of donkey meat obtained from slaughter of non-castrated males at 15 months of age and reported that the meat contained a good amount of protein (22.8%) and lower fat (2.02%) and cholesterol (68.7 mg/100 g) content. The meat contained appreciable amounts of minerals such as potassium (343 mg/100 g), phosphorus (212 mg/100 g), sodium (52 mg/100 g), magnesium (24 mg/100 g) and calcium (8.65 mg/100 g), iron (3.80 mg/100 g) and zinc (3.67 mg/100 g). While comparing the nutritional profile of the processed meat products, bresaola and salami, prepared from donkey meat with that of traditional meats such as beef and pork, Marino et al. (2015) found substantially higher PUFA, specifically ω3 fatty acids, and lower saturated fatty acids for donkey meat products compared to beef and pork. The donkey meat products showed highest content of arachidonic, oleic, and eicosapentaenoic acids and the lowest amounts of palmitic and myristic acid, compared to beef and pork products. The donkey meat products also contained higher amounts of most of the essential amino acids compared to beef and pork ones.

These results were supported by the findings of Polidori et al. (2009) who studied the composition of two muscles viz. *Longissimus* (L) and *Biceps femoris* (BF) obtained from the Martina Franca breed of donkey. The authors reported a higher content of PUFA in the intramuscular fat and higher percentages of essential amino acids compared with the total amino acid content in both muscles (52.88% in L and 51.26% in BF). The higher PUFA/SFA ratio and the total content of essential amino acids exceeded 50% of the total amino acids, that indicated the nutritional potential of donkey meat as an alternative healthy red meat.

8.5.2 Horse

Considered as a delicacy in some cultures in some countries such as Italy, Spain, Belgium, China, Mexico and France (Franco & Lorenzo, 2014; Gill, 2005; Lorenzo et al., 2017), horsemeat is attracting attention due to its nutritional value as the meat is leaner than beef and contains a lower percentage of fat and a favourable fatty acid profile, rich in omega-3 (Badiani et al., 1997; Lorenzo et al., 2010). Franco and Lorenzo (2014) studied the meat composition of foals slaughtered at 15 months of age and reported a substantial protein and haem iron content of 22.34% and 2.46 mg/100 g, respectively, compared to meat from other species. Intramuscular fat content ranged from 0.15 to 1.83% and the total omega 3 content was 14.73% with 1.10 PUFA/SFA ratio. While oleic, palmitoleic and linoleic acid were the most abundant fatty acids, the highest ratio of essential/non-essential amino acids recorded was found to be 0.856 and the meat contained good amounts of several minerals such as potassium (243 mg/100 g), phosphorous (202 mg/100 g) and magnesium (26 mg/100 g). These results are in agreement with the findings of other studies (Lorenzo et al., 2013b; Lorenzo et al., 2013a) who also studied the composition of horse meat. The nutritional profile of horse meat makes it an attractive red meat alternative (Lorenzo et al., 2017; Lorenzo et al., 2014). Compared to the composition of conventional meats, such as pork, beef or poultry, horse meat is rich in haem iron and contains low levels of fat and cholesterol (about 20% less) (Lorenzo et al., 2014). A 150 g foal meat steak, trimmed of all visible fat, contains 85–93 mg of cholesterol (Lorenzo & Pateiro, 2013), equivalent to 28–31% of the daily dietary cholesterol recommended previously (USDA, 2013).

8.6 NON-TRADITIONAL MEAT FROM GAME ANIMALS

8.6.1 Deer

Deer meat, known as venison, is highly regarded for its nutritional value and favourable fatty acid profile. Deer meat is a rich source of highly bioavailable protein (20–25%) and essential amino acids and contains the highest quantities of the essential amino acids leucine and lysine (Cygan-Szczegielniak & Janicki, 2012; Kwiatkowska et al., 2009; Okuskhanova et al., 2017; Strazdina et al., 2013). Deer meat is mostly lean with low fat content and is a good source of PUFA and various minerals (Jarzyńska & Falandysz, 2011; Okuskhanova et al., 2017; Piaskowska et al., 2015; Quaresma et al., 2012; Russo, 2005). It is a good source of n-3 PUFA with a more favourable n-6/n-3 ratio (2.1–3.3, the recommended ratio is <4) (Kim et al., 2007) in grass-fed animals due to the presence of α-linolenic acid in grass (Bureš et al., 2015; Morgante et al., 2003; Volpelli et al., 2003). The content of n-3 PUFA is substantially higher than that in most breeds of beef (Bureš et al., 2015; Nuernberg et al., 2005; Realini et al., 2004). Current human diets are typically deficient in n-3 fatty acids and the n-6/n-3 ratio of our diets is reported to be often over 10:1 (Poławska et al., 2013). The caloric value of 100 g of traditional meats, such as pork, beef, or poultry, ranges from 114 to 231 kcal, whereas venison contains only 90 to 110 kcal/100 g of muscle tissue (Żochowska-Kujawska et al., 2009; Chizzolini et al., 1999). These nutritional characteristics make deer meat an attractive red meat option.

8.7 NON-TRADITIONAL MEAT FROM RODENTS

8.7.1 CANE RAT

The cane rat (*Thryonomys swinderianus*) is a feral rodent that is widely distributed in the African sub-region, is highly desired, and is the most expensive meat in West and Central Africa (Teye et al., 2020). The meat from cane rat, both feral and now farmed, is consumed for its quality protein and contributes to the export earnings of several countries (Ntiamoah-Baidu, 1998). Farmed and feral cane rat meat differs in sensory and nutritive value, with meat from feral rats preferred over farmed rats. With a carcass yield of about 64%, the meat from feral cane rat contains less fat (5.74%) and a higher protein content (25.72%) compared to farmed rats (9.49% fat, 24.61% protein) (Ajayi & Tewe, 1980; Hoffman, 2008; Teye et al., 2020).

8.7.2 NUTRIA

Nutria (*Myocastor coypus*), also known as coipu, coipo, quiyá and kija, is a large herbivorous South America rodent farmed in many countries mainly for its pelts and the meat is a by-product (Farashi & Najafabadi, 2015; Tůmová et al., 2015). The meat of nutria provides a healthy and nutritional option for consumers who are interested in novel and exotic meats and is considered adequate for human nutrition in terms of amino acid composition, protein and mineral content and has a healthy lipid profile (Saadoun & Cabrera, 2019). A protein content from 19.2 to 25.5% has been reported for nutria meat with no differences observed between feral and farmed varieties and the protein content is reported to be equivalent to other commonly consumed farmed and feral animals (Hoffman & Cawthorn, 2013). Nutria meat is also an excellent source of the most important amino acids for human nutrition, including lysine, methionine, cysteine, phenylalanine and tyrosine (Migdal et al., 2013). While the lipid content of common farmed animal meats varies from 1.4–8.8%, the lipid content of nutria meat, of both young and adult, varies from 1.0–1.6% with no differences observed between the different nutria sub-species (Saadoun & Cabrera, 2019; Tůmová et al., 2015). While the cholesterol content of meat obtained from feral nutria is reported to range from 29 to 41 mg/100 g, the level of cholesterol ranges from 64.4 to 72.7 mg/100 g for farmed nutria that were fed concentrates, both the ranges are of the same order as observed for meats of common farm animals and farmed feral species (Dinh et al., 2011; Piironen et al., 2002; Saadoun & Cabrera, 2008). It is important to mention here that the original dietary limit recommended for cholesterol intake of 300 mg/day for humans is considered to be outdated (USDA, 2015), hence there is increasing interest in the cholesterol content of meat. Not considered anymore as a nutrient of concern for over-consumption, dietary cholesterol consumption seems to have no appreciable relationship with serum cholesterol and there is insufficient evidence to support that limiting dietary cholesterol reduces low-density lipoprotein cholesterol (Carson et al., 2020).

While dietary intake of cholesterol is now considered differently, the fatty acid profile and the fat content for food products such as meat are gaining importance due to the implications of some fatty acids in human cardiovascular diseases (Nettleton et al., 2016), as well as in the consideration of the nutritional value of meat, sensory value, and consumer perception. A range of 33.8 to 42.7% was reported for the saturated fatty acid content of farmed nutria (5–8 months old) fed on concentrates and no differences were recorded with green fed animals (14–16 months-old) who also had similar saturated fatty acid contents (Głogowski et al., 2010; Migdal et al., 2013; Saadoun et al., 2006; Tulley et al., 2000; Tůmová et al., 2015). While these levels were of the same order as reported for chicken meat and less than other meats such as lamb, beef and pork, the nutria meat has a slight advantage over ruminant meat in terms of saturated fat content (Rule et al., 2002; Saadoun & Cabrera, 2008). A range of 27.4 to 43.6% was reported for monounsaturated fatty acids (MUFA) content for farm-raised nutria (5–8 months old) fed on concentrates and the level increased to 49.0% in green fed animals (14–16 months-old) (Głogowski et al., 2010; Migdal et al., 2013; Saadoun et al., 2006; Tulley et al., 2000; Tůmová et al., 2015). Such levels of MUFA are present in meat from traditional farm animals such as sheep, cattle, pigs and chickens (Rule et al., 2002; Saadoun & Cabrera, 2008). Palmitoleic acid (C16:1) and oleic acid (C18:1) are predominantly present in nutria meat (Migdal et al., 2013; Saadoun et al., 2006). These MUFA not only increase the oxidative stability of the foods but can also lower the atherogenicity of low-density lipoproteins (Bonanome et al., 1992; Calder, 2015; Lopez-Bote et al., 1997). A range of 20.5 to 32.2% was reported for the polyunsaturated fatty acid (PUFA) content of farm-raised nutria (5–8 months old) fed on concentrates which is higher than the levels reported for the meat of traditional farm animals (Saadoun et al., 2006). Among the PUFA, linoleic acid is the most abundant in nutria meat followed by alfa-linolenic acid and docosahexaenoic acid (DHA), all of which are precursors to a cascade of various metabolites that regulate metabolism (Wiktorowska-Owczarek et al., 2015). The DHA levels of nutria meat are of the same order as in chicken and higher than that reported in beef (Głogowski et al., 2010; Migdal et al., 2013; Rule et al., 2002). Thus, it can be concluded that nutria meat has a favourable fat profile, is lean and low in saturated fats and rich in PUFA, particularly n-6 PUFA. Nutria also has substantial levels of minerals essential for human nutrition such as zinc, iron, selenium and copper.

8.7.3 Guinea Pig

Guinea pig, also known as cavy, cuy or cobayo, is increasingly being farmed in developing countries, specifically the Andean region, and in some Asian and African countries (Lammers et al., 2009; Ngoula et al., 2017). Higaonna et al. (2008) studied the composition of the meat from several breeds of guinea pig and found a range of 18.80 to 20.36% for protein, 2.7 to 5.1% for fat and 1.1% for ash. Other studies such as Chauca (1995) reported a protein content of 20.3% and a fat content of 7.8% whereas Nuwanyakpa et al. (1997) reported a protein content of 21% and fat content of 8% for guinea pig meat. Similar values were later reported by other workers such as Tandzong et al. (2015). While comparing the chemical composition of meat of several species, Kadim et al. (2008) found that the protein content of guinea pig was very similar to other species but marked differences were observed in the fat content of different species including camel, sheep, alpaca and guinea pig.

Guinea pig meat is attracting attention due to its nutritional characteristics, including a PUFA content of more than 50% of the total fatty acid content (Sánchez-Macías et al., 2018). A guinea pig carcass devoid of skin contains sufficient PUFA to meet 21% of daily dietary n-3 PUFA requirements (Kouakou et al., 2013) and meets more than 21% of daily requirements if the skin is included in the carcass, as the skin is also considered a rich source of n-3 fatty acids (Fu & Sinclair, 2000). While infiltrated fat of young animals has been found to be higher in PUFA compared to older animals, subcutaneous fat of older animals is reported to have a higher content of PUFA (41.8–44.7%) compared to infiltrated fat (Higaonna et al., 2008).

8.7.4 Chinchilla

Chinchilla (*Chinchilla lanigera*) is a medium-sized rodent native to South America and is intensively farmed throughout the world for its fur (Cortés et al., 2002). Farm-raised chinchilla from Lithuania has been reported to contain 19.96% protein, 6.96% fat and 0.98% ash (Vinauskiene et al., 2019). These values are very close to the values reported by Fellenberg et al. (2016) for the meat of chinchilla farmed in Chile. A protein content of 20.03% and a fat content of 11.26% has also been reported for the meat of chinchilla raised in Argentina (Echalar et al., 1998). Thus, the composition of chinchilla meat is very close to that of other rodents, such as nutria and capybara, and is a good source of protein for human nutrition with a range of 19.96–21.4%, similar to the meat of common farm animals, such as pork, beef and chicken (Vinauskiene et al., 2019). Amino acid analysis of chinchilla meat revealed that it is a rich source of lysine (8.67 g/100 g protein), glutamic acid (15.42 g/100 g protein) and methionine (5.43 g/100 g protein). Among the non-essential amino acids, glutamic acid (15.42 ± 0.19 g/100 g protein) was present in the highest amount and tyrosine (3.67 ± 0.08 g/100 g protein) in the lowest amount (Vinauskiene et al., 2019). These values suggest that the amino acid composition of chinchilla meat is similar to that of rabbit and nutria meat with some minor differences (Migdal et al., 2013; Nasr et al., 2017; Simonová et al., 2010). The DIAAS (dietary indispensable amino acid digestibility score) for both chinchilla and nutria meat is reported to be 114% (valine) and 89% (sulphur amino acids), respectively. DIASS values can be used to rank the meat protein sources with values ≥ 100 as 'excellent' and with values 75≤ DIAAS ≤ 99 as 'good' (Vinauskiene et al., 2019).

The fat content (3.66–6.96%) reported in the meat of chinchilla is similar to that of the meat of other rodents and of common farm animals such as chickens, turkeys, pigs and cattle (http://foodbase.azurewebsites.net/). The fatty acid profile of chinchilla meat has been found to contain 36.08% PUFA (dominated by linoleic acid 29.44% and linolenic acid 4.88%), 40.79% MUFA (dominated by oleic acid 30.57% and palmitoleic acid 9.39%) and 24.46% saturated fatty acids (mainly palmitic acid) (Vinauskiene et al., 2019). Thus, the meat of chinchilla has lower saturated fatty acid content and a higher content of PUFA n-3 and n-6 than that reported for other rodent meats such as capybara, nutria, and also compared to rabbit meat (Fellenberg et al., 2016; Migdal et al., 2013; Saadoun & Cabrera, 2008). In addition, chinchilla meat has also been reported to contain a lower amount of sodium (32.65 mg/100 g muscle) (Vinauskiene et al., 2019).

8.7.5 Capybara

Capybara (*Hydrochoerus hydrochaeris*) is the largest rodent on earth and a herbivore that is widely distributed in South America (Moreira et al., 2012). With a carcass yield of 60% (Felix et al., 2014); farmed capybaras produce high-quality meat compared to their feral counterparts (Nogueira-Filho & Nogueira, 2018), partly due to proper slaughtering procedures following animal welfare and public health (Moreira & Pinheiro, 2013). Being lean and high in protein content, meat from capybara is generally considered to be healthier than other red meats, be it feral or farm produced, specifically due to its lower intramuscular fat and cholesterol contents (Nogueira-Filho & Nogueira, 2018; Oda et al., 2004; Oda et al., 2004). The capybara meat is low in saturated fat content and high in polyunsaturated fatty acids with a favourable ratio of ω6: ω3 fatty acids (Bressan et al., 2004; Saldanha et al., 2002), making it a healthier meat option for human nutrition. A linoleic acid (C18:2ω6) content of 18.8 to 19.2% and a protein content of 22.8% with a high digestibility (0.89) and biological value (61.3%) has been reported for the meat obtained from farmed capybara (Bressan et al., 2004; Jardim et al., 2003; Oda et al., 2004). However, the composition and quality of capybara meat is influenced by several factors including gender and production system (Pinheiro & Moreira, 2013).

8.8 NON-TRADITIONAL MEAT FROM REPTILES

8.8.1 Crocodile

The meat from crocodiles has a long tradition of consumption in rural and marginalized areas of Asia and Africa and is often associated with having medicinal properties, in being believed to relieve asthma, strengthen the body, promote longevity and treat several other ailments (Williams et al., 2016; Zhang et al., 2021). In a study conducted on the meat composition of Nile crocodile (*C. niloticus*) of 33–34 months age, Hoffman et al. (2000) reported no difference in the protein (21.1–22.9%) and fat (2.94–9.11%) content between the different body parts of the carcasses. In contrast, Černíková et al. (2015) reported a significant difference in the protein and fat contents of the different parts of the carcasses. The highest values for protein were reported for cheek (17.2–19.6%) and lowest for neck (14.0–16.1%) and the highest values for fat were recorded for tail dorsal (13.3–15.5%) and lowest for shoulder (0.47–1.01%). Significant differences were also observed for the contents of individual amino acids in different carcass parts. The total content of amino acids in individual carcass parts varied from 15.4–18.9% (w/w) and corresponded to the crude protein content, which in turn contained 81.1–86.5% of amino acids. Like other meats, such as beef, pork, poultry, foal and eland the most abundant amino acids observed in crocodile meat were aspartic and glutamic acids followed by lysine and leucine (Barton et al., 2014; Lorenzo & Pateiro, 2013), Thus, crocodile meat is highly nutritious in terms of protein and amino acid profile and has a favourable ratio of PUFA to saturated fatty acids (Hoffman, 2008). While studying the fatty acid composition of tail samples of crocodiles, Hoffman et al. (2000) reported that the total fatty acid content was comprised of 51.1% monounsaturated, 37.7% saturated, and 10.7% polyunsaturated and fatty acids such as palmitic acid (25.4%), stearic acid (9.9%) and linoleic acid (9.1%) were present in higher concentrations. Previous studies have also reported the presence of higher amounts of free fatty acids such as oleic (33.1%), palmitic (22.5%), linoleic (15.2%) and long-chain polyunsaturated fatty acids, such as arachidonic acid (3.6%), in the crocodile meat (Mitchell et al., 1995).

8.8.2 CAIMAN

With organoleptic properties resembling to those of rabbit and chicken meat (Martens, 2010), caiman meat along with other crocodilian meats is gaining popularity among consumers of exotic meats, due to several nutritional advantages. Characterized by a fine flavour and soft texture, caiman meat contains a good proportion of protein (20.5%) and a low amount of intramuscular fat (0.8%) (Simoncini et al., 2020). Caiman meat in general is recognized as having a high-value protein content, low fat and a favourable fatty acid profile that is beneficial to human health compared to other meats such as beef (Hoffman & Cawthorn, 2013; Piña et al., 2016; Vicente Neto et al., 2010). The fatty acid content of caiman tail meat was reported to contain 69.9% unsaturated fatty acids (SFA), 36.8% PUFA, 30.2% saturated fatty acids and a ratio of PUFA/SFA of 1.25 (Simoncini et al., 2020). Studies have reported similar results for protein and fat contents for crocodilian meats (Cossu et al., 2007, Hoffman et al., 2000; Takeuchi Fernandes et al., 2017;). While a ratio of PUFA/SFA of 1.06 has been reported for caiman (*Caiman crocodilus yacare*) meat (Canto et al., 2015), an intermuscular fat content of a 2 to 3% higher value has been reported for larger crocodilians (Morais et al., 2013). Healthy meat for human consumption is characterized by a higher PUFA content and a lower SFA content (Simopoulos, 2016; Swanson et al., 2012). A slightly lower amount of SFA (28%) has been reported for the meat obtained from broad-snouted caiman compared to caiman yacare (34–36%) meat (Vicente Neto et al., 2010) which is higher than that reported for the meat of common farm animals such as lamb (41–48%), beef (43–48%) and pork (35–39%) (Cifuni et al., 2004; Juárez et al., 2009; Mitchaothai et al., 2007). For a healthy diet, the suggested ratio of PUFA/SFA should be ≥ 0.4 (Department of Health 1994) and these conditions are met by the meat from broad-snouted caiman that has a higher PUFA/SFA ratio compared to commonly consumed meats, such as chicken (0.9), beef (0.1) and rainbow trout (0.7) (USDA & USDHHS, 2015). Foods rich in MUFA and PUFA, especially n-3 fatty acids such as eicosapentaenoic acid, alpha linolenic acid and docosahexaenoic acid, are highly beneficial for human health and can help in prevention of several chronic diseases (Del Gobbo et al., 2016; Mir et al., 2018; Siegel & Ermilov, 2012)

8.9 NON-TRADITIONAL MEAT FROM OTHER ANIMALS

8.9.1 Rabbit

With a favourable fatty acid profile and chemical composition, rabbit meat is considered a healthy food and its nutritional profile fits well with the attitude of consumers towards healthy food (Cullere & Dalle, 2018). Rabbit meat is a good source of quality protein (20–21%) and essential amino acids for human nutrition that can play a crucial role in meeting the protein requirements of people in developing countries (Abdel-Azeem et al., 2007). While the lipid composition of rabbit meat varies with production factors, specifically diet, in general, rabbit meat contains low fat and cholesterol contents with low saturated fatty acid content (Dalle Zotte & Szendrő, 2011; Dalle Zotte, 2002). It is an important source of both PUFA and MUFA (Dalle Zotte, 2014). While studying the nutritional composition of rabbit meatballs, Secci et al. (2020) reported that 100 g of the product contained 1.16 g, 0.88 g and 1.15 g of PUFA, MUFA and SFA respectively, and contained important fatty acids such as α-linolenic, oleic, linoleic and arachidonic acids. Because of its high linoleic acid percentage, the n-6/n-3 ratio of rabbit meat is generally very high. A range of 11.6–14.6 has been reported for rabbit meat by different workers (Dalle Zotte, 2002; Liu et al., 2009; Peiretti et al., 2011), however, values as low as 1.1–1.9 have been reported for meat from farmed rabbits fed golden flax seed (Peiretti & Meineri, 2010).

8.10 SAFETY ISSUE CONSIDERATIONS OF NON-CONVENTIONAL MEATS

Non-conventional meats have received considerable interest in recent years as nutritious food components and consequently production and consumption has expanded worldwide. However, there are substantial concerns about the safety and hygienic quality of these foods especially in regard to meat obtained from feral animals (González et al., 2020). Several outbreaks of transmitted diseases have been linked to the trading and consumption of 'bush' meat, and with the recent outbreak of coronavirus (COVID-19), trading and consumption of feral meat in Wuhan, China, has raised the alarm on the safety of such meat sources (Jacob et al., 2020; Koh et al., 2021). To date, non-traditional meats have been considered as potential sources of health-threatening disease agents such as viruses, prions, bacteria, fungi, parasites, veterinary drugs residues, hormones, and heavy metals, particularly game, reptile and rodent meat (European Food Safety Authority, 2007; Krijger, 2020; Magnino et al., 2009; Paulsen et al., 2011). Hepatitis E virus is one of the most common zoonotic diseases worldwide that can be transmitted to humans through not well-cooked meats of pig and wild boar, rabbit and deer, or by direct contact with these animals (Sooryanarain, & Meng, 2019). In addition, it has been hypothesized that the origin of the recent pandemic coronavirus (COVID-19), that causes severe respiratory tract infection (> 107 million infected people) and death (> 2.4 million people), was a seafood market that sold wild animals in Wuhan, China (González et al., 2020; Li et al., 2020). A recent review has indicated the existence of 51 zoonotic pathogens (19 bacteria, 16 viruses, and 16 parasites) in wild meat hunted, traded, and consumed in Malaysia, that have high potential health risks to humans (Cantlay et al., 2017). Nipah virus is reported to be a most dangerous virus that transmitted from wild animals in Malaysia and Bangladesh causing a high death rate (Chua et al., 2002; Luby et al., 2006). In addition, reports indicated the transmission of *Cercopithecine herpesvirus*-1, Rabies virus, ebola virus, foamy viruses, monkey pox, marburg virus, lassa virus, H5N1, and lyssaviruses can transfer from feral animals to humans, which cause several diseases that can be fatal (Cantlay et al., 2017; Favoretto et al., 2001; Gessain et al., 2013; Hanna et al., 2000; Huff & Barry, 2003; Van Vliet et al., 2017; Wolfe et al., 2004). 'Bush' meat can also be a source of pathogenic bacteria dangerous to humans, such as *Brucella* Shiga-toxin producing *Escherichia coli*, *Leptospira*, *Mycobacterium*, *Campylobacter*, *Listeria*, *Salmonella*, and *Yersinia* (Cantlay et al., 2017; Fukushima et al., 2008; Holds et al., 2008; Li et al., 2004; Patrick et al., 2013; Silva et al., 2005; Tu et al., 2004; Van Vliet et al., 2017). The most dominant parasites that are transmitted from feral animal meats to humans include *Sarcocystis, Toxoplasma* and *Trichinella* species (Cantlay et al., 2017; Ramakrishna et al., 2017; Van Vliet et al., 2017). In addition, the zoonotic parasites *Balantidium coli, Cryptosporidia, Entamoeba histolytica,* and *Giardia, Strongyloides fulleborni, Trichuris* sp., *Echinococcus vogeli, Ancylostoma* sp., and *Ascaris* have been reported to be transmitted from game animal meats to humans causing numerous health threatening diseases (Almeida et al., 2013; Cantlay et al., 2017; De Bruyne et al., 2006; Garcıa et al., 2005; Huffman et al., 2013; Kurpiers et al., 2016; Mayor et al., 2015; Meng et al., 2009; Rodríguez et al., 2004; Van Vliet et al., 2017). Non-traditional meats can also contain high levels of toxic heavy metals such as mercury, lead, cadmium, nickel, zinc, aluminium, and silver (Adei & Forson-Adaboh, 2008). In this regard, high concentrations of nickel and cadmium were found in grass cutter (*Thryonomys swinderianus*) meat (Igene et al., 2015; Soewu et al., 2014) and heavy metals found in duiker (Cephalophus spp.) meat (Yemi et al., 2015). A recent study indicated a high toxicity risk when consuming black duiker, brush-tailed porcupine, bushbuck, and Maxwell's duiker meat on daily bases due to their high levels of lead and selenium (Gbogbo et al., 2020). In addition, high concentrations of lead have been found in red-legged partridge and feral rabbit meat (Sevillano-Morales et al., 2020) and game migratory upland bird meat (Sevillano-Cano et al., 2021). High levels of polycyclic hydrocarbons were also found in smoked 'bush' meat in Ghana suggesting a high health risk of these foods (Abdul et al., 2014). Despite the high nutritional quality of non-traditional meats, when derived particularly from feral animals, there is a substantial risk of the transmission of dangerous health-threatening agents to humans and hence this is an important consideration with utilization of these meat types.

8.11 RELIGIOUS ISSUES ASSOCIATED WITH MEAT OBTAINED FROM NON-TRADITIONAL SOURCES

In Christianity and according to the New Testament, no prohibitions are declared in relation to eating meat "[1]*Now the Spirit expressly says that in latter times some will depart from the faith, giving heed to deceiving spirits and doctrines of demons,*[2]*speaking lies in hypocrisy, having their own conscience seared with a hot iron,*[3]*forbidding to marry, and commanding to abstain from foods which God created to be received with thanksgiving by those who believe and know the truth.*[4]*For every creature of God is good, and nothing is to be refused if it is received with thanksgiving;*[5]*for it is sanctified by the word of God and prayer.* Timothy 4:1–5, New King James Version'.

In St. Peter's vision "[9]*The next day, as they went on their journey and drew near the city, Peter went up on the housetop to pray, about the sixth hour.*[10]*Then he became very hungry and wanted to eat; but while they made ready, he fell into a trance*[11]*and saw heaven opened and an object like a great sheet bound at the four corners, descending to him and let down to the earth.*[12]*In it were all kinds of four-footed animals of the earth, wild beasts, creeping things, and birds of the air.*[13]*And a voice came to him, "Rise, Peter; kill and eat."*[14]*But Peter said, "Not so, Lord! For I have never eaten anything common or unclean."*[15]*And a voice spoke to him again the second time, "What God has cleansed you must not call common."*[16]*This was done three times. And the object was taken up into heaven again.,* Acts 10, 9–16, New King James Version" a clear statement of "*all kinds of four-footed animals of the earth, wild beasts, creeping things*" that covers all types discussed in the present chapter (Table 8.16).

However, there are some differences that are found among different sects and groups. For example, while the Niceno-Constantinopolitan Creed (mainstream Christianity, known as Nicene) has no clear objection on the kinds of animals that could be eaten "[4]*For every creature of God is good, and nothing to be refused, if it be received with thanksgiving:*[5]*for it is sanctified by the word of God and prayer.* Timothy 4:4–5, New King James Version" and all what is required is to offer a prayer, some churches such as the Coptic church do not consume meat slaughtered for idols and do not consume camel meat. Some churches may follow the guidelines of the old testament "Talmud"

TABLE 8.16
Meat consumption in various religions and faiths. The list is based on the interpretation of the majority of opinions as there are some differences among various sects and religious branches

Religion	Pork	Beef	Lamb	Chicken	Other	Rodents	Reptiles	Kangaroo	Rabbits	Game	Equidae
Christianity Anglican, Catholic, Lutheran, Methodist, and Orthodox denominations	✓	✓	✓	✓	✓	??	??	✓	✓	✓	✓
Islam	✗	Halal only	Halal only	Halal only	Halal only	✗	✗	Halal only	✓	Halal only	Makruh (detestable)
Sunna									✓		✓
Shia									✗		✗
Hinduism	✗	✗	✓	✓	?	?	?	?	✓	✓	✗
Jain	✗	✗	✗	✗	✗	✗	✗	✗	✗	✗	✗
Judaism	✗	Kosher only	Kosher only	Kosher only	Camels are not kosher	✗	✗	✗	✗	Kosher only	✗
Sikhism	✗	✗	✓	✓	?	?	?	?	?	?	?
Buddhism (strict)*	✗	✗	✗	✗	✗	✗	✗	✗	✗	✗	✗
Seventh-day Adventist Church	✗	✓	✓	✓	✗	✗	✗	✗	✗	✗	✗
Rastafari Movement	✗	✗	✗	✗	✗	✗	✗	✗	✗	✗	✗
Taoism	✓	✓	✓	✓	✓	✓	✓	✓	✓	✓	✓

such as Seventh-day Adventist Church, Armenian Apostolic Church, and several Orthodox churches where kosher rules are applied as it will be discussed later. Therefore, the above information indicates no restrictions on non-tradition meat sources with the exception of some churches that adapted the Jewish dietary rules.

In Islam, Sharia, which provides a framework of guidelines and rules for what is lawful (halal), detestable (makruh), and prohibited (haram) based on the Quran and Prophet Mohammed (ﷺ) teachings. The holy Quran states "Eat from the good things which We have provided for you" Surat Al-Baqara (2:172) and the concept of halal tayyib is deeply rooted in Islam, for example: *"Oh, you people, eat from the earth what is halal and tayyib, and follow not the footsteps of the Shaytan …"*, Surat al-Baqarah (2:168) and ": *O ye who believe! Eat of tayyibat [the good things] wherewith We have provided you and render thanks to Allah if it is (indeed) He Whom ye worship"*, Surat al-Baqarah (2:172). The general rules for meat to be considered halal, is that it must be produced from healthy live animals that are slaughtered according to Sharia. Meat from animals that died in a way that prevented full drainage of their blood (for example animals that had natural death, or died from sickness, or were beaten to death, or were strangled) or died due fights and accidents (falling from high places, animal fights, head-butting or gored to death by horns), or decaying flesh (carrion), or animals that had been partly eaten by beasts) are haram. Animals used for halal meat production are herbivorous clean animals (all cattle, sheep, goats, camels and kangaroo) that are slaughtered according to Sharia. Horse meat is regarded as makruh and only permissible under exceptional circumstances. Swine, carnivorous animals, rodents, reptiles, mules and asses are haram.

For Judaism, only kosher animals that have been slaughtered according to Kashrut laws (these are based on the teachings of the holy book of Judaism "Torah" and compiled oral Jewish laws "Halakha") are considered fit for consumption. The main characteristics required for kosher animals are stated in Leviticus (11:3–8) *"[3]Among the animals, whatever divides the hoof, having cloven hooves and chewing the cud—that you may eat. [4]Nevertheless these you shall not eat among those that chew the cud or those that have cloven hooves: the camel, because it chews the cud but does not have cloven hooves, is unclean to you; [5]the rock hyrax, because it chews the cud but does not have cloven hooves, is unclean to you; [6]the hare, because it chews the cud but does not have cloven hooves, is unclean to you; [7]and the swine, though it divides the hoof, having cloven hooves, yet does not chew the cud, is unclean to you. [8]Their flesh you shall not eat, and their carcasses you shall not touch. They are unclean to you.",* New King James Version, and Deuteronomy (14:4–8) *"[4]These are the animals which you may eat: the ox, the sheep, the goat, [5]the deer, the gazelle, the roe deer, the wild goat, the mountain goat, the antelope, and the mountain sheep. [6]And you may eat every animal with cloven hooves, having the hoof split into two parts, and that chews the cud, among the animals. [7]Nevertheless, of those that chew the cud or have cloven hooves, you shall not eat, such as these: the camel, the hare, and the rock hyrax; for they chew the cud but do not have cloven hooves; they are unclean for you. [8]Also the swine is unclean for you, because it has cloven hooves, yet does not chew the cud; you shall not eat their flesh or touch their dead carcasses."* New King James Version. The main requirements for animals are that they have cloven "completely split" hoof and chew the cud. This description rules all reptiles, rodents, rabbits/ hare, swine, carnivorous animals, camels and Equidae to be not kosher.

Buddhist scriptures advocate the principle of Ahimsa "non-violence" and in some sutras there is clear instruction of avoiding meat consumption. For example, in the Lankavatara Sutra *"So as not to become a source of terror, bodhisattvas established in benevolence should not eat food containing meat…. Meat is food for wild beasts; it is unfitting to eat it…. People kill animals for profit and exchange goods for the meat. One person kills, another person buys — both are at fault."*. Several explanations have been explained in chapter 8:249–251 *"The Blessed One said this to him: For innumerable reasons, Mahamati, the Bodhisattva, whose nature is compassion, is not to eat any meat; I will explain them: Mahamati, in this long course of transmigration here, there is not one living being that, having assumed the form of a living being, has not been your mother, or father, or brother, or sister, or son, or daughter, or the one or the other, in various degrees of* kinship; and when acquiring another form of life may live as a beast, as a domestic animal, as a bird, or as a womb-born, or as something standing in some relationship to you; [this being so] how can the Bodhisattva-Mahasattva who desires to approach all living beings as if they were himself and to practise the Buddha-truths, eat the flesh of any living being that is of the same nature as himself? Even, Mahamati, the Rakshasa, listening to the Tathagata's discourse on the highest essence of the Dharma, attained the notion of protecting [Buddhism], and, feeling pity, (246) refrains from eating flesh; how much more those who love the Dharma! Thus, Mahamati, wherever there is the evolution of living beings, let people cherish the thought of kinship with them, and, thinking that all beings are [to be loved as if they were] an only child, let them refrain from eating meat. So with Bodhisattvas whose nature is compassion, [the eating of] meat is to be avoided by him. Even in exceptional cases, it is not [compassionate] of a Bodhisattva of good standing to eat meat. The flesh of a dog, an ass, a buffalo, a horse, a bull, or man, or any other [being], Mahamati, that is not generally eaten by people, is sold on the roadside as mutton for the sake of money; and therefore, Mahamati, the Bodhisattva should not eat meat."* That provide compassion and loving-kindness to all creatures as the reason for not eating meat.

Taoism emphasis the relationship between human and nature focussing on the natural flow of the Universe in a dynamic way that do not follow rigid and orderly guidelines. Taoism uses the terms Yin and Yang that refers to the positive and negative energies of the Universe. Taoism emphasises the importance of grains in their diet and consider meat is a natural consumption process and restriction of eating meat is unnatural. Taoists consume small amounts of meat. In Taoism, the prohibition of eating buffalo, beef, snake and dog meat could be found in literature. In Hinduism, according to Mrinal Pande (https://scroll.in/article/833393/from-ramayana-to-the-scriptures-its-clear-india-has-a-long-history-of-eating-meat) who discussed the history of meat-eating practices in India and stated that many animals were scarified and used for food. The author stated *"The marketplace had various stalls for vendors of different kinds of meat: gogataka (cattle), arabika (sheep), shookarika (swine), nagarika (deer) and shakuntika (fowl). There were even separate vends for selling alligator and tortoise meat (giddabuddaka). The Rigveda describes horses, buffaloes, rams and goats as sacrificial animals. The 162nd hymn of the Rigveda describes the elaborate horse sacrifice performed by emperors. Different Vedic gods are said to have different preferences for animal meat. Thus Agni likes bulls and barren cows, Rudra likes red cows, Vishnu prefers a dwarf ox, while Indra likes a bull with droopy horns with a mark on its head, and Pushan a black cow. The Brahmanas that were compiled later specify that for special guests, a fattened ox or goat must be sacrificed. The Taittireeya Upanishad praises the sacrifice of a hundred bulls by the sage Agasthya. And the grammarian Panini even coined a new adjective, goghna (killing of a cow), for the guests to be thus honoured."*. Therefore, many of the animals in Table 8.16 may fit well with historical use, but modern times may have different preferences.

8.12 CONCLUSIONS AND FUTURE PERSPECTIVES

It is evident from the information currently available that there is considerable opportunity for developing scale-up of utilization of meat from animals that are not part of the current mass production of commonly farmed animals that has developed in more recent times. Such meat from other animals can be considered as 'non-traditional' and has considerable potential for further development to meet the protein needs of the increasing world population. From the literature available, the majority of these non-traditional meats are of high nutritional value and contain good proportions of health-promoting molecules, besides protein, such as lipids and minerals.

The utilization of 'non-traditional' animals as sources of meat for human consumption originated from scavenging and then subsequently organized hunting of feral animals prior to the development of farmed animal practices. Emphasis likely became focused on animal species that could be readily domesticated and had high meat yield. However, the farming practices that developed into mass production to feed the increasing population are now becoming limited by resources and are contributing to environmental issues. Environmental issues associated with farming practices of commonly farmed animals may in part be overcome by expansion of farming of 'non-traditional' animals for meat production, provided the development of such farming practices is organized appropriately.

Worldwide there is still considerable interest in the consumption of meat derived from feral animals, often referred to as 'bush' meat, in part based on the sporting opportunity to hunt the animals, and in many places, out of sheer necessity, to obtain food sustenance. Consumption of feral meats also carries various health risks as the feral animals live in uncontrolled environments and the processing and distribution of the meats may not be of high standard. These considerations can be overcome in farming environments, provided appropriate practices are put in place and quality assurance is monitored.

The source of the meat and the method of processing can also have religious belief considerations and be subject to consumer perceptions. This is a consideration with meat currently mass-produced and will need to be also considered with future development of meat production from non-traditional sources.

ACKNOWLEDGEMENT

The authors extend their appreciation to the International Scientific Partnership Program ISPP at King Saud University for funding this research work through ISPP-16–73(2).

REFERENCES

Abdel-Azeem, A. S., Abdel-Azim, A. M., Darwish, A. A., & Omar, E. M. (2007). Body weight and carcass traits in four pure breeds of rabbits and their crosses under Egyptian environmental conditions. Proceedings 5th international conference of rabbit production in hot climate Hurghada Egypt (pp. 67–80).

Abdul, I. W., Amoamah, M. O., & Abdallah, A. (2014). Determinants of polycyclic aromatic hydrocarbons in smoked bushmeat. *International Journal of Nutrition and Food Sciences*, *3*, 1–6.

Abu-Tarboush, H. M., Atia, M., & Al-Johany, A. M. (1996). Nutritional quality of Duhb (lizard) meat (*Uromastys aegyptius* Blanford 1874) and characterization of its protein using electrophoretic techniques. *Ecology of Food and Nutrition*, *55*, 272–284.

Adei, E., & Forson-Adaboh, K. (2008). Toxic (Pb, Cd, Hg) and essential (Fe, Cu, Zn, Mn) metal content of liver tissue of some domestic and bush animals in Ghana. *Food Additives and Contaminants, Part B Surveill*, *1*, 100–105.

Adeyeye, E. I., & Adesina, A. J. (2018). Proximate and mineral compositions, Mineral Safety Index (MSI) of ten organs of African giant pouch rat. *International Journal of Pharmacology, Phytochemistry and Ethnomedicine*, *9*, 1–9.

Adeyeye, E. I., & Aremu, M. O. (2011). Amino acid composition of two fancy meats (liver and heart) of African giant pouch rat (*Cricetomys gambianus*). *Oriental Journal of Chemistry*, *27*, 1409–1419.

Adeyeye, E. I., & Falemu, F. A. (2012). Relationship of the amino acid composition of the muscle and skin of African giant pouch rat (*Cricetomys gambianus*). *Elixir Applied Biology*, *43*, 6543–6549.

Adeyeye, E. I., & Jegede, R. O. (2010). Muscle and skin amino acid compositions of the greater cane rat (*Thryonomys swingerianus*). *International Journal of Pharma and Bio Sciences*, *1*, 1–9.

Adeyeye, E. I., Olaofe, O., & Ogunjana, K. E. (2012). Lipid profiles of the skin, muscle and liver of greater cane rat (*Thryonomys swinderianus*): Dietary implications. *Elixir Food Science*, *53*, 11749–11756.

Adeyinka, V. D., Eduvie, L. O., Adeyinka, I. A., Jokthan, E., & Orunmuyi, A. (2007). Effect of progesterone secretion on egg production in grey helmet guinea fowl (*Numidia meleagris* galleatd). *Pakistan Journal of Biological Sciences*, *10*, 998–1000.

Adzitey, F., & Adzitey, S. P. (2011). Duck production: Has a potential to reduce poverty among rural households in Asian communities – A review. *Journal of World's Poultry Research*, *1*, 7–10.

Ajayi, S. S., & Tewe, O. O. (1980). Food preference and carcass composition of the grass cutter (*Thryonomys swinderianus*) in captivity. *African Journal of Ecology*, *18*, 133–140.

Al-Amer, S., Bekhit, A. E. D., Gooneratne, R., & Mason, S. L. (2016). Nutritional composition of Mutton bird (*Puffinus griseus*) meat. *Journal of Food Composition and Analysis, 46*, 22–28.

Almeida, F., Caldas, R., Corrêa, C., Rodrigues-Silva, R., Siqueira, N., & Machado-Silva, J. R. (2013) Coinfections of the cestode *Echinococcus vogeli* and the nematode *Calodium hepaticum* in the hystricomorphic rodent Agouti paca from a forest reserve in Acre, Brazil. *Journal of Helminthology, 87*, 489–493.

Al-Owaimer, A. N., Suliman, G. M., Sami, A. S., Picard, B., & Hocquette, J. F. (2014). Chemical composition and structural characteristics of Arabian camel (*Camelus dromedarius*) m. longissimus thoracis. *Meat Science, 96*, 1233–1241.

Amici, A., Cifuni, G. F., Conto, M., Esposito, L., & Failla, S. (2015). Hunting area affects chemical and physical characteristics and fatty acid composition of wild boar (*Sus scrofa*) meat. *Rendiconti Lincei. Scienze Fisiche e Naturali, 26*, S527–S534.

Antunes, I. C., Coimbra, M. C. P., Ribeiro, A. P., Ferreira, J. D., Abade dos Santos, F., Alves, S. P., Bessa, R. J. B., & Quaresma M. A. G. (2019). Nutritional value of meat lipid fraction from red-legged partridge (*Alectoris rufa*) obtained from wild and farmed specimens. *Poultry Science, 98*, 1037–1046.

Antunes, I. C., Ribeiro, M. F., Pimentel, F. B., Alves, S. P., Oliveira, M. B. P. P., Bessa, R. J. B., & Quaresma M. A. G. (2018). Lipid profile and quality indices of ostrich meat and giblets. *Poultry Science, 97*, 1073–1081.

Aronal, A. P., Huda, N., & Ahmad R. (2012). Amino acid and fatty acid profiles of Peking and Muscovy duck meat. *International Journal of Poultry Science, 11*, 229–236.

Badiani, A., Nanni, N., Gatta, P. P., Tolomelli, B., & Manfredini, M. (1997). Nutrient profile of horsemeat. *Journal of Food Composition and Analysis, 10*, 254–269.

Banjade, J., Devkota, N. R., Yadav, D. K., & Chaudhry, N. P. (2017).Commercial fattening of buffalo calves for economic meat production. *Nepalese Veterinary Journal, 34*, 51–59.

Baeza, E., Salichon, M. R., Marche, G., Wacrenier, N., Dominguez, B., & Culioli J. (2000). Effects of age and sex on the structural, chemical and technological characteristics of mule duck meat. *British Poultry Science, 41*, 300–307.

Baggio, S., Vicente, E., & Bragagnolo, N. (2002). Cholesterol oxides, cholesterol, total lipid, and fatty acid composition in Turkey meat. *Journal of Agricultural and Food Chemistry, 50*, 5981–5986.

Baggio, S. R., Miguel, A. M. R., & Bragagnolo, N. (2005). Simultaneous determination of cholesterol oxides, cholesterol and fatty acids in processed turkey meat products. *Food Chemistry, 89*, 475–484.

Barton, L., Bures, D., Kotrba, R., & Sales, J. (2014). Comparison of meat quality between eland (*Taurotragus oryx*) and cattle (*Bos taurus*) raised under similar condition. *Meat Science, 96*, 346–352.

Bekhit, A. E. D., Al-Amer, S., Gooneratne, R., Mason, S. L. Osman, K. A., & Clucas, L. (2011). Concentrations of trace elementals and organochlorines in Mutton bird (*Puffinus griseus*). *Ecotoxicology and Environmental Safety, 74*, 1742–1746.

Bekhit, A.E.D., & Farouk, M. M. (2013). Nutritive and health value of camel meat. In: *Camel Meat and Meat Products*. I. T. Kadim, O. Mahgoub, B. Faye, and M.M. Farouk (Eds). Bostan, MA, USA: CAB International, pp. 205–223.

Belaunzaran, X., Lavín, P., Barron, Luis J. R., Mantecón, A. R., Kramer, J. K.G., & Aldai, N. (2017). An assessment of the fatty acid composition of horse-meat available at the retail level in northern Spain. *Meat Science, 124*, 39–47.

Belhaj, K., Mansouri F., Ben Moumen, A., Fauconnier, M.-L. Boukharta, M., Caid, H. S., Sindic, M., & Elamrani, A. (2018). Physicochemical and nutritional characteristics of Beni Guil lamb meat raised in eastern Morocco. *Mediterranean Journal of Nutrition and Metabolism, 11*, 175–185.

Betancourt, L., & Jair Diaz, G. (2014). Fatty acid profile differences among the muscle tissue of three rodents (*Hydroahoerus hidrochaeris*, *Cuniculus paca* and *Cavia porcellus*) and one Lagomorph (*Oryctolagus cuniculus*). *Journal of Food and Nutrition Research, 2*, 744–748.

Bivolarski, B., Vachkova, E., Ribarski, S., Uzunova, K., & Pavlov, D. (2011). Amino acid content and biological value of rabbit meat proteins, depending on weaning age. *Bulgarian Journal of Veterinary Medicine, 14*, 94–102.

Bonanome, A., Pagnan, A., Biffanti, S., Opportuno, A., Sorgato, F., Dorella, M., & Ursini, F. (1992). Effect of dietary monounsaturated and polyunsaturated fatty acids on the susceptibility of plasma low density lipoproteins to oxidative modification. *Arteriosclerosis and Thrombosis, 12*, 529–533.

Bressan, M. C., Oda, S. H. I., Cardoso, M. G., Miguel, G. Z., Freitas, R. T. F., Vieira, J. O., & Ferrão, S. P. B. 2004. Composição de ácidos graxos dos cortes comerciais de capivara (*Hydrochaeris L.* 1766). *Ciência e Agrotecnologia, 28*, 1352–1359.

Brudnicki, A., Brudnicki, W., Wach, J., Kulakowska, A., & Pietruszynska, D. (2012). Amino acid composition in the wild boar (*Sus scrofa ferus*) meat originating from different part of carcass. *Journal of Central European Agriculture*, *13*, 662–670.

Bucław M., Majewska D., Szczerbińska D., & Jakubowska M. (2019). Nutritional quality assessment of different muscles derived from 15-year-old female emus (*Dromaius novaehollandiae*): Meat physicochemical traits and sensory scores. *Czech Journal of Animal Science*, *64*, 226–238.

Bureš, D., Bartoň, L., Kotrba, R., & Hakl, J. (2015). Quality attributes and composition of meat from red deer (*Cervus elaphus*), fallow deer (*Dama dama*) and Aberdeen Angus and Holstein cattle (*Bos taurus*). *Journal of the Science of Food and Agriculture*, *95*, 2299–2306.

Cagiltay, F., Erkan, N., Selcuk, O., & Devrim, T. S. (2014). Chemical composition of wild and cultured marsh frog (*Rana Ridibunda*). *Bulgarian Journal of Agricultural Sciences*, *20*, 1250–1254.

Çaklı, Ş., Kışla, D., Cadun, A., Dinçer, T., & Cağlak, E. (2009). Determination of shelf life in fried and boiled frog meat stored in refrigerator in 3.2±1.08 C. *Journal of Fish Aquatic Sciences*, *26*, 115–119.

Calabrò, S., Cutrignelli, M.I., Gonzalez, O.J., Chiofalo, B., Grossi, M., Tudisco, R., Panetta, C., & Infascelli, F. (2014). Meat quality of buffalo young bulls fed faba bean as protein source. *Meat Science*, *96*, 591–596.

Calder, P. C. (2015). Functional roles of fatty acids and their effects on human health. *Journal of Parenteral and Enteral Nutrition*, *39*, 18S–32S.

Caldironi, H. A., & Manes, M.E. (2006). Proximate composition, fatty acids and cholesterol content of meat cuts from tegu lizard Tupinambis merianae. Journal of Food Composition and Analysis, 19, 711–714.

Calik, J., Połtowicz, K., Świątkiewicz, S., Krawczyk, J., & Nowak, J. (2015). Effect of caponization on meat quality of Greenleg Partridge cockerels. *Annals of Animal Science*, *15*, 541–553.

Cantlay, J. Caroline, Ingram, D. J., & Meredith, A. L. (2017). A review of zoonotic infection risks associated with the wild meat trade in Malaysia. *Ecology of Health*, *14*, 361–388.

Canto, A. C. V. C. S., Costa-Lima, B. R. C., Cruz, A. G., Lazaro, C. A., Freitas, D. G. C., Faria, J. A. F., et al. (2012). Effect of high hydrostatic pressure on the color and texture parameters of refrigerated caiman (*Caiman crocodilus* yacare) tail meat. *Meat Science*, *91*, 255–260.

Canto, A. C. V. C. S., Costa-Lima, B. R. C., Suman, S. P., Monteiro, M. L. G., Marsico, E. T., Conte-Junior, C. A., & Silva, T. J. P. (2015). Fatty acid profile and bacteriological quality of caiman meat subjected to high hydrostatic pressure. *LWT-Food Science and Technology*, *63*, 872–877.

Canto, A.C.V.C.S., Lima, B.R.C.C., Suman, S.P., Lazaro, C.A., Monteiro M.L.G., & Cruz, A.G. (2014). Physico-chemical and sensory attributes of low-sodium restructured caiman steaks containing microbial transglutaminase and salt replacers. Meat Science, 96(1), 623–632.

Carson, J. A. S., Lichtenstein, A. H., Anderson, C. A. M., Appel, L. J., Kris-Etherton, P. M., Meyer, K. A., Petersen, K., Polonsky, T., & Horn, L. V. (2020). Dietary cholesterol and cardiovascular risk: A science advisory from the American heart association. *Circulation*, *141*, e39–e53.

Cardinali, R., Cullere, M., Dal Bosco, A., Mugnai, C., Ruggeri, S., Mattioli, S., Castellini, C., Trabalza, M. M., & Dalle Z. A. (2015). Oregano, rosemary and vitamin E dietary supplementation in growing rabbits: Effect on growth performance, carcass traits, bone development and meat chemical composition. *Livestock Science*, *175*, 83–89.

Cawthorn, D.-M., & Hoffman, L. C. (2014). The role of traditional and non-traditional meat animals in feeding a growing and evolving world. *Animal Frontiers*, *4*, 6–12.

Černíková, M., Gál, R., Polášek, Z., Janíček, M., Pachlová, V., & Buňka, F. (2015). Comparison of the nutrient composition, biogenic amines and selected functional parameters of meat from different parts of Nile crocodile (*Crocodylus niloticus*). *Journal of Food Composition and Analysis*, *43*, 82–87.

Chauca, L. (1995). Producción de cuyes (*Cavia porcellus*) en los Paises Andinos. *World Animal Review*, *83*, 9–19.

Chen, C. Y., & Huang, C. H. (2015). Effects of dietary magnesium on the growth, carapace strength and tissue magnesium concentrations of soft-shelled turtle, *Pelodiscus sinensis* (Wiegmann). *Aquatic Research*, *46*, 2116–2123.

Chin, S. F., Liu, W., Storkson, J. M., Ha, Y. L., & Pariza, M. W. (1992). Dietary sources of conjugated dienoic isomers of linoleic acid, a newly recognized class of anticarcinogens. *Journal of Food Composition and Analysis*, *5*, 185–197.

Chizzolini, R., Zanardi, E., Dorigoni, V., & Ghidini, S. (1999). Calorific value and cholesterol content of normal and low-fat meat and meat products. *Trends in Food Science and Technology*, *10*, 119–128.

Cholewa, R., Beutling, D., Mleczek, M., & Arndt, G. (2014). Mineral content in leg muscle and liver of coypu (*Myocastor coypus*). *Aparatura Badawcza i Dydaktyczna*, *19*, 7–14.

Chua, K. B., Lek, K. C., Hooi, P. S., Wee, K.F., Khong, J. H., Chua, B. H., et al. (2002). Isolation of Nipah virus from Malaysian Island flying foxes. *Microbes and Infection*, *4*, 145–151.

Cifuni, G. F., Napolitano, F., Riviezzi, A. M., Braghieri, A., & Girolami, A. (2004). Fatty acid profile, cholesterol content and tenderness of meat from Podolian young bulls. *Meat Science, 67*, 289–297.

Coates, W., & Ayerza, R. (2004). Fatty acid composition of llama muscle and internal fat in two Argentinian herds. *Small Ruminant Research, 52*, 231–238.

Cobos, A., Veiga, A., & Dıaz, O. (2005). Chemical and fatty acid composition of meat and liver of wild ducks (*Anas platyrhynchos*). *Food Chemistry, 68*, 77–79.

Cobos, A., De la Hoz, L., Cambero, M. I., & Ordoñez, J. A. (1995). Chemical and fatty acid composition of meat from Spanish wild rabbits and hares. *Zeitschrift für Lebensmittel- Untersuchung und -Forschung, 200*, 182–185.

Corazzin, M., Del Bianco, S., Bovolenta, S., & Piasentier, E. (2019). Carcass characteristics and meat quality of sheep and goat, In: *More than Beef, Pork and Chicken – The Production, Processing, and Quality Traits of Other Sources of Meat for Human Diet*. Lorenzo, J. M., Munekata, P. E. S., Barba, F. J., & Toldrá, F. (Eds). Cham, Switzerland, Springer Nature Switzerland AG, 119–166.

Cordain, L., Watkins, B. A., Florant, G. L., Kelher, M., Rogers, L., & Li, Y. (2002). Fatty acid analysis of wild ruminant tissues: Evolutionary implications for reducing diet-related chronic disease. *European Journal of Clinical Nutrition, 56*, 181–191.

Cortés, A., Miranda, E., & Jiménez, J. E. (2002). Seasonal food habits of the endangered long tailed chinchilla (*Chinchilla lanigera*): The effect of precipitation. *Mammalian Biology-Zeitschrift fur Saugetierkunde, 67*, 167–175.

Cossu, M. E., González, O. M., Wawrkiewicz, M., Moreno, D., & Vieites, C. M. (2007). Carcass and meat characterization of "yacare overo" (*Caiman latirostris*) and "yacare negro" (*Caiman yacare*) *Brazilian Journal of Veterinary Research and Animal Science, 44*, 329–336.

Costa, H., Mafra, I., Oliveira, M. B. P. P., & Amaral, J. S. (2016). Game: Types and Composition. In: Caballero, B., Finglas, P., and Toldrá, F. (eds.). *The Encyclopedia of Food and Health*, vol. 3, pp. 177–183. Oxford: Academic Press.

Cristofanelli, S., Antonini, M., Torres, D., Polidori, P., & Renieri, C. (2004). Meat and carcass quality from Peruvian llama (Lama glama) and alpaca (Lama pacos). *Meat Science, 66*, 589–593.

Cullere, M., & Dalle Zotte, A. (2018). Rabbit meat production and consumption: State of knowledge and future perspectives. *Meat Science, 143*, 137–146.

Cygan-Szczegielniak, D., & Janicki B. (2012). Amino acids content and basic chemical composition of roe deer (*Capreolus* L.) meat. *Polish Journal of Veterinary Sciences, 15*, 645–649.

Dal Bosco A, Mourvaki, E., Cardinali R., Servili M., Sebastiani B., Ruggeri S, Mattioli S, Taticchi A., Esposto S., & Castellini C. (2012). Effect of dietary supplementation with olive pomaces on the performance and meat quality of growing rabbits. *Meat Science 92*, 783–788.

Dalle Zotte, A. (2002). Perception of rabbit meat quality and major factors influencing the rabbit carcass and meat quality. *Livestock Production Science, 75*, 11–32.

Dalle Zotte, A. (2014). Rabbit farming for meat purposes. *Animal Frontiers, 4*, 62–67.

Dalle Zotte, A., & Szendrő, Z. (2011). The role of rabbit meat as functional food. *Meat Science, 88*, 319–331.

Dalle Zotte, A., & Cullere, M. (2019). Carcass Traits and Meat Quality of Rabbit, Hare, Guinea Pig and Capybara, Lorenzo. J.M., Munekata, P.E.S., Barba, F.J., & Toldrá F. (Eds) More than Beef, Pork and Chicken – The Production, Processing, and Quality Traits of Other Sources of Meat for Human Diet, 167–210.

Daszkiewicz, T., & Mesinger D. (2018). Fatty acid profile of meat (*Longissimus lumborum*) from female roe deer (*Capreolus* L.) and red deer (*Cervus elaphus* L.). *International Journal of Food Properties, 21*, 2276–2282.

De Bruyne, A., Ancelle, T., Vallee, I., Boireau, P., & Dupouy-Camet, J. (2006). Human trichinellosis acquired from wild boar meat: A continuing parasitic risk in France. *Euro Surveillance, 11*, 3048.

Del Gobbo, L. C., Imamura, F., Aslibekyan, S., Marklund, M., Virtanen, J. K., Wennberg, M., & Fretts, A. M. (2016). ω-3 polyunsaturated fatty acid biomarkers and coronary heart disease: Pooling project of 19 cohort studies. *JAMA Internal Medicine, 176*, 1155–1166.

De Palo, P., Maggiolino, A., Centoducati, P., Milella, P., Calzaretti, G., & Tateo, A. (2016). Is meat quality from *Longissimus lumborum* samples correlated with other cuts in horse meat? *Animal Science Journal, 87*, 428–438.

De Palo, P., Tateo, A., Maggiolino, A., Marino, R., Ceci, E., Nisi, A., & Lorenzo, J. M. (2017). Martina Franca donkey meat quality: Influence of slaughter age and suckling technique. *Meat Science, 134*, 128–134.

Dhanda, J. S., Pegg, R. B., & Shand, P. J. (2003). Tenderness and chemical composition of Elk (*Cervus elaphus*) meat: Effects of muscle type, marinade composition, and cooking method. *Journal of Food Science, 68*, 1882–1888.

Dhanda, J. S., Pegg, R. B., Janz, J. A. M., Aalhus, J. L., & Shand, P.J. (2002). Palatability of bison semi-membranosus and effects of margination. *Meat Science*, *62*, 19–26.

Diamond, J. (2002). Evolution, consequences and future of plant and animal domestication. *Nature*, *418*, 700–707.

Dinh, T. T. N., Thompson, L. D., Galyean, M. L., Brooks, J. C., Patterson, K. Y., & Boylan, L. M. (2011). Cholesterol content and methods for cholesterol determination in meat and poultry. *Comprehensive Reviews in Food Science and Food Safety*, *10*, 269–289.

Domaradzki, P., Florek, M., Skałecki, P., Litwińczuk, A., Kędzierska-Matysek, M., Wolanciuk, A., & Tajchman, K. (2019). Fatty acid composition, cholesterol content and lipid oxidation indices of intramuscular fat from skeletal muscles of beaver (Castor fiber L.). *Meat Science*, *150*, 131–140.

Domínguez, R., Borrajo P., Crecente, S., Agregán R., & Lorenzo J. M. (2015). Effect of slaughter age on foal carcass traits and meat quality. *Animal*, *9*, 1713–1720.

Domínguez, R., Pateiro, M., Crecente, S., Ruiz, M., Sarriés, M.V., & Lorenzo J. M. (2018). Effect of linseed supplementation and slaughter age on meat quality of grazing cross-bred Galician x Burguete foals. *Journal of the Science for Food and Agriculture*, *98*, 266–273.

Domínguez, R., Pateiro, M., Munekata, P. E. S., Gagaoua, M., Barba, F. J., & Lorenzo, J. M. (2019). Exotic meats: An alternative food source. In: *More than Beef, Pork and Chicken – The Production, Processing, and Quality Traits of Other Sources of Meat for Human Diet*. Lorenzo, J. M., Munekata, P. E. S., Barba, F. J., & Toldrá, F. (Eds.). Springer Nature Switzerland AG, 385–408.

Echalar, S. R., Jiménez, M. J. M., & Ramón, A. N. (1998). Valor nutritivo y aceptabilidad de la carne de chinchilla. *Archivos Latinoamericanos de Nutrición*, *48*, 77–81.

Engelke, C. F., Siebert, B. D., Gregg, K., Wright, A-D. G., & Vercoel, P. E. (2004). Kangaroo adipose tissue has higher concentrations of *cis* 9, *trans* 11-conjugated linoleic acid than lamb adipose tissue. *Journal of Animal and Feed Sciences*, *13*, 689–692.

European Food Safety Authority (2007). Scientific Opinion of the Panel on Biological Hazards on a request from the European Commission on public health risks involved in the human consumption of reptile meat. *The EFSA Journal*, *578*, 1–55.

Fairfield, T. (2006). The politics of livestock sector policy and the rural poor in Peru. In D. K. Leonard (Ed.), *(Research director), Pro-Poor Livestock Policy Initiative (PPLPI)*, Working Paper No. 32 (70 pp.). Rome, Italy: Food and Agriculture Organization – Animal Production and Health Division.

Fakolade, P. O. (2015). Effect of age on physico-chemical, cholesterol and proximate composition of chicken and quail meat. *African Journal of Food Science*, *9*, 182–186.

Farashi, A., & Najafabadi, M. S. (2015). Modeling the spread of invasive nutrias (*Myocastor coypus*) over Iran. *Ecological Complexity*, *22*, 59–64.

Favoretto, S. R., de Mattos, C. C., Morais, N. B., Araujo, F. A., & de Mattos, C.A. (2001). Rabies in marmosets (*Callithrix jacchus*), Ceara, Brazil. *Emerging Infectious Diseases*, *7*, 1062–1065.

Felix, G. A., Ibiara, C. L. A. P., Piovezan, U., Garcia, R. G., Pinheiro, M. S., Fernandes, A. R. M., Lima, K. A. O., & Rezende, M. A. (2014). Meat and carcass characteristics of free-living capybaras (*Hydrochoerus hydrochaeris*). *Nacameh*, *8*, 23–38.

Fellenberg, A., Mac Cawley, A., & Ivan, P. (2016). Nutritional value of chinchilla meat and its Agroindustrial derivatives. *Carpathian Journal of Food Science and Technology*, *8*, 22–29.

Fernandes, V. R. T., de Souza, M. L. R., Gasparino, E., Coutinho, M. E., Visentainer, J. V., Bérgamo, A. S., & Goes E. S. R. (2017). Commercial cuts of Pantanal caiman meat according to sex. *Ciência Rural*, Santa Maria, *47*, e20160195.

Ferreira, M. M. C., Morgano, M. A., Queiroz, S. C. N., & Mantovani, D. M. B. M. (2000). Relationship of the minerals and fatty acid contents in processed turkey meat products. *Food Chemistry*, *69*, 259–265.

Filgueras, R. S., Gatellier, P., Aubry, L., Thomas, A., Bauchart, D., Durand, D., Zambiazi, R. C., & Santé-Lhoutellier, V. (2010). Colour, lipid and protein stability of *Rhea americana* meat during air- and vacuum-packaged storage: Influence of muscle on oxidative processes. *Meat Science*, *86*, 665–673.

Fitzhenry, L. B. (2016). Yield and meat quality attributes of wild fallow deer (*Dama dama*) in South Africa. MSc Thesis. Department of Consumer Science, University of Stellenbosch, South Africa.

Florek, M., Domaradzki, P., Drozd, L., Skałecki, P., & Tajchman, K. (2017b). Chemical composition, amino acid and fatty acid contents, and mineral concentrations of European beaver (*Castor fiber* L.) meat. *Journal of Food Measurement and Characterization*, *11*, 1035–1044.

Florek, M., Drozd, L., Skałecki, P., Domaradzki, P., Litwińczuk, A., & Tajchman, K. (2017a). Proximate composition and physicochemical properties of European beaver (*Castor fiber* L.) meat. *Meat Science*, *123*, 8–12.

Franco, D., & Lorenzo, J. M. (2013). Meat quality and nutritional composition of pheasants (*Phasianus colchicus*) reared in an extensive system. *British Poultry Science*, *54*, 594–602.

Franco, D., & Lorenzo, J. M. (2014). Effect of muscle and intensity of finishing diet on meat quality of foals slaughtered at 15 months. *Meat Science*, *96*, 327–334.

Fu, Z., & Sinclair, A. J. (2000). Increased α-linolenic acid intake increases tissue α-linolenic acid content and apparent oxidation with little effect on tissue docosahexaenoic acid in the Guinea pig. *Lipids*, *35*, 395–400.

Fukushima, H., Okuno, J., Fujiwara, Y., Hosoda, T., Kurazono, T., Ohtsuka, K., et al. (2008). An outbreak of Salmonella food poisoning at a snapping turtle restaurant. *Journal of the Japanese Association for Infectious Diseases*, *61*, 328.

Galbraith, J. K., Aalhus, J. L., Juárez, M., Dugan, M. E. R., Larsen, I. L., Aldai, N., Goonewardene, L. A., & Okine, E. K. (2016). Meat colour stability and fatty acid profile in commercial bison and beef. *Journal of Food Research*, *5*, 92–101.

Galbraith, J. K., Hauer, G., Helbig, L., Wang, Z., Marchello, M. J., & Goonewardene, L. A. (2006). Nutrient profiles in retail cuts of bison meat. *Meat Science*, *74*, 648–654.

Gálvez, F., Domínguez, R., Pateiro, M., Carballo, J., Tomasevic, I., & Lorenzo, J. M. (2018). Effect of gender on breast and thigh turkey meat quality. *British Poultry Science*, *59*, 408–415.

Garcıa, E., Mora, L., Torres, P., Jercic, M. I., & Mercado, R. (2005). First record of human trichinosis in Chile associated with consumption of wild boar (*Sus scrofa*). *Memorias do Instituto Oswaldo Cruz*, *100*, 17–18.

Gbogbo, F., Rainhill, J. E., Koranteng, S. S., Owusu, E. H., & Dorleku, W.-P. (2020). Health risk assessment for human exposure to trace metals via bushmeat in Ghana. *Biological Trace Element Research*, *196*, 419–429

Geldenhuys, G., Hoffman, L. C., & Muller, N. (2013). Aspects of the nutritional value of cooked Egyptian goose (*Alopochen aegyptiacus*) meat compared with other well-known fowl species. *Poultry Science*, *92*, 3050–3059.

Geldenhuys, G., Hoffman, L. C., & Muller, N. (2015). The fatty acid, amino acid, and mineral composition of Egyptian goose meat as affected by season, gender, and portion. *Poultry Science*, *94*, 1075–1087.

Georgiev, L., Pavlov, A., & Dinkov, D. (2001). Studies upon the composition of Kangaroo meat. *Bulgarian Journal of Veterinary Medicine*, *4*, 115–118.

Gertonson, E. H., Dawson L. E., & Coleman T. H. (1974). Yield, composition and acceptability of meat from chukar partridge. *Poultry Science*, *53*, 1819–1823.

Gessain, A., Rua, R., Betsem, E., Turpin, J., & Mahieux, R. (2013). HTLV-3/4 and simian foamy retroviruses in humans: Discovery, epidemiology, cross-species transmission and molecular virology. *Virology*, *435*, 187–199.

Gill, C. O. (2005). Safety and storage stability of horse meat for human consumption. *Meat Science*, *71*, 506–513.

Girardi, F., Cardozo, R. M., de Souza, V. L. F., de Moraes, G. V., dos Santos, C. R., Visentainer, J. V., et al. (2005). Proximate composition and fatty acid profile of semiconfined young capybara (*Hydrochaeris* L. 1766) meat. *Journal of Food Composition and Analysis*, *18*, 647–654.

Girolami, A., Marsico, I., D'Andrea, G., Braghieri A., Napolitano F., & Cifuni G. F. (2003). Fatty acid profile, cholesterol content and tenderness of ostrich meat as influenced by age at slaughter and muscle type. *Meat Science*, *64*, 309–315.

Giuffrida-Mendoza, M., Arenas De Moreno, L., Uzcátegui-Bracho, S., Rincón-Villalobos, G., & Huerta-Leidenz, N. (2007). Mineral content of longissimus dorsi thoracis from water buffalo and Zebu-influenced cattle at four comparative ages. *Meat Science*, *75*, 487–493.

Głogowski, R., & Panas, M. (2009). Efficiency and proximate composition of meat in male and female nutria (*Myocastor coypus*) in an extensive feeding system. *Meat Science*, *81*, 752–754.

Głogowski, R., Czauderna, M., Rozbicka, A. J., & Krajewska, K. A. (2009). Selected functional characteristics of hind leg muscle of nutria (*Myocastor coypus* Mol.), from an extensive feeding system. *Roczniki Naukowe Polskiego Towarzystwa Zootechnicznego*, *5*, 95–103.

Głogowski, R., Czauderna, M., Rozbicka, A., Krajewska, K. A., & Clauss, M. (2010). Fatty acid profile of hind leg muscle in female and male nutria (*Myocastor coypus* Mol.), fed green forage diet. *Meat Science*, *85*, 577–579.

Gok, V., & Bor, Y. (2016). Effect of marination with fruit and vegetable juice on some quality characteristics of turkey breast meat. *Revista Brasileira de Ci*, *18*, 481–488.

Gonzalez, F., Smulders, F. J. M., Paulsen, P., Skewes, O., & Konig, H. E. (2004). Anatomical investigations on meat cuts of guanacos (*Lama guanicoe*, Muller, 1776) and chemical composition of selected muscles. *Wiener Tierarztliche Monatsschrift*, *91*, 77–84.

González, N., MarquŠs, M., Nadal, M., & Domingo, J. L. (2010-2020). Meat consumption: Which are the current global risks? A review of recent (2010–2020) evidence. *Food Research International, 137,* 109341.

Gordon, I. J. (2018). Review: Livestock production increasingly influences wildlife across the globe. *Animal, 12*(s2), s372–s382.

Hamm, D., & Ang, C. Y. W. (1982). Nutrient composition of quail meat from three sources. *Journal of Food Science, 47,* 1613–1614.

Hanna, J. N., Carney, I. K., Smith, G. A., Tannenberg, A., Deverill, J. E., Botha, J. A., et al. (2000). Australian bat lyssavirus infection: A second human case, with a long incubation period. *The Medical Journal of Australia, 172,* 597–599.

Hassan, M. A., Abdel-Naeem, H. H.S., Mohamed, H. M. H., & Yassien, N. A. (2018). Comparing the physico-chemical characteristics and sensory attributes of imported Brazilian beef meat and imported Indian buffalo meat. *Journal of Microbiology, Biotechnology and Food Science, 8,* 672–677.

Hermida, M., Gonzalez, M., Miranda, M., & Rodrıguez-Otero, J. L. (2006). Mineral analysis in rabbit meat from Galicia (NW Spain). *Meat Science, 73,* 635–639.

Higaonna, O. R., Muscari, G. J., Chauca, F. L., & Astete, F. (2008). Composición química de la carne de cuy (*Cavia porcellus*). INIA. *Investigaciones en cuyes, Trabajos presentados a la Asociación Peruana de Producción Animal.* Lima, Peru: INIA – CE La Molina, Universidad Agraria La Molina, Universidad Peruana Cayetano, Heredia, Aprodes. APPA.

Hoffman, L. C. (2008). The yield and nutritional value of meat from African ungulates, camelidae, rodents, ratites and reptiles. *Meat Science, 80,* 94–100.

Hoffman, L. C., & Ferreira, A.V. (2004). Chemical composition of two muscles of the common duiker (*Sylvicapra grimmia*). *Journal of the Science of Food and Agriculture, 84,* 1541–1544.

Hoffman, L. C., & Cawthorn, D.-M. (2013). Exotic protein sources to meet all needs. *Meat Science, 95,* 764–771.

Hoffman, L. C., Fisher, P. P., & Sales, J. (2000). Carcass and meat characteristics of the Nile crocodile (*Crocodylus niloticus*). *Journal of Science of Food and Agriculture, 80,* 390–396.

Hoffman, L. C., Geldenhuys, G., & Cawthorn, D.-M. (2016). Proximate and fatty acid composition of zebra (*Equus quagga burchellii*) muscle and subcutaneous fat. *Journal of the Science of Food and Agriculture, 96,* 3922–3927.

Hoffman, L. C., Smit, K., & Muller, N. (2008a). Chemical characteristics of blesbok (*Damaliscus dorcas phillipsi*) meat. *Journal of Food Composition and Analysis, 21,* 315–319.

Hoffman, L. C., van Schalkwyk, S., & Muller, N. M. (2008b). Physical and chemical properties of male and female mountain reedbuck (*Redunca fulvorufula*) meat. *South African Journal of Wildlife Research, 38,* 11–16.

Hoffman, L. C., van Schalkwyk, S., & Muller, M. M. (2009). Effect of season and gender on the physical and chemical composition of black wildebeest (*Connochaetus gnou*) meat. *South African Journal of Wildlife Research, 39,* 170–174.

Hoffman, L. C., Kritzinger, B., & Ferreira, A. V. (2005). The effects of region and gender on the fatty acid, amino acid, mineral, myoglobin and collagen contents of impala (*Aepyceros melampus*) meat. *Meat Science, 69,* 551–558.

Hoffman, L. C., Kroucamp, M., & Manley M. (2007a). Meat quality characteristics of springbok (*Antidorcas marsupialis*). 2: Fatty acid composition as influenced by age, gender and production region. *Meat Science, 76,* 762–767.

Hoffman, L. C., Kroucamp, M., & Manley M. (2007b). Meat quality characteristics of springbok (*Antidorcas marsupialis*). 3: Chemical composition of springbok meat as influenced by age, gender and production region. *Meat Science, 76,* 768–773.

Hoffman, L. C., Mostert, A. C., Kidd, M., & Laubscher, L. L. (2009a). Meat quality of kudu (*Tragelaphus strepsiceros*) and impala (*Aepyceros melampus*): Carcass yield, physical quality and chemical composition of kudu and impala Longissimus dorsi muscle as affected by gender and age. *Meat Science, 83,* 788–795.

Hoffman, L. C., Smit, K., & Muller, N. (2010). Chemical characteristics of red hartebeest (*Alcelaphus buselaphus caama*) meat. *South African Journal of Animal Science, 40,* 221–228.

Holds, G., Pointon, A., Lorimer, M., Kiermeier, A., Raven, G., & Sumner, J. (2008). Microbial profiles of carcasses and minced meat from kangaroos processed in South Australia. *International Journal of Food Microbiology, 123,* 88–92.

Horbańczuk, O. K., Moczkowska, M., Marchewka, J., Atanasov, A. G., & Kurek, M. A. (2019). The composition of fatty acids in Ostrich meat influenced by the type of packaging and refrigerated storage. *Molecules, 24,* 4128.

Horbańczuk, O. K., & Wierzbicka, A. (2016). Technological and nutritional properties of ostrich, emu, and rhea meat quality. *Journal of Veterinary Research, 60*, 279–286.

Huang, C. H., & Lin, W. Y. (2004). Effects of dietary vitamin E level on growth and tissue lipid peroxidation of soft-shelled turtle, *Pelodiscus sinensis* (Wiegmann). *Aquaculture Research, 35*, 948–954.

Huang, C.-H., Lin, W.-Y., & Chu, J.H. (2005). Dietary lipid level influences fatty acid profiles, tissue composition, and lipid peroxidation of soft-shelled turtle, Pelodiscus sinensis. *Comparative Biochemistry and Physiology. Part A: Molecular & Integrative Physiology, 142*, 383–388.

Huff, J. L., & Barry, P. A. (2003). B-virus (*Cercopithecine herpesvirus* 1) infection in humans and macaques: potential for zoonotic disease. *Emerging Infectious Diseases, 9*, 246–250.

Huffman, M., Nahallage, C., Hasegawa, H., Ekanayake, S., De Silva, L., & Athauda, I. (2013). Preliminary survey of the distribution of four potentially zoonotic parasite species among primates in Sri Lanka. *Journal of the National Science Foundation of Sri Lanka, 41*, 319–326.

Igene, J. O., Okoro, K. I., Ebabhamiegbebho, P. A., & Evivie, S. E. (2015). A study assessing some metal elements contamination levels in grasscutter (*Thryonomys swinderianus* Temminck) meat. *International Journal of Biotechnology and Food Science, 3*, 63.

Ivanović, S. Pisinov, B., Pavlović, M., & Pavlović I. (2020). Quality of meat from female fallow deer (*Dama dama*) and roe deer (*Capreolus capreolus*) hunted in Serbia. *Annals of Animal Science, 20*, 245–262.

Ivanovic, S., Pavlovic, I., & Pisinov, B. (2016). The quality of goat meat and its impact on human health. *Biotechnology in Animal Husbandry, 32*, 111–122.

Jacob, M. C. M., Feitosa, I. S., & Albuquerque, U. P. (2020). Animal-based food systems are unsafe: severe acute respiratory syndrome coronavirus 2 (SARS-CoV-2) fosters the debate on meat consumption. *Public Health Nutrition, 23*, 3250–3255.

Jankowska, B., Zmijewski, T., Kwiatkowska, A., & Korzeniowski, W. (2005). The composition and properties of beaver (*Castor fiber*) meat. *European Journal of Wildlife Research, 51*, 283–286.

Januškevičius, A., Bukelis, R., Andrulevičiūtė, V., Sinkevičienė, I., Budreckienė, R., & Kašauskas, A. (2015). Dynamics of growth, biochemical blood parameters, carcass and meat characteristics of foddering nutria (*Myocastor coypus*) influenced by proteins diet. *Veterinarija Ir Zootechnika, 71*, 21–25.

Jardim, N. S., Bressan, M. C., Lemos, A. L. S., Thomazini, M., & Ferreira, M. W. (2003). Teor lipídico e perfil de ácidos graxos da carne de capivara (*Hydrochaeris hydrochaeris*). *Ciência e Agrotecnologia, 27*, 651–657.

Jarzyńska, G., & Falandysz, J. (2011). Selenium and 17 other largely essential and toxic metals in muscle and organ meats of red deer (*Cervus elaphus*) - consequences to human health. *Environment International, 37*, 882–888.

Joy, M. (2010). *Why We Love Dogs, Eat Pigs and Wear Cows. An Introduction to Carnism*. Cornari Press, San Francisco.

Joyce, K., Emikpe, B. O., Asare, D. A., Asenso, T. N., Richmond, Y., Jarikre, T. A., & Jagun-Jubril, A. (2016). Effects of different cooking methods on heavy metals level in fresh and smoked game meat. *Journal of Food Processing & Technology, 7*, 617.

Juárez, M., Failla, S., Ficco, A., Pena, F., Avilés, C., & Polvillo, O. (2010). Buffalo meat composition as affected by different cooking methods. *Food and Bioproducts Processing, 88*, 145–148.

Juárez, M., Horcada, A., Alcalde, M. J., Valera, M., Polvillo, O., & Molina, A. (2009). Meat and fat quality of unweaned lambs as affected by slaughter weight and breed. *Meat Science, 83*, 308–313.

Juárez, M., López-Campos, Ó., Prieto, N., Roberts, J., Galbraith, J., Failla, S., & Aalhus, J. L. (2019). Carcass characteristics and meat quality of Bison, Buffalo, and Yak, In JM Lorenzo, PES Munekata, FJ Barba, F Toldrá (eds), More than Beef, Pork and Chicken – The Production, Processing, and Quality Traits of Other Sources of Meat for Human Diet, pp. 95–117, Springer International Publishing, Switzerland.

Kadim, I. T., Mahgoub, O., & Mbaga, M. (2014). Potential of camel meat as a nontraditional high quality source of protein for human consumption. *Animal Frontiers, 4*, 13–17.

Kadim, I. T., Al-Karousi, A., Mahgoub, O., Al-Marzooqi, W., Al-Maqbaly, R., Khalaf, S. K., & Raiymbek, G. (2013). Physical, chemical, quality and histochemical characteristics of infraspinatus, triceps brachii, longissimus thoraces, biceps femoris, semitendinosus, and semimembranosus of dromedary camel (*Camelus dromedaries*) muscles. *Meat Science, 93*, 564–571.

Kadim, I. T., & Purchas, R. (2019). Camel carcass and meat quality characteristics. In JM Lorenzo, PES Munekata, FJ Barba, F Toldrá (eds.), *More than Beef, Pork and Chicken – The Production, Processing, and Quality Traits of Other Sources of Meat for Human Diet*. Springer Nature Switzerland AG, 69–94.

Kadim, I. T., Mahgoub, O., & Purchas, R. W. (2008). A review of the growth, and of the carcass and meat quality characteristics of the one-humped camel (*Camelus dromedaries*). *Meat Science, 80*, 555–569.

Kadim, I.T., Al-Hosni, Y., Mahgoub, O., Al-Marzooqi, W., Khalaf, S. K., Al-Maqbaly, R. S., Al-Sinawi, S. S. H., & Al-Amri, I. S. (2009). Effect of low voltage electrical stimulation on biochemical and quality characteristics of Longissimus thoracis muscle from one-humped Camel (*Camelus dromedaries*). *Meat Science*, *82*, 77–85.

Karadağoğlu, Ö., Şahin, T., Ölmez, M., Ahsan, U., Özsoy, B., & Önk, K. (2019). Fatty acid composition of liver and breast meat of quails fed diets containing black cumin (*Nigella sativa* L.) and/or coriander (*Coriandrum sativum* L.) seeds as unsaturated fatty acid sources. *Livestock Science*, *223*, 164–171.

Kasprzyk, A., Stadnik, J., & Stasiak, D. (2019). Technological and nutritional properties of meat from female wild boars (*Susscrofa scrofa* L.) of different carcass weights. *Archives of Animal Breeding*, *62*, 597–604.

Khalifa, A. H., & Nassar, A. M. (2001). Nutritional and bacteriological properties of some game duck carcasses. *Food Nahrung*, *45*, 286–292.

Kilonzo-Nthenge, A., Nahashon, S. N., Chen, F., & Adefope, N. (2008). Prevalence and antimicrobial resistance of pathogenic bacteria in chicken and Guinea fowl. *Poultry Science*, *87*, 1841–1848.

Kim, S. C., Adesogan, A. T., Badinga, L., & Staples, C. R. (2007). Effects of dietary n-6: n-3 fatty acid ratio on feed intake, digestibility, and fatty acid profiles of the ruminal contents, liver, and muscle of growing lambs. *Journal of Animal Science*, *85*, 706–716.

Kim, S.-W., Kim, K.-W., Park, S.-B., Kim, M.-J., & Yim, D.-G. (2016). Quality characteristics and composition of the *Longissimus* muscle from entire and castrate elk in Korea. *Asian-Australasian Journal of Animal Sciences*, *29*, 709–715.

Knapik, J., Ropka-Molik, K., & Pieszka M. (2017). Genetic and nutritional factors determining the production and quality of sheep meat. *Annals of Animal Science*, *17*, 23–40.

Koh, L. P., Li, Y., & Lee, J. S. H. (2021). The value of China's ban on wildlife trade and consumption. *Nature Sustainability*, *4*, 2–4.

Kokoszyński D., Arpášová, H., Hrnčar, C., Zochowska-Kujawska, J., Kotowicz, M., & Sobczak M. (2020). Carcass characteristics, chemical composition, physicochemical properties, texture, and microstructure of meat from spent Pekin ducks. *Poultry Science*, *99*, 1232–1240.

Kokoszyński, D., Piwczyński, D., Arpášová, H., Hrnčar, C., Saleh M., & Wasilewski R. (2019). A comparative study of carcass characteristics and meat quality in genetic resources Pekin ducks and commercial crossbreds. *Asian-Australasian Journal of Animal Sciences*, *32*, 1753–1762.

Kouakou, N. D., Grongnet, J. F., Assidjo, N. E., Thys, E., Marnet, P. G., Catheline, D., and Kouba, M. (2013). Effect of a supplementation of Euphorbia heterophylla on nutritional meat quality of Guinea pig (*Cavia porcellus* L.). *Meat Science*, *93*, 821–826.

Krijger, I. M. (2020). Rodent-borne health risks in farming systems. Ph.D. thesis, Wageningen University, Netherlands.

Króliczewska, B., Miśta, D., Korzeniowska, M., Pecka-Kiełb, E., & Zachwieja, A. (2018). Comparative evaluation of the quality and fatty acid profile of meat from brown hares and domestic rabbits offered the same diet. *Meat Science*, *145*, 292–299.

Kurpiers, L. A., Schulte-Herbrüggen, B., Ejotre, I., & Reeder, D. A. M. (2016). Bushmeat and emerging infectious diseases: Lessons from Africa. In: *Problematic Wildlife: A Cross Disciplinary Approach*. Angelici, F. M. (Ed.). New York: Springer, 507–551.

Kwiatkowska, A., Żmijewski, T., & Cierach, M. (2009). Utility value of carcass of European deer (*Cervus elaphus*) and its meat evaluation. *Polish Journal of Food and Nutrition Sciences*, *59*, 151–156.

Lammers, P. J., Carlson, S. L., Zdorkowski, G. A., & Honeyman, M. S. (2009). Reducing food insecurity in developing countries through meat production: The potential of the Guinea pig (*Cavia porcellus*). *Renewable Agriculture and Food Systems*, *24*, 155–162.

Lanza, M., Landi, C., Scerra, M., Galofaro, V., & Pennisi P. (2009). Meat quality and intramuscular fatty acid composition of Sanfratellano and Haflinger foals. *Meat Science*, *81*, 142–147.

Lee, M.-K., Moon, J.-H., & Ryu, H.-S. (1994). Nutrient composition and protein quality of giant snail products. *Journal of Korean Society of Food and Nutrition*, *23*, 453–458.

Lehel, J., Laczay, P., Gyurcsó, A., Jánoska, F., Majoros, S., Lányi, K., & Marosán, M. (2016). Toxic heavy metals in the muscle of roe deer (*Capreolus capreolus*)—food toxicological significance. *Environmental Science and Pollution Research*, *23*, 4465–4472.

Leonard, W. R., Snodgrass, J. J., & Robertson, M. L. (2007). Effects of brain evolution on human nutrition and metabolism. *Annual Review in Nutrition*, *27*, 311–327.

Leroy, F., & De Smet, S. (2019). Meat in the Human Diet: A Biosocial Perspective; In; *More than Beef, Pork and Chicken – The Production, Processing, and Quality Traits of Other Sources of Meat for Human Diet*. Lorenzo, J. M., Munekata, P. E. S., Barba, F. J., & Toldrá, F. (Eds.). Springer Nature Switzerland AG, 1–19.

Lesiów, T., & Xiong Y. L. (2004). Up-to-date knowledge on the nutritional composition of poultry meat. *50th*, Helsinki, August 8–13.

Li, Q., Sherwood, J. S., & Logue, C. M. (2004). The prevalence of *Listeria, Salmonella, Escherichia coli* and *E. coli* O157:H7 on bison carcasses during processing. *Food Microbiology, 21*, 791–799.

Li, J., Li (Justin), J., Xie, X., Cai, X., Huang, J., Tian, X., & Zhu, H. (2020). Game consumption and the 2019 novel coronavirus. *The Lancet Infectious Diseases, 20*, 275–276.

Li, Q., Wang, Y., Tan, L., Leng, J., Lu, Q., Tian, S., Shao, S., Duan, C., Li, W., & Mao, H. (2018). Effects of age on slaughter performance and meat quality of Binlangjang male buffalo. *Saudi Journal of Biological Sciences, 25*, 248–252.

Li, S., Zeng, W., Li, R., Hoffman, L. C., He, Z., Sun, Q., & Li, H. (2018). Rabbit meat production and processing in China. *Meat Science, 145*, 320–328.

Liang, H., Tong, M., Cao, L., Li, X., Li, Z., & Zou, G. (2018). Amino acid and fatty acid composition of three strains of Chinese soft-shelled turtle (*Pelodiscus sinensis*). *Pakistan Journal of Zoology, 50*, 1061–1069.

Liu, H. W., Gai, F., Gasco, L., Brugiapaglia, A., Lussiana, C., Guo, K. J., Tong, J. M., & Zoccarato, I. (2009). Effects of chestnut tannins on carcass characteristics, meat quality, lipid oxidation and fatty acid composition of rabbits. *Meat Science, 83*, 678–683.

Löest, C. A., Ferreira, A.V., van der Merwe, H. J., & Fair, M. D. (1997). Chemical and essential amino acid composition of South African mutton Merino lamb carcasses. *South African Journal of Animal Sciences, 27*, 7–12.

Lopez-Bote, C., Rey, A., Ruiz, J., Isabel, B., & Sanz Arias, R. (1997). Effect of feeding diets high in monounsaturated fatty acids and α-tocopheryl acetate to rabbits on resulting carcass fatty acid profile and lipid oxidation. *Animal Science, 64*, 177–186.

López-Pedrouso, M., Cantalapiedra, J., Munekata, P. E. S. Barba, F. J., Lorenzo, J. M., & Franco, D. (2019). Carcass characteristics, meat quality and nutritional profile of pheasant, quail and guinea fowl. In JM Lorenzo, PES Munekata, FJ Barba, F Toldrá (eds.), *More than Beef, Pork and Chicken – The Production, Processing, and Quality Traits of Other Sources of Meat for Human Diet*. Springer Nature Switzerland AG, 269–311.

Lorenzo, J. M., & Pateiro, M. (2013). Influence of type of muscles on nutritional value of foal meat. *Meat Science, 93*, 630–638.

Lorenzo, J. M., Fuciños, C., Purriños, L., & Franco, D. (2010). Intramuscular fatty acid composition of "Galician Mountain" foals breed. Effect of sex, slaughtered age and livestock production system. *Meat Science, 86*, 825–831.

Lorenzo, J. M., Maggiolino, A., Gallego, L., Pateiro, M., Serrano, M. P., Domínguez, R., García, A., Landete-Castillejos, T., & De Palo P. (2019). Effect of age on nutritional properties of Iberian wild red deer meat. *Journal of the Science for Food and Agriculture, 99*, 1561–1567.

Lorenzo, J. M., Maggiolino, A., Sarriés, M. V., Polidori, P., Franco, D., Lanza, M., & De Palo P. (2019). Horsemeat: Increasing quality and nutritional value. In JM Lorenzo, PES Munekata, FJ Barba, F Toldrá (eds.), *More than Beef, Pork and Chicken – The Production, Processing, and Quality Traits of Other Sources of Meat for Human Diet*. Springer Nature Switzerland AG, 31–69.

Lorenzo, J. M., Munekata, P. E. S., Campagnol, P. C. B., Zhu, Z., Alpas, H., Barba, F. J., & Tomasevic, I. (2017). Technological aspects of horse meat products - A review. *Food Research International, 102*, 176–183.

Lorenzo, J. M., Pateiro, M., & Franco, D. (2013a). Influence of muscle type on physicochemical and sensory properties of foal meat. *Meat Science, 94*, 77–83.

Lorenzo, J. M., Sarriés, M. V., & Franco, D. (2013b). Sex effect on meat quality and carcass traits of foals slaughtered at 15 months of age. *Animal, 7*, 1199–1207.

Lorenzo, J. M., Sarriés, M. V., Tateo, A., Polidori, P., Franco, D., & Massimiliano Lanza, M. (2014). Carcass characteristics, meat quality and nutritional value of horsemeat: A review. *Meat Science, 96*, 1478–1488.

Łozicki, A., Olech, W., Dymnicka, M., Florowski, T., Adamczak, L. Arkuszewska, E., & Niemiec, T. (2017). Nutritive value and meat quality of domestic cattle (*Bos taurus*), zubron (*Bos taurus* × *Bison bonasus*) and European bison (*Bison bonasus*) meat. *Agricultural and Food Science, 26*, 118–128.

Luby, S. P., Rahman, M., Hossain, M. J., Blum, L. S., Husain, M. M., Gurley, E., et al. (2006). Foodborne transmission of Nipah virus, Bangladesh. *Emerging infectious diseases, 12*, 1888–1894.

Luo, F., Xing, R., Wang, X., Peng, Q. & Li, P. (2017). Proximate composition, amino acid and fatty acid profiles of marine snail Rapana venosa meat, visceral mass and operculum. *Journal of the Science of Food and Agriculture, 97*, 5361–5368.

Luo, X. L., Tong, Z. B., Wei, Y. P., & Zhao, X. Q. (2006). Meat characteristics of Qinghai yak and semi-wild yak. *Animal Science Journal*, *77*, 230–234.

Madzimure, J., Saina, H., & Ngorora, G. P. K. (2011). Market potential for guinea fowl (*Numidia meleagris*) products. *Tropical Animal Health and Production*, *43*, 1509–1515.

Magnino, S., Colin, P., Dei-Cas, E., Madsen, M., McLauchlin, J., Nöckler, K., et al. (2009). Biological risks associated with consumption of reptile products. *International Journal of Food Microbiology*, *134*, 163–175.

Maheswarappa, N. B., & Kiran M. (2014). Emu meat: New source of healthier meat towards niche market. *Food Reviews International*, *30*, 22–35.

Mamani-Linares, L. W., & Gallo, C. (2013). Meat quality attributes of the *Longissimus lumborum* muscle of the Kh'ara genotype of llama (*Lama glama*) reared extensively in northern Chile. *Meat Science*, *94*, 89–94.

Mamani-Linares, L. W., & Gallo, C. (2014). Meat quality, proximate composition and muscle fatty acid profile of young llamas (*Lama glama*) supplemented with hay or concentrate during the dry season. *Meat Science*, *96*, 394–399.

Marchello, M. J., Slanger, W. D., Hadley, M., Milne, D. B., & Driskell, J. A. (1998). Nutrient composition of bison fed concentrate diets. *Journal of Food Composition and Analysis*, *11*, 231–239.

Mareko, M. H. D., Nsoso, S. J., & Thibelong, K. (2006). Preliminary carcass and meat characteristics of guinea fowl (*Numidia meleagris*) raised on concrete and earth floors in Botswana. *Journal of Food Technology*, *4*, 313–317.

Marino, R., Albenzio, M., della Malva, A., Muscio, A., & Sevi, A. (2015). Nutritional properties and consumer evaluation of donkey bresaola and salami: Comparison with conventional products. *Meat Science*, *101*, 19–24.

Martens, F. M. (2010). Carne de Yacaré: exótica y saludable. Universidad Fasta. Facultad de Ciencias Médicas. *Tesis de Licenciatura en Nutrición*, Mar del Plata.

Mason, S. L., Shi, J., Bekhit, A. E. D., & Gooneratne R. (2014). Nutritional and toxicological studies of New Zealand *Cookia sulcate*. *Journal of Food Composition and Analysis*, *36*, 79–84.

Mayeaux, M. H. (1994). Preliminary culture studies with the common snapping turtle (*Chelydra Serpentina*): Growth, nutrition, and stocking density. Graduate Faculty of the Louisiana State University, Agricultural and Mechanical College, USA, LSU Historical Dissertations and Theses. 5890.

Mayeaux, M. H., Reich, R. C., & Culley, D. (1998). Fatty acid composition of muscle, liver, and depot fat of wild and cultured common snapping Turtles *Chelydra serpentina*. *Journal of The World Aquaculture Society*, *29*, 234–242.

Mayor, P., Baquedano, L. E., Sanchez, E., Aramburu, J., Gomez-Puerta, L. A., Mamani, V. J., & Gavidia, C. M. (2015). Polycystic Echinococcosis in Pacas, Amazon Region, Peru. *Emerging Infectious Diseases*, *21*, 456.

Mazhangara, I. R., Chivandi, E., Mupangwa J. F., & Muchenje, V. (2019). The potential of goat meat in the red meat industry. *Sustainability*, *11*, 3671.

Mazizi, B. E., Erlwanger, K. H., Chivandi, E. (2020). The effect of dietary Marula nut meal on the physical properties, proximate and fatty acid content of Japanese quail meat. *Veterinary and Animal Science*, *9*, 100096.

McClenahan, J. M., & Driskell, J. A. (2002). Nutrient content and sensory characteristics of bison meat. *Historical Materials from University of Nebraska-Lincoln Extension*, 144, NF01–NF502.

McDaniel, J., Askew, W., Bennett, D., Mihalopoulos, J., Anantharaman, S., Fjeldstad, A. S., et al. (2013). Bison meat has a lower atherogenic risk than beef in healthy men. *Nutrition Research*, *33*, 293–302.

Meng, X., Lindsay, D., & Sriranganathan, N. (2009). Wild boars as sources for infectious diseases in livestock and humans. *Philosophical Transactions of the Royal Society: Biological Sciences*, *364*, 2697–2707.

Migdal, L., Barabasz, B., Niedbal, P., Lapińsk, I. S., Pustkowiak, H., vŽivković, B., & Migdal, W. (2013). A comparison of selected biochemical characteristics of meat from nutrias (*Myocastor coypus* Mol.) and rabbits (*Oryctolagus cuniculus*). *Annals of Animal Science*, *13*, 387–400.

Mir, N. A., Tyagi, P. K., Biswas, A. K., Mandal, A. B., Kumar, F., Sharma, D., et al., (2018). Inclusion of flaxseed, broken rice, and distillers dried grains with solubles (DDGS) in broiler chicken ration alters the fatty acid profile, oxidative stability, and other functional properties of meat. *European Journal of Lipid Science and Technology*, *120*, 1700470.

Mitchaothai, J., Yuangklang, C., Wittayakun, S., Vasupen, K., Wongsutthavas, S., Srenanul, P., & Beynen, A. C. (2007). Effect of dietary fat type on meat quality and fatty acid composition of various tissues in growing–finishing swine. *Meat Science*, *76*, 95–101.

Mitchell, G. E., Reed, A. W., & Houlihan, D. B. (1995). Composition of crocodile meat (*Crocodylus porosus* and *Crocodylus johnstoni*). *Food Australian*, *47*, 221–224.

Mohamed, E. H. A. (2013). Fatty acids compositions in the liver and fat oils of the Spiny-Tailed Lizards *Uromastx dispar* and *Uromastx ocellata* (Sauria: Agamidae). *American Journal of Research Communication, 1,* 197–210.

Mohammed, H. H. H., Jin, G., Ma, M., Khalifa, I., Shukat, R., Elkhedir, A. E., et al. (2020). Comparative characterization of proximate nutritional compositions, microbial quality and safety of camel meat in relation to mutton, beef, and chicken. *LWT - Food Science and Technology, 118,* 108714.

Morais, C. S. N., Morais Júnior, N. N., Vicente-Neto, J., Ramos, E. M., Almeida, J., Roseiro, C., & Bressan, M. C. (2013). Mortadella sausage manufactured with Caiman yacare (*Caiman crocodilus yacare*) meat, pork back fat, and soybean oil. *Meat Science, 95,* 403–411.

Morales, J. S., Moreno-Ortega, A., Lopez, M. A. A., Casas, A. A., Cámara-Martos, F., & Moreno-Rojas, R. (2018). Game meat consumption by hunters and their relatives: a probabilistic approach. *Food Additives & Contaminants: Part A, 35,* 1739–1748.

Moreira, J. R., Alvarez, M. R., Tarifa, T., Pacheco, V., Taber, A., Tirira, D. G., & Macdonald, D. W. (2012). Taxonomy, natural history and distribution of the capybara. In J. R. Moreira, K. M. P. M. B. Ferraz, E. A. Herrera, & D. W. MacDonald (Eds.). *Capybara: Biology, use and conservation of an exceptional neotropical species* (pp. 3–39). Nova Iorque, U.S.A.: Springer.

Moreira, J. R., & Pinheiro, M. S. (2013). Capybara production in Brazil: Captive breeding or sustainable management? In: Moreira, J. R., Ferraz, K. M. P. M. B., Herrera E. A., and Macdonald, D. W. (Eds.). *Capybara: Biology, Use and Conservation of an Exceptional Neotropical Species* (pp. 333–344). New York: Springer.

Morgante, M., Valusso, R., Pittia, P., Volpelli, L. A., & Piasentier, E. (2003). Quality traits of fallow deer (Dama dama) dry-cured hams. *Italian Journal of Animal Science, 2,* 557–559.

Mostert, A. C. (2007). Meat quality characteristics of Kudu (*Tragelaphus strepsiceros*) and Impala (*Aepyceros melampus*) meat. MSc Thesis. Department of Consumer Science, University of Stellenbosch, South Africa.

Mostert, R., & Hoffman, L.C. (2007). Effect of gender on the meat quality characteristics and chemical composition of kudu (*Tragelaphus strepsiceros*), an African antelope species. *Food Chemistry, 104,* 565–570.

Munekata, P. E. S., Tomašević, I., Franco, D., Barba, F. J., Gómez, B., & Lorenzo, J. M. (2019). Goose, Duck and Garganey, In: JM Lorenzo, PES Munekata, FJ Barba, F Toldrá (eds.), *More than Beef, Pork and Chicken – The Production, Processing, and Quality Traits of Other Sources of Meat for Human Diet.* Springer Nature Switzerland AG, 313–345.

Mustafa, A. F., Chavarr, E. C., Mantilla, J. G., Mantilla, J. O., & Paredes, M. A. (2019). Effects of feeding flaxseed on performance, carcass trait, and meat fatty acid composition of Guinea pigs (*Cavia procellus*) under northern Peruvian condition. *Tropical Animal Health and Production, 51,* 2611–2617.

Nahashon, S. N., Aggrey, S. E., Adefope, N. A., & Amenyenu, A. (2006). Modeling growth characteristics of meat-type guinea fowl. *Poultry Science, 85,* 943–946.

Nasr, M. A. F., Abd-Elhamid, T., & Hussein, M. A. (2017). Growth performance, carcass characteristics, meat quality and muscle amino-acid profile of different rabbits breeds and their crosses. *Meat Science, 134,* 150–157.

Nanda, A.S., & Nakao, T. (2003). Role of buffalo in the socioeconomic development of rural Asia: Current status and future prospectus. *Animal Science Journal, 74,* 443–455.

Naveena, B. M., Sen. A.R., Muthukumar M., Girish, P. S., Praveen Kumar, Y., & Kiran, M. (2013). Carcass characteristics, compositions, physicochemical, microbial and sensory quality of emu meat. *British Poultry Science, 54,* 329–336.

Ndyoki, F. P. (2018). Physicochemical and microbiological attributes of Black Wildebeest (*Connochaetes gnou*) Muscles. MSc Thesis. Department of Consumer Science, University of Stellenbosch, South Africa.

Neethling, J., Hoffman, L. C., & Muller, M. (2016). Factors influencing the flavour of game meat: A review. *Meat Science, 113,* 139–153.

Neethling, J., Hoffman, L. C., & Britz, T. J. (2014). Impact of season on the chemical composition of male and female blesbok (*Damaliscus pygargus phillipsi*) muscles. *Journal of the Science for Food and Agriculture, 94,* 424–431.

Nettleton, J. A., Lovegrove, J. A., Mensink, R. P., & Schwab, U. (2016). Dietary fatty acids: Is it time to change the recommendations? *Annals of Nutrition & Metabolism, 68,* 249–257.

Ngoula, F., Guemdjo, T. M., Kenfack, A., Tadondjou, T. C., Nouboudem, S., Ngoumtsop, G., & Tsafack, B. (2017). Effects of heat stress on some reproductive parameters of male cavie (Cavia porcellus) and mitigation strategies using guava (*Psidium guajava*) leaves essential oil. *Journal of Thermal Biology, 64,* 67–72.

Nogueira-Filho, S. L. G., & Nogueira, S. S. D. C. (2018). Capybara meat: An extraordinary resource for food security in South America. *Meat Science*, *145*, 329–333.

Ntiamoah-Baidu, Y. (1998). Sustainable Use of Bush meat, in: *Wildlife Development Plan, 1998-2003*, Wildlife Department, Accra, p. 78.

Nuernberg, K., Dannenberger, D., Nuernberg, G., Ender, K., Voigt, J., Scollan, N. D., et al. (2005). Effect of a grass-based and a concentrate feeding system on meat quality characteristics and fatty acid composition of longissimus muscle in different cattle breeds. *Livestock Production Science*, *94*, 137–147.

Nuno, A., Blumenthal, J. M., Austin, T. J., Bothwell, J., Ebanks-Petrie, G., Godley, B. J., & Broderick, A. C. (2018). Understanding implications of consumer behavior for wildlife farming and sustainable wildlife trade. *Conservation Biology*, *32*, 390–400.

Nuwanyakpa, M., Lukefahr, S. D., Gudahl, D., & Ngoupayou, J. D. (1997). The current stage and future prospects of Guinea pig production under smallholder conditions in West Africa; 2. Cameroon case. *Livestock Research for Rural Development*, *9*, 43.

Oblakova, M., Ribarski, S., Oblakov, N., & Hristakieva, P. (2016). Chemical composition and quality of Turkey Broiler meat from crosses of layer light (LL) and meat heavy (MH) Turkey. *Trakia Journal of Sciences*, *2*, 142–147.

Ockerman, H. W., & Basu, L. (2009). Undomesticated food animals hunted and used for food. In: *Agricultural Sciences – Vol. I – Undomesticated food animals hunted and used for food*. Edited by Rattan Lal. Eolss Publishers Co. Oxford, UK. pp: 232–249.

Oda, S. H. I., Bressan, M. C., Freitas, R. T. F., Miguel, G. Z., Vieira, J. O., Faria, P. B., & Savian, T. V. (2004). Efeito do método de abate e do sexo na composição centesimal, perfil de ácidos graxos e colesterol da carne de capivara (*Hydrochaeris L.* 1766). *Ciência e Tecnologia de Alimentação*, *24*, 236–242.

Okuskhanova, E., Assenova, B., Rebezov, M., Amirkhanov, K., Yessimbekov, Z., Smolnikova, F., & Stuart, M. (2017). Study of morphology, chemical, and amino acid composition of red deer meat. *Veterinary World*, *10*, 623–629.

Olmedo, G. G., Farnés, O. C., Martín, M. I., Fernández, R. D., Andreu, G. N., Martínez, C. D., et al. (2004). Cultural, social and nutritional values of sea turtles in Cuba. Research Report. Universidad de La Habana, Cuba.

Onk, K., Yalcintan, H., Sari M., Isik S. A., Yakan A., & Ekiz B. (2019). Effects of genotype and sex on technological properties and fatty acid composition of duck meat. *Poultry Science*, *98*, 491–499.

Ordoñez, G. M., Pereyra, G. S., Gallardo, Z. L., & Cortéz, B. L. (2019). Effect of dietary sacha inchi pressed cake as a protein source on guinea pig carcass yield and meat quality. *Pakistan Journal of Nutrition*, *18*, 1021–1027.

Osthoff, G., Hugo, A., Bouwman, H., Buss, P., Govender, D., Joubert, C. C., & Swarts, J. C. (2010). Comparison of the lipid properties of captive, healthy wild, and pansteatitis-affected wild Nile crocodiles (*Crocodylus niloticus*). *Comparative Biochemistry and Physiology Part A: Molecular & Integrative Physiology*, *155*, 64–69.

Oyarekua, M. A., & Ketiku, A. O. (2010). The Nutrient Composition of the African Rat. *Advance Journal of Food Science and Technology*, *2*, 318–324.

Oz, F., & Yuzer, O. M., (2017). The effects of different cooking methods on the formation of heterocyclic aromatic amines in turkey meat. *Journal of Food Processing and Preservation*, *41*, e13196.

Oz, F., Kizil, M., & Celik, T. (2016). Effect of different cooking methods on the formation of heterocyclic aromatic amines in goose meat. *Journal of Food Processing and Preservation*, *40*, 1047–1053.

Özogul, F., Özogul, Y., Olgunoglu, A. I., & Boga, E. K. (2008). Comparison of fatty acid, mineral and proximate composition of body and legs of edible frog (*Rana esculenta*). *International Journal of Food Science and Nutrition*, *59*, 558–565.

Özoğul, Y., Özoğul, F., & Olgunoğlu, I. A. (2005) Fatty acid profile and mineral content of the wild snail (Helix pomatia) from the region of the south of Turkey. *European Food Research and Technology*, *221*, 547–549.

Patrick, M. E., Gilbert, M. J., Blaser, M. J., Tauxe, R. V., Wagenaar, J. A., & Fitzgerald, C. (2013). Human infections with new subspecies of *Campylobacter fetus*. *Emerging Infectious Diseases*, *19*, 1678–1680.

Paulsen, P., Bauer, A., Vodnansky, M., Winkelmayer, R., & Smulders, F. J. M. (2011). *Game Meat Hygiene in Focus Microbiology, Epidemiology, Risk Analysis and Quality Assurance*. Wageningen Academic Publishers, Wageningen, The Netherlands.

Pegg, R. B., Amarowicz, R., & Code, W. E. (2006). Nutritional characteristics of emu (Dromaius novaehollandiae) meat and its value-added products. *Food Chemistry*, *97*, 193–202.

Peiretti, P. G., & Meineri, G. (2010). Effects of diets with increasing levels of golden flaxseed on carcass characteristics, meat quality and lipid traits of growing rabbits. *Italian Journal of Animal Science, 9*, 372–377.

Peiretti, P. G., Masoero, G., & Meineri, G. (2011). Effects of replacing palm oil with maize oil and *Curcuma longa* supplementation on the performance, carcass characteristics, meat quality, and fatty acid profile of the perirenal fat and muscle of growing rabbits. *Animal, 5*, 795–801.

Peplow, A., Balaban, M., & Leak, F. (1990). Lipid composition of fat trimmings from farm-raised alligator. *Aquaculture, 91*, 339–348758.

Pereira, P. M. C. C., & Vicente, A. F. R. B. (2013). Meat nutritional composition and nutritive role in the human diet. *Meat Science, 93*, 586–592.

Perez, P., Maino, M., Guzman, R., Vaquero, A., Kobrich, C., & Pokniak, J. (2000). Carcass characteristics of llamas (*Lama glama*) reared in Central Chile. *Small Ruminant Research, 37*, 93–97.

Piaskowska, N., Daszkiewicz, T., Kubiak, D., & Janiszewski, P. (2015). The effect of gender on meat (*Longissimus lumborum*) quality characteristics in the fallow deer (*Dama L.*). *Italian Journal of Animal Science, 14*, 389–393.

Piironen, V., Toivo, J., & Lampi, A. M. (2002). New data for cholesterol contents in meat, fish, milk, eggs and their products consumed in Finland. *Journal of Food Composition and Analysis, 15*, 705–713.

Piña, C. I., Lucero, L. E., Simoncini, M., Peterson, G., & Tavella, M. (2016). Influence of flaxseed enriched diet in Broad-snouted caiman (*Crocodylia: alligatoridae*) meat. *Zootecnia Tropical, 34*, 25–33.

Pinheiro, M. S., & Moreira, J. R. (2013). Products and Uses of Capybaras, in: J. R. Moreira, K. M. P. M. B. Ferraz, E. A. Herrera, and D. W. Macdonald (eds), *Capybara: Biology, Use and Conservation of an Exceptional Neotropical Species*. Springer, New York, USA, 211–228.

Pinto, F., Tarricone, S., Marsico, G., Forcelli, M., Celi, R., & Rasulo, A. (2009). Nutritional quality of meats from young fallow deer (*Dama dama*) of different ages. *Progress in Nutrition, 11*, 57–67.

Pobiner, B. (2013). Evidence for meat-eating by early humans. *Nature Education Knowledge, 4*, 1.

Poławska, E., Marchewka, J., Cooper, R. G., Sartowska, K., Pomianowski, J., Jóźwik, A., et al. (2011). The ostrich meat – an updated review. II. *Nutritive value. Animal Science Papers and Reports, 29*, 89–97.

Poławska, E., Cooper, R. G., Jóźwik, A., & Pomianowski, J. (2013). Meat from alternative species - nutritive and dietetic value, and its benefit for human health - a review. *CyTA - Journal of Food, 11*, 37–42.

Polidori, P., Antonini, M., Torres, D., Beghelli, D., & Renieri, C. (2007). Tenderness evaluation and mineral levels of llama (*Lama glama*) and alpaca (*Lama pacos*) meat. *Meat Science, 77*, 599–601.

Polidori, P., Cavallucci, C., Beghelli, D., & Vincenzetti, S. (2009). Physical and chemical characteristics of donkey meat from Martina Franca breed. *Meat Science, 82*, 469–471.

Polidori, P., Pucciarelli, S., Ariani, A., Polzonetti, V., & Vincenzetti, S. (2015). A comparison of the carcass and meat quality of Martina Franca donkey foals aged 8 or 12 months. *Meat Science, 106*, 6–10.

Polidori, P., & Vincenzetti, S. (2013). Meat quality in donkeyfoals. *Italian Journal of Food Science, 25*, 390–393.

Polidori, P., Vincenzetti, S., Cavallucci, C., & Beghelli, D. (2008). Quality of donkey meat and carcass characteristics. *Meat Science, 80*, 1222–1224.

Qiao, Y., Huang, J., Chen, Y., Chen, H., Zhao, L., Huang, M., & Zhou, G. (2017). Meat quality, fatty acid composition and sensory evaluation of Cherry Valley, Spent Layer and Crossbred ducks. *Animal Science Journal, 88*, 156–165.

Quaresma, M.A.G., Pimentel, F.B., Ribeiro, A.P., Ferreira, J.D., Alves, S.P., Rocha, I., & Oliveira, M. B. P. P. (2016). Lipid and protein quality of common pheasant (*Phasianus colchicus*) reared in semi-extensive conditions. *Journal of Food Composition and Analysis, 46*, 88–95.

Quaresma, M. A. G., Trigo-Rodrigues, I., Alves, S. P., Martins, S. I. V., Barreto, A. S., & Bessa, R. J. B. 2012. Nutritional evaluation of the lipid fraction of Iberian red deer (*Cervus elaphus hispanicus*) tenderloin. *Meat Science, 92*, 519–524.

Ramakrishna, C., Vaithiyanathan, S., Muthukumar, M., Chatlod, L. R., Lavanya, P., & Kulkarni, V. V. (2017). Prevalence of Sarcocystosis in Buffalo meat in major cities of India. *Journal of Meat Science, 12*, 66–68.

Ramos, A., Cabrera, M.C., Del Puerto, M., & Saadoun, A. (2009). Minerals. Haem and non-haem iron contents of rhea meat. *Meat Science, 81*, 116–119.

Raut S. S., Sharma D. P., & Yadav S. (2016). Studies on assessment of Emu carcass characteristics and composition of lean meat. *Haryana Veterinary, 55*, 59–61.

Razmaite, V., & Pileckas, V. (2019). Fatty acid composition in maternal and foetal muscle tissues of beaver (*Castor fiber*). *Biologia, 74*, 97–101.

Razmaite, V., Pileckas, V., & Juškiene V. (2019). Effect of muscle anatomical location on fatty acid composition of beaver (*Castor fiber*) females. *Czech Journal of Food Sciences*, 37, 106–111.

Razmaitė, V., Šveistienė, R., & Švirmickas, G. J. (2011). Compositional Characteristics and Nutritional Quality of Eurasian Beaver (*Castor fiber*) Meat. *Czech Journal of Food Sciences*, 29, 480–486.

Realini, C. E., Duckett, S. K., Brito, G. W., Dalla Rizza, M., & De Mattos, D. (2004). Effect of pasture vs. concentrate feeding with or without antioxidants on carcass characteristics, fatty acid composition, and quality of Uruguayan beef. *Meat Science*, 66, 567–577.

Redgrave, T. G., & Jeffery, F. (1981). The lipids of Kangaroo meat. *Lipids*, 16, 626–627.

Rodríguez, P. E., Rodriguez-Ferrer, M., Nieto-Martinez, J., Ubeira, F., & Garate-Ormaechea, T. (2004). Trichinellosis outbreaks in Spain (1990–2001). *Enfermedades infecciosas y microbiologia clinica*, 22, 70–76.

Romanelli, P. F., Trabuco E., Scriboni A. B., Visentainer J. V., & de Souza N. E. (2008). Chemical composition and fatty acid profile of rhea (*Rhea americana*) meat. *Archivos Latinoamericanos De Nutrition*, 58, 201–205.

Roślewska, A., Stanek, M., Janicki, B., Cygan-Szczegielniak, D., Stasiak, K., & Buzała, M. (2016). Effect of sex on the content of elements in meat from wild boars (*Sus scrofa* L.) originating from the Province of Podkarpacie (south- -eastern Poland). *Journal of Elementology*, 21, 823–832.

Rule, D. C., Broughton, K. S., Shellito, S. M., & Maiorano, G. (2002). Comparison of muscle fatty acid profiles and cholesterol concentrations of bison, beef cattle, elk, and chicken. *Journal of Animal Science*, 80, 1202–1211.

Russo, C. (2005). Relazione sulla qualità della carcassa e della carne di daino (*Dama dama*). *Annali Della Facoltà Di Medicina. Veterinária*, 58, 207–212.

Russo, C., Balloni, S., Altomonte, I., Martini, M., Nuvoloni, R., Cecchi, F., et al. (2017). Fatty acid and microbiological profile of the meat (longissimus dorsi muscle) of wild boar (*Sus scropha scropha*) hunted in Tuscany. *Italian Journal of Animal Science*, 16, 1–8.

Saadoun, A., & Cabrera, M. C. (2008). A review of the nutritional content and technological parameters of indigenous sources of meat in South America. *Meat Science*, 80, 570–581.

Saadoun, A., Cabrera, M. C., & Castellucio, P. (2006). Fatty acids, cholesterol and protein content of nutria (*Myocastor coypus*) meat from an intensive production system in Uruguay. *Meat Science*, 72, 778–784.

Saadoun, A., Cabrera, M. C., Terevinto, A., & del Puerto, M. (2014). Why not a piece of meat of rhea, nutria, yacare, or vicugna for dinner? *Animal Frontier*, 4, 25–32.

Saadoun, A., & Cabrera, M. C. (2019). A review of productive parameters, nutritive value and technological characteristics of farmed nutria meat (*Myocastor coypus*). *Meat Science*, 148, 137–149.

Sabow A. B. (2020). Carcass characteristics, physicochemical attributes, and fatty acid and amino acid compositions of meat obtained from different Japanese quail strains. *Tropical Animal Health and Production*, 52, 131–140.

Saina, H., Kusina, N.T., Kusina, J.F., Bhebhe, E., & Lebel, S. (2005). Guinea fowl production by indigenous farmers in Zimbabwe. *Livestock Research for Rural Development*, 17(9): http://www.cipav.org.co/lrrd/lrrd17/9/saina7101.htm.

Salazar-Pressler, F., Melo-Ruíz, V., Sánchez-Herrera, K., López-Naranjo, F., & Gazga-Urioste, C. (2018). Mineral composition of the Donkey (*Equus asinus*) muscle meat. *Journal of Life Sciences*, 12, 100–104.

Saldanha, T., Santana, D. M. N., & Gaspar, A. (2002). Total lipids, fatty acid composition and cholesterol content of capybara (Hydrochoerus hydrochaeris) meat. *Brazilian Journal of Food Technology*, 5, 245–250.

Sales, J., & Hayes, J. P. (1996). Proximate, amino acid and mineral composition of ostrich meat. *Food Chemistry*, 56, 167–170.

Sales, J. (2007). Modelling the Protein and Amino Acid Requirements of the Greater Rhea (Rhea americana). *Turkish Journal of Veterinary and Animal Sciences*, 31, 403–406.

Sales, J., & Kotrba, R. (2013). Meat from wild boar (*Sus scrofa* L.): A review. *Meat Science*, 94, 187–201.

Sales, J., Navarro, J. L., Martella, M. B., Lizurume, M. E., Manero, A., Bellis, L., et al. (1999). Cholesterol content and fatty acid composition of rhea meat. *Meat Science*, 53, 73–75.

Salvá, B. K., Zumalacárregui, J. M., Figueira, A. C., Osorio, M. T., & Mateo, J. (2009). Nutrient composition and technological quality of meat from alpacas reared in Peru. *Meat Science*, 82, 450–455.

Sánchez-Macías, D., Barba-Maggi, L., Morales-delaNuez, A., & Palmay-Paredes, J. (2018). Guinea pig for meat production: A systematic review of factors affecting the production, carcass and meat quality. *Meat Science*, 143, 165–176.

Sari, M., Onk, K., Sisman, T., Tilki, M., & Yakan, A. (2015). Effects of different fattening systems on technological properties and fatty acid composition of goose meat. *European Poultry Science*, 79, 1–12.

Scherf, D. B. (2000). *World Watch List for domestic animal diversity* (3rd ed.). Rome: FAO.

Secci, G., Bovera, F., Musco, N., Husein, Y., & Parisi, G. (2020). Use of mirrors into free-range areas: effects on rabbit meat quality and storage stability. *Livestock Science, 239*, 104094.

Secci, G., Moniello, G., Gasco, L., Bovera F., & Parisi G. (2018). Barbary partridge meat quality as affected by Hermetia illucens and Tenebrio molitor larva meals in feeds. *Food Research International, 112*, 291–298.

Seong, P.-N., Kang, G.-H., Cho, S.-H., Park, B.-Y., Park, N.-G., Kim, J.-H., & Ba, H. V. (2019). Comparative study of nutritional composition and color traits of meats obtained from the horses and Korean native black pigs raised in Jeju Island. *Asian-Australasian Journal of Animal Science, 32*, 249–256.

Seong, P.-N., Kang, G.-H., Cho, S.-H., Park, B.-Y., Park, N.-G., Kim, J.-H., and Ba, H. V. (2016). The Differences in chemical composition, physical quality traits and nutritional values of Horse meat as affected by various retail cut types. *Asian-Australasian Journal of Animal Science, 29*, 89–99.

Sevillano-Cano, J., Camara-Martos, F., Zamora-Díaz, R., & Sevillano–Morales, J. S. (2021) Lead concentration in game migratory upland bird meat: Influence of ammunition impacts and health risk assessment. *Food Control, 124*, 107835.

Sevillano-Morales, J.S., Sevillano-Caño, J., Cámara-Martos, F., Moreno-Ortega, A., Amaro-López, M. A., Arenas-Casas, A., & Moreno-Rojas, R. (2020). Risk assessment of Cd, Cu, and Pb from the consumption of hunted meat: red-legged partridge and wild rabbit. *Biological Trace Element Research*, 10.1007/s12011-020-02290-w.

Shelepov, V.G., Uglov, V.A., Boroday, E.V., & Poznyakovsky, V.M. (2019). Chemical c omposition ofindigenous raw meats. *Foods and Raw Materials, 7*, 412–418.

Shul'gin, R. Y., Prikhod'ko, Y. V., & Shul'gin, Y. P. (2015). Kangaroo meat as a valuable raw material for dietary products. *Bioscience, and Biotechnology Research Asia, 12*, 333–340.

Siegel, G., & Ermilov, E. (2012). Omega-3 fatty acids: Benefits for cardio-cerebro-vascular diseases. *Atherosclerosis, 225*, 291–295.

Silva, E., Rosa, P., Arruda, M., & Rúbio, E. (2005). Determination of duffy phenotype of red blood cells in *Dasypus novemcinctus* and *Cabassous* sp. *Brazilian Journal of Biology, 65*, 555–557.

Simoncini, M. S., Lábaque, M. C., Perlo, F., Fernandez, M. E., Leiva, P. M. L., Paez, A. R., et al. (2020). Caiman latirostris meat characterization: Evaluation of the nutritional, physical and chemical properties of meat from sustainable ranching program in Argentina. *Aquaculture, 515*, 734570.

Simonová, M. P., Chrastinová, L., Mojto, J., Lauková, A., Szabóvá, R., & Rafay, R. (2010). Quality of rabbit meat and phyto-additives. *Czech Journal of Food Science, 28*, 161–167.

Simonová, M.P., Chrastinová, Ľ., Chrenková, M., Formelová, Z., Kandričáková, A., Bino, E., & Lauková, A. (2020). Benefits of Enterocin M and sage combination on the physicochemical traits, fatty acid, amino acid, and mineral content of rabbit meat. *Probiotics & Antimicrobial Protein, 12*, 1235–1245.

Simopoulos, A. P. (2016). Evolutionary aspects of the dietary omega-6/omega-3 fatty acid ratio: Medical implications. In: Alvergne, A., Jenkinson, C., Faurie, C. (Eds.), *Evolutionary Thinking in Medicine. Advances in the Evolutionary Analysis of Human Behaviour*. Springer, Cham, 119–134.

Sinclair, A. J., Mann, N. J. & Kelly, J. (1997). Kangaroo meat for human consumption. *Proceeding of the Nutrition Society of Australia, 21*, 52–57.

Smit, K. (2004). Meat quality characteristics of Blesbok (*Damaliscus dorcas* phillipsi) and Red hartebeest (*Alcelaphus buselaphus* caama) meat. MSc Thesis. Department of Consumer Science, University of Stellenbosch, South Africa.

Smith, M. A., Bush, R. D., van de Ven, R. J., Hall, E. J. S., Greenwood, P. L., & Hopkins, D. L. (2017). The impact of gender and age on the nutritional parameters of alpaca (*Vicugna pacos*) meat, colour stability and fat traits. *Meat Science, 123*, 21–28.

Soewu, D. A., Agbolade, M. O., Oladunjoye, R. Y., & Ayodele, A. I. (2014). Bioaccumulation of heavy metals in cane rat (*Thryonomys swinderianus*) in Ogun State, Nigeria. *Journal of Toxicology, Environment and Health Sciences, 6*, 154–160.

Sooryanarain, H., & Meng, X. J. (2019). Hepatitis E virus: Reasons for emergence in humans. *Current Opinion in Virology, 34*, 10–17.

Strakova E., Suchy P., Herzig I., Marada P., & Vitula F. (2016). Amino acid levels in muscle tissue of six wild feathered species. *Acta Universites Agriculture et Silviculture Mendeliane Brunensis, 64*, 1661–1666.

Strazdina, V., Jemeljanovs, A., & Sterna V. (2012). Fatty acids composition of Elk, Deer, Roe Deer and Wild Boar meat hunted in Latvia. *International Journal of Biological, Bimolecular, Agricultural, Food and Biotechnological Engineering, 6*, 765–768.

Strazdina, V., Jemeljanovs, A., & Sterna V. (2013). Nutritional value of wild animal meat. *Proceedings of the Latvian Academy of Sciences, 67*, 373–377.

Strazdina, V., Jemeljanovs, A., Sterna V. and Vjazevica, V. (2011). Evaluation of Protein Composition of Game Meat in Latvian Farms and Wildlife. *Agronomy Research*, *9*, 469–472.

Strazdina, V., Jemeljanovs, A., Sterna, V., & Ikauniece, D. (2014). Nutritional characteristics of wild boar meat hunted in Latvia. *Food Balt*, *1*, 32–36.

Strazdina, V., Jemeljanovs, A., Sterna, V., & Ikauniece, D. (2013). Nutrition value of deer, wild boar and beaver meat hunted in Latvia. *Proceedings of the Latvian Academy of Sciences*, *67*, 373–377.

Strazdina, V., Sterna, V., Jemeljanovs, A., Jansons, I., & Ikauniece, D. (2015). Investigation of beaver meat obtained in Latvia. *Agronomy Research*, *13*, 1096–1103.

Strmiskova, G., & Strmiska, F. (1992). Contents of mineral substances in venison. *Food/Nahrung*, *36*, 307–308.

Suchy P., Strakova E., Kroupa L., Steinhauser L., & Herzig I. (2010). Values of selected biochemical and mineral metabolism indicators in feathered game. *Acta Verterinaria Brno*, *79*, S9–S12.

Suman, S. P., & McMillin, K.W. (2014). Contributions of non-traditional meat animals to global food security and agricultural economy. *Animal Frontiers*, *4*, 4–5.

Swanepoel, D., Boomker, J. & Kriek, N.P.J. (2000). Selected chemical parameters in the blood and metals in the organs of the Nile crocodile, *Crocodylus niloticus*, in the Kruger National Park. *Onderstepoort Journal of Veterinary Research*, *67*, 141–148.

Swanson, D., Block, R., & Mousa, S. A. (2012). Omega-3 fatty acids EPA and DHA: health benefits throughout life. *Advances in Nutrition*, *3*, 1–7.

Szymczyk, K., & Zalewski K. (2003). Copper, zinc, lead and cadmium content in liver and muscles of Mallards (*Anas Platyrhychnos*) and other hunting Fowl species in Warmia and Mazury in 1999-2000. *Polish Journal of Environmental Studies*, *12*, 381–386.

Tajik, H., Rezaei, S. A., Alamouti, M. R. P., Moradi, M., & Dalir- Naghadeh, B. (2010). Mineral contents of muscle (*longissimus dorsi* thoracis) and liver in river buffalo (*Bubalus bubalis*). *Journal of Muscle Foods*, *21*, 459–473.

Takeuchi Fernandes, V. R., Rodrigues de Souza, M. L., Gasparino, E., Coutinho, M. E., Visentainer, J. V., Spinola Bérgamo, A., & Souza dos Reis Goes, E. (2017). Commercial cuts of Pantanal caiman meat according to sex. *Ciência Rural*, *47*, 1–7.

Tandzong, M. L. C., Mbougueng, P. D., Womeni, H. M., & Mweugang, N. N. (2015). Effect of cassava leaf (*Manihot esculenta*) level in guinea pigs (*Cavia porcellus*) meal on the physico-chemical and technological properties of its meat. *Food and Nutrition Sciences*, *6*, 1408–1421.

Taylor, C. M., Golding, J., & Emond, A. M. (2014). Intake of game birds in the UK: Assessment of the contribution to the dietary intake of lead by women of childbearing age and children. *Public Health Nutrition*, *17*, 1125–1129.

Tesařová, S., Ježek, F., Hulankova, R., Plhal, R., Drimaj, J., Steinhauserova, I., & Borilova, G. (2018). The individual effect of different production systems, age and sex on the chemical composition of wild boar meat. *Acta Veternary Brno*, *87*, 395–402.

Teye, M., Fuseini, A., & Odoi, F. N. A. (2020). Consumer acceptance, carcass and sensory characteristics of meats of farmed and wild cane rats (*Thryonomys swinderianus*). *Scientific African*, *8*, e00461.

Tlhong, T. M. (2008). Meat quality of raw and processed Guineafowl (*Numeda maleagris*). MSc Diss. Stellenbosch University, South Africa.

Thornton, P. K. (2010). Livestock production: recent trends, future prospects. *Philosophical Transactions of the Royal Society B*, *365*, 2853–2867.

Tokur, B., Gürbüz, R. D., & Özyurt, G. (2008). Nutritional composition of frog (*Rana esculanta*) waste meal. *Bioresource Technology*, *99*, 1332–1338.

Trocino, A., Birolo, M., Dabbou, S., Gratta, F., Rigo, N., & Xiccato, G. (2018). Effect of age and gender on carcass traits and meat quality of farmed brown hares. *Animal*, *12*, 864–871.

Tu, Z.-C., Zeitlin, G., Gagner, J.-P., Keo, T., Hanna, B. A., & Blaser, M. J. (2004). *Campylobacter fetus* of reptile origin as a human pathogen. *Journal of clinical microbiology*, *42*, 4405–4407.

Tulley, R. T., Malekian, F. M., Rood, J. C., Lamb, M. B., Champagne, C. M., Redman, S. M., Jr., & Raby, C. T. (2000). Analysis of the nutritional content of *Myocastor coypus*. *Journal of Food Composition and Analysis*, *13*, 117–125.

Tůmová, E., Chodová, D., Svobodová, J., Uhlířová, L., and Volek, Z. (2015). Carcass composition and meat quality of Czech genetic resources of nutrias (*Myocastor coypus*). *Czech Journal of Animal Science*, *60*, 479–486.

Turpeinen, A. M., Mutanen, M., Aro, A., Salminen, I., Basu, S., Palmquist, D. L., & Griinari, J.M. (2002). Bioconversion of vaccenic acid to conjugated linoleic acid in humans. *American Journal of Clinical Nutrition*, *76*(3), 504–510.

USDA & USDHHS. (2015). Dietary Guidelines for Americans 2015-2020, eighth ed. Available at: http://health.gov/dietaryguidelines/2015/guidelines/.
USDA. (2013). National nutrient database for standard reference, Release 20. http://fnic.nal.usda.gov/food-composition (consulted: 19/02/2013).
USDA. (2015). Scientific report of the 2015 dietary guidelines advisory committee. Part D, chapter 1. 17.
Valencak, T., & Gamsjäger, L. (2014). Lipids in tissues of wild game: overall excellent fatty acid composition, even better in free-ranging individuals, In. P Paulsen, A Bauer, & FJM Smulders (eds). Trends in game meat hygiene, Wageningen Academic Publishers, Wageningen, Netherlands, pp. 335–344.
Van Schalkwyk, S. (2004). Meat quality characteristics of three South African game species: Black wildebeest (*Connochaetes gnou*), Blue wildebeest (*Connochaetes taurinus*) and Mountain reedbuck (*Redunca fulvorufula*). MSc Thesis. Department of Consumer Science, University of Stellenbosch, South Africa.
Van Vliet, N., Moreno, J., Gómez, J., Zhou, W., Fa, J. E., Golden, C., Alves, R. R. N., & Nasi, R. (2017). Bushmeat and human health: Assessing the evidence in tropical and sub-tropical forests. *Ethnobiology and Conservation*, 6, 3.
Van Zyl, A., van der Merue, M., & Blignaut, A. S. (1999). Meat quality and carcass characteristics of the vondo, *Thryonomys swingerianus*. *South African Journal of Animal Science*, 29, 120–123.
Van Zyl, L., & Ferreira, A. V. (2004). Physical and chemical carcass composition of springbok (*Antidorcas marsupialis*), blesbok (*Damaliscus dorcas phillipsi*) and impala (*Aepyceros melampus*). *Small Ruminant Research*, 53, 103–109.
Vengušt, G., & Vengušt, A. (2004). Some minerals as well as trace and toxic elements in livers of fallow deer (Dama dama) in Slovenia. *European Journal of Wildlife Research*, 50, 59–61.
Vicente Neto, J., Bressan, M. C., Bitencourt Faria, P., Oliveira e Vieira, J., Cardoso, M. G., de Abreu Glória, M.B., & Telo da Gama, L. (2010). Fatty acid profiles in meat from Caiman yacare (*Caiman crocodilus yacare*) raised in the wild or in captivity. *Meat Science*, 85, 752–758.
Vicenti, A., Ragni, M., di Summa, A., Marsico, G., & Vonghia, G. (2003). Influence of feeds and rearing system on the productive performances and the chemical and fatty acid composition of hare meat. *Food Science and Technology International*, 9, 279–284.
Vinauskiene, R., Leskauskaite, D., & Akromaite, E. (2019). Nutritional composition of farm chinchilla (*Chinchilla lanigera*) meat. *Journal of Food Composition and Analysis*, 84, 103303.
Volpelli, L. A., Valusso, R., Morgante, M., Pittia, P., & Piasentier, E. (2003). Meat quality in male fallow deer (*Dama dama*): Effects of age and supplementary feeding. *Meat Science*, 65, 555–562.
Wang, Q., Wu, J. P., Zhang, S. G., Zhang, Y. B., Zhang, H. X., & Fan, E. (2009). Fatty acid composition analysis from the kidney of yak by gas-chromatography. *Chromatographia*, 69, 139–143.
Wang, Q., Zhao, X., Ren, Y., Fan, E., Chang, H., & Wu, H. (2013). Effects of high-pressure treatment and temperature on lipid oxidation and fatty acid composition of yak (*Poephagus grunniens*) body fat. *Meat Science*, 94, 489–494.
Webb, E.C. (2014). Goat meat production, composition, and quality. *Animal Frontiers*, 4, 33–37.
Webb, E.C., Casey, N. H., & Simela, L. (2005). Goat meat quality. *Small Ruminant Research*, 60, 153–166.
Wiktorowska-Owczarek, A., Berezińska, M., & Nowak, J. Z. (2015). PUFAs: Structures, metabolism and functions. *Advances in Clinical and Experimental Medicine*, 24, 931–941.
Williams, P. (2007). Nutritional composition of red meat. *Nutrition & Dietetics*, 64, S113–S119.
Williams, V. L., Moshoeu, T. J., & Alexander, G. J. (2016). Reptiles sold as traditional medicine in Xipamanine and Xiquelene markets (Maputo, Mozambique). *South African Journal of Science*, 112, 1–9.
Williamson, J., Ryland, D., Suh, M., & Aliani, M. (2014). The effect of chilled conditioning at 4 °C on selected water and lipid-soluble flavor precursors in Bison longissimus dorsi muscle and their impact on sensory characteristics. *Meat Science*, 96, 136–146.
Wolfe, N. D., Switzer, W. M., Carr, J. K., Bhullar, V. B., Shanmugam, V., Tamoufe, U., et al. (2004). Naturally acquired simian retrovirus infections in central African hunters. *The Lancet*, 363, 932–937.
Wood, J. D. (2017). Meat Composition and Nutritional Value, In: Toldera F., 8th edition, *Lawrie's Meat Science*, Woodhead Publishing, Elsevier Ltd., Duxford, CB22 4QH, UK, pp. 635–660.
Wu, G. S., & Huang, C. H. (2008). Estimation of dietary copper requirement of juvenile soft-shelled turtles, *Pelodiscus sinensis*. *Aquaculture*, 280, 206–210.
Yemi, O. R., Asiru, R. A., & Shokoya, D. A. (2015). Heavy metals (Cd, Pb, Cu, Fe, Cr, Mn, Zn) contents in ungulates of Ogun State Agricultural Farm Settlement, Ago-Iwoye, Nigeria. *Journal of Biology and Life Science*, 6, 119–129

Zhang, L., Sun, B., Yu, Q., Ji, Q., Xie, P., Li, H., et al. (2016). The breed and sex effect on the carcass size performance and meat quality of yak in different muscles. *Korean Journal of Food Science and Technology, 36*, 223–229.

Zhang, S. G., Liu, T., Brown, M. A., & Wu, J. P. (2015). Comparison of *longissimus dorsi* fatty acids profiles in Gansu Black Yak and Chinese Yellow Cattle Steers and Heifers. *Korean Journal of Food Science and Technology, 35*, 286–292.

Zhang, X., Armani, A., Giusti, A., Wen, J., Fan, S., & Ying, X. (2021). Molecular authentication of crocodile dried food products (meat and feet) and skin sold on the Chinese market: Implication for the European market in the light of the new legislation on reptile meat. *Food Control, 124*, 107884.

Zi, X. D., Zhong, G. H., Wen, Y. L., Zhong, J. C., Liu, C. L., Ni, Y. A., et al. (2004). Growth performance, carcass composition and meat quality of Jiulong-yak (*Bos grunniens*). *Asian-Australian Journal of Animal Science, 17*, 410–414.

Ziauddin, K. S., Mahendrakar, N. S., Rao, D. N., Ramesh, B. S., & Amla, B. L. (1994). Observations on some chemical and physical characteristics of buffalo meat. *Meat Science, 37*, 103–113.

Żochowska-Kujawska, J., Sobczak, M., & Lachowicz, K. (2009). Comparison of the texture, rheological properties and myofibre characteristics of SM (semimembranosus) muscles of selected species of game animals. *Polish Journal of Food and Nutrition Sciences, 59*, 243–246.

Zomborszky, Z., Szentmihalyi, G., Sarudi, I., Horn, P., & Szabo, C. S. (1996). Nutrient composition of muscles in deer and boar. *Journal of Food Science, 61*, 625–627.

Zygoyiannis, D. (2006). Sheep production in the world and in Greece. *Small Rumin Res., 62*, 143–147.

9 Cultured Meat: Challenges in the Path of Production and 3D Food Printing as an Option to Develop Cultured Meat-Based Products

Zuhaib F. Bhat[1], James D. Morton[2],
Alaa El-Din Ahmed Bekhit[3], Sunil Kumar[1], and Hina F. Bhat[4]
[1]Livestock Products Technology, SKUAST-Jammu, India
[2]Department of Wine, Food and Molecular Biosciences, Faculty of Agriculture and Life Sciences, Lincoln University, New Zealand
[3]Department of Food Science, University of Otago, Dunedin, New Zealand
[4]Animal Biotechnology, SKUAST-Kashmir, India

CONTENTS

- 9.1 Introduction 272
- 9.2 Possibilities for Production 272
- 9.3 3D-Printing of Muscle Products 273
  - 9.3.1 3D-Printed Beef Products 274
  - 9.3.2 3D-Printed Poultry Products 275
  - 9.3.3 3D-Printed Fish/Seafood Products 276
  - 9.3.4 3D-Printing Using Transglutaminase 278
  - 9.3.5 3D-Printed Meat Products for Special Needs 279
  - 9.3.6 3D-Printed Meat Products Using Cultured Meat 280
- 9.4 Challenges in the Path of Cultured Meat 282
  - 9.4.1 Production Challenges 283
  - 9.4.2 Resemblance to Meat in Structure, Sensory Attributes and Nutrition 284
  - 9.4.3 Acceptance Issues 284
  - 9.4.4 Ethical Aspects 285
  - 9.4.5 Sensory Aspects 285
  - 9.4.6 Environmental Considerations 285
  - 9.4.7 Religious Aspects 288
  - 9.4.8 Cost and Affordability 289
  - 9.4.9 Safety Assurance 289
  - 9.4.10 Sustainability Issues 290
  - 9.4.11 Funding and Research 290
  - 9.4.12 Other Risks 290
- 9.5 Conclusion 291
- References 291

9.1 INTRODUCTION

Due to ethical and environmental changes that took place in the 20th century, several established human practices are no longer perceived positively by new generations. One of these practices that is not widely accepted, at least in certain societies, is the farming and slaughtering of animals for food. Environmental factors such as the impact of intensive farming, the carbon footprint of animal production and the use of massive water and land resources for the seemingly inefficient plant to meat conversion have created a debate about the sustainability of animal and, in particular cattle, farming. Furthermore, humane slaughtering and the concept of sacrificing one creature's life for the pleasure of another has been proposed to be animalistic and unfair. Despite the development of legislation that addresses issues about animal welfare and ensures minimal animal suffering, the global philosophical debate over the morality of eating meat and slaughtering animals has been gaining momentum. One of the alternatives that have attracted great publicity and gained global interest is *in vitro* meat. The concept of growing meat from cells has been around for many years with most of the reviews on the topic credit Frederick Edwin Smith and Winston Churchill with the vision of growing meat without the need to slaughter animals. Recent biotechnological development such as the ability of stem cells to proliferate into muscle myotubes *in vitro* (Seale & Rudnicki, 2000) paved the way to make this vision to become a reality. *In vitro* meat, also known as clean meat and cultured meat, as a concept has been progressing at a fast rate and a concise timeline of the significant steps in the development of *in vitro* meat is available in the following link: https://en.wikipedia.org/wiki/Timeline_of_cellular_agriculture. The technology aims to grow tissue from stem cells that have been harvested from a biopsy obtained from a live donor animal, bird or fish (Bhat et al., 2015; Bhat & Bhat, 2011). The stem cells will be grown in a media that contain all required nutrients (including hormones, growth factors and foetal bovine serum) to facilitate cell division and proliferation in a similar fashion to conventional cell culture. The cells will form a network of myotubes that can be transferred into a construct that allows the growth of muscle tissue (Bhat et al., 2014). Culturing meat in a laboratory is a novel and emerging technology that has been proposed to provide meat without involving slaughtering animals and with a relatively small ecological footprint (Bhat et al., 2017). There have been numerous claims and speculations in favour of this new product, as yet unproven and unclear, giving it huge publicity and superiority over conventional meat (Bhat et al., 2019). Cultured meat production is often proposed as one of the solutions to overcome the negative environmental impacts associated with conventional meat production systems. However, recent research has raised a big question mark over this claim (Lynch & Pierrehumbert, 2019). While advanced research has been carried out by companies and various research institutions in this area, there are several challenges that need to be overcome before it can become a commercial reality and as such cultured meat cannot help with the urgent environmental problems that we face currently (Tuomisto, 2019). The first cultured beef burger was prepared by Mark Post who offered the burger to a taste panel in 2013 (the panellists were Josh Schonwald and Hanni Rutzler, a food writer and a nutritionist, respectively). The stem cells used in the preparation were sourced from the thigh of a cattle and an 85 g beef burger was produced at a cost of US$ 330,000 (Fernandes et al., 2019; Post, 2014).

A complementary technology that has been gaining momentum is the use of the 3D printing of stem cells into structures that contain different stem cells for muscle and fat. Similarly, the use of printed meat products has been extensively investigated due to the ability to design foods for special needs that fit seniors and infants as well as having innovative designs.

9.2 POSSIBILITIES FOR PRODUCTION

Recently, Singapore became the first country to give regulatory approval to produce the world's first cultured meat (https://www.theguardian.com/environment/2020/dec/02/no-kill-lab-grown-meat-to-go-on-sale-for-first-time). This approval will pave way for a US-based start-up 'Eat Just' to sell lab-grown chicken, initially in the form of chicken nuggets at a price of 50$ a piece (The BBC, 2020).

Several companies and research institutions are investigating different possibilities for cultured meat production. Scientists of the University of Bath are investigating the development of slaughter-free bacon and are growing pig cells on blades of grass, as a natural and edible scaffold, as a possible option to scale up the process (Briggs, 2019). It may sound equally strange but perhaps an attempt to culture meat within the sterile and nutrient-rich floating environment inside coconuts still on the trees should also be experimented. Cell culture and tissue culture (i.e., use of growth media that contain required nutrients and under sterile environment) are two more traditional methods that have been extensively researched by start-ups and institutions for possible production at commercial scales. While cell culture allows growth and differentiation of stem cells harvested from farm animals in the media in presence of specific chemical and physical stimuli, tissue culture involves expanding the volume of skeletal muscle explants in a medium as self-organizing constructs that results in highly structured meat. Although several stem cells could be used for cell culture, adult tissue-derived myoblasts or satellite cells, obtained from farm animal biopsies, are the preferred cell types. These cells can be grown on a scaffold in a medium within a bioreactor and fuse together to form myotubes which develop into myofibers and could be harvested from the scaffolds to produce processed meat products. While several scaffold designs and materials, such as collagen meshwork and collagen beads, have been proposed, the current scaffold-based methods can only produce thin monocyte layers (100–200 µm) and lack the structure of native skeletal muscle tissue (Bhat et al., 2020; Carrier et al., 1999). The meat produced by tissue culture techniques resembles more closely to farm-produced meat in that it contains all the tissues in the right proportions and by co-culturing with other cell types along with myoblasts, it is feasible to produce highly structured meat (Bhat et al., 2017; Dennis et al., 2001). However, since both of these methods lack a functional circulatory system to deliver oxygen and nutrients to the cells and to eliminate the metabolic waste products, developing muscles at a commercial scale is currently a big challenge. Figure 9.1 suggests a general design for cell culture-based production of cultured meat.

In addition to cell culture and tissue culture, some other speculative methods of production, such as nanotechnology, organ-printing and biophotonics, have also been proposed. Among these technologies, organ-printing appears to be more promising than others and can provide a feasible option for generation of fully structured meat in future. When combined with principles of tissue engineering, three-dimensional (3D) or four-dimensional (4D) bioprinting technologies are able to produce biological tissue constructs that mimic the anatomical, structural, and functional features of native organs or tissues (Gillispie et al., 2019). Since it deposits biomaterials and multiple cell types into a single 3D tissue architecture with high precision, 3D-bioprinting is one of the most powerful and attractive tools for providing functionally and anatomically similar organs or tissues for regenerative tissue and organ clinical applications. Unfortunately, not enough has been achieved in this direction to produce fully structured meat for human consumption. However, studies have been conducted recently to use 3D- or 4D-food printing for the development of several food products including fish and meat products by using food inks and mostly extrusion-based printers. The cultured meat that is produced right now in the laboratories and start-up companies is produced in the form of loose cells or tissues and can only be used for the development of processed/ground meat products such as sausages, patties and nuggets. This 3D-food printing technology can provide an attractive option for the production of meat products from this loose cultured meat and can provide variety and products with complex designs. Since the production of fully structured meat by organ-printing is not possible yet, the remaining discussion in this chapter about 3D-printing will be limited to studies that have used 3D-food printing to produce meat and fish products before returning to the challenges facing cultured meat.

9.3 3D-PRINTING OF MUSCLE PRODUCTS

Due to its numerous advantages, additive manufacturing, also known as 3D printing or solid freeform fabrication, has recently received huge attention from academia and industry (Wang et al., 2018).

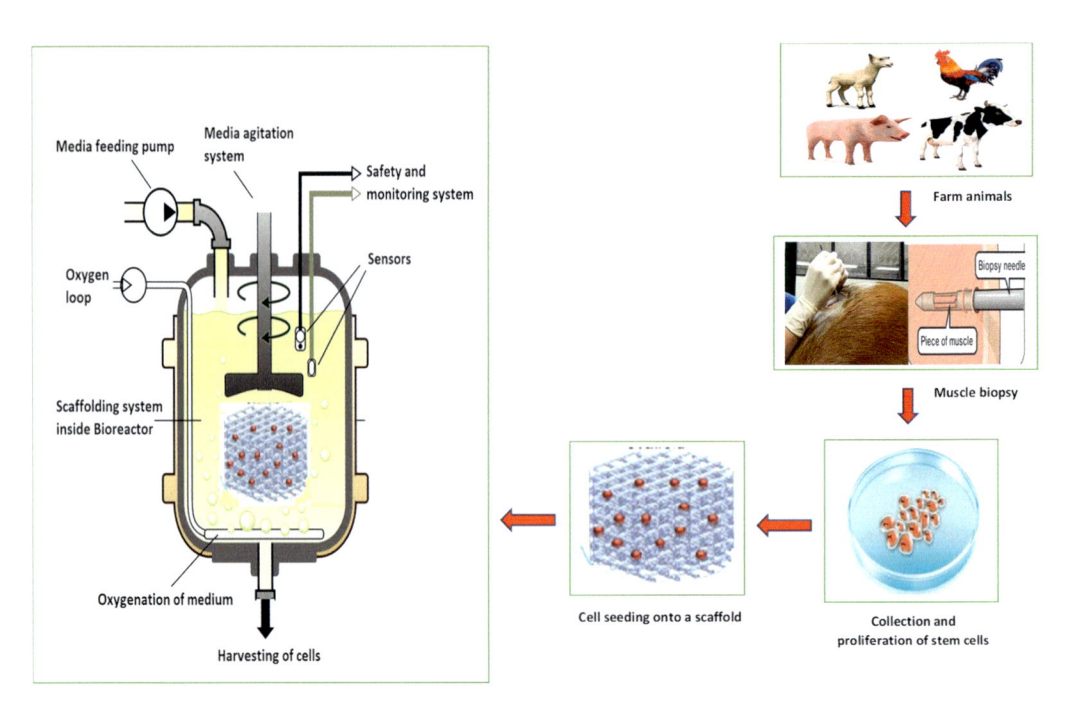

FIGURE 9.1 Cultured meat production system.

This technology has applications in several spheres from biomedical engineering and design science to aeronautics, mechanical engineering, biotechnology, pharmaceuticals and food (Portanguen et al., 2019). This technology uses a computer-aided design model to produce 3D food products and has the potential to revolutionize the food manufacturing processes by offering unmatched levels of customization in terms of nutrition and food appearance (Bhat et al., 2019; Handral et al., 2020). The technology was introduced to the food sector by Cornell university researchers (Periard et al., 2007) and has several environmental and economic benefits. The 3D printing of foods can produce some complex and artistic designs and shapes otherwise difficult to produce by conventional means and offers several advantages to the food sector such as personalized and digitalized nutrition, simplifying supply chain, customized food designs, and broadening the source of available food material (Liu et al., 2017). This technology can cater to personalized needs by tailoring the foods with specific characteristics meeting the requirements of specific individuals such as specific nutritional needs, specific shape, calorie intake, texture, or flavour. Using similar technology, 4D printing is an extension of 3D printing that adds the dimension of transformation over time (Javaid & Haleem, 2018).

Based on their functioning, four different types of printers are currently available for printing foods viz. binder jetting, extrusion, inkjet, and selective sintering. Several food printers have been specifically developed for printing foods such as Foodini, f3d, ChefJet, Choc Creator, NASA printer, Discov3ry Extruder, Cake and Chocolate Extruder, 3D Everything Printer, 3D Fruit Printer, Palatable-Looking Goop Printer, and Original Food Printer (Marsden, 2013; Molitch-Hou, 2014). Extrusion-based 3D printers are most popular for food printing and studies on the development of 3D printed meat and fish products are currently mostly focused on rheological and physical properties.

9.3.1 3D-Printed Beef Products

Dick et al. (2019) studied the integrity of the designed external and internal structures of 3D-printed beef products. A meat paste base was prepared from 85% beef and 15% water to which NaCl (1.5%) and guar gum (0.5%) were added. A rectangular prism design (L × W × H = 40 × 40 × 10 mm) was followed with variation in the fat layers (0, 1, 2 and 3 layers of 1 mm height of lard) within the structure. The layers of the lard were printed in the interior of the structure and were surrounded by the meat paste to avoid fat loss during cooking. A dual nozzle model 3D printer performed the printing process at ambient temperature using a rectilinear infill pattern, and three different infill densities were evaluated (50, 75 and 100%). The study evaluated the effect of infill density and fat content on the quality characteristics of the composite-layer 3D printed beef before and after sous-vide cooking. The developed products were successfully cooked, and the infill density was inversely ($P<0.05$) related to shrinkage and cohesiveness and contributed proportionally ($P<0.05$) to hardness, chewiness, and moisture retention. While no effect of the infill density was observed on the fat retention, the fat content inversely ($P<0.05$) affected the hardness, chewiness, and fat and moisture retention. The fat content proportionally ($P<0.05$) affected the shrinkage, cooking loss and cohesiveness. It is important to highlight that the use of ingredients such as lard, a limited animal resource, will not be feasible for the commercial production of the printed meat products based on cultured meat and will not make a good case for this type of meat products from an animal welfare point of view.

Lindström (2020) studied the effect of ultrasonic-assisted drying of minced beef on 3D printability and rheological properties. The concept behind the study was to develop meat powder from underutilized or inferior cuts of meat for the development of 3D-printed meat products. Beef mince was thermally processed at 85 °C for 10 min in a water bath to extract fat and to render it microbiologically safe. The processed beef mince was dried in an oven at 105 °C for 24 hours or using a new ultrasonic transducer set to increase drying speed (1 or 2 kW, 40 kHz, –15 °C or 40 °C). The food inks were developed for 3D printing of the meat products by using the dried meat powder and two thickening agents viz. xanthan gum and sodium alginate combined with calcium carbonate and an acidifier (lactic acid, 9%). Drying of meat at low temperature (–15 °C) resulted in a more porous product that was easily milled to a lower particle size, one of the necessary requirements for 3D printing. Pastes that were prepared by using meat dried at –15 °C also provided higher viscosity, which was better for 3D printing. Ultrasound processing had no significant effect on the quality of dried beef.

9.3.2 3D-Printed Poultry Products

Wilson et al. (2020) evaluated the development and the feasibility of customized shapes for 3D-printed chicken nuggets. Chicken meat was ground to a fine paste in a domestic mixer grinder and was mixed with different levels of refined wheat flour (1:1, 2:1, and 3:1, w/w) to optimize the processing conditions for the development of 3D-printed chicken nuggets. The settings optimized for printing chicken nuggets using 2:1 formulation were 0.82 mm nozzle size, 0.64 mm nozzle height, 1000 mm/min printing speed, 360 rpm extrusion motor speed, 8.8 mm^3/s extrusion rate, and 4 bar extrusion pressure. The fibrillar protein network of chicken meat made it unsuitable for 3D printing and the addition of refined wheat flour improved the printability of the ground chicken (Wilson et al., 2020). The printed samples were hot-air dried and cooked by deep oil frying. Hot air drying, which was optimized for 10 min at 58 °C, aided in the removal of some moisture and that helped in retaining the structure of the construct during the cooking process. Further, the hot air-drying process reduced oil uptake during subsequent deep oil frying by decreasing the rate of exchange of moisture and oil and therefore, reduced the surface oil of final products (Krishnaraj et al., 2019). The dried constructs were cooked in oil at 175 °C for about 1 min until the colour changed to golden brown due to the Maillard reaction between amino acids of chicken and carbonyl sugar components of the refined wheat flour (Park & Kim, 2016; Rahimi et al., 2018). The cooking resulted in a moisture loss of about 28% from the 3D printed samples and was attributed to the denaturation of the proteins induced by the high-temperature cooking and the loss of moisture binding. The cooking imparted a desirable crispy texture and gave a characteristic flavour and taste to the 3D-printed chicken nuggets. Fat retention and the percentage shrinkage of the cooked product was found to be 77% and 10%, respectively. This significant shrinkage was attributed to the loss of moisture during high-temperature cooking due to the differences in partial pressure of the cooking oil and the printed chicken nuggets. Fat displacement during cooking (heat treatment) resulted in a porous structure that contributed a characteristic texture to the 3D-printed chicken nuggets (Dick et al., 2019). The fat retention during deep oil frying, which depends on the total time of the cooking and the temperature of the oil, is due to the exchange of moisture with the fat.

The acceptance of the cooked 3D-printed nuggets was assessed by a sensory evaluation and the mean score of 7.38 was obtained for overall acceptability of the nuggets which is much higher than the 4.0–5.5 cut-off score for acceptance and marketability of the product (Severini et al., 2017), indicating the potential of the 3D printed nuggets for commercialization. Thus, 3D printed cooked chicken nuggets that had crispy texture, 56% moisture, 22% carbohydrates, 19% protein, 0.76% fat and an energy value of 166 kcal/100 g were successfully developed in different customized shapes.

Lipton et al. (2010) evaluated the development of multi-material 3D constructs with a complex internal structure suitable for cooking methods such as broiling, baking, and frying. Different shaped 3D products were successfully printed using turkey meat with the aid of transglutaminase. The developed turkey meat constructs were cooked by the sous-vide method and were sensorily evaluated and approved by expert chefs for taste and texture.

9.3.3 3D-Printed Fish/Seafood Products

Wang et al. (2018) evaluated the possibility of using fish surimi gel as a food material for 3D printing. Fresh silver carp fillets were minced, washed twice with cold water (mince: water = 1:3 v/w, 4 °C) and centrifuged (700 g at 4 °C) for 15 min and the obtained surimi mince had a moisture content of 82% and pH of 6.8. The surimi mince was mixed with different levels of NaCl (0–2.0% w/w) in a mixer to evaluate its effect on quality characteristics of the surimi gel such as gel strength, rheological property, water holding capacity and microstructure. The 3D printing system used for extrusion of surimi samples onto a polished transparent plastic polymer plate had three major components viz. an X-Y-Z positioning system, an extrusion system and a feed hopper with auger mixer and conveyor. The printing process was done at room temperature using nozzles of circular shape with diameters of 0.8, 1.5 and 2.0 mm. With increased shear rate, the significantly decreasing viscosity indicated that the surimi gels are shear-thinning and pseudoplastic fluids. Further, a general decrease was observed in the viscosity of the gel with an increased concentration of NaCl, suggesting that it would aid in the flow of the gel through the nozzle and after deposition would become vicious to hold the shape of the construct. The lower values of the loss modulus (G″) than the storage modulus (G′) in the linear viscoelastic region indicated its potential to form a gel-like structure or elastic gel. With increasing oscillatory frequency, both loss modulus (G″) and the storage modulus (G′) increased progressively, inducing an increase in the internal friction of the material. With increasing concentration of NaCl from 0 to 1.5 g/100 g, both G″ and G′ decreased significantly and continuously at any oscillatory frequency, which was attributed to the denaturation of the light meromyosin (myosin tail), which induced the redistribution of intra- and inter-molecular forces (Wang et al., 2018) and increased the fluidity of the surimi while weakening the elastic component of the pre-gel structure (Tahergorabi & Jaczynski, 2012). Ideally, the surimi slurry should be mixable and printable within the range of the extrusion pressure of the printer and should be able to retain its shape after extrusion and capable of fusing with earlier printed layers. Based on the rheological analysis of the study, surimi gels containing 1.5 g NaCl/100 g can be successfully used for 3D printing and the addition of NaCl helped the flow of the slurry from the printer nozzle in time and to retain the shape of the construct. The study also optimized the printing parameters for geometrical accuracy and dimensions of the printed construct. For the given printer, a nozzle height of 5.0 mm, a nozzle diameter of 2.0 mm, a nozzle moving speed of 28 mm/s and an extrusion rate of 0.003 cm^3/s resulted in samples accurately matching the targeted geometry with fine resolution, no compressed deformation and fewer point defects.

Chen et al. (2021) studied the effect of different concentrations of NaCl and water on the rheological properties and 3D printability of surimi gels. The study also evaluated the suitability of low field nuclear magnetic resonance parameters (LF-NMR) and dielectric characteristics (at 915 and 2450 MHz) to rapidly predict the rheological properties and estimate the printability of the surimi gels. Frozen silver carp surimi was cut into small pieces after thawing and chopped for 2 min in a mixer, followed by the addition of NaCl at 0, 1, 2, and 3 g/100 g and again chopped for 5 min. Water was added in the form of ice to adjust the water content of the samples to 76.5, 80.0, 83.5 and 87.0 g/100 and the samples were equilibrated at 4 °C for 12 h before printing. Based on the printing performance and the results of hierarchical cluster analysis of rheological parameters, surimi gels with different concentrations of water and NaCl were classified into four categories viz. difficult formation, good extrusion but poor self-supporting, good extrusion and self-supporting and difficult extrusion. The shear-thinning behaviour of the surimi samples was evident from the decreasing viscosities of all the samples with the increasing shear rates, indicating the pseudoplastic nature of the surimi gels. Similar findings have also been reported by previous studies (Huang et al., 2019; Wang et al., 2018). Among the two monitoring techniques used in the study, partial least squares regression models based on LF-NMR showed better accuracy and robustness for predicting main rheological properties whereas discriminant analysis using LF-NMR showed a higher classification accuracy of printability in samples. These results suggest the importance of LF-NMR in estimating the printability and predicting the rheological properties of surimi gels.

Gudjonsdottir et al. (2019) studied the effect of processing methods (conventional washing vs. the pH-shift method), salt concentration (0–3%), storage time before 3D printing (0–7 days) and steam cooking on the quality of 3D printed surimi using low field nuclear magnetic resonance (LF-NMR) and chemometrics. The salt induced a gelling effect in the pH-shift processed surimi whereas the myofibrillar swelling was observed with an increasing salt concentration in the conventionally prepared surimi. While both disadvantages and advantages of the two processing methods were revealed by the LF-NMR analysis, the authors concluded that there was a stabilizing effect of increasing salt concentration on the surimi and recommended the 3D printing of fresh raw materials.

Dong et al. (2019) studied the effect of sweet potato starch on the physical properties and the microstructure of 3D printed surimi. The *Scomberomorus niphonius* fish fillets were minced and washed twice using cold water (4 °C) and 0.2% NaCl solution, which was followed by the removal of excess surface water. For the preparation of the surimi gel, 2.5% NaCl solution (w/w) was added to the surimi, mixed well for 5 min and then sweet potato starch was added at different levels (0–10%, w/w). The mixture was mixed for 5 min and incubated at 40 °C for 30 min that was followed by heating at 90 °C for 20 min. The apparent viscosity of the surimi gel decreased with both increasing shear rate and level of starch in the gel, indicating the pseudoplastic behaviour of the gel. While the gel strength and water holding capacity increased significantly with the increasing level of starch in the gel, the cooking losses showed a significant decrease in the starch-containing gels. The addition of starch significantly increased the texture characteristics such as hardness, springiness, cohesiveness, chewiness, and resilience whereas decreased the colour values (L*, a*, b* and Whiteness). The addition of starch was found to increase the number of molecules per unit volume of the gel resulting in the formation of a dense network structure due to increased chances of intermolecular hydrogen bonding (Nunes et al., 2006). As surimi filler (Kong et al., 2016), starch has been widely reported to enhance the mechanical and physical properties of fish products (Dong et al., 2019). By absorbing the available water, the starch granules expand and increase pressure in the gel matrix that increases the gel strength and can help in supporting the 3D construct. Based on the reported results, surimi gel containing 8.0 g/100 g sweet potato starch showed most favourable physical characteristics and network structure that improved the quality of 3D printed surimi products. The optimized settings of 1 mm nozzle diameter, 15 mm^3/s extrusion rate and 20 mm/s printing speed were most suitable for producing best 3D printed surimi products. The authors concluded that the 3D printed surimi products were softer than those prepared by traditional methods and could meet the requirements of special groups of the population such as the elderly, children or people who have special needs such as suffering from dysphagia.

Wu et al. (2021) developed high internal phase emulsions stabilized by cod myofibers with excellent 3D printing properties. The cod myofibers endowed strong and elastic mechanical properties to these emulsions making them a suitable candidate for 3D printing of foods with tailorable rheological and textural properties. The authors stated that the exquisite injectability of these emulsions gives them the ability to be programmed for different types of 3D constructions and the excellent cohesion of cod myofibers conferred great moulding ability to the developed inks, attributing customizability and flexibility for fabricating structures with arbitrary shapes.

Lipton et al. (2010) successfully printed multi-material 3D constructs with complex internal structures using scallops and transglutaminase. The scallop-based products were cooked by deep frying, sensorily evaluated and approved by expert chefs.

9.3.4 3D-Printing Using Transglutaminase

Zhao et al. (2021) studied the effect of microwave 3D print and transglutaminase on the moulding quality of 3D printed surimi constructs. They tried to improve the moulding quality of the surimi by the synergistic effect of transglutaminase and a microwave 3D print to optimize the rheological properties and solid-like behaviour for sufficient mechanical strength to resist any post-processing deformation or disturbances due to self-gravity. The salt and water were added to the frozen surimi in the amounts to obtain a 3% final concentration of salt (w/w) and 78% moisture content. This was followed by the addition of transglutaminase at a concentration of 5 U/g and the mixture was mixed in a vacuum chopper at 4 °C. A microwave 3D printer was used to produce 3D surimi and had different components such as 3D printer, microwave source (400 W output power, 2450 MHz frequency, 260 °C maximum heating temperature), control system, and a barrel coupled with a microwave heating cavity. An increasing range of microwave power from 0–60 W/g was used along with the following printing settings viz. 1 mm layer height, 1.2 mm nozzle diameter, 7.2 mm shell thickness (1.2 mm for cylindrical samples), 0% fill density (80% with a rectilinear fill pattern for cylindrical samples), 50 mm/s reaction speed, 40 mm/s print speed, and 120% flow. By changing the temperature distribution of surimi in the nozzle, an effect of the microwave power was obvious on the extrudability and was reflected in the printing results. When a microwave power of less than 60 W/g was applied, a shear-thinning behaviour was exhibited by the surimi and the addition of transglutaminase resulted in the solid gels with large protein aggregates and better shape fidelity at a power of 40 and 50 W/g, indicating that microwave activated transglutaminase promoted self-gelation of the surimi. Microwave printing along with transglutaminase at 40 and 50 W/g induced sufficient mechanical strength to resist deformation from cutting and stacking. The short-term heating characteristics of the microwave-assisted 3D printing and the rapid extrusion process suggested that 3D printing did not leave enough time for the heated proteins to unfold and expose the -SH groups and induce hydrophobic interactions, indicating that the generation of ε-(γ-Glu)-Lys by the synergetic action of microwave and transglutaminase be the possible mechanism behind the self-gelation process of the surimi. Further, the microwave-induced hydrogen bond formation was another important factor attributed to water retention capacity and the mechanical strength of the surimi. Thus, the study successfully reported a microwave-assisted 3D printing for surimi-based products with improved moulding quality/mechanical strength to withstand the deformations due to self-gravity and during processing such as cooking.

Dong et al. (2020) studied the effect of microbial transglutaminase on physical properties and the microstructure of 3D printed surimi. The meat from *S. niphonius* was chopped in a grinder and was washed three times in ice-cold water (4 °C) or 0.5% NaCl aqueous solution (w/w, third time), followed by removal of excess water. For the preparation of the gel, surimi was chopped for 1 min, 2.5% NaCl (w/w) and 15% cold water were added and chopped for 5 min. The microbial transglutaminase was added at different levels (0–0.4% w/w) and mixed for 5 min. For 3D printing of the surimi, an extrusion-based printer was used with a pressure system having a stainless extruder tube and a syringe pump to extrude the surimi gel. The 3D printing was performed at room temperature and the printing settings used were 1 mm nozzle diameter, 15 mm^3/s extrusion rate and 20 mm/s printing speed. The raw surimi constructs were subjected to two successive heating processes in a water bath viz. 40 °C for 60 min, to provide an optimal temperature and reaction time for microbial transglutaminase, which was followed by 90 °C for 20 min for cooking. The glutamine transaminase, a calcium-dependent endogenous protease present in fish muscle fibres, catalyses the cross-linking formation in myosin heavy chain that mostly determines the gel formation in surimi (Benjakul et al., 2003; Kumazawa et al., 1995). It induces the formation of nondisulphide covalent bonds between the γ-carboxyamide groups of glutamine residue and the ε-amino groups of lysine residue on myosin heavy chains (Dondero et al., 2006). The added microbial transglutaminase also catalyses the formation of more ε-(γ-glutamyl) lysine covalent bonds that reinforce the strength of the gel after subsequent heating at above 80 °C.

Two important aspects about the 3D printing of foods are the ability of the food inks to extrude and to maintain the shape and structure of the construct after printing. This is where the role of physical properties of food inks come into play with storage modulus (G′), adhesiveness and gel strength important for the supporting capacity and flow properties and the loss modulus (G″) for extrusion performance (Yang et al., 2018). In agreement with the previous studies (Wang et al., 2018), Dong et al. (2020) reported a significant decrease in the viscosity of the surimi gel with increasing shear rate indicated the pseudoplastic behaviour of the gel. The viscosity of food inks affects the printing accuracy by affecting the stackable ability between layers when the viscosity is too low whereas too high a viscosity results in a slower extrusion rate thereby causing an uneven extrusion and affecting the smoothness of the surface. The surimi developed from *S. niphonius* is generally of low viscosity and the addition of microbial glutaminase increased its viscosity at the same shear rate, which positively affected its 3D printing ability (Dong et al., 2020), however, an excessive increase in viscosity can negatively affect printing accuracy. The microbial transglutaminase can help in the formation of crosslinked structure in the protein gels, which has been reported to increase the apparent viscosity (Liu et al., 2018). Analysis of the printing and rheological results revealed that adding 0.2% or 0.3% microbial transglutaminase to surimi not only facilitated the extrusion process but also helped in maintaining the appearance and shape of the printed constructs owing to its high storage modulus. A significant increase was also observed in the gel strength and textural characteristics, such as hardness, cohesiveness, and resilience, of the printed gels incorporated with microbial transglutaminase. NMR analysis revealed the enhanced ability of the gels to retain residual water due to the modifications in the gel microstructure that became a more uniform and denser network compared to irregular distribution of control samples. Interestingly, an increase in the cooking loss was recorded with increasing concentration of the microbial transglutaminase. The authors concluded that the addition of microbial transglutaminase significantly improved the 3D printability and accuracy of the surimi gels by positively affecting the viscoelastic and mechanical properties and the gel microstructure.

9.3.5 3D-Printed Meat Products for Special Needs

Kouzani et al. (2017) attempted the development of 3D printed tuna for people with swallowing difficulties. A pureed form of tuna, pumpkin and beetroot was used to develop the 3D printed product for people who have special needs. The pumpkin and beetroots were cooked for 15 min in water in a microwave and then pureed in a blender. Canned tuna was also pureed in a blender for 5 min and all the three purees were loaded into the three different barrels of a printer (EnvisionTEC GmbH Bioplotter) that can create a physical object from a 3D computer-aided design (CAD) model by using pressure-controlled extrusion technology. A wide range of viscous liquids or pastes are suitable for use in these printers and are placed inside standard 30CC barrels with a precision tip and a piston top. The pressure is applied to the barrel with a piston top using pressure from an external nitrogen source that extrudes the print material/ink onto the print bed to produce a 3D construct. A 3D CAD model of the tuna fish having dimensions of 14 cm × 14 cm with 1 cm thickness was created and loaded into the bioplotter control software and a 3D tuna was successfully fabricated. The developed 3D tuna was compared for taste with a similar product developed by a skilled cook using the same ingredients in the same form and the taste of both the products was found to be the same. Several valuable observations were made during the fabrication of the 3D tuna-based product. While aluminium foil and greaseproof paper did not allow a successful attachment of the first printed layer due to little surface friction, a transparent film of cellulose acetate was highly suitable for both printing and cooking. A very low pressure in the range of 0.2–0.3 bar was used for the extrusion of the materials and the viscosity of the purees was adjusted so that the extrusion was prevented during the rest period as a result of the residual pressure from the printing barrel.

Dick et al. (2021) studied the textural characteristics and printability of modified-texture cooked beef pastes for dysphagia patients. Beef blade roast was cooked in water (meat: water = 2:1) at 150°C for 5 h in an electric oven. The cooked meat was crumbled and minced in a food processor. Minced cooked meat was used for the preparation of meat paste base which contained 60% meat and 40% water. The cooked beef pastes were prepared by adding 1% NaCl and 0.5 or 1% of xanthan gum, guar gum, k-carrageenan, or locust bean gum individually or as blends (on equal ratio basis). These cooked beef pastes were 3D printed using a syringe-based-extrusion 3D printer at 23 °C and the printing setting used were 1 mm layer height, 1.2 mm diameter nozzle, 15 mm/s printing speed, 10 mm/s travel speed, 100% flow rate, 100% infill density, and a concentric infill pattern. Compared to other infill patterns, such as grids or lines, the concentric infill pattern exhibits lower tensile strength (Kim et al., 2021) that favoured the purpose of the study 'developing the product for dysphagia patients'. Based on the results of the International Dysphagia Diet Standardisation Initiative testing methods and the Texture Profile Analysis, the developed formulations qualified in the category of modified-texture foods.

The viscosities of the beef pastes ranged from 108–350 Pa.s. at rest and from 4.3–11.6 Pa.s. at a shear extrusion rate of 50 s^{-1}. Samples with negligible or minimal printing dimensional deviation showed constant or decreased phase angles across frequencies, denoting higher shape stability over time whereas the samples with higher printing dimensional deviation showed increasing phase angles, denoting less shape stability over time. In a similar study, Dick et al. (2020) developed a hydrocolloid incorporated 3D printed pork for dysphagia patients and studied its textural, rheological, and microstructural properties. Pork leg was cooked at 150 °C for 65 min in distilled water (meat: water = 65:35) and was ground in a grinder. The pork paste was developed by using ground cooked pork, distilled water, NaCl, xanthan gum and/or guar gum. Samples without any added hydrocolloids served as control samples. A significantly lower apparent viscosity was observed for the control samples at rest compared to the samples containing hydrocolloids, indicating that the addition of hydrocolloids improved the stability of the matrix, however, no significant difference in the stability was recorded among the samples containing hydrocolloids. While no significant differences were recorded for the dynamic viscoelastic properties of all the samples at room temperature, a shear-thinning behaviour was observed for all the samples, which suggests their suitability for applications for extrusion purposes. Significant differences were observed in the texture of the samples heated at 100 °C for 7 min, frozen at –18 °C and cooled at 37 °C. The 3D printed samples with hydrocolloids showed lower mean values for chewiness, hardness and cohesiveness compared to the control samples. While the control samples showed a denser microstructure and more elastic-like behaviour, the samples with hydrocolloids showed a more viscous-like behaviour and the microstructure presented an extended network with heterogeneous cavities. Based on the rheological and textural results, the 3D printed pork products were in the category of transitional foods according to the International Dysphagia Diet Standardisation Initiative Framework and were suitable for dysphagia patients with chewing and swallowing difficulties.

9.3.6 3D-Printed Meat Products Using Cultured Meat

The current 3D-food printing technology mostly uses viscous liquids or purees as food inks to develop the 3D constructs mostly by extrusion technology. These food inks are developed by using a minced paste of meat and hydrocolloids/other additives and unlike organ-printing, the developed products, although 3 dimensional, are very close to emulsion-based and ground meat products. The technology can, however, aim at creating a product close to 3D fully structured meat by producing cultured muscle fibres using cell culture or tissue culture techniques and gluing them together by using a binding paste of adipose tissues, meat glue, and extracellular matrices which could be cultured separately. Such a printer should allow the extrusion of intact fibrous muscle cells constructed in a parallel fashion and binding them together with a binding paste. While microbial transglutaminase can provide a suitable option as a meat glue to bind the meat paste, other similar food-grade materials with binding properties, such as hydrocolloids, need to be explored experimentally as alternatives. To make it as close possible to the real 3D meat, the extracellular matrices should contain some form of connective tissues such as collagen/elastin/reticulin which could be initially harvested from animal by-products, such as pigskin or poultry skin and offal's (not sustainable in the long run) or be cultured separately. The addition of small amounts of blood (poultry/animal) or synthetic haem may help in the development of flavour and colour.

Liu et al. (2017) proposed a 3D printer for printing fibrous meat materials. The printer was reported to model a desired shape or pattern with the help of computer animation modelling software and computer-aided design. The food inks were extruded gradually through the nozzle to form the desired shape layer by layer based on the design profile. The printer was capable of printing a wide range of meat materials on the constructs without mixing flavours due to the presence of multiple nozzles contributing separate components in the structure. The authors reported that the technology could also help developing products for people with special dietary needs such as elderly people who might have problems in mastication of food. The presence of a pressurized tank with soft piping was reported to solve the problem of solid-liquid separation of fibrous meat materials. The printer was capable of producing appealing different food shapes and patterns using food inks of different viscosities due to volume- and time-controlled feeding by a peristaltic pump.

Lupton and Turner (2018) studied consumer responses and their attitudes to the idea of 3D printing of meat products using cultured meat. The study involved an online discussion group with Australian participants. While the respondents recognized the potential benefits of 3D-printed meat products based on cultured meat for society, their own food consumption choices centred more on the qualities of health, taste, and naturalness. The respondents expressed their uneasiness towards the degree of processing cultured meat undergoes and considered it to be 'unnatural', not nutritious, or lacking taste and potentially harmful. These results suggest that the success of the 3D-printed products based on cultured meat will have to overcome major cultural barriers in countries like Australia.

Based on the findings of all the above studies, it can be concluded that the 3D printing of meat products is in its infancy and there is a long way to go before the production of acceptable 3D-printed products based on cultured meat can be realized. The printers that can produce meat products that would resemble the actual meat are either under development or currently not available, the food inks currently available/formulated are developed using meat tissues by grounding them together with some hydrocolloids and the constructs are frozen or dried before cooking. Future focus should be on developing food inks that can produce meat products closer to actual meat by using existing meat technologies such as 'meat restructuring' that uses small bits and fibres to reconstruct the intact meats. The 'tearing and forming method' used for the production of restructured meats can be attempted by using torn apart muscle fibres (or cultured muscle fibres) by tumbling them for a long time in the presence of salt and other additives to extract the salt soluble proteins (myofibrillar and sarcoplasmic proteins), which will act as a cementing material and will provide the required viscosity for printing the constructs. While 3D printing is currently used to produce designer meat products, one must take caution while using this technology for the production of complex shaped/designed meat products because the cooking of such products/designs may affect the sensory attributes such as juiciness and texture which have a marked effect on the acceptance of the meat products. The race for designing highly complex shapes for meat products should not override the sensory and nutritional appeal of the products.

9.4 CHALLENGES IN THE PATH OF CULTURED MEAT

Figure 9.2 presents some merits and challenges of cultured meat in comparison to farm meat production.

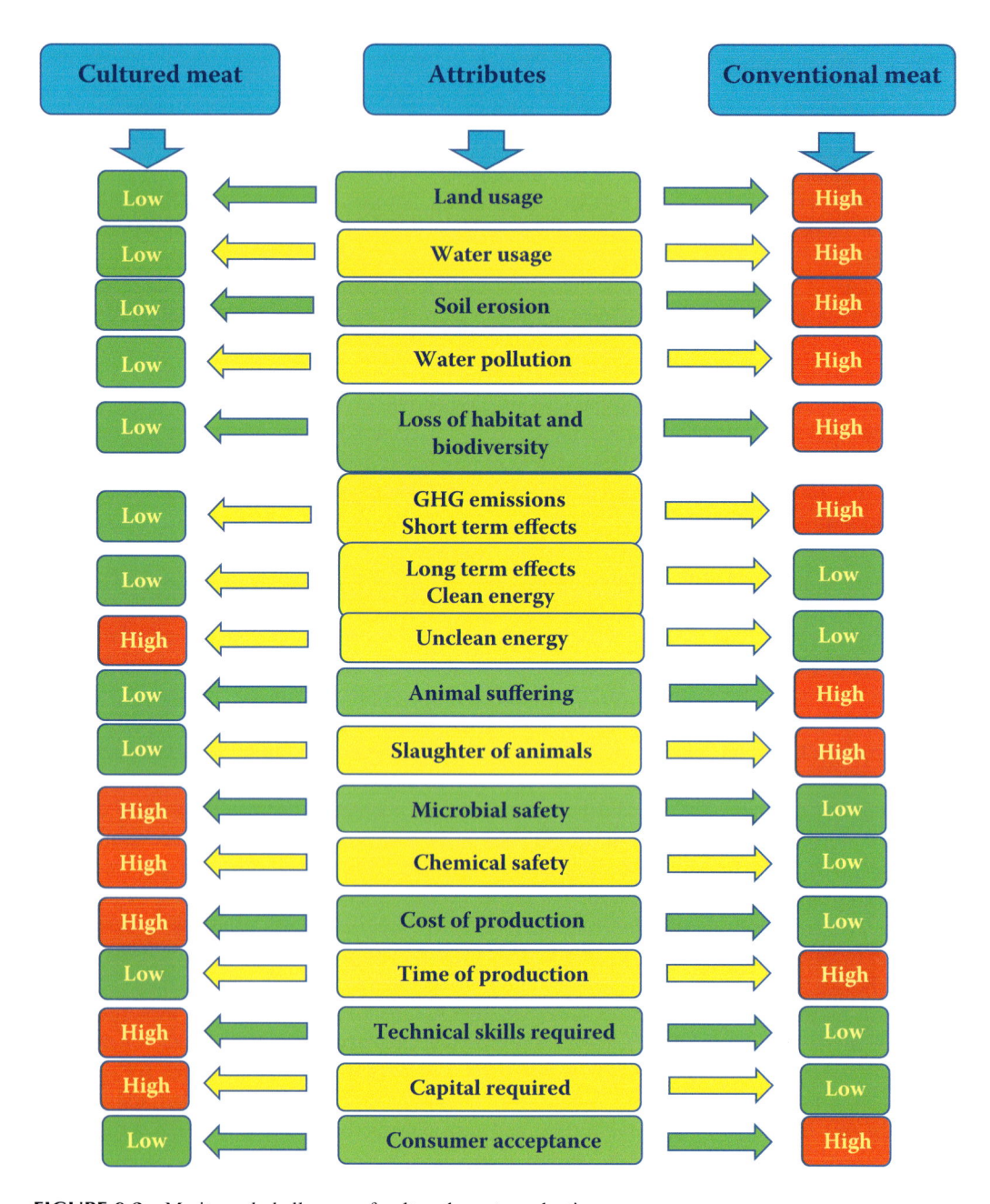

Cultured meat	Attributes	Conventional meat
Low	Land usage	High
Low	Water usage	High
Low	Soil erosion	High
Low	Water pollution	High
Low	Loss of habitat and biodiversity	High
Low	GHG emissions Short term effects	High
Low	Long term effects Clean energy	Low
High	Unclean energy	Low
Low	Animal suffering	High
Low	Slaughter of animals	High
High	Microbial safety	Low
High	Chemical safety	Low
High	Cost of production	Low
Low	Time of production	High
High	Technical skills required	Low
High	Capital required	Low
Low	Consumer acceptance	High

FIGURE 9.2 Merits and challenges of cultured meat production.

9.4.1 Production Challenges

The currenate the metabolic waste products. While cell culture uses stem cells to proliferate, grow and differentiate on scaffolds in a media in the presence of specific stimuli to produce myofibers which are used for production of meat products, tissue culture allows expanding the volume of skeletal muscle explants in a medium as self-organizing constructs to produce highly structured meat. Due to the static cultural conditions, scaffold-based methods can only produce thin monocyte layers that lack the structure of native skeletal muscle tissue (Carrier et al., 1999). Although cultured meat produced by tissue culture can closely resemble farm produced meat in that it contains all the tissues present, it is difficult to scale up the process for industrial-scale production due to the diffusional limitations of the process. Meat produced by current methods also lack other elements such as nerves, blood and adipose tissue and do not consider some of the important factors developed during conversion of muscle to meat which significantly affect the sensory characteristics of the meat.

Currently, the biggest challenge in the production of cultured meat is the scaling of cell production and that of subsequent production of tissues. These steps are currently manual and are not only laborious and expensive but also increase safety risks and the chances of contamination. Thankfully, full automated systems already exist in tissue engineering facilities for medical purposes where all these steps are done under sterile and closed environment (Post & Hocquette, 2017). Due to a poor surface-to-volume ratio, the traditional ways of culturing cells in cell culture flasks or Petri dishes, where cells get nutrients from medium above them and remain attached to the bottom, are not suitable for scale up to the industrial levels for commercial purposes. Myoblasts can also be grown using suspension methods by providing attachment surfaces in the medium in the form of suspended small spheres or carrier beads for cell growth. However, currently, the maximum available capacity for growth of myoblasts has been reported to be 1.5 L stirred bioreactors or stirred flasks (Post Purslow, 2017). Similar suspension methods are used to grow yeasts and bacteria at industrial level with a maximum available capacity of 25,000 L.

Other challenges associated with cultured meat are source of initial cells, culture media and composition of scaffolds. It is not clear which tissue, breed and specie will result in optimal cell source as the starting material and would require extensive research. Obtaining tissue biopsies and harvesting the primary cells present in them is a likely option that would require maintaining a small herd of animals. Using cell lines as the starting material is another promising option, however, there are some associated concerns such as sub-culturing, passaging, misidentification and continuous evolution (Stephens et al., 2018). Media used for culturing cells also poses some serious challenges, including the cost, production scale and its animal origin as well as issues of waste management. Culture media used for growing meat is currently available for biomedical research and is very expensive and available in limited volumes. Use of animal components such as foetal calf serum or horse serum in culture media, required at 0.5–2% at the differentiation stage of skeletal muscle (Burattini et al., 2004; Chiron et al., 2012), raises a big question mark on the humane claim of the production and will also affect the acceptance of cultured meat. Other components of concern, which are traditionally present in culture media and serum are antibiotics, antimitotics and a wide range of growth factors, growth inhibitors and hormones (Aswad et al., 2016; Brunner et al., 2010). In addition to ethical issues, serum-based media can become a major limiting factor for industrial-scale production and can increase the chances of contamination and disease and the variation between different batches. No serum-free media has been developed for myoblasts yet.

Due to the close resemblance with their natural physiological niche, animal-origin materials, such as collagen, provide an optimal scaffolding for differentiating myoblasts to form a muscle fibre (Langelaan et al., 2010) and most of the successful experiments aimed at producing cultured meat have used collagen-based scaffolding systems (Snyman et al., 2013). Several attempts to use alternative synthetic materials for scaffolding have failed to achieve required tissue contraction

(Bian & Bursac, 2009). Using an animal-based material for industrial-scale production is simply not feasible and sustainable and there would be other issues such as variation in batches and acceptance concerns. Several natural biomaterials possess properties of an ideal scaffolding, such as they are non-toxic, available at an industrial scale and form a suitable matrix, however, these materials often lack functionality and fail to provide an adherable surface to myoblasts. Separation of cultured meat from scaffolding system is another challenge that conventionally involves the use of enzymes or mechanical separation that often damages the muscle cells as well as the extracellular matrix (Canavan et al. 2005). Further, in absence of any external support surface after separation of scaffolding system, the muscle cells collapse into multicellular detached spheroids due to the aggregation resulting from contractile forces of the muscle cells (Lam et al., 2009).

9.4.2 Resemblance to Meat in Structure, Sensory Attributes and Nutrition

There are two viewpoints about the characteristics of cultured meat. If it is projected as an alternative to meat it must be as close to meat as possible having similar sensory and nutritional characteristics and meeting the expectations of consumers as an alternative to meat. However, if it is projected as a unique product and not as an alternative, it should have separate and unique characteristics of its own. As a successful meat alternative, cultured meat must be spun with sensorial properties like that of farm-produced meat because consumers are particular about attributes such as texture, flavour, and juiciness when it comes to meat. Currently, the technologies available for cultured meat production can only produce loose muscle cells in the form of mince and fail to produce a fully structured 3D meat such as a steak. Further, due to the absence of other components present in conventional meat such as haemoglobin, nerves, adipose tissues, and given that thousands of fat-derived and water-soluble components are responsible for the flavour of meat (Sharma et al., 2015), biochemical composition, sensory and nutritional profile of cultured meat is expected to be different in absence of processing interventions. The colour of fresh meat, which is used as a freshness indicator by consumers and is one of the determinants for the repeat purchase of meat, tends to be less reddish or pinkish and towards more yellowish side in cultured meat due to suppressed myoglobin expression under ambient oxygen conditions (USDA, 1998). The absence of an ageing period also adds to the variation in sensorial attributes and quality of meat. Co-culturing (growing different cells together), proposed as a solution to some of these problems, is experimentally challenging due to differential nutritional and maturational demands of different cells and several test conditions.

9.4.3 Acceptance Issues

Western media has overemphasized cultured meat and events associated with it, such as the cultured meat burger tasting that took place in London in 2015, and has not highlighted the challenges for this novel product in the path to commercial production and consumer acceptance (Bhat et al., 2019; Hopkins, 2015). Studies on consumers acceptance and reaction to cultured meat have reported a low level of acceptance along with feelings of disgust and unnaturalness (Siegrist et al., 2018; Verbeke et al., 2015a). How consumers are going to see this novel meat in relation to farm produced meat will have a significant impact on its commercial success (Bekker et al., 2017b), although, sustainability and positive perception about cultured meat will also have an influence on its success and consumer acceptance (Bekker et al., 2017a). A few studies (Bekker et al., 2017b; Verbeke et al., 2015b) have reported a positive perception of consumers about the acceptance and market of cultured meat, however, most of the studies (Hocquette et al., 2015; Siegrist & Sütterlin, 2017; Verbeke et al., 2015a; 2015b) are less optimistic and educated consumers (scientists and students) do not believe that cultured meat is a solution for problems of farm-produced meat (Hocquette et al., 2015). Only 11% of the respondents chose to purchase a cultured meat-based burger in a choice experiment with hypothetical conditions that prices were equal, and the burgers tasted the same (Slade, 2018). Lack of naturalness is believed to affect the acceptance of cultured meat to the extent that it can override the positive benefits of the production system (Siegrist & Sütterlin, 2017). Despite the marketing of higher environmental benefits and lower risks, consumer acceptance may be a big concern with novel food technologies (Siegrist & Sutterlin, 2016; Siegrist et al., 2016). Table 9.1 presents the main findings of the studies on different aspects of consumer acceptance of cultured meat.

9.4.4 Ethical Aspects

Although, it is believed that cultured meat will reduce animal suffering and slaughter significantly, current methods of production are still dependent on farm animals and involve some level of animal suffering and death. Small herds must be maintained to harvest biopsies for initial cells and if no successful serum-free media are developed for the production in future, it will require a continuous supply of blood from foetuses for growth media that has both ethical and sustainability considerations.

Current technology of culturing meat can produce processed meat products only. There is growing evidence against red meat consumption in general and processed meats in specific and promoting consumption of cultured meat is seen by some as unethical as it promotes consumption of unhealthy food, which will not only retain the centrality of meat in human diet but will subdue the efforts of health departments to discourage the consumption of foods that have a negative impact on human health.

Culturing meat will require obtaining cells and foetus bovine serum from donor animals. The foetus bovine serum may represent an ethical issue since its obtained from dead or slaughtered calves. It also presents a massive practical issue as it is already an extremely limited resource that requires a continuation of the animal slaughter industry.

Diverting resources to grow meat, which is not an efficient nutrient conversion system in comparison to plants, could also be unethical if allowed on the pretext that cultured meat would be necessary to feed growing human population in future. Simply diverting the resources towards growing plant-based crops would be more effective in solving the widespread hunger and famine problems in future. The possibility of cannibalism and perceived unnaturalness are some other ethical considerations.

9.4.5 Sensory Aspects

It is already well established that the sensory properties of meat dictate its value and acceptability. Sensory aspects such as texture, colour and flavour are important at various stages of purchase and consumption of fresh meat. The particular organization of muscle with its various types of proteins (myofibrillar, connective and sarcoplasmic) contributes to the sensory aspects of meat. The different structures of various muscle groups contribute to a range of attributes that generate varying and desirable eating qualities that are characteristic to those meat cuts. For example, the anatomical location and the variation in meat biochemistry, structure and physicochemical properties of different muscles/ meat cuts results in different levels of tenderness that require different cooking styles and produce different flavours. This choice of flavour and texture may not be replicated by cultured meat. For example, several reviews stated that the beef burger made by Mark Post was bland and was yellowish but tasted like meat which required the addition of colourants (red beet juice and saffron) to bring a meat-like appearance (Chriki & Hocquette, 2020). The variety of meat cuts, flavours and utility of meat are still a long way from being replicated by cultured meat.

9.4.6 Environmental Considerations

All the buzz about cultured meat was invariably based on its low environmental footprint, however, this was marketing and speculation and was not based on scientific experimentation and data.

TABLE 9.1
Main findings of various studies elucidating consumer aspects of cultured meat

Authors	Aspects Studied	Findings
Weinrich et al. (2020)	Conducted a survey on attitudes previously found to be important in the literature. The survey included 713 German consumers.	The results of the survey suggested that the German consumers were only moderately prepared to accept cultured meat.
Mancini and Antonioli (2019)	Conducted a study involving 525 Italian consumers about their willingness to try and pay for cultured meat.	About 54% of the respondents were willing to try this new bioengineered product. The respondents who wanted to try cultured meat were young, highly educated, a meat consumer, mostly familiar with this novel production and willing to reduce meat consumption.
Mohorčich and Reese (2019)	The study discussed the choices and strategies that can affect the adoption of novel food technologies including cultured meat.	Based on the history of GMO adoption in the USA and Europe, the study concluded that the adoption of cultured meat will be slower, harder, and more complicated than predicted by its supporters. The challenges highlighted in the way of this production were unnaturalness, safety, industry structure, funding, and intellectual property control.
Wilks et al. (2019)	Explored a range of psychological mechanisms by using an attitude roots model to decipher the mechanisms that may underpin cultured meat.	In terms of negative intentions and attitudes towards cultured meat, the most powerful predictors were distrust of food scientists, food neophobia and political conservatism. Whereas food neophobia, food and hygiene disgust sensitivity subscales, and conspiratorial ideation were the strongest predictors when it came to absolute opposition to cultured meat.
Bryant et al. (2019)	The study analysed the efficacy of some messages created to address the concerns of consumers about the naturalness of cultured meat.	The study revealed that arguing that conventional meat is unnatural was more persuasive to increase the acceptance of cultured meat in comparison to other messages whereas challenging the appeal to nature and arguing that cultured meat is natural were less persuasive.
Lupton and Turner (2018)	Studied the attitudes of the Australian consumers and their responses towards the concept of 3D-printing of cultured meat.	While the respondents recognized the potential benefits of 3D-printed cultured meat for society, their own food consumption choices centred more on the qualities of health, taste, and naturalness. The respondents considered cultured meat to be 'unnatural', not nutritious or lacking taste and potentially harmful.
Slade (2018)	Studied the consumer preferences for cultured meat burgers in a hypothetical choice experiment.	If prices were equal and burgers tasted the same, only 11% consumers would purchase the cultured meat burger and 65% of consumers would purchase the regular beef burger.
Siegrist et al. (2018)	How acceptance of cultured meat is influenced by perceived naturalness and evoked disgust.	To increase the acceptance of cultured meat, authors emphasized the significance of a non-technical way that should not be production oriented but product oriented giving the merits of the product.

TABLE 9.1 (Continued)
Main findings of various studies elucidating consumer aspects of cultured meat

Authors	Aspects Studied	Findings
Bryant et al. (2019)	Authors conducted a systematic review of the available literature for consumer acceptance of cultured meat.	The study highlights common consumer objections, factors that affect acceptance and its demographic variations, areas of uncertainty and perceived benefits. Authors concluded that while consumers certainly perceive the advantages of cultured meat in terms of environmental benefits and animal welfare, these issues are not going to be the central to influence their buying decisions.
Stephens et al. (2018)	The study evaluated the socio-political, technical, and regulatory challenges in the area of cultured meat, based on interviews with seventy experts, available literature and professional experience of the authors.	The study highlighted the key technical challenges associated with this technology including culture media, cell source, synthetic and animal-derived materials, mimicking the in-vivo myogenesis environment, and commercial-scale production. Authors emphasized there is a need to recognize the significance of the institutional and political forms a cultured meat industry might take.
Bekker et al. (2017a)	The study evaluated the effect of information provision on the explicit and implicit attitude towards cultured meat to understand the consumer acceptance.	The results showed that the information about a positively perceived sustainable product and the sustainability of this production system can influence the explicit attitude towards this new product. This effect was not merely affect-based but was shown to be content-based.
Bekker et al. (2017b)	A cross-cultural study was conducted to investigate how study participants from the Netherlands, Ethiopia and China operationalize the concept of meat and to evaluate the extent to which *in-vitro* meat fits or does not fit into this operationalization.	Cultured meat was positioned across the symbolic boundaries of meat and was viewed as a technology for the future.
Siegrist and Sütterlin (2017)	Significance of perceived naturalness for acceptance of cultured meat.	Although cultured meat was more humane and environmentally friendly, lack of naturalness associated with this production system might reduce the acceptability of the risk associated with such a product. While evaluating foods, consumers rely on symbolic information that may lead to biased decisions and judgments.
Verbeke et al. (2015a)	Studied attitude formation and reactions of consumers towards cultured meat through online deliberations and focus group discussions involving 179 meat consumers from the United Kingdom, Portugal and Belgium.	While learning about the cultured meat, initial reactions were underpinned by considerations of unnaturalness and feelings of disgust that induced some kind of fear of the unknown. The consumers acknowledged the possible benefits of this technology at the global level and envisaged some direct personal benefits.

(Continued)

TABLE 9.1 (Continued)
Main findings of various studies elucidating consumer aspects of cultured meat

Authors	Aspects Studied	Findings
Verbeke et al. (2015b)	Study on the prospects and challenges for consumer acceptance of cultured meat.	While vegetarians may not be the ideal primary target group for this novel product as a meat alternative, sensory expectations and price are major obstacles.
Hocquette et al. (2015)	A study was conducted to evaluate the various assumptions associated with cultured meat. Study involved educated people, mainly students and scientists, 865 French people, 817 persons worldwide interviewed online and 208 persons (mainly scientists) interviewed after an oral presentation about cultured meat.	Educated respondents think that cultured meat is not going to solve the problems associated with conventional meat production. Majority of consumers did not believe cultured meat would be tasty and healthy. Only a minority of respondents (5 to 11%) would accept to eat or recommend cultured meat.

Whether this will hold true on commercial and industrial scales is not clear and will depend on several factors including the energy efficiency of the production and source of energy. Since there are more long-term effects of carbon dioxide, the main greenhouse gas of cultured meat production, in comparison to the short-term effects of methane, the main green-house gas of farm meat production, a few researchers have raised concerns that this novel meat production may cause more long-term damage to environment and will worsen the climate change (Cockburn, 2019; McGrath, 2019). Comparing the impact of beef cattle production (three different beef production systems) and cultured meat (four synthetic meat GHG footprints available in the literature) at all times to 1,000 years in the future, Lynch and Pierrehumbert (2019) reported that the impact of cultured meat on the climate is unclear and will depend on specific environmental footprints and the type of energy used in the production in future. Thus, the carbon footprint of cultured meat production will depend on energy revolution and what level of decarbonized energy generation could be achieved in future. The authors emphasized the need for comprehensive and transparent life cycle assessment of real cultured meat production and warned that this novel meat production does not give license for unrestrained meat consumption.

9.4.7 Religious Aspects

Currently, the meat industry also caters to the religious requirements of some communities by following their ritual rites during the slaughtering of animals. To tap the available market, the cultured meat industry will have to produce ritual options, such as *Halal* and *Kosher* meats, which forms a significant part of the global meat market. Author Bekhit contacted several Islamic centres and Rabbinical authorities to obtain a formal *Fatwa* or declaration regarding the religious views from Islamic and Jewish perspectives. However, no formal response was received and this 'sitting on the fence' response appears to be due to the high hype related to the potential benefits of cultured meat.

All Ibrahimic faiths (Judaism, Christianity and Islam) provide clear guidelines that only healthy and beneficial foods should be consumed. For example, the Holy Bible stated *'Why do you spend money for what is not bread, And your wages for what does not satisfy? Listen carefully to Me, and eat what is good, And let your soul delight itself in abundance'* Isaiah 55:2, New King James Version. Similarly, the Holy Quran stated *'Eat from the good things which We have provided for you'* Surat Al-Baqara (2:172). So far, the nutritional value of cultured meat has not been evaluated or compared with conventional meat, due to the cost associated with its production. Therefore, a clear evaluation of healthiness compared to the alternative is yet to be established. Meat is not protein only; other important minerals and nutrients contribute to its healthiness.

For Muslims, ritual slaughtering in the form of Qurbani or korban (sacrifice or offering) is required in several cases such as during performing Haj (visiting El-kaba in Makkah to perform rituals that are regarded as the fifth pillar of Islam. Haj is required once for any Muslim if they can afford it or physically capable of performing it). Also, required the wealthy Muslims to offer a sacrifice in Eid Al-Adha (A four-day holiday observed by Muslims worldwide every year, and it honours the willingness of Prophet Ibrahim (Peace and blessing of Allah on him) to obey God's command of sacrifice his son Ismael. Also, it is preferred to offer a sacrifice for a childbirth (*Aqiqa*). It must be mentioned that all these acts encourage charitable and kind relationships as the meat of slaughtered animals is meant to be distributed to the poor, needy, neighbours and family members regardless of their faith. Similarly, Jews are also required to make offerings in atonement for transgression or errors, childbirth, following recovery from serious illness and Passover as well as other occasions. Therefore, the act of slaughter has a significant religious significance other than the production of 'meat for food' concept that cannot be fulfilled by cultured meat. Further, the definition of 'meat' in biochemical sense is only applicable to muscles that have been through rigor and experienced the 'muscle to meat' conversion. This is not clearly the case with cultured meat. In addition, the use of foetal bovine serum, which is normally obtained from dead calves, is prohibited in both Judaism and Islam.

An argument in Islam that may support the use of cultured meat is the axiom 'La darar wa la dirar' that means it is not allowed to cause harm on others, whether to begin or to retaliate it. This can be interpreted as 'if cultured meat will alleviate greater problems such as malnutrition, then it will be permissible to prevent a greater damage'. Similarly, in Judaism the concept of 'heavenly meat' meat that was not obtained from an animal is acceptable (Shurpin, 2018).

Few Islamic scholars have stated that *Halal* status of cultured meat can be resolved by identifying the source of initial cells and the culturing media (Billinghurst, 2013; Hamdan et al., 2018). The initial cells used for the production must be extracted from a *Halal* slaughtered animal and does not involve use of blood or serum in the process (Hamdan et al., 2018). Although, there is no consensus among religious certifying bodies, some rabbis agree that cultured meat will be *Kosher* if initial cells were harvested from animals slaughtered according to Jewish law (Friedrich, 2017; JTA, 2018; Shurpin, 2018). Currently available technology uses blood serum in the growth medium and slaughtering the animals before the harvest of initial cells does not sound much different from farm meat production.

9.4.8 Cost and Affordability

One of the main factors that will decide the success of cultured meat is its affordability. Future Meat Technologies™, an Israel based-start-up, aimed to start selling cultured meat around $363 a pound in 2018 (Peters, 2018). According to Dutch-based company 'Mosa Meat™' and Spain-based 'Biotech Foods™', the average cost of producing a kilogram of cultured meat is about €100 now (Axworthy, 2019).

9.4.9 Safety Assurance

The risks and dangers associated with this novel production are totally unknown and could only be speculated from similar production settings in biomedical sciences and from meat industry setups. The possible health hazards involved are chemical or microbial contamination of cell lines, serum, or scaffolds during production phase and after the harvest of muscle cells, the hazards are pretty much like that of conventional meat plants and could be dealt accordingly. There are some new areas of risks currently unknown to meat industry such as the media components (Dilworth & McGregor, 2015) and genetic instability of multiple cell divisions (Hocquette, 2016). No study has been conducted till date regarding the induced allergenicity, toxicity and long-term effects of consumption of cultured meat and it's hard to predict what hazards this novel product could bring to human health.

Since cultured meat is not produced or available commercially in any part of the world and is limited to research only, the regulatory framework has not been established. Because meat production by culturing is novel and more complex than farm meat production, it would require higher safety standards and a more comprehensive review system to ensure safety and consumer confidence. Since the end product is essentially a food commodity, food safety authorities seem to have a role in monitoring the production, however, a combined role of medical and food safety authorities is also possible. A combined role of the USDA and the US FDA was suggested for the regulatory framework in a meeting recently held on cultured meat production in the USA (US FDA, 2018). Once meat is produced, the safety standards applicable thereafter would be similar as that applicable for a regular meat setting, however, the initial steps involving collection of cells, growth of cells in bioreactors using media and scaffolds, and industrial production of media and scaffolds would require comprehensive and specialized safety details. Cultured meat system is believed to be free of microbial infections and contaminations, but this will involve money and resources to maintain sterile and aseptic production environment. This system of production will involve more capital in terms of checks and monitors and specialized human resources to ensure safe production of meat. A regular monitoring to check the genetic instability of cells due to large number of proliferations and traceability of the ingredients used in the production of media should be in place.

9.4.10 Sustainability Issues

The environmental impacts of livestock agriculture are huge; however, the world will continue to have meat and farm animals for the foreseeable future. With increasing human population, it seems more rational and feasible to combine existing highly efficient animal production systems with modern innovations, such as cellular agriculture, to complement and expand meat production to meet the nutritional requirements of world population in future and to mitigate the global impact of meat production. However, the methods and alternatives proposed for such massive endeavours must have scientifically proven sustainability. The true sustainability of this novel meat production system is unclear and undetermined with several unanswered questions. Haunted with the feelings of disgust and unnaturalness, there is no clarity regarding the acceptance of cultured meat, the cost of production under commercial settings is totally unknown, animal-free and cost-effective media are yet to be developed, only speculative data is available about the energy consumption and process efficiency at industrial scale, waste production and management is not clear, all forms of risks (genetic, allergenicity, use of additives such as antibiotics, chemical and microbial contamination) associated with the production need to be assessed at industrial scale, and the long term impact of production on climate change are yet to be identified.

9.4.11 Funding and Research

There are no focused institutions or disciplines that are dedicated to research in the area of cellular agriculture including cultured meat and those working in the area often struggle for funding for the basic biotechnological research required for industrial scale production of cultured meat (Bhat et al., 2019; Rorheim et al., 2016).

9.4.12 Other Risks

There are some other related risks and dangers associated with cultured meat production. This production system can be established in any place near the cities and can make the meat importing countries self-sufficient in meat. This will affect the economy of those countries which are agriculture based and are dependent on meat export and can shift job opportunities from rural areas to cities. Since culturing of meat is a sophisticated and skilled enterprise, it will employ more skilled employees and in large scale set-ups robotic production will take over. Since cultured meat system is focused on production of meat alone, it is likely to affect some other associated traditional businesses such as wool and leather-based industries.

9.5 CONCLUSION

Production of meat by culturing the cells inside bioreactors within factories has long been proposed as a solution to the problems of livestock production which is associated with several environmental and animal welfare issues. However, the environmental benefits of this novel system are unclear and unknown and need comprehensive scientific research under industrial setup before arriving at any conclusion. Current technology can produce processed meat products only at an unaffordable cost and involves the use of foetal calf serum and other animal components. Cell culture and tissue culture are the two feasible methods that can produce cultured meat good enough to produce meat products only. 3D-food printing is an attractive option to produce novel designer culture meat-based products with complex shapes and designs, however, this technology is in its infancy and extensive research is required before it can become a commercial reality. Safety, allergenicity and toxicity trials of this novel product are still pending, and the sustainability of the system is unproven. There are concerns about the acceptance of this novel meat often associated with feelings of disgust and unnaturalness. Much required safety monitoring systems and suitable regulatory framework are missing. In summary, there is a large amount of research and development needed to turn the marketing dream into a practical reality.

REFERENCES

Aswad, H., Jalabert, A., & Rome, S. (2016). Depleting extracellular vesicles from foetal bovine serum alters proliferation and differentiation of skeletal muscle cells *in vitro*. *BMC Biotechnology*, *16*, 32.

Axworthy, N. (2019). Price of lab-grown meat to plummet from $280,000 to $10 per patty by 2021. https://vegnews.com/2019/7/price-of-lab-grown-meat-to-plummet-from-280000-to-10-per-patty-by-2021

Bekker, G. A., Fischer, A. R. H., Tobi, H., & van Trijp, H. C. M. (2017a). Explicit and implicit attitude toward an emerging food technology: The case of cultured meat. *Appetite*, *108*, 245–254.

Bekker, G. A., Tobi, H., & Fischer, A. R. H. (2017b). Meet meat: An explorative study on meat and cultured meat as seen by Chinese, Ethiopians and Dutch. *Appetite*, *114*, 82–92.

Benjakul, S., Chantarasuwan, C., & Visessanguan, W. (2003). Effect of medium temperature setting on gelling characteristics of surimi from tropical fish. *Food Chemistry*, *82*(4), 567–574.

Bhat, Z. F., Bhat, H., & Pathak, V. (2014). Prospects for *in vitro* cultured meat - A future harvest. In: *Principles of Tissue Engineering*, 4th Edition. Lanza, R., Langer, R., Vacanti, J. (Eds). Boston, MA: Academic Press, 1663–1683.

Bhat, Z. F., Kumar, S., & H. Bhat. (2017). *In-vitro* meat: a future animal-free harvest. *Critical Reviews in Food Science and Nutrition*, *57*(04), 782–789.

Bhat, Z. F., Morton, J. D., Mason, S. L., Bekhit, A. E. A. D., & Bhat, H. F. (2019). Technological, regulatory and ethical aspects of *In vitro* meat: A future slaughter-free harvest. *Comprehensive Reviews in Food Science and Food Safety*, *18*(4), 1192–1208.

Bhat Z. F., Kumar, S., & Bhat, H. (2015). *In-vitro* meat production: Challenges and benefits over conventional meat production. *Journal of Integrative Agriculture*, *14*(2), 60345–60347.

Bhat, Z. F., & Bhat, H. (2011). Prospectus of cultured meat-advancing meat alternatives. *Journal of Food Science and Technology*, *48*(2), 125–140.

Bhat, Z. F., Bhat, H. F., & Kumar, S. (2020). Cultured meat - A humane meat production system. In: *Principles of Tissue Engineering*, 5th Edition. Lanza, R., Langer, R., Vacanti, J., & Atala, A. (Eds). Boston, MA: Academic Press, 1369–1384.

Bian, W., & Bursac, N. (2009). Engineered skeletal muscle tissue networks with controllable architecture. *Biomaterials*, *30*, 1401–1412.

Billinghurst, T. (2013). Is 'shmeat' the answer? In vitro meat could be the future of food *Gulf News*. Retrieved November 10, 2018. https://gulfnews.com/going-out/is-shmeat-the-answer-in-vitro-meat-could-be-the-future-of-food-1.1176127

Briggs, H. (2019). Artificial meat: UK scientists growing 'bacon' in labs. BBC News. *Science and Environment*. https://www.bbc.com/news/science-environment-47611026. Accessed February 10, 2021.

Brunner, D., Frank, J., Appl, H., Schöffl, H., Pfaller, W., & Gstraunthaler, G. (2010). Serum-free cell culture: The serum-free media interactive online database. *ALTEX, 27*, 53–62.

Bryant, C. J., Anderson, J. E., Asher, K. E., Green, C., & Gasteratos, K. (2019). Strategies for overcoming aversion to unnaturalness: The case of clean meat. *Meat Science, 154*, 37–45.

Burattini, S., Ferri, P., Battistelli, M., Curci, R., Luchetti, F., & Falcieri, E. (2004). C2C12 murine myoblasts as a model of skeletal muscle development: Morpho-functional characterization. *European Journal of Histochemistry, 48*, 223–233.

Canavan, H. E., Cheng, X., Graham, D. J., Ratner, B. D., & Castner, D. G. (2005). Cell sheet detachment affects the extracellular matrix: A surface science study comparing thermal lift off, enzymatic, and mechanical methods. *Journal of Biomedical Materials Research A, 75*(1), 1–13.

Carrier, R. L., Papadaki, M., Rupnick, M., Schoen, F. J., Bursac, N., Langer, R., Freed, L. E., & Vunjak-Novakovic, G. (1999). Cardiac tissue engineering: Cell seeding, cultivation parameters and tissue construct characterization. *Biotechnology and Bioengineering, 64*(5), 580–589.

Chen, H.-Z., Zhang, M., & Yang, C.-H. (2021). Comparative analysis of 3D printability and rheological properties of surimi gels via LF-NMR and dielectric characteristics. *Journal of Food Engineering, 292*, 110278.

Chiron, S., Tomczak, C., Duperray, A., Lainé, J., Bonne, G., Eder, A., Hansen, A., Eschenhagen, T., Verdier, C., & Coirault, C. (2012). Complex interactions between human myoblasts and the surrounding 3D fibrin-based matrix. *PLoS One, 7*, e36173.

Chriki, S., & Hocquette, J.-F. (2020). The myth of cultured meat: A review. *Frontiers of Nutrition, 7*, 7. doi:10.3389/fnut.2020.00007

Cockburn, H. (2019). Lab grown meat could cause more environmental damage than the real thing, scientists warn. https://www.independent.co.uk/environment/lab-grown-meat-artificial-cultured-environment-impact-cattle-beef-oxford-university-a8786576.html. Accessed April 15, 2019.

Dennis, R., Kosnik, 2nd P., Gilbert, M., & Faulkner, J. (2001). Excitability and contractility of skeletal muscle engineered from primary cultures and cell lines. *American Journal of Physiology: Cell Physiology, 280*(2), C288–C295.

Dick, A., Bhandari, B., & Prakash, S. (2019). Post-processing feasibility of composite-layer 3D printed beef. *Meat Science, 153*, 9–18.

Dick, A., Bhandari, B., & Prakash, S. (2021). Printability and textural assessment of modified-texture cooked beef pastes for dysphagia patients. *Future Foods, 3*, 100006.

Dick, A., Bhandari, B., Dong, X., & Prakash, S. (2020). Feasibility study of hydrocolloid incorporated 3D printed pork as dysphagia food. *Food Hydrocolloids, 107*, 105940.

Dilworth, T., & McGregor, A. (2015). Moral steaks? Ethical discourses of *in vitro* meat in academia and Australia. *Journal of Agricultural and Environmental Ethics, 28*, 85–107.

Dondero, M., Figueroa, V., Morales, X., & Curotto, E. (2006). Transglutaminase effects on gelation capacity of thermally induced beef protein gels. *Food Chemistry, 99*(3), 546–554.

Dong, X., Huang, Y., Pan, Y., Wang, K., Prakash, S., & Zhu, B. (2019). Investigation of sweet potato starch as a structural enhancer for three-dimensional printing of *Scomberomorus niphonius* surimi. *Journal of Texture Studies, 50*, 316–324. doi:10.1111/jtxs.12398

Dong, X., Pan, Y., Zhao, W., Huang, Y., Qu, W., Pan, J., Qi, H., & Prakash, S. (2020). Impact of microbial transglutaminase on 3D printing quality of *Scomberomorus niphonius* surimi. *LWT-Food Science and Technology, 124*, 109123.

Fernandes, A. M., Fantinel, A. L., de Souza, Â. R. L., & Révillion, J. P. P. 2019). Trends in cultured meat: A bibliometric and sociometric analysis of publication. *Brazilian Journal of Information Science: Research Trends, 13*, 56–67.

Friedrich, B. (2017). Why clean meat is kosher. https://www.gfi.org/why-clean-meat-is-kosher. Accessed December 4, 2018.

Gillispie, G. J., Park, J., Copus, J. S., Pallickaveedu, A. K., Asari, R., Yoo, J. J., Atala, A., & Lee, S. J. (2019). Three-Dimensional tissue and organ printing in regenerative medicine. In: *Principles of Regenerative Medicine*, 3rd Edition., Cambridge, MA, United States, Academic Press, 831–852.

Gudjonsdottir, M., Napitupulu, R. J., & Petty Kristinsson, H. T. (2019). Low field NMR for quality monitoring of 3D printed surimi from cod by-products: Effects of the pH-shift method compared to conventional washing. *Magnetic Resonance in Chemistry*, 57(9), 638–648.

Hamdan, M. N., Post, M. J., Ramli, M. A., & Mustafa, A. R. (2018). Cultured meat in Islamic perspective. *Journal of Religion and Health*, 57(6), 2193–2206.

Handral, H. K., Tay, S. H., Chan, W. W., & Choudhury, D. (2020). 3D printing of cultured meat products. *Critical Reviews in Food Science and Nutrition*, 1–10. https://doi-org.ezproxy.lincoln.ac.nz/10.1080/10408398.2020.1815172

Hocquette, A., Lambert, C., Sinquin, C., Peterolff, L., Wagner, Z., Bonny, S. P. F., Lebert, A., & Hocquette, J. F. (2015). Educated consumers don't believe artificial meat is the solution to the problems with the meat industry. *Journal of Integrative Agriculture*, 14(2), 273–284.

Hocquette, F. (2016). Is *in vitro* meat the solution for the future? *Meat Science*, 120, 167–176.

Hopkins, P. D. (2015). Cultured meat in western media: The disproportionate coverage of vegetarian reactions, demographic realities, and implications for cultured meat marketing. *Journal of Integrative Agriculture*, 14(2), 264–272.

Huang, M.-S., Zhang, M., & Bhandari, B. (2019). Assessing the 3D printing precision and texture properties of Brown rice induced by infill levels and printing variables. *Food Bioprocess Technology*, 12(7), 1185–1196.

Javaid, M., & Haleem, A. (2018). 4D printing applications in medical field: A brief review. *Clinical Epidemiology and Global Health*. doi: 10.1016/j.cegh.2018.09.007

JTA. (2018). Rabbi: Lab-grown pork could be kosher for Jews to eat – with milk. *Times of Israel*. Retrieved March 22, 2018.https://www.timesofisrael.com/rabbi-meat-from-cloned-pig-could-be-eaten-by-jews-with-milk/

Kim, S.M., Kim, S. W., & Park, H. J. (2021). Preparation and characterization of surimi-based imitation crab meat using coaxial extrusion three-dimensional food printing.*Innovative Food Science & Emerging Technologies*, 71, 102711.

Kouzani, A. Z., Adams, S., Whyte, D. J., Oliver, R., Hemsley, B., Palmer, S., & Balandin, S. (2017). 3D printing of food for people with swallowing difficulties. In: *The International Conference on Design and Technology*, KEG, 23–29. doi: 10.18502/keg.v2i2.591

Kong, W., Zhang, T., Feng, D., Xue, Y., Li, Z., Yang, W., & Xue, C. (2016). Effects of modified starches on the gel properties of Alaska Pollock surimi subjected to different temperature treatments.*Food Hydrocolloids*, 56, 20–28.

Krishnaraj, P., Anukiruthika, T., Choudhary, P., Moses, J. A., & Anandharamakrishnan, C. (2019). 3D extrusion printing and postprocessing of fibre-rich snack from indigenous composite flour. *Food and Bioprocess Technology*, 12(10), 1776–1786.

Kumazawa, Y., Numazawa, T., Seguro, K., & M. Motoki (1995). Suppression of surimi gel setting by transglutaminase inhibitors. *Journal of Food Science*, 60(4), 715–717.

Lam, M. T., Huang, Y. C., Birla, R. K., & Takayama, S. (2009). Microfeature guided skeletal muscle tissue engineering for highly organized three-dimensional free-standing constructs. *Biomaterials*, 30(6), 1150–1155.

Langelaan, M. L., Boonen, K. J., Polak, R. B., Baaijens, F. P., Post, M. J., & Van Der Schaft D. W. 2010). Meet the new meat: tissue engineered skeletal muscle. *Trend in Food Science and Technology*, 21, 59–66.

Lindström, V. (2020). *Ultrasonic Assisted Drying and Its Effect on 3D Printability of Minced Beef and Other Foods*. Lund University. http://lup.lub.lu.se/student-papers/record/9001595

Lipton, J., Arnold, D., Nigl, F., Lopez, N., Cohen, D., Norén, N., & Lipson, H. (2010). Multi-material food printing with complex internal structure suitable for conventional post-processing. http://citeseerx.ist.psu.edu/viewdoc/summary?doi=10.1.1.375.7717

Liu, C., Ho, C., & Wang, J. (2017). The development of 3D food printer for printing fibrous meat materials. *Materials Science and Engineering*, 284, 012019. doi: 10.1088/1757-899X/284/1/012019

Liu, Z., Zhang, M., & Bhandari, B. (2018). Effect of gums on the rheological, microstructural and extrusion printing characteristics of mashed potatoes. *International Journal of Biological Macromolecules*, 117, 1179–1187.

Liu, Z., Zhang, M., Bhandari, B., & Wang, Y. (2017). 3D printing: Printing precision and application in food sector. *Trends in Food Science & Technology*, 69, 83–94.

Lupton, D., & Turner, B. (2018). Food of the future? Consumer responses to the idea of 3d-printed meat and insect-based foods. *Food and Foodways*, 26, 4269–4289.

Lynch, J., & Pierrehumbert, R. (2019). Climate impacts of cultured meat and beef cattle. *Frontiers in Sustainable Food Systems*. doi: 10.3389/fsufs.2019.00005

Mancini, M. C., & Antonioli, F. (2019). Exploring consumers' attitude towards cultured meat in Italy. *Meat Science*, *150*, 101–110.

Marsden, R. 2013). Print your own food: 3D technology brings a personal touch to pizzas, pasta and cakes. http://www.dailymail.co.uk/news/article-2521606/Print-food.html

McGrath, M. (2019). Cultured lab meat may make climate change worse. https://www.bbc.com/news/science-environment-47283162. Accessed on April 15, 2019.

Mohorčich, J., & Reese, J. (2019). Cell-cultured meat: Lessons from GMO adoption and resistance. *Appetite*, *143*, 104408.

Molitch-Hou, M. (2014). 11 food 3D printers to feed the future. http://3dprintingindustry.com/news/11-food-3d-printers-36052/

Nunes, M. C., Raymundo, A., & Sousa, I. (2006). Rheological behaviour and microstructure of pea protein/κ-carrageenan/starch gels with different setting conditions. *Food Hydrocolloids*, 20,106–113.

Park, J. M., & Kim, J. M. (2016). Monitoring of used frying oils and frying times for frying chicken nuggets using peroxide value and acid value. *Korean Journal for Food Science of Animal Resources*, *36*(5), 612–616.

Periard, D., Schaal, N., Schaal, M., Malone, E., & Lipson, H. (2007). Printing food. In: *Proceedings of the 18th Solid Freeform Fabrication Symposium*, Austin TX: Citeseer, 564–574.

Peters, A. (2018). Lab-grown meat is getting cheap enough for anyone to buy. https://www.fastcompany.com/40565582/lab-grown-meat-is-getting-cheap-enough-for-anyone-to-buy. Accessed November 10, 2018.

Portanguen, S., Tournayre, P., Sicard, J., Astruc, T., & Mirade, P.-S. (2019). Toward the design of functional foods and biobased products by 3D printing: A review. *Trends in Food Science and Technology*, *86*, 188–198.

Post, M. J. (2014). Cultured beef: medical technology to produce food. *Journal of Science of Food and Agriculture*, *94*, 1039–1041.

Post, M. J., & Hocquette, J. F. (2017). New sources of animal proteins: Cultured meat. In: *New Aspects of Meat Quality: From Genes to Ethics*. Purslow, P. (Ed). United Kingdom: Woodhead Publishing.

Rahimi, D., Kashaninejad, M., Ziaiifar, A. M., & Mahoonak, A. S. (2018). Effect of infrared final cooking on some physicochemical and engineering properties of partially fried chicken nugget. *Innovative Food Science and Emerging Technologies*, *47*, 1–8.

Rorheim, A., Mannino, A., Baumann, T., & Caviola, L. (2016). Cultured meat: an ethical alternative to industrial animal farming. *Policy Paper by Sentience Politics*, *1*, 1–14.

Seale, P., & Rudnicki, M. A. (2000). A New Look at the origin, function, and "stem-cell" status of muscle satellite cells. *Developmental Biology*, *218*(2), 115–124.

Severini, C., Derossi, A., Ricci, I., Caporizzi, R., & Fiore, A. (2017). Printing a blend of fruit and vegetables. New advances on critical variables and shelf life of 3D edible objects. *Journal of Food Engineering*, *220*, 89–100.

Sharma, S., Thind, S. S., & Kaur, A. (2015). In vitro meat production system: Why and how? *Journal of Food Science and Technology*, *52*, 7599–7607.

Shurpin, Y. (2018). Is the lab-created burger kosher? https://www.chabad.org/library/article_cdo/aid/2293219/jewish/Is-the-Lab-Created-Burger-Kosher.htm. Accessed December 4, 2018.

Siegrist, M., & Sutterlin, B. (2016). People's reliance on the affect heuristic may result in a biased perception of gene technology. *Food Quality and Preference*, *54*, 137–140.

Siegrist, M., & Sütterlin, B. (2017) Importance of perceived naturalness for acceptance of food additives and cultured meat. *Appetite*, *113*, 320–326.

Siegrist, M., Hartmann, C., & Sütterlin, B. (2016) Biased perception about gene technology: How perceived naturalness and affect distort benefit perception. *Appetite*, *96*, 509–516.

Siegrist, M., Sütterlin, B., & Hartmann, C. (2018) Perceived naturalness and evoked disgust influence acceptance of cultured meat. *Meat Science*, *139*, 213–219.

Slade, P. (2018). If you build it, will they eat it? Consumer preferences for plant-based and cultured meat burgers. *Appetite*, *125*, 428–437.

Snyman, C., Goetsch, K. P., Myburgh, K. H., & Niesler, C. U. (2013). Simple silicone chamber system for in vitro three-dimensional skeletal muscle tissue formation. *Frontiers in Physiology*, *4*, 349.

Stephens, N., Silvio, L. D., Dunsford, I., Ellis, M., Glencross, A., & Sexton, A. (2018). Bringing cultured meat to market: Technical, socio-political, and regulatory challenges in cellular agriculture. *Trends in Food Science and Technology*, *78*, 155–166.

Tahergorabi, R., & Jaczynski, J. (2012). Physicochemical changes in surimi with salt substitute. *Food Chemistry*, *132*, 1281–1286.

The BBC. (2020). Singapore approves lab-grown 'chicken' meat. https://www.bbc.com/news/business-55155741. Accessed February 10, 2021.

Tuomisto, H. L. (2019) Vertical farming and cultured meat: Immature technologies for urgent problems. *One Earth, 1*(3), 275–277.

US FDA. (2018). https://www.fda.gov/NewsEvents/Newsroom/PressAnnouncements/ucm626117.htm. Accessed November 23, 2018.

USDA, FSAIS. (1998). The color of meat and poultry. http://dwb.unl.edu/teacher/ nsf/c10/c10links/www.fsis.usda.gov/oa/pubs/mpcolor.htm

Verbeke, W., Marcu, A., Rutsaert, P., Gaspar, R., Seibt, B., Fletcher, D., & Barnett, J. (2015a). 'Would you eat cultured meat?': Consumers' reactions and attitude formation in Belgium, Portugal and the United Kingdom. *Meat Science, 102*, 49–58.

Verbeke, W., Sans, P., & Loo, E. J. V. (2015b). Challenges and prospects for consumer acceptance of cultured meat. *Journal of Integrative Agriculture, 14*(2), 285–294.

Wang, L., Zhang, M., Bhandari, B., & Yang, C. (2018). Investigation on fish surimi gel as promising food material for 3D printing. *Journal of Food Engineering, 220*, 101–108.

Weinrich, R., Strack, M., & Neugebauer, F. (2020). Consumer acceptance of cultured meat in Germany. *Meat Science, 162*, 107924.

Wilks, M., Phillips, C. J. C., Fielding, K., & Hornsey, M. J. (2019). Testing potential psychological predictors of attitudes towards cultured meat. *Appetite, 136*, 137–145.

Wilson, A., Anukiruthika, T., Moses, J. A., & Anandharamakrishnan, C. (2020). Customized shapes for chicken meat-based products: Feasibility study on 3D-printed nuggets. *Food and Bioprocess Technology, 13*, 1968–1983.

Wu, C., Na, X., Ma, W., Ren, C., Zhong, Q., Wang, T., & Du, M. (2021). Strong, elastic, and tough high internal phase emulsions stabilized solely by cod myofibers for multidisciplinary applications. *Chemical Engineering Journal, 412*, 128724.

Yang, F., Zhang, M., Prakash, S., & Liu, Y. (2018). Physical properties of 3D printed baking dough as affected by different compositions. *Innovative Food Science & Emerging Technologies, 49*, 202–210. doi:10.1016/j.ifset.2018.01.001.

Zhao, Z., Wang, Q., Yan, B., Gao, W., Jiao, X., Huang, J., Zhao, J., Zhang, H., Chen, W., & Fan, D. (2021). Synergistic effect of microwave 3D print and transglutaminase on the self-gelation of surimi during printing. *Innovative Food Science and Emerging Technologies, 67*, 102546.

10 Bioconversion of Marine By-Products into Edible Protein

Abdo Hassoun[1], Turid Rustad[2], and Alaa El-Din Ahmed Bekhit[3]

[1]Agriculture and Food security, Syrian Academic Expertise (SAE), 27200 Gaziantep, Turkey
[2]Department of Biotechnology and Food Science, NTNU-Norwegian University of Science and Technology, NTNU, NO-7491 Trondheim, Norway
[3]Department of Food Science, University of Otago, Dunedin, New Zealand

CONTENTS

10.1 Introduction 297
10.2 Marine By-Products: Potential Sources and Volumes 300
10.3 Handling, Industrial Processing, and Impact of Processing Conditions 301
    10.3.1 Production of Protein Isolate 303
    10.3.2 Production of Protein Hydrolysates and Peptides...............................303
        10.3.2.1 Chemical Methods..303
        10.3.2.2 Enzymatic Hydrolysis...306
        10.3.2.3 Fermentation 307
    10.3.3 Extraction Other Protein-Based Products (e.g., Collagen, Enzymes) 307
10.4 Analytical Methods Used to Monitor Processing of Marine By-Products 308
    10.4.1 Emerging Technologies for Extraction and Separation 308
    10.4.2 Emerging Technologies for Analysis 309
10.5 Composition, Nutritional Value and Potential Health Benefits......................310
10.6 Utilization of Marine Proteins and Protein-Derived Products........................311
    10.6.1 Use of Marine By-Products for Producing Feeds and Fertilizers 312
    10.6.2 Food Applications 312
    10.6.3 Medical, Pharmaceutical and Cosmetic Industries..............................313
10.7 Consumer Acceptance and Religious Aspects 313
10.8 Challenges and Future Trends 315
References..316

10.1 INTRODUCTION

Fish and other marine products are important protein sources in human nutrition and contain a range of several nutritional components such as proteins with a high content of essential amino acids, vitamins, minerals, lipids with a high content of omega-3 polyunsaturated fatty acids. Above all, seafood plays a significant role in global food safety and security; indeed, food safety and security has become a major concern, especially during the current pandemic, with the COVID-19 crisis raging around the world, affecting every aspect of life, including consumer food choices and nutrition habits (Eftimov et al., 2020; FAO, 2020a; Hassoun et al. 2020; 2020; Li et al. 2020).

In 2018, the total global production of fish from aquaculture and capture fisheries was estimated to be around 179 million tonnes, including 96.4 million tonnes from the capture fisheries and 82.1 million tonnes from aquaculture (FAO, 2020b). For the last three decades, the production from capture fisheries has been stable due to the fact that most fisheries are already fully or over-exploited. On the other hand, a significant increase has been recorded in the production of the aquaculture sector, although feed availability remains a challenging factor that could limit growth and development in the aquaculture sector in the future (Figure 10.1).

The rapid growth in the world population has increased the need for improving the utilization of existing protein sources and the development of new and sustainable food production (Nguyen et al., 2020a). This has led to a huge effort to be invested in recent years into finding new protein sources along with reducing food waste. According to the United Nations food agency, one-third of all food produced for human consumption goes to waste (Gustavsson et al., 2011), which explains the emergence of several initiatives focusing on the reduction of food waste. Thus, alternative protein sources such as by-products from the agro-industrial sector (Coelho et al., 2020; Gençdağ et al., 2020), insects, livestock and marine by-products (Baiano, 2020; Gasco et al., 2020; Ojha et al., 2020; Shen et al., 2019) have emerged as interesting solutions. Especially marine wastes have received much attention in recent years as the fisheries and aquaculture sectors are among the most wasteful industrial activities. In these sectors, more and more quantities of waste are generated each year due to the growth in aquaculture activities and the large, industrial-scale processing operations (Gehring et al., 2011; Khawli et al., 2019; Villamil et al., 2017). Figure 10.2 shows the increasing number of publications on marine waste/marine by-products in the last two decades.

The term 'marine waste' refers, in general, to heads, bones, skin, shells and viscera that are unsuitable for human consumption, as well as the by-catch. Another term that is commonly used is 'by-product' describing all the leftovers of fish and shellfish after primary processing. In some studies, the terms 'rest raw materials' or co-streams are used instead of the term by-products (Hjellnes et al., 2020; Penven et al., 2013; Rustad et al., 2011; Shahidi & Ambigaipalan, 2019). However, the term 'by-product' is the most common and will be used in this chapter as a collective term to describe by-catch and marine processing waste. According to Rustad et al., (2011), the term 'by-products' appears to be appropriate to encompass all raw material, edible and inedible, that remains after the production of the main products (Rustad et al., 2011; Stevens et al., 2018).

Catch and seafood processing generate large amounts of marine by-products, which are either discarded, causing a considerable disposal cost and environmental problems, or used to produce low-value products, such as animal feed and fertilizers (Hjellnes et al., 2020; Nguyen et al., 2020a). Better management of marine biomass by exploiting these by-products in protein recovery and extraction of other valuable products will save natural bioresources and address the financial

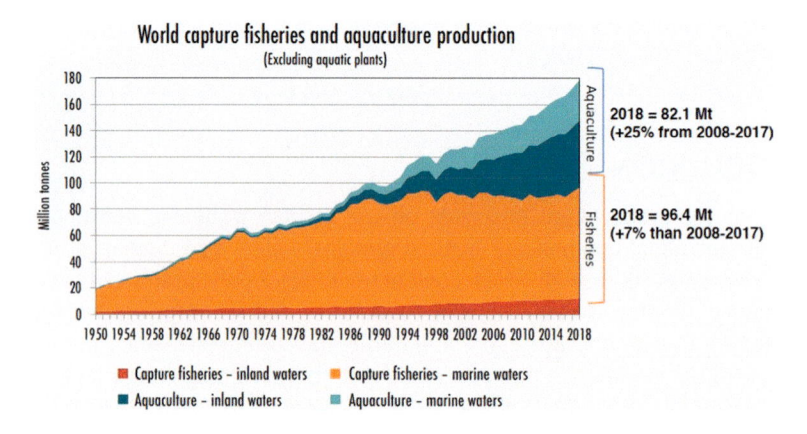

FIGURE 10.1 World capture fisheries and aquaculture production. Adapted from FAO (2020b).

Bioconversion of Marine By-Products 299

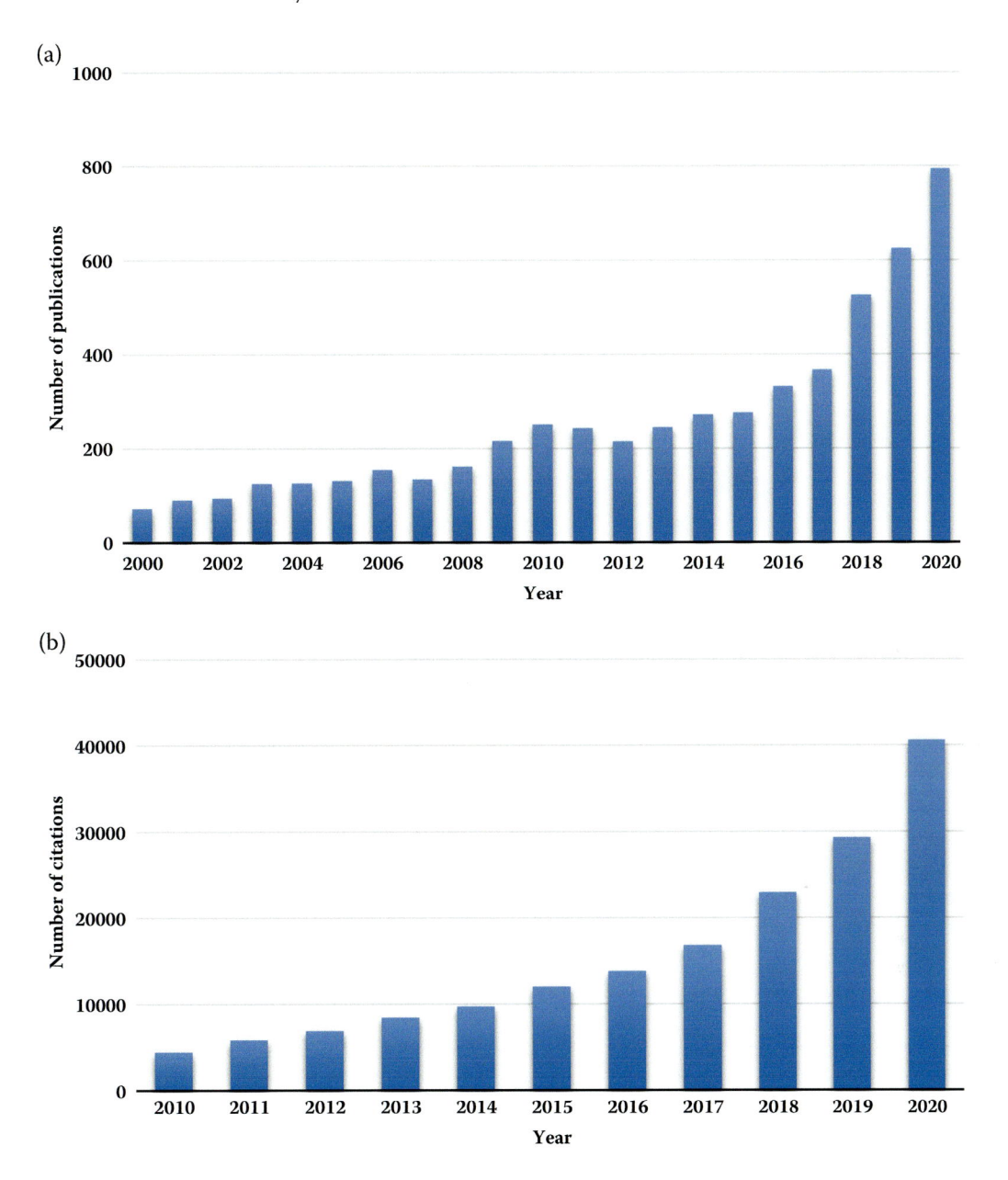

FIGURE 10.2 Publications indexed in Scopus dealing with topics related to marine waste: (a) number of publications, (b) number of citations. (Search criteria: Keywords; marine waste AND/OR marine by-products). The search was performed in November 2020.

and environmental burdens of biowaste, enabling a greener production system and a circular economy. Thus, efficient utilization of marine by-products will contribute to achieving the United States sustainable development goal 14, namely to conserve and sustainably use the oceans, seas and marine resources for sustainable development (Gilman et al., 2020; Hjellnes et al., 2020; Nguyen et al., 2020a). Several recent studies have demonstrated that most of these by-products are good sources of valuable compounds that can be used in many applications (Figure 10.3) (Khawli et al., 2019; Shahidi & Ambigaipalan, 2019; Stevens et al., 2018; Utne-Palm et al., 2020). For

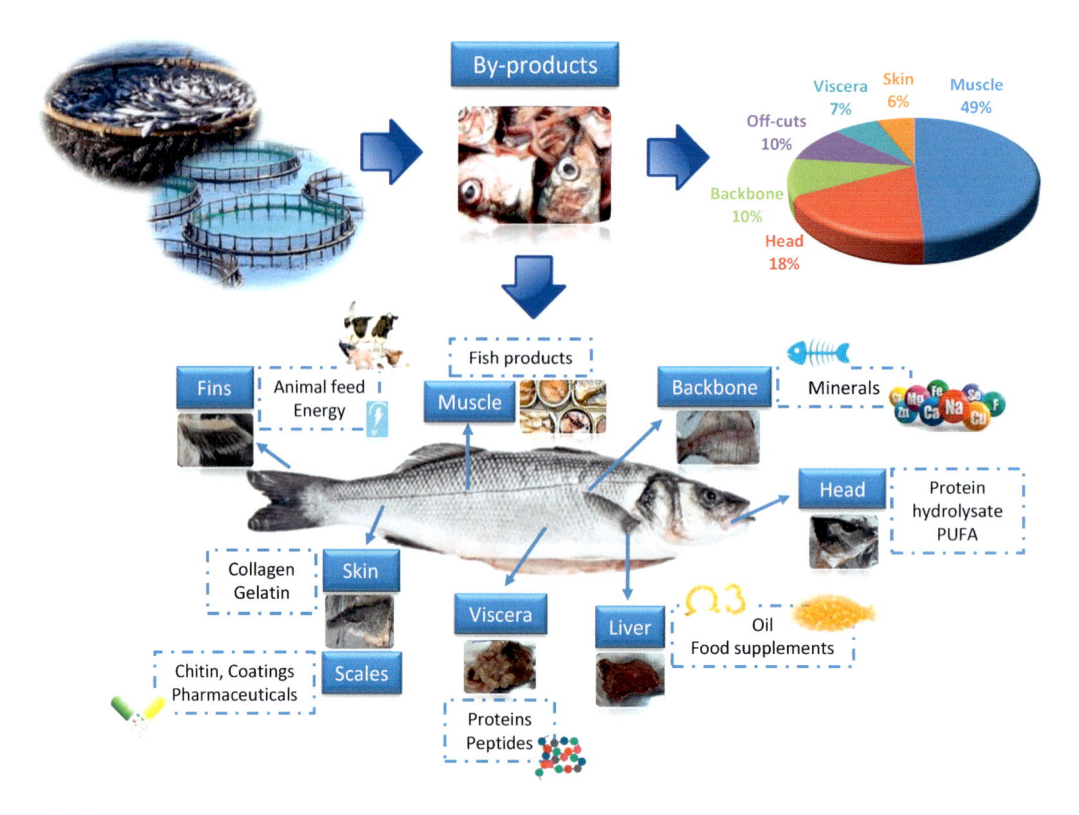

FIGURE 10.3 Fish by-products generated during processing and their end-use applications (Khawli et al. 2019).

example, skin, bones, scales, and other seafood by-products can be a good source of collagen, while crab and shrimp shells can be used to extract chitin (Kaur & Dhillon, 2015; Senadheera et al., 2020; Uranga et al., 2020).

10.2 MARINE BY-PRODUCTS: POTENTIAL SOURCES AND VOLUMES

There are different estimates as to how much waste is generated from fisheries and aquaculture, but most references report huge amounts of loss and by-products that are affected by many factors occurring along the production chain (primary production, post-production, processing, distribution and consumption) and value chain activities (catch or harvest methods, handling, transport, storage, preparation) (Figure 10.4). Globally, in fisheries and aquaculture, around 30–35% of the total harvest is lost or wasted every year (FAO, 2020b).

Seafood pre-processing operations, including beheading, de-shelling, skinning, gutting, removal of fins and scales, filleting, and washing lead to significant raw material weight losses (Ideia et al., 2020; Sasidharan & Venugopal, 2020). Taking Atlantic salmon by-products as an example, it was estimated that the viscera (guts) represent 12.5%, head 10%, frames (bones with attached flesh) 10%, skin 3.5%, trimmings 2%, blood 2%, belly flaps 1.5% (Stevens et al., 2018). Besides fish, crustacean and mollusc production results in huge quantities of by-products. For example, it was reported that during shrimp processing, approximately 50–60% of solid waste is generated as by-products, including the head, viscera, and shell. In some species, the waste percentage could be even higher; for example, in Antarctic krill, only 10–15% of the meat can be recovered. Generally speaking, the discards from shellfish represent from 50% to 80% (Ambigaipalan & Shahidi, 2017; Gehring et al., 2011; Nirmal et al., 2020; Shahidi & Ambigaipalan, 2019). Further processing of

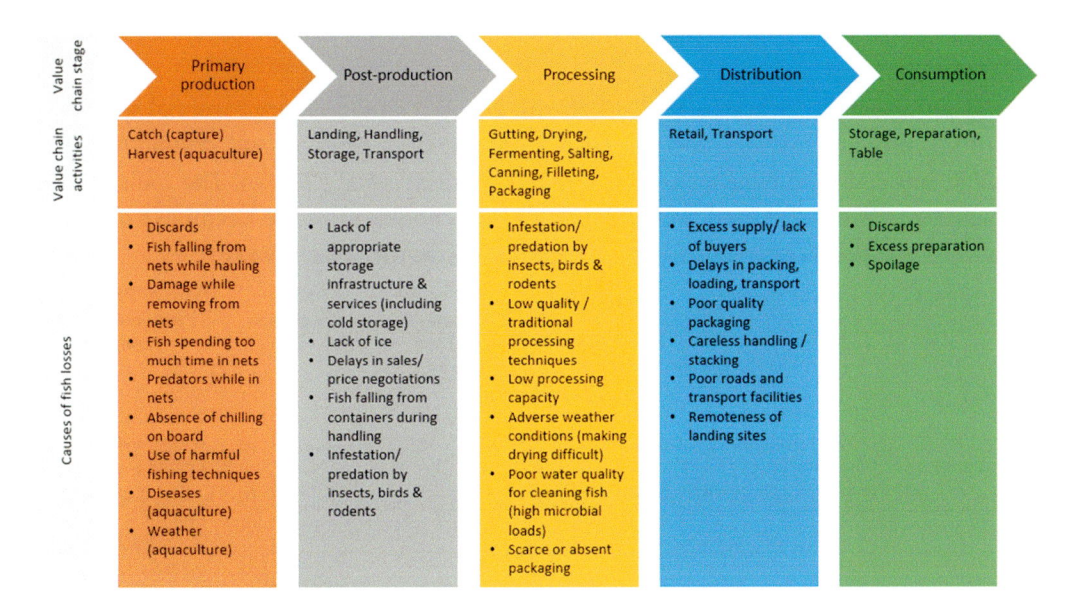

FIGURE 10.4 Fish loss and waste along the value chain: stages and causes (Kruijssen et al. 2020).

fish and other seafood, such as smoking, canning and salting, will generate additional amounts of waste (Ferraro et al., 2010; Rustad et al., 2011; Sasidharan & Venugopal, 2020).

In addition to by-products originating from the processing of fish and shellfish (crustaceans and molluscs), discards from by-catch represent a significant part of the marine waste. The by-catch is the portion of the catch that was not originally targeted, maybe due to undesirable species/size, leading to the generation of underutilized commercial species. Some or all the by-catch may be returned to the sea as discard, which is contrary to responsible fishing practices. That is why fisheries were subject to Landing Obligations at the beginning of 2015, and by 2019, all EU fisheries were required to land the entire catch of all species (Iñarra et al., 2019; Gasco et al., 2020; Kruijssen et al., 2020; Shahidi & Ambigaipalan, 2019; Vázquez et al., 2019b).

These fishery by-products are traditionally considered to be of low value and discarded or used in the production of feed or fertilizers (Olsen et al., 2014; Shahidi & Ambigaipalan, 2019). However, in recent times, considerable research in different has been done to explore new and advanced applications of ingredients or compounds originating from marine by-products, e.g., food, functional food, pharmaceuticals, cosmetics, biodiesel production, among others (Ferraro et al., 2010; Harnedy & FitzGerald, 2012; Shahidi & Ambigaipalan, 2019). A summary of potential content and type of protein materials recovered from seafood processing by-products is shown in Table 10.1.

10.3 HANDLING, INDUSTRIAL PROCESSING, AND IMPACT OF PROCESSING CONDITIONS

Marine by-products, similar to all marine products, are highly perishable and require rapid hygienic handling or adequate preservation methods after the catch or harvest. In fact, marine products and by-products may require strict handling and care since physical treatments carried out during processing and handling can exert physical damage and trigger undesirable chemical and biochemical changes. Onboard handling, sorting, and monitoring of marine by-products are recommended to prevent microbial spoilage, enzymatic reactions, and lipid oxidation. Most of the fishing vessels are small and do not have enough space to ensure proper onboard handling of all

TABLE 10.1

Seafood processing by-products (SPBs) generated from common marine animal species, their ratios, protein contents, and potential for recovery of proteins and protein-based products. Sourced from Nguyen and co-workers (Nguyen et al., 2020a). The table is from open access article distributed under the terms and conditions of the Creative Commons Attribution (CC BY) license (http://creativecommons.org/licenses/by/4.0/)

Marine Groups	Typical Species	By-Product Types	Ratio of By-Products (%) of Total Weight	Protein Contents (%)	Type of Proteins or Protein-Derived Products
Finfish	Pollock, cod, hake, haddock, salmon, tuna, herring, mackerel, and among many others	Heads	15–20	11.9–12.9 a	Proteins, protein hydrolysates, peptides
		Frames	10–15	11.5–17.5 a	Collagen, gelatin, protein hydrolysates, peptides
		Skins and fins	1–3	24.8–27.0 a	Collagen, gelatin, protein hydrolysates, peptides
		Bones	9–15	36.3–56.8 b	Collagen, gelatin, protein hydrolysates, peptides
		Scales	3–5	41–81 b	Ichthylepidin and collagen, biopeptides
		Viscera (livers, roes, and milts)	15–20	12.9–14.8 a	Enzymes, protein hydrolysates, peptides, peptides
		Blood	2–7	0.8–5.7 a	Plasma proteins, active amino acids, enzyme inhibitors
Crustacean	Krill, shrimp, crap, crayfish, lobster	Shells, tails	15	29–40 b	Shell proteins, caroteno-proteins
		Heads	25	43.5–54.4 b	Shell and meat proteins
		Viscera (livers, roes)	5	41 b	Enzymes, protein hydrolysates, peptides
Mollusc	Oyster, mussel, clam, scallop	Shells	75–80	1–5 b	Bioactive peptides
		Body parts and organs		58.7 b	Enzyme, protein hydrolysate, biopeptide, flavour
	Cuttlefish, squid, octopus	Ink bags, organs, and non-edible portions	25–44.3	5–22 a	Enzymes, bioactive peptides, food flavours, taurine
Coelenterate and echinoderm	Sea urchin	Shells, viscera	40.7–77.9	4.1–5.0 b	Bioactive proteins for self-assembly of skeletal structure
	Sea cucumber	viscera		4.5 a	Enzymes, protein hydrolysate, bioactive peptides
	Jelly fish			3–7 a	Protein hydrolysate, bioactive peptides, collagen, gelatin

catches. However, modern, large-scale fishing vessels are normally equipped with chilling and freezing systems to maintain the quality of products/co-products before further processing. In the absence of advanced preservation technologies, fish silage can be produced by adding acids, lactic acid bacteria, and antibiotics in some cases to the raw material at ambient temperature. The resulting fish silage can be used directly as feed, mixed with other feed ingredients, or used as fertilizer (Toppe & Penarubia, 2018). However, economics plays a major role in retaining the co-products or not as they are in direct competition with primary products (e.g., fish muscle) for space and use of facilities.

10.3.1 Production of Protein Isolate

Several methods can be used for protein extraction from marine by-products. Isoelectric solubilization/precipitation (or pH shift) is the most common method due to cost. The technique is based on the change of electrostatic charge of proteins at different pH values. First, the pH will be either increased using alkali or decreased using acids in order to solubilize the muscle proteins, then bones, scales, neutral lipids, and disrupted cellular membranes will be removed by separation (centrifugation). The last step is the precipitation of the proteins at their isoelectric point (pH 5.2–5.5). The pH-shift process is performed at low temperatures in order to avoid excessive protein denaturation, and high yields of recovered proteins can be achieved that can range between 40% and 90% depending on the starting material and the process/extraction conditions (pH, temperature, pressure, time and solid: liquid ratio) (Gehring et al., 2011; Nguyen et al., 2020a; Sasidharan & Venugopal, 2020; Surasani, 2018; Tian et al., 2017; Zhong et al., 2016).

Isoelectric precipitation has been used in several studies to recover protein isolates from several seafood by-products. For example, the technique was used to recover high-quality proteins and lipids from rainbow trout processing by-products using basic and acidic pH treatments (Chen et al., 2007). The results showed high contents of essential amino acids in the isolate obtained by basic pH treatment. This technique was also used successfully in the recovery of fish proteins from silver carp processing by-products (Zhong et al., 2016). Recently, fish protein isolates were successfully extracted from catfish by-products by alkaline extraction and salt extraction (Tan et al., 2019b).

10.3.2 Production of Protein Hydrolysates and Peptides

Marine protein hydrolysate is a mixture of cleaved proteins obtained by hydrolysing proteins into peptides and amino acids. Protein hydrolysis is commonly used to increase protein recovery and the yield of valuable components (Aspevik et al., 2017; Vang et al., 2018). Protein hydrolysates can be performed chemically (use of acid or alkali treatment), biochemically (use of enzymes) or bacterially (fermentation). An early review paper by Kristinsson and Rasco described the various techniques used for manufacturing fish protein hydrolysates (Kristinsson & Rasco, 2000). Table 10.2 shows some relevant examples of the different methods used to produce protein hydrolysates or related compounds.

10.3.2.1 Chemical Methods

Chemical agents (acid or alkali treatment) are used at extreme working conditions (high temperature and sometimes at high pressure) to cleave the bonds between different amino groups in the protein sequence, and to obtain peptides of various sizes. Acid hydrolysis is more common in the marine industry than is alkaline hydrolysis, and the resulting acid hydrolysed proteins can be used to produce fertilizers or organic acids (lactic and acetic acids) (Vang et al., 2018; Vázquez et al., 2020a).

Chemically hydrolysed proteins have both advantages and disadvantages. Indeed, although chemical hydrolysis is simple and inexpensive, the process is difficult to control and causes indiscriminate cleavage of chemical bonds. This results in protein hydrolysates of poor nutritional

TABLE 10.2
Examples of studies reporting on the use of marine by-products to produce protein hydrolysates

Marine Product	By-Products	Enzyme/ Microorganisms/ Chemical	Recovered Products	Activities/ Studied Properties	References
Shrimp (*Penaens vannamei*)	Heads	Endogenous enzymes (autolysis)	Protein hydrolysates	Amino acid composition	Cao et al. (2008)
Black scabbardfish (*Aphanopus carbo*)	Heads, viscera, frames, skin, and trimmings	Protamex™	Protein hydrolysates	Antioxidant activities	Batista et al. (2010)
Sardinella (*Sardinella aurita*)	Heads and viscera	Microbial proteases	Protein hydrolysates	Antioxidant activities	Bougatef et al. (2010)
Horse mackerel (*Magalaspis cordyla*) and croaker (*Otolithes ruber*)	Skins	Pepsin, trypsin and a-chymotrypsin	Protein hydrolysates	Antioxidative activity	Sampath Kumar et al. (2012)
Tuna	Tuna dark muscle by-products	Alcalase	Protein hydrolysates, peptides	Nutritional value	Saidi et al. (2014)
Atlantic holothurian *Cucumaria frondosa*	Aquapharyngeal bulb and internal organs	Nine different proteases	Protein hydrolysates	Antiherpetic activities	Tripoteau et al. (2015)
Bluefin leatherjacket (*Navodon septentrionalis*)	Skins	Trypsin, flavourzyme, neutrase, papain, alcalase, and pepsin	Peptides from protein hydrolysates	Antioxidant activities	Chi et al. (2015)
Bluefin leatherjacket	Heads	Papain	Peptides from protein hydrolysates	Antioxidant properties	Chi et al. (2015)
Atlantic salmon (*Salmo salar*)	Heads and backbones	Alcalase 2.4L, Promod 671L and Protex 7L	Protein hydrolysates	Sensory, surface-active, and chemical properties	Aspevik et al. (2016)
Australian Rock Lobster (*Jasus edwardsii*)	Shells	Alcalase	Protein hydrolysates	Functional properties (solubility, emulsification and foaming capacities…)	Nguyen et al. (2016)
Small-spotted catshark (*Scyliorhinus canicula*)	*S. canicula* muscle by-products	Alcalase, Esperase, and Protamex	Protein hydrolysates	Antioxidant and antihypertensive activities	Vázquez et al. (2017)
Atlantic salmon	Viscera	Flavourzyme, formic acid, lactic acid bacteria	Protein hydrolysates	Antioxidant activity	Subin et al. (2018)
Salmon	Viscera	Autolysis, Alcalase, papain	Protein hydrolysates	Protein recovery, molecular weight distribution, amino acid profile	Lapeña et al. (2018)

TABLE 10.2 (Continued)
Examples of studies reporting on the use of marine by-products to produce protein hydrolysates

Marine Product	By-Products	Enzyme/ Microorganisms/ Chemical	Recovered Products	Activities/ Studied Properties	References
Megrim, hake, boarfish, grenadier, and Atlantic horse mackerel	Skins and heads	Alcalase, lactic acid bacteria	Gelatin, oils, fish protein hydrolysates, and peptones	Antioxidant and antihypertensive activities	Vázquez et al. 2019)(2019b)
Salmon	Frames	Alcalase, Papain	Protein hydrolysates	Antioxidant properties	Idowu et al. (2019)
Squid (*Dosidicus gigas*)	Fins and arms	Protease XIV	Collagen peptides	Antioxidant, antimutagenic, and Antiproliferative activities	Suárez-Jiménez et al. (2019)
Channel catfish (*Ictalurus punctatus*)	Heads and frames	Papain, ficin, bromelain, neutrase, alcalase, protamex, novo-proD and thermolysin	Hydrolysates of proteins and lipids	Emulsifying and foaming properties	Tan et al. (2019a)
Rainbow trout (*Oncorhynchus mykiss*)	Head, viscera, fins, and backbone	Alcalase	Protein hydrolysates	Antioxidant activity	Nikoo et al. (2019)
Snakehead (*Channa argus*)	Skin	Pepsin	Collagen	Structural and physicochemical properties	Liu et al. (2019)
Micropogonias furnieri and *Paralonchurus brasiliensis*	Muscle and skin samples	Alcalase, Protamex	Protein hydrolysates	Antioxidant properties	Rocha Camargo et al. (2021)
Several bycatch species	Fish discard by-products	Alcalase	Protein hydrolysates and fish oil, bioactive peptides and fish peptones	Chemical and functional properties	Vázquez et al. 2020)(2020b)
Serra Spanish mackerel (*Scomberomorus brasiliensis*)	Bones and crushed scales	Alcalase and Flavourzyme	Protein hydrolysates	Technological and nutritional properties	Lima et al. (2020)
Red Tilapia (*Oreochromis spp.*)	Viscera	Alcalase	Protein hydrolysates	Iron-binding activity; iron bioavailability	Gómez et al. (2020)
Blue shark (*Prionace glauca*)	Skins	Alcalase	Gelatin	Antioxidant activity	Limpisophon et al. (2020)

and functional qualities due to the partial or total destruction of valuable amino acids such as cysteine, serine and threonine, and the possible formation of toxic substances with alkaline hydrolyses, such as lysinoalanine, ornithinoalanine, and lanthionine (Özyurt & Özkütük, 2019; Patraşcu & Aprodu, 2017; Vang et al., 2018).

10.3.2.2 Enzymatic Hydrolysis

Enzymatic hydrolysis of marine by-products has been extensively investigated in recent years as a better biotechnological solution that allows more profitable and sustainable uses of protein sources. In this process, endogenous or added (commercial) enzymes have been used to cleave peptide bonds between amino acids. However, the commercial proteases (extracted from animals, plants, or microbial sources) are most often a mixture of several enzymes that could have different specificities and hydrolytic rates (Aspevik et al., 2017; Wubshet et al., 2019).

The enzymatic hydrolysis by endogenous enzymes (called autolysis) generally takes a long time and can be difficult to standardize and control since endogenous enzymes depend on many factors (e.g., age and maturity of the host, environment and diet). Although autolysis has traditionally been used to produce fish sauce and silage, some studies have shown that good protein hydrolysates can be obtained under optimized conditions. For example, protein hydrolysates obtained by autolysis method from shrimp heads at pH 7.85 and 50 °C for 3 hours gave protein hydrolysates of a high degree of hydrolysis (close to 45%) with enhanced functional properties (Cao et al., 2008). In a recent study (Derouiche Ben Maiz et al., 2019), autolysis was used to produce bullet tuna viscera protein hydrolysates as an alternative to the more costly enzymatic hydrolysis (using expensive well-characterized commercial enzymes).

Enzymatic protein hydrolysis using exogenous enzymes has several advantages over autolysis or chemical hydrolysis such as high selectivity and specificity, mild reaction conditions, and controllable hydrolysis. In addition, the bioactive and functional properties of proteins can be improved by the action of enzymes, and the resulting protein hydrolysates can be used in various ways because of their well-balanced nutritional value (Aspevik et al., 2017; Lopes et al., 2018; Senadheera et al., 2020; Zamora-Sillero et al., 2018).

The enzymatic protein hydrolysis is a versatile technology that involves several steps, as shown in Figure 10.5.

The process starts when marine by-products are homogenized and suspended in an appropriate amount of water or buffer. Then, the processing conditions (e.g., temperature and pH) are adjusted and a selected protease (or enzyme mixtures) is added to initiate protein hydrolysis. After a specific hydrolysis time, the hydrolysis is deactivated by heating or adjusting the pH value to a level that inactivates the enzyme. Finally, the reaction mixture is pumped into a unit that separates it into three fractions: solid, liquid, and oil (Nguyen et al., 2020a; Wubshet et al., 2018; 2019). An emulsion phase is also often obtained. The enzymes used in the process can be classified into exopeptidases and endopeptidases, depending on whether they hydrolyse the polypeptide at the side chain or the interior part of the protein molecule, respectively (Petrova et al., 2018; Välimaa et al., 2019; Wubshet et al., 2019; Zamora-Sillero et al., 2018).

Enzymatic protein hydrolysis is a complex process, and multiple factors are usually involved in the production of hydrolysed proteins, including among others the quality of raw materials, the

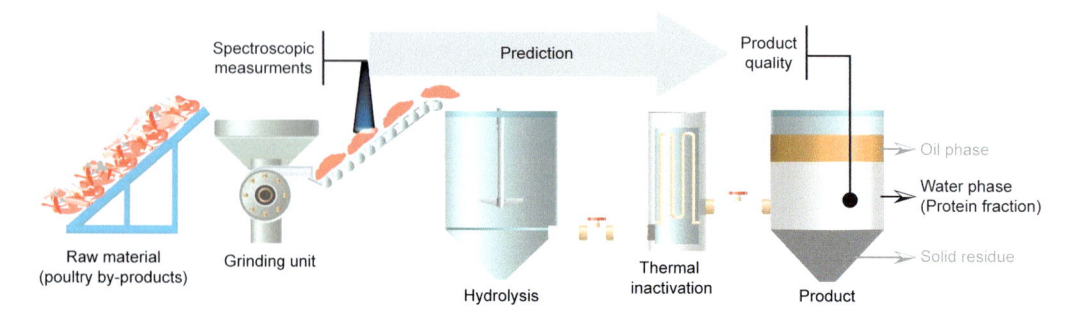

FIGURE 10.5 The main processing stages in enzymatic protein hydrolysis of by-products (Wubshet et al., 2019).

enzymes used, and other processing conditions, such as temperature and pH. By optimizing these factors, hydrolysates with desired molecular structures, functional properties, and bioactive functions can be obtained.

Several parameters can be used to measure the success of given enzymatic protein hydrolysis, such as the product yield and the degree of hydrolysis. Considerable research has been put into developing a successful enzymatic protein hydrolysis process based on various protein-rich by-products. Most studies have used response surface methodology to optimize operating conditions using the degree of hydrolysis or certain activity as the evaluation criterion. Response surface methodology was used to optimize the hydrolysis conditions of viscera hydrolysates for red tilapia (*Oreochromis* spp.) using the degree of hydrolysis and the effect of molecular weight distribution on iron-chelating activity (Gómez et al., 2020). A similar approach was used to determine optimized conditions for producing protein hydrolysates from turbot by-products (heads, viscera, and trimmings + frames), with high nutritional quality (balanced composition of amino acids and high digestibility) and good antioxidant and antihypertensive properties (Vázquez et al., 2020c). Generally, most of the reported studies were conducted in order to find process conditions that are optimized for different raw material properties so that the industry can deliver products with well-defined properties.

Despite the promising potential of protein from fish co-products generated by enzymatic treatments, there are some obstacles that prevent the widespread application of enzymatic protein hydrolysis. The bitter taste of the resulting hydrolysates and the complexity of the process as well as multiple factors that determine the quality of the product are considered the main limitations (Petrova et al., 2018). It is well known that marine raw material (or rest raw material/by-products) are characterized by huge variability due to differences in marine species, age, fishing area, season, feeding regime, etc. The high heterogeneity of the raw material makes it challenging to produce the maximum possible yield of a high-quality product within required specifications and with limited or no batch-to-batch variations. In addition, most of the studies have been conducted at a laboratory scale with well-defined operating conditions. However, the transition from laboratory-scale experiments to industrial applications might face some challenges (e.g., cost, processing issues), and consumer acceptance is not well investigated. Hence, the demonstration phase of innovative products is an important consideration that allows a cost assessment and the ability to test new products in the market before the products are commercialized on a large scale (Aspevik et al., 2017).

10.3.2.3 Fermentation

Bacterial fermentation has been proposed as an alternative, safe, environment-friendly, and low-cost energy method for producing protein hydrolysates (Marti-Quijal et al., 2020). Fish sauce is the major fermented fish product consumed worldwide. The process of production of fish sauce is similar to that of fish silage but the pH is neutral instead of acidic. Lactic acid bacteria are the main group that has been widely used for the fermentation of foods (Djellouli et al., 2020; Marti-Quijal et al., 2020). Three different proteolytic lactic acid bacteria (*Enterococcus faecium, Pediococcus acidilactici* and *Pediococcus acidilactici* FD3) have resulted in the recovery of bioactive protein hydrolysates from fish heads (Ruthu et al., 2014). The degree of hydrolysis ranged between 29% and 38%, and the resulting hydrolysates showed promising bioactive properties (antioxidant and antimicrobial). In another study, Choksawangkarn and others extracted bioactive peptides from fermented fish sauce made from by-products (Choksawangkarn et al., 2018).

10.3.3 Extraction Other Protein-Based Products (e.g., Collagen, Enzymes)

In addition to protein hydrolysates and peptides, other protein-derivative compounds (such as collagen, enzymes) can be recovered from marine by-products.

Collagen is a structural protein that is found in the skin and bones of all animals and constitutes ~30% of the total protein content. Collagen from marine origin has interesting properties compared to livestock collagen (e.g., excellent biocompatibility with food regulations, and it has no religious issues), hence the increased research interest in recent times (Kim et al., 2013; Nguyen et al., 2020a; Senadheera et al., 2020; Subhan et al., 2020). Several studies have indicated that by-products resulting from seafood and other marine products can be a potential source of collagen that can be used across a wide range of applications in various industries (Kumar & Rani, 2017; Maschmeyer et al., 2020; Pal & Suresh, 2016; Senadheera et al., 2020). Extensive research has been conducted comparing different methods of extraction, isolation, characterization, properties and applications. Examples of this work include extraction of collagen from the skin of tilapia (*Oreochromis niloticus*) (Li et al., 2018), Northern snakehead (*Channa argus*) (Duan et al., 2018; Liu et al., 2019), sea bass (*Lateolabrax japonicus*) (Kim et al., 2013), and by-products of squid (*Dosidicus gigas*) (Suárez-Jiménez et al., 2019).

Marine enzymes from marine products and seafood by-products are characterized by unique features such as tolerance to high salt concentrations and extreme temperatures, making them of great interest for applications in many fields (Ferraro et al., 2010; Shahidi & Ambigaipalan, 2019; Suresh & Prabhu, 2014; Venugopal, 2016). Most marine origin enzymes are extracted from aquatic invertebrates and internal organs of fish (viscera) and the shells of crustaceans. Proteases, such as pepsin, trypsin and chymotrypsin, and collagenase are among the most extensively studied enzymes from marine sources. Other types of enzymes, such as lipases, carbohydrases, transglutaminases and other enzymes have been successfully isolated from various marine by-products (Suresh & Prabhu, 2014; Venugopal, 2016). More details concerning marine enzymes from seafood by-products and advances in enzyme technology and relevant applications in seafood processing can be found in the literature (Barba et al., 2019; Fernandes, 2016; Morrissey & Okada, 2007).

10.4 ANALYTICAL METHODS USED TO MONITOR PROCESSING OF MARINE BY-PRODUCTS

In recent years, both innovative extraction technologies and analytical methods have been investigated as interesting alternatives to conventional methods.

10.4.1 EMERGING TECHNOLOGIES FOR EXTRACTION AND SEPARATION

Conventional extraction techniques of protein, peptides, collagen and other protein-related compounds present several shortcomings, such as high energy consumption, possible degradation of the extracted compounds due to high temperatures, low extraction yield, etc. To overcome these limitations, several techniques, including pulsed electric field (Gómez et al., 2019), ultrasound and supercritical fluid extraction, among others have recently been developed (Khawli et al., 2019; Nguyen et al. 2020a; Ojha et al. 2020). Some examples of these emerging techniques will be presented here; however, the reader is referred to other references in the literature for a more thorough overview (Bruno et al., 2019; Ciko et al., 2018).

Pulsed electric field (Gómez et al., 2019) has attracted considerable interest in the food industry and academia as an innovative processing approach. PEF refers to the application of high voltage (up to 80 kV/cm) in the form of short pulses over a short duration (in the order of microseconds) with the aim of creating electropores in cells that leads to several beneficial effects. Several studies have indicated that PEF technology is advantageous compared with conventional treatments. Li and co-authors applied a PEF-assisted process to extract protein from abalone (*Haliotis Discus Hannai Ino*) viscera (Li et al., 2016). The results showed the highest extraction yield when the solvent (phosphate buffer solution) to material ratio was 1 to 4 and the PEF was applied for 600 μs at an intensity strength of 20 kV/cm. In addition, the PEF-assisted enzymatic extraction resulted in full hydrolysation and good functional properties (increased solubility and decreased viscosity) of the extracted products compared to traditional enzymatic extraction.

Recently, ultrasound-assisted extraction has gained considerable attention due to several advantages that it offers, such as increased mass transfer rates and enhanced extraction yields with minimal or no damage to the quality of extracted compounds. The basic principle behind ultrasound is the use of high-frequency sound waves (in a range of 20–1000 kHz), generating bubble cavitation in the biological matrix (Benjakul et al., 2020; Khawli et al., 2019; Ojha et al., 2020). Ultrasound is applied in many areas in the food industry, including the recovery of value-added compounds from seafood processing by-products, activation or deactivation of enzymes, mixing and homogenization (Benjakul et al., 2019; Gallo et al., 2018). The use of ultrasound increased the extraction yield of acid-soluble collagen from sea bass skin (Kim et al., 2012). The yield increased then the amplitude of the ultrasound treatment was increased from 20% to 80 %, requiring a lower amount of acid and a shorter time for the treatment. In another study, acid and pepsin soluble collagens were extracted with the aid of ultrasonication (Ali et al., 2018). The results showed that the ultrasound treatment coupled with pepsin increased the yield of collagen markedly. Recently, protein was extracted from Australian Rock lobster head by-products by ultrasound (Nguyen et al., 2020b). The results showed that protein yields of up to 99% can be achieved with ultrasonic extraction under alkaline conditions (pH 13).

Microwave-assisted extraction is another promising method that has been developed to enhance the industrial extraction of several commercial ingredients (Bruno et al., 2019; Ciko et al., 2018; Nguyen et al., 2016). Several studies have shown that the use of microwave-assisted extraction of proteins and other biomolecules from marine by-products leads to shorter extraction time, higher extraction yield, and less solvent consumption (Nguyen & Zhang, 2020).

Another innovative alternative extraction technology is supercritical fluid extraction that has attracted much attention in the food industry in the last decade and is considered to be a green technology. Due to its safety and affordability, carbon dioxide (CO_2) is the most widely used supercritical fluid extraction solvent in food applications (Coelho et al., 2020; Khawli et al., 2019). However, up to now, much of the effort has been devoted to the extraction of pigments, lipid-soluble compounds, chitosan, phenolic compounds and carotenoids, while little effort has been focused on protein extraction (Bruno et al., 2019; Ciko et al., 2018; Khawli et al., 2019). Other new approaches have also been developed, such as extrusion–hydro-extraction (Huang et al., 2016) and membrane-based technologies (Castro-Muñoz et al., 2020; Soufi-Kechaou et al., 2017).

10.4.2 Emerging Technologies for Analysis

Marine by-products are usually characterized by large variability, making it challenging to produce a stable and consistent product. The characterization of raw materials is of ultimate importance to obtain robust processes and products with defined quality. Several offline instruments and methods have been applied for this purpose. For example, the Kjeldahl nitrogen method and chromatographic methods have been used frequently for the determination of protein and amino acid composition, respectively. Electrophoretic techniques (such as SDS-PAGE, and 2D-SDS-PAGE) have also been used on proteins or hydrolysed proteins to characterize them by molecular weight and follow the degradation of native proteins. Other commonly used methods include instruments to determine colour, texture, zeta potential, functional properties, such as water and oil holding capacities, oxidation products, and volatile compounds. Although most of these methods are considered to be reference methods, they have many well-known limitations, such as the fact that measurements cannot be performed in real-time, they are time-consuming, and they require the use of solvents and other chemicals (Aspevik et al., 2017; Landgrebe et al., 2010; Limpisophon et al., 2020; Tan et al. 2019b; Wubshet et al., 2019).

Recently, a new generation of analytical methods based on spectroscopy and other approaches has been developed for easy and accurate monitoring of the whole production chain, including the raw materials, the process itself (e.g., enzymatic protein hydrolysis), and the final product (e.g., protein hydrolysates, collagen). These techniques are innovative and considered green and sustainable technologies, making them cost-effective and environmentally friendly (Duarte et al., 2014; Ideia et al., 2020; Oliveira et al., 2021; Wubshet et al., 2019).

In this context, Fourier-transform infrared (FTIR) spectroscopy is the vibrational spectroscopic technique that has been used the most, especially for the investigation of changes in the secondary structure of proteins, which are induced, for example, during enzymatic hydrolysis (Böcker et al., 2017). In this line, the potential of using FTIR for characterization of protein chain reductions in enzymatic hydrolysed protein (salmon and chicken) was investigated and the results showed a strong relationship between changes in the FTIR spectral signatures and hydrolysis time (Böcker et al. 2017). In a similar study, the technique was used to predict the average molecular weight of protein hydrolysates produced from protein-rich by-products from the food industry using commercial enzymes (Kristoffersen et al., 2019). Additionally, FTIR technique provided useful information during: (i) extraction of collagens with the aid of ultrasonication (Ali et al., 2018), (ii) debittering of salmon frame protein hydrolysates (Singh et al. 2020a), and (iii) composition and conformation of peptide fractions obtained from the hydrolysis of squid (*Dosidicus gigas*) by-products collagen (Suárez-Jiménez et al., 2019). More examples about the application of FT-IR for studying chemical structure properties of collagen can be found in the literature (Riaz et al., 2018).

Nuclear magnetic resonance (NMR) spectroscopy is the second most used technique and has a broad range of versatile applications (Wubshet et al., 2019). One of the relevant applications of NMR spectroscopy is its application to probe differences in the metabolite composition of hydrolysates as a function of processing parameters, enabling real-time monitoring of protein hydrolysis (Steinsholm et al., 2020; Sundekilde et al., 2018). For example, the potential prediction of the sensory properties of protein hydrolysates from cod, salmon and chicken, based on proton (^{1}H) NMR metabolomic profiling was confirmed in a recent study (Steinsholm et al., 2020). In a similar study (Anderssen & McCarney, 2020), a benchtop NMR spectroscopy was found to be a promising method for real-time monitoring of enzymatic hydrolysis reactions on red cod, salmon, and shrimp.

It can be concluded that spectroscopic techniques provide online process control, allowing active monitoring and optimization of the process by collecting continuous data during processing (Wubshet et al., 2019). However, little work has been done using other spectroscopic techniques (e.g., fluorescence and Raman) in regard to marine waste-derived protein and other compounds (Djellouli et al., 2020; Nekvapil et al., 2019; Oliveira et al., 2021; Vorob'ev, 2019; Wubshet et al., 2018). Therefore, further research and development can be expected in this area.

10.5 COMPOSITION, NUTRITIONAL VALUE AND POTENTIAL HEALTH BENEFITS

Fish and other seafood, as well as their by-products, are highly desirable nutritionally primarily due to their high nutritional quality protein in terms of both the composition of amino acids and their bioavailability (Aspevik et al., 2017; Hjellnes et al., 2020; Nguyen et al. 2020a). It is well-known that marine products and their by-products are also a good source of other nutrients, such as omega-3 fatty acids and vitamins, but this chapter will focus on the protein components. The amount of protein depends on the species and the part of the fish used (frame, head, etc.). Chalamaiah and co-authors reviewed the approximate composition, amino acid composition and properties of fish protein hydrolysates extracted from fish muscle and different fish by-products (skin, head, viscera, frame, and bone) (Chalamaiah et al., 2012). Marine by-products also constitute an important source of protein-derived bioactive peptides.

In recent years, Vázquez and co-workers studied the possibility of recovering protein substrates and other valuable compounds from various marine by-products (Valcarcel et al., 2020; Vázquez et al., 2019a; 2019b; 2019c; 2020c; 2020d). Both the by-products (starting raw material) and the recovered compounds (e.g., collagen and protein hydrolysates) showed high protein and essential amino acids contents. For example, the heads, frames and trimmings, and viscera from seabass and seabream contained about 30% organic matter, mainly as proteins and lipids (Valcarcel et al., 2020). The same by-products generated from salmonid (rainbow trout and salmon) processing contained between 30% and 34% organic matter (mainly protein and lipids) (Vázquez et al., 2019c). In another study conducted by the same research team, protein hydrolysates, obtained from skins and heads of five by-catch species (megrim, hake, boarfish, grenadier, and Atlantic horse mackerel) showed degrees of hydrolysis higher than 13%, with soluble protein concentrations greater than 27 g/L and *in vitro* digestibility superior to 90% (Vázquez et al., 2019b). Li and co-workers reported that rainbow trout heads and skipjack tuna heads contained about 18g/100g and 29g/100g fresh weight protein, respectively (Li et al., 2019).

In addition to fish, crustacean species usually contain significant amounts of protein. For example, it was found that Australian rock lobster shells contain 29% protein (Nguyen et al., 2016), while shrimp and crab shells contain from 20–40% (Yan & Chen, 2015). More detailed information about the nutritional composition of marine by-products and their end products can be found in the literature (Siddik et al., 2020).

Besides the protein content, amino acid composition and digestibility are important nutritional quality parameters. Balanced amino acid composition and high digestibility of proteins and hydrolysates prepared from marine by-products have been widely reported in the literature. For example, high digestibility and remarkable amounts of essential amino acids were observed in protein hydrolysates from monkfish by-products (Vázquez et al. 2020c). Generally, the amino acid profile of protein hydrolysates depends on several factors, including the type of raw material, the enzyme used, and the hydrolysis conditions. Among all the amino acids, glutamic and aspartic acids were found to be higher in most of the reported fish protein hydrolysates (Chalamaiah et al., 2012; Idowu et al., 2019; Valcarcel et al., 2020; Vázquez et al. 2020b; 2019c). In a recent study conducted by Pateiro and co-authors (Pateiro et al., 2020), gilthead seabream by-products (fishbone, gills, guts, heads, liver, and skin) were found to be rich in high-quality protein (10–25%) in terms of its composition of essential amino acids, especially lysine, leucine, and arginine.

A tremendous amount of research has been published during the last ten years describing in detail the potential bioactivities and biological properties of protein, protein hydrolysates and bioactive peptides extracted from marine by-products. Functional properties, such as emulsification, water holding and oil holding capacities, and biological properties, such as antioxidant, antimicrobial, and antihypertensive activities, are among the most studied parameters (Abuine et al., 2019; Ambigaipalan & Shahidi, 2017; Atef & Mahdi Ojagh, 2017; Harnedy & FitzGerald, 2012; Ishak & Sarbon, 2018; Najafian & Babji, 2012; Odeleye et al., 2019; Olatunde & Benjakul, 2020; Samarakoon et al., 2014; Sánchez & Vázquez, 2017; Sila & Bougatef, 2016; Venkatesan et al., 2017; Villamil et al., 2017; Zamora-Sillero et al., 2018). For example, antioxidative properties, and antihypertensive and antidiabetic effects of fish protein hydrolysates, extracted from defatted salmon backbones, were studied using eight different commercial enzymes (Slizyte et al., 2016). The results showed that trypsin, bromelain + papain and Protamex gave the most bioactive hydrolysates.

10.6 UTILIZATION OF MARINE PROTEINS AND PROTEIN-DERIVED PRODUCTS

Compared to terrestrial life, marine life is characterized by a long evolutionary period with massive biodiversity, leading to a broad spectrum of biological constituents. This made marine by-products a promising potential source for a wide range of applications in both edible (e.g., food ingredients, health-promoting compounds) and nonedible (e.g., fertilizer, cosmetics, biofuels) products. As previously mentioned, most of the marine by-products are turned into low-value fish meals or fertilizers. However, huge potential exists for the use of these marine waste in more valuable applications, such as food applications and pharmaceutical products, as will be discussed in the following section.

10.6.1 Use of Marine By-Products for Producing Feeds and Fertilizers

One of the main utilizations of marine by-products is the production of animal feeds for aquaculture or livestock. Nowadays, approximately 33% of the world's fish meal production comes from by-products (FAO, 2020b; Marti-Quijal et al., 2020). Some studies demonstrated that animals fed with fish meal or silage of marine by-products showed improved growth performance and increased survival rate (Nirmal et al., 2020; Shabani et al., 2018; Shahidi & Ambigaipalan, 2019). Several marine by-products have been used recently to produce different types of fish silage using various production methods (fermentation with lactic acid bacteria, autolysis, use of acid) (Ozyurt et al., 2020; Özyurt et al., 2019; Toppe & Penarubia, 2018). In a recent review, Ahuja and co-authors presented an overview of knowledge relevant to the utilization of waste resulting from captured fish in the production of fertilizers in organic farming (Ahuja et al., 2020).

10.6.2 Food Applications

Recovered products from marine by-products have demonstrated promise as valuable functional food ingredients and nutraceuticals (Li-Chan, 2015; Shahidi, 2019; Samarakoon et al., 2014). Protein, hydrolysates, collagen and gelatin, chitin, chitosan, fish oil, peptides, amino acids, pigments, vitamins, enzymes, and many other related compounds are examples of functional ingredients and nutraceuticals that have been widely extracted and studied (Naik & Hayes, 2019; Shahidi et al., 2019; Shahidi & Ambigaipalan, 2015; Singh et al. 2020b). For example, the antioxidant activity of gelatin hydrolysates extracted from blue shark (*Prionace glauca*) by-products was demonstrated in a recent study (Limpisophon et al., 2020). In another study, gelatin hydrolysates with enhanced functional properties (antioxidant activity and flavour) were obtained from grass carp (*Ctenopharyngodon idellus*) scales combined with Maillard reaction products (Chen et al., 2019). Extraction of flavours from marine by-products is another interesting application for the valorization of these wastes (Suresh et al., 2018). In this context, by-products from the fish industry (fish powder) were used to generate fish flavour formulations using different proteases and heating in the presence of glucose and/or fish oil (Peinado et al., 2016). In this study, the authors used a combination of various enzymes to release different amounts of free amino acids, especially lysine, leucine, glutamic acid, and alanine, influencing the characteristic compounds derived from the Maillard reaction. In another study, flavoured-functional protein hydrolysates with a high amount of glutamic acid were produced from squid by-products (Sukkhown et al., 2018).

Chitin and its derivative (chitosan) can be extracted from crustacean by-products (such as the shells from shrimp, crabs, etc.). The use of these polysaccharide polymers as edible films with antimicrobial properties has been extensively investigated to improve safety and extend the shelf life of the treated products (Hamed et al., 2016). For example, Gómez-Estaca and co-authors developed edible films based on water-soluble fish muscle proteins resulted from shrimp processing wash water (Gómez-Estaca et al., 2018). The same research team prepared edible films from shrimp demineralization extract blended with chitosan to be used for raw salmon wrapping (Gómez-Estaca et al., 2019). Quality changes of the treated salmon were studied during chilled storage of 19 days. The results showed higher chemical and microbial quality of treated samples compared to unwrapped salmon. In a recent study, fish gelatin obtained from fish skin and chitin (extracted from squid pens) were used to prepare porous materials to be employed as bioactive carriers and moisture scavengers (Uranga et al., 2020). In a comprehensive review paper published by Halim and others, it was reported that the recovered compounds from marine by-products (e.g., proteins, hydrolysates, bioactive peptides, collagen and gelatin) have substantial potential as value-added ingredients for commercial food products (Halim et al., 2016). More utilization of marine by-products for food applications has been recently reviewed, focusing on the importance of fisheries by-products for fortification, especially the effect of these by-products on the texture of food, colour, nutritional value and sensorial characteristics (Nawaz et al., 2020).

10.6.3 MEDICAL, PHARMACEUTICAL AND COSMETIC INDUSTRIES

Protein hydrolysates, bioactive peptides, collagen, chitin, chitosan, and other related compounds extracted from marine sources have found many applications in the medical, biomedical, pharmaceutical, and cosmeceuticals industries (Alves et al., 2020; Atef & Mahdi Ojagh 2017; Hamed et al., 2016; Özyurt & Özkütük, 2019). As previously mentioned, most of these compounds exhibit various functions, including antioxidant, antimicrobial, antihypertensive, antidiabetic, anticancer, anti-inflammatory, hypocholesterolemic, and multifunctional properties (Benjakul et al., 2014; Fu et al. 2019a; Halim et al., 2016; Udenigwe & Aluko, 2012; Zamora-Sillero et al., 2018).

The biomedical and pharmaceutical industries were pioneers in exploring oceans to find possible novel drugs. Up to now, extensive research has been carried out, demonstrating that marine bioactive peptides and related compounds (e.g., collagen and gelatin) exhibit a wide range of positive health effects. For example, peptides from herring milt hydrolysate were shown to have in-vitro anti-inflammatory activity (Durand et al., 2020), while antiherpetic activities was demonstrated on enzymatic hydrolysates of aquapharyngeal bulb (Tripoteau et al., 2015).

Collagen is widely used in the biomedical and pharmaceutical fields due to its biocompatibility and biodegradability, and its wide range of biological activities (antioxidant, anti-microbial, wound healing, anti-aging, anti-coagulant, anti-tumour). It is especially used as a drug carrier in the form of membranes and in wound dressing materials (Ahmed et al., 2020; Coppola et al., 2020; Lim et al., 2019). An example of such applications is a recent study that investigated the possibility of using collagen derived from sea urchin waste as an alternative to skin grafts to repair wounds and injuries (Ferrario et al., 2020). Similar applications have been reported for chitin and chitosan and their derivative products (Hamed et al., 2016; Özogul et al., 2019; Shahidi & Ambigaipalan, 2015; Wang et al., 2020).

In addition, marine oil, derived from by-products that are rich in polyunsaturated fatty acids (PUFAs), and especially the omega-3 PUFAs, such as eicosapentaenoic acid (EPA; C20:5) or docosahexaenoic acid (DHA; C22:6), are known for their capacity to prevent various diseases such as blood pressure, coronary heart disease, inflammation, and cancer (Shahidi et al., 2019).

The demand for cosmetic products from marine origins has increased in recent times due to increased consumer awareness of the importance of natural products as well as the unique properties of marine organisms compared to terrestrial sources. Therefore, many compounds with cosmetic applications are currently produced from marine-derived products. The term 'cosmeceuticals' has emerged in recent years as a combination of cosmetics and pharmaceuticals, referring to cosmetic products with drug-like benefits (Alves et al., 2020; Özyurt & Özkütük, 2019; Venkatesan et al., 2017). Again, collagen extracted from marine by-products plays an important role in this context. For instance, marine-derived collagen extracted from salmon and codfish skins was investigated to evaluate its ability to be used as a component in cosmetic formulations (Alves et al., 2017). The results demonstrated that the extracted collagen has a good moisturizing effect through water absorption, preventing skin dehydration with no irritation or inflammatory effects.

10.7 CONSUMER ACCEPTANCE AND RELIGIOUS ASPECTS

The recovery of meat from fish frames (up to 45% of the frame weight) via the use of mechanical deboning machines or water jet deboning techniques provides a valuable means to recover flesh that remains on fish frames/skins after filleting (Wendel et al., 2002). The recovered meat has been traditionally used in surimi production and in restructured fish meat that could be used in formed fish products (imitation crab meat, imitation shrimp and fish fingers).

The acceptability of fish protein in food products depends on the food products that the protein is added to. Generally, the use of protein from fatty fish can lead to undesirable sensory notes due to oxidative processes during storage, which limits the amount of fish protein to be incorporated into the product and the shelf life of the products.

Oliveira et al. (2020) investigated the use of protein from surimi production recovered using ultrafiltration (Polyethersulfone membrane with a 30 kDa cut off) in fish burgers made of tilapia surimi at 5% and 10% addition levels. The recovered protein, which was spray-dried, had 66.49% amino acids and contained all the essential amino acids. The addition of the recovered protein improved the colour appearance and acceptability of the fish burger as reported in a sensory analysis conducted by 52 untrained panelists. Furthermore, the nutritional properties (higher protein content) were improved by the addition of the recovered protein.

Similarly, protein isolate obtained from tuna fish dark meat was used in a silver carp mince burger and the optimum ratio (20% tuna protein isolate and 50% silver carp) provided the best sensory attributes as determined by trained panelists (5 and 9 members). The study indicated that this ratio produced a highly stable product for 6 months at −18 °C, and the product had a 10% higher protein content compared to the silver carp mince control.

Fish protein isolate was used in meals and compared with control proteins (provided by beef, chicken, eggs or liver) at 12% to 15% of the total energy and provided to children aged 6–38 months (n = 441) (Ochoa et al., 2017). No differences in growth performance (weight and height gain) or acceptability were observed between the treatments, and the fish protein was more economical at 20–40% lower cost compared to the controls. Fish flour prepared from labeobarbus fillets by solar drying for 3 days was used as a flour replacement in bread at 5, 10, 15 and 20% and compared to 100% wheat flour (Zebib et al., 2020). The samples were evaluated for their compositions, and the sensory attributes were examined by a rather small consumer panel (n = 10). The supplementation of the fish flour improved the protein content by 1.37, 3.13, 4.77 and 6.45% for the 5, 10, 15 and 20% supplementations, respectively. The addition of fish flour increased the Ca, Zn, Fe and P contents by 40–180%, 30–90%, 20–60% and 70–130%, respectively. Fish flour addition at 5% and 10% improved the taste and flavour scores compared to control samples and were not different in terms of colour, texture and overall acceptability. The authors concluded that 10% addition of labeobarbus flour was the best level of fortification. Similar findings have been reported for protein extracts obtained from tilapia (Adeleke & Odedeji, 2010), wastes of Red-tailed Brycon (*Brycon cephalus*) (Bastos et al., 2014) and fish protein/fish hydrolysate (Cercel et al., 2016) in baked products, where lower levels of inclusion resulted in better sensory attributes compared with non-treated control samples, and lower sensory scores were obtained at high supplementation levels (>10%).

The use of fish products in ice cream has been experimented with in several commercial and research trials. Shaviklo et al. (2011c) reported the use of several fish species (crab (*Kani Aisu*), eel (*Unagi Aisu*), saury fish (*Sanma Aisu*), octopus (*Taco Aisu*), and shrimp (*sakura Ebi Aisu*)) in Japanese ice cream products as well as in other Iranian and Indian ice cream products. Sensory aspects of ice cream suggested that the inclusion of fish protein isolate at a concentration level of ≤10 g/kg did not affect the sensory attributes for 2 months.

Several other food applications of fish protein (isolate/hydrolysates) have been reported, such as protein mix, rice-fish extruded snacks, fish crackers, mayonnaise, high protein corn snacks and fish cutlet mix (Chavan et al., 2008; Gogoi et al., 1996; Sathivel et al., 2005; Shaviklo et al., 2011a; 2011b; 2013).

Unlike baked products, the addition of fish protein isolate in fish burgers, sausages and other fish products appears to improve the sensory aspects of the products as well as the nutritional value at incorporation levels >10%. Fish protein has been utilized from Pangas processing waste (Surasani et al., 2020), tilapia viscera (Cavenaghi-Altemio et al., 2013), and threadfin bream to make surimi (Santana et al., 2015). For example, whole small tilapia was used to produce fish protein isolate by isoelectric solubilization/precipitation method and used to supplement fish and meatballs (Ibrahim, 2015). The supplementation of the fish isolate at 25% of the meat and fish balls increased the protein contents in the products by 6% and 14%, respectively. This also resulted in substantial increases in the Ca, P, Na, and Mn contents of cooked meat and fish balls. Supplementation resulted in increased levels of Mg, Fe and Zn in cooked meatballs, whereas these same minerals were decreased in cooked fish balls by supplementation. A sensory evaluation of the products was carried out using a trained panel (n = 10), which scored the supplemented samples higher for odour and texture and lower for flavour and overall acceptability.

In terms of religious restrictions on fish protein consumption, Abrahamic faiths present various rulings according to religious laws described in their respective scriptures. Generally, there are no restrictions against seafood in Christianity. Clear statements in the new Testaments such as 'What God has made clean, do not call common'. Acts 10:15 and 'Then are you also without understanding? Do you not see that whatever goes into a person from outside cannot defile him, since it enters not his heart but his stomach, and is expelled?' Mark 7:18–19 have declared all foods as clean.

In Judaism, Halacha 'the Jewish religious laws collected from written and oral Torah' provide a clear description for permissible and forbidden seafoods. For example, Leviticus 11:9–12 'These you may eat, of all that are in the waters. Everything in the waters that has fins and scales, whether in the seas or in the rivers, you may eat. But anything in the seas or the rivers that has no fins and scales, of the swarming creatures in the waters and of the living creatures that are in the waters, is detestable to you. You shall regard them as detestable; you shall not eat any of their flesh, and you shall detest their carcasses. Everything in the waters that has not fins and scales is detestable to you.' and Deuteronomy 14:9–10 'Of all that are in the waters you may eat these: whatever has fins and scales you may eat. And whatever does not have fins and scales you shall not eat; it is unclean for you.' state that seafood that do not have fins and scales are not regarded as kosher. Various lists of fish and seafood species that are considered as kosher or non-kosher are available in books (Garfunkel, 1997; Carter et al., 2000) and websites (https://www.ka.org.au/consumer-resources/common-kosher-and-non-kosher-fish and https://mk.ca/kosher-guide/fish-guide-2/). Specifically, the declaration 'you shall not eat any of their flesh, and you shall detest their carcasses' suggests that not only the meat, but all carcass components are forbidden.

The Islamic sharia is based on two pillars, guidelines declared in Quran (the holy book of Muslims) and authentic Hadith (confirmed record of sayings and traditions of Prophet Muhammed (ﷺ)). The Quran has no specific prohibition against seafood, but the clear prohibition against the consumption of carrion (dead animals), which does not apply to fish. According to a Hadith narrated by Abdullah bin Umar that the Messenger of Allah (ﷺ) said: 'Two kinds of dead meat and two kinds of blood have been permitted to us. The two kinds of dead meat are fish and locusts, and the two kinds of blood are the liver and spleen.' – [Collected by Sunan ibn Majah]. This clearly shows that no restrictions against fish and their products. However, an important consideration for permissible foods in sharia, and in many other religions, is the safety and healthiness of the food. This requires assurances regarding the safety of long-term use of any products generated from the use of the co-products.

10.8 CHALLENGES AND FUTURE TRENDS

Based on scientific literature, there has been a growing interest from both academia and industry in marine by-products. Indeed, protein hydrolysates, bioactive peptides, and other valuable related compounds extracted from marine by-products have been the object of many studies and industrial applications in the past decade. The increase in world population and the global increase in the demand for protein, along with the growing awareness of consumers towards benefits associated with natural ingredients and products are some of the reasons that explain this tremendous interest in marine resources. Several examples of successful applications on the translation of research into commercial products have been already reported. Marealis AS, a Norwegian marine biotechnology company focusing on the development and commercialization of natural health products from marine peptides, Polybait AS, a Norwegian company producing a range of sustainable baits, based on hydrolysed marine by-products, and Calanus AS, a bio-marine company pioneering the use of the crustacean Calanus finmarchicus are examples of such applications (Vang et al., 2018).

However, several challenges must be overcome in order to achieve a wider industrial-scale production and successful commercialization of the recovered products. The high perishability of marine by-products is one of the most challenging aspects of implementing an appropriate waste management system. As fish and other marine products deteriorate rapidly and easily (due mainly to their high moisture content), it is important to minimize the time spent between catching and processing. Likewise, marine by-products must be processed immediately after the production in order to ensure the high quality of the recovered products (protein, gelatin, chitin, etc.). Lack of appropriate technologies and processing facilities (such as onboard freezing and refrigeration) is still a barrier to profitable production and further processing of marine by-products (Olsen et al., 2014; Rustad et al., 2011).

Lack of consumer knowledge and consumer acceptance is another issue that limits the recovery of protein and protein-derived products from marine by-products. Not all consumers are aware that fish by-products contain the same valuable components as the fish itself. In addition, the sensory properties of the recovered products are the main obstacle in the road to fully exploiting marine by-products. For example, the bitter taste of fish protein hydrolysates is one of the well-known limitations that highly affects consumer acceptance. The bitter taste perception of protein hydrolysates is mainly due to the presence of bitter peptides comprising hydrophobic amino acids, but other factors, such as the amino acid peptide sequence, spatial structure, peptide length, and the degree of hydrolysis can also contribute to this undesirable taste. In addition to the bitter taste, protein hydrolysates could have flavours related to the raw material, i.e., fish (Aspevik et al., 2017; Fu et al. 2019b; Rustad et al., 2011). To mask initial fish odours and to overcome the limitation of the bitterness of protein hydrolysate, several debittering strategies have been investigated in the last few years, including the use of exopeptidase treatment, Maillard reaction, encapsulation technology, among others (Aspevik et al., 2016; Cardinal et al., 2020; Fu et al. 2019b; Li-Chan, 2015; Peinado et al., 2016; Singh et al. 2020a).

The successful transfer of technology to the market requires both more advanced extraction methods and analytical techniques. Several environment-friendly extraction techniques (e.g., microwave-, ultrasonic- and enzyme-assisted extractions) have been developed recently based on the concept of green technology, allowing rapid extraction, high recovery rate, low use of chemicals, high economic benefit, and high quality of the recovered products (Coelho et al., 2020; Khawli et al., 2019). The current industrial strategy for monitoring the different processing stages as well as the quality of the final products is based on classical well-established analytical methods. However, progress in spectroscopic technologies offers a great opportunity in this context. For example, much research is now being carried out to use such non-destructive methods as valuable tools for industrial production of protein hydrolysates. Enzymatic protein hydrolysis is a complex process, which is affected by a variety of variables, including hydrolysis time, pH, temperature, type and amount of enzyme, in addition to the initial variation in the rest raw material. Despite this complexity, the use of an adequate analytical strategy, consisting of characterization of the raw material and adjusting processing parameters accordingly, allows producing hydrolysis products of the desired quality (Wubshet et al., 2019). Although the use of some spectroscopic techniques (such as FTIR) has been well documented, the potential of other spectroscopic techniques is still to be investigated. For example, NIR, Raman, and fluorescence spectroscopy have been used to monitor and optimize the protein recovery process from poultry by-products (Wubshet et al., 2018), but very limited work has been found on the use of these spectroscopic techniques for marine by-products.

Finally, there is a need to gain approval from the regulatory authorities for the specific health claims for proteins, bioactive peptides and the other related compounds extracted from marine by-products.

REFERENCES

Abuine, R., Rathnayake, A. U., & Byun, H. G. (2019). Biological activity of peptides purified from fish skin hydrolysates. *Fisheries and Aquatic Sciences*, *22*(1), 1–14. doi:10.1186/s41240-019-0125-4

Adeleke, R., & Odedeji, J. (2010). Acceptability studies on bread fortified with tilapia fish flour. *Pakistan Journal of Nutrition*, *9*(6), 531–534. doi:10.3923/pjn.2010.531.534

Ahmed, M., Verma, A. K., & Patel, R. (2020). Collagen extraction and recent biological activities of collagen peptides derived from sea-food waste: A review. *Sustainable Chemistry and Pharmacy, 18*(September), 100315. doi:10.1016/j.scp.2020.100315

Ahuja, I., Dauksas, E., Remme, J. F., Richardsen, R., & Løes, A. K. (2020). Fish and fish waste-based fertilizers in organic farming – With status in Norway: A review. *Waste Management, 115*, 95–112. doi:10.1016/j.wasman.2020.07.025

Ali, A. M. M., Kishimura, H., & Benjakul, S. (2018). Extraction efficiency and characteristics of acid and pepsin soluble collagens from the skin of golden carp (*Probarbus jullieni*) as affected by ultrasonication. *Process Biochemistry, 66*(January), 237–244. doi:10.1016/j.procbio.2018.01.003

Alves, A. L., Marques, A. L. P., Martins, E., Silva, T. H., & Reis, R. L. (2017). Cosmetic potential of marine fish skin collagen. *Cosmetics, 4*, 29. doi:10.3390/cosmetics4040039

Alves, A., Sousa, E., Kijjoa, A., & Pinto, M. (2020). Marine-derived compounds with potential use as cosmeceuticals and nutricosmetics. *Molecules, 25*(2536). doi:10.3390/molecules25112536

Ambigaipalan, P., & Shahidi, F. (2017). Bioactive peptides from shrimp shell processing discards: Antioxidant and biological activities. *Journal of Functional Foods, 34*, 7–17. doi:10.1016/j.jff.2017.04.013

Anderssen, K. E., & McCarney, E. R. (2020). Online monitoring of enzymatic hydrolysis of marine by-products using benchtop nuclear magnetic resonance spectroscopy. *Food Control, 112*, 107053. doi:10.1016/j.foodcont.2019.107053

Aspevik, T., Oterhals, Å., Rønning, S. B., Altintzoglou, T., Wubshet, S. G., Gildberg, A., et al. (2017). Valorization of proteins from co- and by-products from the fish and meat industry. *Topics in Current Chemistry, 375*(3). doi:10.1007/s41061-017-0143-6

Aspevik, T., Totland, C., Lea, P., & Oterhals, Å. (2016). Sensory and surface-active properties of protein hydrolysates based on Atlantic salmon (*Salmo salar*) by-products. *Process Biochemistry, 51*(8), 1006–1014. doi:10.1016/j.procbio.2016.04.015

Atef, M., & Mahdi Ojagh, S. (2017). Health benefits and food applications of bioactive compounds from fish byproducts: A review. *Journal of Functional Foods, 35*, 673–681. doi:10.1016/j.jff.2017.06.034

Baiano, A. (2020). Edible insects: An overview on nutritional characteristics, safety, farming, production technologies, regulatory framework, and socio-economic and ethical implications. *Trends in Food Science and Technology, 100*, 35–50. doi:10.1016/j.tifs.2020.03.040

Barba, F. J., Soto, E. R., Brncic, M., Rodriquez, J. M. L., Vázquez, J. A., Durán, A. I., et al. (2019). Tailor-made process to recover high added value compounds from fishery by-products. In: *Green Extraction and Valorization of By-Products from Food Processing*, 1st Edition. Francisco, J. M. L. R., Barba, J., Soto, E. R., & Brncic, M. (Eds). Boca Raton: CRC Press, 91–140. doi:10.1201/9780429325007-4

Bastos, S. C., Tavares, T., Pimenta, M. E. D. S. G., Leal, R., Fabrício, L. F., Pimenta, C. J., & Pinheiro, A. C. M. (2014). Fish filleting residues for enrichment of wheat bread: Chemical and sensory characteristics. *Journal of Food Science and Technology, 51*(9), 2240–2245. doi:10.1007/s13197-014-1258-1

Batista, I., Ramos, C., Coutinho, J., Bandarra, N. M., & Nunes, M. L. (2010). Characterization of protein hydrolysates and lipids obtained from black scabbardfish (*Aphanopus carbo*) by-products and antioxidative activity of the hydrolysates produced. *Process Biochemistry, 45*(1), 18–24. doi:10.1016/j.procbio.2009.07.019

Benjakul, S., Muhammed, A., Ali, M., & Singh, A. (2019). Application of ultrasonication in seafood processing. In: *Innovative Technologies in Seafood Processing*. Özogul, Y. (Ed). Boca Raton: CRC Press, 131–154.

Benjakul, S., Sae-leaw, T., & Simpson, B. K. (2020). Byproducts from fish harvesting and processing. In: *Byproducts from Agriculture and Fisheries: Adding Value for Food, Feed, Pharma, and Fuels*. Simpson, B. K., Aryee, A. N., & Toldrá, F. (Eds). John Wiley & Sons Ltd, 179–217. doi:10.1002/9781119383956.ch9

Benjakul, S., Yarnpakdee, S., Senphan, T., Halldorsdottir, S. M., & Kristinsson, H. G. (2014). Fish protein hydrolysates: Production, bioactivities, and applications. In: *Antioxidants and Functional Components in Aquatic Foods*. Kristinsson, H. G. (Ed). Chichester, UK: John Wiley & Sons, Ltd, 237–281.

Böcker, U., Wubshet, S. G., Lindberg, D., & Afseth, N. K. (2017). Fourier-transform infrared spectroscopy for characterization of protein chain reductions in enzymatic reactions. *Analyst, 142*(15), 2812–2818. doi:10.1039/c7an00488e

Bougatef, A., Nedjar-Arroume, N., Manni, L., Ravallec, R., Barkia, A., Guillochon, D., & Nasri, M. (2010). Purification and identification of novel antioxidant peptides from enzymatic hydrolysates of sardinelle (*Sardinella aurita*) by-products proteins. *Food Chemistry, 118*(3), 559–565. doi:10.1016/j.foodchem.2009.05.021

Bruno, S. F., Ekorong, F. J. A. A., Karkal, S. S., Cathrine, M. S. B., & Kudre, T. G. (2019). Green and innovative techniques for recovery of valuable compounds from seafood by-products and discards: A review. *Trends in Food Science and Technology*, *85*, 10–22. doi:10.1016/j.tifs.2018.12.004

Cao, W., Zhang, C., Hong, P., & Ji, H. (2008). Response surface methodology for autolysis parameters optimization of shrimp head and amino acids released during autolysis. *Food Chemistry*, *109*(1), 176–183. doi:10.1016/j.foodchem.2007.11.080

Cardinal, M., Chaussy, M., Donnay-moreno, C., Cornet, J., Rannou, C., Fillonneau, C., et al. (2020). Use of random forest methodology to link aroma profiles to volatile compounds: Application to enzymatic hydrolysis of Atlantic salmon (*Salmo salar*) by-products combined with Maillard reactions. *Food Research International*, *134*, 109254. doi:10.1016/j.foodres.2020.109254

Carter, E. P., Flick, Jr., G. J., Davis, L. M., Martin, R. E. (2000). *Marine and Freshwater Products Handbook*. CRC Press, Boca Raton, FL.

Castro-Muñoz, R., Boczkaj, G., Gontarek, E., Cassano, A., & Fíla, V. (2020). Membrane technologies assisting plant-based and agro-food by-products processing: A comprehensive review. *Trends in Food Science and Technology*, *95*, 219–232. doi:10.1016/j.tifs.2019.12.003

Cavenaghi-Altemio, A. D., Alcade, L. B., & Fonseca, G. G. (2013). Low-fat frankfurters from protein concentrates of tilapia viscera and mechanically separated tilapia meat. *Food Sciences and Nutrition*, *1*, 445–451.

Cercel, F., Burluc, R. M., & Alexe, P. (2016). Nutritional effects of added fish proteins in wheat flour bread. *Agriculture and Agricultural Science Procedia*, *10*, 244–249. doi:10.1016/j.aaspro.2016.09.060

Chalamaiah, M., Dinesh Kumar, B., Hemalatha, R., & Jyothirmayi, T. (2012). Fish protein hydrolysates: Proximate composition, amino acid composition, antioxidant activities and applications: A review. *Food Chemistry*, *135*(4), 3020–3038. doi:10.1016/j.foodchem.2012.06.100

Chavan, B. R., Basu, S., & Kovale, S. R. (2008). Development of edible texturised dried fish granules from low-value fish croaker (*Otolithus argenteus*) and its storage characteristics. *Chiang Mai University Journal of Natural Sciences*, *1*, 173–182.

Chen, K., Yang, X., Huang, Z., Jia, S., Zhang, Y., Shi, J., & Hong, H. (2019). Modification of gelatin hydrolysates from grass carp (*Ctenopharyngodon idellus*) scales by Maillard reaction: Antioxidant activity and volatile compounds. *Food Chemistry*, *295*, 569–578. doi:10.1016/j.foodchem.2019.05.156

Chen, Y. C., Tou, J. C., & Jaczynski, J. (2007). Amino acid, fatty acid, and mineral profiles of materials recovered from rainbow trout (*Oncorhynchus mykiss*) processing by-products using isoelectric solubilization/precipitation. *Journal of Food Science*, *72*(9), C527–C535. doi:10.1111/j.1750-3841.2007.00522.x

Chi, C. F., Wang, B., Hu, F. Y., Wang, Y. M., Zhang, B., Deng, S. G., & Wu, C. W. (2015). Purification and identification of three novel antioxidant peptides from protein hydrolysate of bluefin leatherjacket (*Navodon septentrionalis*) skin. *Food Research International*, *73*, 124–129. doi:10.1016/j.foodres.2014.08.038

Chi, C. F., Wang, B., Wang, Y. M., Zhang, B., & Deng, S. G. (2015). Isolation and characterization of three antioxidant peptides from protein hydrolysate of bluefin leatherjacket (Navodon septentrionalis) heads. *Journal of Functional Foods*, *12*, 1–10. doi:10.1016/j.jff.2014.10.027

Choksawangkarn, W., Phiphattananukoon, S., Jaresitthikunchai, J., & Roytrakul, S. (2018). Antioxidative peptides from fish sauce by-product: Isolation and characterization. *Agriculture and Natural Resources*, *52*(5), 460–466. doi:10.1016/j.anres.2018.11.001

Chung, Y. C., Ho, M. L., Chyan, F. L., & Jiang, S. T. (2000) Utilization of freeze dried mackerel (*Scomber australasicus*) muscle proteins as a binder in restructured meat. *Fisheries Science*, *66*, 130–135.

Ciko, A. M., Jokić, S., Šubarić, D., & Jerković, I. (2018). Overview on the application of modern methods for the extraction of bioactive compounds from marine macroalgae. *Marine Drugs*, *16*(10). doi:10.3390/md16100348

Coelho, M. C., Pereira, R. N., Rodrigues, A. S., Teixeira, J. A., & Pintado, M. E. (2020). The use of emergent technologies to extract added value compounds from grape by-products. *Trends in Food Science and Technology*, *106*(September), 182–197. doi:10.1016/j.tifs.2020.09.028

Coppola, D., Oliviero, M., Vitale, G. A., Lauritano, C., Ambra, I. D., Iannace, S., & Pascale, D. D. (2020). Marine collagen from alternative and sustainable sources: Extraction, processing and applications. *Molecules*, *18*, 214.

Derouiche Ben Maiz, H., Guadix, E. M., Guadix, A., Gargouri, M., & Espejo-Carpio, F. J. (2019). Valorisation of tuna viscera by endogenous enzymatic treatment. *International Journal of Food Science and Technology*, *54*(4), 1100–1108. doi:10.1111/ijfs.14009

Djellouli, M., López-Caballero, M. E., Arancibia, M. Y., Karam, N., & Martínez-Alvarez, O. (2020). Antioxidant and antimicrobial enhancement by reaction of protein hydrolysates derived from shrimp by-products with glucosamine. *Waste and Biomass Valorization, 11*(6), 2491–2505. doi:10.1007/s12649-019-00607-y

Duan, R., Zhang, J., Wu, J., & Wang, J. (2018). Preparation and characterization of collagens from the skin of Northern Snakehead (*Channa argus*). *Journal of Polymers and the Environment, 26*(3), 867–872. doi:10.1007/s10924-017-1005-6

Duarte, K., Justino, C. I. L., Pereira, R., Freitas, A. C., Gomes, A. M., Duarte, A. C., & Rocha-Santos, T. A. P. (2014). Green analytical methodologies for the discovery of bioactive compounds from marine sources. *Trends in Environmental Analytical Chemistry, 3*, 43–52. doi:10.1016/j.teac.2014.11.001

Durand, R., Pellerin, G., Thibodeau, J., Fraboulet, E., Marette, A., & Bazinet, L. (2020). Screening for metabolic syndrome application of a herring by-product hydrolysate after its separation by electrodialysis with ultrafiltration membrane and identification of novel anti-inflammatory peptides. *Separation and Purification Technology, 235*, 116205. doi:10.1016/j.seppur.2019.116205

Eftimov, T., Popovski, G., Petković, M., Seljak, B. K., & Kocev, D. (2020). COVID-19 pandemic changes the food consumption patterns. *Trends in Food Science and Technology, 104*, 268–272. doi:10.1016/j.tifs.2020.08.017

FAO. (2020a). How is COVID-19 affecting the fisheries and aquaculture food systems. Rome. https://doi.org/10.4060/ca8637en.

FAO. (2020b). The state of world fisheries and aquaculture. Sustainability in action.Rome . https://doi.org/10.4060/ca9229en

Fernandes, P. (2016). Enzymes in fish and seafood processing. *Frontiers in Bioengineering and Biotechnology, 4*, 1–14. doi:10.3389/fbioe.2016.00059

Ferrario, C., Rusconi, F., Pulaj, A., Landini, P., Paroni, M., Colombo, G., et al. (2020). From food waste to innovative biomaterial: Sea urchin-derived collagen for applications in skin regenerative medicine. *Marine Drugs, 18*, 414.

Ferraro, V., Cruz, I. B., Jorge, R. F., Malcata, F. X., Pintado, M. E., & Castro, P. M. L. (2010). Valorisation of natural extracts from marine source focused on marine by-products: A review. *Food Research International, 43*(9), 2221–2233. doi:10.1016/j.foodres.2010.07.034

Fu, Y., Chen, J., Bak, K. H., & Lametsch, R. (2019a). Valorisation of protein hydrolysates from animal by-products: perspectives on bitter taste and debittering methods: A review. *International Journal of Food Science and Technology, 54*(4), 978–986. doi:10.1111/ijfs.14037

Fu, Y., Therkildsen, M., Aluko, R. E., & Lametsch, R. (2019b). Exploration of collagen recovered from animal by-products as a precursor of bioactive peptides: Successes and challenges. *Critical Reviews in Food Science and Nutrition, 59*(13), 2011–2027. doi:10.1080/10408398.2018.1436038

Gallo, M., Ferrara, L., & Naviglio, D. (2018). Application of ultrasound in food science and technology: A perspective. *Foods, 7*(10), 1–18. doi:10.3390/foods7100164

Garfunkel, T. (1997). *Kosher for Everybody: The Complete Guide to Understanding, Shopping, Cooking, and Eating the Kosher Way*. Carol Publishing Group, Secaucus, NJ.

Gasco, L., Acuti, G., Bani, P., Dalle Zotte, A., Danieli, P. P., De Angelis, A., et al. (2020). Insect and fish by-products as sustainable alternatives to conventional animal proteins in animal nutrition. *Italian Journal of Animal Science, 19*(1), 360–372. doi:10.1080/1828051X.2020.1743209

Gehring, C. K., Gigliotti, J. C., Moritz, J. S., Tou, J. C., & Jaczynski, J. (2011). Functional and nutritional characteristics of proteins and lipids recovered by isoelectric processing of fish by-products and low-value fish: A review. *Food Chemistry, 124*(2), 422–431. doi:10.1016/j.foodchem.2010.06.078

Gençdağ, E., Görgüç, A., & Yılmaz, F. M. (2020). Recent advances in the recovery techniques of plant-based proteins from agro-industrial by-products. *Food Reviews International*, 1–22. doi:10.1080/87559129.2019.1709203

Gilman, E., Perez Roda, A., Huntington, T., Kennelly, S. J., Suuronen, P., Chaloupka, M., & Medley, P. A. H. (2020). Benchmarking global fisheries discards. *Scientific Reports, 10*(1), 1–8. doi:10.1038/s41598-020-71021-x

Gogoi, B. K., Oswalt, A. J., & Choudhury, G. S. (1996). Reverse screw elements and feed composition effects during twin-screw extrusion of rice flour and fish muscle blends. *Journal of Food Science, 3*, 590–595

Gómez-Estaca, J., Alemán, A., López-caballero, M. E., Baccan, G. C., Montero, P., & Gómez-guillén, M. C. (2019). Bioaccessibility and antimicrobial properties of a shrimp demineralization extract blended with chitosan as wrapping material in ready-to-eat raw salmon. *Food Chemistry, 276*(October), 342–349. doi:10.1016/j.foodchem.2018.10.031

Gómez-Estaca, J., Montero, P., & Gómez-Guillén, M. C. (2018). Chemical characterization of wash water biomass from shrimp surimi processing and its application to develop functional edible films. *Journal of Food Science and Technology*, *55*(10), 3881–3891. doi:10.1007/s13197-017-2532-9

Gómez, B., Munekata, P. E. S., Gavahian, M., Barba, F. J., Martí-Quijal, F. J., Bolumar, T., et al. (2019). Application of pulsed electric fields in meat and fish processing industries: An overview. *Food Research International*, *123*(April), 95–105. doi:10.1016/j.foodres.2019.04.047

Gómez, L. J., Gómez, N. A., Zapata, J. E., López-Garciá, G., Cilla, A., & Alegriá, A. (2020). Optimization of the red tilapia (*Oreochromis* spp.) viscera hydrolysis for obtaining iron-binding peptides and evaluation of in vitro iron bioavailability. *Foods*, *9*(7). doi:10.3390/foods9070883

Gustavsson, J., Cederberg, C., & Sonesson, U. (2011). Global food losses and food waste. *Food Loss and Food Waste: Causes and Solutions*. doi:10.4337/9781788975391

Halim, N. R. A., Yusof, H. M., & Sarbon, N. M. (2016). Functional and bioactive properties of fish protein hydolysates and peptides: A comprehensive review. *Trends in Food Science and Technology*, *51*, 24–33. doi:10.1016/j.tifs.2016.02.007

Hamed, I., Ozogul, F., & Regenstein, J. M. (2016). Industrial applications of crustacean by-products (chitin, chitosan, and chitooligosaccharides): A review. *Trends in Food Science & Technology*, *48*, 40–50. doi:10.1016/j.tifs.2015.11.007

Harnedy, P. A., & FitzGerald, R. J. (2012). Bioactive peptides from marine processing waste and shellfish: A review. *Journal of Functional Foods*, *4*(1), 6–24. doi:10.1016/j.jff.2011.09.001

Hassoun, A., Carpena, M., Prieto, M. A., Simal-Gandara, J., Özogul, F., Özogul, Y., et al. (2020). Use of spectroscopic techniques to monitor changes in food quality during application of natural preservatives: A review. *Antioxidants*, *9*(9), 882. doi:10.3390/ANTIOX9090882

Hassoun, A., Ojha, S., Tiwari, B., Rustad, T., Nilsen, H., Heia, K., et al. (2020). Monitoring thermal and non-thermal treatments during processing of muscle foods: A comprehensive review of recent technological advances. *Applied Sciences*, *10*(19). doi:10.3390/app10196802

Hjellnes, V., Rustad, T., & Falch, E. (2020). The value chain of the white fish industry in Norway: History, current status and possibilities for improvement – A review. *Regional Studies in Marine Science*, *36*, 101293. doi:10.1016/j.rsma.2020.101293

Huang, C. Y., Kuo, J. M., Wu, S. J., & Tsai, H. T. (2016). Isolation and characterization of fish scale collagen from tilapia (*Oreochromis* sp.) by a novel extrusion-hydro-extraction process. *Food Chemistry*, *190*, 997–1006. doi:10.1016/j.foodchem.2015.06.066

Ibrahim, H. M. I. (2015). Chemical composition, minerals content, amino acids bioavailability and sensory properties of meat and fish balls containing fish protein isolate. *International Journal of Current Microbiology and Applied Science*, *4*, 917–933.

Ideia, P., Pinto, J., Ferreira, R., Figueiredo, L., Spínola, V., & Castilho, P. C. (2020). Fish processing industry residues: A review of valuable products extraction and characterization methods. *Waste and Biomass Valorization*, *11*(7), 3223–3246. doi:10.1007/s12649-019-00739-1

Idowu, A. T., Benjakul, S., Sinthusamran, S., Sookchoo, P., & Kishimura, H. (2019). Protein hydrolysate from salmon frames: Production, characteristics and antioxidative activity. *Journal of Food Biochemistry*, *43*(2), 1–12. doi:10.1111/jfbc.12734

Iñarra, B., Bald, C., Cebrián, M., Antelo, L. T., Franco-Uría, A., Vázquez, J. A., & Jaime, Z. (2019). What to do with unwanted catches: Valorisation options and selection strategies. In: *The European Landing Obligation*. Uhlmann, S. S., Ulrich, C., & Kennelly, S. J. (Eds). Springer Open, 333–359. doi:10.1007/978-3-030-03308-8

Ishak, N. H., & Sarbon, N. M. (2018). A review of protein hydrolysates and bioactive peptides deriving from wastes generated by fish processing. *Food and Bioprocess Technology*, *11*(1), 2–16. doi:10.1007/s11947-017-1940-1

Kaur, S., & Dhillon, G. S. (2015). Recent trends in biological extraction of chitin from marine shell wastes: A review. *Critical Reviews in Biotechnology*, *35*(1), 44–61. doi:10.3109/07388551.2013.798256

Khawli, F. A., Pateiro, M., Domínguez, R., Lorenzo, J. M., Gullón, P., Kousoulaki, K., et al. (2019). Innovative green technologies of intensification for valorization of seafood and their by-products. *Marine Drugs*, *17*(12), 1–20. doi:10.3390/md17120689

Kim, H. K., Kim, Y. H., Kim, Y. J., Park, H. J., & Lee, N. H. (2012). Effects of ultrasonic treatment on collagen extraction from skins of the sea bass *Lateolabrax japonicus*. *Fisheries Science*, *78*(2), 485–490. doi:10.1007/s12562-012-0472-x

Kim, H. K., Kim, Y. H., Park, H. J., & Lee, N. H. (2013). Application of ultrasonic treatment to extraction of collagen from the skins of sea bass *Lateolabrax japonicus*. *Fisheries Science*, *79*(5), 849–856. doi:10.1007/s12562-013-0648-z

Kristinsson, H. G., & Rasco, B. A. (2000). Fish protein hydrolysates: Production, biochemical, and functional properties. *Critical Reviews in Food Science and Nutrition*, 40(1), 43–81. doi:10.1080/10408690091189266

Kristoffersen, K. A., Liland, K. H., Böcker, U., Wubshet, S. G., Lindberg, D., Horn, S. J., & Afseth, N. K. (2019). FTIR-based hierarchical modeling for prediction of average molecular weights of protein hydrolysates. *Talanta*, 205(January), 120084. doi:10.1016/j.talanta.2019.06.084

Kruijssen, F., Tedesco, I., Ward, A., Pincus, L., Love, D., & Thorne-Lyman, A. L. (2020). Loss and waste in fish value chains: A review of the evidence from low and middle-income countries. *Global Food Security*, 26, 100434. doi:10.1016/j.gfs.2020.100434

Kumar, B., & Rani, S. (2017). Technical note on the isolation and characterization of collagen from fish waste material. *Journal of Food Science and Technology*, 54(1), 276–278. doi:10.1007/s13197-016-2443-1

Landgrebe, D., Haake, C., Höpfner, T., Beutel, S., Hitzmann, B., Scheper, T., et al. (2010). On-line infrared spectroscopy for bioprocess monitoring. *Applied Microbiology and Biotechnology*, 88(1), 11–22. doi:10.1007/s00253-010-2743-8

Lapeña, D., Vuoristo, K. S., Kosa, G., Horn, S. J., & Eijsink, V. G. H. (2018). A comparative assessment of enzymatic hydrolysis for valorization of different protein-rich industrial by-products. *Journal of Agricultural and Food Chemistry*, 66(37), 9738–9749. doi:10.1021/acs.jafc.8b02444

Li, J., Wang, M., Qiao, Y., Tian, Y., Liu, J., Qin, S., & Wu, W. (2018). Extraction and characterization of type I collagen from skin of tilapia (*Oreochromis niloticus*) and its potential application in biomedical scaffold material for tissue engineering. *Process Biochemistry*, 74, 156–163. doi:10.1016/j.procbio.2018.07.009

Li, M., Lin, J., Chen, J., & Fang, T. (2016). Pulsed electric field-assisted enzymatic extraction of protein from abalone (*Haliotis discus hannai Ino*) viscera. *Journal of Food Process Engineering*, 39(6), 702–710. doi:10.1111/jfpe.12262

Li, N., Wu, X., Zhuang, W., Xia, L., Chen, Y., Wu, C., et al. (2020). Fish consumption and multiple health outcomes: Umbrella review. *Trends in Food Science and Technology*, 99, 273–283. doi:10.1016/j.tifs.2020.02.033

Li, W., Liu, Y., Jiang, W., & Yan, X. (2019). Proximate composition and nutritional profile of Rainbow trout (*Oncorhynchus mykiss*) heads and Skipjack tuna (*Katsuwonus pelamis*) heads. *Molecules*, 24(17). doi:10.3390/molecules24173189

Li-Chan, E. C. Y. (2015). Bioactive peptides and protein hydrolysates: Research trends and challenges for application as nutraceuticals and functional food ingredients. *Current Opinion in Food Science*, 1(1), 28–37. doi:10.1016/j.cofs.2014.09.005

Lim, Y., Ok, Y., Hwang, S., Kwak, J., & Yoon, S. (2019). Marine collagen as a promising biomaterial for biomedical applications. *Marine Drugs*, 17, 467.

Lima, D. A. S., Santos, M. M. F., Duvale, R. L. F., Bezerra, T. K. A., Araújo, Í. B. S., Madruga, M. S., & da Silva, F. A. P. (2020). Technological properties of protein hydrolysate from the cutting byproduct of Serra Spanish mackerel (*Scomberomorus brasiliensis*). *Journal of Food Science and Technology*, in press. doi:10.1007/s13197-020-04797-5

Limpisophon, K., Shibata, J., Yasuda, Y., Tanaka, M., & Osako, K. (2020). Optimization of hydrolysis conditions for production of gelatin hydrolysates from Shark skin byproduct and evaluation of their antioxidant activities. *Journal of Aquatic Food Product Technology*, 29(8), 736–749. doi:10.1080/10498850.2020.1799469

Liu, W., Zhang, Y., Cui, N., & Wang, T. (2019). Extraction and characterization of pepsin-solubilized collagen from snakehead (*Channa argus*) skin: Effects of hydrogen peroxide pretreatments and pepsin hydrolysis strategies. *Process Biochemistry*, 76, 194–202. doi:10.1016/j.procbio.2018.10.017

Lopes, C., Antelo, L. T., Franco-Uría, A., Alonso, A. A., & Pérez-Martín, R. (2018). Chitin production from crustacean biomass: Sustainability assessment of chemical and enzymatic processes. *Journal of Cleaner Production*, 172, 4140–4151. doi:10.1016/j.jclepro.2017.01.082

Marti-Quijal, F. J., Remize, F., Meca, G., Ferrer, E., Ruiz, M. J., & Barba, F. J. (2020). Fermentation in fish and by-products processing: An overview of current research and future prospects. *Current Opinion in Food Science*, 31, 9–16. doi:10.1016/j.cofs.2019.08.001

Maschmeyer, T., Luque, R., & Selva, M. (2020). Upgrading of marine (fish and crustaceans) biowaste for high added-value molecules and bio(nano)-materials. *Chemical Society Reviews*, 49(13), 4527–4563. doi:10.1039/c9cs00653b

Morrissey, M. T., & Okada, T. (2007). Marine enzymes from seafood by-products. In: *Maximising the Value of Marine By-Products*. Shahidi, F. (Ed.) Woodhead Publishing Series in Food Science, Technology and Nutrition, Amsterdam, The Netherlands, 374–396.

Naik, A. S., & Hayes, M. (2019). Trends in food science & technology bioprocessing of mussel by-products for value added ingredients. *Trends in Food Science & Technology*, *92*, 111–121. doi:10.1016/j.tifs.2019.08.013

Najafian, L., & Babji, A. S. (2012). A review of fish-derived antioxidant and antimicrobial peptides: Their production, assessment, and applications. *Peptides*, *33*(1), 178–185. doi:10.1016/j.peptides.2011.11.013

Nawaz, A., Li, E., Irshad, S., Xiong, Z., Xiong, H., Shahbaz, H. M., & Siddique, F. (2020). Valorization of fisheries by-products: Challenges and technical concerns to food industry. *Trends in Food Science and Technology*, *99*, 34–43. doi:10.1016/j.tifs.2020.02.022

Nekvapil, F., Aluas, M., Barbu-Tudoran, L., Suciu, M., Bortnic, R. A., Glamuzina, B., & Pinzaru, S. C. (2019). From blue bioeconomy toward circular economy through high-sensitivity analytical research on waste blue crab shells. *ACS Sustainable Chemistry and Engineering*, *7*(19), 16820–16827. doi:10.1021/acssuschemeng.9b04362

Nguyen, T. T., Heimann, K., & Zhang, W. (2020a). Protein recovery from underutilised marine bioresources for product development with nutraceutical and pharmaceutical bioactivities. *Marine Drugs*, *18*(8). doi:10.3390/MD18080391

Nguyen, T. T., Luo, X., Su, P., Balakrishnan, B., & Zhang, W. (2020b). Highly efficient recovery of nutritional proteins from Australian rock lobster heads (*Jasus edwardsii*) by integrating ultrasonic extraction and chitosan co-precipitation. *Innovative Food Science and Emerging Technologies*, *60*, 102308. doi:10.1016/j.ifset.2020.102308

Nguyen, T. T., & Zhang, W. (2020). Techno-economic feasibility analysis of microwave-assisted biorefinery of multiple products from Australian lobster shells. *Food and Bioproducts Processing*, *124*, 419–433. doi:10.1016/j.fbp.2020.10.002

Nguyen, T. T., Zhang, W., Barber, A. R., Su, P., & He, S. (2016). Microwave-intensified enzymatic de-proteinization of Australian rock lobster shells (*Jasus edwardsii*) for the efficient recovery of protein hydrolysate as food functional nutrients. *Food and Bioprocess Technology*, *9*(4), 628–636. doi:10.1007/s11947-015-1657-y

Nikoo, M., Benjakul, S., Yasemi, M., Ahmadi Gavlighi, H., & Xu, X. (2019). Hydrolysates from rainbow trout (*Oncorhynchus mykiss*) processing by-product with different pretreatments: Antioxidant activity and their effect on lipid and protein oxidation of raw fish emulsion. *LWT*, *108*, 120–128. doi:10.1016/j.lwt.2019.03.049

Nirmal, N. P., Santivarangkna, C., Rajput, M. S., & Benjakul, S. (2020). Trends in shrimp processing waste utilization: An industrial prospective. *Trends in Food Science and Technology*, *103*, 20–35. doi:10.1016/j.tifs.2020.07.001

Ochoa, T. J., Baiocchi, N., Valdiviezo, G., Bullon, V., Campos, M., & Llanos-Cuentas, A. (2017). Evaluation of the efficacy, safety and acceptability of a fish protein isolate in the nutrition of children under 36 months of age. *Public Health Nutrition*, *20*(15), 2819–2826

Odeleye, T., White, W. L., & Lu, J. (2019). Extraction techniques and potential health benefits of bioactive compounds from marine molluscs: A review. *Food and Function*, *10*(5), 2278–2289. doi:10.1039/c9fo00172g

Ojha, K. S., Aznar, R., O'Donnell, C., & Tiwari, B. K. (2020). Ultrasound technology for the extraction of biologically active molecules from plant, animal and marine sources. *Trends in Analytical Chemistry*, *122*. doi:10.1016/j.trac.2019.115663

Ojha, S., Bußler, S., & Schlüter, O. K. (2020). Food waste valorisation and circular economy concepts in insect production and processing. *Waste Management*, *118*, 600–609. doi:10.1016/j.wasman.2020.09.010

Olatunde, O. O., & Benjakul, S. (2020). Antioxidants from Crustaceans: A Panacea for lipid oxidation in marine-based foods. *Food Reviews International*, *00*(00), 1–31. doi:10.1080/87559129.2020.1717522

Oliveira, D. L. d., Grassi, T. L. M., Bassani, J. S., Diniz, J. C. P., Paiva, N. M., Ponsano, E. H. G. (2020). Enrichment of fishburgers with proteins from surimi washing water. *Food Science and Technology (Campinas)*, *40*(4), 822–826.

Oliveira, V. d. M., Assis, C. R. D., Costa, B. d. A. M., Neri, R. C. d. A., Monte, F. T., Freitas, H. M. S. d. C. V., et al. (2021). Physical, biochemical, densitometric and spectroscopic techniques for characterization collagen from alternative sources: A review based on the sustainable valorization of aquatic by-products. *Journal of Molecular Structure*, *1224*. doi:10.1016/j.molstruc.2020.129023

Olsen, R. L., Toppe, J., & Karunasagar, I. (2014). Challenges and realistic opportunities in the use of by-products from processing of fish and shellfish. *Trends in Food Science and Technology*, *36*(2), 144–151. doi:10.1016/j.tifs.2014.01.007

Özogul, F., Hamed, I., Özogul, Y., & M.Regenstein, J. (2019). Crustacean by-products. In: *Encyclopedia of Food Chemistry*. Laurence Melton, P. V., & Shahidi, F. (Ed). Amsterdam, The Netherlands: Academic Press, 33–38.

Ozyurt, C. E., Boga, E. K., Ozkutuk, A. S., Ucar, Y., Durmus, M., & Ozyurt, G. (2020). Bioconversion of discard fish (*Equulites klunzingeri* and *Carassius gibelio*) fermented with natural lactic acid bacteria; the chemical and microbiological quality of ensilage. *Waste and Biomass Valorization, 11*(4), 1435–1442. doi:10.1007/s12649-018-0493-5

Özyurt, G., & Özkütük, A. S. (2019). Advances in discard and by-product processing. In: *Innovative Technologies in Seafood Processing*. Özoğul, Y. (Ed). Boca Raton: CRC Press Taylor & Francis Group, 323–350. doi:10.1201/9780429327551-16

Özyurt, G., Ozogul, Y., Kuley Boga, E., Özkütük, A. S., Durmuş, M., Uçar, Y., & Ozogul, F. (2019). The effects of fermentation process with acid and lactic acid bacteria strains on the biogenic amine formation of wet and spray-dried fish silages of discards. *Journal of Aquatic Food Product Technology, 28*(3), 314–328. doi:10.1080/10498850.2019.1578314

Pal, G. K., & Suresh, P. V. (2016). Sustainable valorisation of seafood by-products: Recovery of collagen and development of collagen-based novel functional food ingredients. *Innovative Food Science and Emerging Technologies, 37*(Part B), 201–215. doi:10.1016/j.ifset.2016.03.015

Patraşcu, L., & Aprodu, L. (2017). Processing of low-value fish, coproducts, and by-catch. In: *Trends in Fish Processing Technologies*. Daniela Borda, P. R., & Nicolau, A. I. (Eds). Boca Raton: CRC Press, 101–121.

Pateiro, M., Munekata, P. E. S., Wang, M., Barba, F. J., Berm, R., & Lorenzo, J. M. (2020). Nutritional profiling and the value of processing by-products from Gilthead sea bream (*Sparus aurata*). *Marine Drugs, 18*(101), 1–18.

Peinado, I., Koutsidis, G., & Ames, J. (2016). Production of seafood flavour formulations from enzymatic hydrolysates of fish by-products. *LWT - Food Science and Technology, 66*, 444–452. doi:10.1016/j.lwt.2015.09.025

Penven, A., Perez-Galvez R, B. J.-P., & Bergé, J.-P. (2013). By-products from fish processing: Focus on French industry. In: *Utilization of Fish Waste*. Galvez, R. P., & Berge, J.-P. (Eds). Boca Raton: CRC Press, 1–25.

Petrova, I., Tolstorebrov, I., & Eikevik, T. M. (2018). Production of fish protein hydrolysates step by step: Technological aspects, equipment used, major energy costs and methods of their minimizing. *International Aquatic Research, 10*(3), 223–241. doi:10.1007/s40071-018-0207-4

Riaz, T., Zeeshan, R., Zarif, F., Ilyas, K., Safi, S. Z., Rahim, A., et al. (2018). FTIR analysis of natural and synthetic collagen. *Applied Spectroscopy Reviews, 53*(9), 703–746. doi:10.1080/05704928.2018.1426595

Rocha Camargo, T., Ramos, P., Monserrat, J. M., Prentice, C., Fernandes, C. J. C., Zambuzzi, W. F., & Valenti, W. C. (2021). Biological activities of the protein hydrolysate obtained from two fishes common in the fisheries bycatch. *Food Chemistry, 342*, 128361. 10.1016/j.foodchem.2020.128361

Rustad, T., Storrø, I., & Slizyte, R. (2011). Possibilities for the utilisation of marine by-products. *International Journal of Food Science and Technology, 46*(10), 2001–2014. 10.1111/j.1365-2621.2011.02736.x

Ruthu, Murthy, P. S., Rai, A. K., & Bhaskar, N. (2014). Fermentative recovery of lipids and proteins from freshwater fish head waste with reference to antimicrobial and antioxidant properties of protein hydrolysate. *Journal of Food Science and Technology, 51*(9), 1884–1892. doi:10.1007/s13197-012-0730-z

Saidi, S., Deratani, A., Belleville, M. P., & Amar, R. Ben. (2014). Production and fractionation of tuna by-product protein hydrolysate by ultrafiltration and nanofiltration: Impact on interesting peptides fractions and nutritional properties. *Food Research International, 65*(PC), 453–461. doi:10.1016/j.foodres.2014.04.026

Samarakoon, K. W., Elvitigala, D. A. S., Lakmal, H. H. C., Kim, Y. M., & Jeon, Y. J. (2014). Future prospects and health benefits of functional ingredients from marine bio-resources: A review. *Fisheries and Aquatic Sciences, 17*(3), 275–290. doi:10.5657/FAS.2014.0275

Sampath Kumar, N. S., Nazeer, R. A., & Jaiganesh, R. (2012). Purification and identification of antioxidant peptides from the skin protein hydrolysate of two marine fishes, horse mackerel (*Magalaspis cordyla*) and croaker (*Otolithes ruber*). *Amino Acids, 42*(5), 1641–1649. doi:10.1007/s00726-011-0858-6

Sánchez, A., & Vázquez, A. (2017). Bioactive peptides: A review. *Food Quality and Safety, 1*, 29–46. doi:10.1093/fqs/fyx006

Santana, P., Huda, N., & Yang, T. A. (2015). Physicochemical properties and sensory characteristics of sausage formulated with surimi powder. *Journal of Food Science & Technology, 52*, 1507–1515.

Sasidharan, A., & Venugopal, V. (2020). Proteins and co-products from seafood processing discards: Their recovery, functional properties and applications. *Waste and Biomass Valorization, 11*(11), 5647–5663. doi:10.1007/s12649-019-00812-9

Sathivel, S., Bechtel, P. J., Babbitt, J. K., Prinyawiwatkul, W., & Patterson, M. (2005). Functional, nutritional and rheological properties of protein powders from arrow tooth flounder and their application in mayonnaise. *Journal of Food Science, 70*(2), 57–63.

Senadheera, T. R. L., Dave, D., & Shahidi, F. (2020). Sea cucumber derived type I collagen: A comprehensive review. *Marine Drugs, 18*(9), 11–13. doi:10.3390/md18090471

Shabani, A., Boldaji, F., Dastar, B., Ghoorchi, T., & Zerehdaran, S. (2018). Preparation of fish waste silage and its effect on the growth performance and meat quality of broiler chickens. *Journal of the Science of Food and Agriculture, 98*(11), 4097–4103. doi:10.1002/jsfa.8926

Shahidi, F. & Ambigaipalan, P. (2019). Bioactives from seafood processing by-products. In: *Encyclopedia of Food Chemistry*. Melton, P. V. L., & Shahidi, F. (Eds). Academic Press, 280–288.

Shahidi, F., & Ambigaipalan, P. (2015). Novel functional food ingredients from marine sources. *Current Opinion in Food Science, 2*, 123–129. doi:10.1016/j.cofs.2014.12.009

Shahidi, F., Varatharajan, V., Peng, H., & Senadheera, R. (2019). Utilization of marine by-products for the recovery of value-added products. *Journal of Food Bioactives, 6*, 10–61. doi:10.31665/jfb.2019.6184

Shaviklo, A. R., Moradinezhad, N., Abolghasemi, S. J., Motamedzadegan, A., Kamali-Damavandi, N., & Rafipour, F. (2016). Product optimization of fish burger containing Tuna protein isolates for better sensory quality and frozen storage stability. *Turkish Journal of Fisheries and Aquatic Sciences, 16*, 923–933.

Shaviklo, G. R., Olafsdottir, A., Sveinsdottir, K., Thorkelsson, G., & Rafipour, F. (2011a). Quality characteristics and consumer acceptance of a high fish protein puffed corn-fish snack. *Journal of Food Science & Technology, 48*(6), 668–676, doi:10.1007/s13197-010-0191-1

Shaviklo, G. R., Thorkelsson, G., Sigurgisladottir, S., & Pourreza, F. (2013). Studies on processing, consumer survey and storage stability of a ready-to-reconstitute fish cutlet mix. *Journal of Food Science & Technology, 50*(5), 900–908.

Shaviklo, G. R., Thorkelsson, G., Sigurgisladottir, S., & Rafipour, F. (2011b). Quality changes during storage of extruded puffed corn snacks incorporated with freeze dried saithe (*Pollachius virens*) protein and stabilized minces from rainbow trout (*Oncorhynchus mykiss*) and silver carp (*Hypophthalmichthys molitrix*). *Journal of the Science of Food and Agriculture, 91*(5), 886–893. doi:10.1002/jsfa.4261.

Shaviklo, G. R., Thorkelsson, G., Sigurgisladottir, S., & Rafipour, F. (2011c). Chemical properties and sensory quality of ice cream fortified with fish protein. *Journal of the Science of Food and Agriculture, 91*(7), 1199–1204.

Shen, X., Zhang, M., Bhandari, B., & Gao, Z. (2019). Novel technologies in utilization of byproducts of animal food processing: A review. *Critical Reviews in Food Science and Nutrition, 59*(21), 3420–3430. doi:10.1080/10408398.2018.1493428

Siddik, M. A. B., Howieson, J., Fotedar, R., & Partridge, G. J. (2020). Enzymatic fish protein hydrolysates in finfish aquaculture: A review. *Reviews in Aquaculture*, 1–25. doi:10.1111/raq.12481

Sila, A., & Bougatef, A. (2016). Antioxidant peptides from marine by-products: Isolation, identification and application in food systems. A review. *Journal of Functional Foods, 21*, 10–26. doi:10.1016/j.jff.2015.11.007

Singh, A., Idowu, A. T., Benjakul, S., Kishimura, H., Aluko, R. E., & Kumagai, Y. (2020a). Debittering of salmon (*Salmo salar*) frame protein hydrolysate using 2-butanol in combination with β-cyclodextrin: Impact on some physicochemical characteristics and antioxidant activities. *Food Chemistry, 321*(March), 126686. doi:10.1016/j.foodchem.2020.126686

Singh, A., Mittal, A., & Benjakul, S. (2020b). Full utilization of squid meat and its processing by-products: Revisit. *Food Reviews International, 00*(00), 1–25. doi:10.1080/87559129.2020.1734611

Slizyte, R., Rommi, K., Mozuraityte, R., Eck, P., Five, K., & Rustad, T. (2016). Bioactivities of fish protein hydrolysates from defatted salmon backbones. *Biotechnology Reports, 11*, 99–109. doi:10.1016/j.btre.2016.08.003

Soufi-Kechaou, E., Derouiniot-Chaplin, M., Ben Amar, R., Jaouen, P., & Berge, J. P. (2017). Recovery of valuable marine compounds from cuttlefish by-product hydrolysates: Combination of enzyme bioreactor and membrane technologies fractionation of cuttlefish protein hydrolysates by ultrafiltration: Impact on peptidic populations. *Comptes Rendus Chimie, 20*(9–10), 975–985. doi:10.1016/j.crci.2016.03.018

Steinsholm, S., Oterhals, Å., Underhaug, J., Måge, I., Malmendal, A., & Aspevik, T. (2020). Sensory assessment of fish and chicken protein hydrolysates. Evaluation of NMR metabolomics profiling as a new prediction tool. *Journal of Agricultural and Food Chemistry*, *68*(12), 3881–3890. doi:10.1021/acs.jafc.9b07828

Stevens, J. R., Newton, R. W., Tlusty, M., & Little, D. C. (2018). The rise of aquaculture by-products: Increasing food production, value, and sustainability through strategic utilisation. *Marine Policy*, *90*(January), 115–124. doi:10.1016/j.marpol.2017.12.027

Suárez-Jiménez, G. M., Burgos-Hernández, A., Torres-Arreola, W., López-Saiz, C. M., Velázquez Contreras, C. A., & Ezquerra-Brauer, J. M. (2019). Bioactive peptides from collagen hydrolysates from squid (*Dosidicus gigas*) by-products fractionated by ultrafiltration. *International Journal of Food Science and Technology*, *54*(4), 1054–1061. doi:10.1111/ijfs.13984

Subhan, F., Hussain, Z., Tauseef, I., Shehzad, A., & Wahid, F. (2020). A review on recent advances and applications of fish collagen. *Critical Reviews in Food Science and Nutrition*, *61*(6), 1027–1037. doi:10.1080/10408398.2020.1751585

Subin, S. R., Mohan, A., Khiari, Z., Udenigwe, C. C., & Mason, B. (2018). Yield, physicochemical, and antioxidant properties of Atlantic salmon visceral hydrolysate: Comparison of lactic acid bacterial fermentation with Flavourzyme proteolysis and formic acid treatment. *Journal of Food Processing and Preservation*, *42*(6), 1–11. doi:10.1111/jfpp.13620

Sukkhown, P., Jangchud, K., & Lorjaroenphon, Y. (2018). Food hydrocolloids flavored-functional protein hydrolysates from enzymatic hydrolysis of dried squid by-products: Effect of drying method. *Food hydrocolloids*, *76*, 103–112. doi:10.1016/j.foodhyd.2017.01.026

Sundekilde, U. K., Jarno, L., Eggers, N., & Bertram, H. C. (2018). Real-time monitoring of enzyme-assisted animal protein hydrolysis by NMR spectroscopy – An NMR reactomics concept. *LWT*, *95*(January), 9–16. doi:10.1016/j.lwt.2018.04.055

Surasani, V. K. R. (2018). Acid and alkaline solubilization (pH shift) process: a better approach for the utilization of fish processing waste and by-products. *Environmental Science and Pollution Research*, *25*(19), 18345–18363. doi:10.1007/s11356-018-2319-1

Surasani, V. K. R., Raju, C. V., Shafiq, U., Chandra, M.V., & Lakshmisha, I. P. (2020). Influence of protein isolates from Pangas processing waste on physicochemical, textural, rheological and sensory quality characteristics of fish sausages. *LWT - Food Science and Technology*, *117*, 108662.

Suresh, P. V., Kudre, T. G., & Johny, L. C. (2018). Sustainable valorization of seafood processing by-product/discard. In: *Waste to Wealth. Energy, Environment, and Sustainability*. Singhania, S. R., Agarwal, R., & Kumar, R. (Eds). Singapore: Springer, 111–139. doi:10.1007/978-981-10-7431-8_7

Suresh, P. V., & Prabhu, N. G. (2014). Seafood. In: *Valorization of Food Processing By-Products*. Chandrasekaran, M. (Ed). Boca Raton, USA: CRC Press, 685–736.

Tan, Y., Chang, S. K. C., & Meng, S. (2019a). Comparing the kinetics of the hydrolysis of by-product from channel catfish (*Ictalurus punctatus*) fillet processing by eight proteases. *LWT*, *111*, 809–820. doi:10.1016/j.lwt.2019.05.053

Tan, Y., Gao, H., Chang, S. K. C., Bechtel, P. J., & Mahmoud, B. S. M. (2019b). Comparative studies on the yield and characteristics of myofibrillar proteins from catfish heads and frames extracted by two methods for making surimi-like protein gel products. *Food Chemistry*, *272*, 133–140. doi:10.1016/j.foodchem.2018.07.201

Tian, Y., Wang, W., Yuan, C., Zhang, L., Liu, J., & Liu, J. (2017). Nutritional and digestive properties of protein isolates extracted from the muscle of the common carp using pH-shift processing. *Journal of Food Processing and Preservation*, *41*(1). doi:10.1111/jfpp.12847

Toppe, J., & Penarubia, O. (2018). *Production and Utilization of Fish Silage: A Manual on How to Turn Fish Waste into Profit and a Valuable Feed Ingredient or Fertilizer*. Food and Agriculture Organisation of the United Nations, Rome.

Tripoteau, L., Bedoux, G., Gagnon, J., & Bourgougnon, N. (2015). In vitro antiviral activities of enzymatic hydrolysates extracted from byproducts of the Atlantic holothurian *Cucumaria frondosa*. *Process Biochemistry*, *50*(5), 867–875. doi:10.1016/j.procbio.2015.02.012

Udenigwe, C. C., & Aluko, R. E. (2012). Food protein-derived bioactive peptides: Production, processing, and potential health benefits. *Journal of Food Science*, *77*(1). doi:10.1111/j.1750-3841.2011.02455.x

Uranga, J., Etxabide, A., Cabezudo, S., de la Caba, K., & Guerrero, P. (2020). Valorization of marine-derived biowaste to develop chitin/fish gelatin products as bioactive carriers and moisture scavengers. *Science of the Total Environment*, *706*, 135747. doi:10.1016/j.scitotenv.2019.135747

Utne-Palm, A. C., Bogevik, A. S., Humborstad, O. B., Aspevik, T., Pennington, M., & Løkkeborg, S. (2020). Feeding response of Atlantic cod (Gadus morhua) to attractants made from by-products from the fishing industry. *Fisheries Research*, 227, 105535. doi:10.1016/j.fishres.2020.105535

Valcarcel, J., Sanz, N., & Vázquez, J. A. (2020). Optimization of the enzymatic protein hydrolysis of by-products from seabream (*Sparus aurata*) and seabass (*Dicentrarchus labrax*), chemical and functional characterization. *Foods*, 9, 1503.

Välimaa, A. L., Mäkinen, S., Mattila, P., Marnila, P., Pihlanto, A., Mäki, M., & Hiidenhovi, J. (2019). Fish and fish side streams are valuable sources of high-value components. *Food Quality and Safety*, 3(4), 209–226. doi:10.1093/fqsafe/fyz024

Vang, B., Altintzoglou, T., Måge, I., Wubshet, S. G., Afseth, N. K., & Whitaker, R. D. (2018). Nofima: Peptide recovery and commercialization by enzymatic hydrolysis of marine biomass. In: Gonzalo de Gonzalo, Pablo Domínguez de María (ed)*Biocatalysis: An Industrial Perspective*.

Vázquez, J. A., Blanco, M., Massa, A. E., Amado, I. R., & Pérez-Martín, R. I. (2017). Production of fish protein hydrolysates from *Scyliorhinus canicula* discards with antihypertensive & antioxidant activities by enzymatic hydrolysis & mathematical optimization using response surface methodology. *Marine Drugs*, 15(10), 1–15. doi:10.3390/md15100306

Vázquez, J. A., Durán, A. I., Menduíña, A., Nogueira, M., Gomes, A. M., Antunes, J., et al. (2020a). Bioconversion of fish discards through the production of lactic acid bacteria and metabolites: Sustainable application of fish peptones in nutritive fermentation media. *Foods*, 9(9), 1–17. doi:10.3390/foods9091239

Vázquez, J. A., Fernández-Compás, A., Blanco, M., Rodríguez-Amado, I., Moreno, H., Borderías, J., & Pérez-Martín, R. I. (2019a). Development of bioprocesses for the integral valorisation of fish discards. *Biochemical Engineering Journal*, 144(January), 198–208. doi:10.1016/j.bej.2019.02.004

Vázquez, J. A., Fraguas, J., Mirón, J., Valcárcel, J., Pérez-Martín, R. I., & Antelo, L. T. (2020b). Valorisation of fish discards assisted by enzymatic hydrolysis and microbial bioconversion: Lab and pilot plant studies and preliminary sustainability evaluation. *Journal of Cleaner Production*, 246. doi:10.1016/j.jclepro.2019.119027

Vázquez, J. A., Meduíña, A., Durán, A. I., Nogueira, M., Fernández-Compás, A., Pérez-Martín, R. I., & Rodríguez-Amado, I. (2019b). Production of valuable compounds and bioactive metabolites from by-products of fish discards using chemical processing, enzymatic hydrolysis, and bacterial fermentation. *Marine Drugs*, 17(3). doi:10.3390/md17030139

Vázquez, J. A., Menduíña, A., Nogueira, M., Durán, A. I., Sanz, N., & Valcarcel, J. (2020c). Optimal production of protein hydrolysates from Monkfish by-products: Chemical features and associated biological activities. *Molecules*, 25(18). doi:10.3390/molecules25184068

Vázquez, J. A., Rodríguez-Amado, I., Sotelo, C. G., Sanz, N., Pérez-Martín, R. I., & Valcárcel, J. (2020d). Production, characterization, and bioactivity of fish protein hydrolysates from aquaculture turbot (*Scophthalmus maximus*) wastes. *Biomolecules*, 10(2), 1–13. doi:10.3390/biom10020310

Vázquez, J. A., Sotelo, C. G., Sanz, N., Pérez-Martín, R. I., Rodríguez-Amado, I., & Valcarcel, J. (2019c). Valorization of aquaculture by-products of salmonids to produce enzymatic hydrolysates: Process optimization, chemical characterization and evaluation of bioactives. *Marine Drugs*, 17(12), 1–15. doi:10.3390/md17120676

Venkatesan, J., Anil, S., Kim, S. K., & Shim, M. S. (2017). Marine fish proteins and peptides for cosmeceuticals: A review. *Marine Drugs*, 15(5), 1–18. doi:10.3390/md15050143

Venugopal, V. (2016). *Enzymes from Seafood Processing Waste and Their Applications in Seafood Processing. Advances in Food and Nutrition Research*, 1st Edition, Vol. 78. Elsevier Inc. doi:10.1016/bs.afnr.2016.06.004

Villamil, O., Váquiro, H., & Solanilla, J. F. (2017). Fish viscera protein hydrolysates: Production, potential applications and functional and bioactive properties. *Food Chemistry*, 224, 160–171. doi:10.1016/j.foodchem.2016.12.057

Vorob'ev, M. M. (2019). Proteolysis of β-lactoglobulin by trypsin: Simulation by two-step model and experimental verification by intrinsic tryptophan fluorescence. *Symmetry*, 11(2). doi:10.3390/sym11020153

Wang, S., Nguyen, V. B., Doan, C. T., & Tran, T. N. (2020). Production and potential applications of bioconversion of chitin and protein-containing fishery byproducts into prodigiosin: A review. *Molecules*, 25, 1–23.

Wendel, A., Park, J. W., & Kristbergsson, K. (2002). Recovered meat from Pacific Whiting frame. *Journal of Aquatic Food Product Technology*, 11(1), 5–18

Wubshet, S. G., Lindberg, D., Veiseth-Kent, E., A.Kristoffersen, K., Böcker, U., E.Washburn, K., & K.Afseth, N. (2019). Bioanalytical aspects in enzymatic protein hydrolysis of by-products. In: Galanakis, C. M. (ed). *Proteins: Sustainable Source, Processing and Applications.* Cambridge, MA, USA: Academic Press. (pp. 225–258).

Wubshet, S. G., Wold, J. P., Afseth, N. K., Böcker, U., Lindberg, D., Ihunegbo, F. N., & Måge, I. (2018). Feed-forward prediction of product qualities in enzymatic protein hydrolysis of poultry by-products: A spectroscopic approach. *Food and Bioprocess Technology, 11*(11), 2032–2043. doi:10.1007/s11947-018-2161-y

Yan, N., & Chen, X. (2015). Don't waste seafood waste: Turning cast-off shells into nitrogen-rich chemicals would benefit economies and the environment. *Nature, 524,* 155–157.

Zamora-Sillero, J., Gharsallaoui, A., & Prentice, C. (2018). Peptides from fish by-product protein hydrolysates and its functional properties: An overview. *Marine Biotechnology, 20*(2), 118–130. doi:10.1007/s10126-018-9799-3

Zebib, H., Teame, T., Aregawi, T., & Meresa, T. (2020). Nutritional and sensory acceptability of wheat bread from fish flour. *Cogent Food & Agriculture, 6,* 1714831.

Zhong, S., Liu, S., Cao, J., Chen, S., Wang, W., & Qin, X. (2016). Fish protein isolates recovered from silver carp (*Hypophthalmichthys molitrix*) by-products using alkaline pH solubilization and precipitation. *Journal of Aquatic Food Product Technology, 25*(3), 400–413. doi:10.1080/10498850.2013.865282

11 Meat Co-products

Reshan Jayawardena[1], James David Morton[1], Charles S. Brennan[1], Zuhaib Fayaz Bhat[1], and Alaa El-Din Ahmed Bekhit[2]

[1]Department of Wine Food and Molecular Biosciences, Lincoln University, Lincoln, New Zealand
[2]University of Otago, Department of Food Science, Dunedin, New Zealand

CONTENTS

11.1	Introduction	329
11.2	Global Co-product Market	331
11.3	Co-products as Part of the Solution for Global Malnutrition	332
11.4	Co-products for Treatment of Iron Deficiency "Anaemia"	343
11.5	Other Minerals in Co-products	344
11.6	Health Effect of Protein Bio-active Protein	345
11.6	Co-product Processing	346
	11.6.1 Extrusion Cooking	346
	11.6.2 Drying of Co-products	347
	11.6.3 Co-product Hydrolysates	348
11.7	Cooking Effect on Co-products	349
11.8	Consumer Aspects of Co-product Utilisation	350
11.9	Conclusions	354
References		355

11.1 INTRODUCTION

Meat plays a major role in the human diet and fills an essential nutritional requirement by providing quality protein. Based on the amino acid profile, animal protein can supply complete protein with high biological value and bioavailability. World meat consumption has increased continuously during the last two decades. Global meat consumption increased from 204 million tonnes in 1997 to 313 million tonnes in 2017 due to the increasing population, and annual individual consumption has increased from 35.33 to 42.57 kg (Herrero et al., 2013a). The global demand for meat is growing continuously in many parts of the world (i.e., Asia, Middle East and South America), and increasing need of high-quality meat for the growing population has necessitated an expansion of production to meet this need. However further increase in production is hindered by environmental constraints. For instance, ruminants used 3.7 billion tonnes of the 4.7 billion tonnes of feed biomass consumed by livestock globally, while pigs and poultry consumed the remaining 1 billion tonnes of biomass in 2000 (Herrero et al., 2013a). Further, it is estimated that they are responsible for a large portion of the total livestock non-CO_2 greenhouse gas emission (FAOSTAT, 2018). These environmental issues are critical, and the livestock industry needs to focus on increasing its efficiency by co-product usage rather than by just increasing the number of animals. Using a larger proportion of each animal, i.e., adopting nose to tail use as in many developing countries, is a possible alternative to slaughtering more or larger animals.

Carcasses of cattle, sheep and pigs are about 45% to 60%, 40 to 45% and 74%, respectively, of the live animal weight (Boler, 2014; Leonard, 2011; Thomson et al., 2010). The remaining parts are either considered as waste or co-products. Better utilisation of these co-products could significantly increase production efficiency (Albertí et al., 2008; Lynch et al., 2018) and preserve a greater portion of the animal protein within the human food chain.

Consumption of meat co-products (Figure 11.1) is a culturally bound food habit in certain nations and communities and often much less popular than muscle meat in certain societies (mostly Western countries). However, processing meat co-products into extracts, powdered form and pressed and hybrid products could modify the sensory characteristics and possibly allow it to be

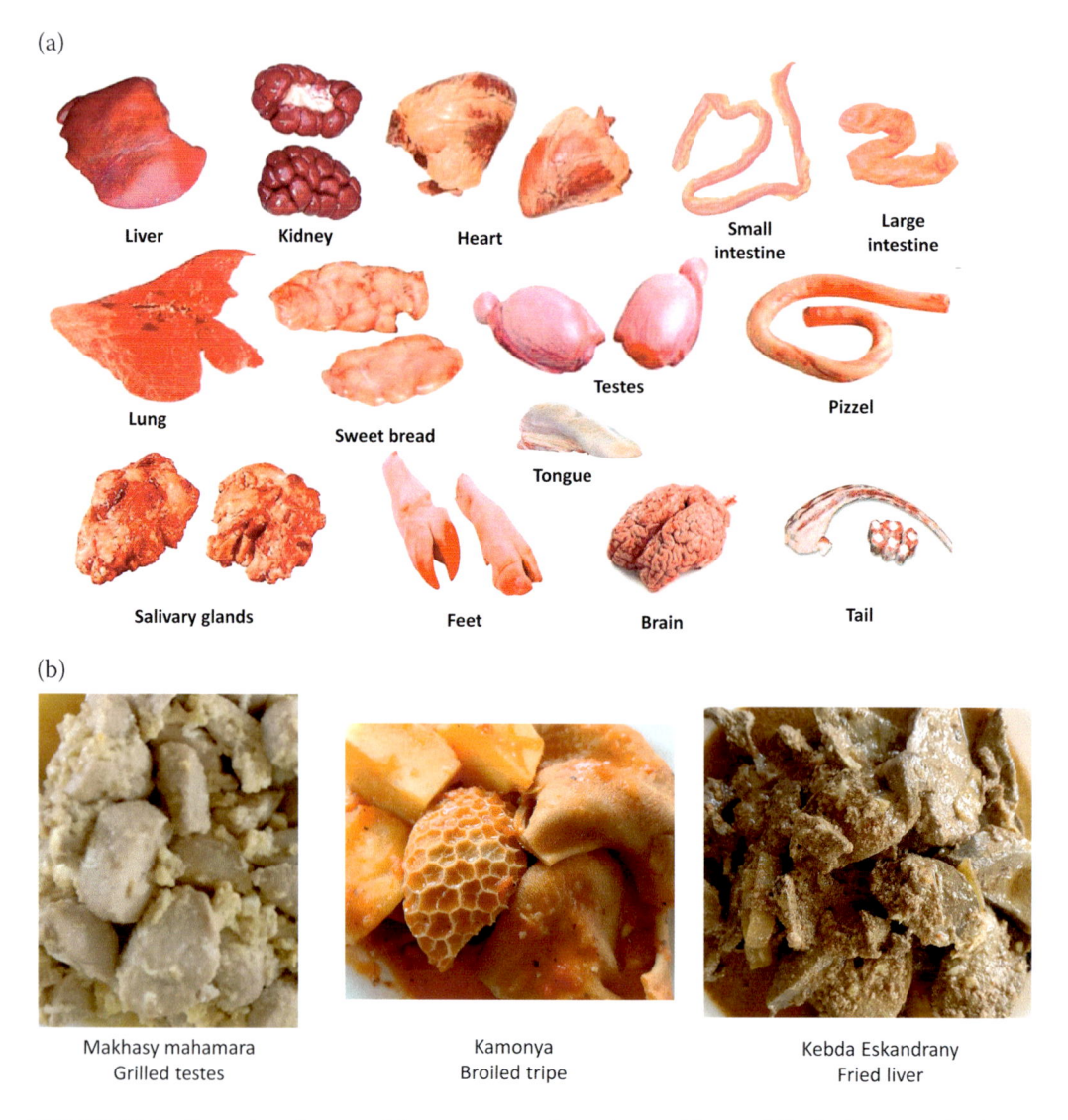

FIGURE 11.1 Examples of some of the meat co-products that could potentially be harvested for human food chain (A) and examples of traditional Middle Eastern dishes utilizing some of these co-products (B). The examples are not exhaustive as there are several items such as tendons, blood, head and so on that have been traditionally harvested for food in many parts of the world.

incorporated into widely consumed foods to attract consumers. A considerable portion of non-carcass mass can be obtained as edible offal and protein products, which would bring a considerable amount of nutritious material to the consumer's food plate. High meat-producing countries like the US, New Zealand and Australia do not use these nutritious organs as edible food but rather repurpose it as pet food or a component of low value meat and bone meal. In some cases, the co-products are harvested and sold as low value exports to developing countries.

The major meat producing countries typically have a low demand for co-products, while other parts of the world suffer from protein deficiency. These latter countries always struggle to fulfil their energy requirement rather than focusing on nutrition requirements. The World Food Program's hunger map (Mullen et al., 2017) illustrated severely malnourished countries, where more than 35% of their population is undernourished. Therefore, they are more prone to have protein-energy malnutrition. The income level of these hunger-stricken countries is at the bottom level of developing countries, and they are unable to purchase expensive animal meat. Globally, the price of meat is higher than plant commodities, and there is an obvious purchasing problem for low-income countries to obtain high quality protein. Having low price animal protein affordable could help fulfil their protein requirements. Underutilised co-products of the meat industry have enormous potential as a protein supplement and provider of other important nutrients. So, there is an opportunity to bridge this gap by utilising the accumulating animal co-products in higher meat producing countries and at the same time, fulfil the nutrition requirement of malnourished communities.

11.2 GLOBAL CO-PRODUCT MARKET

World meat consumption has increased continuously during the last several years. The increase in meat production means that there is also a parallel increase in potential co-products. Identification and quantification of global co-products and their wastage are beneficial for the purpose of evaluating their potential and applications. The current literature does not clearly distinguish the animal source of co-products and wastage. FAO statistics in 2019 provides the world production of co-products, but it does not differentiate particular co-products or species. USDA data provided livestock statistics until mid-2019 and forecast for 2020, but offal statistics were not available. Local meat production in New Zealand was reported by the Meat Industry Association (MIA) annual report, but it does not differentiate the edible offal figures according to animal species.

The importation and export of edible offal increased rapidly from 1993 to 2013. Both import and export quantities of edible offal were around 1 million tonnes in 1993 worldwide and had grown to 4.9 million tonnes exported and 3.8 million tonnes imported in 2013 (FAOSTAT, 2018). World total edible offal exports for different regional markets were as follows; 52.8%-Europe, 30.7%-America, 10.7%-Asia, 5.4%-Oceania and 0.4%-Africa; importation was reported as 48%-Asia, 31.3% Europe, 10.3%-Africa, 10.2%-America and 0.1% Oceania in 2013. In 2017, edible offal import-export market, values and quantities were derived by region from the FAOSTAT (2018) database (Table 11.1). Global total edible offal export quantity was reported as 5,798,582 tonnes with a market value of 9,957,040 thousand (*1000) US$ in 2017 and average offal value was 0.6 US$/Kg including edible offal of cattle, sheep, pig, goat and liver of chicken, duck and geese. According to O'Sullivan et al. (2017), edible pig offal is the most highly demanded edible offal in the world. Germany exported the largest quantity of pig offal in 2016 (668,632 tonnes) and the highest total quantity was imported by China-Mainland (1.35 million tonnes). The top five importers of beef and offal were Hong Kong, China, Egypt, Vietnam, Russian Federation and Japan. Hong Kong imported 272,502 tonnes of cattle offal and was the largest importer in 2016 (Darine et al., 2011) and the USA supplied 280,805 tonnes of cattle edible offal as the largest supplier followed by Australia, Brazil, Ireland and Argentina.

Edible offal can also include material traded for meat and bone meal (MBM) or animal feed. These underutilised co-products produce a very low-price margin. The identification of underutilised edible co-products from edible co-products is important to increase production efficiency and identify

TABLE 11.1
World edible offal market importation and exportation by region (2017). FAOSTAT (2018)

Export quantity of edible offal (tonnes)

Region	Cattle	Chicken	Duck	Geese	Pigs	Sheep	Total (%)
Africa	9,700	7,172	72	33	462	1,331	0.3
Americas	646,167	1,023	30	58	777,091	720	24.6
Asia	135,656	4,023	57	185	558,692	6,183	12.2
Europe	528,540	738,665	14,092	2,114	2,090,960	22,187	58.6
Oceania	192,485	NA	91	NA	6,641	54,151	4.4
World	1,512,548	750,883	14,343	2,389	3,433,847	84,572	100

Export value of edible offal (1000 US$)

Region	Cattle	Chicken	Duck	Geese	Pigs	Sheep	Total (%)
Africa	16,441	6,301	113	48	754	2,942	0.3
Americas	1,682,359	1,264	371	212	1,274,769	1,832	29.7
Asia	322,449	10,800	182	412	1,386,496	16,006	17.4
Europe	1,026,788	640,543	133,865	19,100	2,632,030	40,590	45.1
Oceania	614,512	NA	112	NA	8,842	116,905	7.4
World	3,662,550	658,907	134,644	19,774	5,302,890	178,275	100

Import quantity of edible offal (tonnes)

Region	Cattle	Chicken	Duck	Geese	Pigs	Sheep	Total (%)
Africa	506,929	60,650	93	134	97,920	9,313	13.4
Americas	164,841	32,110	20	94	263,385	5,184	9.2
Asia	584,618	54,048	320	1,122	2,043,856	43,608	54.0
Europe	262,533	298,395	8,963	1,559	578,756	19,238	23.2
Oceania	7,253	30	30	NA	1,619	2,914	0.2
World	1,526,174	445,232	9,426	2,908	2,985,536	80,259	100

Import value of edible offal (1000 US$)

Region	Cattle	Chicken	Duck	Geese	Pigs	Sheep	Total (%)
Africa	530,739	54,089	301	229	83,234	10,665	7.6
Americas	510,140	38,622	295	431	310,764	10,687	9.7
Asia	2,312,777	61,212	7,713	18,425	3,526,791	105,649	67.5
Europe	541,894	188,248	125,300	18,832	412,578	41,715	14.9
Oceania	13,814	59	809	2	2,522	7,044	0.3
World	3,909,364	342,230	134,418	37,919	4,335,888	175,760	100

*NA= Data not available

areas of urgent research need. The general categorising of popular and underutilised co-products varies with countries. The preference for co-products and their usage are entirely affected by the culture and country where they are produced (Darine et al., 2010). However, liver, heart, spleen, pancreas, thymus co-products are accepted by most communities. Liver is the most popular co-product, and the UN-FAO separately categorised liver in the database of FAOSTAT (2018). Thymus and pancreas are used as sweetbread in culinary dishes (Cardoso-Santiago & Arêas, 2001).

11.3 CO-PRODUCTS AS PART OF THE SOLUTION FOR GLOBAL MALNUTRITION

Protein Energy Malnutrition (PEM) contributes to half of the deaths of children in developing countries (Chávez-Jáuregui et al., 2003). The World Health Organisation (WHO) estimated in 2000 that 32% of children under-five were malnourished in developing countries. Recent figures are indicating this category encompass 52 million children, and the situation is very alarming in certain regions according to Dr Francesco Branca, Director of the Department of Nutrition for Health and Development at the World Health Organization (WHO). According to Dr. Branca *"in South Asia one in four, and approximately 45% of deaths among children under five, are linked to undernutrition. These deaths often occur in low- and middle-income countries"* (https://www.who.int/news/item/26-09-2019-malnutrition-is-a-world-health-crisis). Cardoso-Santiago and Arêas (2001) reported that one in nine people faces hunger in the world, and Africa is the region with the highest hunger prevalence, as 1 in 5 people are hungry. These figures have not changed and are still current (https://www.who.int/news/item/15-07-2019-world-hunger-is-still-not-going-down-after-three-years-and-obesity-is-still-growing-un-report), which is a great disappointment, as significant advances in science in both agriculture and food processing do not appear to have alleviated this situation. While political instability in the Middle East, Asia and Africa can be a contributing factor for this unchanged situation, it clearly demonstrates the inability of current food production systems to meet sudden changes in food production and demand. The World Food Program's hunger map (Toldrá et al., 2012) illustrates severely malnourished countries, where more than 35% of the population is undernourished. Macro and micronutrient deficiencies are apparent in those groups, and they are more prone to have protein-energy malnutrition.

Two severe malnutrition syndromes in children are marasmus and kwashiorkor. According to USDA-FAS (2018), those suffering from marasmus have severe muscle wasting and minimal adipose tissue. A key symptom of kwashiorkor is nutritional oedema which is a swelling of body tissues in legs and arms by accumulating body fluid. Lack of protein in the diet causes this problem by lowering the plasma albumin concentration and reducing the osmotic pressure, which leads to fluid accumulation in the tissues. A lack of antioxidants also contributes to oedema as damage to the cell membranes from free radicals causes an increase in vascular permeability (USDA-FAS, 2018).

Treatment for severely malnourished children begins with ready to use therapeutic food (RUTF). These RUTFs are high energy and protein-enriched food with other micronutrients. Although, at initial stages of severely malnourishment children are not given iron (Fe) rich foods to prevent the production of free radicals, macronutrients including iron, can be provided from 2 to 6 weeks during the rehabilitation period (WHO, 2013). Co-products like lung, heart, and kidney are rich in highly bio-available proteins, and lungs and spleen contain high amounts of iron (FAOSTAT, 2018; MIA, 2018). So, these co-products could provide the macronutrients and protein at a low cost for use in rehabilitation (FAOSTAT, 2018).

There is potential to select appropriate co-products according to nutritional requirements and based on their composition tables (Tables 11.2 to 11.4). These tables for cattle, sheep, and pig illustrate the variety of nutrition composition in coproducts. These compositions were derived from the USDA (2020) and are expressed per 100g of wet sample. Though most publications have reported the food composition on a dry weight basis or protein basis, the varying moisture content of coproducts makes it difficult to compare the nutritional value of the same weight of food. So, these tables can be used to identify the nutritional content of wet co-products, and portion sizes can then be calculated.

The highest protein content of cattle co-products is recorded in lungs (20.4g/100g on a wet basis) and liver, heart and spleen are recorded as the next highest levels (Table 11.2). The lowest protein content was recorded in cattle suet at 1.5g/100g. The essential amino acids are the most critical aspect of protein nutrition since humans are unable to synthesis them endogenously, and thus essential amino acid content determines protein quality. Cattle lung and liver contain the highest proportion of essential amino acids (arginine, histidine, isoleucine, leucine, lysine, methionine, phenylalanine, threonine, tryptophan and valine), except for histidine. The highest histidine content is found in cattle heart and spleen (Table 11.2).

Cattle suet is the coproduct with the highest fat content and is composed of more than 90% lipid (Table 11.2 to 11.4). Cattle thymus contains the second-highest fat level (20.45g/100g), and the lowest fat content is reported in cattle spleen. Saturated fat is problematic from a nutritional point

TABLE 11.2
Composition of beef co-products (per 100g raw sample)

Compound	Unit	Lung	Brain	Heart	Kidney	Liver	Pancreas	Spleen	Suet	Thymus	Tongue	Tripe
Water	g	70.8	76.3	78.1	77.9	70.8	65.2	77.2	4	67.8	64.5	84.12
Energy	kcal	135	143	105	99	135	235	105	854	236	224	85
Energy	kJ	564	600	438	413	564	983	439	3573	987	937	355
Protein	g	20.4	10.9	18.5	17.4	20.2	15.7	18.3	1.5	12.2	14.9	12.1
Total lipid (fat)	g	3.6	10.3	3.4	3.1	3.6	18.6	3.0	94.0	20.45	16.1	3.7
Ash	g	1.31	1.51	1.02	1.33	1.31	1.3	1.38	0.1	1.38	0.8	0.55
Carbohydrate, by difference	g	3.9	1.1	–	0.29	3.9	–	–	–	–	3.7	–
Fibre, total dietary	g	–	–	–	–	–	–	–	–	–	–	–
Sugars, total	g	–	–	–	–	–	–	–	–	–	–	–
Calcium, Ca	mg	5	43	4	13	5	9	9	2	7	6	69
Iron, Fe	mg	4.9	2.6	4.4	4.6	4.9	2.2	44.6	0.17	2.1	3.0	0.59
Magnesium, Mg	mg	18	13	22	17	18	18	22	1	14	16	13
Phosphorus, P	mg	387	362	209	257	387	327	296	15	393	133	64
Potassium, K	mg	313	274	275	262	313	276	429	16	360	315	67
Sodium, Na	mg	69	126	86	182	69	67	85	7	96	69	97
Zinc, Zn	mg	4.0	1.0	1.5	1.9	4.0	2.6	2.1	0.22	2.1	2.9	1.4
Copper, Cu	mg	9.8	0.29	0.37	0.43	9.8	0.06	0.17	0.01	0.05	0.17	0.07
Manganese, Mn	mg	0.31	0.03	0.03	0.14	0.31	0.15	0.07	0.001	0.12	0.03	0.09
Selenium, Se	μg	39.7	21.3	9.0	141	39.7	24.7	62.2	0.2	18.1	9.4	12.5
Vitamin C, total ascorbic acid	mg	1.3	10.7	–	9.4	1.3	13.7	45.5	–	34	3.1	–
Thiamine	mg	0.19	0.09	0.25	0.36	0.19	0.14	0.05	0.01	0.11	0.13	0.06
Riboflavin	mg	2.8	0.20	0.68	2.84	2.8	0.45	0.37	0.01	0.35	0.34	0.88
Niacin	mg	13.2	3.6	4.4	8.0	13.2	4.5	8.4	0.3	3.5	4.2	0.23
Pantothenic acid	mg	7.2	2.0	1.8	4.0	7.2	3.9	1.1	0.06	3.03	0.65	0.23
Vitamin B-6	mg	1.08	0.23	0.16	0.67	1.08	0.20	0.07	0.03	0.16	0.31	0.01
Folate, total	μg	290	3	–	98	290	3	4	1	2	7	5
Choline, total	mg	333	–	–	–	333	–	–	5.6	–	–	194.8
Betaine	mg	4.4	–	–	–	4.4	–	–	0.3	–	–	–

Vitamin B-12	μg	59.3	9.5	10.8	27.5	59.3	14.0	5.68	0.27	2.13	3.79	1.39
Vitamin A, RAE	μg	4968	7	10	419	4968	–	–	–	–	–	–
Retinol	μg	4948	–	10	419	4948	–	–	–	–	–	–
Carotene, beta	μg	232	88	–	–	232	–	–	–	–	–	–
Carotene, alpha	μg	11	–	–	–	11	–	–	–	–	–	–
Cryptoxanthin, beta	μg	13	–	–	–	13	–	–	–	–	–	–
Vitamin A, IU	IU	16898	147	34	1400	16898	–	–	–	–	–	–
Lycopene	μg	–	–	–	20	–	–	–	–	–	–	–
Vitamin E (alpha-tocopherol)	mg	0.38	0.99	1.22	0.22	0.38	–	–	1.5	–		0.09
Tocopherol, gamma	mg	0.07	0.05	–	0.02	0.07	–	–	–	–	–	0.02
Tocotrienol, alpha	mg	–	–	–	–	–	–	–	–	–	–	0.02
Vitamin D (D2 + D3), International Units	IU	49	–	6	45	49	–	–	–	–	–	–
Vitamin D (D2 + D3)	μg	1.2	–	0.2	1.1	1.2	–	–	–	–	–	–
Vitamin D3 (cholecalciferol)	μg	1.2	–	0.2	1.1	1.2	–	–	–	–	–	–
Vitamin K (phylloquinone)	μg	3.1	–	–	0	3.1	–	–	3.6	–	–	–
Fatty acids, total saturated	g	1.2	2.3	0.86	0.87	1.2	6.41	1	52.3	7.0	7.0	1.3
10:0	g	–	–	0.001	–	–	–	–	–	–	0.02	–
12:0	g	–	–	0.001	–	–	–	0.01	0.07	–	0.09	–
14:0	g	0.02	0.03	0.02	0.02	0.02	0.15	0.07	2.8	0.16	0.57	0.07
15:0	g	0.01	–	–	0.01	0.01	–	–	–	3.8	–	0.02
16:0	g	0.31	0.92	0.32	0.39	0.31	3.43	0.53	22.6	–	4.2	0.64
17:0	g	0.03	0.03	0.03	0.02	0.03	–	–	–	–	–	0.08
18:0	g	0.86	1.27	0.47	0.37	0.86	2.4	0.38	24.7	2.63	2.1	0.46
20:0	g	–	0.02	0.004	0.012	–	–	–	–	–	–	0.004
22:0	g	0.01	0.03	0.003	0.04	0.01	–	–	–	–	–	0.006
24:0	g	–	–	0.003	–	–	–	–	–	–	–	–
Fatty acids, total monounsaturated	g	0.48	1.89	0.53	0.59	0.48	6.44	0.78	31.5	7.05	7.24	1.53
14:1	g	–	–	0.001	0	0	–	–	–	–	–	0.02
15:1	g	–	–	0.01	0	0	–	–	–	–	–	–
16:1	g	0.04	0.02	0.04	0.04	0.04	1.11	0.12	2.18	1.22	0.55	0.09
16:1 c	g	–	–	0.03	–	–	–	–	–	–	–	–
17:1	g	0.01	–	–	–	0.01	–	–	–	–	–	–

(Continued)

TABLE 11.2 (Continued)
Composition of beef co-products (per 100g raw sample)

Compound	Unit	Lung	Brain	Heart	Kidney	Liver	Pancreas	Spleen	Suet	Thymus	Tongue	Tripe
18:1	g	0.42	1.65	0.48	0.54	0.42	5.33	0.68	28.9	5.83	6.55	1.41
18:1c	g	–	–	0.44	–	–	–	–	–	–	–	–
20:1	g	0.01	0.22	0.003	0.01	0.01	–	–	–	–	0.14	0.02
24:1 c	g	–	–	0.002	–	–	–	–	–	–	–	–
Fatty acids, total polyunsaturated	g	0.47	1.59	0.58	0.55	0.47	3.47	0.22	3.17	3.8	0.90	0.18
18:2	g	0.30	0.04	0.26	0.29	0.30	2.03	0.22	2.15	2.22	0.58	0.12
18:2 n-6	g	0.299	–	0.251	–	0.299	–	–	–	–	–	–
18:2 CLAs	g	–	–	0.01	–	–	–	–	–	–	–	–
18:3	g	0.02	–	0.07	0.01	0.02	0.13	0	0.86	0.14	–	0.01
18:3 n-3 (ALA)	g	0.01	–	0.06	0.01	0.01	–	–	–	–	–	0.01
18:3 n-6	g	0.01	–	–	0.01	0.01	–	–	–	–	–	–
18:4	g	0	–	–	–	–	–	–	–	–	–	–
20:2 n-6	g	0.01	–	–	0.01	0.01	–	–	–	–	–	0.01
20:3	g	0	–	0.03	–	–	–	–	–	–	–	–
20:3 n-6	g	–	–	0.03	–	–	–	–	–	–	–	–
20:4	g	0.14	0.32	0.11	0.23	0.14	0.80	–	–	–	0.31	0.048
20:4 n-6	g	–	–	0.11	–	–	–	–	–	–	–	–
20:5 n-3 (EPA)	g	–	–	0.06	–	–	–	–	–	–	–	–
22:5 n-3 (DPA)	g	–	0.37	0.03	–	–	–	–	–	–	–	–
22:6 n-3 (DHA)	g	–	0.85	–	–	–	–	–	–	–	–	–
Fatty acids, total trans	g	0.17	0.61	0.06	0.10	0.17	–	–	–	–	–	0.15
Fatty acids, total trans-monoenoic	g	–	–	0.06	–	–	–	–	–	–	–	–
16:1 t	g	–	–	0.01	–	–	–	–	–	–	–	–
18:1 t	g	–	–	0.042	–	–	–	–	–	–	–	–
Cholesterol	mg	275	3010	124	411	275	205	263	68	223	87	122
Tryptophan	g	0.26	NA	0.19	NA	0.26	0.20	0.19	0.01	0.09	0.11	NA
Threonine	g	0.87	NA	0.67	NA	0.87	0.73	0.72	0.06	0.44	0.65	NA
Isoleucine	g	0.97	NA	0.77	NA	0.97	0.79	0.71	0.07	0.42	0.64	NA

Leucine	g	1.91	NA	1.40	NA	1.91	1.23	1.62	0.12	0.81	1.11	NA
Lysine	g	1.61	NA	1.47	NA	1.61	1.16	1.32	0.13	1.01	1.15	NA
Methionine	g	0.54	NA	0.61	NA	0.54	0.28	0.34	0.04	0.17	0.32	NA
Cystine	g	0.38	NA	–	NA	0.38	0.20	0.53	0.02	0.16	0.20	NA
Phenylalanine	g	1.08	NA	0.72	NA	1.08	0.65	0.74	0.06	0.35	0.62	NA
Tyrosine	g	0.81	NA	0.62	NA	0.81	0.69	0.52	0.05	0.53	0.48	NA
Valine	g	1.26	NA	0.82	NA	1.26	0.84	1.10	0.07	0.53	0.71	NA
Arginine	g	1.24	NA	1.22	NA	1.24	0.90	1.06	0.10	0.80	0.95	NA
Histidine	g	0.63	NA	0.67	NA	0.63	0.31	0.66	0.05	0.21	0.39	NA
Alanine	g	1.16	NA	0.96	NA	1.16	0.80	1.42	0.09	0.62	0.86	NA
Aspartic acid	g	1.93	NA	–	NA	1.93	1.51	1.29	0.137	1.17	1.36	NA
Glutamic acid	g	2.61	NA	2.58	NA	2.61	1.32	1.67	0.225	1.02	2.05	NA
Glycine	g	1.16	NA	1.01	NA	1.16	0.96	1.11	0.09	0.74	0.89	NA
Proline	g	0.96	NA	0.60	NA	0.96	0.80	1.11	0.07	0.62	0.70	NA
Serine	g	0.91	NA	0.65	NA	0.91	0.63	0.63	0.06	0.49	0.60	NA
Hydroxyproline	g	0.05	NA	–	NA	0.05	–	–	0.02	–	–	NA

- Data derived from USDA (2020)
- NA= data not available
- "–" value not detectable

TABLE 11.3
Composition of pig co-products (per 100g raw sample)

Element	Unit	Lung	Brain	Heart	Kidney	Liver	Pancreas	Spleen	Tripe	Tail	Tongue	Jowl	Feet	Ears
Water	g	79.5	78.4	76.2	80.1	71.1	67.2	78.4	73.5	46.1	65.9	22.2	65.0	61.3
Energy	kcal	85	127	118	100	134	199	100	159	378	225	655	212	234
Energy	kJ	356	531	494	418	561	833	418	665	1582	941	2741	889	979
Protein	g	14.1	10.3	17.3	16.5	21.4	18.6	17.9	16.9	17.8	16.3	6.4	23.2	22.5
Total lipid (fat)	g	2.7	9.2	4.4	3.3	3.7	13.2	2.6	10.1	33.5	17.2	69.6	12.6	15.1
Ash	g	0.80	1.13	0.84	1.17	1.44	1.12	1.53	0.63	0.50	0.90	0.32	0.68	0.60
Carbohydrate, by difference	g	0	0	1.33	0	2.47	0	0	0	0	0	0	0	0.60
Calcium, Ca	mg	7	10	5	9	9	11	10	11	18	16	4	70	21
Iron, Fe	mg	18.9	1.6	4.7	4.9	23.3	2.1	22.3	1.0	1.0	3.4	0.4	0.6	2.4
Magnesium, Mg	mg	14	14	19	17	18	17	13	11	8	18	3	6	7
Phosphorus, P	mg	196	282	169	204	288	234	260	130	50	193	86	75	41
Potassium, K	mg	303	258	294	229	273	197	396	140	349	243	148	63	55
Sodium, Na	mg	153	120	56	121	87	44	98	75	63	110	25	132	191
Zinc, Zn	mg	2.0	1.3	2.8	2.8	5.8	2.6	2.5	1.9	2.3	3.0	0.84	0.76	0.19
Copper, Cu	mg	0.08	0.24	0.41	0.62	0.68	0.09	0.13	0.17	0.08	0.07	0.04	0.07	0.01
Manganese, Mn	mg	0.02	0.09	0.06	0.12	0.34	0.16	0.07	0.04	0.01	0.01	0.01	–	0.01
Selenium, Se	µg	17.8	15.9	10.4	190	52.7	40.8	32.8	31.1	2.7	10.4	1.5	23.3	4.3
Vitamin C, total ascorbic acid	mg	12.3	13.5	5.30	13.3	25.3	15.3	28.5	–	–	4.40	–	–	–
Thiamine	mg	0.09	0.16	0.61	0.34	0.28	0.11	0.13	0.05	0.21	0.49	0.39	0.026	0.08
Riboflavin	mg	0.43	0.28	1.19	1.70	3.01	0.46	0.30	0.20	0.11	0.49	0.24	0.11	0.11
Niacin	mg	3.35	4.28	6.77	8.21	15.3	3.45	5.87	2.48	2.06	5.30	4.54	1.13	0.78
Pantothenic acid	mg	0.90	2.80	2.52	3.13	6.65	4.56	1.06	1.22	0.67	0.64	0.25	0.30	0.07
Vitamin B-6	mg	0.10	0.19	0.39	0.44	0.69	0.46	0.06	0.03	0.37	0.24	0.09	0.05	0.02
Folate, total	µg	3	6	4	42	212	3	4	3	5	4	1	10	–
Choline, total	mg	–	–	–	–	–	–	–	194.8	–	–	–	–	–
Vitamin B-12	µg	2.75	2.19	3.79	8.49	26.0	16.4	3.26	0.3	0.88	2.84	0.82	0.52	0.07
Retinol	µg	–	–	8	59	6502	–	–	–	–	–	3	–	–
Vitamin A, IU	IU	–	–	25	198	21650	–	–	–	–	–	9	–	–

Meat Co-products

Vitamin E (alpha-tocopherol)	mg	–	–	0.63	–	–	–	0.04	–	0.29	0.29	0.02	–
Fatty acids, total saturated	g	0.96	2.08	1.16	1.04	1.17	4.58	4.03	11.6	5.96	25.3	3.57	5.39
10:0	g	–	–	–	–	–	–	–	–	0.02	0.05	0.011	–
12:0	g	–	–	0.01	0.01	–	–	–	–	0.09	0.15	–	0.01
14:0	g	0.02	0.04	0.08	0.04	0.02	0.11	0.13	0.53	0.31	0.88	0.15	0.20
16:0	g	0.63	1.03	0.59	0.58	0.44	2.45	2.26	7.60	3.82	15.2	2.46	3.38
17:0	g	–	–	–	–	–	–	0.03	–	–	–	0.02	–
18:0	g	0.29	1.00	0.45	0.41	0.70	1.72	1.59	3.51	1.73	8.94	0.910	1.8
20:0	g	–	–	–	–	–	–	0.02	–	–	–	0.01	–
Fatty acids, total monounsaturated	g	0.61	1.66	1.02	1.07	0.52	4.60	3.59	15.8	8.13	32.9	6.29	6.86
16:1	g	0.05	0.12	0.1	0.09	0.03	0.79	0.20	1.22	0.64	2.16	0.49	0.43
18:1	g	0.56	1.07	0.9	0.97	0.46	3.81	3.32	14.60	7.3	30.2	5.682	6.43
20:1	g	0.01	–	0.02	0.02	–	–	0.07	–	–	0.56	0.11	–
Fatty acids, total polyunsaturated	g	0.34	1.43	1.12	0.26	0.87	2.48	0.89	3.68	1.78	8.11	1.09	1.61
18:2	g	0.12	0.09	0.77	0.17	0.35	1.45	0.72	3.19	1.70	7.45	0.93	1.41
18:3	g	–	0.12	0.08	0.01	0.03	0.09	0.02	0.28	0.08	0.58	0.04	0.13
18:3 n-3 (ALA)	g	–	–	–	–	–	–	0.02	–	–	–	0.04	–
20:2 n-6	g	–	–	–	–	–	–	0.04	–	–	–	0.05	–
20:3	g	0.18	0.47	0.27	0.08	0.44	0.57	–	–	–	–	0.01	–
20:4	g	–	–	–	–	–	–	0.11	0.21	–	0.08	0.05	0.07
20:5 n-3 (EPA)	g	0.01	–	–	–	–	–	–	–	–	–	–	–
22:5 n-3 (DPA)	g	0.03	0.22	–	–	0.03	–	–	–	–	–	–	–
22:6 n-3 (DHA)	g	0.01	0.45	–	–	0.02	–	–	–	–	–	–	–
Fatty acids, total trans	g	–	–	–	–	–	–	0.13	–	–	–	–	–
Cholesterol	mg	320	2195	131	319	301	193	223	97	101	90	88	82
Tryptophan	g	0.12	0.13	0.20	0.21	0.30	0.41	NA	0.09	0.19	0.02	NA	0.04
Threonine	g	0.50	0.48	0.76	0.68	0.91	0.84	NA	0.55	0.69	0.21	NA	0.63
Isoleucine	g	0.56	0.48	0.83	0.88	1.09	0.97	NA	0.41	0.74	0.17	NA	0.49
Leucine	g	1.09	0.90	1.56	1.48	1.91	1.39	NA	0.91	1.31	0.45	NA	1.17
Lysine	g	1.03	0.81	1.43	1.19	1.65	1.28	NA	1.01	1.33	0.53	NA	1.05
Methionine	g	0.23	0.20	0.442	0.35	0.53	0.31	NA	0.32	0.37	0.10	NA	0.13
Cystine	g	0.22	–	0.31	0.36	0.40	0.24	NA	0.23	0.24	0.06	NA	0.20

(*Continued*)

TABLE 11.3 (Continued)
Composition of pig co-products (per 100g raw sample)

Element	Unit	Lung	Brain	Heart	Kidney	Liver	Pancreas	Spleen	Tripe	Tail	Tongue	Jowl	Feet	Ears
Phenylalanine	g	0.59	0.52	0.76	0.78	1.05	0.80	0.76	NA	0.48	0.68	0.24	NA	0.72
Tyrosine	g	0.40	0.43	0.59	0.59	0.73	0.78	0.50	NA	0.32	0.50	0.10	NA	0.40
Valine	g	0.84	0.59	0.91	0.95	1.32	1.00	0.97	NA	0.52	0.85	0.31	NA	0.83
Arginine	g	0.73	0.54	1.16	1.01	1.32	1.07	0.97	NA	1.19	1.01	0.66	NA	1.861
Histidine	g	0.36	0.28	0.44	0.40	0.58	0.36	0.43	NA	0.30	0.41	0.07	NA	0.27
Alanine	g	0.89	–	1.11	1.04	1.28	0.95	1.15	NA	1.28	0.86	0.38	NA	2.22
Aspartic acid	g	1.27	1.03	1.56	1.55	1.94	1.78	1.57	NA	1.38	1.52	0.59	NA	1.66
Glutamic acid	g	1.46	1.20	2.77	1.96	2.78	1.53	2.05	NA	2.13	2.05	0.99	NA	2.81
Glycine	g	1.03	0.49	0.94	1.04	1.24	1.13	1.14	NA	2.36	1.21	0.29	NA	4.40
Proline	g	0.90	–	0.80	1.02	1.15	0.95	1.00	NA	1.51	0.86	0.24	NA	2.85
Serine	g	0.62	–	0.812	0.87	1.16	0.74	0.78	NA	0.69	0.68	0.26	NA	0.94

TABLE 11.4
Composition of sheep co-products (per 100g raw sample)

Element	Unit	Lung	Brain	Heart	Kidney	Liver	Pancreas	Spleen	Tongue
Water	g	79.7	79.2	76.7	79.2	71.4	73.8	78.2	66.6
Energy	kcal	95	122	122	97	139	152	101	222
Energy	kJ	397	510	510	406	582	636	423	929
Protein	g	16.7	10.4	16.5	15.74	20.4	14.8	17.2	15.7
Total lipid (fat)	g	2.6	8.6	5.7	3.0	5.0	9.8	3.1	17.2
Ash	g	1.1	1.3	0.9	1.3	1.4	1.4	1.3	0.9
Carbohydrate, by difference	g	–	–	0.21	0.82	1.78	–	–	–
Calcium, Ca	mg	10	9	6	13	7	8	9	9
Iron, Fe	mg	6.4	1.8	4.6	6.4	7.4	2.3	41.9	2.7
Magnesium, Mg	mg	14	12	17	17	19	21	21	21
Phosphorus, P	mg	219	270	175	246	364	400	280	184
Potassium, K	mg	238	296	316	277	313	420	358	257
Sodium, Na	mg	157	112	89	156	70	75	84	78
Zinc, Zn	mg	1.8	1.2	1.9	2.24	4.0	1.9	2.8	2.3
Copper, Cu	mg	0.25	0.24	0.40	0.45	7.0	0.06	0.12	0.21
Manganese, Mn	mg	0.02	0.04	0.05	0.12	0.18	0.04	0.05	0.05
Selenium, Se	µg	17.7	9.0	32	126.9	82.4	34.3	32.4	15.0
Vitamin C, total ascorbic acid	mg	31	16	5	11	4	18	23	6
Thiamine	mg	0.05	0.13	0.37	0.62	0.34	0.03	0.05	0.15
Riboflavin	mg	0.24	0.3	0.99	2.24	3.63	0.25	0.35	0.38
Niacin	mg	4.12	3.90	6.14	7.51	16.1	3.70	7.90	4.65
Pantothenic acid	mg	–	0.92	2.63	4.22	6.13	1.00-		0.97
Vitamin B-6	mg	0.11	0.29	0.39	0.22	0.90	0.07	0.11	0.18
Folate, total	µg	12	3	2	28	230	13	4	4
Vitamin B-12	µg	3.93	11.3	10.3	52.4	90.1	6.0	5.3	7.2
Vitamin A, RAE	µg	27	–	–	95	7391	–	–	–
Vitamin A, IU	IU	89	–	–	316	24612	–	–	–
Fatty acids, total saturated	g	0.89	2.19	2.25	1.0	1.94	4.44	1.03	6.63
4:0	g	–	–	–	–	–	–	–	0.03
6:0	g	–	–	–	–	–	–	–	0.48
8:0	g	–	–	–	–	–	–	–	3.29
10:0	g	–	–	–	–	–	–	–	2.52
12:0	g	–	0	0.02	0.01	–	0.06	–	–
14:0	g	–	0.04	0.13	0.03	0.05	0.42	–	–
16:0	g	–	1.06	0.86	0.42	0.68	1.88	–	–
18:0	g	–	1.07	1.16	0.52	1.12	1.94	–	–
Fatty acids, total monounsaturated	g	0.67	1.55	1.6	0.63	1.05	3.54	0.81	8.46
14:1	g	–	–	–	–	–	0.22	–	–
16:1	g	–	0.05	0.07	0.04	0.13	–	–	0.43
18:1	g	–	1.29	1.38	0.55	0.92	3.21	–	7.82
20:1	g	–	0.12	–	–	–	–	–	–
22:1	g	–	0	0.04	0.01	–	–	–	0.19
Fatty acids, total polyunsaturated	g	0.35	0.88	0.55	0.55	0.75	0.48	0.23	1.06
18:2	g	–	0.03	0.24	0.21	0.32	0.18	–	0.48
18:3	g	–	–	0.13	0.07	0.07	0.19	–	0.51

(Continued)

TABLE 11.4 *(Continued)*
Composition of sheep co-products (per 100g raw sample)

Element	Unit	Lung	Brain	Heart	Kidney	Liver	Pancreas	Spleen	Tongue
20:4	g	–	0.23	0.09	0.14	0.36	0.11	–	0.06
20:5 n-3 (EPA)	g	–	–	0.04	0.05	–	–	–	–
22:5 n-3 (DPA)	g	–	0.13	0.03	0.04	–	–	–	–
22:6 n-3 (DHA)	g	–	0.49	0.03	0.03	–	–	–	–
Cholesterol	mg	–	1352	135	337	371	260	250	156
Tryptophan	g	0.17	0.11	0.18	0.212	0.24	0.19	0.19	0.16
Threonine	g	0.61	0.47	0.78	0.74	0.88	0.55	0.70	0.71
Isoleucine	g	0.53	0.41	0.71	0.63	0.88	0.52	1.09	0.61
Leucine	g	1.34	0.81	1.40	1.18	1.67	0.95	1.53	1.12
Lysine	g	1.08	0.67	1.24	1.02	1.10	1.28	1.33	1.11
Methionine	g	0.30	0.21	0.36	0.32	0.44	0.21	0.33	0.33
Cystine	g	0.26	0.11	0.14	0.18	0.21	0.19	0.22	0.17
Phenylalanine	g	0.69	0.50	0.71	0.73	0.91	0.50	0.78	0.59
Tyrosine	g	0.47	0.38	0.51	0.55	0.73	0.36	0.50	0.47
Valine	g	0.92	0.50	0.82	0.92	1.12	0.64	1.12	0.75
Arginine	g	1.01	0.70	1.08	0.91	1.14	0.88	1.09	1.03
Histidine	g	0.42	0.28	0.38	0.40	0.48	0.43	0.57	0.35
Alanine	g	1.05	0.59	1.00	0.85	1.02	0.76	1.11	0.90
Aspartic acid	g	1.32	0.87	1.42	1.36	1.76	1.02	1.49	1.40
Glutamic acid	g	1.80	1.23	2.10	1.71	2.20	2.07	2.00	2.03
Glycine	g	1.41	0.49	0.80	0.92	0.99	0.93	1.12	1.02
Proline	g	1.07	0.45	0.75	0.80	0.97	0.76	0.96	0.83
Serine	g	0.67	0.54	0.64	0.73	0.88	0.59	0.75	0.62

- Data derived from USDA (2020)
- NA= data not available
- " –" value not detectable

of view since it increases cardiovascular disease risk and is considered unhealthy fat (Liu et al., 2016). Saturated fatty acids are higher in suet (52.3g/100g), thymus (7g/100g) and tongue (7g/100g) than in other cattle co-products, and the lowest value is recorded as 0.8g/100 g in cattle heart and kidney (Table 11.2). Monounsaturated fatty acids and polyunsaturated fatty acids are considered healthy fatty acids responsible for reducing cardiovascular disease risk and improving the overall health condition. In cattle co-products, suet, tongue, thymus, and pancreas have the highest proportion of monounsaturated fatty acids. Polyunsaturated fatty acids are higher in pancreas, thymus, and suet than in other co-products and are the lowest in the cattle lungs. Eicosapentaenoic acid (EPA) and docosahexaenoic acid (DHA) are well known essential polyunsaturated omega-3 fatty acids that are responsible for a range of health benefits. EPA is found only in cattle heart (0.06g/100g) whereas DHA is recorded only in cattle brain (0.85g/100g).

In pig co-products, the highest amount of protein is found in pig feet (23.2g/100g), ears (22.5g/100g) and liver (21.4g/100g) compared to other co-products, whereas the lowest protein content is found in pig jowl (6.4g/100g). The pig liver has been reported to have the highest essential amino acid content for all essential amino acids except tryptophan. The highest tryptophan content has been reported in pig pancreas (0.41g/100g) and the second highest level is found in pig liver (0.3g/100g).

High fat content has been recorded in pig jowl (69.6g/100g) and tail (33.5g/100g) while the lowest fat content is recorded in pig spleen (2.6g/100g). The pig jowl has the highest saturated fatty acid contents (25.3g/100g) followed by the tail (11.6g/100g) whereas the lowest amount of saturated fatty acids is reported in liver (0.86g/100g). The beneficial polyunsaturated fatty acids and monounsaturated fatty acids are reported at high levels in the jowl and tail in pig co-products. The highest DHA amount was reported in the pig brain (0.45g/100g), and the second highest amount is found in pig liver (0.02g/100g). Both EPA and DHA are reported at the same concentrations in pig lungs (0.01g/100g).

Table 11.4 shows the nutritional composition of sheep lung, brain, heart, kidney, liver, pancreas, spleen and tongue. All values are presented on a 100g of wet sample basis. The liver has been reported to have the highest protein content (20.4 g/100 g), and the lowest protein content was reported in the brain (10.4g/100g). The highest proportion of essential amino acids is reported in sheep liver, except for isoleucine, lysine, and histidine. The sheep's spleen has the highest amino acid levels for isoleucine (1.09g/100g), lysine (1.33g/100g), and histidine (0.57g/100g). The lowest essential amino acid content is reported in the sheep brain since the sheep brain has the lowest total protein content on a wet sample basis.

The highest total fat content was reported in sheep tongue (17.2g/100g), and the lowest fat content was reported in sheep lungs (2.6g/100g). Unhealthy saturated fatty acids were high in sheep tongue (6.63g/100g) and the lowest content was reported in sheep lungs (0.89g/100g). The highest monounsaturated fatty acids and polyunsaturated fatty acids were reported in sheep tongue (8.46 and 1.06g/100g), whereas the lowest contents were reported in lungs and spleen, respectively. EPA was reported in sheep heart (0.04g/100g), and kidney (0.05g/100g), and the highest DHA content was reported in the brain (0.49g/100g), which is similar to cattle and pig co-products.

11.4 CO-PRODUCTS FOR TREATMENT OF IRON DEFICIENCY "ANAEMIA"

Anaemia is a Greek word which means "without blood", describing the low levels of red blood cells containing haemoglobin. Haemoglobin is a protein with a tightly bound iron-containing haem group. The haemoglobin in red blood cells is responsible for transporting oxygen from the lungs and returning carbon dioxide to the lungs.

All mammals, including humans, have advanced mechanisms to regulate blood iron concentration. Body iron regulation proceeds with the help of iron stores in the body, mostly in the liver, bone marrow and spleen. A low protein diet decreases the formation of red blood cells and depletes iron reserves (Borelli et al., 2007). This demonstrates the strong relationship between protein-energy malnutrition and anaemia.

A WHO survey from 1993 to 2005 reported that 25% of the world population was anaemic, and anaemia was the most abundant global nutritional disorder (Albertí et al., 2008). Further, preschool children, pregnant women and non-pregnant women were reported as highly anaemic prevalence groups, and 47.4%, 41.8% and 30.2% were anaemic, respectively. Anaemia is mainly centred in Africa and South-East Asia and higher in all countries which suffer from malnutrition.

Many co-products contain significant levels of iron and many other micronutrients compared with muscle tissue. Beef loin muscle tissue contains 1.61 mg iron in 100g sample (USDA, 2020) and cattle co-products contain more iron than does muscle, with the exception of tripe (Table 11.2. The highest iron content is recorded in cattle spleen (44.6mg/100g) and the lowest is reported in cattle tripe (0.59g/100g). A recent report (FAOSTAT, 2018) also showed that cattle lung, liver, heart and kidney contain high amounts of iron compared with the loin and semitendinosus muscle. In terms of pig co-products, the highest iron content is reported for liver (23.3 mg/100g) and the next highest iron content is found in the spleen (22.3mg/100g). When pig co-products are compared with premium meats, pork loin muscle has 0.97mg/100g iron content (USDA, 2019), and this value is less than all pig co-products, except for the pig jowl and feet (Table 11.3). Table 11.4 shows the iron content of sheep co-products. Sheep spleen has the highest iron content (41.9 mg/100 g) while sheep brain has the lowest (1.87mg/100g). Sheep muscle (loin) iron content is reported at 1.6mg/100g, and the iron content of all co-products is higher than the iron content in lamb loin.

Iron absorption could be impaired by the fat content of the food. According to Chung et al., (2011), mice intervention studies revealed that a high-fat diet impaired iron metabolism and diminished intestinal iron uptake. The high-fat diet elevated the hepcidin level in the body, which regulates iron metabolism and restricts iron absorption. The cattle, pig and sheep co-products with the highest iron content had less than 4% fat content. So, it is possible to produce healthy low-fat food with high micronutrient availability from these underutilised co-products.

11.5 OTHER MINERALS IN CO-PRODUCTS

In addition to iron, other micronutrients play vital roles in human nutrition. The composition of co-products makes them potentially useful as mineral supplements. The macro and micronutrient compositions of different offal are shown in Tables 11.2 to 11.4.

Calcium is an essential element in human nutrition and is in high demand during the growth period, and throughout pregnancy and lactation. Calcium is necessary for muscle contraction, building strong bones and teeth, blood clotting, nerve impulse transmission and fluid balance (Piste et al., 2012). Calcium is highly available in cattle tripe (69mg/100g) and cattle brain (43mg/100g). The highest calcium level reported is in pig feet (70mg/100g) among cattle, pig and sheep co-products (Tables 11.2 to 11.4). The sheep co-product with the highest level of calcium was kidney (13mg/100g), and all other co-products showed low calcium levels. The high demand muscles of cattle (loin), pork (loin) and lamb (loin) showed only 6mg/100g, 6mg/100g and 15mg/100g of calcium, respectively.

Magnesium is essential in aerobic and anaerobic energy metabolism, and more than 300 enzymes use it as a cofactor (Tenrisanna, 2015). Magnesium deficiency causes electrolyte disturbances, muscle spasms, poor coordination and loss of appetite (FAOSTAT, 2018). The highest magnesium content of offal was recorded as 22mg/100g in the cattle spleen and heart, and all co-products were reported to have magnesium contents above 10mg/100g, with the exception of suet. Pork heart was reported to contain the highest amount of magnesium at 19mg/100g and the second highest level was reported as 18mg/100g in liver and tongue among the pig co-products. The greatest magnesium level was 21mg/100g in sheep pancreas, spleen and tongue within the other sheep co-products. However, beef and pork muscle were reported to have higher levels of magnesium (24 and 27mg/100g, respectively) than their co-products. The upper level of magnesium intake is 400mg/day, according to Awan et al. (2015), and consumption of these co-products is unlikely to exceed the safe intake level.

Zinc and copper metal ions are present at high levels in the liver of cattle, pig and sheep than in other types of offal. Cattle, pig and sheep liver were reported to have 4, 5.8 and 4mg/100g of zinc and 9.6, 0.68 and 7mg/100g of copper, respectively. Zinc is an important metal ion, and deficiencies affect the nervous, skeletal, immune and reproduction systems. These zinc deficiencies are widely prevalent in high cereal and low animal food consuming areas (FSIS, 2015). Copper is responsible for many physiological functions in the human body, such as angiogenesis, the regulation of gene expression, brain development and proper functioning of the immune system. More than 95% of copper in the blood plasma interacts with ceruloplasmin copper-enzyme, which is involved in iron metabolism (Hellman & Gitlin, 2002).

The functions of selenium overlaps with those of vitamin E (BLN, 2017), and low selenium intake leads to Keshan disease, which cause bone deformations in children (Cardoso-Santiago et al., 2001). This vital mineral is more abundant in beef kidney (139mg/100g), spleen (62.2mg/100g), lung (44.3mg/100g) and liver (39mg/100g) than in semitendinosus and loin muscle meat. Similarly, the kidney and liver of pig and sheep contain higher amounts of selenium than does premium pork or lamb.

11.6 HEALTH EFFECT OF PROTEIN BIO-ACTIVE PROTEIN

Proteins are the source of amino acids, and amino acid composition varies from protein to protein. Essential amino acids are not synthesised in the human body, but they are obtained from dietary protein sources. The human body requires these essential amino acids at different ratios and different quantities throughout the life span. The amino acid reference pattern represents the required amino acid ratios for the different life stages (Prohl et al., 2014), and this pattern helps to rate the quality of a protein. The amino acid composition of inferior quality proteins partially matches with these ratios and complete proteins align with this. Proteins are rated using the indispensable amino acid score (IAAS) using reference patterns, and higher amino acid scores refer to complete proteins. In addition to the IAAS, protein digestibility is considered to contribute to the quality of protein, and it is crucial to evaluate the accessibility of amino acids to the human body. Animal-based proteins have more appropriate essential amino acid proportions than do plant-based proteins, and the digestibility of animal protein is more than 90%, while plant-based protein digestion remains around 80% (Cardoso-Santiago & Arêas, 2001). Animal co-products are rich in essential amino acids (Cardoso-Santiago et al., 2001). Dried beef lung protein has been reported to be more than 90% digestible (USDA, 2020). So, beef lungs have high potential to provide highly digestible essential amino acids as a nutritious food.

In addition to being a source of amnio acids, it has been recently recognised that peptides derived from dietary protein exert various other functions which play a beneficial modulatory role in human body systems. The different sequences of peptides engage with different bioactive functions in the human body, and these are identified as bioactive peptides. Bioactive substances have been defined as "food component that can affect biological processes or substrates and, hence, have an impact on body function or condition and ultimately health" (Lynch et al., 2018). This definition was further refined by Francis and Thomas (1975) who stated that the "bioactive" should be a dietary substance which has a measurable biological effect at a physiologically feasible level. Furthermore, "bioactivity" should measure a health beneficial effect and not a damaging effect. Following the definition, animal protein-derived bioactive peptides are capable of influencing the human physiological role by working on a positive health condition. In recent years, a number of bioactive peptides have been studied that have originated from animal proteins, but there is a lack of studies for the bioactivity of co-product peptides.

The most abundant animal protein is collagen, and it is the primary constituent of many co-products, including bone, cartilage and skin (Fornias, 1996). Collagen contains a poor amino acid profile, as a large proportion of the amino acids are the three non-essentials glycine, proline and hydroxyproline(Jayawardena et al., 2019a). However, researchers have focused on bioactive peptides from the collagen-rich co-products rather than nutrition supplements. Pig skin collagen has been hydrolysed by Li et al. (2007) with different protease enzymes to derive a Gln-Gly-Ala-Arg bioactive peptide with proven antioxidant activity. Chicken bone collagen hydrolysate has been produced by Zhang et al. (2010) and were shown to exhibit a cholesterol-lowering effect which might act to prevent atherosclerosis as well as acting as an anti-inflammatory agent. Collagen from chicken legs (yellowish keratinised parts with nails) was hydrolysed by Aspergillus fungal protease to produce antihypertensive peptide with an angiotensin 1 converting enzyme (ACE) inhibitory assay (Saiga et al., 2008). This study obtained the octapeptide sequence (Gly-Ala-Hyp-Gly-Leu-Hyp-Gly-Pro), which showed strong ACE inhibitory activity, and the results were confirmed by rat bioassay. The peptide was administered to spontaneously hypertensive rats and significantly lowered their blood pressure. Around 25% of the protein in bovine lung is collagen (FAO, 2019b) and there is a high possibility to produce bioactive peptides by enzymatic digestion.

ACE inhibitory peptides are among the most extensively studied bioactive peptides derived from different protein sources. Most of these bioactive peptides have been derived from milk proteins, and their antihypertensive effect was confirmed by *in vivo* rat studies and human trials (Bester et al., 2018; Chávez-Jáuregui et al., 2003; FAO, 2019a, 2019b; FAOSTAT, 2018; Haddad et al., 2015; Perignon et al., 2018; Scallan et al., 2010; Walton & Allen, 2011; WFP, 2019; WHO,

TABLE 11.5
Publications on the production of bioactive peptides from offal

Co-product	Processing method	Bioactive compound	References
Bovine lungs	Protein extraction by extraction buffer and column chromatography	Purified bio-Active compound (Soluble guanylate cyclase)	(Fitzsimons & Brock, 2001)
Bovine lungs	Enzymatic hydrolysis with high pressure pre-treatment	Hydrolysates with DPP-IV, PEP inhibitors	(Wilson et al., 2004)
Bovine lung	Enzymatic hydrolysis	Anti-inflammatory agent	(De Benoist et al., 2008)
Bovine, porcine hearts	Ammonium sulphate precipitation, Cation-exchange and affinity chromatography	Isolation of heparin-binding growth factors	(Biel et al., 2019)
Porcine Intestinal mucosa	Hydrolysate of intestinal mucosa, anion exchange	Production of heparin	(Chung et al., 2011)
Duck skin	Enzymatic hydrolysis and RP-HPLC purification	Anti-oxidative peptide	(Piste et al., 2012)
Chicken bone	Enzymatic hydrolysis	angiotensin I-converting enzyme inhibitory peptide	(Jahnen-Dechent & Ketteler, 2012)
chicken legs (yellowish keratinised parts with nails)	Enzymatic hydrolysis with fungal proteases and membrane filtration	angiotensin I-converting enzyme inhibitory peptide	(Saiga et al., 2008)
Bovine blood plasma	Enzymatic hydrolysis and RP-HPLC purification	angiotensin I-converting enzyme inhibitory peptide	(Baghurst, 2006)
Porcine aorta	Solubilisation in salt solution and membrane filtration	Anti-cholesterol peptide	(Roohani et al., 2013)
Bovine tendon	Acid extraction and salt precipitation. Purified by ion-exchange and gel filtration chromatography	angiotensin I-converting enzyme inhibitory peptide	(Hellman & Gitlin, 2002)
Sheep brain	Buffer extraction and purified by ion-exchange and gel-filtration chromatography	Calmodulin Methyltransferase	(Strain & Cashman, 2009)
Porcine brain	Acid extraction with pre-heat treatment and purified by series of chromatographic methods	Galanin-like Peptide	(Hartikainen, 2005)

2013). But studies of bioactive peptides from animal co-products are comparatively limited, and no human intervention studies were reported. Bioactive peptides need to go through the intestinal lumen to show their effect and these *in vivo* studies are very important.

Some researchers argue that only di- and tri-peptides are absorbed through the intestinal lumen to the bloodstream (Walton & Allen, 2011). In contrast, Bernát (1983); Borelli et al. (2007) reported that some peptides even longer than tri-peptides have shown bioactivity during an *in vivo* study. A summary of bioactive compounds derived from co-products are listed on Table 11.5

11.6 CO-PRODUCT PROCESSING

11.6.1 EXTRUSION COOKING

Extrusion is a versatile and very efficient technology that is broadly used in food and feed processing. Extrusion utilises 100% input materials from the feeding end of the extruder barrel (input) to the product formation end (output). The processing steps, i.e., mixing, shearing, temperature and pressure building, metering, formation, expansion and cooling, all take place inside the barrel to produce the extruded products (Biel et al., 2019; USDA, 2019). According to the FAO (2011), ingredients with a lower fat content enhance the extrusion cooking behaviour and overall expansion of the directly expanded products. Thus, co-products that are low in fat would have good potential to produce extruded products.

The limiting factor for the utilisation of many co-products in the human food chain is their poor texture quality and low aesthetic appeal (FAO, 2011). Extruded products have altered organoleptic properties, but they have been reported to potentially be able to enhance the nutritional accessibility and availability of proteins (Berrazaga et al., 2019; Jayawardena et al., 2019a; Mullen et al., 2017).

In 2011 Meat and Livestock Australia (MLA) initiated a project to produce extruded meat using low-cost materials using high moisture extruded cooking (HMEC) (MLA, 2011). Extruded products with better texture were obtained by using 36% trimmed red meat with standard HMEC, and it was further indicated to be possible to produce extruded products with 67% meat (MIA, 2018). It should be possible to substitute co-products to produce retextured meat using high moisture extruded cooking. Although the literature on extrusion is dominated by cereal-based products, high moisture extruded cooking has excellent potential to process high moisture (>40%) materials like meat (Gómez-Guillén et al., 2011; Möller et al., 2008; Schrezenmeir et al., 2000) and has the potential to convert offal to retextured meat. Mechanically deboned chicken was used to prepare a meat analogue by Gómez-Guillén et al. (2011) using high moisture extrusion. Low moisture extrusion was reported to produce fortified snacks with beef lungs in Brazil (Li et al., 2007). These beef lung fortified snacks significantly reduced the prevalence of iron deficiency anaemia in preschool children. A series of beef lung protein extrusion projects was conducted with de-fatted beef lungs and successfully produced nutritious snacks with better textural characteristics (Hata et al., 1996; Lynch et al., 2018; Masuda et al., 1996; Nakamura et al., 1995; Saiga et al., 2008; Zhang et al., 2010).

Nakamura et al. (1995) replaced soy protein with extruded rumen protein in different food products, and the sensory acceptability was evaluated by consumer panellists. Extruded rumen protein improved the flavour of pork sausage, and the incorporation of rumen protein was feasible based on the sensory results. Bovine and porcine lungs and bovine tripe proteins were mixed together by Sipola et al. (2002) and extruded with soy grits to make 20% to 30% highly incorporated snacks. Seppo et al. (2003) prepared beef snacks using extruded beef cardiac muscle, and improved binding ability was demonstrated with non-binding ingredients. Further microbiologically safer snacks were prepared by combining extrusion coupling with electron beam irradiation. This produced safer beef snacks with lower screw speed and low steam injection levels (Mizushima et al., 2004). Extrusion is therefore a viable unit operation to produce snacks by converting unfavourable textural characteristics to a favourable state.

Cold extrusion is used in pasta processing (Aihara et al., 2005) and this mechanism can also be used to incorporate co-products into starchy food. Meat emulsion was prepared by calf meat and incorporated into durum wheat pasta (Jauhiainen et al., 2005) and (Jayawardena et al., 2019a) produced dried bovine lungs incorporated into pasta with durum wheat. Co-product incorporation significantly lowered the glycaemic response similar to calf meat incorporation into durum wheat pasta.

11.6.2 Drying of Co-products

Drying is an ancient method of food preservation and processing (Korhonen, 2009; Miner-Williams et al., 2014). The water is removed from materials by evaporation or sublimation (Mirdhayati et al., 2016), and this restricts the growth of micro-organisms (Saiga et al., 2008). Dried products have increased shelf life, require less storage space, are easier to transport and, most importantly, have the potential to be stored without refrigeration in developing countries with hot and humid conditions (Lafarga & Hayes, 2017; Mathis et al., 2008). Meat co-products are highly perishable foods, and they are prone to microbial contamination and increased safety issues (O'Sullivan et al., 2017), so it is desirable to preserve these using drying technologies. Different ethnic groups in the world use meat co-products for their traditional food plates (Quinkler et al., 1989), and it is challenging to maintain the cold chain in the remote areas where many populations reside. Furthermore, meat co-products like beef lungs exhibit poor textural characteristics (Griffin et al., 1995), and drying also positively affects the textural modification of co-products. Currently, beef jerky and biltong are popular meat dried products with premium meat cuts, and ample research is available on these products (Banerjee & Shanthi, 2012; Cheng et al., 2008; Chernukha et al., 2015; Han et al., 1993; Lee et al., 2012; Ohtaki et al., 1999; Saiga et al., 2008; Wanasundara et al., 2002). However, there are few studies available on offal drying. In a recent study, bovine lungs were minced and air oven dried by Jayawardena et al. (2019a, b) and produced protein powder with a high amino acid score. This lung powder was successfully incorporated into pasta to enrich the protein quality and lower the glycaemic response. Similarly, bovine lungs were air oven dried by Ilo et al. (2000) to produce extruded snacks with a high iron content. Though there is a lack of studies on co-product drying in the human food chain, drying of animal co-products is popular in the pet food industry, and US patents are available with different drying conditions for pet food (Patent US4020187A, US5045339A).

11.6.3 Co-product Hydrolysates

Protein hydrolysates are produced by hydrolysing protein sources to be used for several applications, such as ingredients in nutritional and health products, infant formulas, medical and dietary supplements and flavouring agents (Chávez-Jáuregui et al., 2003).

Traditionally, hydrolysates were produced using concentrated acids (6N HCl), and then generally used for amino acid analysis (Bastos & Arêas, 1990). This method has a list of drawbacks, such as destroying tryptophan, partial destruction of serine and threonine, and conversion of asparagine and glutamine to their acids. Alteration of these amino acids affects the nutritional quality of hydrolysates. Enzyme digestion prevents these drawbacks and produces protein hydrolysates. Enzymatic digestions of protein sources have been extensively studied in the food industry due to the advantages of low energy consumption, a lower enzyme to substrate ratio, and the ease of controlling the reaction. Furthermore, changing enzyme type and hydrolysing time produces varieties of hydrolysates which create a wide range of product diversity from the same protein source.

Different enzymes behaviours are explained in the study of hydrolysing bovine lung tissues with papain, pepsin and Alcalase enzymes to produce lung hydrolysate (Santiago et al., 2001). Among the proteases, Alcalase enzyme hydrolysates displayed anti-inflammatory activity by significant suppression of cytokine production in RAW264.7 cells, while other hydrolysates had no significant effect. Meat co-products can be used to produce food ingredients. The safety of the food ingredients should be ensured before introducing them to the human food chain. Safe flavour enhancer was produced from a chicken bone extract using enzymatic hydrolysis (Osen, 2017). In this study, proteins were extracted by a hot pressure extraction method, and the proteins were hydrolysed with the Flavourzyme enzyme. Safety measures were studied by in-*vivo* rat study, and there was no significant toxicity observed with 13-week administration.

Sheep visceral mass was hydrolysed using fungal proteases to produce a nutritious hydrolysate (Akdogan, 1999). The visceral mass protein digestibility corrected amino acid score (PDCAAS) reached a high level (0.93), corresponding to adult nutrition status. These studies suggest that slaughterhouse co-products have the potential to produce nutritional supplements through protein hydrolysis.

Different processing methods for co-products are illustrated on Table 11.6 with relevant publications.

TABLE 11.6
Publications on the processing of co-products

Co-product	Processing method	Advantage/end product	Reference
Bovine Lungs	Oven-dried, defatted and extrusion cooking	High iron bioavailable snacks	(Cheftel et al., 1992)
Bovine Lungs	Freeze-dried, defatted, extrusion with bacon flavour	High consumer acceptability	(Megard et al., 1985)
Bovine Lungs	Freeze-dried defatted extrusion with chickpea and corn	snacks to prevent anaemia in preschool children	(Moreira-Araújo et al., 2008)
Bovine lungs	Oven-dried and incorporated into pasta	Protein-rich pasta with low glycaemic response	(Arêas & Lawrie, 1984)
Bovine lungs	alkaline solubilisation and PI precipitation	Protein extract with high emulsifying activity and forming property	(Santiago et al., 2001), (Cardoso-Santiago & Arêas, 2001)
Bovine and porcine lungs	Alkali solubilisation and PI precipitation	High protein yield	(Moreira-Araújo et al., 2008)
Bovine lung, liver, spleen and blade-bone	All co-products steamed with cassava and wheat flour, slicing, air oven drying	Snack with high consumer acceptability	(Campos & Arêas, 1993)
Bovine lung, spleen, heart, porcine lung, liver	Protein extraction with low ionic buffer	30% to 75% of extracted protein	(Cardoso-Santiago & Arêas, 2001)
Bovine & porcine lung and bovine tripe	Protein extracted and extruded with soy grits	Extruded snacks with 20% to 30% of co-products	(Conti-Silva et al., 2011)
bovine rumen	Defatted, air oven dried and extrusion	Protein ingredient with high consumer acceptability	(Mittal & Lawrie, 1984)
Bovine heart	Protein extraction by acid solubilisation and salt precipitate	Low fat protein	(Garcia Zepeda et al., 1997)
Bovine heart and lips	Protein extraction by Salt solubilisation	High water holding capacity and emulsion stability	(Garcia Zepeda et al., 1997)
Bovine liver	Enzymatic hydrolysis and membrane filtration	Hydrolysate with antioxidant activity	(Le Roux et al., 1995)
Calf head	Meat emulsion incorporated into pasta	Protein rich pasta with low glycaemic response	(Liu et al., 2016)
Porcine liver	Protein extraction by salt solubilisation	Low-cost protein	(Jayawardena, Morton, et al., 2019b)
Sheep intestine and stomach	Sterilising, enzymatic hydrolysis (fungal protease)	Protein hydrolysate	(Verardo et al., 2009)
Chicken bone	Hot pressure extraction, concentration with vacuum condenser, enzymatic hydrolysis	Safe meaty flavour enhancer	(Lemes et al., 2012)
Buffalo rumen and heart	Emulsion preparation and incorporate into sausages.	High consumer acceptable sausages	(Filip & Vidrih, 2015)

11.7 COOKING EFFECT ON CO-PRODUCTS

Cooking at >60 °C decreases the toughness of animal tissues by breaking down the strength of single muscle fibres (Christensen et al., 2000), and this increases the palatability of animal tissues. Cooking technique have a significant effect on consumer acceptance of the final meat quality.

Traditionally different communities have used different cooking processes for meat co-products. Different cooking techniques could change the chemical composition of the final cooked product.

Table 11.7 shows how chemical composition changes co-products produced with different cooking methods. This table illustrates the correlation between increasing fat content of the cooked food and increasing total energy level. Pan-frying involves adding extra oil, which may increase the sheep liver, sheep brain and cattle brain fat content. Table 11.7 illustrates the minor fluctuation in the amino acid profile and mineral profile, which could be due to the reduction in the moisture level.

11.8 CONSUMER ASPECTS OF CO-PRODUCT UTILISATION

People look for a variety of novel foods in their eating routine for health reasons and to fulfil a need for new food experiences. But consumers are concerned for their health and safety, so they are always attentive to this before experiencing an unfamiliar co-product (Al-Shawaf et al., 2015). Willingness to experience novel foods, yet avoid novelty leads to the term "Neophilia" and "Neophobia" (Veeck, 2010) which are the most crucial consumer impediments to the consumption of co-products. Neophobia could be due to various reasons including fear of consuming toxins and other pathogens. Food neophobia tends to be stronger for animal products than for non-animal products. A study in Canada reported that school students' willingness to taste unfamiliar animal food was not increased even with the positive nutrition information compare to nonmeat food (Martins et al., 1997).

Though meat co-products are considered delightful in some nations, consumers in developed nations have less experience with these foods, and most of them have never tasted many coproducts. These consumers often have a perception of these co-products as being unhealthy or disgust towards co-products (Frewer & Gremmen, 2007).

Three primary motives have been identified that lead to consumer rejection: perceived danger, poor sensory properties, and "ideation". Perceived danger and negative sensory properties are major factors that affect real demand. Danger perception rejects the food irrespective of any other benefit, and sensory attribute is the second critical aspect for rejection. Ideation relates to knowledge of the nature and origin of the food. Furthermore, this attribute generates the feel of disgust, whereby foods are then rejected. The next ideational reason is an inappropriateness. This reason raises the doubt of edibility due to coproducts not being identified as a food within a given culture (Henchion et al., 2016).

Further processing can convert co-products to an unrecognisable state, and the degree of processing relates to a positive influence towards product preference. Gmuer et al. (2016) reported that consumer preferences and the processing state of cricket presented as deep-fried bites, flour, and snack mix with tortilla determined the. The consumers preferred deep fried bites. This research revealed the positive relationship of degree of processing and willingness to eat insects.

Comparable efforts have been made to attract consumers to meat co-products using the same strategy (Henchion et al., 2016). Szocs and Lefebvre (2016) illustrated how the physical state of food influenced the psychological state and importance to the ultimate consumption decision. Changing the physical attributes resulted in a "de-animalising" perception, and some consumers were able to shift from negative psychological ideational factors and consider beneficial aspects instead (Henchion et al., 2016). They further suggested that meat co-products should be processed as ingredients rather than finished products. This concept provides the opportunity to incorporate co-products into common foods to better market the unfamiliar animal co products.

Food habits are nurtured from childhood, and it is a socially, culturally bound phenomenon. So, changes in negative preference towards the unfamiliar offal could be a challenging task for some consumers. Still, the role of experts, celebrity chefs and intimates can greatly influence the process by providing evidence to convince consumers that the co-products are safe and socially acceptable (Mullen et al., 2017).

TABLE 11.7
Effect of different cooking methods on the composition of liver and brain of cattle and sheep (USDA, 2020)

Element	Unit	Cattle liver Raw	Cattle liver Pan fried	Cattle liver Braised	Sheep liver Raw	Sheep liver Pan fried	Sheep liver Braised	Cattle brain Raw	Cattle brain Pan fried	Cattle brain Simmered	Sheep brain Raw	Sheep brain Pan Fried	Sheep brain Braised
Water	g	70.8	62.0	58.8	71.4	56.2	56.7	76.3	70.8	74.9	79.2	60.7	75.7
Energy	kcal	135	175	191	139	238	220	143	196	151	122	273	145
Energy	kJ	564	734	801	582	996	920	600	820	630	510	1142	607
Protein	g	20.4	26.5	29.1	20.4	25.5	30.6	10.9	12.6	11.7	10.4	17.0	12.6
Total lipid (fat)	g	3.63	4.68	5.26	5.02	12.7	8.81	10.3	15.8	10.5	8.58	22.2	10.2
Ash	g	1.31	1.63	1.74	1.44	1.83	1.42	1.51	1.58	1.46	1.33	1.82	1.36
Carbohydrate, by difference	g	3.89	5.16	5.13	1.78	3.78	2.53	1.05	–	1.48	–	–	–
Calcium, Ca	mg	5	6	6	7	9	8	43	9	9	9	21	12
Iron, Fe	mg	4.90	6.17	6.54	7.37	10.2	8.28	2.55	2.22	2.30	1.75	2.04	1.68
Magnesium, Mg	mg	18	22	21	19	23	22	13	15	12	12	22	14
Phosphorus, P	mg	387	485	497	364	427	420	362	386	335	270	495	337
Potassium, K	mg	313	351	352	313	352	221	274	354	244	296	358	205
Sodium, Na	mg	69	77	79	70	124	56	126	158	108	112	157	134
Zinc, Zn	mg	4	5.23	5.3	4.66	5.63	7.89	1.02	1.35	1.09	1.17	2	1.36
Copper, Cu	mg	9.8	14.6	14.3	7.00	9.83	7.07	0.29	0.22	0.23	0.24	0.48	0.21
Manganese, Mn	mg	0.31	0.36	0.36	0.18	0.59	0.52	0.03	0.03	0.03	0.04	0.07	0.06
Selenium, Se	µg	39.7	32.8	36.1	82.4	116.1	111.4	21.3	26.0	21.8	9.00	12.0	12.0
Vitamin C, total ascorbic acid	mg	1.30	0.70	1.90	4.00	13.0	4.00	10.7	3.30	10.5	16.0	23.0	12.0
Thiamine	mg	0.19	0.18	0.19	0.34	0.35	0.23	0.09	0.13	0.07	0.13	0.17	0.11
Riboflavin	mg	2.76	3.43	3.43	3.63	4.59	4.03	0.20	0.26	0.22	0.3	0.37	0.24
Niacin	mg	13.2	17.5	17.53	16.1	16.7	12.2	3.55	3.78	3.62	3.90	4.55	2.47
Pantothenic acid	mg	7.17	6.94	7.11	6.13	6.33	3.96	2.01	0.57	1.21	0.92	1.56	0.99
Vitamin B-6	mg	1.08	1.03	1.02	0.9	0.95	0.49	0.23	0.39	0.14	0.29	0.23	0.11
Folate, total	µg	290	260	253	230	400	73	3	6	5	3	7	5
Choline, total	mg	333	418	426	–	–	–	–	–	491	–	–	–

(Continued)

TABLE 11.7 (Continued)
Effect of different cooking methods on the composition of liver and brain of cattle and sheep (USDA, 2020)

Element	Unit	Cattle liver Raw	Cattle liver Pan fried	Cattle liver Braised	Sheep liver Raw	Sheep liver Pan fried	Sheep liver Braised	Cattle brain Raw	Cattle brain Pan fried	Cattle brain Simmered	Sheep brain Raw	Sheep brain Pan Fried	Sheep brain Braised
Betaine	mg	4.4	6.3	5.6	–	–	–	–	–	–	–	–	–
Vitamin B-12	µg	59.3	83.1	70.6	90.1	85.7	76.5	9.51	15.2	10.1	11.3	24.1	9.25
Vitamin A, RAE	µg	4968	7744	9442	7391	7782	7491	7	–	6	–	–	–
Retinol	µg	4948	7728	9428	7391	7777	7491	–	–	–	–	–	–
Carotene, beta	µg	232	182	162	–	–	–	88	–	70	–	–	–
Carotene, alpha	µg	11	11	11	–	–	–	0	–	0	–	–	–
Cryptoxanthin, beta	µg	13	21	11	–	–	–	0	–	0	–	–	–
Vitamin A, IU	IU	16898	26088	31714	24612	25998	24945	147	–	117	–	–	–
Vitamin E (alpha-tocopherol)	mg	0.38	0.46	0.51	–	–	–	0.99	–	1.67	–	–	–
Tocopherol, gamma	mg	0.07	0.06	0.06	–	–	–	0.05	–	0.06	–	–	–
Vitamin D (D2 + D3), International Units	IU	49	49	49	–	–	–	–	–	–	–	–	–
Vitamin D (D2 + D3)	µg	1.2	1.2	1.2	–	–	–	–	–	–	–	–	–
Vitamin D3 (cholecalciferol)	µg	1.2	1.2	1.2	–	–	–	–	–	–	–	–	–
Vitamin K (phylloquinone)	µg	3.1	3.9	3.3	–	–	–	–	–	0.1	–	–	–
Fatty acids, total saturated	g	1.23	2.53	2.95	1.94	4.90	3.41	2.30	3.74	2.394	2.19	5.67	2.60
14:0	g	0.02	0.04	0.04	0.05	0.14	0.1	0.03	0.07	0.03	0.04	0.09	0.04
15:0	g	0.01	0.01	0.01	–	–	–	–	–	–	–	–	–
16:0	g	0.31	0.72	0.79	0.68	1.72	1.2	0.92	1.98	0.974	1.06	2.74	1.25
17:0	g	0.03	0.06	0.07	–	–	–	0.03	–	0.03	–	–	–
18:0	g	0.86	1.68	2.02	1.12	2.82	1.96	1.27	1.62	1.31	1.07	2.78	1.27
20:0	g	–	–	–	–	–	–	0.02	–	0.02	–	–	–
22:0	g	0.01	0.02	0.02	–	–	–	0.03	–	0.04	–	–	–
Fatty acids, total monounsaturated	g	0.48	1.11	1.12	1.05	2.64	1.84	1.89	3.98	1.88	1.55	4.02	1.84
16:1	g	0.04	0.09	0.08	0.13	0.32	0.22	0.02	0.11	0.02	0.05	0.13	0.06
17:1	g	0.013	0.021	0.022	–	–	–	–	–	–	–	–	–
18:1	g	0.42	0.99	1.02	0.92	2.33	1.62	1.65	3.47	1.67	1.29	3.33	1.53

20:1	g	0.01	0.01	–	–	–	–	0.22	0.24	0.19	0.12	0.32	0.15
Fatty acids, total polyunsaturated	g	0.47	1.02	1.11	0.75	1.89	1.31	1.59	2.31	1.63	0.88	2.28	1.04
18:2	g	0.30	–	–	0.32	0.81	0.57	0.04	0.84	0.04	0.03	0.07	0.03
18:2 n-6	g	0.30	0.62	0.66	–	–	–	–	–	–	–	–	–
18:3	g	0.02	0.04	–	0.07	0.17	0.12	–	0.05	–	–	–	–
18:3 n-3 (ALA)	g	0.01	0.02	0.02	–	–	–	–	–	–	–	–	–
18:3 n-6	g	0.01	0.02	0.03	–	–	–	–	–	–	–	–	–
20:2 n-6	g	0.01	0.02	0.01	–	–	–	–	–	–	–	–	–
20:4	g	0.14	0.31	0.40	0.36	0.9	0.63	0.32	0.29	0.36	0.23	0.60	0.27
22:5 n-3 (DPA)	g	–	–	–	–	–	–	0.37	0.29	0.38	0.13	0.33	0.15
22:6 n-3 (DHA)	g	–	–	–	–	–	–	0.85	0.67	0.86	0.49	1.28	0.59
Fatty acids, total trans	g	0.17	0.34	0.37	–	–	–	0.61	–	0.51	–	–	–
Cholesterol	mg	275	381	396	371	493	501	3010	1995	3100	1352	2504	2043
Tryptophan	g	0.26	0.34	0.37	0.24	0.30	0.36	NA	0.10	NA	0.11	0.18	0.13
Threonine	g	0.87	1.11	1.22	0.88	1.10	1.32	NA	0.60	NA	0.47	0.76	0.56
Isoleucine	g	0.97	1.23	1.35	0.888	1.1	1.32	NA	0.49	NA	0.41	0.68	0.50
Leucine	g	1.91	2.44	2.67	1.67	2.09	2.50	NA	0.94	NA	0.81	1.33	0.98
Lysine	g	1.61	2.05	2.25	1.10	1.38	1.65	NA	0.75	Na	0.67	1.09	0.81
Methionine	g	0.54	0.69	0.76	0.44	0.55	0.66	NA	0.26	NA	0.21	0.34	0.25
Cystine	g	0.38	0.48	0.53	0.21	0.27	0.32	NA	0.22	NA	0.11	0.18	0.13
Phenylalanine	g	1.08	1.38	1.52	0.91	1.14	1.37	NA	0.64	NA	0.50	0.82	0.61
Tyrosine	g	0.81	1.03	1.13	0.73	0.91	1.09	NA	0.45	NA	0.38	0.62	0.46
Valine	g	1.26	1.61	1.76	1.12	1.41	1.68	NA	0.62	NA	0.50	0.81	0.60
Arginine	g	1.24	1.58	1.74	1.14	1.43	1.71	NA	0.69	NA	0.70	1.14	0.85
Histidine	g	0.63	0.80	0.88	0.48	0.60	0.72	NA	0.32	NA	0.28	0.45	0.33
Alanine	g	1.16	1.48	1.63	1.02	1.28	1.53	NA	0.70	NA	0.59	0.96	0.71
Aspartic acid	g	1.93	2.46	2.69	1.76	2.20	2.64	NA	1.13	NA	0.87	1.42	1.05
Glutamic acid	g	2.61	3.33	3.65	2.20	2.75	3.30	NA	1.53	NA	1.23	2.01	1.49
Glycine	g	1.16	1.48	1.63	0.99	1.23	1.48	NA	0.59	NA	0.49	0.80	0.59
Proline	g	0.96	1.23	1.34	0.97	1.22	1.46	NA	0.52	NA	0.45	0.73	0.54
Serine	g	0.91	1.15	1.27	0.88	1.10	1.32	NA	0.73	NA	0.54	0.88	0.65
Hydroxyproline	g	0.05	0.05	0.05	–	–	–	NA	–	NA	–	–	–

In terms of religious restrictions or believes that might affect the consumption of the meat co-products, there are no restrictions in Christianity, as the new testament declared "nothing is unclean in itself". For Muslims, all meat co-products are permissible as long as they are derived from halal slaughtered animals, with the exception of blood that is considered Haram - "not permissible". Carnivore animals and birds of prey are not halal. Pigs and any of its products as well as animals that are found dead, offered or sacrificed to idols, meat of animals that are sacrificed in a name other than God (slaughtered in the name of a person alive or dead, any deity or idol) are not halal. For proper halal slaughtering of animals, a set of rules need to be followed as highlighted by Islamic council of Victoria (Australia):

- The slaughterer must be a sane adult Muslim.
- The slaughterer must say the name of God before making the cut.
- The name of God is said in order to emphasise the sanctity of life and that the animal is being killed for food with God's consent.
- The animal must be killed by cutting the throat with one continuous motion of a sharp knife.
- The cut must sever at least three of the trachea, oesophagus, and the two blood vessels on either side of the throat.
- The spinal cord must not be cut.
- Animals must be well treated before being killed.
- Animals must not see other animals being killed.
- The knife must not be sharpened in the animal's presence.
- The knife blade must be free of blemishes that might tear the wound.
- The animal must not be in an uncomfortable position.
- The animal must be allowed to bleed out and be completely dead before further processing.

For the Jewish faith followers, meat co-products must be from kosher animals and birds (discussed in detail in Chapter 8). If the co-products are in a processed form, the kosher laws regarding use of processing lines that adapt kosher status (i.e., no mixing of meat products with dairy products or with *trayf* seafood ingredients) need to be maintained. The blood must be removed from the organs before consumption, probably using the same principles of *kashering* (koshering the meat using salt and water in various soaking and rinsing). Organs that contain high amounts of blood (i.e., liver, kidney and spleen) should be cooked in a way that does not allow retention of released blood in the final meal, such as broiling or cooked on open fire where blood will run free from the edible portions.

Chelev are animal fats that are found on the kidneys and the stomach (commonly known as Suet). This fat is forbidden to be eaten by the Jews and Israelites ["Speak to the children of Israel, saying: 'You shall not eat any fat of ox or sheep or goat.", Leviticus 7:23, New King James version) and "For whoever eats the fat of the animal of which men offer an offering made by fire to the LORD, the person who eats it shall be cut off from his people.", Leviticus 7:25, New King James version]. This fat is removed by trained kosher butcher "*Shechita*" and the prohibition of *Chelev* is not applied to fat from birds and certain animals such as deer.

Animals used in halal and kosher slaughtering must be free from diseases and be alive at the time of slaughtering according to the Islamic *Sharia* and Jewish *Kashrut*. The main principles behind these rules are the healthiness and safety of the consumed food. Therefore, it is reasonable to conclude that any issues regarding any environmental pollutants and toxic chemicals that could be harmful to people (normally declared in food standards) could render meat co-products unfit for consumption if they exist at a higher level than maximum allowable levels.

11.9 CONCLUSIONS

There are potential opportunities to use meat co-products to gain extra value from the meat processing chain. The yield of animals can be increased through better utilisation of underutilised co-products, and processing of co-products ensures better nutritional and economical value. Efficient production with minimal wastage is also a driver, as the meat industry strives for sustainable practices to meet the global protein demand while minimising its environmental footprint.

REFERENCES

Aihara, K., Kajimoto, O., Hirata, H., Takahashi, R., & Nakamura, Y. (2005). Effect of powdered fermented milk with Lactobacillus helveticus on subjects with high-normal blood pressure or mild hypertension. *Journal of the American College of Nutrition, 24*(4), 257–265.

Akdogan, H. (1999). High moisture food extrusion. *International Journal of Food Science & Technology, 34*(3), 195–207.

Al-Shawaf, L., Lewis, D. M., Alley, T. R., & Buss, D. M. (2015). Mating strategy, disgust, and food neophobia. *Appetite, 85*, 30–35.

Albertí, P., Panea, B., Sañudo, C., Olleta, J. L., Ripoll, G., Ertbjerg, P., & Christensen, M. (2008). Live weight, body size and carcass characteristics of young bulls of fifteen European breeds. *Livestock Science, 114*(1), 19–30. doi:10.1016/j.livsci.2007.04.010

Arêas, J., & Lawrie, R. (1984). Effect of lipid-protein interactions on extrusion of offal protein isolates. *Meat Science, 11*(4), 275–299.

Awan, Z., Tariq, M., Muhammad, A., Satti, N., Mukhtar, T., Akram, W., & Yasin, M. F. (2015). Edible by-products of meat. *Veterinaria, 3*(1), 33–36.

Baghurst, K. (2006). *Nutrient reference values for Australia and New Zealand: including recommended dietary intakes*. Canberra: National Health and Medical Research Council.

Banerjee, P., & Shanthi, C. (2012). Isolation of novel bioactive regions from bovine Achilles tendon collagen having angiotensin I-converting enzyme-inhibitory properties. *Process Biochemistry, 47*(12), 2335–2346.

Bastos, D., & Arêas, J. (1990). Lung proteins: effect of defatting with several solvents and extrusion cooking on some functional properties. *Meat Science, 28*(3), 223–235.

Bernát, I. (1983). Protein-Deficiency Anemia. In I. Bernát (Ed.), *Iron Metabolism* (pp. 299–300). Boston, MA: Springer US. Retrieved from 10.1007/978-1-4615-7308-1_21. doi:10.1007/978-1-4615-7308-1_21

Berrazaga, I., Micard, V., Gueugneau, M., & Walrand, S. (2019). The Role of the Anabolic Properties of Plant- versus Animal-Based Protein Sources in Supporting Muscle Mass Maintenance: A Critical Review. *Nutrients, 11*(8), 1825. doi:10.3390/nu11081825

Bester, M., Schonfeldt, H. C., Pretorius, B., & Hall, N. G. (2018). The nutrient content of selected South African lamb and mutton organ meats (offal). *Food Chemistry, 238*, 3–8. 10.1016/j.foodchem.2017.05.075.

Biel, W., Czerniawska-Piątkowska, E., & Kowalczyk, A. (2019). Offal Chemical Composition from Veal, Beef, and Lamb Maintained in Organic Production Systems. *Animals, 9*(8), 489.

BLN. (2017). *Export cattle slaughter New Zealand year* Beef + Lamb New Zealand Economic Service. Retrieved from https://beeflambnz.com/sites/default/files/data/files/Cattle%20Slaughter%20Trend.pdf

Boler, D. D. (2014). Pigs. In *Encyclopedia of Meat Sciences* (pp. 363–368): Elsevier Inc.

Borelli, P., Blatt, S., Pereira, J., de Maurino, B. B., Tsujita, M., & de Souza, A. C. (2007). Reduction of erythroid progenitors in protein-energy malnutrition. *British Journal of Nutrition, 97*(2), 307–314. doi:10.1017/s0007114507172731

Campos, M. A., & Arêas, J. G. (1993). Protein nutritional value of extrusion-cooking defatted lung flour. *Food Chemistry, 47*(1), 61–66. doi:10.1016/0308-8146(93)90303-W

Cardoso-Santiago, R., & Arêas, J. A. G. (2001). Nutritional evaluation of snacks obtained from chickpea and bovine lung blends. *Food Chemistry, 74*(1), 35–40. doi:10.1016/S0308-8146(00)00335-6

Cardoso-Santiago, R. A., Moreira-Araújo, R. S. R., Pinto e Silva, M. E. M., & Arêas, J. A. G. (2001). The potential of extruded chickpea, corn and bovine lung for malnutrition programs. *Innovative Food Science & Emerging Technologies, 2*(3), 203–209. doi:10.1016/S1466-8564(01)00038-8

Chávez-Jáuregui, R. N., Cardoso-Santiago, R. A., Silva, M. E. P. E., & Arêas, J. A. (2003). Acceptability of snacks produced by the extrusion of amaranth and blends of chickpea and bovine lung. *International Journal of Food Science & Technology, 38*(7), 795–798.

Cheftel, J., Kitagawa, M., & Queguiner, C. (1992). New protein texturization processes by extrusion cooking at high moisture levels. *Food Reviews International, 8*(2), 235–275.

Cheng, F.-Y., Liu, Y.-T., Wan, T.-C., Lin, L.-C., & Sakata, R. (2008). The development of angiotensin I-converting enzyme inhibitor derived from chicken bone protein. *Animal Science Journal, 79*(1), 122–128. doi:10.1111/j.1740-0929.2007.00507.x

Chernukha, I. M., Fedulova, L. V., & Kotenkova, E. A. (2015). Meat by-product is a Source of Tissue-specific Bioactive Proteins and Peptides against Cardio-vascular Diseases. *Procedia Food Science, 5*, 50–53. doi:10.1016/j.profoo.2015.09.013

Christensen, M., Purslow, P. P., & Larsen, L. M. (2000). The effect of cooking temperature on mechanical properties of whole meat, single muscle fibres and perimysial connective tissue. *Meat Science, 55*(3), 301–307.

Chung, J., Kim, M. S., & Han, S. N. (2011). Diet-induced obesity leads to decreased hepatic iron storage in mice. *Nutrition Research, 31*(12), 915–921. doi:10.1016/j.nutres.2011.09.014

Conti-Silva, A. C., Pinto e Silva, M. E. M., & Arêas, J. A. G. (2011). Sensory acceptability of raw and extruded bovine rumen protein in processed meat products. *Meat Science, 88*(4), 652–656. doi:10.1016/j.meatsci.2011.02.024

Darine, S., Christophe, V., & Gholamreza, D. (2010). Production and functional properties of beef lung protein concentrates. *Meat Science, 84*(3), 315–322.

Darine, S., Christophe, V., & Gholamreza, D. (2011). Emulsification properties of proteins extracted from beef lungs in the presence of xanthan gum using a continuous rotor/stator system. *LWT-Food Science and Technology, 44*(4), 1179–1188.

De Benoist, B., Cogswell, M., Egli, I., & McLean, E. (2008). *Worldwide prevalence of anaemia 1993-2005*; WHO Global Database of anaemia.

FAO. (2011). *Dietary protein quality evaluation in human nutrition: report of an fao expert consultation.* Auckland, New Zealand. Retrieved from http://www.fao.org/ag/humannutrition/35978-02317b979a686a57aa4593304ffc17f06.pdf

FAO. (2019a). *OECD-FAO Agricultural Outlook 2019-2028*. OECD Publishing, Paris. Retrieved from https://www.oecd-ilibrary.org/content/publication/agr_outlook-2019-en. doi:10.1787/agr_outlook-2019-en

FAO, &. (2019b). *The State of Food Security and Nutrition in the World 2019. Safeguarding against economic slowdowns and downturns* Rome, FAO.

FAOSTAT. (2018). *Food and Agriculture Organization of the United Nations.* FAOSTAT Database. Retrieved January 02, 2020.

Filip, S., & Vidrih, R. (2015). Amino acid composition of protein-enriched dried pasta: is it suitable for a low-carbohydrate diet? *Food Technology and Biotechnology, 53*(3), 298–306.

Fitzsimons, E., & Brock, J., &. (2001). The anaemia of chronic disease: Remains hard to distinguish from iron deficiency anaemia in some cases. *British Medical Journal, 322*, 811–812. https://doi.org/10.1136/bmj.322.7290.811

Fornias, O. V. (1996). Edible by-products of slaughter animals. In *FAO Animal Production and Health Paper 123*. Rome: FAO.

Francis, G., & Thomas, J. (1975). Isolation and chemical characterization of collagen in bovine pulmonary tissues. *Biochemical Journal, 145*(2), 287–297.

Frewer, L. J., & Gremmen, B. (2007). Consumer interests in food processing waste management and co-product recovery. *In Handbook of waste management and co-product recovery in food processing* (pp. 21–35): Woodhead Publishing.

FSIS. (2015). *Slaughter inspection training - livestock postmortem inspection.* Retrieved from https://www.fsis.usda.gov/wps/wcm/connect/ad2cab87-9bf9-4ead-969a-cec2d4753c30/LSIT_PostMortem.pdf?MOD=AJPERES

Garcia Zepeda, C. M., Kastner, C. L., Wolf, J. R., Boyer, J. E., Kropf, D. H., Hunt, M. C., & Setser, C. S. (1997). Extrusion and low-dose irradiation effects on destruction of Clostridium sporogenes spores in a beef-based product. *Journal of Food Protection, 60*(7), 777–785.

Gmuer, A., Guth, J. N., Hartmann, C., & Siegrist, M. (2016). Effects of the degree of processing of insect ingredients in snacks on expected emotional experiences and willingness to eat. *Food Quality and Preference, 54*, 117–127.

Gómez-Guillén, M. C., Giménez, B., López-Caballero, M. E., & Montero, M. P. (2011). Functional and bioactive properties of collagen and gelatin from alternative sources: A review. *Food Hydrocolloids, 25*(8), 1813–1827. doi:10.1016/j.foodhyd.2011.02.007

Griffin, C. C., Linhardt, R. J., Van Gorp, C. L., Toida, T., Hileman, R. E., Schubert, R. L., & Brown, S. E. (1995). Isolation and characterization of heparan sulfate from crude porcine intestinal mucosal peptidoglycan heparin. *Carbohydrate Research, 276*(1), 183–197. doi:10.1016/0008-6215(95)00166-Q

Haddad, L. J., Hawkes, C., Achadi, E., Ahuja, A., Ag Bendech, M., & Bhatia, K. (2015). *Global Nutrition Report 2015: Actions and accountability to advance nutrition and sustainable development.* Washington, USA: International Food Policy Research Institute.

Han, C. H., Richardson, J., Oh, S. H., & Roberts, D. M. (1993). Isolation and kinetic characterization of the calmodulin methyltransferase from sheep brain. *Biochemistry*, *32*(50), 13974–13980. doi:10.1021/bi00213a030

Hartikainen, H. (2005). Biogeochemistry of selenium and its impact on food chain quality and human health. *Journal of Trace elements in Medicine and Biology*, *18*(4), 309–318.

Hata, Y., Yamamoto, M., Ohni, M., Nakajima, K., Nakamura, Y., & Takano, T. (1996). A placebo-controlled study of the effect of sour milk on blood pressure in hypertensive subjects. *The American Journal of Clinical Nutrition*, *64*(5), 767–771.

Hellman, N. E., & Gitlin, J. D. (2002). Ceruloplasmin metabolism and function. *Annual Review of Nutrition*, *22*(1), 439–458.

Henchion, M., McCarthy, M., & O'Callaghan, J. (2016). Transforming Beef By-products into Valuable ingredients: Which spell/recipe to Use? *Frontiers in Nutrition*, *3*, 53.

Herrero, M., Havlík, P., Valin, H., Notenbaert, A., Rufino, M. C., & Thornton, P. K. (2013a). Biomass use, production, feed efficiencies, and greenhouse gas emissions from global livestock systems. *Proceedings of the National Academy of Sciences*, *110*(52), 20888–20893.

Herrero, M., Havlík, P., Valin, H., Notenbaert, A., Rufino, M. C., Thornton, P. K., ... Obersteiner, M. (2013b). Biomass use, production, feed efficiencies, and greenhouse gas emissions from global livestock systems. *Proceedings of the National Academy of Sciences*, *110*(52), 20888–20893.

Ilo, S., Schoenlechner, R., & Berghofe, E. (2000). Role of lipids in the extrusion cooking processes. *Grasas y Aceites*, *51*(1-2), 97–110.

Jahnen-Dechent, W., & Ketteler, M. (2012). Magnesium basics. *Clinical Kidney Journal*, *5*(Suppl 1), i3–i14. doi:10.1093/ndtplus/sfr163

Jauhiainen, T., Vapaatalo, H., Poussa, T., Kyrönpalo, S., Rasmussen, M., & Korpela, R. (2005). Lactobacillus helveticus fermented milk reduces blood pressure in 24-h ambulatory blood pressure measurement. *American Journal of Hypertension*, *18*, 1600–1605.

Jayawardena, S. R., Morton, J. D., Brennan, C., Bhat, Z. F., & Bekhit, A. E. D. A., &. (2019a). *Effect of drying temperature on the quality and in vitro protein digestion of beef-lung protein powder*. Proceedings of Fifth International Conference on Food Structures, Digestion and Health, Rotorua, New Zealand. Retrieved from http://icomst-proceedings.helsinki.fi/papers/2018_06_43.pdf.

Jayawardena, S. R., Morton, J. D., Brennan, C. S., & Bekhit, A. E. A. (2019b). Utilisation of beef lung protein powder as a functional ingredient to enhance protein and iron content of fresh pasta. *International Journal of Food Science & Technology*, *54*(3), 610–618. doi:10.1111/ijfs.13927

Korhonen, H. (2009). Milk-derived bioactive peptides: From science to applications. *Journal of Functional Foods*, *1*(2), 177–187.

Lafarga, T., & Hayes, M. (2017). Effect of pre-treatment on the generation of dipeptidyl peptidase-IV-and prolyl endopeptidase-inhibitory hydrolysates from bovine lung. *Irish Journal of Agricultural and Food Research*, *56*(1), 12–24.

Le Roux, D., Vergnes, B., Chaurand, M., & Abécassis, J. (1995). A thermomechanical approach to pasta extrusion. *Journal of Food Engineering*, *26*(3), 351–368. doi:10.1016/0260-8774(94)00060-M

Lee, S. J., Kim, Y.-S., Hwang, J.-W., Kim, E.-K., Moon, S.-H., Jeon, B.-T., & Jeon, Y.-J. (2012). Purification and characterization of a novel antioxidative peptide from duck skin by-products that protects liver against oxidative damage. *Food Research International*, *49*(1), 285–295. doi:10.1016/j.foodres.2012.08.017

Lemes, A. C., Takeuchi, K. P., Carvalho, J. C. M. D., & Danesi, E. D. G. (2012). Fresh pasta production enriched with spirulina platensis biomass. *Brazilian Archives of Biology and Technology*, *55*(5), 741–750.

Leonard, B. (2011). *USDA Agricultural Projections To 2017*: DIANE Publishing.

Li, B., Chen, F., Wang, X., Ji, B., & Wu, Y. (2007). Isolation and identification of antioxidative peptides from porcine collagen hydrolysate by consecutive chromatography and electrospray ionization–mass spectrometry. *Food Chemistry*, *102*(4), 1135–1143. doi:10.1016/j.foodchem.2006.07.002

Liu, T., Hamid, N., Kantono, K., Pereira, L., Farouk, M. M., & Knowles, S. O. (2016). Effects of meat addition on pasta structure, nutrition and in vitro digestibility. *Food Chemistry*, *213*, 108–114. doi:10.1016/j.foodchem.2016.06.058

Lynch, S. A., Álvarez, C., O'Neill, E. E., Keenan, D. F., & Mullen, A. M. (2018). Optimization of protein recovery from bovine lung by pH shift process using response surface methodology. *Journal of the Science of Food and Agriculture*, *98*(5), 1951–1960.

Martins, Y., Pelchat, M. L., & Pliner, P. (1997). "Try it; it's good and it's good for you": Effects of taste and nutrition information on willingness to try novel foods. *Appetite*, *28*(2), 89–102.

Masuda, O., Nakamura, Y., & Takano, T. (1996). Antihypertensive peptides are present in aorta after oral administration of sour milk containing these peptides to spontaneously hypertensive rats. *The Journal of Nutrition, 126*(12), 3063–3068.

Mathis, K. J., Emmons, T. L., Curran, D. F., Day, J. E., & Tomasselli, A. G. (2008). High yield purification of soluble guanylate cyclase from bovine lung. *Protein Expression and Purification, 60*(1), 58–63.

Megard, D., Kitabatake, N., & Cheftel, J. (1985). Continuous restructuring of mechanically deboned chicken meat by HTST extrusion-cooking. *Journal of Food Science, 50*(5), 1364–1369.

MIA. (2018). *Meat industry association annual report*Retrieved from https://www.mia.co.nz/resources/current/circulars-2/

Miner-Williams, W. M., Stevens, B. R., & Moughan, P. J. (2014). Are intact peptides absorbed from the healthy gut in the adult human? *Nutrition Research Reviews, 27*(2), 308–329.

Mirdhayati, I., Hermanianto, J., Wijaya, C. H., Sajuthi, D., & Arihara, K. (2016). Angiotensin converting enzyme (ACE) inhibitory and antihypertensive activities of protein hydrolysate from meat of Kacang goat (Capra aegagrus hircus). *Journal of the Science of Food and Agriculture, 96*(10), 3536–3542.

Mittal, P., & Lawrie, R. A. (1984). Extrusion studies of mixtures containing certain meat offals: Part 1—Objective properties. *Meat Science, 10*(2), 101–116. doi:10.1016/0309-1740(84)90063-9

Mizushima, S., Ohshige, K., Watanabe, J., Kimura, M., Kadowaki, T., Nakamura, Y., & Tochikubo, O. (2004). Randomized controlled trial of sour milk on blood pressure in borderline hypertensive men. *American Journal of Hypertension, 17*(8), 701–706.

MLA. (2011). Final Report: Evaluation and Development of High Moisture Extruded Red Meat Trim Products, Sydney, Australia. Retrieved from https://www.mla.com.au/contentassets/3e834ef8e4754-d9ab54220f6fbf971ab/a.mpt.0033_final_report.pdf

Möller, N. P., Scholz-Ahrens, K. E., Roos, N., & Schrezenmeir, J. (2008). Bioactive peptides and proteins from foods: indication for health effects. *European Journal of Nutrition, 47*(4), 171–182.

Moreira-Araújo, R. S., Araújo, M. A., & Arêas, J. A. (2008). Fortified food made by the extrusion of a mixture of chickpea, corn and bovine lung controls iron-deficiency anaemia in preschool children. *Food Chemistry, 107*(1), 158–164.

Mullen, A. M., Álvarez, C., Zeugolis, D. I., Henchion, M., O'Neill, E., & Drummond, L. (2017). Alternative uses for co-products: Harnessing the potential of valuable compounds from meat processing chains. *Meat Science, 132*, 90–98.

Nakamura, Y., Yamamoto, N., Sakai, K., Okubo, A., Yamazaki, S., & Takano, T. (1995). Purification and characterization of angiotensin I-converting enzyme inhibitors from sour milk. *Journal of Dairy Science, 78*(4), 777–783.

Nakamura, Y., Yamamoto, N., Sakai, K., & Takano, T. (1995). Antihypertensive effect of sour milk and peptides isolated from it that are inhibitors to angiotensin I-converting enzyme. *Journal of Dairy Science, 78*(6), 1253–1257.

O'Sullivan, S. M., Lafarga, T., Hayes, M., & O'Brien, N. M. (2017). Bioactivity of bovine lung hydrolysates prepared using papain, pepsin, and Alcalase. *Journal of Food Biochemistry, 41*(6), e12406.

Ohtaki, T., Kumano, S., Ishibashi, Y., Ogi, K., Matsui, H., Harada, M., ... Fujino, M. (1999). Isolation and cDNA cloning of a novel galanin-like peptide (GALP) from porcine hypothalamus. *Journal of Biological Chemistry, 274*(52), 37041–37045.

Osen, R. (2017). *Texturization of pea protein isolates using high moisture extrusion cooking.* München, Germany: Technische Universität München. Retrieved from https://d-nb.info/116838026X/34

Perignon, M., Barré, T., Gazan, R., Amiot, M.-J., & Darmon, N. (2018). The bioavailability of iron, zinc, protein and vitamin A is highly variable in French individual diets: Impact on nutrient inadequacy assessment and relation with the animal-to-plant ratio of diets. *Food Chemistry, 238*, 73–81. doi:10.1016/j.foodchem.2016.12.070

Piste, P., Sayaji, D., & Avinash, M. (2012). Calcium and its Role in Human Body. *Int J Res Pharm Biomed Sci, 4*, 2229–3701.

Prohl, A., Ostermann, C., Lohr, M., & Reinhold, P. (2014). The bovine lung in biomedical research: visually guided bronchoscopy, intrabronchial inoculation and in vivo sampling techniques. *Journal of Visualized Experiments: JoVE* (89), 51557. doi:10.3791/51557

Quinkler, W., Maasberg, M., Bernotat-Danielowski, S., Lüthe, N., Sharma, H. S., & Schaper, W. (1989). Isolation of heparin-binding growth factors from bovine, porcine and canine hearts. *European Journal of Biochemistry, 181*(1), 67–73. doi:10.1111/j.1432-1033.1989.tb14694.x

Roohani, N., Hurrell, R., Kelishadi, R., & Schulin, R. (2013). Zinc and its importance for human health: An integrative review. *Journal of Research in Medical Sciences, 18*(2), 144–157.

Saiga, A., Iwai, K., Hayakawa, T., Takahata, Y., Kitamura, S., Nishimura, T., & Morimatsu, F. (2008). Angiotensin I-Converting Enzyme-Inhibitory Peptides Obtained from Chicken Collagen Hydrolysate. *Journal of Agricultural and Food Chemistry*, 56(20), 9586–9591. doi:10.1021/jf072669w

Santiago, R. C., Moreira-Araújo, R. S. D. R., e Silva, M. P., & Arêas, J. (2001). The potential of extruded chickpea, corn and bovine lung for malnutrition programs. *Innovative Food Science & Emerging Technologies*, 2(3), 203–209.

Scallan, J., Huxley, V. H., & Korthuis, R. J. (2010). *Capillary fluid exchange: regulation, functions, and pathology*. Morgan & Claypool Publishers. Symposium conducted at the meeting of the Colloquium Lectures on Integrated Systems Physiology- From Molecules to Function

Schrezenmeir, J., Korhonen, H., Williams, M., Gill, H., & Shah, N. (2000). Foreword. *The British Journal of Nutrition*, (S1):1, 84.

Seppo, L., Jauhiainen, T., Poussa, T., & Korpela, R. (2003). A fermented milk high in bioactive peptides has a blood pressure–lowering effect in hypertensive subjects. *The American Journal of Clinical Nutrition*, 77(2), 326–330.

Sipola, M., Finckenberg, P., Korpela, R., Vapaatalo, H., & Nurminen, M.-L. (2002). Effect of long-term intake of milk products on blood pressure in hypertensive rats. *Journal of Dairy Research*, 69(1), 103–111.

Strain, J. S., & Cashman, K. D. (2009). Minerals and trace elements. In M. J. Gibney, S. A. Lanham-New, A. Cassidy, & H. H. Vorster(eds). *Introduction to Human Nutrition*, West Sussex, UK: Wiley Blackwell. (pp. 188–237).

Szocs, C., & Lefebvre, S. (2016). The blender effect: Physical state of food influences healthiness perceptions and consumption decisions. *Food Quality and Preference*, 54, 152–159.

Tenrisanna. (2015). *Offal and beef demand in indonesia and Australia's trade prospects*. University of Southern Queensland.

Thomson, B. C., Muir, P. D., Davison, R., & Clark, H. (2010). *Review of population models within the national methane inventory (2010)*. Technical paper prepared for the Ministry of Agriculture and Forestry by On-Farm Research. Wellington: Ministry of Agriculture and Forestry.

Toldrá, F., Aristoy, M.-C., Mora, L., & Reig, M. (2012). Innovations in value-addition of edible meat by-products. *Meat Science*, 92(3), 290–296.

USDA-FAS. (2018). Livestock and poultry: world markets and trade. Washington, USA: United States Department of Agriculture, Foreign Agricultural Service. Retrieved from https://downloads.usda.library.cornell.edu/usda esmis/files/73666448x/mg74qq69r/j6731729p/livestock_poultry.pdf

USDA. (2019). National Nutrient Database for Standard Reference. Retrieved 2020/01/19 https://ndb.nal.usda.gov/ndb/foods/show/13328?n1=%7BQv%3D1%7D&fgcd=&man=&lfacet=&count=&max=25&sort=default&qlookup=Beef%2C+variety+meats+and+by-products%2C+lungs%2C+raw&offset=&format=Full&new=&measureby=&Qv=1&ds=&qt=&qp=&qa=&qn=&q=&ing=

USDA. (2020). USDA food data central. Available from USDA Agricultural Research Service Retrieved 2020/10/01 https://fdc.nal.usda.gov/

Veeck, A. (2010). Encounters with extreme foods: Neophilic/neophobic tendencies and novel foods. *Journal of Food Products Marketing*, 16(2), 246–260.

Verardo, V., Ferioli, F., Riciputi, Y., & Iafelice, G. (2009). Evaluation of lipid oxidation in spaghetti pasta enriched with long chain n− 3 polyunsaturated fatty acids under different storage conditions. *Food Chemistry*, 114(2), 472–477.

Walton, E., & Allen, S. (2011). Malnutrition in developing countries. *Paediatrics and Child Health*, 21(9), 418–424. doi:10.1016/j.paed.2011.04.004

Wanasundara, P. K. J. P. D., Ross, A. R. S., Amarowicz, R., Ambrose, S. J., Pegg, R. B., & Shand, P. J. (2002). Peptides with Angiotensin I-Converting Enzyme (ACE) Inhibitory Activity from Defibrinated, Hydrolyzed Bovine Plasma. *Journal of Agricultural and Food Chemistry*, 50(24), 6981–6988. doi:10.1021/jf025592e

WFP, &. (2019). *Hunger map 2019* Rome, Italy: World Food Programme.

WHO. (2013). *Pocket book of hospital care for children: guidelines for the management of common childhood illnesses*. Geneva, Switzerland: World Health Organization.

Wilson, A., Reyes, E., & Ofman, J. (2004). Prevalence and outcomes of anemia in inflammatory bowel disease: a systematic review of the literature. *Am J Med*, 116(7), 44–49. doi:10.1016/j.amjmed.2003.12.011

Zhang, W., Xiao, S., Samaraweera, H., Lee, E. J., & Ahn, D. U. (2010). Improving functional value of meat products. *Meat Science*, 86(1), 15–31.

12 Food Safety Risks Associated with Novel Proteins

Malik Altaf Hussain
Food Safety Unit, The Victorian Department of Health, Melbourne, Australia

CONTENTS

12.1 Introduction 361
12.2 Food Safety Hazards and Assessment of Novel Protein Source 362
12.3 Food Safety Risks of Specific Emergent Protein Sources 364
    12.3.1 Insects 364
    12.3.2 Seaweed (Macroalgae) 367
    12.3.3 Duckweed 368
    12.3.4 Rapeseed 369
    12.3.5 Single Cell Protein 369
    12.3.6 Microalgae 370
    12.3.7 Cultured Meats 371
12.4 Control of Food Safety Hazards 371
    12.4.1 Risk Assessments 371
    12.4.2 Good Manufacturing Practices (GMPs) 372
    12.4.3 Food Safety Plans 373
12.5 Conclusion and Key Food Safety Concerns 373
Acknowledgement and declaration 373
References 373

12.1 INTRODUCTION

Novel and alternative proteins sources are rapidly entering into global food supply chains. Like conventional protein sources (such as meat, fish, milk, and eggs) for human consumption, the new protein sources (such as single cell protein, insects, duckweed, and rapeseed) could also pose food-safety risks to the consumers. However, food-safety risks of these novel protein sources are not well-documented at this stage (van der Spiegel et al., 2013). Risk-assessment reports highlight that hazards associated with the new protein sources are diverse and complex. Potential food safety hazards may include contaminants such as heavy metals, mycotoxins, pesticide residues, as well as microbial pathogens and parasites (EFSA, 2015; van der Fels-Klerx et al., 2018). Some hazards are intrinsic in nature and associated with a specific novel protein source or product. Whereas many potential hazards are extrinsic that can be introduced by production methods and processing conditions.

The current risk-assessment models and methods consider various types of hazards including physical, chemical, microbiological, and allergens. Some foodborne pathogens can be present in a novel protein source due to its food matrix that promotes the growth of specific microflora. Many other known foodborne pathogens can pose a food safety risk due to processing technology and cross-contamination. The novel protein sources can carry chemical contaminants such as toxic plant proteins, mycotoxins, heavy metals, and acrylamide. Moreover, the inclusion of alternative

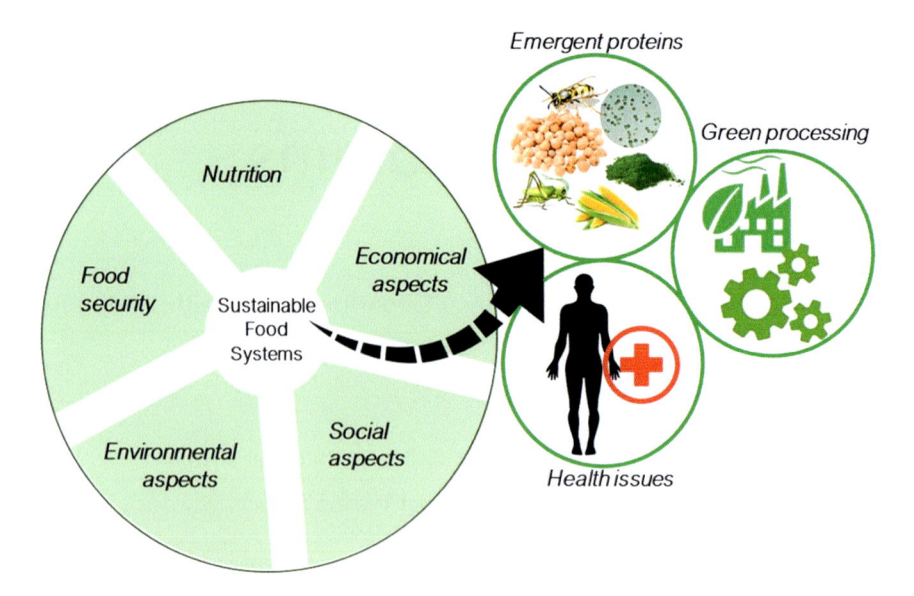

FIGURE 12.1 An overview of the emergent protein sources and their relationship with sustainable and innovative food systems as well as human health issues. The figure is from Fasolin et al. (2019) and re-used with the kind permission of Elsevier Ltd under permission number 5065740258510.

proteins in the diet could increase the risk of developing food allergies in the general population. The allergenicity aspect of the novel protein sources is discussed in Chapter 13.

Scientifically, it is understandable that the introduction of new foods in the food supply chain can also bring potential new food-safety risks. For example, food-safety risks related to newly developed products from insects, the use of genetically modified microorganisms, superfoods, edible flowers, and other sources can be unique and specific. Fasolin et al. (2019) assumed that novel protein sources will be broadly used in future food products, therefore, metabolic mechanisms (e.g., digestion and bioavailability) of these proteins in the human gastrointestinal tract must be assessed. It is important to clearly demonstrate their safety for consumers. An overview of the most promising alternative protein sources and their applications in the future food systems as well as impact on human health is presented in Figure 12.1.

It must be noted that rapidly evolving diversity in novel protein innovation presents a real challenge for food safety risk assessors. In most cases, the important information and required scientific evidence are lacking to conduct a comprehensive risk assessment. This chapter focuses on the food safety hazards and risks associated with novel protein sources.

12.2 FOOD SAFETY HAZARDS AND ASSESSMENT OF NOVEL PROTEIN SOURCE

Like any other food product, microbiological, chemical, and physical hazards, as well as allergens, are considered in the food safety assessment of novel protein sources (Figure 12.2). Microbiological hazards include bacterial pathogens, mycotoxins (fungal), viruses, parasites, and marine biotoxins (algae). Heavy metals, pesticide residues, cleaning agents, and biocides are potential chemical hazards that could be present in novel protein products. Glass, metal, wood, and other foreign materials are examples of physical hazards. Food safety hazards can enter, survive, and persist throughout the food chain. Risks associated with allergenicity, antinutritional factors (ANFs) and natural toxic chemicals are discussed in Chapter 13.

There are reports that provide an overview of potential hazards in novel protein sources such as insects, microalgae, seaweed, duckweed, and rapeseed (Banach et al., 2020; van der Spiegel et al., 2013).

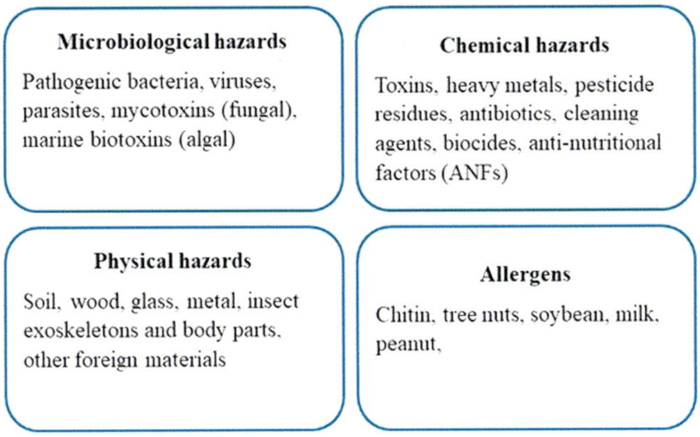

Food Safety Risks of Novel Proteins

Microbiological hazards
Pathogenic bacteria, viruses, parasites, mycotoxins (fungal), marine biotoxins (algal)

Chemical hazards
Toxins, heavy metals, pesticide residues, antibiotics, cleaning agents, biocides, anti-nutritional factors (ANFs)

Physical hazards
Soil, wood, glass, metal, insect exoskeletons and body parts, other foreign materials

Allergens
Chitin, tree nuts, soybean, milk, peanut.

FIGURE 12.2 General overview of food safety hazards associated with novel proteins.

TABLE 12.1
Summary of potential food safety hazards in selected novel protein sources

Potential Hazard	Type	Insects	Microalgae	Seaweed	Duckweed	Rapeseed	SCP	Cultured Meat
Microbiological hazards	Bacterial pathogens	Yes	Yes		Yes		Yes	Yes
	Mycotoxins	Yes						
Chemical hazards	Heavy metals	Yes	Yes	Yes	Yes	Yes		
	Pesticides	Yes	Yes	Yes	Yes			
	ANFs				Yes	Yes		
	Toxins		Yes				Yes	
	Natural toxins	Yes						
Physical hazards		Yes	Yes	Yes	Yes	Yes	Yes	Yes
Allergens		Yes	Yes	Yes		Yes		

Modified from van der Spiegel et al. (2013) using additional information from Ritala et al. (2017) and Specht et al. (2018).

Table 12.1 shows that heavy metals and processing contaminants are potential hazards in selected emergent protein sources whereas pesticides, pathogens, and allergens can be present in most protein sources (van der Spiegel et al., 2013). For example, insects and seaweed could have specific hazards present like ANFs, mycotoxins, and dioxins.

Risk analysis of any novel food source is generally carried out using universally accepted risk-assessment approaches. The Codex risk-assessment framework is commonly used. It has four key steps: hazard identification, hazard characterization, exposure assessment, and risk characterization (FAO/WHO, 2008). A risk-assessment process uses the best available scientific evidence to identify any food-safety hazard that could pose a threat to public health and safety (FAO/WHO, 2006; FSANZ, 2007). Then, this information is used for analyzing and characterizing food-related health risks. A comprehensive risk assessment is required for each novel food or ingredient to estimate the likelihood and severity of an adverse health effect occurring from exposure to a hazard. Food risk assessments look at novel food sources, nutritive substances, and the impact of new technologies as well as substances deliberately added to food and substances that occur inadvertently in food. The outcomes of risk assessments are useful to design mitigation strategies for any health and safety concerns related to a particular food. Therefore, a similar food risk assessment must be applied for an assessment of the hazard(s) and an assessment of exposure which together enable characterization of the risk posed by a novel protein source.

12.3 FOOD SAFETY RISKS OF SPECIFIC EMERGENT PROTEIN SOURCES

Food safety aspects of the emergent and novel protein sources are not well elucidated at this stage; therefore, a comprehensive risk assessment is needed (Figure 12.3) to create certainty in the decision-making process. This exercise is crucial to classify new protein sources into low- or high-risk food groups and make informed decisions to protect public health and safety. Risk assessment reports of the potential hazards in the novel protein sources would be highly useful to consider their risk profile in a particular food application. Table 12.2 provides an overview of food safety hazards detected in specific novel protein sources. The potential hazards in relation to selected novel protein sources are discussed in the sections to follow.

12.3.1 Insects

The long history of insect use as food in some parts of the world suggests that insects harvested for human consumption do not cause many risks to health and safety. According to United Nation statistics, insects make up part of the diet for around 2 billion people globally (FAO, 2013). However, insect consumption is not common in Western countries and they could suffer health risks being an unexposed population. Many food safety hazards could be present in edible insects or insect protein products including different naturally occurring chemicals such as allergens, mycotoxins, antinutritive factors, and environmental contaminants, such as heavy metals, pesticide residues, and pathogens (Van Huis et al., 2013). Like most novel foods, regulatory frameworks of edible insects are pre-mature, and in most cases no pathways are in place to specifically address safety and wholesomeness issues (Chapter 14).

Food-safety concerns need to be carefully assessed and addressed before offering edible insects and/or edible insect-derived foods for consumption by unexposed human populations, such as western consumers. This suggests that food safety issues associated with non-European insects should be identified and assessed before allowing these insects into the European markets (van der Spiegel et al., 2013). It is important to implement food safety and hygiene practices in the entire edible insect value chain to mitigate any public health and safety risks (Imathiu, 2020). An initial risk assessment of the European Food Safety Authority to use insects as a source of protein for human consumption concluded that biological and chemical hazards could be present in food

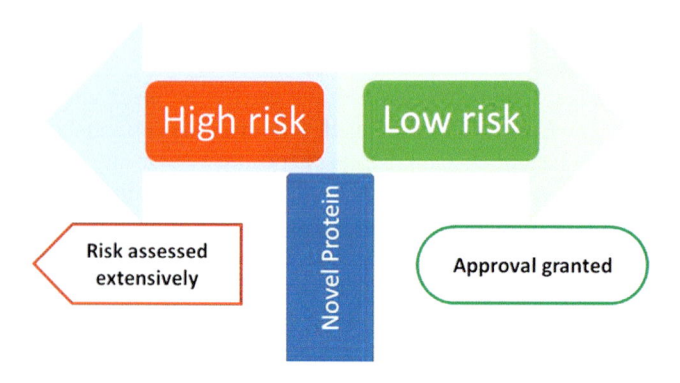

FIGURE 12.3 Comprehensive food safety risk assessment is required for each emergent protein source to classify into low- or high-risk group foods.

TABLE 12.2
Examples of specific food safety hazards associated with selected alternative protein sources

Alternative Protein Source	Hazard Type	Detailed
Insects	Microbial	Bacterial pathogens: *Staphylococcus, Micrococcus, Bacillus, Salmonella, Shigella, Clostridium*
		Parasites: *Dicrocoelium dendriticum, Entamoeba histolytica, Giardia lamblia, Toxoplasma* spp.
	Chemical	Heavy metals: Mercury, lead, cadmium, arsenic
		Toxins: Carboxylic acids, alcohols, aldehydes, alkaloids, ketones, esters, lactones, phenols, 1,4-quinones, hydrocarbons, and steroids
	Physical	Insect exoskeletons, barbs and body parts, injury from stings
	Allergens	Chitin
Microalgae	Microbial	Bacterial pathogens: General microbial contamination
	Chemical	Pesticides: Fenamiphos
	Physical	General
	Allergens	Reports on food allergy are available but more work is required
Seaweed (macroalgae)	Microbial	Bacterial pathogens: *Staph. aureus, Escherichia coli, Salmonella, Bacillus, Listeria,* or *Vibrio* spp.
	Chemical	Heavy metals: Mercury, lead, cadmium, arsenic
		Toxic substances: Dioxins such as polychlorinated dibenzo-p-dioxins
	Physical	General
	Allergens	Reports on food allergy are available but more work required
Duckweed	Microbial	Bacterial pathogens: *Escherichia coli, Clostridium botulinum*
	Chemical	Heavy metals: Cadmium, selenium, copper, chromium, nickel, lead, arsenic
		Pesticides: Organophosphorus
		Toxic substances: Phenols
	Physical	Micro- and nanoplastics
	Allergens	Not well documented
Rapeseed	Microbial	Bacterial pathogens: *Salmonella* spp., *Bacillus cereus*
	Chemical	Heavy metals: Lead, cadmium, chromium, zinc, copper
		Antinutritional factors: Erucic acid, glucosinolates
	Physical	General
	Allergens	2S storage proteins (napins)
Single cell protein	Microbial	Bacterial pathogens: Bacterial endotoxins
	Chemical	Heavy metals: Feedstock dependent
		Toxins: Mycotoxins
	Physical	General
	Allergens	Not well documented
Cultured meats	Microbial	Bacterial pathogens: General microbial contamination
	Chemical	Heavy metals: Not well documented
		Pesticides: Not well documented
		Toxins: Not well documented
	Physical	General
	Allergens	Not well documented

Based on information extracted from van der Spiegel et al. (2013), Ritala et al. (2017), Caporgno and Mathys (2018) and Barkia et al. (2019).

products derived from insects (EFSA, 2015). The prevalence and concentration of contaminants in insects and insect-derived foods depend on the production method, insect species, the stage of the life cycle at harvesting, the substrate (feed) of insects, and the method of further processing. Many reports highlighted the lack of scientific research and knowledge for rearing and use of insects as food to ensure food safety (Schlüter et al., 2017). Risk assessment of edible insects and new food products derived from insects is going to be an ongoing activity.

Current risk-assessment reports suggest that contamination of insects and insect proteins with pathogenic microorganisms, chemical and pesticide residues depend on farming practices or source (wild harvest) (EFSA, 2015). Food safety hazards, such as microbiological and chemical can be introduced or formed in concentrations that may be harmful for public health. Potential hazards of the insects include bacterial pathogens, chemical contaminants, pesticides, and allergens. One of the primary sources of the hazards is feed for insects (vegetables, and waste products) that can be contaminated with mycotoxins, natural toxins, heavy metals, veterinary residues (including antibiotics), pesticides, and pathogens. Insects can convert or accumulate contaminants present in their feed or environment, which can result in degradation or increase of the concentration of toxic substances (van der Fels-Klerx et al., 2018). Therefore, the development and enforcement of legislation for edible insect farming and harvesting as well as insect-derived food production facilities are urgently needed (Chapter 14).

Microbiological risk assessment data on the prevalence of spoilage and pathogenic microorganisms on edible insects or insect-derived foods is limited. However, it is a growing area of interest in food safety research. The pathogen contamination depends on many factors, including insect type (farmed or wild harvest), processing methods, handling and hygiene practices (Rumpold & Schluter, 2013). Several microbial pathogens, including *Staphylococcus aureus*, *Escherichia coli*, *Bacillus*, *Pseudomonas*, *Micrococcus*, *Acinetobacter*, *Proteus*, *Enterobacteriaceae* species, virus, fungi, and protozoa have been identified in insects (Klunder et al., 2012; Mezes, 2018; Vega & Kaya, 2012). *Salmonella* and *Campylobacter* species were also reported to be present in edible insects. Many harmful humans parasites, such as flukes, nematodes, *Entamoeba histolytica*, *Giardia lamblia* and *Toxoplasma* species were isolated from insects (Boye et al., 2012). Edible insects could be vectors of trypanosomiasis and ingesting fly eggs can lead to intestinal myiasis, these are also public health issues.

Microbial pathogens isolated from edible insects are known to cause many foodborne diseases and are commonly associated with outbreaks. Some scientific publications reported microbial foodborne infections and intoxications due to entomophagy (Schabel, 2010), highlighting the need for good hygiene practices in the entire edible insect food value chain to protect the health of the consumers. The prevalence of microbial pathogens is usually lower as compared to other alternative and nonprocessed animal protein sources. Hazeleger et al. (2008) found that *Campylobacter jejuni* had no active replication in the intestinal tract of insects.

Investigations into the role of edible insects in transmitting parasitic foodborne diseases are very limited. Wild-harvested insects are thought to have a higher potential in transmitting parasitic diseases to humans than that the farmed insects. This is primarily as wild insects are grown naturally under uncontrolled conditions such as their feeding habits. Entomophagy is reported to have the potential of foodborne transmission of parasites (Chai et al., 2009), the transmission of a zoonotic parasite *Dicrocoelium dendriticum* through consumption of ants, and *Entamoeba histolytica*, *Giardia lamblia,* and *Toxoplasma* spp. have been isolated in insects such as cockroaches (Boye et al., 2012). There is a lack of evidence data to link farm-reared insects to foodborne parasite transmission. Therefore, more investigations are needed to identify potential food safety risks in farmed insects and products containing insect proteins. Some examples of food safety risks identified in specific products containing insect proteins include pathogenic bacteria and their toxins, viruses, and metabolites in Mealworm (*Tenebrio molitor*) flour (Kooh et al., 2020), and spore-forming bacteria, heavy metals bioaccumulation and allergenicity are risks linked to the house cricket (*Acheta domesticus*) (SLU, 2018).

Chemical hazards are acquired by insects in two major ways. Insects produce many defensive secretions that may be reactive, irritating, or toxic. These secretions are defense chemicals such as toxins and toxic metabolites and include carboxylic acids, alcohols, aldehydes, alkaloids, ketones, esters, lactones, phenols, 1,4-quinones, hydrocarbons, and steroids. Phytochemicals sequestered by various insects include phenolics, flavin, tannins, terpenoids, polyacetylenes, alkaloids, cyanogens, glucosinolates, and mimetic amino acids (Wirtz, 1984). Insects accumulate toxic chemicals by sequestering phytochemicals directly from the food plant in higher concentrations than acceptable levels for food consumption (Schabel, 2008; Wirtz, 1984; Yen, 2008). Accumulation of heavy metals in insects depends on many factors, including the metal type, the metal concentration in the substrate, the insect species, and the growth phase of the insect (EFSA 2015; van der Fels-Klerx et al., 2016). Examples include accumulation of arsenic in *Bogong* moth and selenium in *T. molitor* from agricultural sprays, such as the herbicide monosodium methylarsenate (Green et al., 2001; Hogan & Razniak, 1991). Dolan et al. (2010) reported that toxic substances can be produced by chemical reactions of substrates of insects and other ingredients, such as heterocyclic aromatic amines, acrylamide, chloropropanols, and furans during food processing.

Physical hazards have also been identified and linked to insect consumption. Examples of such hazards include choking on insect exoskeletons and injury from stings, barbs, and body parts that contain toxins. Therefore, it is important for the food processing industry to manage physical hazards through a food-safety plan for edible insect production.

Allergic reactions due to natural allergens that may be present in some insect species pose a food safety and health risk to consumers. The reports of cross-reactions between house dust mite sensitivity and yellow mealworms create public health concerns (Verhoeckx et al., 2014). Chitin, a known allergen, is found in the exoskeletons of many insects (Zainol Abidin et al., 2020). Consumer health and safety could be managed through proper labeling of edible insect products and educating consumers on insect allergy issues (Chapter 13).

12.3.2 Seaweed (Macroalgae)

Seaweed is another promising alternative protein source that has the potential to fulfil the anticipated protein shortage challenges due to a growing world population. The current information and knowledge on the presence of food safety hazards in seaweed are scattered and limited. In a recent study, Banach et al. (2020) systematically reviewed food safety hazards in seaweed and risk to human health. They identified 22 food safety hazards in seaweed and ranked them as major (4), moderate (5), and minor (13) hazards. Seaweed type, physiology, season, harvest and cultivation environment, the location of cultivation, and further processing are the key factors that affect the presence of a hazard in seaweed. They reported arsenic, cadium, iodine, and *Salmonella* as four major hazards in seaweed influenced by intrinsic factors (such as seaweed type and physiology) and extrinsic factors (such as cultivation and harvest season, environment, geography). In general, food safety hazards of seaweed include microbial pathogens, heavy metals, pesticides contaminants, radioactive isotopes, ammonium, dioxins, iodine, ANFs, and allergens.

Microbiological hazards such as *Staph. aureus*, *E. coli*, *Salmonella*, *Bacillus*, *Listeria* and *Vibrio* spp. can contaminate seaweed during the cultivation or processing. Seaweed can become contaminated during growth, cultivation, harvest, and handling as well as further processing into food products, such as rolled sushi. Health risks could be higher when seaweed is consumed raw and without any kill step. Foodborne outbreaks related to *Salmonella* were reported to be linked to the contaminated seaweed (Beach, 2016; Nichols et al., 2017). Studies on the microbiological quality assessment of seaweed during processing and storage detected spore-forming bacteria such as *B. cereus*, *B. licheniformis* and *B. pumilus* (Blikra et al., 2019; Choi et al., 2014). Norovirus and the hepatitis E virus (HEV) may also contaminate seaweed during the cultivation or processing. A scientific report suggested that the presence of human norovirus in aquatic environments could increase the potential of outbreaks (Kim et al., 2016). Therefore, EFSA (2017) assessed the norovirus contamination of seaweed as a potentially emerging hazard.

In terms of chemical hazards, seaweeds can accumulate heavy metals (primarily arsenic, cadmium, mercury and lead) whereas types and levels of metals found in seaweed vary with species, collection time, growth phase, and collection site (Bouga & Combet, 2015; Desideri et al., 2016; Murphy, 2007; Ortega-Calvo et al., 1993; Rubio et al., 2017; Smith et al., 2010). Different seaweed species (red, green, and brown) may contain high levels of iodine (*Laminaria*) and ANFs such as low levels of lectins, tannins, and phytic acid, and high levels of trypsin inhibitors and amylase inhibitors (de Oliveira et al., 2009; Van Netten et al., 2000). A range of other chemical hazards, including accumulation of ammonium, dioxins such as polychlorinated dibenzo-p-dioxins (PCDDs) and polychlorinated dibenzofurans (PCDFs), pesticides such as azametiphos, diflubenzuron, teflubenzuron, propoxurand organic micropollutants such as polychlorinated biphenyls (PCBs), chlorinated pesticides, polycyclic aromatic hydrocarbons (PAHs) (Cheney, 2016; Hashimoto & Morita 1995; Lorenzo et al., 2012; Pavoni et al., 2003; Rees, 2003).

The reports of allergic reactions from the consumption of seaweed are available in the literature. Thomas et al. (2019) reported food allergy to seaweed in a clinical study through positive skin prick tests for red seaweeds such as *Porphyra*, *C. crispus*, and *P. palmata*. Seaweeds such *Ulva* spp. and *U. pinnatifida* showed negative skin prick tests. There is need to explore the allergenicity of seaweed (Chapter 13).

12.3.3 DUCKWEED

Duckweed is also an emerging source of protein for human food products. It is attractive to the food industry due to its high protein content and environmentally friendly production properties. One of the challenges for successful inclusion of duckweed in the diet is to increase the consumer's acceptability. The acceptability could be higher if sensory profiles of duckweed products fit with consumer expectations (de Beukelaar et al., 2019). Apart from the acceptability challenge, food safety hazards, such as the presence of microbial pathogens, heavy metals, phenols, pesticides, and dioxins, associated with duckweed consumption need to be addressed.

Many microbiological hazards could contaminate duckweed biomass including bacteria, viruses, fungi, algae, and microscopic invertebrates during the production in open greenhouse pools (Adeduntan, 2005). Hoving et al. (2011) reported that bacterial pathogens like *E. coli* or *Clostridium botulinum* in duckweed. Islam et al. (2004) studied the fecal coliform contamination of duckweed grown on hospital-based wastewater and found that wastewater-treated duckweed may be safely used as fish feed.

Many chemical hazards including heavy metals, phenols, pesticides, and dioxins were detected in duckweed. Zayed et al. (1998) demonstrated that duckweed is a good accumulator of cadmium, selenium, and copper, a moderate accumulator of chromium, and a poor accumulator of nickel and lead. However, the uptake and rate of accumulation of metals depends on factors such as the chemical form present and on the life form of the macrophytes (floating, free-floating, well rooted, or rootless) (Chandra & Kulshreshtha, 2004). Water contaminated with heavy metals increases the accumulation risk of cadmium, selenium, copper, chromium, nickel, lead, arsenic, and others (Arrhenius et al., 2006; Derksen & Zwart, 2010; Kanoun-Boulé et al., 2009; Zayed et al., 1998).

A range of other chemical hazards can be present in duckweed species phenols (Fujisawa et al., 2010) and pesticides, including organophosphorus pesticides (malathion, demeton-S-methyl, and crufomate) (Gao et al., 2000), lipophilic compounds (De Carvalho et al., 2007), 3-methyl-4-nitrophenol, 3,5-dichloroaniline, 3-phenoxybenzoic acid (Fujisawa et al., 2010), dimethomorph (Dosnon-Olette et al., 2010; Olette et al., 2008), copper sulphate and flazasulfuron (Olette et al., 2008), xenobiotics (chlorophenols) (Day & Saunders, 2004), oxalic acid (Adeduntan, 2005) and dioxins (Holshof et al., 2009). Sikorski et al. (2019) showed that glyphosate was taken up by *Lemna minor* and the plants exposed to 3 µM of glyphosate for 7 days had 10-fold of glyphosate content than the acceptable

Maximum Residue Level (MRL). It is important to develop mitigation strategies to avoid the contamination of protein products of duckweed with heavy metals, phenols, pesticides, and microbial pathogens (Hoving et al., 2011; Stomp, 2005). Sree et al. (2019) reported that duckweed had no detectable anti-proliferative or cytotoxic effects as human food.

12.3.4 Rapeseed

Key food safety hazards for rapeseed may include microbiological pathogens, chemical contaminants, heavy metals, ANFs, and allergens. Microbiological hazards such as *Salmonella* spp. and *B. cereus* could be present in the rapeseed protein isolate. However, the risk of microbial growth is considered low due to physical properties of rapeseed protein isolate being a low moisture food (as defined by the Codex Alimentarius Commission). The water activity of the rapeseed protein isolate inhibits the growth of pathogens including *Salmonella* spp. and *B. cereus* when stored under suitable storage conditions. Furthermore, rapeseed protein isolate is used as an ingredient in cooked foods such as bakery products and the microbiological growth risk is also low. Microbiological assessment to investigate prevalence and risk are required to understand safety of new applications of rapeseed in food products.

The chemical contaminants that may present in rapeseed and rapeseed protein products include pesticide residues, solvent residues, heavy metals, dioxins, aflatoxins, PAHs, and acrylamides. Rossi et al. (2004) showed that *Brassica napus* accumulated zinc and copper in the different edible parts of the plants. Another study also reported that heavy metals contaminants in the soil can accumulate in the roots, plant, and seeds of rapeseeds (Angelova et al., 2008). For example, most of lead and zinc from the soil can accumulate in the roots of *B. napus L.* whereas small amounts of them move through the conductive system to the seeds. On other hand, cadmium accumulates in higher concentrations at the top of the plant as it can easily move from root to stem. Environmental and growing conditions such as treatment with sewage water or use of greenhouse also found to increase the heavy metals (lead, cadmium, chromium, zinc, and copper) accumulation and concentrations in soil, forage, and the seed of *Brassica napus L.* (Ahmad et al., 2011; Brunetti et al., 2011). Rapeseeds are also known to contain several ANFs such as erucic acid, glucosinolates, phytic acid, phenolics such as sinapine and tannins, and high fibre content (Aider & Barbana, 2011; Bonnardeaux, 2007; Burel et al., 2000; EFSA Panel, 2016; Mejia et al., 2009).

Allergenic 2S storage proteins (napins) in rapeseed show cross-reactivity with related *Brassica* species such as mustard. These proteins have great sequence similarity with 2S albumins from different seeds (Focke et al., 1998; Monsalve et al., 2001; Poikonen et al., 2006). According to Directive 2006/142/EC of the EU, mustard is listed among the 14 allergenic foods and requires a declaration on food labels of pre-packaged foods (Chapter 13).

12.3.5 Single Cell Protein

The single-cell protein (SCP) is a concept to use the massive growth of microorganisms for human or animal consumption (Chapter 3). SCP is a generic term that describes the production of crude or refined protein from bacteria, yeasts, molds, or algae. These microorganisms usually contain more than 40% of crude protein on dry-weight bases. The advantages of SCP include considerably shorter production time, the small land requirement, and not being impacted by the weather conditions (Ritala et al., 2017). The human consumption of SCP has some food safety concerns that include RNA content, toxins, harmful substances, and allergens (Nangul & Bhatia, 2013; Scrimshaw & Murray, 2008).

Toxins production by microorganisms (production hosts or contaminants) is a major food safety hazard. Anupama and Ravindra (2000) reported that some fungi produce mycotoxins that make unacceptable to use for SCP production. The fungal toxins are very harmful and could cause allergy, cancer, and death. For example, commercial SCP product Quorn™ mycoprotein was extensively investigated for the presence of mycotoxins or other toxic compounds prior to food use approval (Wiebe, 2004). Similarly, the fungus *Y. lipolytica* was also extensively assessed for safety to use as a source of SCP (Groenewald et al., 2014). The ability of many bacterial species to produce toxins (endotoxins or exotoxins) also makes it difficult to use as SCP. For example, the potential bacterial candidates of SCP such as *Pseudomonas* spp. and *Methylomonas methanica* are endotoxins producers that cause febrile reactions (Rudravaram et al., 2009). A careful selection of the production organism, and optimized process conditions and the product formulation are important to resolve the toxins production issue.

High nucleic acid (RNA) content in SCP products could pose health risks to consumers. For instance, bacterial SCP products may contain up to 16% of nucleic acids on dry weight basis. Calloway (1974) reported that consumption of more than 2 g of nucleic acid daily could cause kidney stone formation and gout. Research has been carried out to decrease RNA contents and methods are in use at an industrial scale (Abou-Zeid et al., 1995; Lewis et al., 1982). Moreover, harmful substances such as heavy metals derived from the feedstock, biomass hydrolysates or waste streams in particular, could pose health risks to consumers (Wiebe, 2004). The food safety aspects of SCP are challenging and must be carefully considered before introducing SCPs in human diets.

12.3.6 MICROALGAE

Microalgae is regarded as an alternative protein source to meet growing protein demand in the future. This promising protein source offers several advantages over traditional protein sources: more sustainable, lower environmental footprint, and provides bioactive compounds with potential benefits for human health (Caporgno & Mathys, 2018). However, the food industry is facing several challenges to exploit microalgae as a source of protein (bulk protein) due to the underdeveloped technologies and processes currently available for microalgae processing. One of the major challenges is the scalability of protein extraction from algae that is still very much in its infancy (Matos, 2019). In general, food safety hazards related to microalgae consumption may include microbial pathogens, heavy metals, pesticides, toxins, undefined biochemicals, and allergens (Barkia et al., 2019; Kerkvliet, 2001). However, similar to other novel protein sources, the food safety hazards and health risks associated with the consumption of microalgae are not well documented (Caporgno & Mathys, 2018).

Kerkvliet (2001) reported that microbiological pathogens could be present in spirulina and chlorella that are cultivated in open basins due to cross-contamination from birds, insects, and rodents. Chemical hazards such as heavy metals, pesticides, and toxins are associated with microalgae consumption. Microalgae may accumulate heavy metals, especially sludge-grown algae contain rather substantial amounts of heavy metals that may impose adverse effects on higher trophic organisms (Hung et al., 1996; Wong et al., 1996). The accumulation of heavy metals could be species-dependent, for example, spirulina accumulates more heavy metals than chlorella (Kerkvliet, 2001). Some microalgae, such as *Pseudokirchneriella subcapitata* and *Chlorococcum* spp., can transform and accumulate the metabolites of the pesticide fenamiphos that adversely impact the food chain and associated biota through contamination of natural environments (Caceres et al., 2008). Toxic microcystines were detected in *Aphanizomenon flos-aqua* whereas no toxins were found in spirulina and chlorella (Heussner et al., 2012; Kerkvliet 2001). Barkia et al. (2019) highlighted that more scientific research is needed on the content, acceptability, and safety of microalgal products for human consumption.

Allergic reactions from microalgal species including the green algal genus *Chlorella* as well as airborne cyanobacteria *Phormidium fragile* and *Nostoc muscorum* were reported (Sharma & Rai, 2008; Tiberg & Einarsson, 1989). The potential of food allergy due to microalgae is discussed in Chapter 13.

12.3.7 CULTURED MEATS

The predicted protein shortage for human consumption also encouraged scientists and entrepreneurs to explore new technologies for food production. The concept of laboratory-grown or cultured meat is to grow muscle tissue from animal cells through replication under *in vitro* conditions. Chapter 9 discusses *in vitro* meats and technologies used in detail. The advocates of cultured meat technology talk about potential environmental, ethical, and safety benefits compared to traditional animal farming. Last year, Singapore became the first country to grant regulatory approval to sell "chicken nuggets" manufactured using plant-based ingredients and cultured chicken in its market (SFA, 2020a). However, Singapore Food Agency acknowledges that the science for producing cultured meat is still at an early stage.

Scientific opinion on food safety risks associated with cultured meat is not firm. Challenges to conducting independent risk assessments of cultured meats or products include unavailability of commercial products and confidentiality of innovating companies. According to Specht et al. (2018) cultured meat production technologies use similar recombinant growth factors (proteins and hormones) that are naturally found in meat and therefore it would not pose a novel protein risk. On other hand, cultured meat has physio-chemical properties that are similar to an animal muscle that is highly susceptible to microbial contamination, therefore, temperature control to limit the growth of pathogens would be necessary. Some industry experts believe that cultured meat production facilities operate using high environmental and hygiene control, therefore, the risk of bacterial contamination is low (King, 2019). However, it must be noted that like all food, the safety of cultured meat depends on the food safety assessment and control of potential hazards along the production process.

It is important to note that the substances used during cultured meat production and the final composition of the product is important in assessing the safety status.. For example, a cultured meat product could contain a mixture of cultured meat and other ingredients and additives, then each ingredient will need to be evaluated for safety. However, at this stage, it seems impossible to predict what hazards (if any) this new technology could bring to human health until the food matrix and manufacturing process are well known.

12.4 CONTROL OF FOOD SAFETY HAZARDS

Introduction of a novel protein source for human consumption put the responsibility on food producer to control any potential food safety hazard associated with the new product. Food producers are responsible to demonstrate that their products are safe. A novel protein source could have some intrinsic food safety aspects whereas many potential hazards can be controlled through the implementation of processing controls and Good Manufacturing Practices (GMPs). The best way to manage intrinsic safety concerns is by selecting a species or a variety of the protein source that can affect safety due to differences in allergenicity, metabolism, and composition. For example, the selection of rapeseed varieties containing less ANFs (erucic acid and glucosinlates) is the only effective control measure to use it as a protein source safely.

12.4.1 RISK ASSESSMENTS

Food safety risk assessments are important scientific tools to assess the health and safety concerns associated with novel protein sources. The outputs of food safety assessments provide information on the type and nature of hazards that could pose a health risk to consumers. Therefore, the results facilitate the decision-making process on a risk management approach. The risk assessment and risk management approaches are designed to protect the health of consumers by controlling risk.

Risk assessments are used for multiple purposes. For instance, producers of novel proteins are responsible to prepare dossiers and conduct risk-assessments of their new products to demonstrate the safety and no adverse effect on the consumer's health. Whereas food regulatory agencies use food safety assessments to grant approval to a novel protein source. Generally, regulatory risk assessments are comprehensive and take many aspects into considerations to inform about potential food safety hazards, risk management approaches, public health policy guidance, consumer behaviors, and economic and regulatory inputs (FAO/WHO, 2007). Many factors including the objectives of the assessor could affect the risk assessment outputs; therefore, results need to be considered and interpreted within the context of available information. In the EU, risk assessments of novel foods are carried out by European Food Safety Authority (EFSA) to ensure harmonized scientific assessment and outputs.

It is important that the criteria for the assessment of the safety risks arising from novel foods should also be clearly defined and laid down. Therefore, it is not surprising to see differences in the requirements and information needed by regulatory agencies in each country or territory. For example, much scientific and technical information is required by SFA to assess a product application that may change based on the developments in the science of producing cultured meat (Table 12.3).

12.4.2 Good Manufacturing Practices (GMPs)

GMPs play a vital role in controlling food safety and minimizing the risk of contamination. Generally, GMPs requirements offer a practical way to develop a controlled production system for novel proteins. Processing conditions of novel protein products can also affect the safety of novel

---

TABLE 12.3

Information (criteria) to be submitted to Singapore Food Authority for the safety assessment of cultured meat

i. A description of the overall manufacturing process.
ii. Characterization of the cultured meat product, including nutritional composition, and comparison of residual growth factors against levels in published literature.
iii. Information related to the cell lines used, including:
   a. Identity and source of cell lines.
   b. Description of methods used for selection and screening of cells.
   c. Information on how the cell lines are prepared and banked following their extraction from animals.
   d. Description of the modifications and adaptions made to the cell lines, and how these relate to the expression of substances that may result in food safety risk.
iv. Information related to the culture media used, including:
   a. Composition of media, including identities and purity of all added substances. Companies should indicate whether the purity of individual substances used in culture media comply with specifications recommended by the Joint FAO/WHO Expert Committee on Food Additives (JECFA, British Pharmacopoeia, European Pharmacopoeia or Food Chemical Codex).
   b. Clarification on whether the culture media remains in the finished cultured meat product, or is removed completely. Where culture media is removed completely, companies should provide information demonstrating removal.
v. Information related to the scaffolding materials, if used, including:
   a. Identities and purity of scaffolding materials used.
vi. Information on how your company ensures the purity and genetic stability of cell culture during the manufacturing process.
   a. Where genetic differences between starter cell lines and finished cultured meat are observed, companies should investigate the differences to determine whether these would result in food safety risks (e.g. upregulation of metabolite production).
vii. Safety assessment covering possible hazards arising from the manufacturing of the cultured meat.
viii. Other relevant studies to support safety such as digestibility assays, allergen profiling, genetic sequencing, etc.

Source: SFA, 2020b.

proteins in many ways, for example, heating of products containing novel proteins can result in the formation of hazardous compounds like acrylamide. The use of solvent-extraction techniques for novel protein products can also affect food safety. Therefore, it is necessary to consider the manufacturing aspects of novel protein products during the product development stage.

Many regulatory agencies are applying GMPs as a tool to control food safety hazards in novel foods. Under EU regulations, the Good Manufacturing Practice (GMP) Regulation (EC) No 2023/2006 obliges any producer to define aspects of quality assurance that ensure that materials and articles are consistently produced and controlled to ensure conformity with the rules applicable to them and with the quality standards appropriate to their intended uses by not endangering human health.

12.4.3 Food Safety Plans

Implementation of a food safety management system such as HACCP could also be a useful tool to proactively monitor, and control hazards associated with the production of a novel protein product. A food-safety plan helps in identifying the critical control points (CCPs) in a process to manage a particular hazard that may enter a food product. For example, in the case of insect protein production, the feed of insects may contain several contaminants that insects may metabolize and accumulate and become a health risk for consumers. Therefore, the selection of feed is regarded as a CCP and it is important to provide contaminant-free feed to insects. Similarly, contaminated water resources to produce microalgae, seaweed, duckweed, and rapeseed could lead to the accumulation of heavy metals from the environment. Therefore, the use of controlled conditions to produce microalgae, seaweed, duckweed, and rapeseed can be considered as a CCP.

12.5 CONCLUSION AND KEY FOOD SAFETY CONCERNS

Consumption of novel proteins, such as plant-based, insects, and algae, is predicted to increase in the world as replacers for animal-derived proteins. Food-safety hazards associated with novel protein sources are like other proteins and include microbiological, chemical, physical and allergens. Scientific and technical information is emerging at this stage; in many cases, possible food safety hazards associated with the use of novel proteins are hardly known. Novel protein sources are reported to carry a range of contaminants including allergens, microbial pathogens, heavy metals, mycotoxins, and pesticide residues. The presence of safety hazards depends on the novel protein source and production methods. Food-safety assessment of emergent proteins is of utmost importance to inform about the nature of risk(s) and management approaches. Therefore, more attention should be directed towards the risk assessment of novel protein sources and developing food safety hazards control strategies to ensure public health and safety.

ACKNOWLEDGEMENT AND DECLARATION

The author declares no conflict of interest. The views and opinions expressed in this chapter are the author's own and do not reflect the position of the Victorian Department of Health.

REFERENCES

Abou-Zeid, A. A., Khan, J. A., & Abulnaja, K. O. (1995). On methods for reduction of nucleic acids content in a single-cell protein from gas oil. *Bioresource Technology, 52*, 21–24.

Adeduntan, S. A. (2005). Nutritional and antinutritional characteristics of some insects foraging in Akure Forest Reserve Ondo State, Nigeria. *Journal of Food Technology, 3*(4), 563–567.

Ahmad, K., Ejaz, A., Azam, M., Khan, Z. I., Ashraf, M., Al-Qurainy, F., Fardous, A., Gondal, S., Bayat, A. R., & Valeem, E. E. (2011). Lead, cadmium and chromium contents of canola irrigated with sewage water. *Pakistan Journal of Botany, 43*(2), 1403–1410.

Aider, M., & Barbana, C. (2011). Canola proteins: Composition, extraction, functional properties, bioactivity, applications as a food ingredient and allergenicity – A practical and critical review. *Trends in Food Science and Technology, 22*(1), 21–39.

Angelova, V., Ivanova, R., Todorov, G., & Ivanov, K. (2008). Heavy metal uptake by rape. *Communications in Soil Science and Plant Analysis, 39*(3-4), 344–357.

Anupama, & Ravindra, P. (2000). Value-added food: Single cell protein. *Biotechnology Advances, 18*, 459–479. doi:10.1016/S0734-9750(00)00045-8

Arrhenius, Å., Backhaus, T., Grönvall, F., Junghans, M., Scholze, M., & Blanck, H. (2006). Effects of three antifouling agents on algal communities and algal reproduction: Mixture toxicity studies with TBT, Irgarol, and Sea-Nine. *Archives of Environmental Contamination and Toxicology, 50*(3), 335–345.

Banach, J. L., Hoek-van den Hil, E. F. & van der Fels-Klerx, H. L. (2020). Food safety hazards in the European seaweed chain. *Comprehensive Reviews in Food Science and Food Safety, 19*, 332–364.

Barkia, I., Saari, N., & Manning, S. R. (2019). Microalgae for high-value products towards human health and nutrition. *Marine Drugs, 17*(5), 304. doi:10.3390/md17050304

Beach, C. (2016). Seaweed farm linked to *Salmonella* outbreak recalls products [Press release]. https://www.foodsafetynews.com/2016/11/seaweed-farm-linked-to-salmonella-outbreak-recalls-products/. Accessed March 25, 2021.

Blikra, M. J., Løvdal, T., Vaka, M. R., Roiha, I. S., Lunestad, B. T., Lindseth, C., & Skipnes, D. (2019). Assessment of food quality and microbial safety of brown macroalgae (*Alaria esculenta* and *Saccharina latissima*). *Journal of the Science of Food and Agriculture, 99*(3), 1198–1206.

Bonnardeaux, J. (2007). *Uses for Canola Meal. State of Western Australia*. Department of Agriculture and Food, Western Australia.

Bouga, M., & Combet, E. (2015). Emergence of seaweed and seaweed-containing foods in the UK: Focus on labeling, iodine content, toxicity and nutrition. *Foods, 4*(2), 240–253.

Boye, J., Danquah, A. O., Thang, C., & Zhao, X. (2012). Food allergens. *Clinical Reviews in Allergy & Immunology, 3*, 798–819.

Brunetti, G., Farrag, K., Soler-Rovira, P., Nigro, F., & Senesi, N. (2011). Greenhouse and field studies on Cr, Cu, Pb and Zn phytoextraction by *Brassica napus* from contaminated soils in the Apulia region, Southern Italy. *Geoderma, 160*(3-4), 517–523.

Burel, C., Boujard, T., Escaffre, A. M., Kaushik, S. J., Boeuf, G., Mol, K. A., der Geyten, S. V., & Kühn, E. R. (2000). Dietary low-glucosinolate rapeseed meal affects thyroid status and nutrient utilization in rainbow trout (*Oncorhynchus mykiss*). *British Journal of Nutrition, 83*, 653–664.

Caceres, T., Megharaj, M., & Naidu, R. (2008). Toxicity and transformation of fenamiphos and its metabolites by two micro algae *Pseudokirchneiriella subcapitata* and *Chlorococcum* sp. *Science of the Total Environment, 398*(1-3), 53–59.

Calloway, D. H. (1974). The place of single cell protein in man's diet. In: *Single Cell Protein*. Davis, P. (Ed). New York: Academic Press, 129–146.

Caporgno, M. P. & Mathys, A. (2018). Trends in microalgae incorporation into innovative food products with potential health benefits. *Frontiers in Nutrition, 5*, 58.

Chai, J. Y., Shin, E. H., Lee, S. H., & Rim, H. J. (2009). Foodborne intestinal flukes in Southeast Asia. *Korean Journal of Parasitology, 47*, S69–S102.

Chandra, P., & Kulshreshtha, K. (2004). Chromium accumulation and toxicity in aquatic vascular plants. *The Botanical Review, 70*(3), 313–327.

Cheney, D. (2016). Toxic and harmful seaweeds. In: *Seaweed in Health and Disease Prevention*. Fleurence, J., & Levine, I. (Eds). London, UK: Elsevier, 407–421.

Choi, E. S., Kim, N. H., Kim, H. W., Kim, S. A., Jo, J. I., Kim, S. H., … Rhee, M. S. (2014). Microbiological quality of seasoned roasted laver and potential hazard control in a real processing line. *Journal of Food Protection, 77*(12), 2069–2075.

Day, J. A., & Saunders, F. M. (2004). Glycosidation of chlorophenols by *Lemna minor*. *Environmental Toxicology and Chemistry, 23*(3), 613–620.

De Carvalho, R. F., Bromilow, R. H., & Greenwood, R. (2007). Uptake of pesticides from water by curly waterweed *Lagarosiphon major* and lesser duckweed *Lemna minor*. *Pest Management Science, 63*(8), 789–797.

de Beukelaar, M. F. A., Zeinstra, G. G., Mes, J. J., & Fischer, A. R. H. (2019). Duckweed as human food. The influence of meal context and information on duckweed acceptability of Dutch consumers. *Food Quality and Preference, 71*, 76–86.

de Oliveira, M. N., Freitas, A. L. P., Carvalho, A. F. U., Sarnpaio, T. M. T., Farias, D. F., Teixeira, D. I. A., Gouveia, S. T., Pereira, J. G., & de Sena, M. (2009). Nutritive and non-nutritive attributes of washed-up seaweeds from the coast of Ceara, Brazil. *Food Chemistry, 115*(1), 254–259.

Derksen, H., & Zwart, L. (2010). Eendenkroos als nieuw eiwit- en zetmeelgewas: Haalbaarheidsstudie November 2010, eindrapport. s.l.: Stichting Sustenable Forum.

Desideri, D., Cantaluppi, C., Ceccotto, F., Meli, M. A., Roselli, C., & Feduzi, L. (2016). Essential and toxic elements in seaweeds for human consumption. *Journal of Toxicology and Environmental Health A, 79*(3), 112–122.

Dolan, L. C., Matulka, R. A., & Burdock, G. A. (2010). Naturally occurring food toxins. *Toxins, 2*(9), 2289–2332.

Dosnon-Olette, R., Couderchet, M., El Arfaoui, A., Sayen, S., & Eullaffroy, P. (2010). Influence of initial pesticide concentrations and plant population density on dimethomorph toxicity and removal by two duckweed species. *Science of the Total Environment, 408*(10), 2254- 2259.

EFSA. (2015). Risk profile related to production and consumption of insects as food and feed. https://www.efsa.europa.eu/en/efsajournal/pub/4257. Accessed April 18, 2021.

EFSA, Afonso, A., García Matas, R., Maggiore, A., Merten, C., & Robinson, T. (2017). *EFSA's Activities on Emerging Risks in 2016*. Parma, Italy: EFSA. https://efsa.onlinelibrary.wiley.com/doi/10.2903/sp.efsa.2017.EN-1336. Accessed April 19, 2021.

EFSA Panel on Contaminants in the Food Chain (CONTAM), Knutsen, H. K., Alexander, J., Barregård, L., Bignami, M., Brüschweiler, B., Ceccatelli, S., Dinovi, M., Edler, L., Grasl-Kraupp, B., Hogstrand, C., Hoogenboom, L (Ron)., Nebbia, C. S., Oswald, I., Petersen, A., Rose, M., Roudot, A. C., Schwerdtle, T., Vollmer, G., Wallace, H., Cottrill, B., Dogliotti, E., Laakso, J., Metzler, M., Velasco, L., Baert, K., Ruiz, J. A. G., Varga, E., Dörr, B., Sousa, R., & Vleminckx, C, (2016). Scientific Opinion on erucic acid in feed and food. *EFSA Journal, 14*(11), 4593.

FAO. (2013). *Edible Insects: Future Prospects for Food and Feed Security*. Food and Agriculture Organization of the United Nations. http://www.fao.org/3/i3253e/i3253e.pdf. Accessed April 19, 2021.

FAO/WHO. (2006). *Food Safety Risk Analysis - Part I - An Overview and Framework Manual*, Provisional Edition. Food and Agriculture Organization of the United Nations, Rome. https://www.fsc.go.jp/sonota/foodsafety_riskanalysis.pdf Accessed April 19, 2021.

FAO/WHO. (2007). *Working Principles for Risk Analysis for Food Safety for Application by Governments (Codex alimentarius)*, First Edition. Rome, Food and Agriculture Organization of the United Nations. http://www.fao.org/3/a1550t/a1550t.pdf. Accessed April 19, 2021.

FAO/WHO. (2008). *Codex Alimentarius Commission Procedural Manual*, 18th Edition. Rome, Food and Agriculture Organization of the United Nations, Codex Alimentarius Commission. ftp://ftp.fao.org/codex/Publications/ProcManuals/ Manual_18e.pdf. Accessed April 19, 2021.

Fasolin, L. H., Pereira, R. N., Pinheiro, A. C. Martins, J. T. Andrade, C. C. P. Ramos, O. L. & Vicente, A. A. (2019). Emergent Food Proteins - Towards Sustainability, Health and Innovation. *Food Research International, 25*, 108586.

Focke, M., Hemmer, W., Kriechbaumer, N., Gotz, M., & Jarisch, R. (1998). Common allergens in pollen and seeds from oilseed rape (*Brassica napus*) and demonstration of cross-reacting proteins in seeds from other plant families. *The Journal of Allergy and Clinical Immunology, 101*(1), S200.

FSANZ (2007). Safety Assessment of Genetically Modified Foods – Guidance Document. http://www.foodstandards.gov.au/consumer/gmfood/safety/documents/GM%20FINAL%20Sept%2007L%20_2_.pdf. Accessed March 25, 2021.

Fujisawa, T., Ichise-Shibuya, K., & Katagi, T. (2010). Uptake and transformation of phenols by duckweed (*Lemna gibba*). *Journal of Pesticide Science, 35*(4), 456–463.

Gao, J., Garrison, A. W., Hoehamer, C., Mazur, C. S., & Wolfe, N. L. (2000). Uptake and phyto-transformation of organophosphorus pesticides by axenically cultivated aquatic plants. *Journal of Agricultural and Food Chemistry, 48*(12), 6114–6120.

Green, K., Broome, L., Heinze, D., & Johnston, S. (2001). Long distance transport of arsenic by migrating Bogong moths from agricultural lowlands to mountain ecosystems. *Victorian Naturalist, 118*(4), 112–116.

Groenewald, M., Boekhout, T., Neuvéglise, C., Gaillardin, C., van Dijck, P. W. M., & Wyss, M. (2014). *Yarrowia lipolytica*: Safety assessment of an oleaginous yeast with a great industrial potential. *Critical Reviews in Microbiology, 40*, 187–206.

Hashimoto, S., & Morita, M. (1995). Analysis of PCDDs, PCDFs, planar and other PCBs in seaweed from Japanese coast. *Chemosphere, 31*(8), 3887–3897.

Hazeleger, W. C., Bolder, N. M., Beumer, R. R., & Jacobs-Reitsma, W. F. (2008). Darkling beetles (*Alphitobius diaperinus*) and their larvae as potential vectors for the transfer of *Campylobacter jejuni* and *Salmonella enterica* serovar paratyphi B variant Java between successive broiler flocks. *Applied and Environmental Microbiology, 74*(22), 6887–6891.

Heussner, A. H., Mazija, L., Fastner, J., & Dietrich, D. R. (2012). Toxin content and cytotoxicity of algal dietary supplements. *Toxicology and Applied Pharmacology, 265*(2), 263–271.

Hogan, G. R., & Razniak, H. G. (1991). Selenium-induced mortality and tissue distribution studies in *Tenebrio molitor* (Coleoptera: Tenebrionidae). *Environmental Entomology, 20*(3), 790–794.

Holshof, G., Hoving, I. E., & Peeters E. T. H. M. (2009). *Eendenkroos: van afval tot veevoer*. Lelystad: Livestock Research Wageningen.

Hoving, I. E., Van Schooten, H. A., Holshof, G., Van Houwelingen, K. M., & Van de Geest, W. (2011). *Inkuilen van eendenkroos als veevoer met verschillende additieven*. Livestock Research Wageningen UR, Lelystad.

Hung, K. M., Chiu, S. T., & Wong, M. H. (1996). Sludge-grown algae for culturing aquatic organisms: Part 1. Algal growth in sludge extracts. *Environmental Management, 20*(3), 361–374.

Imathiu, S. (2020). Benefits and food safety concerns associated with consumption of edible insects. *NFS Journal, 18*, 1–11.

Islam, M. S., Kabir, M. S., Khan, S. I., Ekramullah, M., Nair, G. B., Sack, R. B., & Sack, D. A. (2004). Wastewater-grown duckweed may be safely used as fish feed. *Canadian Journal of Microbiology, 50*(1), 51–56.

Kanoun-Boulé, M., Vicente, J. A. F., Nabais, C., Prasad, M. N. V., & Freitas, H. (2009). Ecophysiological tolerance of duckweeds exposed to copper. *Aquatic Toxicology, 91*(1), 1–9.

Kerkvliet, J. D. (2001). Algen en zeewieren als levensmiddel: een overzicht. *De Ware(n)chemicus, 31*, 77–104.

Kim, M. S., Koo, E. S., Choi, Y. S., Kim, J. Y., Yoo, C. H., Yoon, H. J., ... Kirk, M. E. (2016). Distribution of human norovirus in the coastal waters of South Korea. *PLoS One, 11*(9), e0163800.

King, T. (2019). Meat re-imagined: Alternative proteins and what they mean for *Australia. Food Australia, 2019*, 24–27.

Klunder, H. C., Wolkers-Rooijackers, J., Korpela, J. M. & Nout, M. J. R. (2012). Microbiological aspects of processing and storage of edible insects. *Food Control, 26*, 628–631.

Knudsen, I., Søborg, I., Eriksen, F., Pilegaard, K., & Pedersen, J. (2005). *Risk Assessment and Risk Management of Novel Plant Foods: Concepts and Principles*. Nordic Council of Ministers, Copenhagen, Denmark.

Kooh, P., Jury, V., Laurent, S., Audiat-Perrin, F., Sanaa, M., Tesson, V., Federighi, M., & Boué, G. (2020). Control of biological hazards in insect processing: Application of HACCP method for yellow mealworm (*Tenebrio molitor*) powders. *Foods, 9*, 1528. doi:10.3390/foods9111528

Lewis, P. N., Lawford, H. G., Kligerman, A., & Lawford, G. R. (1982). A novel method for reducing the RNA content of single cell protein isolates. *Biotechnology Letters, 4*, 441–446. doi:10.1007/BF01134593

Lorenzo, R. A., Pais, S., Racamonde, I., Garcia-Rodriguez, D., & Carro, A. M. (2012). Pesticides in seaweed: Optimization of pressurized liquid extraction and in-cell clean-up and analysis by liquid chromatography-mass spectrometry. *Analytical and Bioanalytical Chemistry, 404*(1), 173–181.

Matos, A. P. (2019). Microalgae as a potential source of proteins in proteins. In: *Sustainable Source, Processing and Applications*. Galanakis, C. M. (Ed). Academic Press, Elsevier Inc, 63–96.

Mejia, L. A., Korgaonkar, C. K., Schweizer, M., Chengelis, C., Marit, G., Ziemer, E., Grabiel, R., & Empie, M. (2009). A 13-week sub-chronic dietary toxicity study of a cruciferin-rich canola protein isolate in rats. *Food Chemistry and Toxicology, 47*(10), 2645–2654.

Mezes, M. (2018). Food safety aspects of insects: A review. *Acta Alimentaria, 47*, 513–522.

Monsalve, R. I., Villalba, M., & Rodríguez, R. (2001). Allergy to mustard seeds: The importance of 2S albumins as food allergens. *Internet Symposium on Food Allergens, 3*(2), 57–69.

Murphy, V. (2007). An investigation into the mechanisms of heavy metal binding by selected seaweed species. Doctorate thesis, Waterford Institute of Technology, Waterford City, Ireland.

Nangul, A., & Bhatia, R. (2013) Microorganisms: A marvelous source of single cell proteins. *Journal of Microbiology, Biotechnology and Food Sciences, 3*, 15–18.

Nichols, C., Ching-Lee, M., Daquip, C.-L., Elm, J., Kamagai, W., Low, E., ... & Park, S. Y. (2017). Outbreak of salmonellosis associated with seaweed from a local aquaculture farm—Oahu, 2016. Paper presented at the CSTE, Boise, ID. https://cste.confex.com/cste/2017/webprogram. Accessed April 10, 2021.

Olette, R., Couderchet, M., Biagianti, S., & Eullaffroy, P. (2008). Toxicity and removal of pesticides by selected aquatic plants. *Chemosphere, 70*(8), 1414–1421.

Ortega-Calvo, J. J., Mazuelos, C., Hermosin, B., & Saizjimenez, C. (1993). Chemical-composition of *Spirulina* and eukaryotic algae food-products marketed in Spain. *Journal of Applied Phycology, 5*(4), 425–435.

Pavoni, B., Caliceti, M., Sperni, L., & Sfriso, A. (2003). Organic micropollutants (PAHs, PCBs, pesticides) in seaweeds of the lagoon of Venice. *Oceanologica Acta, 26*(5-6), 585–596.

Poikonen, S., Puumalainen, T. J., Kautiainen, H., Burri, P., Palosuo, T., Reunala, T., & Turjanmaa, K. (2006). Turnip rape and oilseed rape are new potential food allergens in children with atopic dermatitis. *Allergy, 61*(1), 124–127.

Rees, T. A. V. (2003). Safety factors and nutrient uptake by seaweeds. *Marine Ecology Progress Series, 263*, 29–42.

Ritala, A., Hakkinen, S.T., Toivari, M., & Wiebe, M. G. (2017). Single cell protein-state-of-the-art, industrial landscape and patents 2001-2016. *Frontiers in Microbiology, 8*(Oct), art. no. 2009.

Rossi, G., Figliolia, A., & Socciarelli, S. (2004). Zinc and copper bioaccumulation in *Brassica napus* at flowering and maturation. *Engineering in Life Sciences, 4*(3), 271–275.

Rubio, C., Napoleone, G., Luis-González, G., Gutiérrez, A. J., González-Weller, D., Hardisson, A., & Revert, C. (2017). Metals in edible seaweed. *Chemosphere, 173*, 572–579.

Rudravaram, R., Chandel, A. K., Rao, L. V., Hui, Y. Z., & Ravindra, P. (2009). Bio (single cell) protein: Issues of production, toxins and commercialisation status. In: *Agricultural Wastes*. Ashworth, G. S., & Azevedo, P. (Eds). New York, NY: Hauppage, 129–153.

Rumpold, B. A. & Schluter O. K. (2013). Nutritional composition and safety aspects of edible insects. *Molecular Nutrition & Food Research, 57*, 802–823.

Schabel, H. G. (2008). Forest insects as food: A global review. In: *Forest Insects as Food: Humans Bite Back*. Durst, P. B., Johnson, D. V., Leslie, R. N., & Shono, K. (Eds). Proceedings of a Workshop on Asia-Pacific Resources and Their Potential for Development. RAP Publication 2010/02, February 19–21, 2008, Chiang Mai, Thailand, 1–4.

Schabel, H. G. (2010). *Forest Insects as Food: Humans Bite Back*. FAO, Bangkok, Thailand, 37–64.

Schlüter, O., Rumpold, B., Holzhauser, T., Roth, A., Vogel, R. F., Quasigroch, W., Vogel, S., Heinz, V., Jäger, H., Bandick, N., Kulling, S., Knorr, D., Steinberg, P., & Engel, K. (2017). Safety aspects of the production of foods and food ingredients from insects. *Molecular Nutrition & Food Research, 61*, 1600520.

Scrimshaw, N., & Murray, E. (2008). Nutritional Value and Safety of "Single Cell Protein". In: *Biotechnology: Enzymes, Biomass, Food and Feed*. Rehm, H.-J., & Reed, G. (Eds). VCH Verlagsgesellschaft mbH, 221–237.

SFA. (2020a). Safety of Alternative Protein. https://www.sfa.gov.sg/food-information/risk-at-a-glance/safety-of-alternative-protein Accessed April 20, 2021.

SFA. (2020b). Requirements for the Safety Assessment of Novel Foods. https://www.sfa.gov.sg/docs/default-source/food-import-and-export/Requirements-on-safety-assessment-of-novel-foods_23-Nov-2020.pdf. Accessed April 20, 2021.

Sharma, N. K., & Rai, A. K. (2008). Allergenicity of airborne cyanobacteria *Phormidium fragile* and *Nostoc muscorum*. *Ecotoxicology and Environmental Safety, 69*(1), 158–162.

Sikorski, Ł., Baciak, M., Bęś, A., & Adomas, B. (2019). The effects of glyphosate-based herbicide formulations on *Lemna minor*, a non-target species. *Aquatic Toxicology, 209*, 70–80.

SLU, Swedish University of Agricultural Sciences, Department of Biomedical Sciences and Veterinary Public Health, Fernandez-Cassi, X., Supeanu, A., Jansson, A., Boqvist, S., & Vagsholm, I. (2018). Novel foods: A risk profile for the house cricket (*Acheta domesticus*). *EFSA Journal, 16*(Suppl 1), e16082. doi:10.2903/j.efsa.2018.e16082

Smith, J. L., Summers, G., & Wong, R. (2010). Nutrient and heavy metal content of edible seaweeds in New Zealand. *New Zealand Journal of Crop and Horticultural Science, 38*(1), 19–28.

Specht, E. A., Welch, D. R., Clayton, E. M. R., & Lagally, C. D. (2018). Opportunities for applying biomedical production and manufacturing methods to the development of the clean meat industry. *Biochemical Engineering Journal, 132*, 161–168.

Sree, K. S., Dahse, H. M., Chandran, J. N., Schneider, B., Jahreis, G., & Appenroth, K. J. (2019). Duckweed for human nutrition: No cytotoxic and no anti-proliferative effects on human cell lines. *Plant Foods for Human Nutrition, 74*, 223–224. doi:10.1007/s11130-019-00725-x

Stomp, A. M. (2005). The duckweeds: A valuable plant for biomanufacturing. *Biotechnology Annual Reviews, 11*, 69–99.

Thomas, I., Siew, L. Q. C., Watts, T. J., & Haque, R. (2019). Seaweed allergy. *The Journal of Allergy and Clinical Immunology: In Practice*, 7(2), 714–715.

Tiberg, E., & Einarsson, R. (1989). Variability of allergenicity in 8 strains of the green algal genus *Chlorella*. *International Archives of Allergy and Immunology*, 90(3), 301–306.

van der Fels-Klerx, H. J., Camenzuli, L., Belluco, S., Meijer, N. & Ricci, A. (2018). Food safety issues related to uses of insects for feeds and foods. *Comprehensive Reviews in Food Science and Food Safety*, 17, 1172–1183.

van der Fels-Klerx, H. J., Camenzuli, L., van der Lee, M. K., & Oonincx, D. G. A. B. (2016). Uptake of cadmium, lead and arsenic by *Tenebrio molitor* and *Hermetia illucens* from contaminated substrates. *PloS One*, 11, e0166186.

van der Spiegel, M., Noordam, M. & van der Fels-Klerx, H. (2013). Safety of novel protein sources (insects, microalgae, seaweed, duckweed, and rapeseed) and legislative aspects for their application in food and feed production. *Comprehensive Reviews in Food Science and Food Safety*, 12, 662–678.

Van Huis, A., Van Itterbeeck, J., Klunder, H., Mertens, E., Halloran, A., Muir, G. & Vantomme, P. (2013). Edible insects: Future prospects for food and feed security. FAO Forestry Paper 171, FAO, Rome. http://www.fao.org/docrep/018/i3253e/i3253e00.htm. Accessed March 25, 2021.

Van Netten, C., Cann, S. A. H., Morley, D. R., & Van Netten, J. P. (2000). Elemental and radioactive analysis of commercially available seaweed. *Science of the Total Environment*, 255(1-3), 169–175.

Vega, F. E. & Kaya, H. K. (2012). *Insect Pathology*. London: Academic Press.

Verhoeckx, K. C., van Broekhoven, S., den Hartog-Jager, C. F., Gaspari, M., de Jong, G. A., Wichers, H. J., van Hoffen, E., Houben, G. F., & Knulst, A. C. (2014). House dust mite (Der p 10) and crustacean allergic patients may react to food containing Yellow mealworm proteins. *Food Chemistry and Toxicology*, 65, 364–673.

Wiebe, M. G. (2004). Quorn^{TM} Myco-protein – Overview of a successful fungal product. *Mycologist*, 18, 17–20.

Wirtz, R. A. (1984). Allergic and toxic reactions to non-stinging arthropods. *Annual Reviews in Entomology*, 29(1), 47–69.

Wong, M. H., Hung, K. M., & Chiu, S. T. (1996). Sludge-grown algae for culturing aquatic organisms: Part II. Sludge-grown algae as feeds for aquatic organisms. *Environmental Management*, 20(3), 375–384.

Yen, A. L. (2008). Edible insects and other invertebrates in Australia: Future prospects. In: *Forest Insects as Food: Humans Bite Back*. Durst, P. B., Johnson, D. V., Leslie, R. N., & Shono, K. (Eds). Proceedings of a Workshop on Asia-Pacific Resources and Their Potential for Development. RAP Publication 2010/02, February 19–21, 2008, Chiang Mai, Thailand, 65–84.

Zainol Abidin, N. A., Kormin, F., Zainol Abidin, N. A., Mohamed Anuar, N. A. F., & Abu Bakar, M. F. (2020). The potential of insects as alternative sources of chitin: An overview on the chemical method of extraction from various sources. *International Journal of Molecular Sciences*, 21(14), 4978.

Zayed, A., Gowthaman, S., & Terry, N. (1998). Phytoaccumulation of trace elements by wetland plants: I. Duckweed. *Journal of Environmental Quality*, 27(3), 715–721.

13 Allergenicity Risks Associated with Novel Proteins and Rapid Methods of Detection

Mostafa Gouda PhD[1,2] and Alaa El-Din Bekhit PhD[3]
[1]College of Biosystems Engineering and Food Science, Zhejiang University, Hangzhou 310058, China
[2]Department of Nutrition & Food Science, National Research Centre, Dokki 12622, Giza, Egypt
[3]Department of Food Science, Otago University, Dunedin 9054, New Zealand

CONTENTS

13.1 Introduction 380
13.2 Main Protein Alternatives and Novel Sources and Their Risk Factors 381
    13.2.1 Plant-Based Novel Protein Sources and Their Risks 381
    13.2.2 Microalgae Proteins 382
    13.2.3 Insects as Novel Protein Sources 383
    13.2.4 Fungal Mycoprotein 383
13.3 Risks Associated with Phytotoxins in the Novel Protein Sources 384
    13.3.1 Risks Associated with Lectins 384
    13.3.2 Risks Associated with Aflatoxins 384
    13.3.3 Risks Associated with Alkaloids 385
    13.3.4 Risks Associated with Cyanogenic Glycosides 385
13.4 Risks Associated with the Mineral Bioavailability of Novel Proteins 386
13.5 Methods for the Identification of Novel Protein Risk Assessment 387
    13.5.1 Mass Spectrometry Method 387
    13.5.2 Chromatographic Approach for Novel Protein Risk Assessment 387
    13.5.3 Gel-Based Proteomics Approach for Novel Protein Risk Assessment 388
    13.5.4 Spectroscopic Methods for Novel Protein Secondary Structure 389
        13.5.4.1 Fourier Transform IR Spectroscopy (FTIR) in the Structural Characterization of Proteins 389
        13.5.4.2 Surface-Enhanced Raman Scattering Technique 390
        13.5.4.3 X-Ray and NMR 390
13.6 Bottom-Up Protein Risk and Allergen Assessments 392
    13.6.1 Enzyme-Linked Immunosorbent (ELISA) and the Proximity Ligation Assay (PLA) 392
    13.6.2 Polymerase Chain Reactions and Risk Assessment of Novel Proteins 393
13.7 Allergenicity Prediction Methods of Novel Food Proteins 395

DOI: 10.1201/9780429299834-13

	13.7.1 Immune-Mediated Adverse Reactions for Novel Proteins Method	395
	13.7.2 Steps for Novel Protein Risk Assessment by IgE-Mediated Methods	397
13.8	Conclusion and Future Prospective	397
Acknowledgements		397
References		398

13.1 INTRODUCTION

'Protein alternatives' is a rather general term that refers to proteins obtained from sources other than traditional animal protein sources, such as plant-based (legumes, including soybeans and peas), *in vitro* cell-based sources, microalgae (e.g., *Chlorella vulgaris* and *Spirulina platensis*), fungal fermentation-based proteins (mycoproteins), or proteins isolated from insect sources (Caparros et al., 2016; Finnigan et al., 2019; Grahl et al., 2020). Animal-based food production challenges (their negative impact on the environment from the use of natural resources and their low production efficiency, their perceived negative health effects, and ethical issues surrounding meat production) have motivated many consumers to reduce the amount of animal protein in their diets and switch to plant and other protein sources (Sanchez-Sabate & Sabate, 2019). Legume-based products, either in their fermented (e.g., tempeh, natto, dawadawa and oncom) or unfermented (soy protein extract and concentrate) forms have been used for decades and are now enjoying rapid market expansion. In particular, fermented products have a meat-like chewable characteristic and are considered beneficial to health (Anzani et al., 2020; Finnigan et al., 2019; Sanlier et al., 2019; Sha & Xiong, 2020). However, their production still faces several challenges (Souza Filho et al., 2019) and is still not widely accepted by consumers who are not familiar with these products and as a result, still prefer meat. A balanced approach that has been gaining much research interest is the development of hybrid products that contain meat and plant proteins (Anzani et al., 2020; Taylor et al., 2020), and many traditional meat and poultry companies are developing their own brands of plant-based products (Sha & Xiong, 2020).

Plant-based proteins can be directly used to produce meat analogues, where they can partially or fully substitute the protein in animal products (Sha & Xiong, 2020). The use of proteins from plant and fungal sources provides the opportunity to add pigments, vitamins, and important minerals to improve the nutritional and health characteristics of these products (Dekkers et al., 2018).

While plant-based proteins represent a good source of alternative protein, their competitive use as feed in poultry and fish production puts pressure on their availability for human use and creates serious implications from economic, technical, and environmental standpoints (Burr et al., 2012). Therefore, to meet future protein demands, new protein sources need to be explored. Over the last 20 years, scientific research conducted in the public and private sectors has focused on protein sources from algae (Ahmad et al., 2020; Mark Ibekwe et al., 2017), insects (Barbi et al., 2020; Parolini et al., 2020), microbial proteins, such as *Candida utilis, Candida lipolytica, Chaetomium celluloliticum, Fusarium graminearum, Brevibacterium* and *Methylophilus methylitropous* (Kieliszek et al., 2017; Nasseri et al., 2011; Upadhyaya et al., 2016), and *in vitro* muscle cells (Bhat et al., 2019; Kadim et al., 2015). Despite all the ethical, environmental and economic benefits associated with these protein sources, there are concerns over their safety due to the possible bioaccumulation of toxic contaminants, their microbiological safety, the deficiency of some essential amino acids, and protein digestibility (Barbi et al., 2020; Sha & Xiong, 2020).

These concerns have been recognized, and it has been recommended that a comprehensive risk assessment, as directed in EC regulation no. 258/97 and EU recommendation 97/618 EC, be carried out on novel proteins. Food regulations, such as (EU 2015/2283), provide standard and well-defined methods for the assessment of nutritional, microbial, and toxicological risks. Among the potential risks, protein allergens are considered a significant public health issue. Upon the consumption of proteins from certain foods, an immunological tolerance level is assessed, and consumers can then safely consume these foods, if acceptable. However, in some individuals, insufficient tolerance may result in reactivity upon re-exposure to the specific protein in a process known as 'sensitization' (Westerhout et al., 2019). Then, when the individual is exposed to the specific protein(s), an adverse clinical reaction may occur. This immune response is called 'elicitation'. Sometimes, different proteins with high similarity to the sensitizing protein (s) can also elicit an allergic reaction, during a process known as 'cross-reactivity'. Therefore, a food protein that causes an allergic reaction may not necessarily be the sensitizing protein. Sensitization to proteins can take place in the gastrointestinal tract, the oral cavity, the skin and occasionally in the respiratory system. This potentially complicates the assessment of the allergenic potential of novel foods (Sampson et al., 2018).

This chapter discusses the risks associated with novel protein alternatives and their risk assessments with a focus on rapid detection methods. Furthermore, analytical methods applied for this risk assessment will be summarized, and recent advances in the methodology will be highlighted.

13.2 MAIN PROTEIN ALTERNATIVES AND NOVEL SOURCES AND THEIR RISK FACTORS

13.2.1 Plant-Based Novel Protein Sources and Their Risks

Proteins have been extracted from different plants parts (seeds, roots, etc.). For instance, nowadays, many processed animal products have soy protein additives as some of their main compositional ingredients. Soy and pea proteins (pulses or legumes) are the most widely used building blocks for alternative plant protein products. Of the plant proteins, soybean provides more than a quarter of the total global production of protein for human food use (Liu et al., 2020). Also, rice and mung bean proteins are often used along with legume proteins to produce a nutritionally balanced amino acid profile in plant-based food products (Migala & Nied, 2019). Soy and pea proteins are also the two principal protein sources utilized in plant-based alternative meat product manufacture. In these, the albumin and globulin fractions account for as much as 90% of the total protein present. However, the native legume protein structure cannot support a meat-like fibrous texture. Therefore, disruptive processes, such as fiber spinning and thermal extrusion, which form filamentous aggregates, make legume proteins easier to use in the plant-based protein production process. Also, wheat gluten, which contributes to meat-like chewiness is used in some soy or pea protein-based products (Chiang et al., 2019; Sha & Xiong, 2020).

Vicilin and β-conglycinin are the principal proteins in soybeans, and glycinin and legumin are the principal proteins found in peas. Vicilin and β-conglycinin are structurally similar in that they are trimer proteins with molecular masses of approximately 150–200 kDa (Lam et al., 2016). Glycinin and legumin exist as hexamers with molecular masses of 300–350 kDa (Utsumi et al., 1997). Each of the three subunits consists of an acidic polypeptide and a basic polypeptide linked by a disulfide bond. These proteins contribute several important functionalities, such as solubility, gelation, and emulsification during food processing, which cause individual globulin subunits to dissociate, unfold, and re-aggregate (Nishinari et al., 2018).

The β-conglycinin exists in the form of a water-soluble glycoprotein, and it has been found to provide nutritional and health benefits to humans. For example, β-conglycinin has the potential to increase satiety and reduce hunger feelings by increasing cholecystokinin secretion (Hira et al., 2009). Moreover, a daily intake of β-conglycinin has been found to reduce total and low-density lipoprotein (LDL) cholesterol and the incidence of atherosclerosis (Ferreira Ede et al., 2011). In contrast, β-conglycinin can cause a food allergenic reaction, with up to 3% of infants are reportedly being affected by soy proteins (Masilamani et al., 2011; Sicherer & Sampson, 2006). Chen et al. (Chi et al., 2011) found that β-conglycinin at dosages >200 μg caused redness and inflammation in piglets.

Glutenin and gliadins are wheat proteins, and their elasticity and extensibility characteristics impart importance to them as alternatives to animal proteins in food products (Sha & Xiong, 2020).

However, gluten sensitivity or celiac disease (CD) has been widely documented, and gluten intolerance is not only found in wheat, but in barley, rye, and some types of oats as well. Gluten sensitivity affects both children and adults at various frequencies, with an estimated prevalence of 6% in the US population (Kagnoff, 2007; Sapone et al., 2011). The risks associated with the use of these proteins have led to extensive efforts that are focused on finding alternative protein sources. Gil-Humanes et al. (2014) used a reduced gliadin wheat bread as an alternative to a gluten-free diet for people who have celiac disease and who are sensitive to gluten-related ingredients. Gliadin itself was reduced as a specific gluten protein, and it was found that flour and bread with reduced levels of these gliadins would be safer for gluten-intolerant consumers. Soybean leghemoglobin, a hemoprotein with a bloody appearance, was approved by FDA as a colour additive for meat analogs (FDA, 2019). The evaluation of the potential risks of soy leghemoglobin demonstrated that foods that contain this protein are unlikely to present an unacceptable risk of allergenicity or toxicity to consumers (Jin et al., 2018).

Physical treatments like ultrasound or high-temperature treatment of protein foods could have various effects (Gouda et al., 2021b). On the one hand, it could generate toxicants and carcinogens, such as heterocyclic aromatic amines (Barzegar et al., 2019), which could be generated during high-temperature frying, grilling, and baking (Jiang & Xiong, 2016; Lu et al., 2018). On the other hand, the allergenicity of certain proteins could be decreased by the heating process, such as when soy glycinin is heated at 100 °C, its allergenicity is decreased (Huang et al., 1998).

13.2.2 Microalgae Proteins

Global interest, new consumption and nutrition trends, and the market for dietary protein supplements have greatly increased the focus on microalgae proteins in recent decades. Commercially available food supplements based on microalgae, such as Spirulina (Cyanobacteria) are becoming increasingly popular (Gouda et al., 2021a; Rzymski et al., 2015). Microalgae are rich in important nutrients and possible nutraceutical compounds. For example, Spirulina contains phycocyanin, a phycobiliprotein with potent antioxidant and anti-cancer activity (Gouda et al., 2021; Jiang & Xiong, 2016), other phytochemicals, vitamins, and minerals, all of which are known to positively impact human health. There are only a few microalgae that are considered Generally Recognized As Safe (GRAS) by the FDA. These include *Spirulina platensis, Auxenochlorella prothothecoides, Chlorella vulgaris* (Chlorophyta)*, Dunaliella bardawil, and Euglena gracilis*, which are commonly consumed in the USA, Canada, China, the EU, India and Japan (Torres-Tiji et al., 2020). These approved microalgae do not have toxic metabolites, and they have a long history of safe use through human consumption in many countries (Yang et al., 2011). However, serious concerns have been raised against some products manufactured from these microalgae due to their contamination with cyanotoxins (Draisci et al., 2001), toxic metals (Al-Dhabi, 2013), or inorganic arsenic (Hedegaard et al., 2013). Also, a case report of an allergic reaction to Spirulina microalgae as a nutritional supplement was reported and considered as a primary de novo sensitization (Le et al., 2014).

Some other natural hazardous compounds could exist as shown by a recent study that reported two cases of human poisoning following the simultaneous use of Spirulina and Chlorella products (Rzymski et al., 2015).

A multidisciplinary approach to evaluate microalgae safety was carried out, and it included cytotoxic tests using *in vitro* human whole-blood, fluorescent-based flow cytometry (Rzymski et al., 2015), analytical screening of 30 elements, and determination of cyanotoxins, such as anatoxin-A, cylindrospermopsin, and microcystin. They used two models to calculate toxicity related to metals: the Food Supplement Metal Index (FSMI) and the Toxic Elements Contamination Index (TECI). The aqueous extract of chlorella with high levels of FSMI and TECI (69.8 and 2.9, respectively) showed a median share of necrotic cells in the samples (5%). However, chlorella with lower FSMI and TECI (38.2 and 1.8, respectively) did not demonstrate any cytotoxicity in the assessed model, as the viability of neutrophils was not found to be altered. The authors concluded that the microalgae source is the most important factor when considering a harmful effect on human health (Rzymski et al., 2015). One of the common reasons for serious contamination in microalgal products comes from improper culture media purity and, specifically, the presence of toxic cyanobacteria (Vichi et al., 2012). Microcystins, cyclic peptides that are produced by certain cyanobacteria, such as *Microcystis aeruginosa*, are the most common protein-peptide toxins that adversely affect microalgae safety. They are powerful hepato-toxins, and they have been found to cause liver cancer in mammals by inhibiting acetylcholinesterase activity, which is needed for cell regulation (Scoglio, 2018).

13.2.3 INSECTS AS NOVEL PROTEIN SOURCES

Recent interest in insects as a source of edible novel protein has emerged (Baiano, 2020; Fitches & Smith, 2018; Gravel & Doyen, 2020), with a wide range of insects, including crickets, locusts, and grasshoppers, being under consideration (van Hui, 2013). The recent novel foods EC Regulation 258/97, which came into effect on 1 January 2018, clarifies the status of insects as novel foods across the EU and means that approvals will take place through a centralized procedure (EC-258/97, 2018). Insect-containing food manufacturers will need to have approval for marketing such food products. One of the major concerns of novel proteins extracted from insects is their potential to cause immune-mediated adverse reactions or food allergies (Pali-Scholl et al., 2019). Grasshoppers used as animal feed were reported to induce allergic asthmatic reactions in a pet keeper (Jensen-Jarolim et al., 2015).

Edible insects might pose the risk of causing cross-allergenic reactions in patients allergic to shrimp or house dust mites as shown in instances of allergic reactions to yellow mealworm or crickets (Broekman et al., 2016; Srinroch et al., 2015). The phylogenetic relationships between the different classes of arthropods may explain sequence homologies and structural similarities that constitute B cell epitopes in common allergens (pan-allergens), and these may be responsible for the cross-allergies that exist between edible insects and other known allergens (Turck et al., 2016). For instance, Verhoeckx et al. (2014) showed that the cross-reactivity of yellow mealworm (*Tenebrio molitor*) protein with crustaceans and house dust mites was mostly caused by tropomyosin and arginine kinase allergens (Verhoeckx et al., 2014). Furthermore, Broekman et al. (2016) showed that primary sensitization to mealworm occurred in mealworm breeders, leading to a food allergy against mealworm. None of these breeders were initially allergic to shrimp or any other food, indicating that new allergies may be introduced along with the inclusion of novel proteins (Broekman et al., 2016; Pali-Schöll et al., 2019).

13.2.4 FUNGAL MYCOPROTEIN

Mycoprotein is a filamentous fungal protein that can be consumed as an alternative protein source to animal proteins. This protein can provide a meat-like texture along with other sensory properties. Due to these inherent properties, the replacement of meat by mycoprotein is considered to be a more realistic approach to substituting or replacing meat compared to protein-rich plants (Souza Filho et al., 2019). Many fungal products are already approved as GRAS by the FDA (Denny et al., 2008).

Mycoprotein is a low-fat, high-protein, and high-fiber food material. However, the high content of RNA in fungal biomass (~10% dry weight) raises some concerns (Schweiggert-Weisz et al., 2020; Souza Filho et al., 2019). Comparatively, edible offal such as beef liver and heart contain approximately 2 and 0.6% of RNA, respectively, and meat contains even less (Jonas et al., 2001). The consumption of excessive quantities of RNA can lead to an increased amount of uric acid in the body, which leads to the risk of gout development. Also, the iron and vitamin B12 contents of mycoprotein are low compared to red meat (Denny et al., 2008; Jonas et al., 2001). A mycoprotein product that has high commercial success is Quorn, which is made of protein from *Fusarium venenatum* as well as a binding protein that shows adverse gastrointestinal reactions after its consumption (Hoff et al., 2003). A 60S acidic ribosomal protein P2 in this mold was suggested to be the reason for the severe hypersensitivity reactions reported with Quorn (Hoff et al., 2003). Other reports documented sensitivity to Quorn (Jacobson, & DePorter, 2018). Apart from the negative aspects of mycoprotein, its fiber is composed of two-thirds β-glucan and one-third chitin, creating a 'fibrous chitin–glucan matrix' with low water solubility (88% insoluble) (Bottin et al., 2016), which will affect the protein utility and functionality. The chitin is a polymer formed by N-acetylglucosamine monomers not commonly present in the human diet, but it has positive health effects, including the relief of osteoarthritic joint pain and the stimulation of beneficial bacteria in the colon (Sadler, 2004). Jacobson and DePorter (2018) studied adverse reactions linked to Quorn food. They analysed 1,752 reactions which showed that the ingestion of Quorn products results in emergent allergic and gastrointestinal signals. However, 4% of the population studied did not show evidence of gastrointestinal symptoms after the first consumption of Quorn foods.

13.3 RISKS ASSOCIATED WITH PHYTOTOXINS IN THE NOVEL PROTEIN SOURCES

Phytotoxins are chemicals produced by plants that can be toxic to humans. Some of these chemicals are secondary metabolites, such as alkaloids, and cyanides (Chen et al., 2019). In this section, we will discuss some of these proteins and other phytotoxins which may alert the industry to these novel proteins.

13.3.1 Risks Associated with Lectins

Lectins are proteins with a high degree of stereospecificity and which have the ability to specifically bind sugars (Mishra et al., 2019). Numerous lectins have been isolated from various sources of living organisms, and they can be grouped according to their species of origin, such as algal lectins, fungal lectins, plant lectins, and legume lectins. Phycolectins are algal in origin, and they show specificity for glycoproteins rather than monosaccharides. These lectins are used in biomedical research for their anti-inflammatory, antiviral, and anti-tumour properties, and they are cost-effective (Singh et al., 2015). Also, fungal lectins show high specificity toward mucins and N-acetyl galactosamine residues (Kobayashi & Kawagishi, 2014). The legume lectin family displays a broader range of specificity than does any other lectin family. Most legume lectins are mature protomers (30 kDa) that are composed of a single polypeptide chain of nearly 250 amino acid residues (Mishra et al., 2019). Lectin structures differ according to their origin. Thus, they may be classified based on their structure and evolution, as described in Figure 13.1.

Several reports exist on the potential allergenicity of plant lectins (Gruber et al., 2005). Kaushik et al. (2018) classified lectins as protein antinutritional factors (ANFs). Also, peanut lectin and other legume lectins have been characterized as potential allergens for patients who are allergic to edible legume seeds (Rouge et al., 2010). With few exceptions, most assayed legume lectins have been shown to interact more or less strongly with IgE-containing sera from patients allergic to peanut in various immune experiments (Gruber et al., 2005). Immunity experiments have revealed that the majority of tested sera samples from peanut-sensitive patients contain a high level of IgE lectin-binding capability even after heat treatment. The tightly packed dimeric and tetrameric structures of legume lectins are extremely resistant to heat denaturation (cooking) and proteolytic activity by pepsin and trypsin (Morari et al., 2008).

13.3.2 Risks Associated with Aflatoxins

Aflatoxins are a group of secondary fungal metabolites which are produced by fungi of the *Aspergillus* genus. There are four compounds produced by *Aspergillus flavus* that belong to the

Allergenicity Risks with Novel Protein 385

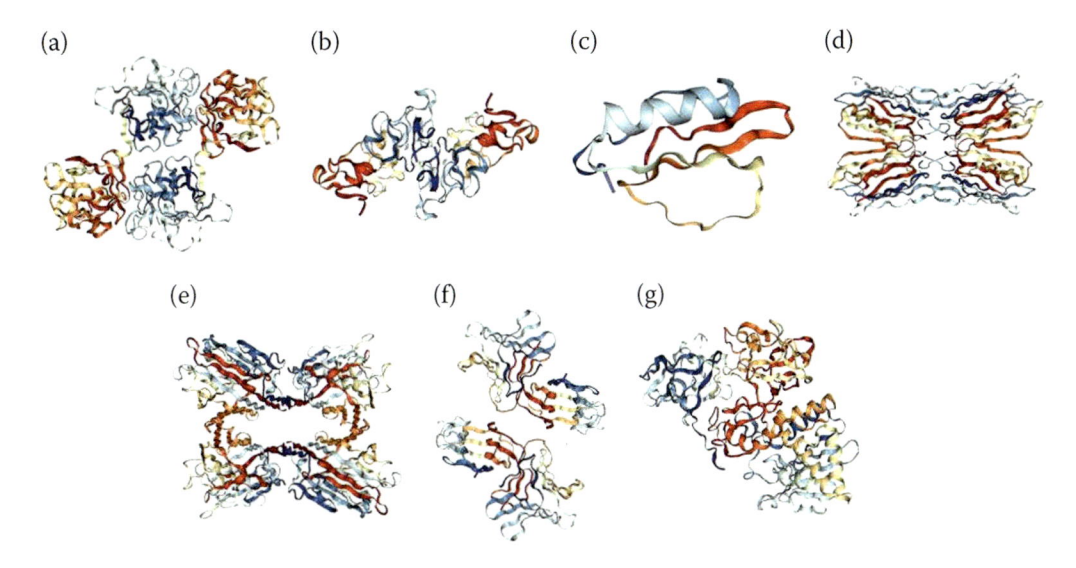

FIGURE 13.1 Structural classifications of lectins using Ribbon drawing models. (a) Amaranthin family; (b) Chitin binding lectin family; (c) *Cucurbitaceae phloem* lectin family; (d) Jacalin-related lectins family; (e) Legume lectin family; (f) Mannose-binding lectin family; (g) Type-2 ribose inactivating lectin family (Mishra et al., 2019) (License Number: 491754077497).

aflatoxin class: aflatoxin B1, aflatoxin B2, aflatoxin G1, and aflatoxin G2 (Rushing & Selim, 2019). Aflatoxin B1 is the most carcinogenic aflatoxin, and it contaminates a wide range of plants, including peanuts, rice, and corn (Ahmed et al., 2010). Heat is increasing total aflatoxin concentration in many alternative protein sources, such as soybeans (Gupta & Venkitasubramanian, 1975b). The availability of zinc in soybeans (which stimulates aflatoxin production) is affected by its binding with soy phytic acid. Heating increases aflatoxin production due to the destruction of phytic acid (Gupta & Venkitasubramanian, 1975a; Wee et al., 2016).

13.3.3 Risks Associated with Alkaloids

Plant alkaloids represent an additional concern within the realm of novel proteins. Two percent of all plant species have the potential to severely poison people, and alkaloids are the major causative factor (Morandini, 2010). Alkaloids are a diverse group of heterocyclic compounds, with a constituent nitrogen atom within the ring structure, and they are mainly present in lupins (Kaushik et al., 2018). They are one of the largest groups of chemical compounds synthesized by plants, and they generally are found as the salts of several plant acids, such as malic or tartaric. Alkaloids are synthesized from amino acids (Figure 13.2) (Aniszewski, 2015; Sato, 2020), and they cause neurological and gastrointestinal disorders (Chen et al., 2019). For instance, the consumption of high tropane alkaloids have been shown to produce both heart disorders and paralysis (Fernando et al., 2012).

13.3.4 Risks Associated with Cyanogenic Glycosides

The cyanogenic glycosides are plant secondary metabolites that are found in many legumes, such as Lima beans (*P. lunatus*) (Lai et al., 2020). Cyanogenic glucosides (α-hydroxynitrile glucosides) are derived from five amino acids (Leucine, Phenylalanine, Valine, Isoleucine, and Tyrosine) and from the nonproteinogenic amino acid cyclopentenyl glycine. Lima beans, as a legume with a high

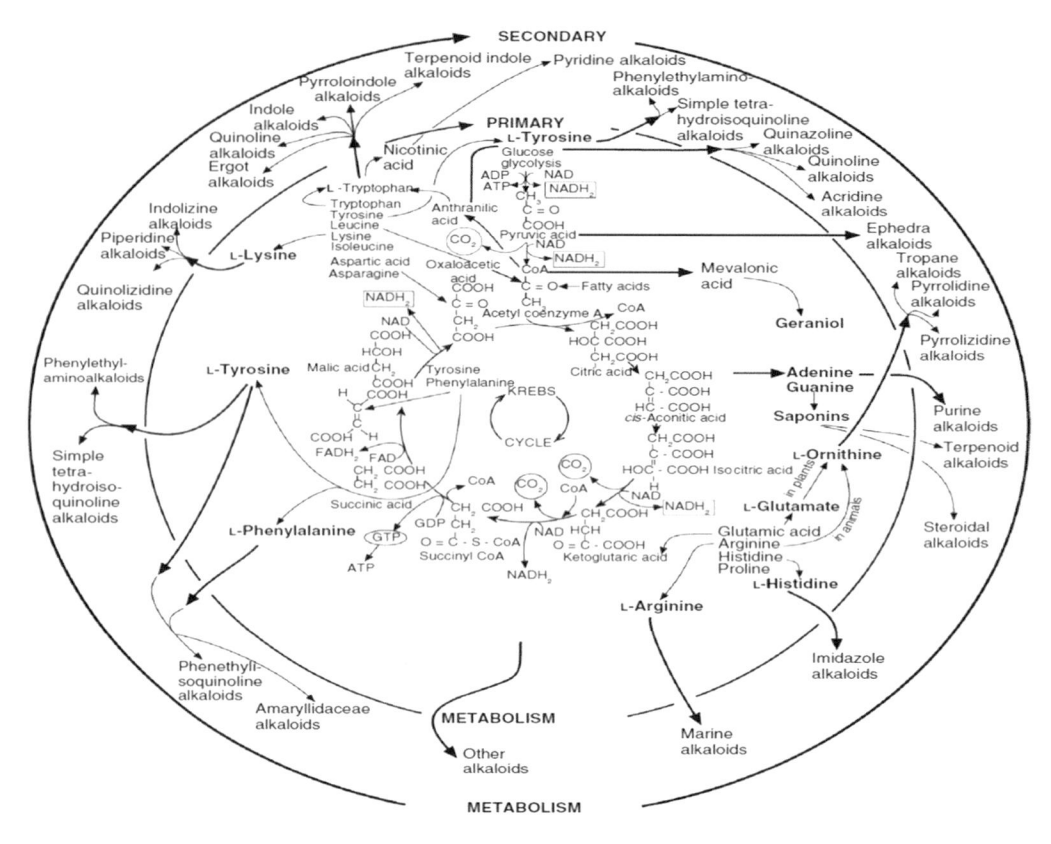

FIGURE 13.2 Alkaloid biosynthesis from amino acids (Aniszewski, 2015) (License Number: 4918560487930).

protein content, releases toxic hydrogen cyanide (HCN) as a hydrolytic product, which has harmful effects on the human body (Gleadow & Moller, 2014). The existence of biosynthetic gene clusters for cyanogenic glucosides has been identified in the genomes of cassava, barley, and sorghum (Ahn et al., 2007; Aouida et al., 2019; Darbani et al., 2016; Knoch et al., 2016). When any of these plant products is consumed, the cyanide ions bind to cytochrome enzymes and inhibit the mitochondrial electron transport chain. As a consequence, neuropathy, toxicity, and death may occur in extreme cases (Kaushik et al., 2018).

13.4 RISKS ASSOCIATED WITH THE MINERAL BIOAVAILABILITY OF NOVEL PROTEINS

One of the presumed advantages of using protein alternatives over meat and animal products is to improve the overall diet of the population, from a health perspective. Currently, there are few nutritional studies available to support the specific health benefits that are claimed for protein alternatives as compared to animal protein sources. For instance, it is not clear whether inorganic minerals added to the product formulations are of biological equivalence to the organic heme iron, zinc, selenium, and other trace minerals that are present in muscle tissue (Sha & Xiong, 2020). Also, the effect of pre-processing treatments to remove antinutritional factors in soy-based formulations on mineral bioavailability should be considered. As an example, treatment with phytase may reduce the content of phytic acid in soy protein isolates from 8.4 mg/g protein to 0.01 mg/g protein (Hurrell et al., 1992), thus improving the availability of phosphorus and other minerals.

13.5 METHODS FOR THE IDENTIFICATION OF NOVEL PROTEIN RISK ASSESSMENT

As mentioned above, health concerns regarding the use of novel proteins have been reported, and the appropriate risk assessments and interventions to avoid exposure should be established. Of particular interest is the risk of allergenicity that has been reported for certain insect proteins and mycoproteins. A promising strategy for cross-reactivity assessment is using bioinformatics that provides a fast prediction tool for protein allergenicity. A potential limitation is the lack of reference structures for some proteins; therefore, analytical methods for allergenic risk assessment should be used.

13.5.1 Mass Spectrometry Method

The determination of the primary sequence of novel proteins using mass spectrometry and proteomics is a very promising approach and a fast method for the multi-detection of proteins and in-depth characterization of their physicochemical properties (Cunsolo et al., 2014). These analyses can determine a protein's primary sequence, post-processing modifications, molecular interactions, and other structural details. This information may help to identify allergens and modifications in protein structure due to processing (e.g., thermal and non-thermal treatments, processing or storage under modified environments, etc.). The primary sequence of a protein is determined using a mass spectrometer (MS), which is composed of an ion source, a mass analyser, and detector, and which is available in various designs and with different modes of action and applications. Electrospray ionization (ESI) and matrix-assisted laser desorption ionization (MALDI) are the most common mass spectrometers used for proteomic studies (Monaci & Visconti, 2009).MALDI technology utilizes singly charged ions, whereas ESI generally induces multiply charged ionic states. Surface-enhanced laser desorption ionization (SELDI) is a modification of the MALDI technology that introduces a further purification step to the probe surface before MS analysis (Rawel et al., 2005). There are five types of mass analysers which are commonly used to study novel proteins and their allergens, including time-of-flight (TOF), ion traps (IT), quadrupoles (Q), Orbitraps, and Fourier transform ion cyclotron resonance (FTICR) analysers (Aebersold & Mann, 2003; Domon & Aebersold, 2006; Guerrera & Kleiner, 2005). The mass analysers can be combined in a tandem MS (MS-MS), such as Q-TOF, Q-IT, TOF-TOF, and ITFTICR (Han et al., 2008). Recent advanced techniques and their relationship to mass spectrometry are illustrated in Figure 13.3.

Advanced sequencing methods combine sequencing experiments on digested proteins that were treated with proteases (e.g., trypsin) to generate peptides with database searches of the obtained sequences. The detection, identification, and localization of allergen modifications require different activation techniques for the purified proteins to enhance the MS fragmentation capability. Recent developments in Multiple Reaction Monitoring mass spectrometry (MRM–MS) have resulted in significant progress in novel protein risk assessment and quantification of allergenicity. Specific peptide signatures derived from allergens can be quantified by MRM and the use of internally labelled peptide standards (Picotti & Aebersold, 2012). For example, soybeans contain at least ten proteins that are allergenic to humans, and these have been identified and characterized by Houston et al. (2011) from twenty commercial soybean varieties using mass spectrometric approaches. Relative and absolute quantification of the allergens was achieved using multiple reaction monitoring (MRM) with isotope-labelled peptides as internal standards. Eight of the 10 quantified allergens were present at concentrations of up to 5.7 µg/mg of the total soy protein.

13.5.2 Chromatographic Approach for Novel Protein Risk Assessment

Chromatography enables researchers to separate the components of a mixture, identify their properties, and determine their amounts. Preparation of the proteins through the elimination of contaminants and separation of complex mixtures before mass spectrometric analysis is required to reduce the complexity

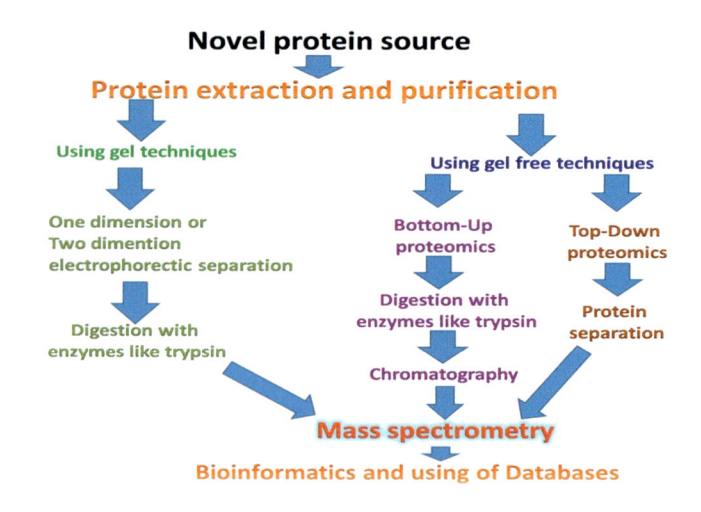

FIGURE 13.3 General flowchart of techniques used to detect and identify proteins.

of the matrix. Over the last decade, there has been an increasing number of publications describing the use of LC-MS methods in proteomics for the characterization of proteins and novel single proteins (Faeste et al., 2011; Wen et al., 2020). The LC–MS/MS technique is a powerful approach for proteomics analysis. The technique has been used to successfully identify a large number of protein allergens in yellow mealworm protein extracts, such as tropomyosin and arginine kinase (Verhoeckx et al., 2014). An *in silico* analysis of the chromatographic spectra of amino acid sequences obtained from yellow mealworm, using databases that apply a criteria of >35% identity, indicated several hits for known insect and mite allergens (Verhoeckx et al., 2014). Subsequent *in vivo* testing confirmed that the allergenicity of novel insect proteins could be predicted. The use of chromatography enables fast detection of allergens. For instance, Concepcion Garcia et al. (2007) reported that β-conglycinin in soy protein could rapidly be detected by HPLC in just 3 min. In that study, two proteins (7S and 11S globulins) that are responsible for soy protein allergenicity were identified. Furthermore, Jia et al. (2019) developed a chromatographic method for the identification of Gly m5.0101, the alpha subunit of β-conglycinin. This method quantified Gly m5.0101 using the MRM technique and a synthetic peptide NPFLFGSNR as the external standard. The analysis used trypsin digestion and liquid chromatography-tandem mass spectrometry to quantify the residue and, subsequently, the β-conglycinin. The authors mentioned that the selected peptide exhibited a detection limit of 0.48 ng/mL.

Other chromatography examples (e.g., ion exchange chromatography) allow separation based on the charge of molecules. Elution is carried out by changing the ionic strength of the mobile phase, either by modifying pH or increasing the salt concentration. Reverse-phase chromatography is based on repulsive hydrophobic forces from interactions among a polar carrier solvent, a nonpolar separated compound, and a nonpolar stationary phase. Sample proteins are denatured at acidic pH, during which hydrophobic regions facilitate separation by polarity. Nonpolar or hydrophobic regions are retained longer in the column and are eluted later than polar (hydrophilic) regions. Another example is affinity chromatography, which is used when specific antibodies are available, and the target protein is only available at low concentration. Once the allergen protein has been isolated and purified, the identity and the level of purity need to be assessed. In this regard, amino-terminal sequencing (increasingly obsolete) and identification by peptide mass fingerprinting and MS are the most frequently used techniques (Poms et al., 2004).

13.5.3 GEL-BASED PROTEOMICS APPROACH FOR NOVEL PROTEIN RISK ASSESSMENT

Proteomics technology has been used to detect novel protein allergens based on a gel separation approach. Sodium dodecyl sulphate polyacrylamide gel electrophoresis (SDS-PAGE) can be carried out in one (1D) and two dimensions (2D), followed by immunoblotting or spectroscopic methods to identify the separated proteins. Several studies have reported the successful detection of wheat beer and rice protein allergens using 2D immunoblotting systems (Golias et al., 2013; Hoffmann-Sommergruber, 2016; Picariello et al., 2015).The reactivity of the separated proteins are then checked against allergen databases to obtain information about the allergens' characteristics (e.g., www.allergen.org) which can then be used for allergenic risk assessment. Most common plant protein allergens belong to the 2S albumin family, which is mainly found in sunflower and sesame seeds, hazelnuts, walnuts, and peanuts. A plant non-specific lipid transfer protein (nsLTPs) is the main allergen found in fruits (e.g., peach and apple). Furthermore, 7/8S globulins and 11S globulins are found in tree nut and seeds, and a pathogenesis-related PR-10 protein is related to the rolamin and cupin superfamilies (Hoffmann-Sommergruber, 2016; Radauer et al., 2008). Gel-based proteomic methods can easily be used to confirm similarities of new proteins to these known allergens. Gubesch et al. (2007) investigated the presence of allergens in three exotic vegetables from South America, Africa and Asia; water spinach, hyacinth bean and Ethiopian eggplant. The authors applied a stepwise approach that involved three confirmation steps. The first was an investigation of the presence of allergens (Bet v 1 homologous proteins, profilins and nonspecific lipid transfer proteins) in the vegetable extracts, which were analysed using an immunoblot assay. This was followed by an investigation of IgE-binding of the allergens in the vegetable extracts by immunoblot analysis using sera from subjects with IgE-reactivity to known allergens (birch tree, grass and mugwort pollen; soy, peanut, tomato, and nonspecific lipid transfer proteins). Finally, an *in vivo* skin prick test was used followed by open oral food challenges. The authors identified various allergenic structures by gel based-immunoblot analysis, which verified the *in vitro* IgE-binding capacity of these structures, and by the use of *in vivo* tests. This supported the authors' approach as being a viable method to be used for the allergenicity testing of natural novel foods.

13.5.4 Spectroscopic Methods for Novel Protein Secondary Structure

Spectroscopic approaches, such as Circular Dichroism (CD) and Fourier Transform IR (FTIR) Spectroscopy, have become very useful techniques to obtain information on proteins structures and their interactions (Gouda et al., 2018; Sheng et al., 2018; Tang et al., 2019). For instance, CD spectra can provide information about the composition percentages of the secondary structures α-helix, β-sheet, β-turn, and random coil. Different types of secondary structures give rise to characteristic CD spectra below 250 nm (Whitmore & Wallace, 2008). Various empirical methods have been developed to analyse protein CD spectra for the quantitative estimation of the secondary structure content. Reference protein CD spectra database sets can be used as markers for the novel proteins. These reference databases are very important and contribute to the quality of the CD spectra analyses for the prediction of protein secondary structure (Lees et al., 2006).

The CD spectra in the region between 260 and 320 nm characterize the aromatic amino acids. The shape and magnitude of the spectrum at the UV region of a protein depend on the number of the aromatic amino acids, their mobility, and their positions in the protein. The near UV spectrum of a protein CD can be used to compare the novel protein with known proteins (Stojadinovic et al., 2014). Also, it can give insights into the effects of processing on protein structure and confirmation, which may clarify changes in the protein's toxicity. For instance, CD was used to evaluate the effect of high-intensity ultrasound treatment on the folding and structure of β-lactoglobulin, a known milk protein allergen, and it confirmed the significance of ultrasound on β-lactoglobulin fold and stability (Stojadinovic et al., 2014).

13.5.4.1 Fourier Transform IR Spectroscopy (FTIR) in the Structural Characterization of Proteins

Fourier Transform IR (FTIR) Spectroscopy is another nondestructive technique that is employed to characterize protein and polypeptide structure (Gouda et al., 2018; Sheng et al., 2018). The FTIR spectra of proteins are interpreted as vibrations of structural repeat units. The protein units can define nine characteristic absorption bands (amides A, B and I–VII). Amide I bands (1700–1600 cm^{-1}) are related to the protein secondary structural components. This method is commonly used for the assessment of conformational changes, secondary structure and structural dynamics, protein stability, and aggregation, all which have direct influence on novel protein allergenicity (Baltacioglu et al., 2017). For instance, it has been shown that increasing temperature affects the shape of the FTIR amide I band, which indicates the formation of β-structures of the peanut Ara h 1 protein allergen. This change in the Ara h 1 structure indicates the protein's aggregation by heat, which subsequently will affect its solubility and the quality of measurement by other methods, such as CD spectra. FTIR is regarded as one of the best non-destructive techniques for confirming protein structural features of aggregated or insoluble proteins (Gomaa & Boye, 2015; Vissers et al., 2011; Yasar et al., 2020).

13.5.4.2 Surface-Enhanced Raman Scattering Technique

The high sensitivity surface-enhanced Raman Spectroscopy (SERS) technique uses Raman scattering (the inelastic scattering of photons) to plot the relationship between light intensity, expressed in arbitrary units versus the frequency of scattered light in frequency units. The technique has attracted considerable interest for use in the bio-detection of proteins, due to its nondestructive and ultrasensitive features (Ma et al., 2020). Also, SERS technology has been used to detect biotoxins, such as poisonous proteins and microcystin (Neng et al., 2020). This technique provides a 'molecular fingerprint' that can be used to identify a molecule or verify its presence in a sample using its intrinsic signals. The technique has been found to have significant advantages, which include high affinity binding, high sensitivity, and fingerprint resolution, all which enhance signal strength by up to 10 orders of magnitude (Almehmadi et al., 2019). Due to these favourable characteristics, SERS has been applied to a number of immunoassays available to detect proteins and protein allergens (Lin & He, 2019; Ma et al., 2017). For this type of application, glass-coated slides with nanoparticles (e.g., silver nanoparticles) are used due to their wide utility as immunoassay matrices and their good adsorption and fixation capacities for antibodies (Figure 13.4) (Song et al., 2009).

He et al. (2011) developed a method based on nano-silver particles for the detection of allergenic proteins using Raman Spectroscopy. They focused on the detection of Ricin toxin protein, which is naturally present in the castor bean plant (*Ricinus communis*) by using an aptamer (artificial ssDNA antibody that is generated from the randomized nucleic acid) and nano-silver. The authors established a 'two-step' aptamer-based surface-enhanced Raman scattering (SERS) detection assay for ricin in liquid foods. Ricin B chain was first captured from the food matrices by aptamer conjugated silver dendrites, and the spectrum was then read directly on the silver dendrites (Figure 13.5). Also, they mentioned that SERS can detect concentrations of this protein as low as 100 ng/mL. Zhu et al. (2012) determined the feasibility of using the SERS immunoassay to rapidly detect the microcystin heptapeptide. In that work, gold nanoparticles were assembled into nanorod chains to allow the ultra-sensitive detection of microcystin, with a limit of detection as low as 5 pg/mL and a short assay time of less than 15 min. Moreover, a double antibody sandwich method for the rapid detection of β-conglycinin by Raman enhanced immunoassay with colloidal gold as the active substrate was established (Xi & Yu, 2020). In that study, the authors developed a flow immunoassay strip test based on surface-enhanced Raman spectroscopy coupled with gold nanoparticles for the rapid detection of β-conglycinin as a soybean allergen (Xi & Yu, 2020).

13.5.4.3 X-Ray and NMR

X-ray crystallographic and NMR spectroscopic approaches could be used as tools to study protein tertiary structure. Although X-ray crystallography is the most powerful method available to obtain information about the tertiary structure of proteins at the atomic level (Sheng et al., 2018), it is not always possible to obtain crystals of appropriate quality to use this method of analysis. Fortunately, NMR offers a reasonable alternative to X-ray crystallography for low-molecular-weight proteins (Bax, 1989). The X-ray structures of molecular complexes allow the identification of atoms involved in interactions between those the molecules in allergens and those in cells of the immune

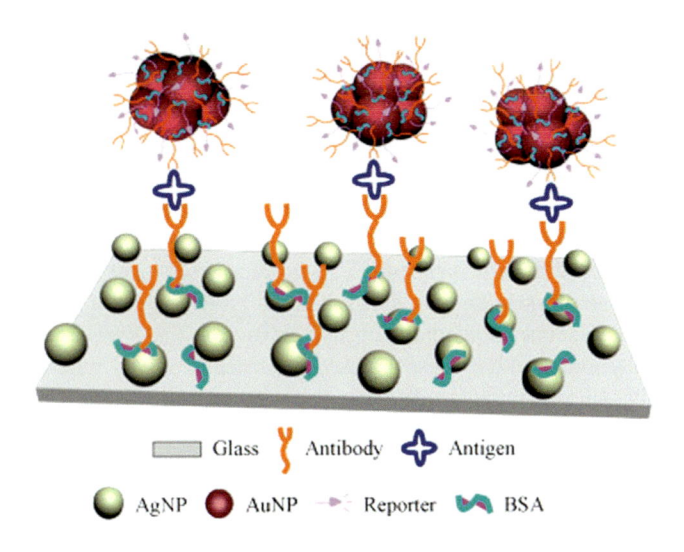

FIGURE 13.4 Sketch map of the standard sandwich protocol the SERS-based immunoassay (Song et al., 2009) (License Number: 4917461299113).

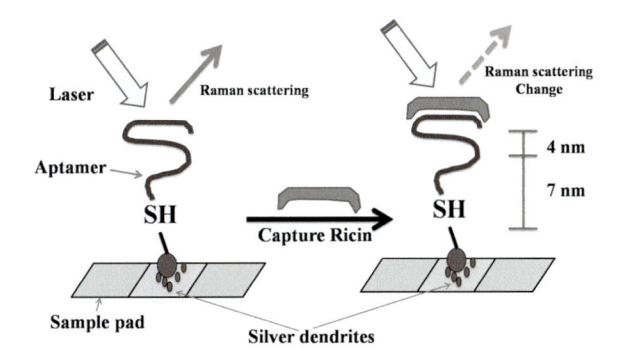

FIGURE 13.5 Illustration of the 'two-step' aptamer-based SERS assay modification, as described by He et al. (2011). (Copyright permission is confirmed by Royal Society of Chemistry.)

system. These complexes include peptides presented by MHC class II molecules (Kusano et al., 2014), cytokines bound to their receptors (LaPorte et al., 2008), and allergen–antibody complexes (Mueller et al., 2014). X-ray crystallography was used to elucidate the structure of the *Alternaria alternata* protein allergen (Alt-a-1) which is found in fungi species (Chruszcz et al., 2012). The results showed that the protein has a unique β-structure that forms a 'butterfly-like' dimer.

Allergenicity of some plant proteins, such as soy (IgE-binding G4 glycinin), is a well-recognized risk factor. Clinical cross-reactivity and IgE-binding studies for G4 glycinin have confirmed its suitability for the study of immune responses (Verhoeckx et al., 2015). Similarly, wheat gluten protein intolerance is a common allergenicity and the cause of Celiac disease (McClain et al., 2014). Only 2% of all classes of proteins cause allergenicity (Radauer et al., 2008). The structures of most of these proteins have been studied and well documented in many scientific databases, such as Allergen Online (http://www.allergenonline.org), Allergome (http://www.allergome.org/), IUIS allergen database (www.allergen.org) and ALLFam (http://www.meduniwien.ac.at/allfam/) (Pomes et al., 2018). For instance, Allergen Online provides access to a peer-reviewed allergen list, and it sequences searchable databases intended for the identification of proteins that may present a potential risk of allergenic cross-reactivity. Also, the IUIS database is a domain supervised by a committee that provides updates on systematic allergen taxonomy. The Allergome database, on the other hand, is a non-peer-reviewed database that provides a wide range of information about allergenic proteins. In the ALLFam database, protein allergens are categorized according to their characteristics (Radauer et al., 2014). In this database, 123 fungi allergens from 42 allergenic protein families are reported on, according to their biological function (Caraballo et al., 2020). Also, parvalbumin (a finfish allergen) and tropomyosin (a shellfish allergen) are two of the largest classes of animal-derived allergens, according to the allergen database AllFam (Fu et al., 2019). The risk assessment carried out using the various databases requires an analysis of the target protein sequence or potential sequence that will be compared for similarity to well-known allergens included in these databases. This *in silico* assessment uses an alignment criterion between the unknown novel protein and an already known protein allergen, using an 80 amino acid sequence representing 35% sequence identity (EFSA, 2010). The FAO/WHO guideline to assess allergenicity of genetically modified crops uses relaxed sequence similarity criteria. A protein is identified as a potential allergen if it harbors >35% identity with a known allergen over a window of 80 amino acids or if it has six contiguous amino acids that are also found in a known allergen. These criteria are implemented in most of the allergen databases and tools (Dang & Lawrence, 2014). Sequence similarity between novel proteins and known allergens is often established by using Basic Local Alignment Search Tool (BLAST) or FAST-All (FASTA) algorithms. It has been noted that allergenic proteins generally have a relatively low molecular weight, exist in high abundance, are highly water soluble, and are strongly resistant to heat and digestion (Vickery et al., 2011). Westerhout et al. (2019) employed a machine learning approach to develop an *in silico* model to predict protein allergenicity, based on their physicochemical and biochemical similarities, by using Random Forest, a well-known machine learning algorithm. The Random Forest model can be used to identify predictive properties by ranking the importance of various properties in a regression or classification problem. Such a prediction model could be used to complement the current weight-of-evidence approach for predicting the allergenicity of novel proteins. The applicability of the model was tested with insect proteins. Results showed a robust model performance with a sensitivity, specificity and accuracy each greater than ≥85%. In conclusion, the model developed in this study improves the predictability of the allergenicity of new or modified proteins, as demonstrated for insect proteins.

13.6 BOTTOM-UP PROTEIN RISK AND ALLERGEN ASSESSMENTS

A bottom-up method is used for the development of allergen sequence databases, where curation allows additional criteria to be applied to rank the clinical relevance of the allergens, including their proven ability to act as triggers of an allergic reaction. Such a robust, reliable, and verifiable database will allow risk assessors to calibrate and frame the risk assessment around defined public health objectives. However, the allergen sequence databases used for allergenicity risk assessment still do not provide systematic data concerning their allergenic potential. For example, while peanut protein allergens (Ara h 5) can be identified by gene expression screening in the database library for peanuts, these proteins are very similar to the birch protein allergen Bet v 2, and they share a similar structure (Wang et al., 2013). Given that care can be taken when contacting peanuts, this particular protein may pose a low risk to individuals with this allergenicity, however, this may be more of importance for individuals with pollen allergies (Becker et al., 2018). More metadata should be added in relation to allergen sequence databases to improve the usefulness of the bioinformatic analyses.

13.6.1 ENZYME-LINKED IMMUNOSORBENT (ELISA) AND THE PROXIMITY LIGATION ASSAY (PLA)

Competitive enzyme-linked immunosorbent assay (ELISA) is an immune-based technique, which uses monoclonal antibodies to identify allergens. For example, 3B7, 6G4, and 5F10 antibodies have been used for the identification of β-conglycinin, and they show an IC_{50} of 4.7 ng/mL with a detection limit of 2.0 ng/mL (You et al., 2008).

These monoclonal antibodies against β-conglycinin can be generated from chicken ovalbumin using a synthetic peptide that corresponds to one epitope sequence of β-conglycinin as the immunogen. A competitive ELISA is then developed to evaluate antibody specificity and determine immunoreactivity to a specific antigen (protein allergen). Currently, there are several ELISA kits in the market for specific protein allergen detection, like the Tepnel Bio-Systems kit (Elisa Technologies, FL, USA), which is used to detect renatured soy proteins with a detection limit of <5000 ng/mg of food product (You et al., 2008). Also, there is an Elisa Systems kit (ELISA Systems, Windsor, Australia) available which is based on the sandwich ELISA principle for the soy Kunitz trypsin inhibitor with a sensitivity of 1 ng/mg of food product (Liu et al., 2012; You et al., 2008).

Takagi et al. (2006) described an improved human antigen-specific IgE ELISA method to monitor novel proteins in genetically modified foods. The authors found that ELISA is one of the most convenient methods available for this purpose. With this method, the levels of recombinant protein IgE, phosphinothricin-N-acetyltransferase (PAT) protein, and Cry9C protein are determined by ELISA using the sera of patients who are allergic to known allergens. The assay is then used to test the binding capacity of serum IgE to novel proteins, to investigate the cross-reactivity of specific IgE antibodies of known allergens and novel proteins, and to assess the possibility of acquiring novel IgE through the ingestion process.

One of the major challenges in using ELISA for novel protein risk assessment is its sensitivity in detecting low-abundance proteins. Therefore, scientists have combined ELISA with a proximity ligation assay (PLA), resulting in the modified ELISA–PLA method. The PLA technology has attracted attention due to its high sensitivity and specificity in many fields; e.g., cancer biomarker screening and the discovery of histone modifications (Feinberg, 2013; Gomez et al., 2013). PLA utilizes two to four types of antibodies labelled with DNA strands. When the antibodies bind to the target protein, the oligonucleotides are brought into proximity and thus the ligation of multiple oligonucleotides can begin and be amplified by DNA ligase (Gullberg et al., 2004; Schallmeiner et al., 2007; Tavoosidana et al., 2011). The combined ELISA and PLA system has the advantages of rapidness, accuracy, and convenience offered by ELISA as well as the sensitivity and specificity of PLA. The limit of detection (LOD) is two orders of magnitude lower than the traditional ELISA method (Figure 13.6) (Tong et al., 2016).

13.6.2 Polymerase Chain Reactions and Risk Assessment of Novel Proteins

The development of fast and effective allergen detection methods for new proteins is very important in achieving timely and accurate assessment of risk. Polymerase chain reaction (PCR) methods are indirect techniques that detect the DNA of allergens. PCR can be combined with other techniques, such as capillary electrophoresis, to simultaneously detect protein allergens from different plant sources (e.g., wheat, soybean, hazelnut, oat, sesame, peanut) (Lian & Zeng, 2017). The LOD of this method is as low as 0.005% (w/w) of the plant source weight. Detection methods targeting nucleic acids are an interesting approach for the detection of novel protein allergenicity.

Although several protein allergens are not suitable for PCR analysis (for example, milk and eggs), conventional PCR and quantitative real-time PCR techniques can be used for risk assessment of protein allergens from nuts, peanuts, and fish (Brezna et al., 2010). Compared to protein-based detection methods, PCR offers the advantages of low impact of temperature on assay sensitivity (because it is targeting the gene codes), high specificity, and low interference with other matrixes (Fuchs et al., 2013). Moreover, PCR is not limited by the lack of antibodies for specific proteins, as with ELISA assays. Despite of these advantages, there are challenges involved in allergen detection using this method, such as the DNA extraction and purification from the source protein that may not be a straightforward process with novel proteins. To overcome this problem, multiplex PCR (MPCR) combined with agarose gel electrophoresis (AGE) was developed to detect multiple allergen genes in a single reaction (Poms et al., 2004). Capillary gel electrophoresis

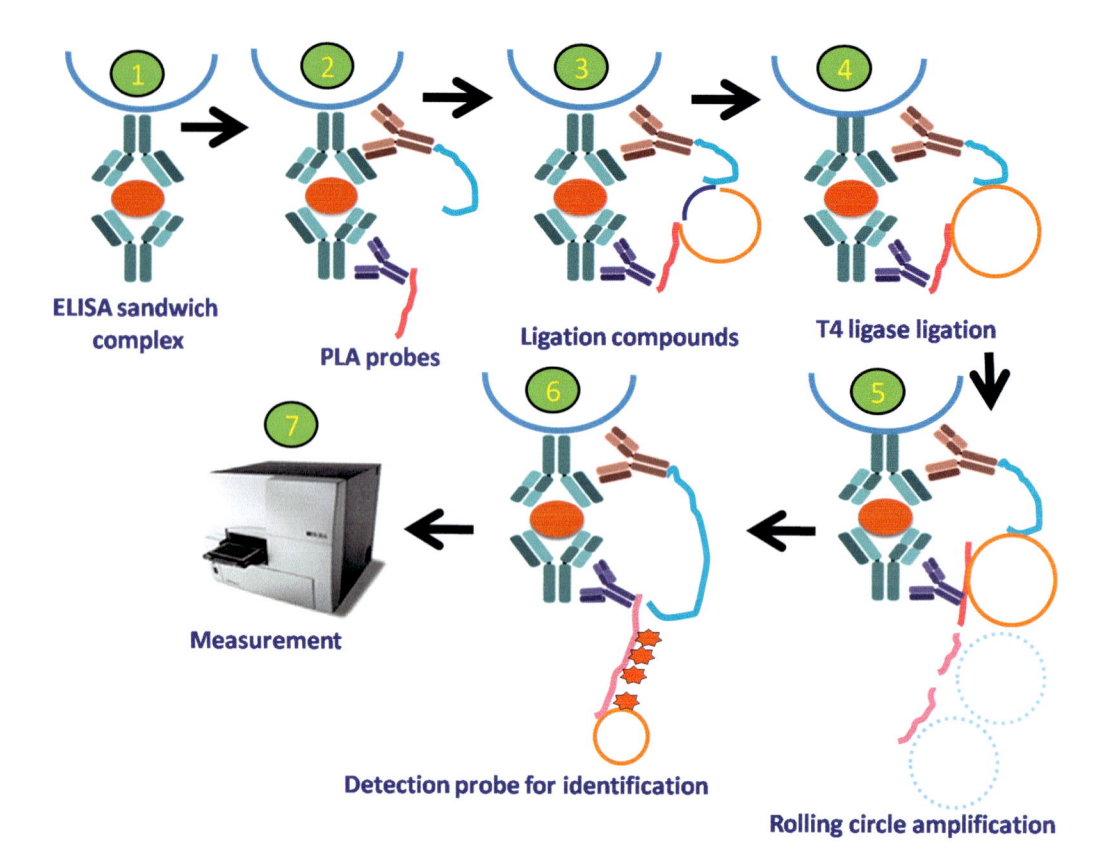

FIGURE 13.6 The workflow of the ELISA–PLA method for novel protein and allergen detection. (1) A primary antibody is adsorbed and recognized by ELISA targets. (2) Two PLA probes combine with the corresponding primary antibodies. (3) ConnectorDNA probes are added to form a circle with the help of both priming PLA and non-priming PLA probes. (4) The sticky end of the circle probes is ligated by T4 DNA ligase to form a circular DNA. (5) Rolling circle amplification by using the DNA template. (6) Labelling with detection probes. (7) Detection of the amplified products. The figure is adapted from Tong et al. (2016) (License Number: 4917451361871).

(CGE) was subsequently proposed in place of AGE to improve separation resolution (Guo et al., 2011) and PCR stability and sensitivity (Cheng et al., 2016). Cheng et al. (2016) developed a decaplex polymerase chain reaction capillary electrophoresis (PCR-CE) assay that os capable of simultaneously detecting 10 allergens from hazelnut, pistachio, oat, sesame, peanut, cashew, barley, wheat, soybean, and pecan, with a detection limit of 0.005%. A method employing capillary electrophoresis-systematic ligand evolution by exponential enrichment (CE-SELEX) (Tran et al., 2013), using low pH CE-SELEX (Li et al., 2014), was developed to specifically and sensitively select an aptamer that binds the peanut allergen Ara h 1, and this aptamer was used to detect Ara h 1 protein (Tran et al., 2013). A detection limit of 0.001% was achieved by using this method, which was better than the detection limits of qPCR or protein-based methods, indicating that PCR-CE may be a superior analytical tool for allergen detection (Lian & Zeng, 2017).

Tachibana et al. (2015) used a continuous-flow polymerase chain reaction (CF-PCR) in microfluidic devices for onsite detection of various pathogens. They developed a self-propelled CF-PCR (SP-CF-PCR) in a microfluidic device which requires no external pumps to control the flow. And they mentioned that this chip could be used for rapid food inspection (Figure 13.7).

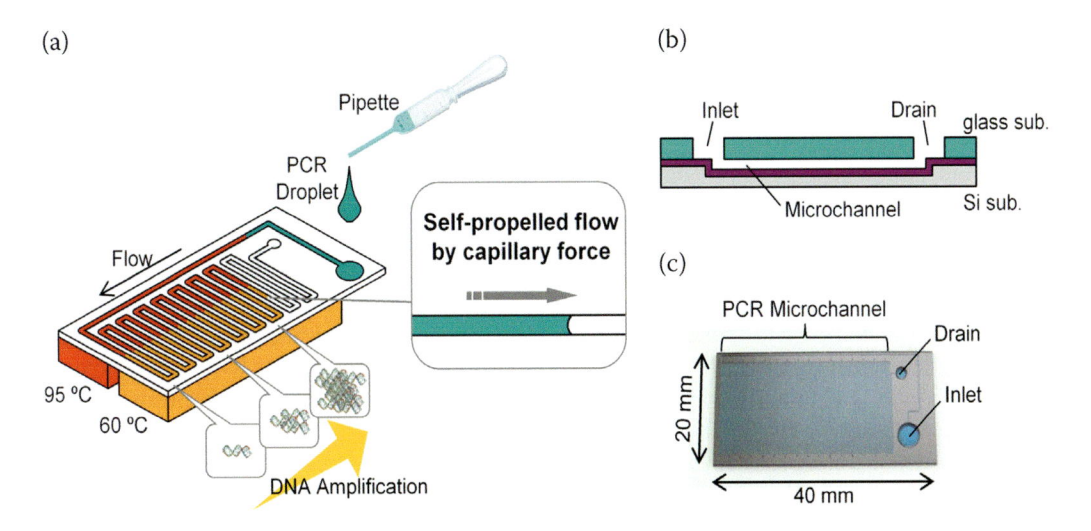

FIGURE 13.7 Schematic of a Self-propelled continuous-flow PCR (SP-CF-PCR) microfluidic device (Tachibana et al., 2015) (License Number: 4916980531990). (a) The microfluidic device, which has a meandering-shaped microchannel, was fixed on aluminium blocks. Panels (b) and (c) show the cross-sectional schematic and photo of the microfluidic device, respectively. The device was 40 × 20 mm in size and composed of a double-layer of Si and a glass substrate.

13.7 ALLERGENICITY PREDICTION METHODS OF NOVEL FOOD PROTEINS

Allergenicity prediction is a challenging task (Fernandez et al., 2020). There are no validated tests available to predict the sensitization potential of food proteins (Dearman & Kimber, 2009). Most available tests focus on sequence similarity, which may elucidate a cross-reactive potency but not *de novo* sensitization (Remington et al., 2018). Our understanding of what causes a protein to be allergenic is incomplete (Remington et al., 2018). Therefore, risk assessment of novel proteins relies on a weight-of-evidence approach (Codex, 2009; EFSA, 2017) and history of exposure if a specific protein in question is expressed in existing foods or in the environment. For many years, a key assessment process for cross-reactivity has relied on bioinformatics. In addition to sequence identity and gene source comparison, *in vitro* digestibility studies and IgE binding studies may be performed as part of the weight-of-evidence data collection. Current approaches are applied to assess potential allergenicity by bioinformatics to compare the sequence of a novel protein with known allergen proteins that cause allergic reactions (EFSA, 2011; 2017). Novel protein sequences can be compared with known allergens using alignment algorithms such as FASTA by threshold values and amino acid sequence alignments. This way to distinguish allergens from non-allergens in developing more advanced *in silico* algorithm tools (e.g., using the machine and deep learning) to predict the potential risk of novel food proteins to human health appears to be promising (Dimitrov et al., 2014).

13.7.1 IMMUNE-MEDIATED ADVERSE REACTIONS FOR NOVEL PROTEINS METHOD

The need for food and health authorities to conduct novel protein safety assessment is critical since immune-mediated adverse reactions in susceptible individuals can often be life-threatening. IgE-mediated allergies are a relevant health concern and affect a significant fraction of the population. For example, Nwaru et al. (2014) reported that up to 3.2% of adults and 5.7% of children in Europe have adverse IgE-mediated responses to food allergens. Anvari et al. (2019) reported even a higher prevalence (5% and 8% in adults and children, respectively), but self-reporting suggests that up to one-third of the population could have these allergies (Anvari et al., 2019). Given this estimate, safety assessments should be performed on new foods, especially those containing novel proteins, before they are placed on the market. Several aspects are used to reduce uncertainty and enhance the reliability of predictions (EFSA, 2011). There is only a limited number of foods that have to date been identified that can induce an immune response in predisposed individuals (Anvari et al., 2019). These include soy, milk, egg, fish, peanut, tree nuts, wheat, and sesame.

A reliable strategy for the risk assessment of new proteins involves several steps. An initial gene sequence is checked for potential sequence and/or structural similarity to known allergens. Then, *in vitro* assays are used to investigate IgE binding capacity in the serum of well-known allergic donors. The stability of novel protein structure during gastric digestion is then analysed, as high protein stability implies persistent allergenic activity. Protein structures vary in their stability when exposed to physical or chemical treatments, which necessitates the evaluation of processing effects on their resistance and allergenic risk (Verhoeckx et al., 2016). Overall, the risk assessment strategy for proteins is derived from classical risk assessment for chemicals. However, this strategy has some important limitations when applied to proteins. There is evidence that gastrointestinal digestion can affect the immunogenicity of dietary proteins in relation to both IgE and non-IgE-mediated adverse immune reactions to food (Pali-Scholl et al., 2018; Pekar et al., 2018). Therefore, the fate of a novel protein in the environment of the gastrointestinal tract and its presentation to the gut mucosa are key considerations that need to be established during the risk assessment process. Interactions among novel proteins and their digestion byproducts and how they are processed by the intestinal mucosa should also be considered.

In vivo testing for the sensitizing capacity of allergens using animals or cell culture systems has been used, but several challenges remain, including considerations for species and strains, diet, route of administration, relevant controls, and endpoint measurements (NASEM, 2017). Cellular systems, such as the dendritic cell activation assays, have been used to investigate the interaction of proteins with immune cells to determine sensitization or tolerance induction (Song et al., 2016).

A system to determine Immune-Mediated Adverse Reactions (IMAR) in Celiac disease was developed to assess the risk that novel proteins may cause. This is a comprehensive evidence-based strategy that was developed to assess whether novel proteins are related to the development of other diseases, in addition to celiac disease. It can predict a protein's ability to cause adverse effects with a higher degree of assurance compared to other traditional tools, such as those currently in use for the risk assessment of immune reactions. However, unlike Celiac disease, IgE-IMAR are not currently able to define a reliable predictive approach for other IgE-mediated food allergies because other environmental factors are involved. Therefore, a series of informative and elegant genome-wide association studies, using a large cohort of subjects from different geographical origins, has been used to characterize peanut allergens (Hong et al., 2015), the major shrimp allergen (tropomyosin – Pen a 1), and the major peach allergen (lipid transfer protein) in a specific gene region called HLA-DR/DQ (Khor et al., 2018). These HLA alleles predispose individuals to IgE-mediated food allergies to particular allergens by affecting antigen presentation events. This information could support the future development of more powerful tools for the risk assessment of novel proteins with regards to IgE-mediated protein allergies by developing sequence identity (for cross-reactivity) through validation of the bioinformatics' approach and consideration of amino-acid physico-chemical properties (Fernandez et al., 2019).

Several databases have been developed and are currently in use for IgE food allergy risk-assessment purposes. Under the current models, the follow-up risk assessment methods are used to analyse the quality of the specific similarity regions between the allergen and the novel protein. However, there are no clear guidelines on how such an allergenic potency should be assigned for risk classification. Therefore, an alternative approach is currently used whereby clinically relevant trials are conducted to link and characterize the potential allergen with specific follow-up actions to be undertaken if the problem has occurred (Fernandez et al., 2020).

13.7.2 STEPS FOR NOVEL PROTEIN RISK ASSESSMENT BY IgE-MEDIATED METHODS

With IgE-mediated methods, the first step is to generate a protein extract from a parent protein that has been subjected to common processing and preparatory steps that may have altered the protein's allergenicity. In most instances, simple buffers, such as tris(hydroxymethyl)aminomethane (TRIS, pH 7.4) or phosphate-buffered saline (PBS, pH 7.0), are used to extract the proteins; however, proteins display a range of characteristics, and therefore, the proper selection of the pH and/or the salt concentration of the extraction buffer is crucial. For example, extraction with PBS pH 7.0 usually yields 80–90% of soluble protein, leaving 10–20% unaccounted for (Blaauboer et al., 2016). Furthermore, during the purification of target proteins, chemical modifications of allergens may occur, leading to erroneous information. Plant seed proteins, such as oleosins, and wheat proteins have been found to undergo structural changes during their purification processes. Therefore, it is important to know the nature of the target novel protein to be isolated and then design the least harmful purification protocol. It is advised that a series of different extraction and chromatographic techniques be used to isolate the new proteins to streamline the extraction process (Poms et al., 2004).

The extracted purified protein could be subsequently produced in relatively large amounts (in the mg to g range) using heterologous expression systems, such as a cloning process, with the same biological activity as the natural protein. Cloning and expressing the protein encoded gene in bacteria (e.g., *E. coli*), yeast (e.g., *Saccharomyces cerevisiae*), or other eukaryotic cell systems, is usually practiced. Following the expression step, a purification protocol needs to be developed to obtain a highly purified homogenous protein batch. This is crucial since the purification process of the expressed proteins itself could add contaminants that then cause allergenicity (Lorence, 2012).

The purified protein is subsequently subjected to chromatographic and/or spectroscopic methods to characterize the purified proteins. The purity level needs to be established, and the potential isoforms that may have varying IgE binding capacity should be defined as a reference set of proteins (Levin et al., 2015). The presence of recombinant protein contaminants (e.g., lipopolysaccharide) could affect subsequent immunization/sensitization studies (Mazzucchelli et al., 2018).

13.8 CONCLUSION AND FUTURE PROSPECTIVE

Novel proteins are valuable alternatives to traditional animal proteins, as they meet certain consumer and vegetarian requirements. Nevertheless, there are challenges that must be faced in meeting safety and nutritional quality requirements for novel proteins. A systematic scientific approach to investigate the safety of these novel proteins, their functionalities, their biological interactions and the influence of processing conditions on their functionalities will need to be established before using them at an industrial scale. Novel protein alternatives from sustainable sources, such as plants, microalgae, insects, and fungi have the potential to meet the increase in global protein demand, but they may carry with them some health concerns. Novel proteins should be utilized only after consideration of their allergenicity and inherent risk factors.

The use of sensitive, fast, and quantitative detection systems for risk assessment of novel proteins is currently afforded by methods implementing mass spectrometry, immunoassays, and spectroscopic techniques. The reduction of matrix interferences and increased method throughput are future research goals. Quantitative mass spectrometry has been successfully used in several research studies, and it has the potential to be used for routine simultaneous detection of multiple allergens in the future.

ACKNOWLEDGEMENTS

The authors acknowledge all publishers including Elsevier and the Royal Society of Chemistry for their help regarding copyright permissions.

REFERENCES

Aebersold, R., & Mann, M. (2003). Mass spectrometry-based proteomics. *Nature*, *422*(6928), 198–207.

Ahmad, F., Nasr, M., Guldhe, A., Kumar, S., Rawat, I., & Bux, F. (2020). Techno-economic feasibility of algal aquaculture via fish and biodiesel production pathways: A commercial-scale application. *Science of the Total Environment*, *704*, 135259. doi:10.1016/j.scitotenv.2019.135259.

Ahmed, S., Bacha, N., & Alharazi, T. (2019). Detection of total aflatoxins in groundnut and soybean samples in Yemen using enzyme-linked immunosorbent assay. *Journal of Food Quality*, *2019*, 1–7.

Ahn, Y. O., Saino, H., Mizutani, M., Shimizu, B., & Sakata, K. (2007). Vicianin hydrolase is a novel cyanogenic beta-glycosidase specific to beta-vicianoside (6-O-alpha-L-arabinopyranosyl-beta-D-glucopyranoside) in seeds of *Vicia angustifolia*. *Plant and Cell Physiology*, *48*(7), 938–947.

Al-Dhabi, N.A. (2013). Heavy metal analysis in commercial Spirulina products for human consumption. *Saudi Journal of Biological Sciences*, *20*(4), 383–388.

Almehmadi, L. M., Curley, S. M., Tokranova, N. A., Tenenbaum, S. A., & Lednev, I. K. (2019). Surface enhanced Raman spectroscopy for single molecule protein detection. *Scientific Reports*, *9*(1), 12356.

Aniszewski, T. (2015). Alkaloid chemistry. In: *Alkaloids*, 2nd Edition. T. Aniszewski (Ed). Netherlands: Elsevier B.V., 99–193.

Anvari, S., Miller, J., Yeh, C. Y., & Davis, C. M. (2019). IgE-mediated food allergy. *Clinical Reviews in Allergy & Immunology*, *57*(2), 244–260.

Anzani, C., Boukid, F., Drummond, L., Mullen, A. M., & Álvarez, C. (2020). Optimising the use of proteins from rich meat co-products and non-meat alternatives: Nutritional, technological and allergenicity challenges. *Food Research International*, *137*, 109575. doi:10.1016/j.foodres.2020.109575.

Aouida, M., Rook, F., Bianca Maimann, A., Sánchez-Pérez, R., Abid, G., Fauconnier, M. L., Jebara, M., & Link, W. (2019). Polymorphisms in cyanogenic glucoside and cyano-amino acid content in natural accessions of common vetch (*Vicia sativa*, L.) and selection for improved agronomic performance. *Plant Breeding*, *138*(3), 348–359.

Baiano, A. (2020). Edible insects: An overview on nutritional characteristics, safety, farming, production technologies, regulatory framework, and socio-economic and ethical implications. *Trends in Food Science and Technology*, *100*, 35–50.

Baltacioglu, H., Bayindirli, A., & Severcan, F. (2017). Secondary structure and conformational change of mushroom polyphenol oxidase during thermosonication treatment by using FTIR spectroscopy. *Food Chemistry*, *214*, 507–514.

Barbi, S., Macavei, L. I., Fuso, A., Luparelli, A. V., Caligiani, A., Ferrari, A. M., Maistrello, L., & Montorsi, M. (2020). Valorization of seasonal agri-food leftovers through insects. *Science of the Total Environment*, *709*, 136209. doi:10.1016/j.scitotenv.2019.136209.

Barzegar, F., Kamankesh, M., & Mohammadi, A. (2019). Heterocyclic aromatic amines in cooked food: A review on formation, health risk-toxicology and their analytical techniques. *Food Chemistry*, *280*, 240–254.

Bax, A. (1989). Two-dimensional NMR and protein structure. *Annual Review of Biochemistry*, *58*, 223–256.

Becker, W. M., Petersen, A., & Jappe, U. (2018). Peanut allergens: New consolidated findings on structure, characteristics, and allergome. *Allergol Select*, *2*(1), 67–79.

Bhat, Z. F., Morton, J. D., Mason, S. L., & Bekhit, A. E. A. (2019). Current and future prospects for the use of pulsed electric field in the meat industry. *Critical Reviews in Food Science and Nutrition*, *59*(10), 1660–1674.

Blaauboer, B. J., Boobis, A. R., Bradford, B., Cockburn, A., Constable, A., Daneshian, M., Edwards, G., Garthoff, J. A., Jeffery, B., Krul, C., & Schuermans, J. (2016). Considering new methodologies in strategies for safety assessment of foods and food ingredients. *Food and Chemical Toxicology*, *91*, 19–35.

Bottin, J. H., Swann, J. R., Cropp, E., Chambers, E. S., Ford, H. E., Ghatei, M. A., & Frost, G. S. (2016). Mycoprotein reduces energy intake and postprandial insulin release without altering glucagon-like peptide-1 and peptide tyrosine-tyrosine concentrations in healthy overweight and obese adults: A randomised-controlled trial. *British Journal of Nutrition*, *116*(2), 360–374.

Brezna, B., Dudasova, H., & Kuchta, T. (2010). A novel real-time polymerase chain reaction method for the detection of Brazil nuts in food. *Journal of Association of Official Analytical Chemists International*, *93*(1), 197–201.

Broekman, H., Verhoeckx, K. C., den Hartog Jager, C. F., Kruizinga, A. G., Pronk-Kleinjan, M., Remington, B. C., Bruijnzeel-Koomen, C. A., Houben, G. F., & Knulst, A. C. (2016). Majority of shrimp-allergic patients are allergic to mealworm. *Journal of Allergy and Clinical Immunology*, *137*(4), 1261–1263.

Burr, G. S., Wolters, W. R., Barrows, F. T., & Hardy, R. W. (2012). Replacing fishmeal with blends of alternative proteins on growth performance of rainbow trout (*Oncorhynchus mykiss*), and early or late stage juvenile Atlantic salmon (*Salmo salar*). *Aquaculture, 334*, 110–116.

Caparros, R., Gierts, C., Blecker, C., Brostaux, Y., Haubruge, É., Alabi, T., & Francis, F. (2016). Consumer acceptance of insect-based alternative meat products in Western countries. *Food Quality and Preference, 52*, 237–243.

Caraballo, L., Valenta, R., Puerta, L., Pomes, A., Zakzuk, J., Fernandez-Caldas, E., Acevedo, N., Sanchez-Borges, M., Ansotegui, I., Zhang, L., van Hage, M., Fernandez, E., Arruda, L., Vrtala, S., Curin, M., Gronlund, H., Karsonova, A., Kilimajer, J., Riabova, K., Trifonova, D., & Karaulov, A. (2020). The allergenic activity and clinical impact of individual IgE-antibody binding molecules from indoor allergen sources. *World Allergy Organization Journal, 13*(5), 100118. doi:10.1016/j.waojou.2020.100118.

Chen, Q., Zhu, L., Chen, J., Jiang, T., Ye, H., Ji, H., Tsang, S., Zhao, Z., Yi, T., & Chen, H. (2019). Recent progress in nanomaterial-based assay for the detection of phytotoxins in foods. *Food Chemistry, 277*, 162–178.

Cheng, F., Wu, J., Zhang, J., Pan, A., Quan, S., Zhang, D., Kim, H., Li, X., Zhou, S., & Yang, L. (2016). Development and inter-laboratory transfer of a decaplex polymerase chain reaction assay combined with capillary electrophoresis for the simultaneous detection of ten food allergens. *Food Chemistry, 199*, 799–808.

Chiang, J. H., Loveday, S. M., Hardacre, A. K., & Parker, M. E. (2019). Effects of soy protein to wheat gluten ratio on the physicochemical properties of extruded meat analogues. *Food Structure-Netherlands, 19*, 100102. doi:10.1016/J.Foostr.2018.11.002.

Chi, C. C., Tai, L. T., Bin, H. C., Wei, H. C., & Bi, Y. (2011). Associations of allergenic soybean proteins with piglet skin allergic reaction and application of polyclonal antibodies.*Animal Production Science*, 51, 1008–1014. https://doi.org/10.1071/AN11142.

Chruszcz, M., Chapman, M. D., Osinski, T., Solberg, R., Demas, M., Porebski, P. J., Majorek, K. A., Pomes, A., & Minor, W. (2012). *Alternaria alternata* allergen Alt a 1: A unique beta-barrel protein dimer found exclusively in fungi. *Journal of Allergy and Clinical Immunology, 130*(1), 241–247.

Codex .(2009). Foods Derived from Modern Biotechnology: Second edition, FAO&WHO. 16, 1–85.

Concepcion Garcia, M., Heras, J. M., & Marina, M. L. (2007). Simple and rapid characterization of soybean cultivars by perfusion reversed-phase HPLC: Application to the estimation of the 11S and 7S globulin contents. *Journal of Separation Science, 30*(4), 475–482.

Cunsolo, V., Muccilli, V., Saletti, R., & Foti, S. (2014). Mass spectrometry in food proteomics: A tutorial. *Journal of Mass Spectrometry, 49*(9), 768–784.

Dang, H. X., & Lawrence, C. B. (2014). Allerdictor: Fast allergen prediction using text classification techniques. *Bioinformatics, 30*(8), 1120–1128.

Darbani, B., Motawia, M. S., Olsen, C. E., Nour-Eldin, H. H., Moller, B. L., & Rook, F. (2016). The biosynthetic gene cluster for the cyanogenic glucoside dhurrin in Sorghum bicolor contains its co-expressed vacuolar MATE transporter. *Scientific Reports, 6*, 37079.

Dearman, R.J., & Kimber, I. (2009). Animal models of protein allergenicity: Potential benefits, pitfalls and challenges. *Clinical and Experimental Allergy, 39*(4), 458–468.

Dekkers, B. L., Boom, R. M., & van der Goot, A. J. (2018). Structuring processes for meat analogues. *Trends in Food Science and Technology, 81*, 25–36.

Denny, A., Aisbitt, B., & Lunn, J. (2008). Mycoprotein and health. *Nutrition Bulletin, 33*(4), 298–310.

Dimitrov, I., Naneva, L., Doytchinova, I., & Bangov, I. (2014). AllergenFP: Allergenicity prediction by descriptor fingerprints. *Bioinformatics, 30*(6), 846–851.

Domon, B., & Aebersold, R. (2006). Mass spectrometry and protein analysis. *Science, 312*(5771), 212–217.

Draisci, R., Ferretti, E., Palleschi, L., & Marchiafava, C. (2001). Identification of anatoxins in blue-green algae food supplements using liquid chromatography-tandem mass spectrometry. *Food Additives and Contaminants, 18*(6), 525–531.

EC-258/97. (2018). Regulation (EC) No 258/97 of the European Parliament and of the Council of 27 January 1997 concerning novel foods and novel food ingredients. *EC-Official Journal, L043*, 1–6.

EFSA. (2010). Scientific Opinion on the assessment of allergenicity of GM plants and microorganisms and derived food and feed. *European Food Safety Authority Journal, 8*(7), 1700.

EFSA. (2011). Scientific opinion on guidance for risk assessment of food and feed from genetically modified plants. *European Food Safety Authority Journal,9*(5), 2150.

EFSA. (2017). Guidance on allergenicity assessment of genetically modified plants. *European Food Safety Authority Journal*, 15(6), 4862.. https://www.efsa.europa.eu/en/efsajournal/pub/4862.

FDA. (2019). Listing of Color Additives Exempt from Certification; Soy Leghemoglobin FDA Federal Register, 84(244), 69620–69626.

Faeste, C. K., Ronning, H. T., Christians, U., & Granum, P. E. (2011). Liquid chromatography and mass spectrometry in food allergen detection. *Journal of Food Protection*, 74(2), 316–345.

Feinberg, A. P. (2013). A third-generation method reveals cell lineage ancestry. *Nature Methods*, 10(2), 117–118.

Fernandez, A., Mills, C., Koning, F., & Moreno, J. (2019). Safety assessment of immune-mediated adverse reactions to novel food proteins. *Trends in Biotechnology*, 37(8), 796–800.

Fernandez, A., Mills, E. N. C., Koning, F., & Moreno, F. J. (2020). Allergenicity assessment of novel food proteins: What should be improved? *Trends in Biotechnology*, 39(1), 4–8.

Fernando, R., Pinto, M., & Pathmeswaran, A. (2012). Goitrogenic food and prevalence of goitre in Sri Lanka. *International Journal of Internal Medicine*, 1(13), 1076–1081.

Ferreira Ede, S., Silva, M. A., Demonte, A., & Neves, V. A. (2011). Soy beta-conglycinin (7S globulin) reduces plasma and liver cholesterol in rats fed hypercholesterolemic diet. *Journal of Medicinal Food*, 14(1-2), 94–100.

Finnigan, T. J. A., Wall, B. T., Wilde, P. J., Stephens, F. B., Taylor, S. L., & Freedman, M. R. (2019). Mycoprotein: The future of nutritious nonmeat protein, a symposium review. *Current Developments in Nutrition*, 3(6), nzz021. doi:10.1093/cdn/nzz021.

Fitches, E.C., & Smith, R. (2018) PROteINSECT: Insects as a Sustainable Source of Protein. In: Halloran, A., Flore, R., Vantomme, P., Roos, N. (eds) Edible Insects in Sustainable Food Systems. Switzerland, Cham, Springer. https://doi.org/10.1007/978-3-319-74011-9_26.

Fu, L., Wang, C., Zhu, Y., & Wang, Y. (2019). Seafood allergy: Occurrence, mechanisms and measures. *Trends in Food Science and Technology*, 88, 80–92.

Fuchs, M., Cichna-Markl, M., & Hochegger, R. (2013). Development and validation of a duplex real-time PCR method for the simultaneous detection of celery and white mustard in food. *Food Chemistry*, 141(1), 229–235.

Gil-Humanes, J., Piston, F., Altamirano-Fortoul, R., Real, A., Comino, I., Sousa, C., Rosell, C. M., & Barro, F. (2014). Reduced-gliadin wheat bread: an alternative to the gluten-free diet for consumers suffering gluten-related pathologies. *PLoS One*, 9(3), e90898. doi:10.1371/journal.pone.0090898.

Gleadow, R. M., & Moller, B. L. (2014). Cyanogenic glycosides: Synthesis, physiology, and phenotypic plasticity. *Annual Review of Plant Biology*, 65, 155–185.

Golias, J., Humlova, Z., Halada, P., Habova, V., Janatkova, I., & Tuckova, L. (2013). Identification of rice proteins recognized by the IgE antibodies of patients with food allergies. *Journal of Agricultural and Food Chemistry*, 61(37), 8851–8860.

Gomaa, A., & Boye, J. (2015). Impact of irradiation and thermal processing on the immunochemical detection of milk and egg allergens in foods. *Food Research International*, 74, 275–283.

Gomez, D., Shankman, L. S., Nguyen, A. T., & Owens, G. K. (2013). Detection of histone modifications at specific gene loci in single cells in histological sections. *Nature Methods*, 10(2), 171–177.

Gouda, M., Chen, K., Li, X., Liu, Y., & He, Y. (2021a). Detection of microalgae single-cell antioxidant and electrochemical potentials by gold microelectrode and Raman micro-spectroscopy combined with chemometrics. *Sensors and Actuators B: Chemical*, 329, 129229. doi:10.1016/j.snb.2020.129229.

Gouda, M., El-Din Bekhit, A., Tang, Y., Huang, Y., Huang, L., He, Y., & Li, X. (2021b). Recent innovations of ultrasound green technology in herbal phytochemistry: A review. *Ultrasonics Sonochemistry*, 73, 105538 10.1016/j.ultsonch.2021.105538.

Gouda, M., Zu, L., Ma, S., Sheng, L., & Ma, M. (2018). Influence of bio-active terpenes on the characteristics and functional properties of egg yolk. *Food Hydrocolloids*, 80, 222–230.

Grahl, S., Strack, M., Mensching, A., & Mörlein, D. (2020). Alternative protein sources in Western diets: Food product development and consumer acceptance of spirulina-filled pasta. *Food Quality and Preference*, 84, 103933. doi:10.1016/j.foodqual.2020.103933.

Gravel, A., & Doyen, A. (2020). The use of edible insect proteins in food: Challenges and issues related to their functional properties. *Innovative Food Science & Emerging Technologies*, 59, 102272. doi:10.1016/j.ifset.2019.102272.

Gruber, P., Becker, W. M., & Hofmann, T. (2005). Influence of the maillard reaction on the allergenicity of rAra h 2, a recombinant major allergen from peanut (*Arachis hypogaea*), its major epitopes, and peanut agglutinin. *Journal of Agricultural and Food Chemistry*, 53(6), 2289–2296.

Gubesch, M., Theler, B., Dutta, M., Baumer, B., Mathis, A., Holzhauser, T., Vieths, S., & Ballmer-Weber, B. K. (2007). Strategy for allergenicity assessment of 'natural novel foods': Clinical and molecular investigation of exotic vegetables (water spinach, hyacinth bean and Ethiopian eggplant). *Allergy*, 62(11), 1243–1250.

Guerrera, I. C., & Kleiner, O. (2005). Application of mass spectrometry in proteomics. *Bioscience Reports*, *25*(1-2), 71–93.

Gullberg, M., Gustafsdottir, S. M., Schallmeiner, E., Jarvius, J., Bjarnegard, M., Betsholtz, C., Landegren, U., & Fredriksson, S. (2004). Cytokine detection by antibody-based proximity ligation. *Proceedings of the National Academy of Sciences*, *101*(22), 8420–8424.

Guo, J., Yang, L., Chen, L., Morisset, D., Li, X., Pan, L., & Zhang, D. (2011). MPIC: A high-throughput analytical method for multiple DNA targets. *Analytical Chemistry*, *83*(5), 1579–1586.

Gouda, M., Huang, Z., Liu, Y., He, Y., & Li, X. (2021). Physicochemical impact of bioactive terpenes on the microalgae biomass structural characteristics. *Bioresource Technology*, 1, 334. doi: 10.1016/j.biortech.2021.125232.

Gupta, S. K., & Venkitasubramanian, T. A. (1975a). The effect of zinc and phytic acid on the incorporation of 1-14C-acetate into aflatoxin by resting mycelia of *Aspergillus parasiticus*. *Zeitschrift für Lebensmittel-Untersuchung und Forschung*, *159*(2), 107–111.

Gupta, S. K., & Venkitasubramanian, T. A. (1975b). Production of aflatoxin on soybeans. *Appl Microbiol*, *29*(6), 834–836.

Han, X., Aslanian, A., & Yates, J. R., 3rd. (2008). Mass spectrometry for proteomics. *Current Opinion in Chemical Biology*, *12*(5), 483–490.

He, L. L., Lamont, E., Veeregowda, B., Sreevatsan, S., Haynes, C. L., Diez-Gonzalez, F., & Labuza, T. P. (2011). Aptamer-based surface-enhanced Raman scattering detection of ricin in liquid foods. *Chemical Science*, *2*(8), 1579–1582.

Hedegaard, R. V., Rokkjaer, I., & Sloth, J. J. (2013). Total and inorganic arsenic in dietary supplements based on herbs, other botanicals and algae: A possible contributor to inorganic arsenic exposure. *Analytical and Bioanalytical Chemistry*, *405*(13), 4429–4435.

Hira, T., Maekawa, T., Asano, K., & Hara, H. (2009). Cholecystokinin secretion induced by beta-conglycinin peptone depends on Galphaq-mediated pathways in enteroendocrine cells. *European Journal of Nutrition*, *48*(2), 124–127.

Hoff, M., Trueb, R. M., Ballmer-Weber, B. K., Vieths, S., & Wuethrich, B. (2003). Immediate-type hypersensitivity reaction to ingestion of mycoprotein (Quorn) in a patient allergic to molds caused by acidic ribosomal protein P2. *Journal of Allergy and Clinical Immunology*, *111*(5), 1106–1110.

Hoffmann-Sommergruber, K. (2016). Proteomics and its impact on food allergy diagnosis. *EuPA Open Proteom*, *12*, 10–12.

Hong, X., Hao, K., Ladd-Acosta, C., Hansen, K. D., Tsai, H. J., Liu, X., Xu, X., Thornton, T. A., Caruso, D., Keet, C. A., Sun, Y., Wang, G., Luo, W., Kumar, R., Fuleihan, R., Singh, A. M., Kim, J. S., Story, R. E., Gupta, R. S., Gao, P., Chen, Z., Walker, S. O., Bartell, T. R., Beaty, T. H., Fallin, M. D., Schleimer, R., Holt, P. G., Nadeau, K. C., Wood, R. A., Pongracic, J. A., Weeks, D. E., & Wang, X. (2015). Genome-wide association study identifies peanut allergy-specific loci and evidence of epigenetic mediation in US children. *Nature Communications*, *6*, 6304. doi:10.1038/ncomms7304.

Houston, N. L., Lee, D. G., Stevenson, S. E., Ladics, G. S., Bannon, G. A., McClain, S., Privalle, L., Stagg, N., Herouet-Guicheney, C., MacIntosh, S. C., & Thelen, J. J. (2011). Quantitation of soybean allergens using tandem mass spectrometry. *Journal of Proteome Research*, *10*(2), 763–773.

Huang, L., Mills, E. N. C., Carter, J. M., & Morgan, M. R. A. (1998). Analysis of thermal stability of soya globulins using monoclonal antibodies. *Biochimica et Biophysica Acta (BBA) - Protein Structure and Molecular Enzymology*, *1388*(1), 215–226.

Hurrell, R. F., Juillerat, M. A., Reddy, M. B., Lynch, S. R., Dassenko, S. A., & Cook, J. D. (1992). Soy protein, phytate, and iron absorption in humans. *American Journal of Clinical Nutrition*, *56*(3), 573–578.

Jacobson, M. F., & DePorter, J. (2018). Self-reported adverse reactions associated with mycoprotein (Quorn-brand) containing foods. *Annals of Allergy, Asthma & Immunology*, *120*(6), 626–630.

Jensen-Jarolim, E., Pali-Scholl, I., Jensen, S. A. F., Robibaro, B., & Kinaciyan, T. (2015). Caution: Reptile pets shuttle grasshopper allergy and asthma into homes. *World Allergy Organization Journal*, 8. doi:1 0.1186/s40413-015-0072-1.

Jia, H., Zhou, T., Zhu, H., Shen, L., & He, P. (2019). Quantification of gly m 5.0101 in soybean and soy products by liquid chromatography-tandem mass spectrometry. *Molecules*, *24*(1). doi:10.3390/molecules24010068.

Jiang, J., & Xiong, Y. L. (2016). Natural antioxidants as food and feed additives to promote health benefits and quality of meat products: A review. *Meat Science*, *120*, 107–117.

Jin, Y., He, X., Andoh-Kumi, K., Fraser, R. Z., Lu, M., & Goodman, R. E. (2018). Evaluating potential risks of food allergy and toxicity of soy leghemoglobin expressed in *Pichia pastoris*. *Molecular Nutrition and Food Research*, *62*(1), 1700297. doi:10.1002/mnfr.201700297.

Jonas, D. A., Elmadfa, I., Engel, K. H., Heller, K. J., Kozianowski, G., Konig, A., Muller, D., Narbonne, J. F., Wackernagel, W., & Kleiner, J. (2001). Safety considerations of DNA in food. *Annals of Nutrition and Metabolism*, *45*(6), 235–254.

Kadim, I. T., Mahgoub, O., Baqir, S., Faye, B., & Purchas, R. (2015). Cultured meat from muscle stem cells: A review of challenges and prospects. *Journal of Integrative Agriculture*, *14*(2), 222–233.

Kagnoff, M. F. (2007). Celiac disease: Pathogenesis of a model immunogenetic disease. *Journal of clinical investigation*, *117*(1), 41–49.

Kaushik, G., Singhal, P., & Chaturvedi, S. (2018). Food Processing for Increasing Consumption: The Case of Legumes. Grumezescu, A. M., Holban, A. M. (Eds), Handbook of Food Bioengineering, Food Processing for Increased Quality and Consumption, Academic Press, Elsevier, Netherland, pp 1-28, https://doi.org/10.1016/B978-0-12-811447-6.00001-1.

Khor, S. S., Morino, R., Nakazono, K., Kamitsuji, S., Akita, M., Kawajiri, M., Yamasaki, T., Kami, A., Hoshi, Y., Tada, A., Ishikawa, K., Hine, M., Kobayashi, M., Kurume, N., Kamatani, N., Tokunaga, K., & Johnson, T. A. (2018). Genome-wide association study of self-reported food reactions in Japanese identifies shrimp and peach specific loci in the HLA-DR/DQ gene region. *Scientific Reports*, *8*(1), 1069.

Kieliszek, M., Kot, A. M., Bzducha-Wróbel, A., Błażejak, S., Gientka, I., & Kurcz, A. (2017). Biotechnological use of Candida yeasts in the food industry: A review. *Fungal Biology Reviews*, *31*(4), 185–198.

Knoch, E., Motawie, M. S., Olsen, C. E., Moller, B. L., & Lyngkjaer, M. F. (2016). Biosynthesis of the leucine derived alpha-, beta- and gamma-hydroxynitrile glucosides in barley (*Hordeum vulgare* L.). *Plant Journal*, *88*(2), 247–256.

Kobayashi, Y., & Kawagishi, H. (2014). Fungal lectins: A growing family. *Methods in Molecular Biology*, *1200*, 15–38.

Kusano, S., Kukimoto-Niino, M., Satta, Y., Ohsawa, N., Uchikubo-Kamo, T., Wakiyama, M., Ikeda, M., Terada, T., Yamamoto, K., Nishimura, Y., Shirouzu, M., Sasazuki, T., & Yokoyama, S. (2014). Structural basis for the specific recognition of the major antigenic peptide from the Japanese cedar pollen allergen Cry j 1 by HLA-DP5. *Journal of Molecular Biology*, *426*(17), 3016–3027.

Lai, D., Maimann, A. B., Macea, E., Ocampo, C. H., Cardona, G., Picmanova, M., Darbani, B., Olsen, C. E., Debouck, D., Raatz, B., Moller, B. L., & Rook, F. (2020). Biosynthesis of cyanogenic glucosides in *Phaseolus lunatus* and the evolution of oxime-based defenses. *Plant Direct*, *4*(8), e00244. doi:10.1002/pld3.244.

Lam, A. C. Y., Can Karaca, A., Tyler, R. T., & Nickerson, M. T. (2016). Pea protein isolates: Structure, extraction, and functionality. *Food Reviews International*, *34*(2), 126–147.

LaPorte, S. L., Juo, Z. S., Vaclavikova, J., Colf, L. A., Qi, X., Heller, N. M., Keegan, A. D., & Garcia, K. C. (2008). Molecular and structural basis of cytokine receptor pleiotropy in the interleukin-4/13 system. *Cell*, *132*(2), 259–272.

Le, T. M., Knulst, A. C., & Rockmann, H. (2014). Anaphylaxis to Spirulina confirmed by skin prick test with ingredients of Spirulina tablets. *Food and Chemical Toxicology*, *74*, 309–310.

Lees, J. G., Miles, A. J., Wien, F., & Wallace, B. A. (2006). A reference database for circular dichroism spectroscopy covering fold and secondary structure space. *Bioinformatics*, *22*(16), 1955–1962.

Levin, M., Otten, H., von Wachenfeldt, C., & Ohlin, M. (2015). A folded and immunogenic IgE-hyporeactive variant of the major allergen Phl p 1 produced in *Escherichia coli*. *BMC Biotechnology*, *15*, 52. doi:10.1186/s12896-015-0150-z.

Li, Q., Zhao, X., Liu, H., & Qu, F. (2014). Low pH capillary electrophoresis application to improve capillary electrophoresis-systematic evolution of ligands by exponential enrichment. *Journal of Chromatography A*, *1364*, 289–294.

Lian, D.-S., & Zeng, H.-S. (2017). Capillary electrophoresis based on nucleic acid detection as used in food analysis. *Comprehensive Reviews in Food Science and Food Safety*, *16*(6), 1281–1295.

Lin, Z., & He, L. (2019). Recent advance in SERS techniques for food safety and quality analysis: A brief review. *Current Opinion in Food Science*, *28*, 82–87.

Liu, B., Teng, D., Yang, Y., Wang, X., & Wang, J. (2012). Development of a competitive ELISA for the detection of soybean α subunit of β-conglycinin. *Process Biochemistry*, *47*(2), 280–287.

Liu, Y., Du, H., Li, P., Shen, Y., Peng, H., Liu, S., Zhou, G. A., Zhang, H., Liu, Z., Shi, M., Huang, X., Li, Y., Zhang, M., Wang, Z., Zhu, B., Han, B., Liang, C., & Tian, Z. (2020). Pan-genome of wild and cultivated soybeans. *Cell*, *182*(1), 162–176.

Liu, Y., & Wu, F. (2010). Global burden of aflatoxin-induced hepatocellular carcinoma: a risk assessment. *Environmental health perspectives*, *118*(6), 818–824.

Lorence, A. (2012). Recombinant gene expression. *Methods in Molecular Biology*, *824*, 209–223.

Lu, F., Kuhnle, G. K., & Cheng, Q. (2018). The effect of common spices and meat type on the formation of heterocyclic amines and polycyclic aromatic hydrocarbons in deep-fried meatballs. *Food Control*, *92*, 399–411.

Ma, H., Han, X. X., & Zhao, B. (2020). Enhanced Raman spectroscopic analysis of protein post-translational modifications. *Trends in Analytical Chemistry*, *131*, 116019. doi:10.1016/j.trac.2020.116019.

Ma, H., Sun, X., Chen, L., Cheng, W., Han, X. X., Zhao, B., & He, C. (2017). Multiplex immunochips for high-accuracy detection of afp-l3% based on surface-enhanced Raman scattering: Implications for early liver cancer diagnosis. *Analytical Chemistry*, *89*(17), 8877–8883.

Mark Ibekwe, A., Murinda, S. E., Murry, M. A., Schwartz, G., & Lundquist, T. (2017). Microbial community structures in high rate algae ponds for bioconversion of agricultural wastes from livestock industry for feed production. *Science of the Total Environment*, *580*, 1185–1196.

Masilamani, M., Wei, J., Bhatt, S., Paul, M., Yakir, S., & Sampson, H. A. (2011). Soybean isoflavones regulate dendritic cell function and suppress allergic sensitization to peanut. *Journal of Allergy and Clinical Immunology*, *128*(6), 1242–1250 e1.

Mazzucchelli, G., Holzhauser, T., Cirkovic Velickovic, T., Diaz-Perales, A., Molina, E., Roncada, P., Rodrigues, P., Verhoeckx, K., & Hoffmann-Sommergruber, K. (2018). Current (food) allergenic risk assessment: Is it fit for novel foods? Status quo and identification of gaps. *Molecular Nutrition and Food Research*, *62*(1), 1700278. doi:10.1002/mnfr.201700278.

McClain, S., Bowman, C., Fernandez-Rivas, M., Ladics, G. S., & Ree, R. (2014). Allergic sensitization: food- and protein-related factors. *Clinical and Translational Allergy*, *4*(1), 11. doi:10.1186/2045-7022-4-11.

Migala, J., & Nied, J. (2019). What is the beyond burger and is it healthy? Women's health. *Women's Health*. https://www.womenshealthmag.com/food/a21566428/beyond-meat-burger-ingredients/

Mishra, A., Behura, A., Mawatwal, S., Kumar, A., Naik, L., Mohanty, S. S., Manna, D., Dokania, P., Mishra, A., Patra, S. K., & Dhiman, R. (2019). Structure-function and application of plant lectins in disease biology and immunity. *Food and Chemical Toxicology*, *134*, 110827. doi:10.1016/j.fct.2019.110827.

Monaci, L., & Visconti, A. (2009). Mass spectrometry-based proteomics methods for analysis of food allergens. *Trends in Analytical Chemistry*, *28*(5), 581–591.

Morandini, P. (2010). Inactivation of allergens and toxins. *Nature Biotechnology*, *27*(5), 482–493.

Morari, D., Stepurina, T., & Rotari, V.I. (2008). Calcium ions make phytohemagglutinin resistant to trypsin proteolysis. *Journal of Agricultural and Food Chemistry*, *56*(10), 3764–3771.

Mueller, G. A., Ankney, J. A., Glesner, J., Khurana, T., Edwards, L. L., Pedersen, L. C., Perera, L., Slater, J. E., Pomes, A., & London, R. E. (2014). Characterization of an anti-Bla g 1 scFv: epitope mapping and cross-reactivity. *Molecular Immunology*, *59*(2), 200–207.

NASEM. (2017). Finding a path to safety in food allergy: Assessment of the global burden, causes, prevention, management, and public policy, 574. doi:10.17226/23658.

Nasseri, A. T., Rasoul-Ami, S., Morowvat, M. H., & Ghasemi, Y. (2011). Single cell protein: Production and process. *American Journal of Food Technology*, *6*(2), 103–116.

Neng, J., Zhang, Q., & Sun, P. (2020). Application of surface-enhanced Raman spectroscopy in fast detection of toxic and harmful substances in food. *Biosensors and Bioelectronics*, *167*, 112480. doi:10.1016/j.bios.2020.112480.

Nishinari, K., Fang, Y., Nagano, T., Guo, S., & Wang, R. (2018). Soy as a food ingredient. In: *Proteins in Food Processing*. R. Yada (Ed). Duxford, UK: Woodhead Publishing, 149–186.

Nwaru, B. I., Hickstein, L., Panesar, S. S., Muraro, A., Werfel, T., Cardona, V., Dubois, A. E., Halken, S., Hoffmann-Sommergruber, K., Poulsen, L. K., Roberts, G., Van Ree, R., Vlieg-Boerstra, B. J., Sheikh, A., Allergy, E. F., & Anaphylaxis Guidelines, G. (2014). The epidemiology of food allergy in Europe: a systematic review and meta-analysis. *Allergy*, *69*(1), 62–75.

Pali-Scholl, I., Meinlschmidt, P., Larenas-Linnemann, D., Purschke, B., Hofstetter, G., Rodriguez-Monroy, F.A., Einhorn, L., Mothes-Luksch, N., Jensen-Jarolim, E., & Jager, H. (2019). Edible insects: Cross-recognition of IgE from crustacean- and house dust mite allergic patients, and reduction of allergenicity by food processing. *World Allergy Organization Journal*, *12*(1), 100006. doi:10.1016/j.waojou.2018.10.001.

Pali-Scholl, I., Untersmayr, E., Klems, M., & Jensen-Jarolim, E. (2018). The effect of digestion and digestibility on allergenicity of food. *Nutrients*, *10*(9), 1129.

Pali-Schöll, I., Verhoeckx, K., Mafra, I., Bavaro, S. L., Clare Mills, E. N., & Monaci, L. (2019). Allergenic and novel food proteins: State of the art and challenges in the allergenicity assessment. *Trends in Food Science and Technology*, *84*, 45–48.

Parolini, M., Ganzaroli, A., & Bacenetti, J. (2020). Earthworm as an alternative protein source in poultry and fish farming: Current applications and future perspectives. *Science of the Total Environment*, *734*, 139460. doi:10.1016/j.scitotenv.2020.139460.

Pekar, J., Ret, D., & Untersmayr, E. (2018). Stability of allergens. *Molecular Immunology*, *100*, 14–20.

Picariello, G., Mamone, G., Cutignano, A., Fontana, A., Zurlo, L., Addeo, F., & Ferranti, P. (2015). Proteomics, peptidomics, and immunogenic potential of wheat beer (Weissbier). *Journal of Agricultural and Food Chemistry*, *63*(13), 3579–3586.

Picotti, P., & Aebersold, R. (2012). Selected reaction monitoring-based proteomics: Workflows, potential, pitfalls and future directions. *Nature Methods*, *9*(6), 555–566.

Pomes, A., Davies, J. M., Gadermaier, G., Hilger, C., Holzhauser, T., Lidholm, J., Lopata, A. L., Mueller, G. A., Nandy, A., Radauer, C., Chan, S. K., Jappe, U., Kleine-Tebbe, J., Thomas, W. R., Chapman, M. D., van Hage, M., van Ree, R., Vieths, S., Raulf, M., Goodman, R. E., & Sub-Committee, W. I. A. N. (2018). WHO/IUIS Allergen Nomenclature: Providing a common language. *Molecular Immunology*, *100*, 3–13.

Poms, R. E., Klein, C. L., & Anklam, E. (2004). Methods for allergen analysis in food: A review. *Food Additives and Contaminants*, *21*(1), 1–31.

Radauer, C., Bublin, M., Wagner, S., Mari, A., & Breiteneder, H. (2008). Allergens are distributed into few protein families and possess a restricted number of biochemical functions. *Journal of Allergy and Clinical Immunology*, *121*(4), 847–52 e7.

Radauer, C., Nandy, A., Ferreira, F., Goodman, R. E., Larsen, J. N., Lidholm, J., Pomes, A., Raulf-Heimsoth, M., Rozynek, P., Thomas, W. R., & Breiteneder, H. (2014). Update of the WHO/IUIS allergen nomenclature database based on analysis of allergen sequences. *Allergy*, *69*(4), 413–419.

Rawel, H. M., Rohn, S., Kroll, J., & Schweigert, F. J. (2005). Surface enhanced laser desorptions ionization-time of flight-mass spectrometry analysis in complex food and biological systems. *Molecular Nutrition and Food Research*, *49*(12), 1104–1111.

Remington, B., Broekman, H. C. H., Blom, W. M., Capt, A., Crevel, R. W. R., Dimitrov, I., Faeste, C. K., Fernandez-Canton, R., Giavi, S., Houben, G. F., Glenn, K. C., Madsen, C. B., Kruizinga, A. K., & Constable, A. (2018). Approaches to assess IgE mediated allergy risks (sensitization and cross-reactivity) from new or modified dietary proteins. *Food and Chemical Toxicology*, *112*, 97–107.

Rouge, P., Culerrier, R., Granier, C., Rance, F., & Barre, A. (2010). Characterization of IgE-binding epitopes of peanut (*Arachis hypogaea*) PNA lectin allergen cross-reacting with other structurally related legume lectins. *Molecular Immunology*, *47*(14), 2359–2366.

Rushing, B. R., & Selim, M. I. (2019). Aflatoxin B1: A review on metabolism, toxicity, occurrence in food, occupational exposure, and detoxification methods. *Food and Chemical Toxicology*, *124*, 81–100.

van Huis, A., Van Itterbeeck, J., Klunder, H., Mertens, E., Halloran, A., Muir, G. Vantomme, P. (2013) Edible insects: future prospects for food and feed security. (FAO forestry paper; No. 171). Food and Agriculture Organization of the United Nations. https://edepot.wur.nl/258042.

Rzymski, P., Niedzielski, P., Kaczmarek, N., Jurczak, T., & Klimaszyk, P. (2015). The multidisciplinary approach to safety and toxicity assessment of microalgae-based food supplements following clinical cases of poisoning. *Harmful Algae*, *46*, 34–42.

Sadler, M. J. (2004). Meat alternatives - market developments and health benefits. *Trends in Food Science and Technology*, *15*(5), 250–260.

Sampson, H. A., O'Mahony, L., Burks, A. W., Plaut, M., Lack, G., & Akdis, C. A. (2018). Mechanisms of food allergy. *Journal of Allergy and Clinical Immunology*, *141*(1), 11–19.

Sanchez-Sabate, R., & Sabate, J. (2019). Consumer attitudes towards environmental concerns of meat consumption: A systematic review. *International Journal of Environmental Research and Public Health*, *16*(7), 1220.

Sanlier, N., Gokcen, B. B., & Sezgin, A. C. (2019). Health benefits of fermented foods. *Critical Reviews in Food Science and Nutrition*, *59*(3), 506–527.

Sapone, A., Lammers, K. M., Casolaro, V., Cammarota, M., Giuliano, M. T., De Rosa, M., Stefanile, R., Mazzarella, G., Tolone, C., Russo, M. I., Esposito, P., Ferraraccio, F., Carteni, M., Riegler, G., de Magistris, L., & Fasano, A. (2011). Divergence of gut permeability and mucosal immune gene expression in two gluten-associated conditions: Celiac disease and gluten sensitivity. *BMC Medicine*, *9*, 23. doi:10.1186/1741-7015-9-23.

Sato, F. (2020). Plant alkaloid engineering. In: *Comprehensive Natural Products III*, 3rd Edition. L. Hung-Wen, B. Tadhg (Eds). Netherlands, Amsterdam: Elsevier, 700–755.

Schallmeiner, E., Oksanen, E., Ericsson, O., Spangberg, L., Eriksson, S., Stenman, U. H., Pettersson, K., & Landegren, U. (2007). Sensitive protein detection via triple-binder proximity ligation assays. *Nature Methods*, *4*(2), 135–137.

Schweiggert-Weisz, U., Eisner, P., Bader-Mittermaier, S., & Osen, R. (2020). Food proteins from plants and fungi. *Current Opinion in Food Science*, *32*, 156–162.

Scoglio, S. (2018). Microcystins in water and in microalgae: Do microcystins as microalgae contaminants warrant the current public alarm? *Toxicology Reports, 5*, 785–792.

Sha, L., & Xiong, Y. L. (2020). Plant protein-based alternatives of reconstructed meat: Science, technology, and challenges. *Trends in Food Science and Technology, 102*, 51–61.

Sheng, L., Li, P., Wu, H., Liu, Y., Han, K., Gouda, M., Tong, Q., Ma, M., & Jin, Y. (2018). Tapioca starch-pullulan interaction during gelation and retrogradation. *LWT-Food Science and Technology, 96*, 432–438.

Sicherer, S., & Sampson, H. (2006). Food allergy. *Journal of Allergy and Clinical Immunology, 117*(2), S470–S475.

Singh, R. S., Thakur, S. R., & Bansal, P. (2015). Algal lectins as promising biomolecules for biomedical research. *Critical Reviews in Microbiology, 41*(1), 77–88.

Song, C., Wang, Z., Zhang, R., Yang, J., Tan, X., & Cui, Y. (2009). Highly sensitive immunoassay based on Raman reporter-labeled immuno-Au aggregates and SERS-active immune substrate. *Biosensors and Bioelectronics, 25*(4), 826–831.

Song, J., Huang, Y. F., Zhang, W. J., Chen, X. F., & Guo, Y. M. (2016). Ocular diseases: Immunological and molecular mechanisms. *International Journal of Ophthalmology, 9*(5), 780–788.

Souza Filho, P. F., Andersson, D., Ferreira, J. A., & Taherzadeh, M. J. (2019). Mycoprotein: Environmental impact and health aspects. *World Journal of Microbiology and Biotechnology, 35*(10), 147. doi:10.1007/s11274-019-2723-9.

Srinroch, C., Srisomsap, C., Chokchaichamnankit, D., Punyarit, P., & Phiriyangkul, P. (2015). Identification of novel allergen in edible insect, *Gryllus bimaculatus* and its cross-reactivity with *Macrobrachium* spp. allergens. *Food Chemistry, 184*, 160–166.

Stojadinovic, M., Pieters, R., Smit, J., & Velickovic, T. C. (2014). Cross-linking of beta-lactoglobulin enhances allergic sensitization through changes in cellular uptake and processing. *Toxicological Sciences, 140*(1), 224–235.

Tachibana, H., Saito, M., Tsuji, K., Yamanaka, K., Hoa, L. Q., & Tamiya, E. (2015). Self-propelled continuous-flow PCR in capillary-driven microfluidic device: Microfluidic behavior and DNA amplification. *Sensors and Actuators B: Chemical, 206*, 303–310.

Takagi, K., Teshima, R., Nakajima, O., Okunuki, H., & Sawada, J. (2006). Improved ELISA method for screening human antigen-specific IgE and its application for monitoring specific IgE for novel proteins in genetically modified foods. *Regulatory Toxicology and Pharmacology, 44*(2), 182–188.

Tang, S., Zhou, X., Gouda, M., Cai, Z., & Jin, Y. (2019). Effect of enzymatic hydrolysis on the solubility of egg yolk powder from the changes in structure and functional properties. *LWT-Food Science and Technology, 110*, 214–222.

Tavoosidana, G., Ronquist, G., Darmanis, S., Yan, J., Carlsson, L., Wu, D., Conze, T., Ek, P., Semjonow, A., Eltze, E., Larsson, A., Landegren, U. D., & Kamali-Moghaddam, M. (2011). Multiple recognition assay reveals prostasomes as promising plasma biomarkers for prostate cancer. *Proceedings of the National Academy of Sciences, 108*(21), 8809–8814.

Taylor, J., Ahmed, I. A. M., Al-Juhaimi, F. Y., & Bekhit, A. E. A. (2020). Consumers' perceptions and sensory properties of beef patty analogues. *Foods, 9*(1), 63. doi:10.3390/foods9010063.

Tong, Q. H., Tao, T., Xie, L. Q., & Lu, H. J. (2016). ELISA-PLA: A novel hybrid platform for the rapid, highly sensitive and specific quantification of proteins and post-translational modifications. *Biosensors and Bioelectronics, 80*, 385–391.

Torres-Tiji, Y., Fields, F. J., & Mayfield, S. P. (2020). Microalgae as a future food source. *Biotechnology Advances*, 107536. doi:10.1016/j.biotechadv.2020.107536.

Tran, D. T., Knez, K., Janssen, K. P., Pollet, J., Spasic, D., & Lammertyn, J. (2013). Selection of aptamers against Ara h 1 protein for FO-SPR biosensing of peanut allergens in food matrices. *Biosensors and Bioelectronics, 43*, 245–251.

Turck, D., Bresson, J. L., Burlingame, B., Dean, T., Fairweather-Tait, S., Heinonen, M., Hirsch-Ernst, K. I., Mangelsdorf, I., McArdle, H., Naska, A., Auser-Berthold, M. N., Nowicka, G., Pentieva, K., Sanz, Y., Siani, A., Odin, A. S., Stern, M., Tom, D., Vinceti, M., Willatts, P., Engel, K. H., Marchelli, R., Poting, A., Poulsen, M., Salminen, S., Schlatter, J., Arcella, D., Gelbmann, W., de Sesmaisons-Lecarre, A., Verhagen, H., van Loveren, H., & Nutr, E. P. D. P. (2016). Guidance on the preparation and presentation of an application for authorisation of a novel food in the context of Regulation (EU) 2015/2283. *EFSA Journal, 14*(11), 4594. doi:10.2903/j.efsa.2016.4594.

Upadhyaya, S., Tiwari, S., Arora, N., & Singh, D. (2016). Microbial protein: A valuable component for future food security. In: *Microbes and Environmental Management*. J. Singh, & D. Singh (Eds). USA: Studium Press, 259–277.

Utsumi, S., Matsumura, Y., & Mori, T. (1997). Structure-function relationships of soy proteins. In: *Food Proteins and Their Applications*. Damodaran, A.P.S. S. (Ed). New York: Marcel Dekker Inc, 257–291.

Verhoeckx, K., Broekman, H., Knulst, A., & Houben, G. (2016). Allergenicity assessment strategy for novel food proteins and protein sources. *Regulatory Toxicology and Pharmacology*, 79, 118–124.

Verhoeckx, K., van, S., den, C.F., Gaspari, M., De Jong, G., Wichers, H., Van Hoffen, E., Houben, G., & Knulst, A. (2014). House dust mite (Der p 10) and crustacean allergic patients may react to food containing Yellow mealworm proteins. *Food and Chemical Toxicology*, 65, 364–373.

Verhoeckx, K. C. M., Vissers, Y. M., Baumert, J. L., Faludi, R., Feys, M., Flanagan, S., Herouet-Guicheney, C., Holzhauser, T., Shimojo, R., van der Bolt, N., Wichers, H., & Kimber, I. (2015). Food processing and allergenicity. *Food and Chemical Toxicology*, 80, 223–240.

Vichi, S., Lavorini, P., Funari, E., Scardala, S., & Testai, E. (2012). Contamination by Microcystis and microcystins of blue-green algae food supplements (BGAS) on the Italian market and possible risk for the exposed population. *Food and Chemical Toxicology*, 50(12), 4493–4499.

Vickery, B. P., Chin, S., & Burks, A. W. (2011). Pathophysiology of food allergy. *Pediatric Clinics of North America*, 58(2), 363–376, ix–x.

Vissers, Y. M., Blanc, F., Skov, P. S., Johnson, P. E., Rigby, N. M., Przybylski-Nicaise, L., Bernard, H., Wal, J. M., Ballmer-Weber, B., Zuidmeer-Jongejan, L., Szepfalusi, Z., Ruinemans-Koerts, J., Jansen, A. P., Savelkoul, H. F., Wichers, H. J., Mackie, A. R., Mills, C. E., & Adel-Patient, K. (2011). Effect of heating and glycation on the allergenicity of 2S albumins (Ara h 2/6) from peanut. *PLoS One*, 6(8), e23998. doi:10.1371/journal.pone.0023998.

Wang, Y., Fu, T. J., Howard, A., Kothary, M. H., McHugh, T. H., & Zhang, Y. (2013). Crystal structure of peanut (*Arachis hypogaea*) allergen Ara h 5. *Journal of Agricultural and Food Chemistry*, 61(7), 1573–1578.

Wee, J., Day, D. M., & Linz, J. E. (2016). Effects of zinc chelators on aflatoxin production in *Aspergillus parasiticus*. *Toxins (Basel)*, 8(6), 171. doi:10.3390/toxins8060171.

Wen, C., Zhang, J., Zhang, H., Duan, Y., & Ma, H. (2020). Plant protein-derived antioxidant peptides: Isolation, identification, mechanism of action and application in food systems: A review. *Trends in Food Science and Technology*, 105, 308–322.

Westerhout, J., Krone, T., Snippe, A., Babe, L., McClain, S., Ladics, G. S., Houben, G. F., & Verhoeckx, K. C. (2019). Allergenicity prediction of novel and modified proteins: Not a mission impossible! Development of a random forest allergenicity prediction model. *Regul Toxicol Pharmacol*, 107, 104422. doi:10.1016/j.yrtph.2019.104422.

Whitmore, L., & Wallace, B. A. (2008). Protein secondary structure analyses from circular dichroism spectroscopy: Methods and reference databases. *Biopolymers*, 89(5), 392–400.

Xi, J., & Yu, Q. (2020). The development of lateral flow immunoassay strip tests based on surface enhanced Raman spectroscopy coupled with gold nanoparticles for the rapid detection of soybean allergen β-conglycinin. *Spectrochimica Acta Part A: Molecular and Biomolecular Spectroscopy*, 241, 118640. doi:10.1016/j.saa.2020.118640.

Yang, Y., Park, Y., Cassada, D. A., Snow, D. D., Rogers, D. G., & Lee, J. (2011). In vitro and in vivo safety assessment of edible blue-green algae, Nostoc commune var. sphaeroides Kutzing and *Spirulina plantensis*. *Food and Chemical Toxicology*, 49(7), 1560–1564.

Yasar, S., Tosun, R., & Sonmez, Z. (2020). Fungal fermentation inducing improved nutritional qualities associated with altered secondary protein structure of soybean meal determined by FTIR spectroscopy. *Measurement*, 161, 107895. doi:10.1016/j.measurement.2020.107895.

You, J., Li, D., Qiao, S., Wang, Z., He, P., Ou, D., & Dong, B. (2008). Development of a monoclonal antibody-based competitive ELISA for detection of β-conglycinin, an allergen from soybean. *Food Chemistry*, 106(1), 352–360.

Zhu, Y., Kuang, H., Xu, L., Ma, W., Peng, C., Hua, Y., Wang, L., & Xu, C. (2012). Gold nanorodassembly based approach to toxin detection by SERS. *Journal of Materials Chemistry*, 22(6), 2387–2391.

14 Novel Protein Sources: An Overview of Food Regulations

Malik Altaf Hussain
Food Safety Unit, The Victorian Department of Health, Melbourne, Australia

CONTENTS

14.1 Introduction 407
14.2 Regulatory Framework 408
    14.2.1 Novel Food Regulation 408
    14.2.2 Food Safety Regulation 413
    14.2.3 Other Regulations 418
14.3 Regulatory Examples of Specific Novel Protein Sources 419
    14.3.1 Insects 419
    14.3.2 Microalgae 421
    14.3.3 Seaweed 421
    14.3.4 Duckweed 422
    14.3.5 Rapeseed 422
    14.3.6 Single Cell Protein 423
    14.3.7 Cultured Meats 423
14.4 Need for Harmonized Global Regulations of Novel Protein Sources 423
14.5 Conclusion 424
Acknowledgement and Declaration 424
References 424

14.1 INTRODUCTION

Food laws and standards are key elements of any legal framework to ensure safe food production and supply to consumers. Generally, a set of complex food laws and regulations is used to regulate the production, trade, and handling of foods. These legislations cover the regulation of food control, food safety and relevant aspects of food trade (van der Spiegel et al., 2013; Lähteenmäki-Uutela & Grmelová, 2016; de Boer & Bast, 2018). In recent years, many countries have reviewed their existing food laws to develop modern and effective national food laws and regulations. These food laws generally regard international agreements such as the World Trade Organization (WTO) and Codex Alimentarius standards (Kuik, 2004). The most essential and challenging part of a food regulatory system is to implement food laws and regulations effectively. Countries also face challenges of updating their food laws to meet the pace of rapid growth and innovation taking place at the commercial level (Marinangeli et al., 2017).

Many countries have general legal requirements for the introduction of new foods or ingredients in the market. For example, food business operators that wish to introduce a novel food protein product into the European market should comply with the requirements established in EU and national laws. The novel products, including new protein sources, would need to meet the general legal requirements to be considered as food. This would include novel food regulations, food safety legislation, labelling requirements and other specific legislation that may apply to new protein sources. Under EU regulations, any food that was not consumed 'significantly' prior to May 1997 is considered to be a novel food (European Parliament and the Council, 1997). These regulations are applied to all new foods, food from new sources, new substances used in food, and new technologies for producing food. Similarly, several regulatory agencies include a definition of novel food in their regulations (Table 14.1).

A new protein source can be considered as a novel food or ingredient if it is a newly developed and innovative protein, a protein produced using new technologies and production processes, or foods traditionally eaten outside of a geographical region (https://ec.europa.eu/food/safety/novel_food_en). Cultured meat is an example of a protein produced using new technologies by growing cell lines in artificial media in a laboratory or *in vitro* condition. Cultured meat is a novel food as compared to the production of animals on farm and obtaining meat post-slaughter. There are many reasons to regulate novel protein sources. One of the most important is to manage any potential risks and unknown consequences of new technologies and materials developed to produce food for human consumption (Vapnek et al., 2020). Regulations of novel proteins can be categorized into two major phases that include regulating market access (e.g., regulatory requirements for pre-market assessment and approvals) and regulating the products after approval in the market (e.g., labelling requirements).

This chapter provides an overview of regulatory frameworks that are in force to assess and regulate novel proteins in different parts of the world. Novel food regulations in Australia/New Zealand, Canada, and the European Union are discussed in more detail, as they are more developed. The legislation in all three regions differentiates the traditional protein foods and the novel protein foods because the novel protein foods need to go through a pre-market assessment process. Examples of some specific regulatory requirements for selected novel protein sources are also outlined.

14.2 REGULATORY FRAMEWORK

Current approval processes of novel and alternative protein sources are lacking a universal and harmonized regulatory framework. Several countries with well-established food regulatory systems have developed regulations for novel foods, food safety, and labelling that may apply to a novel protein source. Regulatory approval assessment is generally conducted by a regulatory or standard-setting agency.

14.2.1 Novel Food Regulation

In most countries, novel protein sources are regulated under novel food regulations. However, there is no universally accepted definition of novel food. The description of a novel food or ingredient in the novel food regulations does vary from country to country. The requirement of a pre-market safety assessment for novel foods is a common element of these regulations. Table 14.1 provides an overview of novel food definitions adopted by some selected countries. The EU and Australia/New Zealand novel food legislation considers food with no documented history of food use in the definition of novel foods. Australia/New Zealand use the specific term 'non-traditional food' to describe novel food. The definition of 'novel food' in legislation creates some common understanding, but there is still room for interpretation that can cause confusion and uncertainty in many cases. Therefore, a need exists to develop a more precise definition to diminish any grey areas and create certainty in the novel food assessment process. Novel food assessment applications are handled by national agencies in Australia/New Zealand and Canada. In the EU, handling and processing of novel food applications is now centralized, and it has been assessed by the European Food Safety Authority (EFSA) since 2018.

In Australia and New Zealand, novel foods are regulated by Standard 1.5.1 – Novel Foods of the Australia New Zealand Food Standards Code (Australian Government, 2017a). Standard 1.5.1

TABLE 14.1
Definitions of 'Novel Food' by different regulatory agencies in the world

Country/Region	Novel Food Definition and Description	Source

Australia/New Zealand	In Australia and New Zealand novel foods are regulated by Standard 1.5.1 – Novel Foods of the Australia New Zealand Food Standards Code. Standard 1.5.1 introduced in December 1999 defines non-traditional food and novel food as follows:
	• non-traditional food means a food which does not have a history of significant human consumption by the broad community in Australia or New Zealand.
	• novel food means a non-traditional food for which there is insufficient knowledge in the broad community to enable safe use in the form or context in which it is presented, taking into account –
	  a. the composition or structure of the product; or
	  b. levels of undesirable substances in the product; or
	  c. known potential for adverse effects in humans; or
	  d. traditional preparation and cooking methods; or
	  e. patterns and levels of consumption of the product.
	(Australia New Zealand Food Standards Code, Standard 1.5.1, 'Novel Foods')
		(Australian Government, 2017a; FSANZ, 2010)

Canada	The Canadian Food and Drug Regulations (Health Canada 1999) states that 'novel food' means:
	a. a substance, including a microorganism, that does not have a history of safe use as a food;
	b. a food that has been manufactured, prepared, preserved or packaged by a process that has not been previously applied to that food, and causes the food to undergo a major change; and
	c. a food that is derived from a plant, animal or microorganism that has been genetically modified such that
	  • the plant, animal or microorganism exhibits characteristics that were not previously observed in that plant, animal or microorganism,
	  • the plant, animal or microorganism no longer exhibits characteristics that were previously observed in that plant, animal or microorganism, or
	  • one or more characteristics of the plant, animal or microorganism no longer fall within the anticipated range for that plant, animal or microorganism.
	(Consolidated Regulations of Canada, chapter 870, Food and Drugs Act, Food and Drug Regulations, Part B, 'Foods', Division 28, 'Novel Foods')
		(Department of Justice Canada, 2010)

EU	The EU Regulations define 'novel food' as any food that was not used for human consumption to a significant degree within the Union before 15 May 1997, irrespective of the dates of accession of Member States to the Union, and that falls under at least one of the following categories:	(European Parliament and the Council, 1997)

(Continued)

TABLE 14.1 (Continued)
Definitions of 'Novel Food' by different regulatory agencies in the world

Country/Region	Novel Food Definition and Description	Source
	i. food with a new or intentionally modified molecular structure, where that structure was not used as, or in, a food within the Union before 15 May 1997; ii. food consisting of, isolated from or produced from microorganisms, fungi or algae; iii. food consisting of, isolated from or produced from material of mineral origin; iv. food consisting of, isolated from or produced from plants or their parts, except when the food has a history of safe food use within the Union and is consisting of, isolated from or produced from a plant or a variety of the same species obtained by: - traditional propagating practices which have been used for food production within the Union before 15 May 1997; or - non-traditional propagating practices which have not been used for food production within the Union before 15 May 1997, where those practices do not give rise to significant changes in the composition or structure of the food affecting its nutritional value, metabolism or level of undesirable substances; v. food consisting of, isolated from or produced from animals or their parts, except for animals obtained by traditional breeding practices which have been used for food production within the Union before 15 May 1997 and the food from those animals has a history of safe food use within the Union; vi. food consisting of, isolated from or produced from cell culture or tissue culture derived from animals, plants, micro-organisms, fungi or algae; vii. food resulting from a production process not used for food production within the Union before 15 May 1997, which gives rise to significant changes in the composition or structure of a food, affecting its nutritional value, metabolism or level of undesirable substances; viii. food consisting of engineered nanomaterials ix. vitamins, minerals and other substances used in accordance with Directive 2002/46/EC, Regulation (EC) No 1925/2006 or Regulation (EU) No 609/2013, where: - a production process not used for food production within the Union before 15 May 1997 has been applied (The Regulation (EU) 2015/2283 Regulation (EC) No 258/97)	
Singapore	SFA considers novel foods to be foods and food ingredients that do not have a history of safe use. A history of safe use is defined as substances that have been consumed as an ongoing part of the diet by a significant human population, for a period of at least 20 years and without reported adverse human health effects. Food and food ingredients which are	(SFA, 2020a)

TABLE 14.1 (Continued)
Definitions of 'Novel Food' by different regulatory agencies in the world

Country/Region	Novel Food Definition and Description	Source
	shown to have history of safe use will not be considered to be novel foods. Novel foods may also include compounds that are chemically identical to naturally occurring substances, but produced through advances in technology.	
UK	Novel foods are foods which have not been widely consumed by people in the UK or European Union (EU) before May 1997. This means that the foods don't have a 'history of consumption'. Examples of novel foods include: • new foods, for example, phytosterols and phytostanols used in cholesterol reducing spreads • traditional foods eaten elsewhere in the world, for example, chia seeds, baobab • foods produced from new processes, for example, bread treated with ultraviolet light to increase the level of vitamin D present	(FSA, 2020)
USA	Not generally recognized as safe, including food substances that were not used as food in the USA before January 1, 1958; and/or foods for which no recognition of safety based on scientific procedures exists yet. This also includes processes and breeding/selection applied to GRAS substances so that the characteristics (e.g., composition, levels of toxicants) are changed, such as extracts, isolates, distillates, and reaction products of GRAS substances, as well as synthetic analogues of GRAS substances of biological origin(Federal Food Drug and Cosmetic Act, Chapter II (Definitions), Section 201(s), and Chapter IV (Food), Section 409 (Unsafe Food Additives), Implementing regulations: Code of Federal Regulations, Title 21 (Food and Drugs), Subchapter B (Food for Human Consumption), Part 170 (Food Additives), Sections 170.3 (Definitions) and 170.30 ['Eligibility for classification as generally recognized as safe (GRAS)'].	(Food and Drug Administration U.S., 2004; Food and Drug Administration U.S., 2009)

does not clearly state whether it applies retrospectively. Therefore, a product that was on the market in Australia and/or New Zealand prior to the introduction of the Standard could possibly be considered as 'non-traditional' (Knudsen et al., 2005). Food Standards Australia New Zealand (FSANZ) describes novel foods as non-traditional foods that require an assessment to establish their safety before they are added to the food supply chains in Australia and New Zealand. Food businesses or companies interested in selling a novel food or a novel food ingredient must apply to FSANZ for a pre-market safety assessment and request that the Standard be amended to include a new protein source in the permitted novel foods list (Australian Government, 2017b). Currently, there are two documents developed by the FSANZ to assist in interpreting the Standard as follows:

1. 'Format for applying to amend the Code – Novel Foods' which has a template that can be used when making an application for permission to use a novel food (FSANZ, 2017).

2. 'Guidelines to assist in applying to amend the Australia New Zealand Food Standards Code – Novel Foods' which provides details of the operation of the standard, descriptions of the likely categories of novel foods, a decision tree for determining the novelty of food, data requirements for the assessment of novel foods and a record of views formed in response to inquiries with respect to novelty (FSANZ, 2004).

FSANZ has set up the Advisory Committee on Novel Foods (the ACNF) that represents Australian state and territory jurisdictions and the New Zealand Ministry for Primary Industries (Source: https://www.foodstandards.gov.au/industry/novel/novelcommittee/Pages/default.aspx). Food businesses or companies can send inquiries to the ACNF for an opinion as to whether a food is considered novel or not. The ACNF members consider the information provided by an enquirer to make an assessment as to whether a particular food meets the definition of 'non-traditional food' in the Standard and needs a safety assessment. Then ACNF makes a recommendation about the novelty status of the food in question, and it publishes 'Novel food – Record of views formed in response to inquiries' on the FSANZ website along with necessary information (FSANZ, 2021). The ACNF recommendations are neither legal advice nor have any legal binding, but views of the Committee members to advise enquirers whether they should submit an application seeking to amend the Standard.

The Canadian Novel Food Regulations have a two-step assessment process – first, the determination that something is novel and second, the requirement of a food safety assessment. A pre-market notification of novel foods to Health Canada is a mandatory part of the assessment process. Health Canada describes several groups of foods, including products that do not have a history of safe use as a food, foods resulting from a process not previously used for food, or foods that have been modified by genetic manipulation (also known as genetically modified foods, GM foods, genetically engineered foods or biotechnology-derived foods) as novel foods. The Food Directorate maintains an updated list of novel foods, including genetically modified (GM) foods, where information on safety assessment and findings that supports it to be safe for human consumption, are made publicly available (Health Canada, 2021). There are 226 entries in the list that was updated on 23 April 2021.

The first EU Novel Food Regulation (EC No 258/97) was adopted in 1997 and came into force on 15 May 1997 to protect public health. In the regulation novel food is defined as 'food that had not been consumed to a significant degree by humans in the EU before 15 May 1997'. The original EU Novel Food legislation focused mainly on genetically modified organisms; however, this part was detached from the Novel Food Regulation to introduce the new EC regulation (No. 1829/2003) on genetically modified food and feed in 2003. The remaining part of the Novel Food Regulation (EC No. 258/97) was revised as the Novel Food Regulation (EC No 1852/2001) and remained in force until 31 December 2017. On 1 of January 2018, it was replaced with the new Regulation (EU) 2015/2283 on novel food that is applicable now. The new regulation is developed to promote food innovation by the industry by safeguarding food for consumers in the EU market.

The novel food assessment situation in the UK is interesting and has continued to change with the regional geographic alliance. The legislation changes can be categorized into three periods:

1. In the pre-EU era, the UK reconstituted the Advisory Committee on Irradiated and Novel Foods as the Advisory Committee on Novel Foods and Processes (ACNFP) in 1988. The ACNFP was established as an independent body of experts to advise the central authorities on any matters relating to novel foods and novel food processes (ACNFP, 2003; 2004).
2. As part of the EU, the UK accepted the assessment of novel foods under the regulations of the European Union.
3. Now in the Post-EU era, the novel foods need to be authorized before they can be placed on the market in the UK. The UK retained the EU law on novel foods, Regulation (EU) 2017/2468. Now the UK has developed two authorization routes under the retained EU law on novel food using a traditional food notification or full application.

The EFSA guidance remains relevant to the development of dossiers for the authorization processes in the UK. However, a new application for authorization of a novel food should use a regulated products application service (FSA, 2020). A list of all authorized novel foods that can be sold in accordance with the conditions and protection set out is available online (https://www.legislation.gov.uk/eur/2017/2470/annex/2017-12-20).

In the USA, novels foods are not considered as an individual group of food products. Therefore, there are no specific regulations in place for novel foods. There are two main entry routes for novels foods into the US market. A novel ingredient or substance (food additive) needs pre-market approval by the US Food and Drug Administration (FDA) before it can be added to food or used as food unless its use is generally recognized as safe (GRAS) by qualified experts. A novel ingredient or substance can be sold in the market if it is a prior sanctioned substance (food additive) that the FDA or the US Department of Agriculture (USDA) determined safe for use in food before 1958 (Food and Drug Administration U.S., 2010). FDA has published partial lists of GRAS-approved ingredients including microorganisms and microbial-derived ingredients and enzyme preparations used in food (Food and Drug Administration U.S., 2019a).

In Singapore, new protein sources are assessed by the Singapore Food Agency (SFA) under the novel food regulation. SFA requires food traders who intend to use and/or sell novel foods in its market to submit an application for approval. In 2019, SFA introduced the novel food regulatory framework to require food companies to seek pre-market allowance for novel foods such as alternative protein products (Singapore Food Agency, 2019). The pre-market safety assessment is required for novel protein sources that do not have a history of being consumed as food.

In China, novel foods and ingredients are regulated according to the Administrative Measures for Safety Review of New Food Materials (2013). In Chinese regulations, novel foods are defined as animal, plant, or micro-organisms or substances derived from these sources, food substances with structural changes, or newly developed food materials. The National Health and Family Planning Commission (NHFPC) conducts pre-market approval of novel food materials to be sold in China. In Japan, regulatory requirements are specific to the nature of the new food ingredient. For example, the Ministry of Health, Labour and Welfare (MHLW) does not require a pre-market assessment and authorization for the new food ingredients to be used as food. However, the new food must be compliant with the Food Sanitation Act (Act No. 233, 1947). When the new food ingredient is used as a food additive, then a pre-market assessment and authorization is required prior to entry into the Japanese market.

14.2.2 Food Safety Regulation

The scientific guidelines for performing risk assessments of novel foods are in general poorly harmonized and are still at the development stage. More attention is paid to these foods as more experience about testing methodology is obtained. Therefore, it would be very helpful to develop a common understanding of how such a safety assessment could be carried out based on present-day knowledge. Table 14.2 provides details of the information required to conduct food safety assessments for novel food, such as a new protein source, by selected regulatory agencies.

In Australia and New Zealand, all non-traditional and novel foods go through a pre-market safety assessment as part of the assessment of an application by FSANZ to amend Standard 1.5.1. A risk-based assessment approach is used to make an assessment of the level of knowledge and scientific data about the safe use of non-traditional food in the broad community of Australia and New Zealand. The assessment process is designed to evaluate the public health and safety of a novel food or novel food ingredient and its potential adverse impact on consumers. A range of biological, chemical, toxicological, and nutritional issues related to a novel food are considered to ensure the safety of novel foods before permitting their sale in Australia and New Zealand. The essential information required to make an application to seek permission for the sale of a novel protein source in the Australia New Zealand Food Standards Code (the Code) is available in the

TABLE 14.2
Information required to conduct food safety assessment for novel food approvals by different agencies around the world

Country/Region	Safety Assessment Process	Source
Australia/New Zealand	FSANZ considers following factors in a safety assessment of novel foods: a. the history of use as a food in other countries b. the composition of the novel food, particularly the levels of anti-nutrients and naturally occurring toxins c. the method of preparation and specifications of a novel food ingredient d. potential for allergenicity of the novel food e. metabolism/toxicokinetic studies on the novel food ingredient f. animal toxicity studies on the novel food ingredient g. human toleration studies on the novel food ingredient	(Food Standards Australia New Zealand, 2019)
Canada	Information sufficient to establish that a novel food is safe for consumption are required, Health Canada recommends the safety assessment data packages according to the following headings, as applicable: a. History of use b. Dietary exposure c. Detail of novel process d. History of organism(s) e. Characterization of derived line/strain f. Genetic modification considerations g. Nutritional considerations h. Toxicology considerations i. Allergenicity considerations j. Chemical considerations k. Microbiological considerations	(Health Canada, 2006)
EU	Since the new EU regulation on novel food came into effect in January 2018, the process for scientific risk assessment of a novel food application has been centralized. EFSA performs risk assessments on the safety of a novel food upon request by the European Commission. EFSA carries out its safety assessment based on dossiers provided by applicants. Dossiers need to contain data on the compositional, nutritional, toxicological and allergenic properties of the novel food as well as information on respective production processes, and the proposed uses and use levels. Substances that do not have a history of safe use will be considered to be novel foods.	(EFSA, 2018)
Singapore	SFA takes into consideration the following information: i. the length of consumption/use of the ingredient (i.e., how many years the ingredient has been consumed as food or used in food). ii. extent of use of the ingredient (i.e., whether the ingredient is consumed or used by the general population, sub-population, certain tribes, etc). iii. quantity (i.e., the level of the ingredient consumed as food or used in food).	(SFA, 2020a)

TABLE 14.2 (Continued)
Information required to conduct food safety assessment for novel food approvals by different agencies around the world

Country/Region	Safety Assessment Process	Source

	iv. purpose/context of use (i.e., whether the ingredient is used for ceremonial purposes such as weddings, during famines, etc).
	 v. evidence demonstrating lack of adverse effects to human health attributed to the substance during the specific period of use as food.
	 Singapore Food Agency uses following safety assessment criteria for novel foods food ingredients in general:
	   i. Information on the identity and purity of the novel food, including, percentages of major components and impurities present.
	   ii. Information on the novel food's manufacturing process, and inputs used.
	   iii. Intended use and proposed use levels in food. Novel foods which are intended for consumption by specific population groups should be indicated.
	   iv. Toxicity studies (in-vitro and in-vivo), where relevant. This includes acute, short-term and long-term toxicity studies, carcinogenicity studies, reproductive toxicity studies, developmental toxicity studies and genotoxicity studies.
	   v. Metabolism or toxicokinetics studies, where relevant. These include absorption, distribution, metabolism and excretion (ADME) studies.
	   vi. Any safety assessment reports conducted by food safety authorities in major developed countries (Australia, Canada, New Zealand, Japan, the European Union and the USA)
	 In general, studies referenced in safety assessments should be published in reputable scientific journals. Unpublished studies may be considered if they have been conducted according to Good Laboratory Practice and other relevant guidelines established internationally (such as OECD guidelines).
	 Safety assessments that have been conducted in accordance to the following reference documents published by the US FDA, European Food Safety Authority (EFSA), and FAO/WHO, would be accepted for review.
	 • US FDA Guidance for Industry and Other Stakeholders Toxicological Principles for the Safety Assessment of Food Ingredients, Redbook 2000
	 • EFSA Guidance for submission for food additive evaluations
	 • FAO/WHO Environmental Health Criteria 240 - Principles and Methods for the Risk Assessment of Chemicals in Food	

UK	Food Standards Agency requires specific information to assess the food safety of the novel food: a. identity of the novel food b. production process c. compositional data d. specifications	(FSA, 2020)

(Continued)

TABLE 14.2 (Continued)
Information required to conduct food safety assessment for novel food approvals by different agencies around the world

Country/Region	Safety Assessment Process	Source
	e. the history of use of the novel food and/or of its source f. proposed uses and use levels and anticipated intake g. absorption, distribution, metabolism and excretion h. nutritional information i. toxicological information and allergenicity	
USA	The information critical in determining the safety of a GRAS substance and must be publicly available: • Description of the GRAS substance • Production process • Historical use, regulatory status, and consumer • Intended effect • Analytical methodology • Review of safety data • Safety assessment and GRAS determination	(Food and Drug Administration U.S., 2016b)
	The following information for the food additive is required for a safety assessment: • identity and composition, • proposed use, • use level, • data establishing the intended effect, • quantitative detection method(s) in the intended food, • estimated exposure from the proposed use (in food, drugs, cosmetics, or devices, as appropriate), • full reports of all safety studies, • proposed tolerances (if needed), • environmental information (as required by the National Environmental Policy Act (NEPA), as revised (62 FR 40570; 29 July 1997)) • Consistent information should be presented throughout all sections of the petition, including those pertaining to, • chemistry, • toxicology, • environmental science, and any other pertinent studies (e.g., microbiology)	(FDA, 2019)

Application Handbook (Food Standards Australia New Zealand, 2019). There are several categories of novel foods, and FSANZ requires applicants to provide information on the safety of the novel food (Table 14.2). The information and data required depend on the nature of the novel foods that need to be assessed.

In Canada, novel foods, novel fibres, and food additives must undergo pre-market safety assessments before they can be sold in the market. Novel food safety assessments are conducted by the Food Directorate, Health Products and Food Branch of Health Canada, and a set of regulatory requirements has been developed for this purpose (Table 14.2). As previously described, novel foods are products that do not have a history of safe use as a food, foods resulting from a process not previously used for food, or foods that have been modified by genetic manipulation (also known as genetically modified foods, GM foods, genetically engineered foods or biotechnology-derived foods). The Guidelines for the safety assessment of novel foods that were updated in 2006, were originally produced in 1994 to address the safety of GMO and novel processing technologies (Health Canada, 1994; 2006). These Guidelines help the applicant to prepare a novel food submission and to ensure that sufficient information is available for a safety assessment.

The European Novel Food Regulation has established a system for pre-market approval of novel foods, and the legislation aims to protect public health and safety. Before placing a novel food on the European Union market, the applicant must submit an online application for food safety assessment and authorization. The first Novel Food Regulation of the European Parliament and the Council, Regulation (EC) No 258/97 was adopted in 1997. Until 2018, the applications were assessed by the competent authority of the member state where the product is first to be placed on the market and a copy was sent to the European Commission. The new EU regulation on novel food came into effect in January 2018, which meant that the scientific risk assessment of a novel food application had been centralized. Now it is EFSA's responsibility to perform risk assessments on the safety of a novel food upon request by the European Commission (Ververis et al., 2020). The application must fulfill the requirements set in Article 10 of the Novel Food Regulation. The EU Commission's Implementing Regulation (EU) 2017/2469 has details of administrative and scientific requirements for applications. Since 2018, EFSA has published several risk assessments of different novel foods (Source: https://efsa.onlinelibrary.wiley.com/doi/pdf/10.2903/sp.efsa.2018.EN-1381). These documents contain useful information, checklists, and tables for presenting the scientific data required for food safety assessments and authorizations (Table 14.2). The European Commission, through the Regulation (EU) 2017/2470, maintains an online list of all authorized novel foods, called the Novel Food Catalogue.

For new microorganisms, EFSA conducts assessments to determine the safety status. The EFSA grants a microorganism qualified presumption of safety (QPS) status if the safety assessment concludes that a group of microorganisms does not raise safety concerns. The qualified presumption of safety (QPS) status is based on reasonable evidence (https://www.efsa.europa.eu/en/topics/topic/qualified-presumption-safety-qps). If the QPS status indicates that the biological agents require a safety risk assessment, then that group must undergo a full safety assessment. A list of all notifications received by EFSA since 2007 for inclusion in the QPS list is available (https://zenodo.org/record/4428353#.YIuFwSXivIU), and the next scientific opinion updating the QPS list is planned for December 2022. An application for market authorization of a regulated product that requires a safety assessment needs to be submitted to EFSA for a QPS assessment. A microorganism must meet the following criteria to have a QPS status:

- Its taxonomic identity must be well defined.
- The available body of knowledge must be sufficient to establish its safety.
- A lack of pathogenic properties must be established and substantiated.
- Its intended use must be clearly described.

In the UK, the ACNFP undertook risk assessments of various types of novel foods, such as quorn, lupins, quinoa and passion fruit seed oil, and examples of these novel food risk assessments can be found in the annual reports (ACNFP, 2003; 2004). Current advice by FSA is to follow EFSA guidance on the preparation of dossiers and to present an application for safety assessment and authorization of a novel food (FSA, 2020). FSA requires specific information for the risk assessment element to the novel food (Table 14.2).

In the USA, any new food ingredient is assessed at two different levels, either as a food additive or as being Generally Recognized as Safe (GRAS). For a food additive, a pre-market approval for specific uses is required by the FDA. GRAS approval for specific uses is granted by the consensus of a panel of qualified experts. GRAS status is determined by the history of safe use in food prior to 1958 or using a scientific procedure. The GRAS procedure is a notification procedure that assesses a new food ingredient or product using scientific data and evidence, such as (un)published studies and information (Food and Drug Administration U.S., 2010). Alternatively, a substantial history of consumption for food use by a significant number of consumers is required to make a GRAS assessment (Food and Drug Administration U.S., 2010). A comprehensive set of scientific data, information on the consumption, microbiological safety, pharmacological activities, methods, or principles should be provided to qualified experts to determine that the substance is not harmful (Food and Drug Administration U.S., 2016a).

If a substance is not GRAS or has a prior sanction as substance, then it is considered a food additive and requires a safety assessment. For a mandatory safety assessment of a food additive by the FDA, comprehensive toxicological testing, genetic toxicity, acute oral toxicity, short-term toxicity, (sub)chronic toxicity, and reproduction and developmental toxicity are required (Food and Drug Administration U.S., 2019b). The approach to the safety assessment of food additives is compiled in a publication entitled *Toxicological Principles for the Safety Assessment of Direct Food Additives and Color Additives Used in Food*, commonly known as 'the Redbook' originally published in 1982 and revised in 2000 (Food and Drug Administration U.S., 1982; 2007).

In Singapore, the novel food regulatory framework requires food companies to conduct and submit safety assessments of the novel foods including new protein sources to address potential food safety risks (SFA, 2020a). Provision of detailed information on raw material and ingredients, processes, food safety risks including toxicity, allergenicity, the safety of its production method, and dietary exposure, as well as their preventive control is mandatory. These safety assessments are rigorously reviewed by a Novel Food Safety Expert Working Group established by SFA. The expert group provides scientific advice on the food safety status of a novel protein. Recently, SFA reviewed the safety assessment of Eat Just, Inc.'s cultured chicken and allowed its sale in Singapore as a novel food and alternative protein product (SFA, 2020b).

14.2.3 OTHER REGULATIONS

A range of other regulations such as Food Labelling, Food Hygiene, Food Safety Management, and others could be applicable to novel foods including new protein sources once approved to be sold. These regulations are dependent on the type of novel food or ingredients and legislative requirements of the authorizing agency.

Consumers have the right to know what they are eating and where a particular food came from. Information regarding the species, origin, safety concerns, and any known allergens are also important for consumers to make informed decisions on whether to consume a food or not. Food labelling regulations are set up in different countries to ensure that food manufacturers are providing the required information to their customers. Generally, approval of a novel protein source also includes labelling requirements such as origin labelling, health and nutrition claims, and allergen declarations. The labelling regulations and rules vary from country to country and for different types of food, and the information on labelling requirements is generally described in the Food Act.

In Canada, new regulations on food allergen labelling came into force on 4 August 2012. The food allergens labelling requirements are applied to all pre-packaged foods sold in Canada (Agriculture and Agri-Food Canada, 2021). Food labels must declare specific priority food allergens, gluten sources, and added sulphites either in the list of ingredients or immediately following the list of ingredients. Mustard is a new priority allergen. Many foods or proteins derived from foods are included in the priority food allergens. Peanuts, tree nuts (almonds, brazil nuts, cashews, hazelnuts, macadamia nuts, pecans, pine nuts, pistachios, walnuts), sesame seeds, milk, eggs, seafood (fish, crustaceans and shellfish), soybeans, wheat (including kamut, spelt and triticale) and mustard seeds are included in the priority food allergens.

An example of food labelling requirements has been set up by Singapore for alternative protein products as part of the approval for cultured meat. Food establishments are required to clearly communicate on the true nature of food. The misrepresentation of cultured meat as conventionally produced meat to consumers is not allowed. Food companies that sell pre-packaged alternative protein products in Singapore must label the product packaging with qualifying terms such as 'mock', 'cultured' or 'plant-based' to indicate their true nature. A qualifying labelling term for products made of surimi fish paste is 'imitation crabmeat'. The labelling of alternative meat products as meat is not allowed. This is important so that consumers can decide whether to buy alternative protein products.

The EU Food Hygiene Regulations (Regulation (EC) 852/2003 and (EC) 853/2004) contain general rules on hygiene applied to manufacturers of the foodstuffs including those involved in primary production. According to the Food Hygiene regulations, the food business operator is obliged to notify the competent authorities of its existence (art. 6, 852/2004). For the handling of certain animal-origin products, the food business operator should be approved before the start of operations (art. 4, 853/2004). Similar food hygiene requirements are also set by countries.

14.3 REGULATORY EXAMPLES OF SPECIFIC NOVEL PROTEIN SOURCES

This section covers regulatory approvals and key requirements for novel protein sources by providing some examples from the countries, such as Australia/New Zealand, Canada, Singapore, the UK, and the USA, as well as the EU. More detailed and updated information can be obtained from the regulatory agency's website of the relevant country or region. Table 14.3 lists selected examples of novel protein sources that were assessed for regulatory approvals by different agencies.

14.3.1 INSECTS

The lack of regulations for production, processing, and sale of edible insects in developing countries where entomophagy is traditionally practiced (Dobermann et al., 2017) generally leads to no barriers imposed to their utilization. However, western countries face a different situation, where regulatory approvals are required to introduce a new food source such as edible insects or their products. For example, the EU legislation requires that all insect-based foods meant for human consumption be regarded as novel foods. Novel foods are mainly considered those that do not have a history of consumption by humans in the country/region in question. Therefore, authorization is required to sell edible insects and their products under the Novel Food Regulation (EU) 2015/2283.

If approved, then the general requirements of the food legislation and controls are applied to insect production. For instance, food business operators need to meet the legislative requirements under the Food Act. They are also responsible for implementing process controls, maintaining the microbiological quality, determining the shelf life of the products as well as the safety of their final products. Animal welfare, hygiene practices and the labeling information provided to the customer need to be taken into account (Evira, 2018). According to Merten-Lentz and Commandeur (2018), none of the edible insects were included in the EU novel food list until November 2018. At this stage, more than 20 applications for authorization of edible insects as novel foods have been assessed by the European Commission.

Edible insects such as *Acheta domesticus*, *Aegiale hesperiaris*, *Alphitobius diaperinus* (larvae), *Apis mellifera* (male pupae), *Gryllodes sigillatus*, *Hermetia illucens* (larvae), *Liometopum apiculatum* (larvae and pupae), *Liometopum occidentale* (larvae and pupae), *Locusta migratoria*,

TABLE 14.3
Examples of novel protein assessment and decision by different agencies around the world

Product/Ingredient	The Authority	Decision	Issues/Comments	References
Rapeseed protein isolate	FSANZ	Permitted	FSANZ has permitted the use of rapeseed protein isolate as a novel food, subject to specified conditions of use. The approved draft variation to the Code has a commencement date of 30 June 2021.	(FSANZ, 2020)
Rapeseed powder	EFSA	Authorized	The Panel considers that the rapeseed powder from *Brassica rapa* L. and *Brassica napus* L., is safe at the proposed conditions of use. (Regulation (EU) 2015/2283)	(EFSA NDA Panel, 2020a)
Dried yellow mealworm (*Tenebrio molitor* larva)	EFSA	Authorized	The Panel concludes that the dried yellow mealworm is safe under the proposed uses and use levels. (Regulation (EU) 2015/2283)	(EFSA NDA Panel, 2021)
Freeze-dried alga	Health Canada	Notified	Health Canada assessed and determined that the proposed use of freeze-dried *Tetraselmis chui* strain 8/6 does not pose a risk to consumers. Therefore, Health Canada has no objection to the sale of this product for human food use in Canada.	(Health Canada, 2017)
Lemna protein or water lentil protein (Duckweed)	US FDA	GRAS Approved	Pursuant to the regulatory and scientific procedures established by the regulation at 21 C.F.R.§ 170.225 (c)(5), the intended use of Parabel's LENTEIN Complete and Degreened LENTEIN™ Complete are exempt from premarket approval requirements of the United States Federal Food, Drug and Cosmetic Act. It is determined that such use is GRAS.	(Food and Drug Administration U.S., 2017)
Yarrowia lipolytica yeast biomass (Single cell protein)	EFSA	Approved		(EFSA NDA Panel, 2019)
Cultured chicken nuggets	SFA	Allowed		(SFA, 2020)

Schistocerca gregaria and *Tenebrio molitor* (larvae) are being considered in the applications. After EFSA safety assessment that was planned to be completed in 2020, the European Commission will finalize the decision about the authorization. The EU allowed countries to make individual decisions on edible insects until 2020, the time when EFSA's assessments on edible insect applications are expected to become available. In January 2021, EFSA published its first scientific opinion on an insect-derived food, 'Safety of dried yellow mealworm (*Tenebrio molitor* larva) as a novel food pursuant to Regulation (EU) 2015/2283', and it concluded that there were no safety concerns (EFSA, 2021). The EFSA's endorsements of whole or ground mealworms, lesser mealworms, locusts, crickets, and grasshoppers for human consumption are expected to be released in 2021.

Although edible insect authorizations are pending, some EU countries, including Finland, Denmark, and the United Kingdom, have granted temporary market access to insect foods. The market access is given using the former Novel Food Regulation (EU) 258/97 that had some room for interpretations for animals that are consumed in whole and not slaughtered. In 2018, the Finnish Food Authority (Evira) published guidelines for the food industry in relation to the farming, sales, and preparation of insects for consumption (Evira, 2018). It is the responsibility of insect farmers, manufacturers and sellers to be responsible to ensure that insect-based products are safe for consumers. The guide only applies to farmed insects intended for sale as a whole for human consumption. Wild insects are not permitted to be sold, marketed or presented as food.

In the USA, there is no specific regulation for edible insects. However, edible insects fit the definition of food as described under US Code Title 21, Subchapter II: Definitions, which therefore fall under current legislation. The legislative requirements include the requirement that they must be wholesome, labeled appropriately to declare origin, species and allergen content, toxin-free, and produced under sanitary conditions.

14.3.2 Microalgae

The regulatory bar for marine microalgae to enter the food supply chain is relatively high, and it follows a lengthy process. The existing regulations (such as GRAS, New Dietary Ingredient Notification, Novel Food) generally take from a few months to years to grant approval, and the process involves many complex regulatory challenges. For example, at present, some algae have received approval for their oil, however, the protein from the same algae is not approved. Similarly, some algae are known to be toxigenic, producing neurotoxins. Therefore, any microalgae strain that is selected for the production of food proteins must be non-toxic. In the USA, FDA has five algae included in the GRAS list. In the EU, foods consisting of or derived from algae are considered under the Novel Food Regulation (EU) 2015/2283. Therefore, an application should be filed for authorization to introduce novel algae or the product in the market. There is a need for a fast-track regulatory approval process, simpler evaluation criteria for photosynthetic algae, and guidelines for research and development.

Health Canada approved the sale of freeze-dried algae, *Tetraselmis chui* strain 8/6, as a novel food ingredient in 2017 (Health Canada, 2017). The freeze-dried algae were assessed to be used as a condiment to give flavour to different foods. The assessment was done according to the Guidelines for the Safety Assessment of Novel Foods (Health Canada, 2006) for the safety of the organism, the manufacturing process, the nutritional composition of the final food product, and what the potential is for this product to present a toxic or allergenic concern. The assessment determined that the proposed use of freeze-dried *Tetraselmis chui* strain 8/6 does not pose a risk to consumers, therefore it can be sold for human consumption in Canada.

14.3.3 Seaweed

Seaweeds are macroalgae, and a vast variety of macroalgae species has the potential to be used as raw material for food. Until now, there is no report suggesting marine macroalgae species are harmful to human health. In the EU, all edible macroalgae species are not authorized as food or food supplements but the consumption history of these species is the most important factor that affects their regulatory status. Proteins isolated from macroalgae need authorization, and they are regulated by the Novel Food Regulation (EU) 2015/2283. The European Commission's Novel Food Catalogue lists the status of certain varieties of seaweed to be considered as a novel or not. For instance, according to this catalogue, the brown seaweed *Fucus vesiculosus* is not a novel food whereas the red seaweed *Rhodymenia palmata* L (*P. palmata*) is a novel food because only brown seaweed has a history of use as a food supplement. There were 22 seaweed species listed in the Novel Food Catalogue until the end of 2020 (https://ec.europa.eu/food/safety/novel_food/catalogue_en). When seaweeds are used for human consumption, then MRLs for residues of plant protection products apply. Commission Regulation (EC) No. 1881/2006 sets a maximum limit of 3.0 mg/kg for cadmium in food supplements consisting exclusively or mainly of dried seaweed or of products derived from seaweed.

14.3.4 Duckweed

In the EU, common duckweed (*Lemna minor*) was considered to be a novel food when an application was filed under the Novel Food Regulation (Novel Food Catalogue). Similarly, the novel foods regulation will be applied to other subspecies of duckweed and require authorization prior to marketing as a food. Duckweed is likely to belong to the product group 'fish, fish products, shellfish, molluscs, and other marine and freshwater food products' in Annex I of pesticide residue Regulation (EC) 396/2005. No MRLs for the residues of plant production products have been set for duckweed. Duckweed protein products from the Lemnaceae polygenus, including *Wolffia*, *Lemna*, *Landoltia*, and *Spirodella* were evaluated for safety (Food and Drug Administration U.S., 2017). The products are produced by Parabel and identified as Parabel's LENTEIN Complete and Parabel's degreened version of LENTEIN Complete (LENTEINTM Lean) have been determined to be GRAS based on scientific procedures Pursuant to 21CFR 170.30 (a). Therefore, these products are exempted from pre-market approval requirements of the United States Federal Food, Drug and Cosmetic Act.

14.3.5 Rapeseed

Historically, rapeseed or canola is processed for oil production which is then used as food. Therefore, the oil of rapeseed is not a novel food. In the EU, rapeseed is included in Annex I of Regulation (EC) 396/2005. However, the by-product from rapeseed processing has been used in animal feed but not consumed as human food. The novel foods Regulation (EU) 2015/2283 applies to the proteins derived from rapeseed seeds. Recently, the EFSA assessed the authorization application to place rapeseed powder on the EU market. The scientific opinion on the safety of rapeseed powder from *Brassica rapa* L. and *Brassica napus* L. as a novel food (NF) pursuant to Regulation (EU) 2015/2283 was published in 2020 (EFSA NDA Panel, 2020a). The EFSA Panel on Nutrition, Novel Foods and Food Allergens (NDA) considered the rapeseed powder from *Brassica rapa* L. and *Brassica napus* L. to be safe in the proposed conditions of use. The approved rapeseed powder as a novel protein source is produced using the seeds of non-genetically modified double low (00) cultivars. The *Brassica* varieties have a low erucic acid content and reduced content of glucosinolates.

Food Standards Australia New Zealand (FSANZ) also assessed an application to amend the Australia New Zealand Food Standards Code (the Code) to permit the use of rapeseed protein isolate as a novel food and approved it in 2020 (FSANZ, 2020). This approval is for rapeseed protein isolate sourced from *Brassica* species that are naturally low in the anti-nutritional factors erucic acid and glucosinolates. FSANZ also outlined regulatory requirements and risk management measures to minimize the identified risks with the consumption of rapeseed protein isolate. The identified risks include the potential for microbiological contamination, the potential for allergic reaction in consumers with mustard allergy, and the need to ensure that levels of substances such as phytates and certain metal contaminants are retained as low as reasonably achievable.

14.3.6 Single Cell Protein

In the EU, the novel food regulations apply to the SCP product if the producer strain is not on the QPS list. EFSA has already published several scientific opinions on food safety assessments of SCP products. For example, the EFSA NDA Panel favourably assessed the safety of *Yarrowia lipolytica* yeast biomass as a novel food (EFSA NDA Panel EFSA Panel on Nutrition, Novel Foods and Food Allergens et al., 2019). The yeast, *Y. lipolytica*, is widespread in nature and naturally present in foods high in fat and protein such as cured meat, dairy products, and various types of cheese. There is no history of *Y. lipolytica* biomass consumption, so it is considered a novel food. The biomass of heat-killed *Y. lipolytica* yeast was authorized for placement on the market as a food supplement, excluding food supplements for infants and young children, in 2019 (Commission Implementing Regulation (EU) 2019/7666). In another application, the EFSA NDA Panel assessed the selenium-enriched biomass of *Y. lipolytica* as a novel food (NF) pursuant to Regulation (EU) 2015/2283 and published a scientific opinion in 2020 (EFSA NDA Panel, 2020). The selenium-enriched biomass of the yeast *Y. lipolytica* falls under category (ii), i.e., food consisting of, isolated from or produced from microorganisms, fungi or algae, according to the Article 3(2)(a) of Regulation (EU) No. 2015/2283.

14.3.7 Cultured Meats

Cultured meat is meat produced by cell culture of animal cells *in vitro*. The Singapore Food Agency (SFA) approved the world's first cultured chicken produced by Eat Just, Inc. in December 2020. The SFA reviewed the Eat Just's cultured chicken using the 'novel food' petition against the requirements for the safety assessment of novel foods (SFA, 2020a). This is seen as the beginning of the global regulatory approval process to clear the entry of cultured meats and their products in the food supply chain. Food traders and establishments selling alternative protein products such as cultured meats must label the products with qualifying terms such as 'mock' or 'cultured' to indicate the true nature of the product.

This approval has initiated a legislative discussion in many countries to develop a regulatory framework specifically for cultured meat and cell-based products. For example, a formal agreement to regulate cell-cultured food products from cell lines of livestock and poultry was announced in 2019 by the US FDA (Food and Drug Administration U.S., 2019c). In the EU, novel foods Regulation (EU) 2015/2283 needs an application to authorize cultured meats or cell-based products filed to the EFSA for a scientific assessment. In China, a possible route to obtain approval for cultured meat is through a petition process for approving 'new food ingredients'. According to FSANZ, the Food Regulation System in Australia and New Zealand is equipped to deal with new types of foods including foods produced by new technologies such as cell-based meats (https://www.foodstandards.gov.au/consumer/generalissues/Pages/Cell-based-meat.aspx).

14.4 NEED FOR HARMONIZED GLOBAL REGULATIONS OF NOVEL PROTEIN SOURCES

As discussed in previous sections, foods or food ingredients that do not have a history of use within a country are typically considered as 'novel foods' or 'new food additives'. A pre-market authorization or approval is necessary to assess the safety of novel food for human consumption. There are no harmonized international guidelines to conduct these safety assessments. Many different regulations and pre-market assessment requirements for novel food/ingredient approvals exist in different countries. Therefore, good planning and a solid strategy are needed to deal with the complexities in obtaining approvals for novel proteins and the ever-evolving global regulatory landscape.

Efforts are made to adopt a harmonized assessment approach in some parts of the world. For example, the EU has centralized the assessment process to be carried out by EFSA to ensure the harmonized scientific assessment of novel foods. The EFSA assesses the novel food that may pose a safety risk to human health and provides its opinion to assist the authorization process for EU markets. There is an agreed procedure for authorizing a novel food and updating the European Union's list of authorized novel foods. This could be a model to develop a globally harmonized system to set the regulatory and safety assessment requirements for novel foods and additives, including novel protein sources. This would be useful for food innovation processes and companies to gain approval in multiple markets efficiently and effectively.

14.5 CONCLUSION

Novel protein products are generally required to go through a pre-market safety assessment and approval process prior to placing them in a market. Regulatory agencies in each country or region have developed their own regulatory framework. Most of the countries and regions, including Australia/New Zealand, Canada, the EU, and Singapore use Novel Food legislation to deal with foods with no documented history of food use. The USA uses either GRAS status or a pre-approval process for food additives to enter the market. The novel proteins approval applications are handled by central authorities, for example in Canada it falls within the responsibility of Health Canada, and FSANZ is an authorized agency in Australia/New Zealand. Once approved, a new protein or product must meet the regulatory requirements (such as hygiene regulations, labelling regulations, MRLs, and food safety management) outlined in the Food Act of the particular country or region. Globally, the safety assessment of novel proteins is not harmonized, and international guidelines as to how such assessments should be performed are lacking.

ACKNOWLEDGEMENT AND DECLARATION

The author declares no conflict of interest. The views and opinions expressed in this chapter are the author's own and do not reflect the position of the Victorian Department of Health.

REFERENCES

ACNFP. (2004). Annual Report 2003: Food Standards Agency, London, UK. http://www.food.gov.uk/multimedia/pdfs/acnfp2003.pdf. Accessed April 15, 2021.

Agriculture and Agri-Food Canada. (2021). Canada's Regulatory System for Foods with Health Benefits - An Overview for Industry, Modified 29 March 2021. https://www.agr.gc.ca/eng/canadas-agriculture-sectors/food-products/processed-food-and-beverages/trends-and-market-opportunities-for-the-food-processing-sector/canada-s-regulatory-system-for-foods-with-health-benefits-an-overview-for-industry/?id=1274467299466#b4. Accessed May 2, 2021.

Australian Government. (2017a). Federal Register of Legislation - Australia New Zealand Food Standards Code – Standard 1.5.1 – Novel foods, 13 April 2017. https://www.legislation.gov.au/Details/F2017C00324. Accessed April 29, 2021.

Australian Government. (2017b). Federal Register of Legislation - Australia New Zealand Food Standards Code – Schedule 25 – Permitted Novel Foods, 13 July 2017. https://www.legislation.gov.au/Details/F2017C00543. Accessed April 29, 2021.

de Boer, A., & Bast, A. (2018). Demanding safe foods – Safety testing under the novel food regulation (2015/2283). *Trends Food Science and Technology*, 72, 125–133. doi:10.1016/j.tifs.2017.12.013

Department of Justice Canada. (2010). *Consolidated Regulations of Canada, Chapter 870, Food and Drugs Act, Food and Drug Regulations, Part B (food), Division 28 (Novel Foods)*. Department of Justice Canada, Ottawa, ON. http://laws.justice.gc.ca/eng/C.R.C.-c.870/page-1.html. Accessed April 10, 2021.

Dobermann, D., Swift, J. A., & Field, L. M. (2017). Opportunities and hurdles of edible insects for food and feed. *BNF Nutrition Bulletin*, 42, 293–308.

EFSA NDA Panel (EFSA Panel on Nutrition, Novel Foods and Food Allergens) Turck, D., Castenmiller, J., de Henauw, S., Hirsch-Ernst, K.I., Kearney, J., Maciuk, A...... (2019). Scientific Opinion on the safety of *Yarrowia lipolytica* yeast biomass as a novel food pursuant to Regulation (EU) 2015/2283. *EFSA Journal*, 17(2), 5594.

EFSA NDA Panel (EFSA Panel on Nutrition, Novel Foods and Food Allergens) Turck, D., Castenmiller, J., De Henauw, S., Hirsch-Ernst, K. I., Kearney, J., Maciuk, A., Mangelsdorf, I., McArdle, H. J., Naska, A., Pelaez, C., Pentieva, K., Siani, A., Thies, F., Tsabouri, S., Vinceti, M., Cubadda, F., Engel, K. H., Frenzel, T., Heinonen, M., Marchelli, R., Neuhäuser-Berthold, M., Poulsen, M., Sanz, Y., Schlatter, J. R., van Loveren, H., Ackerl, R., & Knutsen, H. K. (2020). Scientific Opinion on the safety of selenium-enriched biomass of *Yarrowia lipolytica* as a novel food pursuant to Regulation (EU) 2015/2283. *EFSA Journal*, 18(1), 5992.

EFSA NDA Panel (EFSA Panel on Nutrition, Novel Foods and Food Allergens) Turck, D., Castenmiller, J., De Henauw, S., Hirsch-Ernst, K. I., Kearney, J., Maciuk, A., Mangelsdorf, I., McArdle, H. J., Naska, A., Pelaez, C., Pentieva, K., Siani, A., Thies, F., Tsabouri, S., Vinceti, M., Cubadda, F., Frenzel, T., Heinonen, M., Marchelli, R., Neuhäuser-Berthold, M., Poulsen, M., Prieto Maradona, M., Schlatter, J. R., van Loveren, H., Ververis, E., & Knutsen, H. K. (2021). Scientific Opinion on the safety of dried yellow mealworm (*Tenebrio molitor* larva) as a novel food pursuant to Regulation (EU) 2015/2283. *EFSA Journal*, 19(1), 6343. doi:10.2903/j.efsa.2021.6343

European Food Safety Authority (EFSA). (2018). Administrative guidance on the submission of applications for authorisation of a novel food pursuant to Article 10 of Regulation (EU) 2015/2283. Technical Report Approved February 7, 2018. https://efsa.onlinelibrary.wiley.com/doi/10.2903/sp.efsa.2018.EN-1381. Accessed April 30, 2021.

EFSA Panel on Nutrition, Novel Foods and Food Allergens (NDA) Turck, D., Castenmiller, J., De Henauw, S., Hirsch-Ernst, K. I., Kearney, J., Maciuk, A., Mangelsdorf, I., McArdle, H. J., Naska, A., Pelaez, C., Pentieva, K., Siani, A., Thies, F., Tsabouri, S., Vinceti, M., Cubadda, F., Engel, K. H., Frenzel, T., Marchelli, R., Neuhäuser-Berthold, M., Poulsen, M., Schlatter, J. R., van Loveren, H., Dumont, A. F., & Knutsen, H. K. (2020a). Scientific Opinion on the safety of rapeseed powder from *Brassica rapa* L. and *Brassica napus* L. as a Novel food pursuant to Regulation (EU) 2015/2283. *EFSA Journal*, 18(7), 6197. doi:10.2903/j.efsa.2020.6197

European Parliament and the Council. (1997). Regulation (EC) No 258/97 of the European Parliament and of the Council of 27 January 1997 concerning novel foods and novel food ingredients. *Official Journal of the European Union*, L43, 1e7. http://eur-ex.europa.eu/smartapi/cgi/sga_doc?smartapi!celexapi!prod!CELE Xnumdoc&lg¼EN&numdoc¼31997R0258&model¼guichett

Evira. (2018). Insects as food, Evira Guide 10588/2/uk. https://www.ruokavirasto.fi/globalassets/tietoameista/asiointi/oppaat-ja-lomakkeet/yritykset/elintarvikeala/alkutuotanto/eviran_ohje_10588_2_uk.pdf. Accessed April 30, 2021.

Food and Drug Administration (U.S.). (1982). Toxicological Principles for the Safety Assessment of Direct Food Additives and Color Additives Used in Food (also known as Redbook I), U.S. Food and Drug Administration, Bureau of Foods (now CFSAN).

Food and Drug Administration (U.S.). (2007). Guidance for Industry and Other Stakeholders: Redbook 2000 "Toxicological Principles for the Safety Assessment of Food Ingredients", July 2007. https://www.fda.gov/regulatory-information/search-fda-guidance-documents/guidance-industry-and-other-stakeholders-redbook-2000. Accessed April 30, 2021.

Food and Drug Administration (U.S.). (2010). FDA announces start of generally recognized as safe (GRAS) notification pilot program for ingredients in animal food. http://www.fda.gov/AnimalVeterinary/NewsEvents/CVMUpdates/ucm214432.htm. Accessed April 29, 2021.

Food and Drug Administration (U.S.). (2016a). Substances Generally Recognized as Safe. https://www.federalregister.gov/documents/2016/08/17/2016-19164/substances-generally-recognized-as-safe. Accessed April 30, 2021.

Food and Drug Administration (U.S.). (2016b). Guidance for Industry: Frequently Asked Questions About GRAS for Substances Intended for Use in Human or Animal Food, October 2016. https://www.fda.gov/regulatory-information/search-fda-guidance-documents/guidance-industry-frequently-asked-questions-about-gras-substances-intended-use-human-or-animal-food. Accessed April 30, 2021.

Food and Drug Administration (U.S.). (2017). Comprehensive GRAS assessment of LENTEINTM Complete (LC) and Degreened LENTEINTM Complete (DGLC) Food Usage Conditions for General Recognition of Safety, November 2017. https://www.fda.gov/media/113614/download. Accessed May 2, 2021.

Food and Drug Administration (U.S.). (2004). *Federal Food Drug and Cosmetic Act*. Food and Drug Administration, Washington, DC. http://www.fda.gov/regulatoryinformation/legislation/federalfooddrugandcosmeticactfdcact/default.htm. Accessed April 10, 2021.

Food and Drug Administration (U.S.). (2019a). Generally Recognized as Safe (GRAS). https://www.fda.gov/food/food-ingredients-packaging/generally-recognized-safe-gras. Accessed April 29, 2021.

Food and Drug Administration (U.S.). (2009). *Code of Federal Regulations, Title 21 (Food and Drugs), Chapter I (Food and Drug Administration, Department of Health And Human Services), Part 170 (Food additives)*. US Government Printing Office, Washington, DC. http://www.access.gpo.gov/nara/cfr/waisidx_09/21cfr170_09.html. Accessed April 10, 2021.

Food and Drug Administration (U.S.). (2019b). Ingredients, Additives, GRAS & Packaging Guidance Documents & Regulatory Information, 9 June 2019. https://www.fda.gov/food/guidance-documents-regulatory-information-topic-food-and-dietary-supplements/ingredients-additives-gras-packaging-guidance-documents-regulatory-information. Accessed April 30, 2021.

Food and Drug Administration (U.S.). (2019c). USDA and FDA announce a formal agreement to regulate cell-cultured food products from cell lines of livestock and poultry, 7 March 2019. https://www.fda.gov/news-events/press-announcements/usda-and-fda-announce-formal-agreement-regulate-cell-cultured-food-products-cell-lines-livestock-and. Accessed May 3, 2021.

Food Standards Agency (UK). (2020). Novel foods authorisation guidance, updated 31 December 2020. https://www.food.gov.uk/business-guidance/regulated-products/novel-foods-guidance#:~:text=Novel%20foods%20are%20foods%20which,used%20in%20cholesterol%20reducing%20spreads. Accessed April 29, 2021.

Food Standards Australia New Zealand. (2010). *Australia New Zealand Food Standards Code, Part 1.5 (Foods Requiring Pre-market Clearance), Standard 1.5.1 (Novel Foods)*. Food Standards Australia New Zealand, Canberra/Wellington. http://www.foodstandards.gov.au/_srcfiles/Standard_1_5_1_Novel_Foods_v115.pdf

Food Standards Australia New Zealand. (2019). FSANZ Application Handbook, 1 July 2019. https://www.foodstandards.gov.au/code/changes/pages/applicationshandbook.aspx. Accessed April 29, 2021.

Food Standards Australia New Zealand. (2004). General information to assist in applying to amend the Australian New Zealand Food Standards Code – Novel foods, updated April 2004. https://www.foodstandards.gov.au/industry/novel/novelhistory/Pages/default.aspx. Accessed April 15, 2021.

Food Standards Australia New Zealand. (2017). Regulation of novel foods, July 2017. https://www.foodstandards.gov.au/industry/novel/Pages/default.aspx. Accessed April 15, 2021.

Food Standards Australia New Zealand. (2020). Approval Report - Application A1175, rapeseed protein isolate as a novel food, 15 December 2020. https://www.foodstandards.gov.au/code/applications/Documents/A1175%20Approval%20Report.pdf. Accessed April 29, 2021.

Food Standards Australia New Zealand. (2021). Novel food - Record of views formed in response to inquiries, updated 11 March 2021. https://www.foodstandards.gov.au/industry/novel/novelrecs/Pages/default.aspx. Accessed April 29, 2021.

Health Canada. (1994). Guidelines for the Safety Assessment of Novel Foods, September 1994. http://www.hc-sc.gc.ca/fnan/alt_formats/hpfbdgpsa/pdf/legislation/novele_e.pdf

Health Canada. (2006). Guidelines for the Safety Assessment of Novel Foods, June 2006. https://www.canada.ca/en/health-canada/services/food-nutrition/legislation-guidelines/guidance-documents/guidelines-safety-assessment-novel-foods-derived-plants-microorganisms/guidelines-safety-assessment-novel-foods-2006.html. Accessed April 26, 2021.

Health Canada. (2017). Freeze-dried *Tetraselmis chui* strain 8/6 as a novel food, updated on 27 February 2018. https://www.canada.ca/en/health-canada/services/food-nutrition/genetically-modified-foods-other-novel-foods/approved-products/lyophilized-tetraselmis-chui-strain-8-6.html. Accessed April 29, 2021.

Health Canada. (2021). Completed safety assessments of novel foods including genetically modified (GM) foods, updated on 23 April 2021. https://www.canada.ca/en/health-canada/services/food-nutrition/genetically-modified-foods-other-novel-foods/approved-products.html. Accessed April 29, 2021.

Knudsen, I., Søborg, I., Eriksen, F. D., Pilegaard, K., & Pedersen, J. W. (2005). *Risk Assessment and Risk Management of Novel Plant Foods: Concepts and Principles*. Nordic Council of Ministers. TemaNord No. 2005:588.

Kuik, O. (2004). The international regulatory framework for novel protein foods: challenges and opportunities, PROFETAS report. http://citeseerx.ist.psu.edu/viewdoc/download?doi=10.1.1.1022.3608&rep=rep1&type=pdf. Accessed May 10, 2021.

Lähteenmäki-Uutela, A., & Grmelová, N. (2016). European law on insects in food and feed. *European Food and Feed Law Review*, *11*(1), 2–8.

Marinangeli, C. P. F., Foisy, S., Shoveller, A. K., Porter, C., Musa-Veloso, K., Sievenpiper, J. L., & Jenkins, D. J. A. (2017). An appetite for modernizing the regulatory framework for protein content claims in Canada. *Nutrients*, *9*, 921. doi:10.3390/nu9090921

Merten-Lentz, K., & Commandeur, C. (2018). Edible Insects in the EU: The Long Road to Legalization. https://www.foodnavigator.com/Article/2018/11/07/Edible-insects-in-the-EU-the-long-road-to-legalisation. Accessed April 5, 2021.

Singapore Food Agency. (2019). Singapore Food Agency Act 2019 (Act 11 of 2019). https://www.sfa.gov.sg/legislation. Accessed April 29, 2021.

Singapore Food Agency (2020a). Requirements for the safety assessment of novel foods, Version dated 23 November 2020. https://www.sfa.gov.sg/docs/default-source/food-import-and-export/Requirements-on-safety-assessment-of-novel-foods_23-Nov-2020.pdf. Accessed April 29, 2021.

Singapore Food Agency. (2020b). Safety of alternative protein. https://www.sfa.gov.sg/food-information/risk-at-a-glance/safety-of-alternative-protein. Accessed April 29, 2021.

van der Spiegel, M., Noordam, M. & van der Fels-Klerx, H. (2013). Safety of novel protein sources (insects, microalgae, seaweed, duckweed, and rapeseed) and legislative aspects for their application in food and feed production. *Comprehensive Reviews in Food Science and Food Safety, 12*, 662–678.

Vapnek, J., Purnhagen, K., & Hillel, B. (2020). *Regulatory and Legislative Framework for Novel Foods, Bayreuth Working Paper Series Food Law* 03/2020, 5. University of Bayreuth, Germany.

Ververis, E., Ackerl, R., Azzollini, D., Colombo, P. A., da Sesmaisons, A., Dumas, C., Fernandez-Dumont, A., Ferreira da Costa, L., Germini, A., Goumperis, T., Kouloura, E., Matijevic, L., Precup, G., Roldan-Torres, R., Rossi, A., Svejstil, R., Turla, E., & Gelbmann, W. (2020). Novel foods in the European Union: Scientific requirements and challenges of the risk assessment process by the European Food Safety Authority. *Food Research International, 137*, 10951.

Index

3D printed meat, **2**, 274–5, 279–282
3D printing, 8, 272–82, 292–5

acrylamide, 361, 367, 369, 373
aflatoxins, 369, 384–5
aging population, 5–6
algae, 4, 6, 10, 65–80, 134, 137, 164, **190**, 362, 368–370, 373, 380, 382–3, 397, 421, 423, **410**
alkaloids, **365**, 367, 384, 385
allergenicity, 79, 124, 164, 290–1, 362, 366, 368, 371, 379–397, **414**, **416**, 418
allergens, 10–1, 79, 90, 123–4, 163, 165, 167, 170, 361–7, 369–370, 373–7, 380, 383–4, 387–390, 392–405, 418, 422–5
allergy, 10, 15, 79, 83, 165, 168, 170, 365, 367–370, 374–8, 383, 394, 396, 398–401, 403–6, 422
almonds, **2**, 35, **36**, 37, 418
alternative protein, 1–7, 10, 16, 66, 87, 89, 101, *107*, 111, 126–7, 129, 141, 167, 173, 176, 204, 274, 276, 361–2, *365*, 367, 370, 376–7, 380, 382–3, 385, 399–400, 403, 408, 413, 418–9, 423, 426
alternative protein sources, 1–7, 10, 16, 66, 87, 141, 298, 362, *365*, 382, 385, 400, 408
amaranth, **2**, 34–5, 40–1, 355, 385
amino acid, 12–13, 17–20, 22–9, 31, 34–41, 44–7, 66, 68–9, 80–2, 86–8, 90–7, 99–103, 110, 112, 131, 133, 138, 145–6, 166–8, 171–183, 188, 194, 196–201, 203–9, 212–3, 219–221, **223**, **225**, **227–8**, **232**, **235–6**, **239**, 241–7, 252–3, 255–8, 261, 263–4, 266–7, 275, 297, 302–7, 310–2, 316, 318, 320, 323, 329, 333, 342–3, 345, 348, 350, 356, 367, 380–1, 384–6, 388–9, 392, 395–6, 398
anaemia, 343, 347, *349*, 356, 358
animal welfare, **3**, 89, 204, 220, 245, 257, 272, 275, *287*, 291, 419
animal protein, 3, 6, 10, 13, 17, 19–21, 25–6, 40, 86–7, 89, 112, 126, 128, 131, 141, 212, 216, 218–9, 294, 319, 325, 329–331, 345, 366, 380–1, 383, 386, 397
antimicrobial, 43, 85, 96, 111–3, 127–9, 163–6, 168, 194, 202, 209, 260, 267, 307, 311–3, 319, 322–3
antinutrients, 10, 13, 30, 42, 45
antinutritional factors, 17–8, 27–31, 35, 37–9, 41–4, 362, *365*, 384, 386
antioxidant, 31, 36, 38–9, 42, 81, 83, 108, 111–3, 127–9, 132, 155, 165, 170, 173, 175, 178–9, 198, 200, 206, 208, 210–4, 220, 265, **304–5**, 307, 311–3, 317–324, 326, 333, 345, 349, 382, 400–1, 406
aquaculture, *11*, 33, 66, 81, 87, 89, 126–130, 164, 166–8, 171, 258, 262, 264, 267, 269, 298, 300, 312, 319, 324–6, 376, 398–9

aquatic species, 5, 34
availability, 1, 3, 5, 12, 17, 23, 26, 28, 32, 39, 47, 50, 53, 61, 87, 90, 97, 103, 111, 148, 163, 171, 174–6, 178, 209, 298, 344, 347, 380, 385–6

bacteria, 2, 10, 23, 49, 51–3, 55–6, 59, 112–3, 124, 127, 163, 173, 189, 193–4, 205, 207, 210, 212, 247, 260, 283, 303–5, 307, 312, 323, 325–6, 366–9, 397
bamboo borer, **2**
barley, **2**, 18, 32–3, 43–4, 46, 382, 386, 394, 402
beans, **2**, 3, 17, 21, 23, **24**, 27, 29–31, 39, 41, 54, **115**, 385
bee, **2**, 129
beef, 9, **14**, 16, 21, 26, 42, 54, 68, 86, 88–90, 93–4, 111, **121**, 123, 130, 141, 144–6, 170, 218–9, 241–4, 246, **249**, 251, 254–7, 259–263, 265–6, 285–6, 288, 292–4, 271–2, 274–5, 280, 314, 331, *334*, *336*, 343–5, 347–8, 355–7, 359, 383, 405
bioactive peptides, 3, 18, 31, 41, 110, 167, 173, 196, *197*, 198, 200, *302*, *305*, 307, 310–3, 315–321, 323, 325, 345–6, 357–9
biodiversity, 5, 14–5, 43, 86, 169, **282**, 311
biomass, 2, 14, 43, 50–1, 53, 55–62, 71, *74*, 75–6, 80–3, 94, 131, 188, 211, 213, 298, 319–321, 323–4, 326, 329, 357, 383, 401, *420*, 422–5
black beans, **2**, 30
buckwheat, **2**, 34–5, 40, 42–4, 46, 107
buffalo, 19, 123, 215, *217*, 218, **223–4**, 241, 251, 253–4, 257, 259–260, 263, 265, 268, 270, *349*

camel, 216, *217*, **218**, 219, 244, 248, **249**, 250, 252–3, 259, 262
camelids, 215, *217*, **218**, 219–220, **221–2**, 258
cancer, 5–6, 20, 25, 38, 42–7, 147, 170, 206, 313, 369, 383, 393, 404–5
cashew, **2**, 35, 37, 394, 418
cattle, 5, 9, 16, 19–20, 33–4, 79, 86, 89, 94, 96–7, 130, 216, 241, 244–5, 250–1, 253, 257, 261, 263, 266, 269, 272, 288, 292–3, 330–3, 342–4, *351–2*, 355
cell-cultured chicken, **2**
cell-cultured fish, **2**
cell-cultured meat, **2**, 294
cell-cultured prawn, **2**
centipede, **2**
cereals, 18–20, 24–5, 32–5, 39–40, 47, 102, 107–8, 123
challenges, 1, 3–4, 6–9, 14–6, 51, 61, 76, 85–6, 97, 124–5, 127, 130, 201, 216, 271–3, 275, 277, 279, 281–9, 291, 293–5, 297, 307, 315, 319, 321–2, 367–8, 370–1, 380, 389, 393, 396–400, 402–3, 405, 407, 421, 426–7
chemical contaminants, 124, 361, 366, 369
chemical hazards, 123, 362–4, 367–8, 370

429

chia seeds, **2**, 18, 36–7, 45, 411
chickpeas, **2**, 17, 23, **24**, 27–8, 30–1, 39, 47
chitin, 96–7, 99, 104, *105*, 106, 113, 127–8, 312–3, 316, 300, 320–1, 325–6, *365*, 367, 378, 384–5
cholesterol, 13, **14**, 25, 33–4, 57, 96, 133, 141, 145, 155, 167–170, 217, 219–220, *221*, 222, **223**, 224, **225**, **227–8**, 232, **235**, **239**, 241–3, 245, 247, 253–7, 265–6, *336*, *339*, *342*, 345–6, *353*, 381, 411, 426
chromatography, 77, 166, 172, 200, 269, *346*, 357, 376, 387–8, 399–402
chronic disease, 1, 5–6, 170–1, 246, 255, 356
clam, **151**–2, 155, **156**, *302*
clean labels, 4
climate change, 6, 10, 13, 61, 83–4, 86, 164, 204, 288, 290, 294
Codex, 363, 369, 372, 375, 395, 399, 407
collagen, 8, 273, 281, 293, 297–300, *302*, *305*, 307–310, 312–3, 317, 319–323, 325, 345, 355–7, 359
commercial scale, 8, 273, 287, 398
compatibility, 4
consumer acceptance, 3, **7**, 9, 11, 101, 107–8, 125–6, 268, **282**, 284–5, 287–8, 295, 313, 316
consumer health, 3
consumer perception, 220, 243, 252, 297, 307, 313, 316, 324, 349, 399, 400
consumer trends, 2
consumption, 5–6, 9, 11, 14–5, 17–22, 24–6, 30–4, 40, 44–5, 54–5, 57–61, 65–6, 76–7, 79–80, 82, 86–7, 94, 99–101, 107, 110, 113, 123–7, 130, 138, 155, 163–4, 167, 196, 198, 204, 216–7, 219, 241, 243, 245–7, **249**, 250–1, 255–7, 259–262, 267, 273, 281, 285–6, 288, 290, 298, 300, 308–9, 315, 319, 329–331, 344, 348, 350, 354, 359, 361, 364, 366–371, 375–6, 380, 382–5, 402, 404, 408–9, 411–2, 414–5, 418–423
contamination, 8, 51, 54, 59, 89, 124, 158, 162, 168–9, 188, 259, 283, 289, 290, 348, 361, 365–6, 368–372, 374, 406, 382–3, 422
controlled conditions, 8, 366, 373
conventional protein, 3, 10, 58, 68, 109, 361
conversion factors, 4, 78, 80, 82–3
cooking, 8, 17, 21, 26, 28–30, 35, 38–40, 46–7, 102, 108–9, 123, 129, 148, 163, 166, 255, 259, 264, 275–7, 279–281, 285, 294, 319, 329, *346*–7, 349, 350, 355–8, 384, 409
corn, **2**, 18, 20–2, 25, 32–4, 39, **115**, 161, 201, 314, 318, 324, 349, 355, 358–9, 385
cost, 1, **3**–4, 6, **7**–8, 10–1, 14–5, 31, 49–50, 53, 56, 59–61, 70, 75–7, 86, 89, 94, 99, 141, 176, 183, 194, 196, 200, 204, 271–2, 282–3, 288–291, 303, 307, 310, 323, 333, 347, 349, 384
cost competitiveness, **7**
crab, **156**, 293, 300, 311–4, 322
cricket, 10, 13, 16, 85, 89–90, **92**, 94, **95**, 98–9, *101*–4, 106–113, **117**–**8**, 123–4, *125*, 127–132, 350, 366, 377, 383, 420
cross-contamination, 361, 370
cross-reactivity, 124, 131, 381, 383, 387, 391, 395–6, 403, 405

cultivation, 26–7, 41, 50–1, 61, 84, 86, 195, 200, 292, 367
cultural, 4, 6–8, 126, 216, 219, 264, 281, 283, 287
cultured meat, **2**, 8–9, 12, 15–6, 271–5, 277, 279–295, 371–2, 402, 407, 418, 423

dairy protein, 1
dietary habits, 5, 17, 20
dioxins, 363, **365**, 367–9
distribution, 5, **7**, 11, 14, 137, 165, 170–2, 188, 252, 258, 276, 278–9, 300, **304**, 307, 376, *415–6*
dragonfly, **2**
duck, 19, 174, **190**, 216–8, 252–4, 259, 260, 263–5, 331–2, 346, 357
duckweed, 6, 84, 131, 361–3, *365*, 368–9, 373–8, 407, 420, 422, 427
dung beetle, **2**

economic, 2, 4, 10, 14, 41, 46, 50, 53, 55, 59, 65, 70, 82–3, 86–7, 89, 96, 99, 127, 130–1, 174, 204, 253, 274, 303, 314, 316, 355–6, 372, 380
ecosystem, 5, *11*, 16, 58, 133, 137, 148, 375
edible insects, 1, 7, 9–10, 13, 15–6, 89, 90, 103, 112, 123–4, 128–131, 317, 364, 366, 375–8, 383, 398, 400, 403–4, 419, 421, 424, 426
edible offal, 331–2, 383
EFSA, 256, 361, 366–9, 372, 375, 377, 392, 395–6, 399, 405, 413–5, 417, 419–420, 422–5
eicosapentaenoic acid, 63, 148, 241, 246, 313, 342
ELISA, 379, 392–4, 402, 405–6
Entomophagy, 9, 15, 366, 419
environmental, 1–3, 6–7, 9–11, 13–4, 16, 19–20, 41, 46, 50, 58, 61–3, 65, 80–4, 86–7, 89–90, 126, 128, 131, 137–8, 148, 158, 162, 165–6, 168–172, 174–5, 196, 201–2, 204–5, 207–211, 213, 218, 251–3, 260, 268, 271–2, 274, 285, 287–8, 290–2, 298–9, 310, 319, 325, 354–5, 364, 369–371, 374–8, 380, 396, 402, 404–5, 415–6
environmental contaminants, 364
environmental footprint, **3**, *11*, 14, 58, 285, 288, 355, 370
environmental impact, 1, **3**, 9, 11, 86, 174, 201, 272, 290, 405
environmental sustainability, 2, 6, 16, 131
enzymatic hydrolysis, 77, 81, *105*, 109–112, 129–130, 132, 185, **192**, 199, 206, 208, 210, 297, 306, 310, 317–8, 321, 325–6, *346*, 348–9, 405
ethical, 1, 8, 10, 13, 22, 31, 89, 204, 271–2, 283, 285, 291–2, 294, 317, 371, 380, 398
ethical challenges, 8
EU regulations, 373, 408, **409**
Evolution, 8, 21, 42, 44, 47, 54, 172, 216, 250, 255, 260, 267, 283, 384, 394, 402
extrusion, 27, 124, 273–281, 293, 309, 319–320, 326, 346–7, *349*, 355–8, 381

fatty acid, 21, 36, 39, 41, 43, **52**, 58, 61, 89, 96–7, 99–100, 102, 123, 133, 141, 147–8, *149–154*, 164–5, 167–172, 206, 217, 219–221, *222*, *224*, *226*, *230*, *234*, *237–8*, *240*, 241–7, 252–269, 297, 310, 313, 318, 335–6, *339*, 341–3, *352–3*, 359

Index

FDA, 25–6, 290, 295, 382–3, 400, 413, 415–8, 420–1, 423, 425–6
fermentation, 21, 35, 39, 49–54, 60–2, 78, 82, 124, 132, 189, *190–2*, 195, 206, 297, 303, 307, 312, 321, 323, 325–6, 380, 406
fibre, 3, 27, 31, 33, 38–9, 54, 78, 87, 89, 113, *114*, *116–8*, *120*, *122*, 177, 182, **187**, **197**, 201, 209, 279, 281, 283, 293, *334*, 349, 356, 369, 416
filamentous fungi, 2, 54, 57, 59
fish, **2**, 6, 9, 19–20, 27, 32, 38, 40, 54, 56, 79, 86–7, 89, 94, 96–100, 102, 111, 123, 126–7, 130–1, **136**, 137, 158, 162, 165, 167–9, 177, 210, 241, 253, 265, 271–4, 276–7, 279, 291, 295, 297–8, 300–2, 304–5, 307–8, 310–327, 361, 368, 376, 380, 393, 396, 398, 403, 418–9, 422
fish by-products, 297, 300, 310, 316, 319, 323
fisheries, 87, 130, 165, 170, 298, 300–1, 312, 316–320, 322–4, 326
flavour, **3**, 54, 199, 202, 216, 246, 263, 274–5, 281, 284–5, 302, 312, 314–6, 323, 347–9, 421
flaxseed, 2, 106, 262–5
food allergy, 15, 79, *365*, 368, 370, 383, 396, 398, 401, 403–6
food hygiene, 418
food justice, 4
food laws, 407
food neophobia, 9, 16
food production, **3**, 6, 41, 45, 49–50, 53, 56–7, 60, 65–6, 83, 104, **164**, 196, 298, 325, 333, 366, 371, 380, 407, *410*
food regulations, 407
food safety, 1, 11, 42, 84, 123, 131, 247, 255–6, 407–8, 412–3, **414–6**, 417–8, 421–2, 424
 assessment, 412–3, **414–6**, 417, 422
 authority, 247, 256, 364, 372, 408, **415**, 425, 427
 issues, 364, 378
 management, 373, 418, 424
 regulation, 407, 413
 risk, 361, 418
food security, 1–4, 14–6, 42–4, 58, 63, 174, 207, 226, 268, 297, 321, 356, 405
food standards, 354, 407–9, 411–6, 422, 424, 426
food systems, 2–4, 16, 84, 90, 110, 113, 125, 128, 259, 260, 293, 319, 324, 362, 400, 406
food transition, 1, 4
food wastes, 49, 53, 60
foodborne pathogens, 361
FSA, 411, 413–5, 417
FSANZ, 363, 375, 409, 411–4, 416, 420, 422, 424, 426
Fungi, 2, 21, 49, **52**, 53–4, 56–7, 59, 112–3, 173, 189, 193–4, 205, 247, 366–9, 384, 391–2, 397, 399, 404, 410, 423

game, 215–6, *217–8*, 219–220, *227–8*, *230*, 242, 247–8, *249*, 255, 259, 260, 262–4, 267–8, 270
genetic modification, 49, 51, 58, 404, 412
genetically modified, 362, 375, 392–3, 399, 405, 409, 412, 417, 422, 426
global population, 4, 14, 66
GMPs, 361, 371–3
goat, 141, 144, 168–9, 211, 216–8, 250–1, 254, 259, 262, 269, 331, 354, 358

grains, **3**, 17, 19–20, 22, 24–5, 32–4, 38–40, 43–4, 94, 251, 262
GRAS, 382–3, **411**, 413, **416**–8, **420**–2, 424–5
grasshopper, **2**, 10, 85, 90, 94, 102–3, 103, 109, 113, *118–9*, 126–9, 131, 383, 401, 420
greenhouse gas, **3**, 4, 15, 58, 61, 66, 86, 89, 288, 329, 357
guinea fowl, 174, 215, *217–9*, 252, 260–3, 266

HACCP, 373, 376
haemoglobin, 284, 343
halal, 9, 248, **249**, 250, 288–289, 354
health, 1, 2, **3**, *5*, 7, 10, 12, 13, 14, 20, 22, 25, 26, 31, 33, 39, 56, 59, 61, 65, 66, 68, 79, 98, 99, 113, **122**, 123, 126, 134, 138, 147, 157, 162–164, 197, 200, 203, **203**, 204, 245–248, 251, 281, 285, **286**, **288**, 289, 290, 310, 311, 313, 315, 332, 333, 342, 344, 345, 348, 350, 363, 364, 366, 367, 370, 371, 372, 373, 380, 382, 383, 384, 387, 392, 395, **410**, 412, 413, **414–415**, 416, 417, **420**, 421–424
health authorities, 6, 395
health claims, 31, 316
health concerns, 2, 367, 387, 395, 398
health improvement, **3**
health-related risks, 6
healthy choice, 3
healthy products, 7, 416
heart disease, 5, 6, 25, 147, 148, 155, 313
heavy metals, 55, 79, 94, 123, 158, 194, 247, 248, 361, 367–371, 373
heliciculture, 138, 164
hemp seed, **2**
high quality proteins, 1, 3, 6, 12, 26, 31, 39, 87, 99, 108, 134, 220, 303, 311, 331
horse, 8, 34, *119*, 216, *217*, **218**, 219, **225**, **226**, 241, 242, 250, 251, 284, **304**, **305**, 311
housefly, 85, 89, 94, 98, 99, 101–103
hydrolysate, 57, 60, *105*, 108, 110–112, 124, 163, 178, **180**, 183, 185, 188, 194, 196, *198*–202, **302**, 303–316, **346**, 348, 370
hygiene regulations, 419, 424
hygienic conditions/quality, 8, 51, 219, 247, 301

immunoassays, 397
ingredient, 275, 280, 290, 301, 303, 309, 311, 312, 315, 347, 348, 350, 354, 367, 371, 381, 382, 408, 411, 413, **414–415**, 417–418, **420**, 421, 423
ingredient supply, 7
innovation, 2, 3, 4, 6, 50, 290, 309, 310, 362, 407, 412, 424
insect, **2**, 3, 9, 10, 11, 13, 18, 20, 21, 58, 85–126, 162, 196, *197*, 298, 350, 364, **365**, 366, 367, 373, 380, 383, 387, 388, 392, 419, 421
insect proteins, 6, 13, 90, 94, *105*, 106, 108, 110, 111, 364, 366, 373, 387, 388, 392
iron deficiency, 343, 347

keratin, 8, 13, 14, 173–204
keratin hydrolysates, 175, 183, 185, 188, 196, 198
keratinase, 188–189, 193–196, *197*, 198
keratinolytic microorganisms, 173, 188, 189, **190**, **191**, 193, 195, 196, *198*, 199–203
kidney beans, **2**, 29
KnipBio Meal, **2**

labelling, 7, 367, 394, 408, 418–419, 424
laboratory-grown meats, 6, 371
lamb, 21, 79, 90, 141, **144**, 145, **146**, 219, 243, 246, **249**, 344
land snails, 133, 138, **140**, 141, 145, **147**, 148, **149**, **150**, **153**, **154**, 155, **156**, 158, **159**, 162, 163
larvae, 21, 85, 94, 98–100, 103, 107, 109, 112, 113, 123–125, 162, 419
lectin, 13, 30, 368, 384
legumes, 17, 22, 23, **24**, 25, 28, 29, 32, 34–40, 68, 98, 112, 381, 384, 385
lentils, **2**, 3, 18, **24**, 30–32, 39, 106, 107
lima beans, **2**, 29, 385
locust, **2**, 9, 10, 85, 94, **95**, 98, 99, 103, 109, 112, 113, 123, 280, 315, 383
logistic barriers, 4

macroalgae, **67**, 148, **365**, 367, 421
malnutrition, 10, 31, 123, 174, 289, 331–333, 344
marine biotoxins, 362
marine products, 297, 301, 308, 310, 316
marine snails, 133–134, *137*, 138, 140, 141, **142**, 145, 148, 155, **156**, 163
market demand, 124
marketing tactics, 4
mass spectrometry, 387, 388, 397
mealworm, 13, 85, 90, 94, **95**, 98, 99, 100, 101, 103, 106, 107–109, 111–113, **117**, 123, 124, 367, 383, 388, 419, **420**
meat co-products, 87, 329–46
meat cuts, 8, 220, 286, 348
meat in vitro, 7–11
meat protein, 245, **302**
metabolites, 54, 58, 59, 162, 244, 382, 384, 385
microalgae, **2**, 51, **52**, 53, 55, 77, 163, 363, 362, **363**, **365**, 370, 373, 380, 382, 383, 421
microbial, 2, 10, 11, 13, 61, 78, 106, 124, 174–203, 278, 279, 281, **282**, 289, 290, 301, **304**, 306, 310, 313, 371, 373, 380, 413
microbial biomass, 2, 51, 55–6, 60–1, 188
microbial contaminants, 11–12, 188, 289, 290, 348, **365**, 422
microbial pathogens, 361, 366–370
microbial sources, 49, 51, 53, 306
microbiological hazards, 123, 126, 361, **363**
millet, **2**
minerals, 3, 8, 13, 35, 38, 39, 57, 62, 78, 89, 113, 123, 156, **157**, 158, 174, 199, 202, 220, **221**, **223**, **225**, **228**, **229**, **233**, **236**, **239**, 241, 242, 244, 251, 289, 297, 315, 380, 382, 386, **410**
misidentification, 8, 283
mopane worm, 2, **115**
MRLs, 369, 421, 422, 424
mule, *217*, **218**, 219, 220, **226**, 241
mycoproteins, 6, 54, 383, 384
mycotoxins, 57, 59, 123, 361–**365**, 366, 369, 370, 373

navy beans, **2**, 29
new products, 4, 272, **287**, 307, 371
new protein, 2, 4, **7**, 11, 14, 87, 298, 361, 364, 389, 393, 396, 397, 407, 408, 411, 413, 418, 424
NMR spectroscopy, 276, 277, 279, 310, 390
non-animal protein, 6

non-traditional meats, 215–220, **221**–**240**, 241–243, 245–248
non-traditional protein, 2, 251
novel food regulation, 408, 412, 413, 417
novel protein sources, 2, 3, 4, 7, 10–13, **363**, 364, 370, 371–373, 407–409, 413, 418, 419, 422, 423, 424
novel sources, 2, **7**, 9, 12, 381, 383, 384
nucleic acid, 51, 53, 55, 56, 58, 158, 370, 390, 393
nutrition, 2, 8, 50, 56, 57, 87, 163, 164, 174, 176, 196, *197*, 198, 220, 224, 241, 243, 244, 245, 247, 274, 284, 297, 331, 333, 344, 345, 350, 382, 418, 422
nutritional aspects/benefits, 2, 3, 7, 8, 10–14, 22, 24, 26, 27, 31, 37–40, 50, 51, 53, 54, 56, 60, 61, 66, 68, 70, 87, 89, 94, 97, 103, 106, 108, 110, 113, 123, 126, 134, 138, 145, 158, 176, 178, 183, 188, 196–200, 202, 204, 216, 217, 219, 220, 240–248, 251, 274, 282, 284, 288, 297, 303, **304**, 306, 307, 310, 311, 312, 314, 333, 343, 347, 348, 355, **372**, 380, 383, 386, **410**, 413, **414**, **416**, 421
nutritional characteristics, 241, 242, 244, 284
nutritional implications, 2, 14
nutritional quality, 8, 22, 68, 94, 97, 216, 219, 248, 307, 310, 311, 397
nuts, **18**, 35–40, 70, 393, 396, 418

oats, **2**, 21, **32**, 35–37, 40, 100, 382
oyster, 148, **151**, **152**, 155, **156**, **161**, 302

parasites, 10, 162, 167, 247, 361–2, **365**, 366
peanuts, **2**, 21, 35–9, 41, 68, **135**, 385, 389, 392–3, 418
peas, **2**–3, 17, 23, **24**, 26–8, 30–2, 39, 41, 43, 45, 87, 90, 380–1
pesticide residues, 165, 170, 361–2, 364, 366, 369, 373
physical hazards, 126, 361–3, 367
pine nuts, **2**, 418
pistachio, **2**, 418
plant protein, 4–6, 11, 13, 17–21, 23–31, 34, 36, 39–40, 47, 68, 87, 90, 111, 361, 380–1, 389, 391, 405–6
plant-based protein, 2–4, **7**, 14, 17, 20–1, 34–5, 56, 319, 345, 380–1
pork, 21, 42, 89–90, **93**, 108, **121**, 141, **144**, 145, **146**, 166, 218–9, 241–4, 246, **249**, 254–6, 259–263, 280, 292–3, 343–4, 347
poultry, 5–6, 19–22, 33–4, 42, 44, 56, 85–7, 89, 94, 96–8, 100–3, 126–8, 131, 141, 166–7, 174–5, **190**–2, 205, 207–8, 210, 217–9, 242, 246, 252–3, 255–7, 260, 263–4, 266, 271, 275, 281, 295, 316, 327, 329, 359, 380, 403, 423, 426
proteases, 77–9, 85, 109, 111, 176, 188–9, 194, 207, **304**, 306, 308, 312, 325, **345**–6, 348, 387
protein consumption, 6, 14, 17, 19, 25, 40, 87, 315
protein digestibility, 12, 17–8, 22–3, 26–31, 35, 37–41, 44–5, 68, 78–9, 90, 99–100, 109, 129, 178, *197*, 345, 348, 380
protein efficiency, 17, 22, 28, 68, 99, 101
protein extraction, 53, 65, 70–1, 73, 77, 80–3, *105*, 106, 109, 303, 309, **346**, **349**, 370
protein hydrolysates, 41, 62, 85, *105*, 108, 110–2, 128–9, 132, 163, 188, 199–201, 206, 208, 297, 302–7, 310–3, 315–327, **349**, 358
protein quality, 12–3, 17–9, 22–3, 26, 28, 35, 37, 40–2,

Index

44–6, 51, 57, 65, 68, 90, 99, 106, 127, 129, 145, 260, 265, 333, 348, 356
protein supply, 16, 216
proteomics, 379, 387–8, 398–9, 401, 403–4
public health, 2, 5, 245, 256, 259, 268, 322, 363–4, 366–7, 372–3, 377, 380, 392, 404, 412–3, 417
pumpkin seed, **2**, 37, 40, 43

quinoa, **2**, 3, 34–6, 40–2, 46, 417
Quorn products, 382, 417
Quorn^{TM}, **2**, 57, 378

rabbit, 21, 216–9, 239–240, 245–250, 252–5, 258, 260–4, 266–7
rapid growth, 6, 55–6, 61, 298, 407
rapid methods, 379, 387
recovery, 54, 58, 60, 65, 70–1, 75–7, 82–3, 89, 104, 109, 127, 129–130, 194, 289, 298, 302–4, 307, 309, 313, 316, 318–9, 322–4, 326, 356–7
regulations, 124–5, 308, 373, 380, 407–9, 411–3, 418–9, 421–5
regulatory approvals, 2, 419
regulatory authorities, 316
regulatory challenges, **7**, 16, 61, **287**, 294, 421
regulatory framework, **7**, 290–1, 317, 364, 398, 407–8, 413, 418, 423–4, 426
religious, 7–9, 86, 164, 204, 215–6, 219, 248–9, 252, 271, 288–9, 297, 308, 313, 315, 354
religious issues, 215–6, 248, 308
religious restrictions, 7, 9, 86, 164, 315, 354
risk assessments, 2, 371–2, 361, 363, 381, 387, 413–4, 417
rodents, 127, 202, *217*, 215–240, 243–5, 249–250, 253, 258, 370

Saccharomyces cerevisiae, 50, *52*, 397
scallop, 148, **151–2**, 155, **156**, **161**, 170, 278, **302**
seafood, 82, 87, 148, 165, 168, 170, 172, 247, 271, 276, 297–8, 300–3, 308–310, 315, 317–321, 323–7, 354, 400, 418
seeds, 18–20, 23–4, 30, 32, 34–8, 40, 42–6, 81, 259, 369, 375–6, 381, 384, 389, 398, 411, 418, 422
sensory characteristics, 8, 102, 131, 262, 268–9, 283–4, 317, 324, 330
SFA, **222**, **224**, **226**, **231**, **234**, **237**, 240–2, 246–7, 371–2, 377, **410**, 413–4, 418, **420**, 423
Sheep, 14, 21, 79, 86, 89, 202, 216–8, 244, 250–1, 254, 260, 270, 330–3, 341–4, **346**, 348–352, 357
silkworm, 85, **91**, 94, 98–100, 102–4, 108, 110–2, **114**, 124, 127–132
single-cell protein, 2, 20, 49–50, 62, 80, 369, 373

snails, 21, 127, 133–72
social, **3**–4, 6, 16, 219, 264
sorghum, **2**, 18, **32**–5, 41–5, 47, 101, 106, 386, 399
soybean, **2**, 5, 17, 20, 22, 24–6, 34, 36, 41, 44, 47, 66, 68, 83, 86–**8**, 94, 98, 100–1, 111, 148, 155, 199, 201, 213, 262, 380–2, 385, 387, 390, 393–4, 398–9, 401–3, 406, 418
spectroscopy, 309–10, 316, 317, 321, 323, 325, 379, 389–90, 398, 400, 402–3, 406
Spirulina, **2**, 53, 81–2, 84, **67**–8, **69**, **73**, 78, 357, 370, 377, 380, 382, 398, 400, 402, 406
sunflower seeds, **2**, 18, 36
sustainable approach, 4, *5*
synthetic eggs, **2**
synthetic milk, **2**

technological, 1, 4, 13, 16, 106, 124, 129, 165, 253, 258–9, 261, 264, 266, 268, 291, **305**, 320–1, 323, 398
temperature control, 187, 371
terrestrial snails, 133–4, 137, 169
texture, **3**, 15, 27, 54, 97, 100–1, 103–4, 108, 126, 200, 217, 246, 254, 260, 270, 274–7, 280–1, 284–5, 292–3, 309, 312, 314–5, 347, 381, 383
turkey, 26, 28, **138**, 166, 169, 174, *217*, **218**, 241, 345, 353, 356–7, 364, 276

veal, 21
vegan lifestyles, 4
vegetables, **3**, 18–20, 36, 38–9, 94, 100, 257, 294, 366, 389, 400
vegetarian, 2, 4, 6, 9, 17, 19–20, 22–5, 29, 37, 39–41, 44, 293, 397
vitamin E, 133, 155–6, *157*, 165, 170, 172, 254, 258
vitamins, 3, 8, 13, 28, 38–9, 56, 58, 61, 89, 113, 123, 165–6, 220, 297, 310, 312, 380, 382, **410**

walnuts, **2**, 35–7, 389, 418
water usage, **3**–4, *282*
wheat, **2**, 13, 15, 18, 21–2, 28, **32**–4, 41, 44–5, 47, 54–55, 63, 83, **88**, 94, 99–100, 106–8, 111, 127, 130, 170, 201, 275, 314, 317–8, 327, 347, **349**, 381–2, 389, 391, 393–4, 396–7, 399–400, 404, 418
wild rice, 2

X-ray crystallography, 390–1

Yeast, 2, 50–1, 53, 55, 58–9, 62, 283, 369, 402, **420**, 422–4
yuck factor, 7, 9, 125